A Checklist of Pennsylvania Newspapers

Volume I

PHILADELPHIA COUNTY

Prepared by
THE PENNSYLVANIA HISTORICAL SURVEY
Division of Community Service Programs
Work Projects Administration

PENNSYLVANIA HISTORICAL COMMISSION
Harrisburg, 1944

THE PENNSYLVANIA HISTORICAL COMMISSION

Ross Pier Wright, *Chairman*

Frances Dorrance

Edward R. Barnsley

Gregg L. Neel

Francis B. Haas, *ex-officio*
    Superintendent of Public Instruction

Sylvester K. Stevens, *State Historian*

Donald A. Cadzow, *State Anthropologist*

TRUSTEES—EX-OFFICIO

Edward Martin
    Governor of the Commonwealth

F. Clair Ross, *Auditor General*

G. Harold Wagner, *State Treasurer*

FOREWORD

The inception of the project, bearing its first mature fruit in the publication to which this is a foreword, came at the 1932 conference of the Pennsylvania Library Association. Dr. C. Seymour Thompson, Librarian of the University of Pennsylvania, announced that the American Library Association had started a movement to preserve the basic source materials for the social sciences in the various states, a development of the project launched by the Social Service Science Research Council, in cooperation with the Bibliographical Society of America. Dr. A. F. Kuhlman, Chairman of the American Library Association Committee, stated that one of the most important needs would be a bibliography of newspapers published in the various states, since the checklist made for the American Antiquarian Society by Dr. Clarence Brigham listed only American newspapers prior to 1820.

The Pennsylvania Historical Commission decided in May, 1933, to undertake this desirable and constructive piece of work for Pennsylvania. The plan would make available the newspaper holdings in Pennsylvania, indispensable for historical research, by a checklist of all files of newspapers, both local and state wide.

The list prepared by Doctor Brigham covers thoroughly the period up to 1820. The only other checklists available, apparently, were those published by Yale University, containing very few Pennsylvania items; the Library of Congress checklist with only a short Pennsylvania list, and the Pennsylvania State Library list of 1900 which contains only items held by the State Library. This last is a very valuable list but incomplete for the whole state.

The correspondence with Doctor Kuhlman disclosed the plan of the Bibliographical Society of America, to work through the different states on the local files. Some state lists were then complete and ready for publication. At that time the Bibliographical Society was doing nothing in the eastern part of Pennsylvania and the Historical Society of Western Pennsylvania was listing only Western Pennsylvania items, except for a survey of Allegheny County, which was complete.

In view of the above facts, the Historical Commission project was outlined to secure data from existing newspapers and from institutions and individuals on their holdings. The information received was typed on cards under each newspaper. By June, 1934, returns had been received from approximately 70 percent of these sources. In the meantime, the American Bibliographical Society had developed their project into a definite Union List of Newspapers in the libraries of the United States and Canada, under the editorship of Miss Winifred Gregory, the work to be done in the Library of Congress. The Historical Commission immediately got in touch with Miss Gregory, who suggested that the Historical Commission take charge of the work, under direction of the Union List of Newspapers.

About this time, the State Library's project of an historical survey of the entire Commonwealth under Dr. C. W. Garrison, the archivist, was begun, which grew and developed far beyond the vision of its originators. The first project closed, another took up the work, and was followed by others, until it was finished in 1936, and submitted to Miss Gregory. Since then, the successive heads of the Historical Survey have recognized the necessity of making the work as complete as possible, in order to make available to students of Pennsylvania history, the invaluable information in the local newspapers on the growth and history of municipalities, daily events, and contemporary thought. Such a guide, to give the research worker, whether historical, political, economic or social, the information there contained, would be a credit to the organization preparing it.

Great credit is due the Historical Survey for the fruition of their undertaking as exemplified in the first volume of so magnificent a work.

FRANCES DORRANCE,
Pennsylvania Historical Commission.

PREFACE

Thirty-eight years after Charles II granted the Province of Pennsylvania to William Penn, the first newspaper was established. The *American Weekly Mercury* made its appearance on December 22, 1719. This was the third newspaper established on the British-American Continent, the *Boston News-Letter* having been published in 1704. The second newspaper, the *Boston Gazette,* preceded the first Pennsylvania paper by one day—December 21, 1719.

During the period 1704-1775, approximately seventy-eight newspapers were published in the American colonies, of which more than half had been discontinued previous to the outbreak of the American Revolution. At the end of January, 1775, nine newspapers were published in Pennsylvania, more than in any other colony. Massachusetts followed, with seven, Connecticut and New York had four, and South Carolina three, Maryland, Virginia, North Carolina and Rhode Island possessed two each, while only one was published in New Hampshire and Georgia.

Of the nine newspapers published in Pennsylvania in 1775, seven were published in Philadelphia, six in English and one in German. Another German paper was published in Germantown, and the remaining one, published in Lancaster, was in English and German.

The spread of newspaper publications in the English language throughout the Commonwealth during the period 1776-1810 was irregular. Newspapers were established in Carlisle in 1785, at Pittsburgh in 1786, and at York in 1787. During the 1790's, fourteen made their appearance. Beginning at Chambersburg in 1790, Harrisburg followed in 1792, Mifflintown and West Chester in 1794, Uniontown and Washington in 1795, Reading, Wilkes-Barre and Lewistown in 1796, Huntingdon in 1797, and Bristol, Easton, Greensborough and Norristown in 1799. The year 1806 saw their establishment at Doylestown and Gettysburg. Williamsport followed in 1802, Bedford and Meadville in 1805, Beavertown in 1807, Allentown, Downingtown and Erie in 1808. A newspaper was first published at Brownsville in 1809 and at Frankford in 1810.

The large influx of German immigrants was accompanied by the establishment of a large number of newspapers which played an important role in the growth and development of the colony. For a short period, Benjamin Franklin published the *Philadelphische Zeitung* in 1731. Christopher Sower, one of the best known German publishers, founded the Hoch Deutsch, *Pennsylvanische Geschicht-Schreiber* in 1739. By the close of the century, five others had been published in the vicinity of Philadelphia at one time or another. Seven more were published at Ephrata, Lancaster, Reading, Easton, Harrisburg, York, and Hanover, during the same period. Four additional German newspapers were established during the first decade of the next century at Norristown, Somerset, Lebanon and Allentown.

French newspapers in the American colonies were unknown until after the American Revolution. One was published in Philadelphia in the 1780's and three during the 1790's, although they were short-lived and few issues survive today.

In 1800, there were one hundred and fifty newspapers in the United States. There was a marked increase in the next decade, three hundred and sixty-six being published in 1810. Pennsylvania outranked all other States at this time, with seventy-three.

The nineteenth century was an age of rugged individualism, and in no place can this be seen more plainly than in the newspaper field. The same century that saw the small merchant and individual proprietor also saw the individual newspaper publisher. The peak in Philadelphia was reached during the decade 1870-1880, one hundred and five being established during that period. Thereafter, the number of new newspapers waned. The era of combinations in big business has also been reflected in the newspaper field. The influence of the individual publisher over American life has greatly diminished.

The titles of the newspapers have been arranged genealogically, the latest title of any newspaper being entered alphabetically as to the main title, with the date span covering the entire length of the sequence. The frequency, and any political, religious, foreign, or other known affiliation follow. Under the latest title, all titles have been arranged chronologically, with their respective date spans, frequencies, and abbreviations. Any variations in title have also been shown. Each prior title has been cross-indexed alphabetically, in order to indicate its location in the proper sequence. Cross-references that would immediately precede or follow a title are omitted. Publishers and editors are listed under each prior title, followed by the depository symbols and holdings. Only Pennsylvania holdings have been listed. An asterisk beside any title indicates that out-state holdings may be found by consulting Winifred Gregory's *American Newspapers, 1821-1936*. The number sign beside any title indicates that out-state holdings may be located by consulting Clarence M. Brigham's *Bibliography of American Newspapers, 1690-1820*.

Few volumes arranged in this manner have been presented. The period of Pennsylvania's newspaper history, through 1820, has been thoroughly covered by Mr. Brigham. From that date until the establishment of George P. Rowell's *American Newspaper Directory*, in 1869, a period which may well be called "The Dark Ages," ensued. During this period, the surviving newspaper files are the only evidence as to the number of papers that were published in approximately five decades. Every effort has been made to discover newspapers published during this period, but in the absence of an annual newspaper directory, there is always the possibility that some have not been located.

Where conditions permitted, a personal check of the newspaper files in any depository was productive of much information. When a personal

PREFACE vii

check has been made, the symbol ♦ has been placed between the depository symbol and the holding. In all cases in which a personal check was not made, the information was supplied by the individual depository. This checklist provides a tool with which collections in depositories can be profitably checked.

The first Philadelphia Newspaper Checklist, published in 1937, contained 331 newspaper titles. Additional research, including all titles listed in *Rowell* or *Ayer, American Newspaper Annual, 1880-1908, American Newspaper Annual and Directory, 1909-1929, Directory of Newspapers and Periodicals, 1930-1941,* has resulted in the increase in this number to more than 700 newspaper titles. More than 340 of the newspaper titles which are listed have no known Pennsylvania holdings. For purposes of convenience, those with Pennsylvania holdings and those without these holdings have all been grouped together alphabetically, in order to avoid the necessity of referring to more than one list of newspapers.

In several instances, it has been difficult to determine the line of demarkation between newspapers and magazines, particularly those which are of a religious nature. The early publications of various denominations frequently contained news, vital statistics, commercial advertising, and general as well as secular news. Although in recent years they have nearly all developed into religious magazines, they have been included. Copies of all of these publications have not been found.

The volume herewith presented covers all known newspapers which have been published in the area that is now Philadelphia since 1719, including the former villages of Germantown and Frankford. A second volume, which includes the counties constituting the western part of Pennsylvania, is now in preparation. Under the present Pittsburgh will be found grouped the former divisions such as Allegheny; also, some of the contiguous boroughs. The remainder of the State will be published subsequently.

It is to be hoped that unknown files will eventually find their way into the numerous public depositories, thus reducing the number of newspapers listed which have no known Pennsylvania holdings. It should also arouse greater interest in the preservation of newspapers, which constitute such a valuable historical source. Pennsylvania is more fortunate than many States in the wealth of her newspaper files, especially in the early period.

It is to be hoped that eventually the majority of the newspapers in all of the depositories will be microfilmed, for the sake of preservation. Due to their frail character, many existing files are in a bad state of deterioration, particularly during the period following the Civil War, when the supply of rag paper was insufficient, and first esparto, and later wood pulp came into use.

The cooperation of all those who have made this volume possible is gratefully acknowledged. Particular thanks should go to Mr. Franklin

Price, of the Free Library of Philadelphia, N. W. Ayer & Sons, and all the depositories listed in this volume.

Copies of the *Checklist of Pennsylvania Newspapers, Philadelphia,* are published for distribution to important libraries in Pennsylvania and to a limited number of libraries and Government depositories outside the State. Requests for information regarding any of the former activities of the Survey should be addressed to the Pennsylvania Historical Commission.

J. KNOX MILLIGAN,
State Supervisor.

Philadelphia, Pennsylvania,
March, 1942.

ABBREVIATIONS AND SYMBOLS

abol	Abolitionist
assoc	Associate or Associates
asst	Assistant or Assistants
bw	Bi-weekly
calendar	**Jan.** May **Sept.** Sun. Thurs.
	Feb. **June** **Oct.** **Mon.** **Fri.**
	Mar. July Nov. Tues. Sat.
	Apr. Aug. Dec. Wed.
co	Company
col	Collegiate
comm	Commercial
d	Daily
dem	Democrat
ed.	Editor and edition
educ	Educational
evg	Evening
fed	Federalist
finan	Financial
for	Foreign
frat	Fraternal
fs	Free soil
♦	Holdings actually examined
inc	Incorporated
ind	Independent
ir	Irregular frequency
lit	Literary
Ltd	Limited
m	Monthly
morn	Morning
no	Number
non-part	Non-partisan
pol	Political
prop	Proprietor
pub	Publisher
quar	Quarterly
q.v.	Which see
rel	Religious
rep	Republican
sm	Semi-monthly
sun	Sunday
sup	Supplement
sw	Semi-weekly
temp	Temperance
tw	Tri-weekly
vol	Volume
w	Weekly
/	Issue carries both dates
||	Ceased publication, reason unknown
†	To date
-	From the former to and including the latter
♦	No known holdings
( )	Mutilated
[ ]	Incomplete dates
%	Title varies slightly
*	See Gregory Union List of Newspapers for outside holdings
#	See Brigham Bibliography of American Newspapers, 1600-1820, for outside holdings

DEPOSITORY SYMBOLS

P	Pennsylvania State Library, Harrisburg
P-M	Pennsylvania State Library, Miscellaneous Collection, Harrisburg
PAg	Carnegie Free Library of Allegheny, Pittsburgh
PAlC	Allentown Call, Allentown
PAlHi	Lehigh County Historical Society, Allentown
PAlL	Lehigh County Law Library, Allentown
PAlMu	Muhlenberg College, Allentown
PAlR	Chas. R. Roberts, Allentown
PAltHi	Blair County Historical Society, Altoona
PArdL	Lower Merion Junior High School, Ardmore
PAtM	Tioga Point Museum, Athens
PB	Public Library, Bethlehem
PBG	The Globe-Times, Bethlehem
PBK	Wilbur L. King, 417 First Ave., Bethlehem
PBL	Lehigh University, Bethlehem
PBM	Moravian Office, Bethlehem
PBMa	Moravian Archives, Bethlehem
PBelC	Centre County Court House, Bellefonte
PBf	Carnegie Free Library, Beaver Falls
PBiH	Dr. George Hetrich, Birdsboro
PBloHi	Columbia County Historical Society, Bloomsburg
PBridE	Mrs. David Ellis, Bridgeport
PBro	Free Public Library, Brownsville
PBuE	Dr. W. S. Erdman, Buckingham
PByL	J. P. Lamborn, Berwyn
PByW	David Wilson, Berwyn
PCAB	American Baptist Historical Society, Chester
PCC	Crozer Theological Seminary, Chester
PCHi	Delaware County Historical Society, Chester
PCarlHi	Hamilton Library and Cumberland County Historical Society, Carlisle
PChalK	Samuel King, Chalfont
PChalS	William Swartzlander, Chalfont
PCt	Free Library, Coudersport
PDC	Montour County Court House, Danville
PDoC	Bucks County Court House, Doylestown
PDoHi	Bucks County Historical Society, Doylestown
PE	Public Library, Easton
PEC	Northampton County Court House, Easton
PEHi	Northampton County Historical Society, Easton
PEjC	John S. Correll, Easton
PEL	Lafayette College, Easton
PEbHi	Cambria County Historical Society, Ebensburg
PEr	Public Library, Erie
PFgR	Ralph Rockafellow, Forest Grove
PGLS	Lutheran Theological Seminary, Gettysburg
PGrT	Tribune and Review, Greensburg
PHHi	Dauphin County Historical Society, Harrisburg
PHLC	Lutheran Church House, Harrisburg
PHaC	Haverford College, Haverford
PHartD	Anna Darrah, Hartsville
PHi	Historical Society of Pennsylvania, Philadelphia
PHoHi	Blair County Historical Society, Hollidaysburg
PHsHi	Wayne County Historical Society, Honesdale

x

DEPOSITORY SYMBOLS   xi

PJB	R. N. Branager, Johnstown
PJR	Dwight Roberts, Johnstown
PJT	Johnstown Tribune, Johnstown
PJenkT	Times-Chronicle Office, Jenkintown
PJsK	Mrs. J. H. Krom, Jersey Shore
PKiHi	Armstrong County Historical Society, Kittanning
PLaF	Franklin and Marshall College, Lancaster
PLaHi	Lancaster County Historical Society, Lancaster
PLaL	Landis Valley Museum, Lancaster
PLaN	Lancaster Newspapers, Inc., Lancaster
PLanAl	Sarah Allen, Langhorne
PLewL	Linn Collection, Lewisburg
PLhT	R. H. Thompson, Lock Haven
PMcC	Carbon County Court House, Mauch Chunk
PMcT	Times-News, Mauch Chunk
PMe	Public Library, Meadville
PMedD	Delaware County Institute of Science, Media
PMilD	Milford Dispatch, Milford
PMilHi	Pike County Historical Society, Milford
PMilt	Public Library, Milton
PMontHi	Susquehanna Historical Society & Library, Montrose
PNWilW	Westminster College, New Wilmington
PNazHi	Moravian Historical Society, Nazareth
PNeB	Edward R. Barnsley, Newtown
PNeBr	Mrs. Edward Briggs, Newtown
PNhE	Margaret Ely, New Hope
PNhF	Richard Foulke, New Hope
PNo	Norristown Library Company, Norristown
PNoHi	Montgomery County Historical Society, Norristown
PNoM	Mrs. Wm. E. Montague, Norristown
PNorC	Commissioners' Office, Court House, Northumberland
PP	Free Library of Philadelphia, Philadelphia
PPAP	American Philosophical Society Library, Philadelphia
PPAp	Apprentice Free Library, Philadelphia
PPAT	Athenaeum Library, Philadelphia
PPBa	Philadelphia Bar Association, City Hall, Philadelphia
PPBu	Philadelphia Bulletin Office, Philadelphia
PPCo	County Commissioners' Office, Philadelphia
PPCHi	American Catholic Historical Society, Philadelphia
PPCS	Catholic Standard & Times Office, Philadelphia
PPD	Sunday Dispatch Office, 709 Chestnut St., Philadelphia
PPDe	Philadelphia Democrat-Gazette, Philadelphia
PPDr	Dropsie College, Philadelphia
PPEC	Church House (Episcopal), Philadelphia
PPEHi	The Church Historical Society, Episcopal Divinity School, 42nd & Spruce Sts., Philadelphia
PPER	Publication House Evangelical and Reformed Church, Philadelphia
PPF	Franklin Institute, 20th & Parkway, Philadelphia
PPFfHi	Frankford Historical Society, 1505 Orthodox St., Philadelphia
PPFfN	Frankford News Gleaner Publishing Office, Philadelphia
PPFI	Friends' Intelligencer Publishing Office, Philadelphia

PPG	German Society of Pennsylvania, Spring Garden & Marshall Sts., Philadelphia
PPGB	Germantown Bulletin, Philadelphia
PPGHi	Germantown Historical Society, 5214 Germantown Ave., Philadelphia
PPH	Philadelphia Herald Office, 1631 Germantown Ave., Philadelphia
PPI	Philadelphia Inquirer, Philadelphia
PPJ	Jewish Daily Forward, Philadelphia
PPJMj	Philadelphia Jewish Morning Journal and the Jewish Daily News, Philadelphia
PPK	Krauth Memorial Library, Lutheran Theological Seminary, Philadelphia
PPL	Library Company of Philadelphia, Philadelphia
PPLp	United Lutheran Publication House, Philadelphia
PPM	Mercantile Library, 14 South 10 St., Philadelphia
PPN	Philadelphia News Bureau, Philadelphia
PPNw	Northwest News Office, Philadelphia
PPO	L'Opinione Office, Philadelphia
PPOl	Olney Times Publishing Company, Philadelphia
PPP	S. W. Pennypacker Library, Philadelphia
PPPHi	Presbyterian Historical Society, Philadelphia
PPR	Philadelphia Record, Broad & Wood Sts., Philadelphia
PPRD	Recorder of Deeds Office, Philadelphia
PPRE	Reformed Episcopal Seminary, Philadelphia
PPSD	Sunday Dispatch Office, Philadelphia
PPTU	Sullivan Memorial Library, Temple University, Philadelphia
PPYMHA	Young Men's Hebrew Association, Philadelphia
PPenbB	H. F. Beck, Penbrook
PPeS	Schwenkfelder Historical Society, Pennsburg
PPhoR	Harmon Rees, R. D. #2, Phoenixville
PPi	Carnegie Library of Pittsburgh, Pittsburgh.
PPiHi	Historical Society of Western Pennsylvania, Pittsburgh
PPitE	Pitcairn Express, Pitcairn
PPiUD	Darlington Collection, University of Pittsburgh, Pittsburgh
PPiV	Volksblatt Publishing Company, Pittsburgh
PPoHi	Schuylkill County Historical Society, Pottsville
PPoU	C. W. Unger, Pottsville
PPot	Public Library, Pottstown
PPotW	George F. P. Wanger, Pottstown
PPph	Philadelphia Herald Office, Philadelphia
PRHi	Berks County Historical Society, Reading
PSF	Friends' Historical Library, Swarthmore
PScrG	G. A. R. Memorial Hall, Scranton
PSeSu	Susquehanna University, Selinsgrove
PSew	Public Library, Sewickley
PShH	Mrs. K. C. Heffelfinger, Shamokin
PShN	Shamokin News Dispatch, Shamokin
PShW	Mrs. J. E. Weary, Shamokin
PSom	Public Library, Somerset
PStP	Pennsylvania State College, State College
PStrHi	Monroe County Historical Society, Stroudsburg

DEPOSITORY SYMBOLS

PSuCo	Commissioners' Office, Northumberland County, Sunbury
PSuHi	Northumberland County Historical Society, Sunbury
PToF	A. C. Fanning, Towanda
PToHi	Bradford County Historical Society, Towanda
PU	University of Pennsylvania, Philadelphia
PUB	Current Publishers
PUL	Biddle Law Library, University of Pennsylvania, Philadelphia
PUn	Free Public Library, Uniontown
PVC	Villanova College Library, Villanova
PVfHi	Valley Forge Historical Society, Valley Forge
PW	Warren Library Association, Warren
PWC	Warren County Court House, Warren
PWCl	Frank & Alice Clemons, Warren
PWaHi	Washington County Historical Society, Washington
PWalG	Alexander B. Geary, Wallingford
PWbW	Wyoming Historical and Geological Society, Wilkes-Barre
PWcA	George Ashbridge, West Chester
PWcH	Joseph Hergesheimer, West Chester.
PWcHi	Chester County Historical Society, West Chester
PWcL	Daily Local News, West Chester
PWcP	Maurice B. Pratt, West Chester
PWcT	State Teachers College, West Chester
PWet	Tioga County Treasurer's Office, Wellsboro
PWfF	Westfield Free Press, Westfield
PWmT	Ray Thompson, West Middletown
PWpHi	Lycoming County Historical Society, Williamsport
PYHi	York County Historical Society, York

A Checklist of Pennsylvania Newspapers

PHILADELPHIA COUNTY

ABEND POST (1865-1918) d 1865-1908; w 1908-1918 for.
    Pub. 1868-1872   Aschmied & Co.
          1872-1889   Friedlander & Co.
          1889-1897   Post Printing & Publishing Co.
          1897-1904   Central Newspaper Union
          1904-1911   Alfred Schlesinger
          1911-1918   Ernest B. Fortmann
    Ed. 1895-1897   R. Friedlander
          1897-1902   W. Buergermeister
          1902-1908   A. Timm
          1908-1911   Alfred Schlesinger
          1911-1918   Ernest B. Fortmann

ADVANCE, see Twenty First Ward Advance

ADVERTISER AND MONITOR (1871-1872)
    Pub. & Ed. 1871-1872 Charles B. Hart

ADVOCATE (1885-1919) w ind
    Pub. & Ed. 1888-1919 Advocate Publishing Company
    Ed.   1908-1919 H. S. Moore

AFRO-AMERICAN (1902-1904) w Negro rep
    Pub. & Ed. 1902-1904 W. H. McLean

AGE (Nov. 26, 1836-1842||) w
    Pub. & Ed. 1836-1842 William C. Shryock
        PLhT   1841 July 17
                    1842 Aug. 27
        PNoHi   1837 Jan. 7 (Vol. 1, No. 7)

AGE (1863), see Illustrated New Age

ALBUM, AND THE LADIES WEEKLY GAZETTE, THE, see Philadelphia Album and Ladies' Literary Portfolio

ALEXANDER'S EXPRESS MESSENGER, see Family Messenger and National Gleaner

ALEXANDER'S PICTORIAL MESSENGER, see Family Messenger and National Gleaner

ALEXANDER'S WEEKLY MESSENGER, see Family Messenger and National Gleaner

ALL DAY CITY ITEM, see Item

ALL THE NEWS FOR TWO COPPERS, see Pennsylvania Evening Post and Daily Advertiser

ALLIED MERCURY: OR INDEPENDENT INTELLIGENCER
(Oct. 17, 1781-Nov. 1781||) sw ♦ #
Pub. & Ed. 1781 Oct. 17-1781 Nov. 30   George Kline

ALTE UND DIE NEUE WELT, DIE, (Dec. 9, 1833-Dec. 28, 1844) w for * %
    Pub. 1834 Jan. 4-1842 Apr.   2   J. G. Wesselhoeft
          1842 Apr. 9-1843 Feb. 25   J. G. Wesselhoeft & Co.
                                          (C. L. Rademacher)
          1843 Mar. 18-1844 Mar.   9   Schreiber and Schwacke
          1844 Mar. 16-1844 Sept. 28   J. H. Schwacke
    Ed. 1841 June 5-1842 Nov.   5   Wilhelm Langenheim
          1842 Nov. 12-1844 Dec. 28   Dr. Max Schele de Vere
         PPG   1833 Dec. (9) (forecast advertisement)
                 1834 Jan. (4-11)-(25)-Feb. (1)-(22)-Mar. (1-15)-May (3-10)-June 28, July 4, Aug. (2-17)-(30)-Sept. (6)-Oct. [4-11]-Dec. (25)

AMERICA (1911†) d w tw for *
    AMERYKA (1911-1916) w % ♦
    Pub. 1911-1916   Ruthenian Printing House
    Ed. 1911-1916   Anthony Curkowsky
       continued as
    AMERICA (1916-1941) d (1916-1921) tw (1921-1941)
    Pub. 1916-1922   Ruthenian Catholic Association of Providence
         1922-1927   Ukrainian Catholic Association of Providence
         1927-1941   The Providence Association of the Ukrainian Catholics in America
    Ed. 1916-1918   Vladimir B. Lototsky
         1919-1927   Anthony Curkowsky
         1927-1928   Joseph Nazaruk
         1928-1941   Vladimir B. Lototsky
         PUB   1927 Jan. 1†
         PP   1927 Nov. 19†
         PPiHi   1931 Dec. 31-1932 Mar. 31

AMERICAN (1919-1923) w Negro ♦
    Pub. 1920-1923   Philadelphia American Publishing Co.
    Ed. 1920-1923   Arthur W. Lynch

AMERICAN ADVOCATE, THE, (1844-1845), see Native Eagle and American Advocate

AMERICAN BANNER AND NATIONAL DEFENDER (1850-1856) w *
    AMERICAN BANNER (Apr. 13, 1850-Apr. 12, 1856) w
    Pub. 1855-1856   J. H. Jones & Co.
    Ed. 1855-1856   H. Jones
        P-M   1854 Dec. 16
        PBuE   1855 Dec. 15
        PDoHi   1855 June 16
        PHi   1850 Apr. 13, May 4-Aug. 10, 24-1852 Apr. 10
        PShH   1855 Mar. 10

PHILADELPHIA COUNTY 3

continued as
AMERICAN BANNER AND NATIONAL DEFENDER (Apr. 19, 1856-Nov. 1, 1856) w
 Pub. 1856   J. H. Jones & Co.
 Ed. 1856   H. Jones
  PBuE   1856 May 29
  PDoHi 1856 Nov. 1
  PShH   [1856]

AMERICAN CENTINEL, THE, see Evening Bulletin

AMERICAN CENTINEL AND MERCANTILE ADVERTISER, see Evening Bulletin

AMERICAN CITIZEN (1887-1917) w anti-clerical ♦
 Pub. 1916-1917 American Publishing Co.
 Ed. 1916-1917 R. J. Long

AMERICAN CITIZEN AND THE WEEKLY PHILADELPHIAN (1845-1846) w *
 AMERICAN CITIZEN, THE, (Mar. 29, 1845-1846) w
 Pub. & Ed. 1846 W. H. Brisbane
  PHi   1845 Nov. 22 (Vol. 1, No. 34)
       1846 Jan. 24
  PNoHi 1846 June 18

continued as
AMERICAN CITIZEN AND THE WEEKLY PHILADELPHIAN (1846) w
 Pub. & Ed. 1846 W. H. Brisbane
  PNoHi 1846 Dec. 17

AMERICAN DEMOCRATIC HERALD AND COMMERCIAL GAZETTE (1813-1815) tw d #
 VOICE OF THE NATION (PHOEBUS) (Aug. 12, 1813-1814) tw d
 Pub. & Ed. 1813-1814 Henry Bickley
  The word *Phoebus* was centered above the title *Voice of The Nation* and was omitted from the title in the latter part of March, 1814.
  PDoHi 1813 Sept. 2
  PHi ♦ 1813 Sept. 2

continued as
AMERICAN DEMOCRATIC HERALD AND COMMERCIAL GAZETTE (May 9, 1814-1815) d
 Pub. & Ed. 1814-1815 Andrew C. Mitchell
  The *American Democratic Herald and Commercial Gazette,* suspended May 14, 1814, was resumed July 11, 1814, under the same title.
  PDoHi 1814 July 23
  PP   1814 Sept. 24

AMERICAN EAGLE AND PHILADELPHIA COUNTY DEMOCRAT (July 25, 1836) d dem * ♦

AMERICAN FREE PRESS (1940†)   sm tw
  Pub. 1940-1941   American Free Press Publishing Co.
  Ed. 1940-1941   Ernest Pendrell
    PP   tw 1940 Feb. 15-1941 Feb. 1

AMERICAN FRIEND, THE,   (July 19, 1894†) w lit rel
  Pub. 1894 July 19-1912 Dec. 26 The American Friend Publishing Co.
      1913 Jan. 2-1941 June 19 The Friend Publication Board at Richmond, Indiana
  Ed. 1894 July 19-1906 Dec. 27 Rufus M. Jones
      1907 Jan. 3-1918 Dec. Herman Newman
      1919 Jan. 2-1941 June 19 Walter C. Woodward
    PP
      1894 Aug. 2 (Vol. 1, No. 3)
      1900 Jan. 4, Feb. 1, Mar. 8, Apr. 12, May 3, June 7, Oct. 4, Nov. 8
      1901 Feb. 7, Mar. 7, Apr. 4, May 2, June 6, Oct. 10, Nov. 7, Dec. 5
      1902 Jan. 2, Feb. 6, Mar. 6, Apr. 3, May 8
      1911 Jan.-1913 Nov. 27
      1914 May 28-1917 July 19
      1924 May 1, 15, 22, 29, June 5, 12, 26, July 3, 10, 17, 24, 31, Aug. 21, 28, Sept. 4, 11, 18, 25, Oct. 2, Dec. 4, 11, 18, 25
      1926 Jan. 7-1929 Dec. 26
      1930 Jan. 9, 23, Feb. 6, 20, Mar. 6, 20, Apr. 3, 17, May 1, 8, 29, June 12, 26, July 10, 24, Aug. 21, Sept. 4, 18, Oct. 2, 16, 30, Nov. 13, 27, Dec. 11, 25
      1931 Jan. 8, 22, Feb. 5, 19, Mar. 5, Apr. 2, 16, 30, May 14, 28, June 11, July 23, Sept. 17, Oct. 1
      1932 Jan. 21, July 21, Sept. 1, Nov. 10, 24, Dec. 8, 22
      1933 Jan. 5, 19, Feb. 2, 16, 23, Mar. 2, 16, 30, Apr. 6, 20, May 4, 18-Dec. 28
      1936 May 28
    PSF w 1894 July 19-1905 Mar. 9, 30, Apr. 13-Dec. 21
      1906 Jan. 4-Nov. 8, 22-1907 Mar. 14
      1907 Mar. 28-Apr. 25, May 16, 30-July 11, Oct. 31, Nov. 21, Dec. 12
      1908 Jan. 9, Feb. 13-Apr. 16, 30-May 14, June 4-18, July 2, 16-Aug. 20, Sept. 3-Oct. 1, 15-Dec. 3, 17-31
      1909 Jan. 7-Mar. 1, 15-Dec. 30
      1910 Jan. 6-1912 Oct. 31
      1912 Nov. 14-Dec. 5, 19, 26
      1913 Jan. 2-Dec. 25
      1919 Jan. 2-1923 Mar. 29, Apr. 12, 26-May 10, June 14, Oct. 18-Dec. 27
      1924 Jan. 3-Apr. 10, May 8, June 5, 19, Sept. 25
      1925 Jan. 1-1927 May 12
      1927 May 26-1928 June 28
      1928 July 12-Aug. 23, Sept. 6-Nov. 22, Dec. 13-27
      1929 Jan. 3-1933 July 20
    sm 1929 July 27-1941 June 19

PHILADELPHIA COUNTY 5

AMERICAN GUARDIAN (1868-1870) w temp
    Pub. & Ed. 1868-1870 John Moore

AMERICAN HERALD (1901-1908) w Negro
    Pub. 1905-1908 John Clinton, Jr.
    Ed. 1905-1906 Abel P. Caldwell
         1906-1908 John Clinton, Jr.

AMERICAN MECHANIC (1868-1871) w
    Pub. & Ed. 1870-1871 Frank Smith & Co.

AMERICAN MECHANICS ADVOCATE AND WORKINGMAN'S JOURNAL (1847-1850) w
    Pub. 1847-1850 David E. Thompson
    Ed. 1847-1850 David E. Thompson and Charles S. Bailey
        PHi   1849 June 9
        PPFiHi   1847 Nov. 27

AMERICAN NAVAL AND COMMERCIAL REGISTER, see Finlay's American Naval and Commercial Register

AMERICAN PIONEER AND FIREMAN'S CHRONICLE (1830-1833) w Military
    PIONEER, THE, (Mar. 6, 1830-Feb. 26, 1831) w
    Pub. & Ed. 1830-1831 Wm. W. Weeks and J. Perry
        PHi   1830 Mar. 6-1831 Feb. 26
            continued as
    AMERICAN PIONEER AND MILITARY CHRONICLE (Mar. 5, 1831-Dec. 24, 1831) w
    Pub. & Ed. 1831 Wm. W. Weeks and J. Perry
        PHi   1831 Mar. 5-Dec. 24
        PP   1831 Mar. 5-Apr. 9, May 21-June 4, 25, July 9, 23, Aug. 6, 20, 27, Oct. 29, Nov. 9
        PPL   1831 Mar. 5-Dec. 24
            continued as
    AMERICAN PIONEER AND FIREMAN'S CHRONICLE (Dec. 31, 1831-June 15, 1833||) w
    Pub. & Ed. 1831-1833 Wm. W. Weeks and J. Perry
        PHi   1831 Dec. 31-1832 Feb. 25
        PP   1832 Jan. 28, Feb. 11-18, Mar. 10-17, 31, May 5-12, 26, July 7, 21, Aug. 4, 25, Sept. 8-15, Oct. 6, 20, Nov. 3-10, 24-Dec. 8, 29-1833 Jan. 12
                  1833 Jan. 26, June 15
        PPL   1831 Dec. 31-1832 Feb. 25

AMERICAN PRESBYTERIAN, THE (1856-1870) w rel
    AMERICAN PRESBYTERIAN (Sept. 4, 1856-Oct. 29, 1857) w
    Pub. 1856 Sept. 4-1857 Oct. 29 at Philadelphia
    Ed. 1856 Sept. 4-1856 Oct. 30 Benj. J. Wallace
          1856 Nov. 6-1857 Oct. 29 Benj. J. Wallace, John W. Dulles
        P   1857 July 23-Oct. 29
        PHi   1856 Sept. 4

PP   1856 Sept. 4-1857 Oct. 29
PPPHi   1856 Sept. 4-1857 Oct. 29
           merged with *Genessee Evangelist* (of Rochester, N. Y.)
           continued as

AMERICAN PRESBYTERIAN, AND GENESSEE EVANGELIST, THE, (Nov. 5, 1857-Jan. 10, 1867) w

Pub. 1857 Nov. 5-1863 Dec. 31 at Philadelphia
     1864 Jan. 7-1867 Jan. 10 John W. Mears, at Philadelphia
Ed. 1857 Nov. 5-1858 Aug. 26 Benj. J. Wallace, John W. Dulles, D. C. Houghton
     1858 Sept. 2-1860 Feb. 16 D. C. Houghton
     1860 Feb. 23-1860 July 5 D. C. Houghton, John W. Mears
     1860 July 12-1867 Jan. 10 John W. Mears
P   1857 Nov. 5-1867 Jan. 10
PP   1856 Sept. 4-1861 July 18
           1861 Aug. 1, 8, 22-1862 Dec. 29
           1863 Jan. 1-1867 Jan. 10
PPPHi   1857 Nov. 5-1867 Jan. 10
           continued as

AMERICAN PRESBYTERIAN, THE, (Jan. 17, 1867-Feb. 17, 1870) w

Pub. & Ed. 1867 Jan. 17-1870 Feb. 17 John W. Mears
P   1867 Jan. 17-1870 Feb. 17
PP   1867 Jan. 17-1869 Dec. 30
PPPHi   1867 Jan. 17-1870 Feb. 17
           on Feb. 24, 1870, this paper merged with the *New York Evangelist*

AMERICAN REPUBLICAN (1876-1894) sw

PWcHi   1876 July 29-Dec. 30
           1877 Mar. 10-July 3, 7
           1894 [Jan. 5-Dec. 27]

AMERICAN SATURDAY COURIER (1831-1856) w *

SATURDAY COURIER (May 2, 1831-Dec. 12, 1835) w

Pub. 1831-1835   Woodward & Spragg
     1835   Woodward & Clarke
Ed. 1831-1835   Morton McMichael
PBL ♦   1831 Sept. 3
                  1833 Dec. 14
PDoHi   1832 May 20
                  1833 Sept. 14
                  1835 Sept. 26, Oct. 24
PHi   1832 Sept. 1-1835 Dec. 12
PLaF   1832 Apr. 7-Dec. 15
PP   1832 May 26
PPL   1834 Apr. 22
PWcHi   1835 Oct. 24
                  merged with

PHILADELPHIA SATURDAY COURIER (Dec. 19, 1835-Mar. 13, 1843) w

Pub. & Ed. 1835-1843 A. McMakin and E. Holden
PBL ♦   1836 July 30, Aug. 13, Sept. 3, 24-Oct. 15, Nov. 5-Dec. 10, 24
           1837 Jan. 28-Feb. 11, Mar. 11-25, May 6-June 3, 24-July 22, Aug. 5, 26, Sept. 2, 16-Nov. 18, Dec. 2-30
           1838 Jan. 6-Feb. 10, Mar. 10-July 28, Aug. 11, Dec. 15, 22

PHILADELPHIA COUNTY 7

	1839 Feb. 16, Apr. 6, Sept. 7-Nov. 9, 30-Dec. 28
	1840 Jan. 4-18, Feb. 1, 29-Mar. 21, Apr. 4-25, May 16-July 4, Aug. 1
PDoHi	1836 July 2, Aug. 20
	1838 Mar. 10
PHi	1835 Dec. 19-1841 Mar. 13
PMe	1841 Mar. 13
PPCHi	1838 Jan. 20, Sept. 15, Dec. 29
	1839 Oct. 5-Nov. 9, 23, Dec. 7, 14
	1840 Jan. 11, Mar. 14, 28, Apr. 4, May 2, 16, 23, June 13, July 11-Aug. 1, 15-29
PPL	1837 Jan.-1839 Mar. 16
PWcHi	1836 May 14
	continued as

SATURDAY COURIER (Mar. 18, 1843-Mar. 14, 1848) w

Pub. 1843-1845   A. McMakin & E. Holden
     1846   Mrs. E. Holden
     1847-1848   Andrew McMakin
Ed. 1843-1845   A. McMakin & E. Holden
     1847-1848   Andrew McMakin

PBL ♦	1845 Nov. 22
PCt	1841 July 24-1843 Mar. 11
PHi	1841 Mar. 20-1848 Mar. 4
PLhT	1846 Feb. 14
PP	1843 Nov. 25
	1844 May 25
	1845 Feb. 1, June 21
	1847 Jan. 30
PPCHi	1843 Jan. 7-Dec. 30
PPL	1842 Mar. 19-1844 Aug.
	1845 Mar. 15-1846 Feb.
	1846 Mar. 14-1848 Mar. 11
PShH	1836 Oct. 1, 8
PW	1837 July 29
PWcHi	1846 Mar. 28, Apr. 4
	continued as

McMAKIN'S MODEL AMERICAN COURIER (Mar. 18, 1848-Mar. 1, 1851) w

Pub. & Ed. 1848-1851   Andrew McMakin

PCarlHi	1850 Apr. 6, July 20
PDoHi	1849 Feb. 17, 24, Mar. 3, Dec. 29
PHi	1848 Mar. 18-1851 Mar. 1
PNoHi	1850 July 20-1851 Mar. 1
PP	1848 Mar. 25
	1849 Oct. 20
	1850 Oct. 12
PPCHi	1848 Oct. 28
PPL	1848 Mar. 18
	1849 Mar. 10-1851 Mar. 1
	continued as

AMERICAN SATURDAY COURIER (Mar. 8, 1851-Nov. 8, 1856) w

Pub. & Ed. 1851-1856   Andrew McMakin

P-M	1853 Jan. 8
PHi	1852 Jan. 3-Dec. 25
PNoHi	1851 Mar. 8-1853 Dec. 3
	1853 Dec. 17-1854 Aug. 12
	1854 Aug. 26-Nov. 10, 24-1856 Sept. 6

AMERICAN SATURDAY COURIER, continued
        1856 Sept. 20-Nov. 8
    American Saturday Courier was absorbed Nov. 15, 1856, by *The Evening Bulletin.* (q.v.)

AMERICAN SENTINEL, see Evening Bulletin

AMERICAN STAR, THE ("L'Etoile Americaine") (1794) pol Eng. & French tw #
    AMERICAN STAR, or HISTORICAL, POLITICAL, CRITICAL, AND MORAL JOURNAL, THE, (Feb. 1, 1794-Mar. 25, 1794) tw
    Pub. 1794   C. C. Tanguy de la Boissière
        PHi   1794 Feb. 4, 6, 11, 13, 18, 20, 25, Mar. 1-18, 25
    AMERICAN STAR, THE, ("L'Etoile Americaine") (Apr. 1, 1794-May 3, 1794)
    Pub. 1794   C. C. Tanguy de la Boissière
        PHi   Apr. 1, 10, 17, May 1, 3

AMERICAN STATESMAN AND SPIRIT OF THE AGE (Mar. 27, 1840) d * ♦

AMERICAN WEEKLY MERCURY (1719-1746) w #
    Pub. 1719-1720   Andrew Bradford and John Copson
            1720-1739   Andrew Bradford
            1739-1740   Andrew Bradford and William Bradford
            1740-1742   Andrew Bradford
            1742-1743   Cornelia Bradford
            1743-1744   Isaiah Warner and Cornelia Bradford
            1744-1746   Cornelia Bradford
    Ed. 1743-1744   Isaiah Warner
        PDoHi   1719 Dec. 22-1722 Jan. 17
                     1722 Jan. 20-1723 Mar. 28
                     1723 Apr. 11-Dec. 31
                     1743 Mar. 24-30
        PHi   [1725 Jan. 1-1728 Dec. 31]
               1729 Jan. 1-1742 Dec. 31
               1743 Apr. 28
        PLaHi   1721 Dec. 26-1722 Jan. 16
                 1722 Jan. 30-1723 Mar. 28
                 1723 Apr. (11)-Dec. 31
        PP   1719 Dec. 22-1724 Jan. 7
        PPAP   1719 Dec. 22-1723 Dec. 31
                1733 Feb. 28-Aug. 9, 30-1734 Feb. 19
        PPi   1719-1721
        PPL   1719 Dec. 22-1723 Apr. 11-Aug. (1)-1726 Dec. 3
             1726 Dec. 15-1727 May 18
             1727 June 1-1728 Dec. 5
             1728 Dec. 24-1735 Feb. 25
             1735 May 11-Sept. 11, 25-1736 Feb. 24
             1736 Mar. 9-1737 Jan. 25
             1737 Feb. 8-1738 Apr. 20
             1738 May 4, 18-1739 Jan. 11
             1739 Jan. 23-Apr. 5, 19-1740 May 1
             1740 May 15-July 10, 24-Aug. 28, Sept. 11-Nov. 6, 20-1745 Aug. 8
             1745 Aug. 29-1746 Jan. 1

PHILADELPHIA COUNTY 9

    PRHi   1722 Jan. 1-Dec. 31
    PU   1719 Dec. 22-1724 Jan. 7
    PWcHi   1719 Dec. 22, 29 (Reprints)
                 1720 Jan. 5-Mar. 8, 17-Dec. 8, 13-
                 1724 Mar. 3, 12-1725 Dec. 9
                 1725 Dec. 21-1726 Dec. 1
                 1726 Dec. 13-1728 Dec. 5
                 1728 Dec. 18-1730 Feb. 10
                 1730 Feb. 19-1736 Mar. 23
                 1736 Apr. 1
                 1738 Mar. 7, 23-Apr. 20, May 4, 18-1739 Jan. 11
                 1739 Jan. 23-Feb. 28, Mar. 14-1745 Dec. 24
                 1746 Jan. 1-21, 29-Mar. 18, 27-Apr. 24, May 8-22

AMERICAN WEEKLY MESSENGER, see Family Messenger and National Gleaner

AMERICAN WEEKLY SENTINEL, see Native American

AMERIKANISCHER BEOBACHTER, DEM HANDEL UND LANDBAU GEWIDMET (1808-1811) w for #
    Pub. 1808-1811   Conrad Zentler
        PDoHi   1810 June 21

AMERIKANISCHER CORRESPONDENT, see Philadelphia'er Telegraph, Und Deutsches Wochenblatt

AMERIKANSKI SRBOBRAN (1914-1915) w for rel ♪
    Pub. 1914-1915   Servian Orthodox Society
    Ed. 1914-1915   M. Mevosh

AMERYKA, see America

ARGUS (1888-1891) w ind ♪
    Pub. & Ed. 1888-1891 J. Woods Maginley

ARTHUR'S HOME GAZETTE (Sept. 7, 1850-1855) w *
    Pub. & Ed. 1850-1855 T. S. Arthur
        PBL ♪   1852 Apr. 3, May 1, 15
        PP   1852 May 29

ASSOCIATED PHILADELPHIA COMMUNITY NEWSPAPERS
    The following titles are found in their alphabetical order of appearance in the checklist:
    Central City News, Feltonville Weekly, Frankford Dispatch, Frankford Gazette, Frankford News Gleaner, Germantown Courier, Germantown Telegraph, Girard Ave. Home News, Journal of North Philadelphia, Kensington News, Lawndale Press, Lindley-Olney News, Logan Beacon, Manayunk Review, Northeast News, North Philadelphia Globe, North Philadelphia News, Olney Times, Overbrook Mirror, South Philadelphian, West Philadelphia Times, West Philadelphia Tribune, Wynnefield Forum.

AURORA (Oct. 1, 1790-April 25, 1835) d tw w
GENERAL ADVERTISER AND POLITICAL, COMMERCIAL, AGRICULTURAL AND LITERARY JOURNAL (Oct. 1, 1790-Dec. 31, 1790) d #

Pub. & Ed. 1790-1791 Benjamin Franklin Bache
    PHi   1790 Oct. 1-Dec. 31
    PPF   1790 Oct. 2-Dec. 31
    PPL   1790 Oct. 1-Dec. 31
    PRHi   1790 Dec. 25

continued as

GENERAL ADVERTISER AND POLITICAL, COMMERCIAL AND LITERARY JOURNAL, THE (Jan. 1, 1791-Aug. 15, 1791) d

Pub. & Ed. 1791   Benjamin Franklin Bache
    P   1791 Jan. 1-Aug. 15
    PAtM   1791 Jan. 1-Aug. 15
    PHi   1791 Jan. 1-Aug. 15
             Missing:
             1791 Feb. 24, Apr. 19
    PPiUD   1791 Feb. 19-Aug. 15
    PPL   1791 Jan. 1-Apr. 25
             1791 Apr. 27-Aug. 15

continued as

GENERAL ADVERTISER (Aug. 16, 1791-Nov. 7, 1794) d #

Pub. & Ed. 1791-1794 Benjamin Franklin Bache
    P   1791 Aug. 16-1794 Nov. 7
    PAtM   1791 Aug. 16-Dec. 20
    PDoHi   1794 Feb. 19
    PHi   1791 Aug. 16-1794 Nov. 7
    PPF   1791 Oct. (1-3)-Nov. 15, 17-19, 22-26, 29-1792 Mar. 8
             1792 Mar. 10-(16)-May 4, 7-14, 16-June (8)-13, 16-July (2)-Sept. (17)-(22)-Oct. (18)-1793 Jan. (23-24)-25
             1793 Jan. 28-Feb. 15, 18-June 13, 15-July (8)-10, 12-22, 25-30, Aug. 1-(2)-6, 8-27, 30, 31, Sept. 4-6, 9, 10, 13, 16, 19, 23, 26, Nov. 26-Dec. 5, 7-9, 11, 13, 31
    PPiUD   1791 Aug. 16-Nov. 2
             1793 July 1-Dec. 31
    PPL   1791 Aug. 16-1794 Nov. 7
    PWaHi   1792 Jan. 4-Apr. 23
             1793 Apr. 8

continued as

AURORA GENERAL ADVERTISER (Nov. 8, 1794-1824) d tw w *

Pub. 1794 Nov. 8-1798 Sept. 10   Benjamin Franklin Bache
    1798 Nov. 1-1798 Nov. 13   Margaret H. Bache
    1798 Nov. 14-1800 Mar. 7   for the heirs of Benj. Franklin Bache
    1800 Mar. 8-1807 Nov. 2   William Duane
    1807 Nov. 3-1809 Jan. 1   William J. Duane & Co.
    1809 Jan. 2-1810 May 14   Duane & Co.
    1810 May 15-1813 May 3   William Duane
    1813 May 4-1815 June 16   James Wilson

PHILADELPHIA COUNTY 11

        1815 June 17-1822   William Duane
        1822-1824   Richard Penn Smith
        1823   Joseph M. Sanderson
Ed. 1794-1798   Benjamin Franklin Bache
     1798-1822   William Duane
     1822-1824   Richard Penn Smith
     1823   John Sanderson

Tri-Weeklies were published, *Bache's Philadelphia Aurora* (earliest copy located, June 14, 1797); *The Philadelphia Aurora* (March 10, 1800-Nov. 7, 1800); *Aurora For The Country* (Nov. 7, 1800-June 2, 1817); *Aurora* (June 17, 1817-1821). Weekly edition published, *Aurora Weekly* (June 19, 1810-1821).

```
P                  d    1796 Jan. 1-1811 Dec. 31
                        1818 Jan. 1-June 30
                   tw   1799 Aug. 2-1802 Dec. 24
                        1805 Jan. 2-1809 May 10
P-M                     1805 Apr. 30, May 1
                        1807 Apr. 30, May 1
PBelC                   1807 Sept. 7
                        1818 May 28, 29
PBL    ♦           sw   1823 Sept. 17
PBloHi             tw   1803 Jan. 26
PBMa               d    1795 Jan. 29
PCarlHi            d    1802 Feb. 2
                   tw   1801 Jan. 31/Feb. 1, Oct. 10/12
                        1803 Jan. 5/6, 23/24-Dec. 29/30
                        1804 Jan. 3/4-May 10/11
                        1807 May 2/4
                        1808 Jan. 14/15-19/20, Aug. 25/26, Oct. 13/14,
                             27/28, Dec. 17/19
                        1810 May 1/2, Nov. 3/5
                        1811 Jan. 1/2, 12/13, 14/15, Mar. 12/13
                        1812 Aug. 25/26
                        1813 Apr. 10/11-Nov. 25/26
                        1814 Dec. 29/30
                        1815 Mar. 14/15
                        1816 June 1, 6/7-16/17, 22/24
PCHi               d    1795 Oct. 9
PDoHi              d    1795 Jan. (15), Nov. 20
                        1797 Feb. 22
                        1798 Feb. 3, Mar. 30, Nov. 28, Dec. 1, 13, 26
                        1799 Jan. 9
                        1800 Apr. 11, 15, May 8, 21, 22, June 9-14, 20, 21,
                             25, 28, 30, July 1, 3, 4
                        1801 Mar. 6
                        1803 Mar. 9, May 14, Sept. 3
                        1804 Apr. 2
                        1805 Jan. 30
                        1807 Oct. 13
                        1809 Aug. 9
                        1812 Oct. 20-23, Nov. 4, 5, 19, 25, 27, 30, Dec. 3, 4
                        1813 Apr. 22, May 19, June 15, Aug. 12-17, Oct.
                             29, Nov. 4, 16, Dec. 24
                        1814 Jan. 14, May 26, June 9, July 18, 20, Aug. 17,
                             31, Sept. 6, 17, Nov. 10, Dec. 20, 27, 29
                        1815 Jan. 4, 7, 11-13, 17-26, Mar. 1-3, 6
                        1816 Nov. 19
                        1817 May 13, 14, July 4
```

AURORA, *continued*

		1818 May 27, July 30
		1820 Sept. 26
	sw	1823 Sept. 17
	tw	1801 Jan. 1/2-22/23, 27/28-Feb. 5/6, 10/11-21/23, Mar. 14/16, 21/23, Apr. 14/15, May 2/4, 5/6, 9/11-16/18, 21/22-June 2/3, 6/8, 9/10, 23/24, 27/29, 30/July 1, 25/27-Sept. 12/14, Oct. 20/21, 31/Nov. 2, 12/13, 14/16, Dec. 1/2, 10/11, 12/14, 22/23-29/30, 31/-1802 Jan. 1.
		1802 Jan. 2/4-21/22, 26/27-Apr. 13/14, 24/26-29/30, May 8/10, 15/17, 18/19, 22/24, 27/28, June 3/4-July 27/28, Aug. 3/4, Sept. 11/13, 18/20-23/24, Oct. 1/2, 7/8, 26/27, Nov. 4/5, 9/10
		1805 Feb. 9/11
		1806 Mar. 1/3, 4/5, 11/12-25/26, 29/31, Apr. 3/4-26/28, June 10/11, 17/18, 24/25, 28/30, July 8/9, 10/11, 31/Aug. 1-12/13, 16/18, 19/20, 23/25-28/29, Sept. 2/3, 4/5, 9/10, 20/22-Oct. 14/15, 18/20-23/24, Nov. 4/5, 6/7, 11/12, 20/21, 25/26, Dec. 2/3, 13/15-23/24, 30/31
		1807 Jan. 1/2, 6/7-10/12, 15/16-22/23, May 7/8
		1808 May 12/13
		1809 Feb. 23/24
PEC	tw	1812 Sept. 15/16-Dec. 19/21, 26/28, 31/1813 Jan. 1
		1814 Jan. 1/2-May 14/15, 19/20-Dec. 29/30
PHi		1794 Nov. 8-1822 Dec. 31
PHsHi		1808 July 22
PLaHi		1805 Aug. 10-1806 Aug. 30
		1812 Dec. 3-1818 Nov. 11
		1818 Dec. 7-1820 Dec. 4
PNoHi		1797 Dec. 22
		1816 Mar. 5, 6
		1817 Jan. 9, 10
		1818 Oct. 20, 21
		1819 Aug. 20, 21
		1820 Jan. 25, 26
PP		1798 Aug. 28
		1799 May 1, 13, June 28, Aug. 6, 22, 23, Dec. 12
		1800 Jan. 30
		1804 Dec. 19, 20, 22
		1808 July 6
		1813 May 18
		1815 Jan. 17, July 29, Oct. 19
		1816 June 15, Aug. 20
		1817 Feb. 8, 10
		1818 Apr. 2, 3, 23, 24, Aug. 13, 14, Sept. 22, 23
		1819 Nov. 9, 10, 23, 24, Dec. 4, 6-8, 14, 15, 21-29
		1820 Jan. 1, 3, 15, 17, 20, 21, 22, 25-31, Mar. 8, June 24, July 8, 10, Sept. 11, Nov. 22, 28, 29, 30
		1821 Aug. 2, 3
		1824 Nov. 27
		1825 Aug. 8, 16, 19, Sept. 10, 27, Nov. 30
		1826 Nov. 11
		1827 Aug. 20, 21
	tw	1812 Mar. 14/16, Aug. 20/21
		1813 Jan. 2/4
		1815 Jan. 17/18, July 15/17, 29/31, Oct. 19/20
		1816 June 15/17, Aug. 20/21
		1817 Feb. 8/10

PHILADELPHIA COUNTY 13

                    1818 Apr. 2/3, 23/24, Aug. 13/14, Sept. 22/23
                    1819 Oct. 25, Nov. 9/10, 23/24, Dec. 4/6, 7/8, 14/15, 21/22-28/29
                    1820 Jan. 1/3, 15/17, 20/21, 22/23, 25/26-29/31, Feb. 22/23, Mar. 8/9, June 24/25, July 8/10, Nov. 22/23, 28/29, Dec. 22/23, 29/30
                    1821 Aug. 2/3
PPF   d 1795 Jan. 2, 5-10, 13-Feb. 4, 6-18, 20-July 1, 3-9, 11-Aug. 21, 24-Sept. 4, 7-Oct. 9, 12-Nov. 4, 12-30
                    1796 Jan. (6)-Sept. (12)-Dec. 9, 12-31
                    1798 Nov. 1, 3
                    1799 Feb. 1, 4-Apr. 5, 8, May 20, 22-27, 29-31, June 1, 4-18, 20, 21, 24-Aug. 27, 30-Oct. 8, 10-21, 23-Nov. 2, 5-18, 20-Dec. 24, 27-1800 Dec. (8)-(10)-31
                    1802 Jan. 1-Mar. 15, 17-June 23, 25-28, 30-July 13, 15-Aug. 7, 10-(14-15)-26, 28, 31, Oct. 11, 13-18, 20-29, Nov. 3-1805, June (13)
                    1805 June (14)-Aug. (8)-1807 Dec. 28
                    1807 Dec. 31-1808 Jan. 18
                    1808 Jan. 20-Dec. 31
                    1810 Jan. 1-Mar. 9, 12-Sept. (6)-Dec. 31
                    1814 Jan. 1-Dec. 1, 5-8, 10-12, 16-19, 21-26, 29-31
                    1816 Jan. 1-1818 Apr. 4
                    1818 Apr. 7-1820 Mar. (30)-Apr. 11
                    1820 Apr. 13-25, 27-June 29, July 1-Aug. 19, 22-(25)-Sept. 1, 4-1822 Sept. 5
                    1822 Sept. 7, Nov. 18, 20-Dec. (28)-31
            tw 1803 Jan. 25/26-May (5/6)-June (25/26)-July 3/4, 7/8-Sept. 21/22, 24/25-Dec. (14/15)-25/26, 29/31
                    1804 Jan. 5/6-July 3/4, 6/7-Nov. (1/2)-15/16, 20/21-1805 July 3/4
                    1805 July 6/7-(26/27)-Oct. (23/24)-1806 July 3/4
                    1806 July 7/8-Aug. 5/6, 9/11, 12/13, 16/17-(28/29)-Dec. 31
PPFfHi d 1821-1822
PPi   1796 Mar. 3-19, 28-Apr. 7, 9, 10, 12-29, May 3, 5-19, 21-June 9, 11, 16, 18-24, 26-July 4, 6, 8-Aug. 21, Sept. 4-11, 24- Oct. 7, 15-Nov. 14, 19, 25, 27-Dec. 5
                    1798 Aug. 20, 22-24, 26-Sept. 8, Nov. 1, 4-16, 24-Dec. 7, 9-18, 20-25, 27-31
                    1799 Jan. 1-14, 17-30, Feb. 2-Mar. 1, 3, 5-21, 30-Apr. 16, 18-22, 25, May 20, 23-28, 30-July 2, 4, 6, 7, 9-Aug. 7, 10-19, 22-Sept. 4, 26, 27, 29-Oct. 4, 6, 8, 9, 11-16, 19, 20, 22, 24-Nov. 8, 10-15 17, 19-22, 24, 26, Dec. 13, 21-28, 31
                    1800 Jan. 1-3, 5-8, 10, 12-Feb. 11, 13-18, 20, 29, Mar. 10-21, 23, 25, Apr. 11, 13-23
PPiHi   1804 Jan. 3-1805 Jan. (24)-June 18
                    1805 June 20-26, 28-July 4, 7-14, 16-22, 24-30, Aug. 1, 3-13, 15, 17-20, 22, 24-26, Sept. 12, 20-22, 24, 26, Oct. 8, 11-14, 16, 18-24, 26, 27, Nov. 2, 5-10, 14, 22-26, 29-Dec. 2, 5-16, 19-26, 28, 29, 31
                    1809 Jan. 2, 4-30, Feb. 1-Mar. 2, 4-9, 11-13, 16-17, 29-(31)-July 7, 9-Aug. 2, 4-Sept. 21, 23-Oct. 22, 24-Nov. 12, 14-16, 19-Dec. (2)-12, 14-31

AURORA, *continued*

PPiUD   1799 Jan. 1-22, 24-31, Feb. 2-Mar. 11, 19-28, 30-May 13, 15-17, 19-31, June 2, 3, 5-16, 18-21, 23-July 9, 11-Aug. 8, 10-30, Sept. 1-3, 13, 15-(29)-Oct. (4)-7, 17, 25-Nov. 3, 5-8, 10, 20, 22-24, 27-Dec. 16
1812 Nov. 2-1813 Feb. 3
1813 Feb. 6-Mar. 4, 6-Aug. 31, Sept. 2, 3, 5-Oct. 19, 21-Nov. 26, 28-Dec. 31

PPL   1794 Nov. 8-1797 Apr. 29
1797 May 4-Aug. 1, 3-14, 16-21, 23, 26-Oct. 24, 28-1798 Feb. 21
1798 Feb. 23-Mar. 29, 31-Apr. 11, 13-27, 30- June 15, 18-29, July 2-Sept. 7, 10-Nov. 12, 15-1799 Jan. 4
1799 Jan. 7-Aug. 27, 31-Sept. 14, 17-Oct. 21, 24-Dec. 24, 27-1800 June 19
1800 June 21-July 4, 7-31
1801 Jan. 1-Dec. 4, 7-31
1802 Jan. 2-Feb. 17, 19-Mar. 24, 26-Dec. 31
1803 Jan. 1-8, 11-Nov. 16, 18-Dec. 19, 21-31
1804 Jan. 3-30, Feb. 1, 2, 4-13, 15-Apr. 12, 14-June 30, Aug. 1-Dec. 29
1805 Jan. 2-1806 July 4
1806 July 7-Oct. 20, 22-1809 Jan. 31
1809 Feb. 2-1812 Sept. 2
1812 Sept. 4-1817 July 4
1817 July 7-Oct. 23, 25-Dec. 31
1818 Jan. 2-1821 Dec. 31
1822 Jan. 2-1824 Nov. 19

PPM   1798 Mar. 21, 23-Apr. 17, 20-May 17, 21-July 4, 6-14, 18-21, 24-Sept. 3, 6-10, Nov. 1-9, 12-1799 Jan. 14
1799 Jan. 16-23, 26-Feb. 11, 14-Apr. 10, 13- May 2, 7-13, 16, 17, 21, 22, 30-June 13, 18-24, 27-July 4, 6-29, Aug. 1-27, 30-Sept. 23, 26-1800 Mar. 13
1800 Mar. 15-May 13, 15-June 2, 4-July 4, 6-Aug. 10, 12-20, 24-Dec. 31
1805 Jan. 1-22, 24, 26-30, Feb. 1-Mar. 8, 11, 13-Dec. 31
1809 Jan. 2-July 4, 6-Aug. 11, 14-Nov. 18, 21-Dec. 30
1812 Jan. 1-Dec. 31
1816 Jan. 1-June 29

PPot   1795 Aug. 28
1797 Nov. (16)
1799 Dec. 16
1805 Jan. 12, Mar. 12, 13, 16, 18, Apr. 9, 10, May 2-4, 6-10, 12-Dec. 31
1806 Nov. 29
1807 Feb. 24, July 7-10, 15, 18, 20, 28, 29, Sept. 16, Dec. 31
1808 Jan. 1-Dec. 31
1809 Jan. 2-Dec. 29
1811 Jan. 3-Dec. 31

PPoU   tw   [1801-1804]
[1812-1815]

PRHi   d   1798 Nov. 22-1799 Apr. 24
1799 July 20-Nov. 7

PHILADELPHIA COUNTY 15

```
                    1805 Dec. 31-1806 Dec. 30
                    1808 June 7-July 10
PU          tw      1797 Nov. (16)
            d       1797 Feb. 8, 10-16, 18-May 19, 22-Aug. 1, 3-Sept.
                         8, 11-21, 30, Oct. 4-18, 20-Dec. 30
                    1798 Jan. 1-Mar. 31, Apr. 4-June 23, 26-July 27,
                         Aug. 2-15, 17-Sept. 5, Nov. 3-Dec. (31)
                    1799 Jan. 1-14, 16-Feb. (5)-18, 20-Apr. 5, 8-May
                         18, 20-June 29, July 2-23, 25-Aug. 5, 7-27,
                         30-Oct. 8, 10-21, 23, 25-Nov. 12, 15, 16, 19-
                         Dec. 4, 6-24, 27, 28
                    1801 Jan. 1-Mar. 4, 6-July (6)-Dec. 31
                    1803 Jan. 1-8, 11-19, 22-Apr. 1, 4-8, 11-Nov. 28, 30-
                         Dec. 31
                    1804 Jan. 4-Feb. 4, 8-Apr. 16, 18-May 21, 24, 26-
                         June 12, 14-26, 28-July 9, 11-14, (19), 21-24,
                         26, 27, (30)-Aug. (24), 27, 28, 30-Sept. 26,
                         28-Nov. 9, 12, 13, 15-1806 May 27
                    1806 May 29-Dec. 23, 26, 27, 30-1808 Dec. 31
                    1809 Oct. (4)-(9)-17, 19-Nov. 8, 10-(15)-20, 23-
                         (25)-30, Dec. 2-(7)-(9)-21, 23-30
                    1810 Jan. 1-Mar. (6)-9, 12-July (9)-Aug. 21, 23-
                         1811 Jan. 4
                    1811 Jan. (7), 11-23, 25-28, 31-Feb. (1)-(4)-6, 12,
                         13, (16), 18, 25, (28), Mar. (4), 6, (8)-(11),
                         12, 14-19, 21-25, 28, (29), Apr. (1-2)-(22)-
                         (25)-May (1), (2), 6, 8, 13, 17, 18, 22-24,
                         27-31, June 3, 7, (10), 11, (15), 24, 26, 29-July
                         6, 11-15, 19, 20, 26, 27, 31, Aug. 1, 5, 8, 9,
                         12, Sept. 17, 19, 23, 24, 26, (27, 28), Oct. 1, 2,
                         (5), 8, 11, 17, (18), 23, 26, Nov. 6, (7), 9,
                         (13), 19, 20, 22, 25-Dec. 4, 6-9, 11-13, 16-19,
                         21-31
                    1812 Jan. 2-(4)-8, 11-15, 17-22, (24)-(29)- Feb
                         (1)-(5)-19, 21-(24)-(26)-Mar. 11
                    1813 Jan. 1-(20)-(29)-Feb. (5)-(12)-Mar. (4)
                         Apr. 2, 5-(27)-Aug. 4, 6-(19), 21-Sept. 25
                         28-Oct. (12)-Nov. 2, 4-Dec. 10, 13-1814 Aug.
                         31
                    1814 Sept. 2, 5-8, 12-15, 17-Nov. 17, 19-Dec. 12
                         15-(23)-(27)-31
                    1815 Jan. 2-27, 30-Feb. 11, 14-Mar. (29)-July 25
                         27-Nov. 7, 9-16, 18-Dec. 11, 13-21, 23-25, 30
                    1816 Jan. 1-8, 10-June 7-(8)-Dec. 30
                    1817 Jan. 1-24, Feb. 1-25, 27, 28, Mar. 3-24, 26-31,
                         June 20-1818 Apr. 4
                    1818 Apr. 7-1819 Feb. 11
                    1819 Feb. 13-May 11, 13-Sept. 6, 8-17, 20-Oct. 6,
                         8-11, 13-1820 Feb. 10
                    1820 Feb. 12-25, 28-June (20)-July 5, 8-29, Aug.
                         1-16, 18-Sept. 19, 21-Dec. 1, 4-30
                    1823 July 1-Oct. 13, 15-Dec. 31
PUn                 1803 Jan. 27, Dec. 20
                    1806 Mar. 11
PWaHi               1803 May 21
                    1804 Dec. 4, 5
                    1807 Mar. 2
PWcHi       d       1797 Dec. 14
                    1799 Sept. 14
```

AURORA, *continued*

                  1801 May 28
                  1806 Nov. 6
                  1808 May 10
                  1809 Jan. 6
                  1812 Jan. 27
                  1814 July 7
                  1817 July 8
        tw 1800 Sept. 30/Oct. 1
                  1802 Jan. 16/18, Feb. 2/3, 20/22, June 15/16, July 22/23, Aug. 26/27, Oct. 2/4, Nov. 6/8, 9/10, Dec. 14/15, 18/20
                  1803 Feb. 8/9, Apr. 7/8, 12/13, 23/25, June 21/22, (23/24), Aug. 23/24, Oct. 20/21, 22/24, 29/31, Nov. 24/25, 29/30, Dec. 10/12, 13/14
                  1804 Jan. 21/23, Feb. 23/24, Mar. 10/12, 15/16, 20/21, Apr. (5/6), 10/11, 12/13, May 5/7, 10/11, 22/23, June 19/20, 21/22, 23/25, 30/July 2, 5/6-10/11, 26/27, Aug. 14/15, 16/17, Sept. 6/7, 13/14, 22/24, Oct. 13/15, 18/19, Nov. 6/7, 8/9, 29/30, Dec. 13/14, 15/17
                  1805 Jan. 5/7, 22/23-26/28, Feb. 14/15, Apr. 4/5, 9/10, 11/12, 18/19, 30/May 1, 4/6, 7/8, 11/13, 14/15, 21/22, 30/31, June 4/5, 11/12, 20/21, July 23/24, Aug. 1/2, 15/16, 20/21, 31/Sept. 2, 10/11, 19/20, Oct. 12/14
                  1806 Jan. 2/3, 14/15, 21/22, Apr. 1/2, 15/16, May 17/19, June 3/4, July 17/18, Sept. 20/22, 30/Oct. 1, 18/20, Nov. 8/10, 22/24
                  1807 Jan. 3/5, 31/Feb. 2, 14/16, 19/20, 24/25, 26/27, Mar. 28/30, Apr. 11/13, May 2/4, 12/13, 23/25, July 21/22, Sept. 5/7, Oct. 22/23, Nov. 27/28
                  1808 Mar. 1/2, May 3/4, 14/16, June 11/13, July 19/20, 28/29, Sept. 10/12, 24/26, Nov. 5/7, Dec. 6/7, 27/28, 31-1809 Jan. 2
                  1809 Mar. 2/3, Apr. 8/10, June 1/2, Sept. 19/20, Oct. 3/4, Nov. 18/20, 25/27
                  1810 Feb. 6/7, Apr. 10/11, May 17/18, June 12/13, Aug. 25/27, Nov. 15/16, 27/28, 29/30
                  1811 Mar. (12/13), Apr. 9/10, 16/17, Sept. 7/9
                  1812 July 11/13, 30/31, Oct. 29/30
                  1813 Jan. 7/8
                  1814 June 7/8, Dec. 3/5
                  1815 May 13/15
                  1816 Oct. 1/2
       PYHi w [1817-1818]

                  merged with *Franklin Gazette* (q.v.) and continued as

AURORA AND FRANKLIN GAZETTE (1824-1828) d tw w *
                d Nov. 22, 1824-Apr. 13, 1828
              tw Nov.   1824-Aug. 21, 1827||
                w 1824-1828||
Pub. 1824-1828   John Norvell
Ed. 1824-1827   Richard Penn Smith
    1824-1828   John Norvell
    P   1827 Apr. 18-1828 Apr. 13
    PDoHi d 1825 Aug. 26
                 1826 July 11

```
              tw   1825 May 23/24
                   1827 Apr. 20/21
       PEL    d    1828 Feb. 12
       PP     d    1824 Nov. 27
                   1825 Aug. 8, 16, 19, Sept. 10, 27, Nov. 30
                   1826 Nov. 11
                   1824 Dec. 3/4, 20/21, 22/23
              tw
                   1825 Jan. 3/4, 7/8, 10/11-14/15, 17/18, 24/25, 31/
                        Feb. 1, 2/3, Mar. 18/19, 28/29, Apr. 1/2, June
                        1/2, 17/18, 29/30, July 4/7, 8/9, 11/12, 13/14,
                        Nov. 18/19, Dec. 9/10
                   1826 Jan. 4/5, 6/7, 18/19, 23/24, Feb. 3/4, 8/9,
                        17/18, Mar. 6/7, June 28/29, 30/July 1, 3/4,
                        19/20, Sept. 15/16, 20/21, Oct. 4/5-9/10, 16/17,
                        20/21, 23/24, Nov. 1/2, 8/9, 20/21, Dec. 8/9
                   1827 Jan. 10/11, 24/25, 29/30, Feb. 12/13, 16/17,
                        19/20, 21/22, 23/24, Mar. 9/10, 12/13, Apr.
                        9/10, 16/17, 27/28, 30/May 1, 7/8, 9/10, 16/17,
                        23/24, June 15/16, 20/21, 22/23, 25/26, July
                        2/3, 23/24, Aug. 3/4, 20/21
       PPL    d    1824 Nov. 22-1826 Oct. 25
                   1826 Oct. 27-1827 July 4
                   1827 July 6-Dec. 25, 27-1829 Dec. 31
       PRHi        1826 July 13
                   1827 July 27
       continued as
   AURORA AND PENNSYLVANIA GAZETTE (1828-1829) d w *
                   d   Apr. 14, 1828-Dec. 31, 1829
                   w   Apr. 1828-Dec. 31, 1829
   Pub. 1828       John Norvell
        1829       George Taylor & Co.
       P          1828 Apr. 14-1829 Dec. 30
       PHi        1828 Apr. 14-Sept. 28
       PLewL      1829 Mar. 4
       PPL        1828 Apr. 14-1829 Dec. 31
                  Publication suspended from 1830-July, 1834
                  continued as
   AURORA, (July 4, 1834-April 25, 1835||) d w
   Pub. & Ed. 1834-1835  William Duane
       PHHi   w   1834 July 4-1835 Apr. 25
       PHi        1834 July 4-1835 Apr. 18

**BACHE'S PHILADELPHIA AURORA,** see Aurora

**BANNER OF THE CONSTITUTION** (1829-Dec. 31, 1832||) w dem
       Ed. 1829-1832  Coudy Raguet
       In December 1829 the paper was moved to New York City
       and returned to Philadelphia sometime in May of 1831.
       P          1829 Dec. 5-1832 Dec. 31
       PEL        1831 Oct. 5
       PP         1831 Aug. 10
       PUL        1829 Dec. 2-1832 Dec. 31

**BANNER OF THE COVENANT, THE** (Feb. 11, 1860-Feb. 17, 1870)
   sm w rel
          sm 1860 Feb. 11-July 14, 1863 Jan. 3-July 2
          w 1860 July 21-1862 Dec. 27, 1863 July 9-1870 Feb. 17
```

BANNER OF THE COVENANT, *continued*

Pub. 1860 Feb. 11-1870 Feb. 17   Executive Committee of Board of Foreign Missions of the Reformed Presbyterian Church at Philadelphia

Ed. 1860 July 14-1860 Dec. 29   J. M. M. Wilson
    1861 Jan. 26-1863 Apr. 25   Matthew McBride
    1863 May 9-1869 July 8   John W. Mears
    1870 Jan. 6-1870 Feb. 17   C. W. J. Wylie and R. E. Thompson

PHi   1863 June 20
PNazHi   [1847-1855]
         1861-1865
         1866 Jan. 4-Feb. 15, Mar. 1, 23-Oct. 4, 18-Dec. 27
         1867 Jan. 3-Dec. 26
PPPHi   1860 Feb. 11-1870 Feb. 17
         Missing
         1866 Feb. 22, Oct. 11, 1868 June 18, Nov. 19
         NOTE: The issue of July 8, 1869, bears a note that *The Banner* merged in *The American Presbyterian*. There was no issue of the *Banner of the Covenant* on July 15, 1869, *The American Presbyterian* taking its place on that day. From July 22, 1869, until Feb. 17, 1870, the *Banner of the Covenant* again appeared. Apparently the above merger was never effected.
         On Feb. 24, 1870—together with *The American Presbyterian*—it merged with the *New York Evangelist* (the latter however, mentions only *The American Presbyterian*).

BANNER OF THE CROSS   (Jan. 1830-Oct. 31, 1861)   m   w   rel   %

PROTESTANT EPISCOPALIAN AND CHURCH REGISTER (Jan. 1830-Dec. 1837)   m

Pub. 1830 Jan.-1837 Dec.   Jesper Harding, at Philadelphia
Ed.   1830 Jan.-1837 Dec.   An Association of Clergymen
         PHi   1830 Jan.-1833 Dec.
                    1834 Jan.-Mar., June-Dec.
                    1835 Jan.-May, Sept., Nov., Dec.
                    1836 Jan., Mar.-June, Aug.-Nov.
                    1837 Jan.-July, Sept.-Dec.
         PP   1831 Mar.
                    1835 Jan.-1836 Dec.
         PPPHi   1830 Mar., May, June, Aug., Sept.
                    1832 June, July, Sept.
                    continued as

PROTESTANT EPISCOPALIAN, THE, (Jan. 1838-Dec. 1838)   m
Pub. 1838 Jan.-Dec.   John S. Littell
Ed.   1838 Jan.-Dec.   An Association of Clergymen
         PHi   1838 Jan.-Dec.
         PP   1838 Jan.-Dec.
                   continued as

BANNER OF THE CROSS (Jan. 5, 1839-Oct. 31, 1861)   w
Pub. 1839 Jan. 5-1840 July 25   George W. Donohue
      1840 Aug. 1-1844 Apr. 27   R. S. H. George

PHILADELPHIA COUNTY 19

        1844 May 11-1845 July 12 George & Wayne
        1845 July 19-1848 Dec. 30 James S. Newbold
        1849 Jan. 6-1852   King & Baird
        1857 Jan. 8-1859 Aug. 11 H. Hooker & Co.
        1859 Aug. 18-1861 Oct. 31 Herman Hooker
Ed. 1841 July 17-1845 July 12 John Coleman
        1848 Jan. 8-1852   Frederick Ogilby
        1853   -1855 June 30 Frederick Ogilby and John Coleman
        1855 July 7-1856 Apr. 26 John Coleman
        1856 May 3-1857 May 7 Clergymen of Philadelphia
        1857 May 14-1859 Aug. 11 H. Hooker

Beginning Aug. 15, 1841, this paper states that it is the official organ of communication of the Bishops of Pennsylvania, New Jersey, and North Carolina, with their respective dioceses; from June 4, 1842, Maryland is added; from Apr. 29, 1843, Michigan also appears; on Nov. 2, 1844, Pennsylvania is dropped.

About Aug. 1848 the above statement is discontinued altogether.
    PHi ♦   1839 Jan. 5-Dec. 28
              1840 Jan. 4-Dec. 26
              1841 Jan. 2-Dec. 25
              1843 Jan. 7-1844 Dec. 28
              1845 Jan. 4-1846 Dec. 26
              1847 Jan. 2-1848 Dec. 30
              1849 Jan. 6-1850 Dec. 28
              1851 Jan. 4-1852 Dec. 25
              1854 Jan. 14-1855-Dec. 29
              1857 Jan. 1-1858 Dec. 30
              1859 Dec. 15, 22
              1860 Jan. 12, Feb. 16, Apr. 26, May 3, 10, Aug. 9-30, Sept. 13-Oct. 18, Nov. 8-22, Dec. 20
              1861 Apr. 25, Aug. 15-Sept. 12, Oct. 17
    PP   1849 Jan. 6-Dec. 29
    PPEH   1839 Jan. 5-1852 Dec. 25
              1853 Nov. 17
              1854 Jan. 7-1861 Oct. 31
    PPL   1839 Jan. 5-Dec. 28
              1843 Jan. 7-1845 Oct. 27
              1849 Jan. 6-1851 Oct. 25
              1851 Nov. 8-1852 Dec. 25
              1856 Jan. 5-Dec. 25
              1859 Jan. 6-Oct. 6, 20-Dec. 29

BAPTIST COMMONWEALTH (1895-1917) w rel
  COMMONWEALTH (1895-1898) w
    Pub. 1895-1898   The Commonwealth Publishing Co.
    Ed. 1897-1898   Lemuel Moss
        PCAB   [1895 Jan. 1-1898]
                  continued as
  BAPTIST COMMONWEALTH (1899-1917) w
    Pub. 1899-1900   The Commonwealth Publishing Co.
        1900-1908   Harper & Bro. Company
        1908-1917   Baptist Commonwealth Company
    Ed. 1899-1900   Lemuel Moss
        1910-1916   Rev. J. Milnor Wilbur
        1916-1917   R. M. Hunsicker
        PCAB   [1899-1917 July 12]

BAPTIST COMMONWEALTH, *continued*
    PP   1901 Jan. 5-Apr. 18, May 2-23, June 6, 20-July 18,
                 Aug. 1-22
           1904 Mar. 3-1905 Feb. 23
           1905 Sept. 7-1906 Jan. 18
           1906 Feb. 15, 22, Mar. 8-1917 July 12

BAPTIST RECORD, THE (1838-1857) w rel
    Pub. 1838-1857 American Baptist Publication Society
                   (J. M. Allen)
    PDoHi   1841 Nov. 24
                 1843 Oct. 25
    PWbW   1854 Oct.

BATTAGLIA (1898-1905) w for ♦
    Pub. & Ed. 1903-1905 L. DeBenedictis

BATTAGLIA ILLUSTRATA, LA (1898-1906) w for ♦
    Pub. & Ed. 1903-1906 L. DeBenedictis

BAZAAR JOURNAL, THE (Oct. 7, 1845) d
    Published daily at the Bazaar.
    Edited by "The Printer's Devil."
    Printed by "Doctor Faustus."
    PWcHi   1845 Oct. 7

BEACON, THE (Mar. 1, 1940†) w
    Pub. & Ed. 1940 Mar. 1†   Harry C. Osborne, at Logan
                                  Philadelphia
    PUB   1940 Mar. 1†

BEE, THE (May 11, 1870) d
    Pub. 1870 McClintock & Company
    PCHi   1870 July 15 (Vol. 1, No 64)

BEE (1890-1919) w ♦
    BUSY BEE (1890-1894) w comic ♦
    Pub. 1890-1893 Maginn-Dacey Company
           1893-1894 Globe Press Bureau
    Ed. 1893-1894 C. Joseph Dacey
    continued as
    BEE (1895-1919) w ♦
    Pub. 1895-1919   Globe Press Bureau
    Ed. 1895-1919   C. Joseph Dacey

BELL'S REGISTER (1883) d morn ♦
    Pub. 1883 Bell & Dunn
    Ed. 1883 I. P. Benner

BIBLE BANNER (1871-1887) w ♦
    Pub. 1877-1878 A. A. Phelps
         1878-1887 Bible Banner Association

PHILADELPHIA COUNTY 21

    Ed. 1877-1880 A. A. Phelps
          1880-1881 A. A. Phelps and J. D. Brown
          1881-1887 J. D. Brown

BICKNELL'S REPORTER, COUNTERFEIT DETECTOR AND GENERAL PRICES CURRENT (1830-1857) sm w *
    BICKNELL'S COUNTERFEIT DETECTOR AND PENNSYLVANIA REPORTER OF BANK NOTES, BROKEN BANKS, STOCKS, etc. (July 31, 1830-Jan. 17, 1831) sm *
    Pub. 1830-1831   Robert Thaxter Bicknell
        PLewL   1830 July 31-Nov. 8, Dec. 6-20
                   1830 July 31-Dec. 20
                   1831 Jan. 4-17
                   continued as
    BICKNELL'S REPORTER, COUNTERFEIT DETECTOR, AND GENERAL PRICES CURRENT (Jan. 24, 1831-June 30, 1857||) w *
    Pub. 1831-1839   Robert Thaxter Bicknell
          1839-1857   Matthew Miller
        P-M   1832 Jan. 30
        PBL ♦   1833 Dec. 23, 30
                     1834 Jan. 6, 13, 21-Feb. 11, 25-Apr. 15
                     1835 Oct. 27
                     1837 May 23
                     1840 July 21
        PLewL   1831 Jan. 17-Mar. 14, Apr. 25-June 6, July 2-18, Aug. 29-Oct. 3, 17-24, Nov. 7-21, Dec. 7-19
                     1832 Jan. 2, 16-Feb. 20, Mar. 5-19, Apr. 9, 23, May 21-July 9, 23-Sept. 10, 24, Oct. 1, Nov. 5, 26, Dec. 10-31
                     1833 Jan. 7-Feb. 11, 25, June 13
                     1834 Jan. 13, Feb. 11
                     1835 Oct. 27
        PPAP   1834 Apr. 1
        PPM   1832 July 30-1857 June 30
        PShH   1840 July 21
        PW   1831 June 6
                     1833 May 4, 11

BLANCHE'S SUNDAY PRESS (Dec. 11, 1853-Oct. 15, 1854) w * ♦
    Pub. 1853-1854   Louis Blanche

BLUE BOOK, THE (1856) ir
    Pub. N. S. Hurlocke
    Ed. "Edited by a Statesman"
        Campaign paper. Political organ published irregularly during the Buchanan-Fremont Presidential campaign.
        PHi   1856 July 4

BOLLETTINO DELLA SERA, see L'Opinione, Il Progresso Italo-Americano

BOULTON'S WEEKLY (1887-1888) w ind ♦
    Pub. & Ed. Z. A. Boulton

BREEZE OF LOWER MONTGOMERY COUNTY (1927-1938) w
non-part
    Pub. 1936-1938   Blaetz Bros., Inc.
    Ed. 1936-1938   Adelaide M. Blaetz
    PUB   1928†

BREWERYTOWN HERALD, see Weekly Chronicle and Brewerytown Herald

BRITISH-AMERICAN (1887-1919) w ind
    Pub. 1888-1889   Richard G. Hollaman
           1889-1893   British-American, Inc.
           1893-1908   L. Hall
           1908-1919   British-American Publishing Co.
    Ed. 1888-1889   Richard G. Hollaman
           1889-1892   J. Henry Williams
           1892-1893   British-American, Inc.
           1893-1908   L. Hall

BULLETIN, see Evening Bulletin

BUSINESS ADVOCATE (1869-1883) w
    BUSINESS ADVOCATE (1869-1871) w
    Pub. 1869-1870   E. H. Phillips & Co.
           1870-1871   Charles H. Hoovan
       continued as
    BUSINESS ADVOCATE AND PRICE CURRENT (1872-1876) w
    Pub. & Ed. 1872-1875   Charles H. Hoovan
                 1875-1876   Business Advocate Co.
       continued as
    BUSINESS ADVOCATE (1876-1877) w
    Pub. 1876-1877   Advocate Company
    Ed. 1876-1877   C. H. Hoovan
       continued as
    BUSINESS ADVOCATE AND PRICE CURRENT (1877-1881) w
    Pub. & Ed. 1877-1881   C. H. Hoovan
       continued as
    BUSINESS ADVOCATE (1882-1883) w
    Pub. & Ed. 1882-1883   I. H. Stauffer

BUSINESS JOURNAL AND TRAVELER, see United States Journal

BUSY BEE, THE (Jan., 1867-Dec., 1871) m rel
    Pub. 1867 Jan.-1867 Nov.   Orphans' Home at Germantown
          1867 Dec.-1871 Dec.   The Lutheran Association for the Publication of Religious Periodicals at Philadelphia
    PPK   1867 Jan.-1871 Dec.

BUSYBODY AND PHILADELPHIA WHIP (Apr. 9, 1840-June 25, 1842) sw
    PHi   1842 June 25

PHILADELPHIA COUNTY 23

CALL (1883-1904) d evg ind *
    EVENING CALL (1883-1888) d *
           d Sept. 17, 1883-Apr. 18, 1888
           w Dec. 15, 1883-Apr. 1888 as *Weekly Call*
    Pub. & Ed. 1883-1888 Robert S. Davis
        PCHi   d   1888 Mar. 14
        PDoHi d   1885 July 23
        PP   d   1883 Sept. 17-1888 Apr. 18
        PWcHi   1883 Sept. 21
                   1885 Feb. 25, July 30, Aug. 8
                   continued as
    CALL (Apr. 19, 1888-1904) w
           d Apr. 19, 1888-1904
           w Apr. 1888-1895 as *Weekly Call*
             Title varies: *Family Call*
    Pub. & Ed. 1889-1900 Robert S. Davis
        PCHi   d   1900 Nov. 2
        PP   1888 Apr. 19-1900 Sept. 8
        PPiHi   1898 Apr. 12, 28, 29, May 3, 5, 9, 10, 12, 17, 18, June
                   1, 2, 13, 25, July 15, 20, 21, 26, 30, Aug. 6, 16-19,
                   Sept. 19-21, Oct.
                   1899 Jan. 28, Feb. 7, 24, Mar. 27

CAMPAIGN AGE, see Illustrated New Age

CAMPAIGN DIAL (1862-1864) d *
    DIAL, THE, (June 19, 1862-Sept. 8, 1864) d
    Pub. 1862-1864   S. E. Cohen
        PHi   1862 June 19-Dec. 31
                   1863 Jan. 2-Mar. 26
                 continued as
    CAMPAIGN DIAL, THE, (Sept. 8, 1864-Nov. 5, 1864||) d ♦ *
    Pub. 1864 S. E. Cohen
        PHi ♦ 1864 Sept. 8-Nov. 5

CAREY'S DAILY ADVERTISER (1797) #
    DAILY ADVERTISER, THE (Feb. 7, 1797-July 3, 1797) d
    Pub. 1797   James Carey and John Markland
    Ed. 1797   James Carey
        PBuE   1797 June 20
        PDoHi   1797 May 9-June 7, 16, 17, 20
        PHi   1797 Feb. 10-Mar. 18, 20-Apr. 29, May 3-25, 27, 30-
                     July 3
        PPL   1797 Feb. 7-Apr. 13, 15-June 14, 16-28, 30-July 3
                 continued as
    CAREY'S DAILY ADVERTISER (July 5, 1797-Sept. 12, 1797) d
    Pub. & Ed. 1797 James Carey and James Markland
                 1797 James Carey
        PCHi   1797 Aug. 28
        PDoHi ♦ 1797 July 5-27, Aug. 23-Sept. 11
        PHi   1797 July 5-18, 20-26, 28-Aug. 8, 10, 15, 17-23, 25-
                     Sept. 8
        PPL   1797 July 5-Sept. 12

CAREY'S PENNSYLVANIA EVENING HERALD, see Pennsylvania Herald and General Advertiser

CAREY'S PENNSYLVANIA EVENING HERALD AND AMERICAN MONITOR, see Pennsylvania Herald and General Advertiser

CAREY'S UNITED STATES RECORDER (Jan. 23, 1798-Aug.30, 1798)
tw #
   Pub. & Ed. 1798 James Carey
          PDoHi ◆ 1798 Jan. 23-Feb. 20, Mar. 1, June 9-Aug. 16, 23, 28
          PPL   1798 Jan. 23-July 28, Aug. 2-30

CATHOLIC HERALD AND VISITOR, see Universe

C. T. A. NEWS (1887-1899) w temp ♦
   C. T. A. NEWS (1887-1891) w
     Pub. 1887-1891   C. T. A. News Publishing Co.
     Ed. 1888-1891   John H. Campbell
                      continued as
   CATHOLIC T. A. NEWS (1891-1896) w
     Pub. 1891-1894   Bradley Brothers
          1894-1896   C. T. A. Union
     Ed. 1891-1894   Joseph D. Murphy
          1894-1896   Joseph C. Gibbs
                      continued as
   C. T. A. NEWS (1896-1899) w
     Pub. 1896-1899   C. T. A. Union
     Ed. 1896-1899   J. W. Logue & S. A. Moore

CATHOLIC STANDARD AND TIMES (1866†) w rel
   CATHOLIC STANDARD (1866-1895) w
     Pub. 1866-1868   William Pepper & Co.
          1868-1871   Mark Wilcox
          1871-1872   Mark Wilcox & Co.
          1872-1873   Mark Wilcox
          1873-1893   Hardy & Mahony
          1893-1895   Charles A. Hardy
     Ed. 1866-1867   Rev. James Keogh
          1867-1872   Mark F. Vallette
          1872-1895   George D. Wolff
          PPCHi   1866 Apr. (7-1867 Sept. 14)
                        1868 Jan. 4-1870 Dec. 31
          PUB   1866 Jan. (6), (20-Feb. 3), (17-Mar. 31)-July 28, Aug. 11-Oct. (20)-1867 Feb 9
                        1867 Feb. 23-1868 Aug. 8, Sept. 5-Oct. (3)-1870 Mar. 12
                        1870 Mar. 26-1871 Dec. (30)-1872 May 18
                        1872 June 8-1895 Nov. 30
                        merged with *The Catholic Times* to form

PHILADELPHIA COUNTY

CATHOLIC STANDARD AND TIMES (1895†) w
Pub. 1895-1941   Catholic Standard Times Publishing Co.
Ed. 1903-1919   John J. O'Shea
    1919-1923   James A. Dougherty
    1923-1932   John A. Gallagher
    1936-1941   A. K. Ryan
    PHi   1923 June 23
                 1936 Dec. 11
    PUB   1895 Dec. (7-1896 June 20)-27-July (4)-11-(18, 25)-Aug. (15-29)-Sept. (19, 26)-Oct. (17-Nov. 28), Dec. (12)-
                 1897 Nov. (13-27)
                 1898 Jan. (1-Nov. 26)
                 1899 Dec. 2-1911 Nov. 25
                 1912 Dec. 1-1941†
    PP   1927 Dec. 3, 24†

CATHOLIC TIMES, THE (Dec. 3, 1892-Nov. 30, 1895) w rel
Pub. 1892 Dec. 24-1895 Nov. 30   The Catholic Times Publishing Co.
Ed. 1892 Dec. 3-1895 Nov. 30   Rev. L. A. Lanibert
    PUB   1892 Dec. 3-(17)-1893 Jan. (28)-1894 Nov. (24)-1895 Nov. 30
            merged with the *Catholic Standard* to form the *Catholic Standard and Times* (q.v.).

CATHOLIC VISITOR, see Universe

CENT, THE (1830) ↓
Pub. 1830   Dr. Christopher C. Conwell

CENTENNIAL, see Crotzer's Centennial and Journal of the Exposition

CENTENNIAL AND JOURNAL OF THE EXPOSITION, see Crotzer's Centennial and Journal of the Exposition

CENTENNIAL ADVERTISER (1875-1893) sm ↓
Pub. & Ed. 1885-1893   John E. Lonabough

CENTENNIAL GAZETTE AND JOURNAL OF THE EXHIBITION (1873-1876) w
    COMING EVENT AND CENTENNIAL GAZETTE (May 1, 1873-May 3, 1875) w
    Pub. 1874   Mack & Braden
        1875   Centennial Publishing Co.
        P-M   1875 Jan. 8, Feb. 5, 26, Mar. 5, 12, 26, Apr. 2, 9
        PPL   1874 Dec. 11
                continued as
    CENTENNIAL GAZETTE AND JOURNAL OF THE EXHIBITION (May 10, 1875-1876||) w
    Pub. 1875-1876   Centennial Publishing Co.
        P   1876 May 29
        PHi   1875 May 10
        PP   1875 Nov. 22
        PWcHi   1876 Mar. 13

CENTRAL CITY NEWS (Apr. 22, 1940†) w
  Pub. 1940   Len Silverstein, J. C. Kalish, and Harry Steinman
  Ed. 1940   Len Silverstein
  PP   1940 Nov 28† (Vol. 1, No. 32)

CENTRAL NORTH PHILADELPHIA NEWS, see North Philadelphia Press

CENTRAL PHILADELPHIAN (1896-1902) w dem ♦
  Pub. & Ed. 1900-1902   Edward J. Bowen

CHAT OF NORTH PENN, THE (Feb. 16, 1928†) w
  Pub. 1928-1930   William E. Jordan
       1931 June 11   Margaret E. Ocker
       % *Chat, The,* and *North Penn Chat*
  PP   1930 June 12†
  PUB   1928 Feb. 16†

CHELTENHAM ENTERPRISE (1892-1893) w ♦
  Pub. 1892-1893   E. E. Walton & Co.
  Ed. 1892-1893   E. E. Walton

CHESTNUT HILL AND MOUNT AIRY HERALD   (1924-1929) w
  Pub. 1924-1929   Paton & Fetterolf
  Ed. 1924-1929   Edna M. Kneedler
       Merged Jan. 2, 1930, with *Germantown Bulletin* (q. v.).
  PP   1929 Aug. 30, Sept 13-Dec. 20

CHESTNUT HILL TIMES (1894-1902) w ind ♦
  Pub. & Ed. 1898-1902   Curtis E. Blinsinger

CHESTNUT HILL TIMES (Feb. 11, 1931-June 23, 1932||) w
  Pub. 1931-1932   Theodore Marsh
  Ed. 1931-1932   Theodore Marsh
  PP   1931 Feb. 11-1932 June 23

CHESTNUTHILLER WOCHENSCHRIFT, see Philadelphier Wochenblatt

CHRISTIAN, THE (1824) w ♦
  Pub. J. Mortimer

CHRISTIAN BANNER (1888-1820) w rel Negro
  Pub. 1892-1895   Enterprise Publishing Co.
       1895-1918   Christian Banner Publishing Co.
       1918-1920   Warwicks

PHILADELPHIA COUNTY

    Ed. 1892-1918 Rev. G. L. P. Taliaferro
           1918-1920 James E. Warwick
    PHi   1911 Sept. 29, Oct. 20, Nov. 10, Dec. 8

CHRISTIAN CHRONICLE (1846-1863) w rel
    Ed. 1846   Rev. W. B. Jacobs, Rev. James S. Dickerson
    PHsHi   1863 July 16
    United with the *New York Chronicle*, New York, 1863 and published there for both places under the title of *New York Chronicle and Philadelphia Christian Chronicle*.

CHRISTIAN GAZETTE, THE (Mar. 15, 1834-Jan. 16, 1835) w
    Pub. 1834   T. W. Ustick
    Ed. 1834   R. W. Cushman
    PDoHi   1834 Dec. 12

CHRISTIAN GAZETTE AND YOUTH'S HERALD, see Christian Observer

CHRISTIAN INSTRUCTOR AND UNITED PRESBYTERIAN WITNESS (1882-1913) w rel ♦
    CHRISTIAN INSTRUCTOR (1882-1883) w ♦
    Pub. 1882-1883   Collins & Macdill
    Ed. 1882-1883   D. W. Collins, W. W. Barr, A. T. Macdill
                           continued as
    CHRISTIAN INSTRUCTOR AND UNITED PRESBYTERIAN WITNESS (1884-1913) w ♦
    Pub. 1884-1913   Collins & Co.
    Ed. 1884-1899   D. W. Collins, W. W. Barr, J. A. Collins
         1889-1901   Collins & Barr
         1901-1913   J. A. Collins

CHRISTIAN INSTRUCTOR AND WESTERN UNITED PRESBYTERIAN (1859-1872) w rel
    CHRISTIAN INSTRUCTOR, THE (July 6, 1859-July 17, 1861) w
    Pub. 1859 July 6-1861 July 17 William S. Young, at Philadelphia
    Ed. 1859 July 6-1861 July 17 J. B. Dales, J. T. Cooper, G. C. Arnold
    PPPHi ♦   1859 July 6-1861 July 17
                merged with *Western United Presbyterian* under the title of

    THE CHRISTIAN INSTRUCTOR AND WESTERN UNITED PRESBYTERIAN (July 24, 1861-Dec. 28, 1867) w
    Pub. 1861 July 24-1862 Feb. 26 Wm. S. Young, Marion Morrison, at Philadelphia
          1862 Mar. 5-1862 July 12 James M. Ferguson & Co., Marion Morrison, at Philadelphia
          1862 July 19-1867 Dec. 28 James M. Ferguson & Co., at Philadelphia
    Ed. 1861 July 24-1862 Apr. 23 J. B. Dales, J. T. Cooper, G. C. Arnold, Marion Morrison
         1862 Apr. 30-1863 Feb. 28 J. B. Scouller, Marion Morrison

CHRISTIAN INSTRUCTOR AND WESTERN UNITED PRESBYTERIAN, *continued*
    1863 Mar. 7-1863 July 25 James M. Ferguson & Co., Marion Morrison
    1863 Aug. 1-1867 Dec. 28 John B. Dales, Ed., James M. Ferguson, Assoc. Ed., Marion Morrison, Corresp. Ed.
    PPPHi ♦ 1861 July 24-1867 Dec. 28
        article omitted in the title

CHRISTIAN INSTRUCTOR AND WESTERN UNITED PRESBYTERIAN (Jan. 4, 1868-Dec. 25, 1869) w
    Pub. 1868 Jan. 4-1869 Dec. 25 Not expressly stated (apparently James M. Ferguson & Co., at Philadelphia)
    Ed. 1868 Jan. 4-1869 Dec. 25 John B. Dales, Ed., James M. Ferguson, Assoc. Ed., Marion Morrison, Corresp. Ed.
    PPPHi ♦ 1868 Jan. 4-1869 Dec. 25
        The issue of Dec. 25, 1869, contains a note stating that the *Christian Instructor and Western United Presbyterian* has united with the *United Presbyterian* of Pittsburgh, and that the publication of the united paper will be in Pittsburgh with a distinct office in Pittsburgh as well as in Philadelphia. Apparently the two papers separated again on or before March 19, 1870, the paper appearing again under the title of

CHRISTIAN INSTRUCTOR AND WESTERN UNITED PRESBYTERIAN (March 19, 1870-Dec. 28, 1872) w
    Pub. 1870 Mar. 19-1872 Dec. 28 Not expressly stated (apparently James M. Ferguson & Co., at Philadelphia)
    Ed. 1870 Mar. 19-1872 Dec. 28 John B. Dales
    PPPHi ♦ 1870 Mar. 19-1872 Dec. 28 missing
        1870 Jan. 1-Mar. 12, Aug. 6, Nov. 26
        1871 Aug. 26
        The whereabouts of this paper from Jan. 1873 until Dec. 1878 have not been ascertained. Beginning Jan. 2, 1879 or before, the *Christian Instructor and Western United Presbyterian* was published at Chicago, appearing under this title until Dec. 25, 1879. On Jan. 1, 1880, the title was changed to *Christian Instructor*
    PPPHi   1879 Jan. 2-Dec. 25
        1880 Jan. 1-Dec. 23

CHRISTIAN OBSERVER, THE (1813-1861) w rel
    RELIGIOUS REMEMBRANCER, THE, (Sept. 4, 1813-Aug. 16, 1823) w
    Pub. 1813 Sept. 4-1823 Aug. 16 John W. Scott, at Philadelphia
    Ed. 1819 Aug. 28-1823 Aug. 16 John W. Scott
    PP   1813 Sept. 4-1814 Aug. 20
    PPPHi   1813 Sept. 4-1823 Aug. 16
        succeeded by

CHRISTIAN GAZETTE AND YOUTH'S HERALD (ca. 1823-Apr. 30, 1825) w
Pub. 1825 Jan. 1-1825 Apr. 30 S. B. Ludlow, at Philadelphia
    PPPHi   1824 Aug. 21, Sept. 18, 25, Oct. 9, Nov. 6, 13, Dec. 11
                  1825 Jan. 1, 8, Feb. 12, 19, 26, Mar. 26, Apr. 2, 9, 16, 23, 30
                  merged with *Circular,* of Wilmington, Del., and continued as

PHILADELPHIAN, THE (May 6, 1825-Apr. 14, 1836) w *
Pub. 1825 May 6-1829 Nov. 20 S. B. Ludlow
     1829 Nov. 27-1836 Apr. 14 Wm. F. Geddes
Ed. 1825 May 6-1829 Nov. 20 S. B. Ludlow
     1829 Nov. 27-1836 Apr. 14 Ezra Stiles Ely
    PHi   1826 Jan. 6
               1828 May 16
    PPPHi   1825 May 6-1836 Apr. 14
               missing
               1829 Feb. 13, 20, Mar. 6
               succeeded by

PHILADELPHIA OBSERVER (Apr. 21, 1836-Aug. 3, 1837) w *
Pub. & Ed. 1836 Apr. 21-1837 Aug. 3 John M'Knight
    PHi   1837 Sept. 21, 28
               1838 Nov. 17, 24
    PPPHi   1836 Apr. 21-1837 Aug. 3
               missing
               1837 Feb. 23, Apr. 6
               article added to title

PHILADELPHIA OBSERVER, THE (Aug. 10, 1837-Jan. 12, 1839) w *
Pub. 1837 Aug. 10-1839 Jan. 12 at Philadelphia
    PPPHi   1837 Aug. 10-1839 Jan. 12
               merged with *Southern Religious Telegraph* and continued as

RELIGIOUS TELEGRAPH AND OBSERVER (Jan. 24, 1839-Dec. 26, 1839) w
Pub. 1839 Jan. 24-1839 Dec. 26 at Philadelphia
Ed. 1839 Jan. 24-1839 Dec. 26 A. Converse
    PHi   1839 Apr. 18
    PPPHi   1839 Jan. 24-Dec. 26
               missing
               1839 Sept. 19
               succeeded by

CHRISTIAN OBSERVER, THE (Jan. 2, 1840-Nov. 22, 1860) w %
Pub. 1840 Jan. 2-1852 Dec. 25 at Philadelphia
     1853 Jan. 1-1860 Nov. 22 A. Converse, at Philadelphia
Ed. 1840 Jan. 2-1841 Nov. 19 A. Converse
     1841 Nov. 26-1842 Nov. 11 A. Converse, F. Bartlett
     1842 Nov. 18-1852 Dec. 25 A. Converse
     1853 Jan. 1-1853 Dec. 31 A. Converse, Geo. Duffield, Jr.
     1854 Jan. 7-1857 Dec. 31 A. Converse
     1858 Jan. 7-1860 Nov. 22 A. Converse, Ed.; F. B. Converse, Assoc. Ed.

CHRISTIAN OBSERVER, *continued*
    PPPHi   1840 Jan. 2-1860 Nov. 22
                       merged with *The Presbyterian Witness*
                       continued as
    CHRISTIAN OBSERVER (inside title, CHRISTIAN OBSERVER AND PRESBYTERIAN WITNESS) (Nov. 29, 1860) w
    Pub. 1860 Nov. 29-1860 Dec. 27 A. Converse, Philadelphia date line
          1861 Jan. 3-1861 July 25 A. Converse, Philadelphia and Richmond, Virginia, date line
          1861 Aug. 1-1861 Aug. 22 A. Converse, Philadelphia date line
          1861 Sept. 19   A. Converse, Richmond, Virginia, later Louisville, Kentucky
    Ed. 1860 Nov. 29   A. Converse, Ed.; F. B. Converse, Assoc. Ed.
    PPPHi   1860 Nov. 29-1941†
    In 1861, due to the Civil War issue, the *Christian Observer* was confiscated and the editors were compelled to leave Philadelphia. A special issue of the *Christian Observer,* dealing with the confiscation of this paper, was published in Philadelphia on Oct. 24, 1861. This paper is still published in Louisville, Ky.

CHRISTIAN RECORDER (1861-1931) w rel Negro
    Pub. 1868-1869 Rev. Joshua Woodlin
            1869-1872 Rev. A. L. Stanford
            1872-1876 Rev. W. H. Hunter
            1876-1880 Rev. H. M. Hunter
            1880-1884 T. Gould
            1884-1892 Rev. J. C. Embry
            1892-1897 Rev. H. T. Johnson
            1897-1902 T. W. Henderson
            1902-1910 John H. Collett
            1910-1913 R. R. Wright, Jr.
            1913-1916 J. I. Lowe
            1916-1931 R. R. Wright
    Ed. 1868-1884 Rev. Benjamin T. Tanner
            1884-1892 Rev. B. F. Lee
            1892-1910 H. T. Johnson
            1910-1913 R. R. Wright, Jr.
            1913-1916 J. I. Lowe
            1916-1931 R. R. Wright
    PP   1865 Dec. 2, 30

CHRISTIAN REPOSITORY, THE (Jan. 5, 1843-Apr. 8, 1848||) w rel
    Pub. 1848   Orrin Rogers
    Ed. 1847-1848 H. J. Brown and Orrin Rogers
        PHi   1847 Apr. 10, 17, Sept. 4, 11
                         1848 Mar. 11, June 10
        PWcHi   1848 Apr. 8

CHRISTIAN REVIEW (1913†) w Negro
    Pub. 1914-1931 Northern Review Publishing Co.
            1939-1941 Florence M. Johnson

PHILADELPHIA COUNTY 31

  Ed. 1914-1931 Rev. Robert W. Goff
     1939-1940 Rev. M. L. Shepard
     1940-1941 Rev. L. M. Smith
   PUB [1913 Aug.-1925 July]
         1926 Jan.†
   PP   1934 Sept. 20, Oct. 4†

CHRISTIAN STANDARD (1867-1908) w
 CHRISTIAN STANDARD AND HOME JOURNAL (1867-1889) w
 Pub. 1874-1887 National Publishing Association for the Promotion of Holiness
    1887-1889 T. T. Tasker
    1889   Rev. John Thompson
 Ed. 1874-1876 Rev. A. Lowrey
    1876-1884 Rev. John Inskip
    1884-1889 Rev. E. I. D. Pepper
  PP   1876 Apr. 8
         continued as
 CHRISTIAN STANDARD (1890-1908) w rel undenom ♦
 Pub. 1890-1891 Rev. John Thompson
    1891-1895 E. I. D. Pepper
    1895-1908 Christian Standard Co.
 Ed. 1890-1891 E. I. D. Pepper
    1891-1895 George Hughes, E. I. D. Pepper, John Thompson
    1895-1904 E. I. D. Pepper, John Thompson
    1904-1908 E. I. D. Pepper

CHRISTIAN STATESMAN, THE (Sept. 2, 1867-Dec. 19, 1896, or later)
sm w rel %
sm Sept. 2, 1867-Aug. 15, 1872
w Sept. 7, 1872-Dec. 19, 1896, or later
 Pub. 1867 Sept. 2-1879 Aug. 28 at Philadelphia
    1879 Sept. 4-1883 May 31 T. P. Stevenson, David McAllister, at Philadelphia
    1883 June 7-1891 Dec. 25 The Christian Statesman Publishing Co., at Philadelphia
    1892 Jan. 2-1894 Jan. 27 or later Reform Bureau, at Pittsburgh
    1895 Jan. 12-1896 Dec. 19 or before or later The Christian Statesman Co., at Allegheny, Pa. (New York, Philadelphia, Washington, and Pittsburgh also appear on the date line)
 Ed. 1879 Sept. 4-1891 Nov. 12 T. P. Stevenson, David McAllister
    1891 Nov. 19-1893 Dec. 30 Wilbur F. Crafts, J. T. McCrory
    1894 Jan. 6-1894 Jan. 27 or later J. T McCrory
    1895 Jan. 12 -1896 Dec. 19 David McAllister
    or before or later
  PP   1867 Sept. 2-1871 Aug. 15
  PPPHi 1867 Sept. 2-1896 Dec. 19
       missing
       1888 Mar. 15, Apr. 5
       1894 Feb. 3-1895 Jan. 5
       1895 July 13, Aug. 31

CHRISTIAN WORLD, THE (Sept. 1840-Dec. 1842) w
P   1840 Sept.-1842 Dec.

CHRONICLE AND ADVERTISER (Jan. 2, 1869-Oct. 22, 1931) w
(Manayunk) ind
    Pub. 1875-1880   James Milligan
           1880-1893   Milligan & McCook
           1893-1931   Milligan & Co.
    Ed. 1875-1931   James Milligan
    PHi
        1869 Jan. 2-Dec. 25
        1871 Jan. 7-1874 Aug. 8
        1874 Aug. 22-Nov. 7, 28, Dec. 12
        1875 Jan. 2-Dec. 25
        1876 Jan. 8-Dec. 9, 30-1880 Feb. 14
        1880 Feb. 28-1881 Mar. 25
        1881 Apr. 8-1882 Apr. 7
        1882 Apr. 21-1883 May 18
        1883 June 1-1884 Feb. 29
        1884 Mar. 14-May 16, 30-1885 July 31
        1885 Aug. 14-1886 July 23
        1886 Aug. 6-Dec. 17, 31
        1887 Jan. 7-Feb. 25, Mar. 11, Apr. 1-Sept. 9, 23, Nov. 4, 18-1888 Apr. 13
        1888 May 11-June 22, July 27-Dec. 28
        1890 Jan. 3, Mar. 14, May 23, June 8-1891 July 17
        1891 July 31, Aug. 14, 28, Sept. 11-Oct. 2
    PP
        1889 Jan. 4-Mar. 22, Apr. 5-19, Nov. 1, Dec. 13-27
        1892 Sept. 2, 23
        1893 Mar. 10
        1922 Jan. 5-July 20, Aug. 17-Oct. 5, 19-Dec. 28
        1923 Jan. 11, Feb. 15-Apr. 19, May 10, 31, July 26, Aug. 23, 30, Oct. 25-Nov. 22, Dec. 13
        1924 Jan. 10-Feb. 14, Mar. 6, June 19, Sept. 4-Oct. 30, Nov. 13, Dec. 11
        1925 Feb. 19, Mar. 12-Apr. 23, May 21, 28, June 11, 18, Oct. 1-29, Nov. 26, Dec. 17-31
        1926 Jan. 7, 14, Aug. 19, Oct. 14, 21
        1927 Oct. 27, Nov. 10-Dec. 8, 22, 29
        1928 Jan. 5-Feb. 16, Apr. 5-May 3, 31-June 7, July 12-Aug. 9, 23-Sept. 6, 20, Oct. 4-11, 25-Nov. 15, 29, Dec. 13-27
        1929 Jan. 17-Feb. 21, Mar. 7-June 13, 27-July 18, Aug. 1-8, 22-Dec. 26
        1930 Jan. 2-Feb. 6, 27-June 26, Aug. 7-Nov. 6, 20-Dec. 18
        1931 Jan. 15-Apr. 2, 16-30, May 21-Oct. 22

CHRONICLE OF THE TIMES (1821-Nov. 18, 1828||) w
    Ed. 1821-1828   Douglas W. Hyde
    Published for Philadelphia and Reading
    PBL ♦   1828 July 22, Sept. 2, Oct. 28, Nov. 18

CHRONICLE OF WYNNEFIELD, see addenda

CHURCH (1884-1887) w rel
    Pub. 1884-1887   McCalla and Stavely
    Ed. 1884-1887   Rev. A. A. Marple

PHILADELPHIA COUNTY 33

CHURCH MESSENGER, see Lutheran Church Messenger

CHURCH NEWS, THE (1912-1941) m rel
   Official publication of the Protestant Episcopal Church in the Diocese of Pennsylvania
   CHURCH NEWS OF THE DIOCESE OF PENNSYLVANIA, THE (Nov. 1912-Oct. 1924) m (except during summer months)

Pub. 1912 Nov.	-1916 Jan.	By Board of Management, at Philadelphia
1916 Feb.	-1924 Oct.	at Philadelphia
Ed. 1912 Nov.	-1913 June	George G. Bartlett, Arthur Rogers, Francis C. Hartshorne, J. Vaughan Merrick
1913 Oct.	-1914 June	George G. Bartlett, Francis C. Hartshorne, Seaver M. Holden, Royden Keith Yerkes, J. Vaughan Merrick
1914 Oct.	-1915 June	George G. Bartlett, Francis C. Hartshorne, Seaver M. Holden, Henry R. Gummey, Jr., J. Vaughan Merrick
1915 Oct.	-1916 Jan.	Francis C. Hartshorne, Seaver M. Holden, J. Vaughan Merrick
1916 Feb.	-1917 May	John Mockridge, J. Vaughan Merrick
1917 Oct.	-1919 Apr.	Francis C. Hartshorne, Benjamin S. Sanderson
1919 Nov.	-1921 Jan.	William C. Rodgers
1921 Feb.	-1921 Oct.	James Milburn Bennett
1921 Nov.	-1923 Feb.	Frederick E. Seymour, James Milburn Bennett
1923 Mar.	-1924 May	Frederick E. Seymour
1924 Oct.		George Copeland
PP	1912 Nov.-1916 May	
	1916 Oct.-1921 May	
	1921 Oct. 1924-Oct.	
PPEC	1912 Nov.-1924 Oct.	
PPEHi	1912 Nov.-1914 June	
	1915 Oct.-1924 May	

continued as

"THE CHURCH NEWS
   Official publication of the Protestant Episcopal Church in the Diocese of Pennsylvania" title on the cover continuing as *"The Church News of the Diocese of Pennsylvania* Nov. 1924-Oct. 1938 m (except during summer months)

Pub. 1924 Nov.-1938 Oct.		at Philadelphia by the Protestant Episcopal Church Diocese of Pennsylvania
Ed. 1924 Nov.-1938 Oct.		George Copeland
PP	1924 Nov.-1938 Oct.	
PPEC	1924 Nov.-1938 Oct.	
PPEHi	1925 Oct.-1930 May	

continued as

"THE CHURCH NEWS Diocese of Pennsylvania" title inside continuing as *"THE CHURCH NEWS*

CHURCH NEWS, *continued*
Official publication of the Protestant Episcopal Church in the Diocese of Pennsylvania" Nov. 1938-1941 June m (except during summer months)
Pub. 1938 Nov.-1941 June at Philadelphia by the Protestant Episcopal Church Diocese of Pennsylvania
Ed. 1938 Nov.-1941 June George Copeland
PP 1938 Nov.†
PPEC 1938 Nov.-1941 June

CHURCH STANDARD, THE (1892-1908) w rel
Pub. 1892 May 14-1893 Feb. 11 W. E. Hering
1893 Feb. 18-1894 Dec. 8 Church Standard Publishing Co.
1894 Dec. 15-1908 June 27 Church Standard Company
Ed. 1897-1907 John Fulton
1908 George C. Foley
PP 1897 Nov. 6-1908 June 27
PPEHi ♦ 1892 May 14-1893 May 6
1894 May 12-1896 Oct. 31
The last issue, June 27, 1908, contains an editorial note stating that the publication of *The Church Standard* would be discontinued and that its subscription list would be merged with that of *The Churchman*.

CITIZEN SOLDIER (Jan. 7, 1843-Dec. 27, 1843) w
PDoHi 1843 Jan. 7-Dec. 27
United with *Home Journal* to form the *Home Journal and Citizen Soldier* (q.v.)

CITY AND STATE (May 9, 1895-May 26, 1904) w non-part
Pub. & Ed. 1895-1904 Herbert Walsh
PCHi 1895 Sept. 9
PHi ♦ 1895 May 9-1904 May 26
PP 1895 May 9-1904 May 26
PPCHi 1895 Oct. 10
1897 Oct. 14, Dec. 2
1898 Jan. 13
PPL 1895 May 9-1903 Dec. 31

CITY AND STATE (1915-1921) w rep ♦
Pub. & Ed. 1915-1921 Franklin M. Pearce

CITY ITEM FOR TOWN AND COUNTRY, see Item

CITY REGISTER AND DAILY ADVERTISER (May 1823-Oct. 31, 1824) d evg ♦ *
Absorbed by *Freeman's Journal and Philadelphia Mercantile Advertiser* Nov. 1, 1824 (see under *National Palladium and Freeman's Journal*)

CLAN-NA-GAEL (Mar. 4, 1882-Aug. 3, 1896||) w (in Gaelic) rel *
PPCHi 1882 Mar. 4-1887 Nov. 23
1888 Feb. 25, Aug. 12-1889 Feb. 16
1889 Apr. 10-1896 Aug. 3

PHILADELPHIA COUNTY

CLAYPOOLE'S AMERICAN DAILY ADVERTISER, see North American

COHEN'S LOTTERY JOURNAL AND GENERAL REGISTER
(1826) w
    PToHi   1826 June 14

COLONIAL GAZETTE (Oct. 1781)
    Contains account of the surrender of General Cornwallis at Yorktown
    PPot   1781 Oct.

COLONIZATION HERALD (1835-1865) sm m anti-slavery
    COLONIZATION HERALD (Apr. 4, 1835-Dec. 21, 1837) sm
    Pub. 1835-1837   Pennsylvania Colonization Society
        PHi   1835 Apr. 4-Dec. 19
                  1836 Jan. 2-June 11, July 9-Dec. 17
                  1837 Jan. 7-Feb. 18, Mar. 18, Apr. 15-Dec. 16
        PLewL   1835 Apr. 4
        PP   1835 Apr. 4-18, May 16-July 4, 18, Aug. 1-Dec. 26
                  1836 Jan. 7-1837 Dec. 16
        PPL   1835 Apr. 4-1837 Dec. 21
                  1836 Jan. 3-June 11, July 9-Dec. 17
                  1837 Jan. 7-Feb. 18, Mar. 18, Apr. 15-Dec. 16
                  continued as
    COLONIZATION HERALD AND GENERAL REGISTER, THE,
      (Jan. 3, 1838-June 1849) sm m
    Pub. 1838-1849   Pennsylvania Colonization Society
        P   sm 1838 Mar. 13-Dec. 26
        PBL   1838 Jan. 3
        PP   1838 Jan. 17, 24, Mar. 7, 28, May 2, 23-June 13, 27,
                    July 4, 25, Aug. 8, 22, 29, Sept. 12, Nov. 28,
                    Dec. 5, 26
                  1839 Feb.-June
                  1843 July 16, Sept. 13, Dec. 20
                  1844 Jan. 17-Mar. 20
                  1845 Feb. 26-Mar. 19
              m 1848 Mar.
        PPL   1838 Jan. 3-Dec. 26
              m 1848 Mar.
                  1849 Jan. 3-June
        PPPHi   1838 Jan. 3, Dec. 19
              m 1839 Jan.-June
                  1843 Apr. 12-Sept. 27, Oct. 18-1849 June
                  continued as
    COLONIZATION HERALD, THE, (July 1849-1865) m
    Pub. 1849-1865   Pennsylvania Colonization Society
        PBf   1860 Sept., Oct.
                  1861 Feb., June
        PHi   1861 Aug., Oct.
        PP   1849 Sept., Oct.
                  1850 Sept.
                  1851 June, Nov.
                  1852 Jan., Mar., Apr., June, July, Aug., Dec.
                  1853 June-Aug.
                  1854 Jan., Feb., June, Aug., Sept.
                  1855 Jan., Mar.

COLONIZATION HERALD, continued

      1861 Aug.
      1865 Jan.
  PPL   1849 July-Dec.
      1850 Nov.-1855 Nov.
      1856 Jan.-Dec.
  PPPHi 1849 July-Oct.
  PToHi 1853 Jan.-1859 Apr.
  PWcHi 1852 Feb.

COLONO, IL (1900-1904) w ind for ♂

  Pub. & Ed. 1900-1904 Charles Chiantelli

COLORED WORLD (1915-1916) w Negro ♂

  Pub. 1915-1916 Fair Publishing Co.
  Ed. 1915-1916 W. W. Rourk

COLUMBIA ADVERTISER (1900-1903) w ♂

  Pub. & Ed. 1900-1903 C. Keely Hagy

COLUMBIAN CHRONICLE (Jan. 29, 1810-Mar. 20, 1815) sw

  Pub. 1810-1815 William McCorkle
   PBro   1814 Dec. 6, 9
   PCarlHi 1812 Oct. 9
   PEHi   1810 Jan. 30
       1811 Sept. 27, Oct. 11, 22
       1814 July 1
   PRHi   1814 Feb. 24-1815 Mar. 20

COLUMBIAN OBSERVER (1822-1825) d w sw tw dem *

   d Apr. 1, 1822-June 30, 1825||
   w Apr. 6, 1822-July 1822
   sw Aug. 1, 1822-Nov. 1822
   tw Dec. 1822-Aug. 8, 1825
  Pub. & Ed. 1822-1825 Simpson & Conrad (Stephen Simpson & John Conrad)
   PHi d 1825 Feb. 12
   PPL   1825 Jan. 1-Feb. 12, 15-Mar. 1, 3-30, Apr. 1-May 30, June 1-10, 13-30
       merged with the *National Chronicle* 1825 (q. v.).

COMING EVENT (1874-1875) w ♂

  Pub. & Ed. 1874-1875 A. Barrington Irvins & Co.

COMING EVENT AND CENTENNIAL GAZETTE, see Centennial Gazette and Journal of the Exhibition

COMMERCIAL AND MANUFACTURERS GAZETTE (1874-1876)
w ♦
    Pub. 1874-1876   Commercial Publishing Co.
    Ed. 1875-1876   W. C. Nevins

COMMERCIAL AND POLITICAL REGISTER, see Political and Commercial Register

COMMERCIAL BULLETIN (1876-1880) w ♦
    Pub. 1876-1880   W. Channing Nevin
    Ed. 1876-1880   E. L. Townsend

COMMERCIAL CHRONICLE, see United States Gazette

COMMERCIAL HERALD AND PENNSYLVANIA SENTINEL
(1827-1840) d tw w *
    COMMERCIAL HERALD (1827-1837) d w *
    Pub. & Ed. 1827-1829 J. R. Walker
                  1829-1833 N. Sargent
                  1833-1837 Col. Cephas C. Childs, Henry Billington & Co.
                              d, July 3, 1827-July 25, 1837; tw July 1827-July 1837; w Nov. 10, 1827-July 1837 as: *Philadelphia Saturday Herald* or *Saturday Morning Herald;* w Jan. 10, 1835-Aug. 1837
        P   d   [1834 Apr. 28-1837 July 25]
        PEL   1833 Jan. 9, 11-14, 16, 19, 21-29, 31-Feb. 18, 20-Mar. 18, 20, 22, 25, 27, 28, 30-Apr. 15, 17-26, 29-May 14, 16, 17, 20-22, 24, 28-June 11, 13-Aug. 17, 20-Sept. 7, 10-Oct. 26, 29-Nov. 1, 4-Dec. 31
                          1834 Jan. 1-7, 9-23, 25-Feb. 3, 5-19, 21-27, Mar. 1-11, 13-17, 19-Apr. 1, 3-11, 14-19, 22-May 23, 26-June 23, 25-July 4, 7-16, 18-24, 26-Aug. 13, 15-Sept. 3, 5-Nov. 21, 24-Dec. 24, 30
                          1835 Jan. 1-Feb. 23, 25-Mar. 10, 12-24, 27-Apr. 22, 24-May 8, 11-20, 22-27, 29-July 4, 7, 8, 10-31, Aug. 3-8
                          1836 Jan. 2-Feb. 18, 20-23, 25-Mar. 1, 3-Apr. 28, May 3-June 4, 7-9, 11-July 4, 6-14, 16 Aug. 6, 9-24, 26 Sept. 17, 20-28, 30-Nov. 12, 15-Dec. 3
                          1837 Jan. 4-27, 30-Feb. 17, 20-23, 25-Mar. 4, 7-16, 18-Apr. 20, 22-24, 26-28, May 3, 4, 8-18, 20, 24, 25, 29-June 1, 3-16, 19-23, 26-July 3, 6-13, 15-21, 24
        PHi   1833 Mar. 2
        PP   w   [1835 Jan. 10-1837 July]
        PPi   [1833 Apr. 24-1836 Mar. 21]
        PWeT d 1834 Apr. 11, 12, 14, 15
                  Commercial Herald merged with *Pennsylvania Sentinel* July 28, 1837, and

                  continued as

    COMMERCIAL HERALD AND PENNSYLVANIA SENTINEL (1837-1840) d w *
    Pub. & Ed. 1837-1840 Col. Cephas C. Childs, Henry Billington & Co.
                                  d July 26, 1837-May 13, 1840||; w Aug. 1837 as: *Saturday Morning Herald* or *Philadelphia Saturday Herald*

COMMERCIAL HERALD AND PENNSYLVANIA SENTINEL,
continued
        P   d   [1837 July 26-1840 May 12]
              w 1837 Aug.-Dec. 26
        PEL d 1837 July 26, 27, 29
        PHi   1840 Feb. 17, 19
        PP   d 1838 Feb. 20, Mar. 18, May 18, 29, Sept. 3, 6, 7, 10, 17, 19, 22, Oct. 10, 11, 15, 18, 20, 22, 25, 27, 29, Nov. 1, 5, 10, 24, 27
                    1839 Jan. 4, 7, 11, 17, 18, 22, 28, 30, Feb. 1, 6, 13-15, 27, Mar. 5, 8, 9, 11-15, 19, 20, 30, Apr. 12, 18, 22, May 1, 16, July 16, 17, 22, 25, 26, Aug. 5, 22, 27, 28, Sept. 4, 13
                    1840 Apr. 17, 18, 28, May 5, 13
        PPL d 1838 Jan. 1-Feb. 20, 22, Apr. 21, 23-May 31, June 2-Dec. 31
                    1839 Jan. 10, June 15
                    Commercial Herald and Pennsylvania Sentinel was absorbed by the *North American,* 1840 (q.v.)

COMMERCIAL INTELLIGENCER (1830-1834) d
   COMMERCIAL INTELLIGENCER AND LITERARY POLITICAL JOURNAL (Dec. 1830-Feb. 1834)
   Pub & Ed. 1830-1832 Robert T. Conrad
                1832-1834 Edward Conrad
       P   1833 Dec. 2-1834 Feb.
       PBL ◆ 1833 Dec. 18
                continued as
   COMMERCIAL INTELLIGENCER (Feb. 1834-Dec. 1834)
   Pub. & Ed. 1834 Edward Conrad
       P   1834 Feb.-Nov. 20
                merged with *Philadelphia Gazette and Universal Daily Advertiser,* and title changed to *Philadelphia Gazette and Commercial Intelligencer,* Dec. 1, 1834 (q.v.)

COMMERCIAL JOURNAL (1875-1920) w ♦
   Pub. 1909-1920 Ben Frankford
   Ed. 1909-1915   James E. Barnes
         1915-1920   J. George Bucher

COMMERCIAL LIST AND MARITIME REGISTER (May 26, 1827-1934||) sw w *
   PHILADELPHIA PRICE CURRENT (May 26, 1827-Oct. 17, 1829) w *
   Pub. 1827-1829   Billington and Sanderson
                          (Henry Billington)
          PHi   1827 May 26-Dec. 29
              w   1828 Jan. 1-Dec. 31
              sw   1829 Jan. 3-Oct. 17
                    continued as
   PHILADELPHIA PRICE CURRENT AND COMMERCIAL ADVERTISER (Oct. 24, 1829-Jan. 24, 1835) w *
   Pub. 1829-1835   Henry Billington
        PHi sw   1829 Oct. 24-1832 Dec. 15
        PPF sw   1833 Dec. 21-28
                   1834 Jan. 1-1835 Jan. 3-17

PPM sw 1829 Oct. 24-1830 Oct. 23
         continued as
COMMERCIAL LIST AND PHILADELPHIA PRICE CURRENT
(Jan. 24, 1835-Dec. 30, 1848) w *
Pub. 1835-1848   Col. Cephas G. Childs
      PHi   1835 Jan. 24-1848 Dec. 30
      PP   1838 Jan. 13
      PPL   1847 Jan. 2-Mar. 20, Apr. 4-June 19, July 3-Oct 16,
                   30-Dec. 11, 25-31
      PPM   1847 Jan. 2-9, 23-Feb. (13)-Apr. 10, 24-1848 Dec. 31
         continued as
COMMERCIAL LIST AND TRADE AND STATISTICAL REGISTER (Jan. 6, 1849-Nov. 27, 1852) w *
Pub. 1849-1852   Col. Cephas G. Childs
     1850   Stephen N. Winslow
      PHi   1849 Jan. 6-1850 Dec. 31
      PPL   1849 Apr. 21
                 1850 Mar. 2. Apr. 13, Oct. 19, 26, Dec. 14-28
                 1851 Jan. 11-Feb. 15, Mar. 1-15, 29-Apr. 19, May 13-
                   1852 Nov. 27
         continued as
PHILADELPHIA COMMERCIAL LIST AND PRICE CURRENT
(Dec. 4, 1852-Dec. 25, 1922) w *
Pub. 1853   H. G. Leisenring
     1855   William W. Fulton
     1857-1867   Stephen N. Winslow
     1867-1879   S. N. Winslow & Son
                 (Stephen N. Winslow, Jr.)
     1879-1884   S. N. Winslow
     1884-1908   Commercial Publication Co.
     1908-1913   Samuel S. Daniels
     1913-1922   Commercial List Publishing Co.
Ed. 1868-1908   Stephen N. Winslow
     1908-1922   Samuel S. Daniels
      PHi   1864 Dec. 3, 10
                 1865 Apr. 15
                 1868 June 13
      PP   1870 Jan. 1-1888 Dec. 31
                 1890 Jan. 4-1903 Dec. 5
                 1904 Jan. 2-1922 Nov. 25
      PPM   1857 Feb. 28-1859 Dec. 31
      PU   1853 Jan. 1-1856 Dec. 31
                 1860 Jan. 1-Dec. 31
                 1862 Jan. 1-1882 Dec. 31
         continued as
COMMERCIAL LIST AND MARITIME REGISTER (Jan. 1, 1923-1934||) w
Pub. 1923-1934   Commercial List Publishing Co.
Ed. 1923-1934   Harry C. Daniels
      PP   1923 May 19-Nov. 3, 17-1930 Dec. 27
                 1931 Feb. 14-Nov. 14

COMMERCIAL TRAVELER (1870-1871) w ♂
Pub. & Ed. 1870-1871   R. W. Renshaw & Co.

COMMONWEALTH, see Baptist Commonwealth

COMMONWEALTH (May 23, 1874-Feb. 28, 1880) w dem *
    Pub. 1877   Wm. Aydelotte
    Ed. 1874-1879   W. H. Witte
         1879-1880   Charles M. Leisenring
        PHi ♦ 1874 May 23-July 4, 25, Aug. 1, 8, 29, Sept. 19, Oct. 3, 10, 24-Nov. 28, Dec. 26
                1875 Jan. 9, Apr. (3), May 8
                1876 Feb. 5, May 6, 13, 27, June 3, July 1
                1877 May 26
        PPL ♦ 1874 May 23-Nov. 21, Dec. 5-1875 May (15, 22)
                1875 June (12, 19), Sept. 25, Nov. 6, 13, 27, Dec. 11, 25
                1876 Jan. 8, Apr. 23, July 15, Dec. 9, 23
                1877 Jan. 13-Feb. 3, 17, Mar. 3-Apr. 21, Nov. 17
                1878 Jan. 5, 19, Feb. 2-Mar. 30, Apr. 13, Oct. 29, Nov. 16-23, Dec. 7
                1879 Jan. 4, 18, Feb. 1, Mar. 1, 29-Apr. 26, Nov. 22, Dec. 6
                1880 Jan. 3, 17-24, Feb. 28

COMMONWEALTH AND INDEPENDENT DEMOCRAT, THE, (1831-Nov. 1, 1837) w
    Ed. 1837   William Metcalf
        PBL ♦ 1837 Nov. 1

COMMUNITY NEWS (Nov. 15, 1919-Jan. 31, 1920||) w
    Pub. 1919   Fred A. Moone, Executive Director 1919, Community Service of Philadelphia
        PPL ♦ 1919 Nov. 15, Dec. 1, 15
                1920 Jan. 15
        PP   1919 Nov. 15-1920 Jan. 31

COMPLETE COUNTING HOUSE COMPANION (Jan. 25, 1785-Oct. 30, 1790) w #
    Pub. & Ed.   1785   Mathew Carey
                  1785   Carey, Talbot & Spotswood
                  1785-1787   M. Carey & Co.
                  1787-1790   W. Spotswood
                  Complete Counting House Companion was issued as a free supplement of the *Pennsylvania Evening Herald,* and became a separate publication Feb. 5, 1788.
                  See *Pennsylvania Herald and General Advertiser.*
        PHi   1786 July 8, Dec. 9, 23

CONSTITUTIONAL DIARY AND PHILADELPHIA EVENING ADVERTISER (Dec. 2, 1799-Jan. 23, 1800) d ♦ #
    Pub. & Ed.   1799-1800   James Carey

PHILADELPHIA COUNTY 41

CONSTITUTIONAL UNION (June 21, 1862-Mar. 21, 1863) w *
    Pub. & Ed. 1862-1863 Thomas B. Florence & Co.
        PHi   1862 July 26
                  1863 Jan. 17-24
        PWcHi   1862 Nov. 8
                  1863 Jan. 10

CONTINENTAL JOURNAL (1870-1871) w ♦

CORRECTOR AND AMERICAN WEEKLY REVIEW, THE, (1814) w # ♦
    Pub. 1814   James Fullen & Lewis P. Frank

COUNTRY GAZETTE OF THE UNITED STATES, see United States Gazette, The

COUNTRY PORCUPINE, see Porcupine's Gazette

COURANT (1901-1920) w Negro rep ♦
    Pub. 1906-1914   Courant Printing and Publishing Co.
         1914-1920   A. P. Caldwell
    Ed. 1906-1920   A. P. Caldwell

COURIER de L'AMERIQUE (July 27, 1784-Oct. 22, 1784) sw for # ♦
    Pub. 1784   Charles Gist
    Ed. 1784   Daniel Boinod and Gaillard

COURRIER FRANCAIS (Apr. 15, 1794-July 3, 1798) d tw for # ♦
    Pub. 1794-1798   Peter Parent
         1798   Allain, Blocquerst and Wilson
         1798   Allain & Blocquerst

COURRIER POLITIQUE DE LA FRANCE ET DE SES COLONIES
(Oct. 19, 1793-Feb. 13, 1794) # tw for
    Pub. 1793-1794   Philadelphie, de l'Imprimerie de Parker
        PHi   1794 Feb. 13

COVENTRY MERCURY (1793)
    Contains accounts of the execution of Louis XVI, King of France.
        PPotW   1793 Jan. 28

CRACKS (1899-1921) w tw ♦
    Pub. & Ed. 1903-1921 A. B. Clarke

CROTZER'S CENTENNIAL AND JOURNAL OF THE EXPOSITION (1873-1876) m
        CENTENNIAL (Apr. 1873-Mar. 1874) m
      Pub. 1873-1874   H. W. Crotzer
         PHI   ♦ 1873 Apr.-1874 Mar.
         PP   1873 Apr.-1874 Mar.

continued as
CENTENNIAL AND JOURNAL OF THE EXPOSITION (Apr. 1874-Sept. 1875) m
Pub. 1874-1875   H. W. Crotzer
   PHi   1874 Apr.-1875 Sept.
   PP   1874 Apr.-1875 Sept.
continued as
CROTZER'S CENTENNIAL AND JOURNAL OF THE EXPOSITION (Oct. 1875-1876) m
   PHi   1875 Oct.-1876 Mar., May, Aug.
   PP   1875 Oct.-1876 Mar.

CUMMINGS' EVENING BULLETIN, see Evening Bulletin

CUMMINGS' EVENING TELEGRAPHIC BULLETIN, see Evening Bulletin

CUMMINGS' WEEKLY BULLETIN, see Evening Bulletin

CUMMINGS' WEEKLY TELEGRAPHIC BULLETIN, see Evening Bulletin

CYCLONE (1893-1897) see West Philadelphian

DAILY ADVERTISER, THE, (1797) see Carey's Daily Advertiser

DAILY AGE, THE, (1863-1866) see Illustrated New Age

DAILY CHRONICLE (1840-1847) d *
   DAILY CHRONICLE AND GENERAL ADVERTISER (May 4, 1840-1841) d *
   Pub. & Ed. 1840-1841   Charles Alexander and Andrew Scott
      PHoHi   [1840]
      PP   1840 May 8
continued as
DAILY CHRONICLE (1841-1847) d *
Pub. & Ed. 1841-1847   Charles Alexander and Andrew Scott
   PBL   ♦   1843 Mar. 30, Apr. 1, 27, Sept. 4, 22
      1844 Feb. 13, Mar. 4-6, 8, 13, Apr. 4, 6, 8, July 15, Aug. 26, Sept. 7, 9, 10, 24
      1845 Feb. 12, 13, 18, 25, 26, Mar. 11, 19, 26, Apr. 24, May 24, Sept. 17, Nov. 15, 22
      1846 Jan. 12, 17, Apr. 14-18, 21-24, May 8, 11, 13-16, 20, 21, 23-June 2, 4-July 7, 13, 15, 16, 23, 28
      1847 Mar. 17, 24, June 5
   PHi   1841 Dec. 4
      1844 Oct. 11
   PLewL   1844 Apr. 29

DAILY CHRONICLE (1828-34) see Daily Courier

DAILY CHRONICLE (1869-1871), see Philadelphia Evening Chronicle

PHILADELPHIA COUNTY 43

DAILY COURIER (Apr. 7, 1828-June 21, 1834) d *
    DAILY CHRONICLE (Apr. 7, 1828-Apr. 19, 1834) d *
    Pub. & Ed. 1828-1834   Charles Alexander and John Musgrave
        PBL ♦   1828 Oct. 15, 21-30
                  1831 July 28, 30, Aug. 1-4, 8-Sept. 2, 5-Oct. 6, 8, 10-14, 17-21, 24-27, 29, 31-Nov. 3, 5, 8-22, 24, 26, Dec. 5-7, 10, 12-14, 17, 20, 21, 27-29, 31
                  1832 Jan. 2-5, 9-12, 14-19, 21-26, 28, 30, Feb. 1, 2, 4, 8, 9, 11-16, 18-21, 23, 25-Mar. 1, 3, 5, 7, 8, 10-14, 17-22, 24-29, 31-Apr. 5, May 16, 17, 19-21, 28, 30, 31, June 5-7, 9, 12-15, 18, 19, July 4, Sept. 6, 8, 11, 13, 15, 18, 20, 24-27, 29-Oct. 10, 13-18, 23-31, Nov. 3, 5, 8, 13, 15-17, 22, Dec. 1-3, 6, 11, 15, 17, 18, 29
                  1833 Jan. 8, 12, 16, 17, 19, Feb. 4, 7, 9
                  1834 Jan. 6-8, Apr. 15
        PDoHi   1829 June 2, Dec. 31
                  1830 Jan. 7, 14
        PEHi   1831 Jan. 1, 6, 8, 10, 12-Feb. 23, 25-Mar. 2, 4-July 15, 18-20
        PHi   1828 Apr. 17-1829 June 30
                  1831 Jan. 1-1832 Dec. 31
                  1833 Oct. 1-1834 Apr. 19
        PNhE   1830 Apr. 30
                  1831 Feb. 11
        PP   1828 Apr. 7-1833 Dec. 31
        PPCHi 1833 July (12), 15, 17-19, 22, 24-30, Aug. 2, 7-12, 14, 15, 17-23, 26-Sept. 2, 7, 13, 23-27, Oct. 4, 5, 11, 14-16, 30, Nov. 6, Dec. 5, 9
                  1834 Jan. (1), 14, Mar. 3, 6
        PPL ♦   1828 Apr. 7, June 18, 20-Oct. 13, 15-Dec. 20, 23-1829 Feb. 24
                  1829 Feb. 26-Apr. 16, 18-23, 26-1830 Aug. 27
                  1830 Aug. 30-Sept. 3, 6-1831 Oct. 17
                  1831 Oct. 19-1832 Feb. 20-24
                  1832 Feb. 27-July 18, 20-1833 Apr. 3
                  1833 Apr. 6-Aug. 2, 5-Dec. 31
        PPM   1828 Apr. 7-1830 June 30
                  1832 July 2-1833 June 29
        PRHi   1829 June 2, Dec. 3
                  1830 Jan. 7, 14
        PU   1829 Jan. 1-1830 June
                continued as
    DAILY COURIER (Apr. 21, 1834-June 2, 1834||) d
    Pub. & Ed. 1834   James Gordon Bennett
        PBL ♦   1834 Apr. 26, May 14
                Absorbed by the *Pennsylvania Inquirer*, June 2, 1834 (q.v.)
                (See under *Philadelphia Inquirer-Public Ledger*)

DAILY EVENING BULLETIN (1856-1870) see Evening Bulletin

DAILY EXPRESS (Aug. 1, 1832-Sept. 4, 1832||) d *
    Pub. & Ed. 1832   Dr. Edmund Morris
                        The main purpose of this paper was to report on the cholera then raging in Philadelphia
        PPL   1832 Aug. 1-Sept. 4

DAILY FOCUS (1837-1840||) d morn *
  Pub. 1837-1838   Turner, Davis & Valleau
        1838-1840   Davis & Valleau
  Ed. 1837-1838   General Wm. F. Small
       1838-1840   George R. Graham and Charles S. Peterson
          PBL ♦   1838 July 12
          PHi   1838 May 21-July 4, 6-24, 26-28, Aug. 1, 2, 4-30, Sept. 1-Oct. 6, 9-Nov. 3, 6-13, 15-30

DAILY FORUM (1842-1844||) d w pol *
NATIONAL FORUM (Sept. 5, 1842-Jan. 1843) d *
  Pub. 1842-1843   Edward W. Jones & Co.
        1842-1843   Bela Badger
  Ed. 1842-1843   Thomas F. Adams
       1842-1843   James S. Wallace
          PNhF   1842 Sept. 26
                 continued as

PHILADELPHIA NATIONAL FORUM (Jan. 1843-June 3, 1843) d w *
  Pub. 1843   Bela Badger
  Ed. 1843   James S. Wallace
                 Weekly edition entitled *Weekly Forum*
          PBL ♦ d   1843 Jan. 2, 9, Mar. 31, Apr. 1, 17
               w   1843 Feb. 18
          PHi d   1843 Mar. 8-June 3
               continued as

DAILY FORUM (June 4, 1843-Dec. 28, 1844) d *
  Pub. 1843-1844   Bela Badger
  Ed. 1843-1844   James S. Wallace
          PBL ♦   1844 Jan. 26, Mar. 5
          PHi   1843 June 4-Dec. 30
          PWcHi ♦ 1844 June 18 (Extra)

DAILY GLOBE (1868-1869) d
  Pub. 1868-1869   Henry H. Holloway
          PCHi   1868 Oct. 10
          PHi   1868 Oct. 6-Nov. 23

DAILY HERALD AND EVENING CHRONICLE (1885-1887) see Evening Herald

DAILY INDEPENDENT, see Independent Gazette

DAILY INTELLIGENCER (Dec. 10, 1832-Oct. 13, 1833||) d w tw dem *
  Pub. 1832-1833   Robert T. Conrad
          PBL ♦ d 1833 Jan. 23, Mar. 20, July 8, 9, Nov. 1-5
               tw 1833 Sept. 9/10-23/24, 27/28-Oct. 4/5, 9/10-23/24, Nov. 1/2, 4/5, 8/9, 15/16-22/23
          PEL   1833 July 9
          PHi   1832 Dec. 1-1833 June 27
                  1833 June 29-July 1, 3-6, 9, 10, 12-16, 20-Aug. 1
          PPL   1832 Dec. 10-1833 Jan. 23
                  1833 Jan. 25-Feb. 8, 12-18, 20-23, 26-Mar. 15, 21-Apr. 4, 6-13, 16-23
          PWcHi 1833 July 25

PHILADELPHIA COUNTY

DAILY KEYSTONE, THE (1844-July 21, 1847) d *
Pub. 1845-1846 Severns and Magill
1844-1847 Thomas B. Florence and Joseph Severns
Sub-title *And People's Journal* also used
    PBL ♦ 1845 Feb. 6, 7, June 7, 13, Aug. 28, Sept. 13
              1846 Jan. 12, Feb. 4, Mar. 9
    PHi ♦ 1844 Oct. 24 (Vol. 5, No. 4), Nov. 29
              merged with the *Spirit of the Times* (q. v.).

DAILY LEGAL NEWS, THE (1879) d
Pub. & Ed. 1879 Joshua T. Owen
    PUL 1879 Jan. 6-Oct. 13

DAILY MORNING TIMES (Apr. 9, 1855-1856||), see Daily Times

DAILY NEWS (1830-1847, 1848-1858), see Philadelphia Daily News

DAILY NEWS (1879-1915) d rep
  EVENING NEWS (1879-1883) d *
  Pub. & Ed. 1879-1883 Edwin H. Nevin
              1883 Evening News Publishing Co.
    PWcHi 1881 Feb. 21, May 13, Nov. (12)
           1882 Aug. 22, 25
           1883 Aug. 14, 30, 31
           continued as
  DAILY NEWS (1884-1915) d morn evg *
  Pub. 1884-1889 News Publishing Co.
      1889-1892 Daily News Co.
      1892-1902 T. Henry Martin and Henry Starr Richardson
      1902-1915 Daily News Co.
  Ed. 1885-1890 M. P. Handy
      1890-1892 Rufus Road
      1892-1902 T. Henry Martin and Henry Starr Richardson
      1902-1915 Henry Starr Richardson
          Sunday edition published, *Sunday News,* 1884-1889
          Weekly edition published, *Weekly News,* 1885-1908
    PCHi 1885 Oct. 3
          1886 Jan. 25, Feb. 1, 8, 22
    PDoHi 1885 July 23, Dec. 8
           1885 Aug. 9
    PHi 1889 Sept. 5
         1895 Nov. 16
         1910 Jan. 3
    PLaF 1913 May 20, 1914 May 21, July 27, Aug. 3, 6, 17, 24, 27, Sept. 3, 7, 17, 21, Oct. 15-Nov. 12, 19, 27-Dec. 21, 28
          1915 Jan. 4-21, Feb. 1-8, 22, 25
    PPot 1884 Sept. 29, Oct. 31, Nov. 3, 4
         1885 July 25
         1886 Oct. 17
         1888 Nov. 6

DAILY NEWS (1925†) d evg rep
Pub. 1925-1926 Philadelphia Tabloid Publishing Co.
     1926-1932 McFadden Newspaper Corp.

DAILY NEWS, continued
        1932-1937   Lee Ellmaker
        1937-1938   Philadelphia Daily News, Inc.
        1938-1939   Lee Ellmaker
        1939-1940   Philadelphia Publications, Inc.
        1940-1941   Philadelphia Daily News
  Ed. 1928-1934   T. Von Ziekursch
        1934-1936   J. H. Keen
        1936-1941   Lee Ellmaker
        PUB   1925 May 31†
        PP   1927 June 1†

DAILY NEWS AND CHRONICLE (1847-1848), see Philadelphia Daily News

DAILY PENNSYLVANIAN (1855-1857), see Morning Pennsylvanian

DAILY PENNSYLVANIAN (1885†) d w
  PENNSYLVANIAN (1885-1934) w
  Pub. & Ed 1885-1934 Undergraduates of the University of Pennsylvania
      PU   1885-1934
                Missing
                1910 Oct. 12
                1911 May 8, Oct. 9, 19
                1912 Apr. 3, Oct. 4
                1914 Sept. 28
                1915 Jan. 8
                continued as
  DAILY PENNSYLVANIAN, THE (1934†) d
  Pub. & Ed. 1934-1941 Undergraduates of the University of Pennsylvania
      PU   1934†

DAILY REGISTER (1847-1854), see Philadelphia Daily Register

DAILY REPUBLIC, THE (Oct. 8, 1848) d *
  Pub. 1848-1849 William Elder
      PBL   1848 Nov. 1, 3-23, 25-Dec. 19
                1849 Jan. 2, 4, 13
      PLaHi   1848 Oct. 14, 16
      PWcHi   1848 Oct. 9

DAILY STANDARD, THE (Jan. 5, 1840-1841||) d ♦ *
  Pub. 1840-1841 F. J. Grund

DAILY SUN, see Sun (1843-1857)

DAILY TIMES (1855-1857) d *
  DAILY MORNING TIMES (1855-1856) *
  Pub. 1855 Sickles, Jones & Moran
      1856 William Moran
      PHi   1855 June (26)
               1856 Feb. 11, 15, 16, 22, Mar. 3
      PPL   1856 Feb. 28

PHILADELPHIA COUNTY 47

     continued as
  DAILY TIMES (1856-1857) d *
  Pub. 1856   William Moran
    1856-1857 J. Barclay Harding
    % *Philadelphia Daily Times, Philadelphia Morning Times*
    PEHi 1857 July 7, 9, 13, 15, 16, 20, 30, 31
    PHi   1856 Mar. 7, 13, 15, 24-29, Apr. 4, 5, 7-9, 11, June 23,
         July 19, 29-31, Aug. 2, 4-9, Sept. 18, Oct. 13, 17,
         Nov. 5
        1857 Oct. 12
    PPL   1856 Feb. 28, Apr. 19, May 7

DAILY TRANSCRIPT (1835-1836||) d pol ● *
  Pub. & Ed. 1835-1836 William L. Drane
      The Sept. 12, 1836, issue of the *Public Ledger* states that
      the *Daily Transcript* was amalgamated with the *Public
      Ledger.*

DAILY UNION (1856) d
    PPL   1856 Jan. 8

DAY, THE (1869-1881) d morn evg ind *
  DAY, THE, (1869-1874) d morn evg *
  Pub. 1869   Alexander Cummings
    1870-1871 Day Publishing Co.
    1872-1874 Lewis C. Cassidy
    1872-1874 James S. Chambers
  Ed. 1869-1871 M. H. Cobb
    PCHi   1869 Nov. 27
    PHi   1869 Nov. 4
      continued as
  PHILADELPHIA DAY (1875) d evg ●
  Pub. 1875   James S. Chambers
      continued as
  DAY, THE, (1876-1881) d evg *
  Pub. 1876-1881 James S. Chambers
  Ed. 1876-1881 Charles N. Pine, D. Brainard Williamson, Lawrence
          W. Wallace, Harry Brown, Robert A. Wells
    PDoHi   1876 Oct. 7

DEFENDER (1897-1909) w Negro ●
  Pub. 1898-1905 H. C. C. Astwood
    1905-1909 George A. Astwood
  Ed. 1898-1909 H. C. C. Astwood

DEMOCRAT (July 30, 1834) w dem
    PHi   1834 Sept. 3

DEMOCRATIC ARGUS (Oct. 23, 1843-Jan. 22, 1844||) d dem
  Pub. 1843-1844 John Parry
    PHi   1843 Oct. 23-27, 29-Nov. 8, 10-17, 20-22, 24, 25, 28-
         Dec. 14, 16-19, 21, 23, 25, 28-30
        1844 Jan. 1-5, 8-11, 14-18, 22

DEMOCRATIC HERALD AND CHAMPION OF THE PEOPLE
(Jan. 3, 1835) sw *
    Pub. 1835 John B. Dyott & Co.
        PBL ◆ 1835 Feb. 4-Mar. 21, 28, June 20, 27, July 22, 29-Sept. 2, 9-16, 23-Oct. 17
        PHi   1835 Feb. 4 (Vol. 1, No. 10)

DEMOCRATIC HERALD AND COMMERCIAL REGISTER, THE
(1837) tw dem
    Pub.   J. B. Dyott & Company
        PBL ◆ 1837 Jan. 19, Feb. 4

DEMOCRATIC KEYHOLE (Mar. 10, 1934-Apr. 14, 1934||) w dem
    Pub. 1934 Nathan I. Miller
        PP   1934 Mar. 31, Apr. 14

DEMOCRATIC LEADER (Aug. 21, 1862-June 26, 1863||) d dem *
    Pub. 1863 Pine & Lewis
        PHi   1863 June 26 (Vol. I, No. 36)

DEMOCRATIC NEWS (Nov. 1, 1934-Oct. 21, 1935||) w dem
Issue of Nov. 1, 1934 was a special issue
        PArdL   1934 Nov. 1
        PP   1934 Nov. 1
               1935 Oct. 14, 21

DEMOCRATIC PRESS (1807-1829) see Philadelphia Inquirer Public Ledger

DEMOCRATIC PRESS FOR THE COUNTRY (1807-1829) see Philadelphia Inquirer Public Ledger

DEMOCRATIC STANDARD (1836) tw ♦ *

DEMOCRATIC STATESMAN (Sept. 6, 1872) dem
        PWcHi   1872 Sept. 6

DEMOKRAT, DER, see Philadelphia Democrat

DEMOKRAT, UND ANZEIGER DER DEUTSCHEN, DER, see Philadelphia Democrat

DESSERT TO THE TRUE AMERICAN, THE (1798-1799) see True American, The

DEUTSCHE LUTHERANER, DER, see Lutherischer Herold

DEUTSCHE UND ENGLISCHE ZEITUNG, DIE (1751-1752) see Hoch Deutsche Und Englische Zeitung

DEUTSCHE NATIONAL-ZEITUNG (1838) w for ♦ *

DIAL, THE (1862-1864) see Campaign Dial

PHILADELPHIA COUNTY   49

DOLLAR NEWSPAPER (1843-1864) see Philadelphia Home Weekly

DOLLAR WEEKLY (1874-1875) w ind ♪
  Pub. & Ed. 1874-1875 Barnhart & Co.

DOLLAR WEEKLY NEWS (1847-1869) see Philadelphia Daily News

DOLLAR WEEKLY PENNSYLVANIAN (1854-1861) see Morning Pennsylvanian

DOWN TOWN ADVOCATE (1888-1889) w ♪
  Pub. & Ed. 1888-1889 Benjamin Baker

DOWN TOWN NEWS (1894-1903) w rep ♪
  Pub. 1898-1903   M. J. Gibbons
  Ed. 1898-1903   John J. Magan

DOWN TOWN RECORD (1891-1895) w ♪
  Pub. 1894-1895   J. H. Kleefeld
  Ed. 1894-1895   J. Alfred McCaughey

DRAWING-ROOM JOURNAL, THE   (Feb. 2, 1850-Apr. 2, 1853) w
  Pub. 1850-1853   Stephen McHenry
  Ed. 1850-1853   Manuel M. Cooke
       PHi   1850 May 25, June 8-22, July 6-Aug. 3, 17, 31- Sept. 28, Oct. 12, Nov. 2-16, 30-Dec. 21
       PLewL   1853 Apr. 2

DUNLAP AND CLAYPOOLE'S AMERICAN DAILY ADVERTISER (1793-1795) see North American

DUNLAP'S AMERICAN DAILY ADVERTISER (1791-1793) see North American

DUNLAP'S PENNSYLVANIA PACKET OR THE GENERAL ADVERTISER (1773-1777), see North American

DZIENNICK FILADELFIJSKI, see Kuryer Filadelfijski

EAGLE (1897-1923) w local ♪
  Pub. & Ed. 1900-1923 E. T. Tyndall

EAGLE JOURNAL (1880-1881) w ♪
  Pub. 1880-1881 Comegys & Adams
  Ed. 1880-1881 Robert W. Smiley

EDUCATIONAL GAZETTE (1869-1870) m w ed
  Pub. 1869-1870   C. H. Turner & Co.
       PHi   1869 Mar.
                    1870 July (23)

ENTERPRISE (1890-1893) w ♪
  Pub. & Ed. 1890-1893 C. C. Thompson & Co.

EPISCOPAL RECORDER (1823†) w rel

PHILADELPHIA RECORDER (Apr. 5, 1823-March 26, 1831) w

Pub.	1823 Apr.	5-1824 Jan.	3	Sheldon Potter
	1824 Jan.	10- Apr.	3	Potter & Co.
	1824 Apr.	10-1825 Sept.	3	Stavely & Bringhurst
	1825 Sept.	10-1831 Mar.	26	William Stavely
Ed.	1825 Jan.	1-1827 Oct.	20	T. Bedell
	1828 Oct.	4-1830 Oct.	2	B. B. Smith
	1831 Jan.	15- Mar.	26	George A. Smith

PBuE   1829 Oct. 21
PNo   1828 Nov. 29-1829 Feb. (28)
       1829 Dec. 26-1831 Jan. (2)
       1831 Jan. 9-Feb. 19, Mar. 19-26
PPEHi   1823 Apr. 5-1831 Mar. 26
       missing
       1828 Apr. 12, Sept. 13
       1829 Dec. 19
PPi   1829 Aug. 22, Dec. 26
       1830 Jan. 2-Aug. 28, Sept. 11-26, Oct. 9, 23-Dec. 11, 24
PPL   1824 June 5-1825 Dec. 31
PWcHi   1826 July 8, 15, 29, Aug. 5

continued as

EPISCOPAL RECORDER (Apr. 2, 1831-1866) w

Pub.	1831 Apr.	2-1844 Mar.	16	Wm. Stavely
	1844 Mar.	23-1856 Mar.	22	Stavely & McCalla
	1856 Apr.	5-1864 May	28	James McCalla
	1864 June	4-1866 Mar.	17	McCalla & Stavely
		(or later)		
Ed.	1831 Apr.	2-1837 Dec.	30	George A. Smith
	1838 Jan.	6-1840 Nov.	28	James May, John A. Clark, William Suddards, Stephen H. Tyng
	1840 Dec.	5-1843 Sept.	2	J. A. Clark, Wm. Suddards, Stephen H. Tyng
	1843 Sept.	9-1844 Apr.	27	William Suddards and Stephen H. Tyng
	1844 May	4- May	25	William Suddards
	1844 June	2-1845 Feb.	8	G. W. Ridgely and William Suddards
	1845 Feb.	15- Sept.	20	G. W. Ridgely
	1845 Sept.	27-1847 Jan.	2	G. W. Ridgely and William W. Spear
	1847 Jan.	9- Dec.	25	G. W. Ridgely
	1848 Jan.	1- June	3	Association of Clergymen
	1848 June	10-1852 Mar.	20	W. Suddards and H. H. Weld
	1852 Apr.	3-1853 May	21	W. Suddards and G. W. Ridgely
	1853 May	28- Dec.	3	W. Suddards

P   1842 Nov. 26-1846 Jan. 3
PBL♦   1839 Mar. 30-Dec. 28
       1840 Jan. 4-June 20, July 4, Oct. 17, 31-Dec. 26
       1841 Jan. 2-30, Feb. 13-Mar. 20, 27-Apr. 24, May 8-June 12, July 3-Sept. 4, 18-Oct. 9, 23-Nov. 27, Dec. 11-24
       1842 Jan. 1-Mar. 5, 26-Dec. 31
       1843 Jan. 7-Dec. 30

PHILADELPHIA COUNTY 51

                1844 Jan. 6-Mar. 16, 23-Dec. 28
                1845 Jan. 4-Nov. 22, Dec. 6-27
                1846 Jan. 3-31, Feb. 14-Mar. 7, 21-Dec. 26
                1847 Jan. 2, 16-Dec. 23
                1848 Jan. 1-Apr. 1, 15-Nov. 11, 25-Dec. 30
                1849 Jan. 6, 13, Feb. 3-24, Mar. 17-31, Apr. 14-May 26, June 9-Aug. 4, 18-Sept. 8, 22-Dec. 1, 15, 29
PCHi   1844 Apr. 27
Phi ♦   1841 Dec. 4
                1842 Aug. 20
                1846 Jan. 17, 24, Mar. 21, May 30, Aug. 15
                1848 Apr. 29, June (3), Sept. 23, Oct. (14), Nov. 18, 25, Dec. 2, 9, 30
                1849 Feb. 17, May (12)
                1853 Aug. (6)
                1856 July 19
                1858 May 15, July 3, Sept. 25
                1859 Jan. 15, 29, Mar. 12, Aug. 27, Oct. 8, Nov. 12, 26, Dec. 10, 17
                1861 Dec. 28
                1862 Nov. 15
                1864 Feb. 6
PNo   1831 Apr. 2-1832 June 16
                1832 June 30-Aug. 25, Sept. 8-1833 Dec. 21
                1834 Feb. 8-15, Mar. 8-15, June 14-Aug. 30, Oct. 4, 18
PP   1832 Apr. 7-1834 Mar. 29
PPAp   1832 Apr. 7-1834 Mar. 29
PPEHi   1831 Apr. 2-1833 Nov. 9
                1833 Nov. 23-1834 Jan. 18
                1834 Feb. 8-Nov. 15
                1835 Jan. 10, Feb. 28, Apr. 4-1866 Mar. 17 missing
                1838 Jan. 20
                1839 Aug. 10
                1840 Aug. 1, 8, 15, Sept. 5, 12, Oct. 31, Nov. 14, 21
                1841 Jan. 23, 30, Mar. 6, Apr. 24, July 10, 31
                1842 Jan. 15, Mar. 12
                1843 Jan. 7, 28, Mar. 25, Apr. 22, 29, Aug. 19, Nov. 11, 18, Dec. 23
                1844 Mar. 30
                1845 Jan. 11, Feb. 22, Apr. 5, 12, 26, May 3, 10, 17, June 7, July 5, Aug. 9
                1846 Apr. 11, May 16, 23, July 4, Sept. 19, Oct. 3-Dec. 12
                1847 May 15, June 12, Aug. 21, Oct. 30
                1848 Mar. 25
                1849 Jan. 20, Apr. 21, Aug. 11, Oct. 13, 27, Nov. 24-Dec. 29
                1850 Aug. 3, Sept. 21, Oct. 19, Nov. 9, 23
                1851 Feb. 22, July 12
                1855 July 14, Aug. 4
                1856 Jan. 9
                1857 Jan. 31, June 20, July 4, Sept. 19, Dec. 5, 12
                1862 Dec. 20
                1864 June 11, Dec. 10
                1865 Mar. 4, Aug. 5
                1866 Jan. 6, 20, 27, Feb. 11, Mar. 3
PPL   1831 Dec. 3
                1861 Jan. 5, 12-Dec. 26

EPISCOPAL RECORDER, *continued*
    PDoHi   1854 Aug. 8
                1859 May 21, June 25
                1860 May 12
                1861 Sept. 14
    PWcHi   1834 May 31
                1842 Aug. 13-27
                1843 July 5
                continued as

EPISCOPALIAN (1867-1873) w
1867 New York and Philadelphia date line
Pub. & Ed. 1869-1873 Rev. Chas. W. Quick
    PHi   1867 Mar. 16 (Vol. 1, No. 50)
    PPRE   1867-1873
               continued as

EPISCOPAL RECORDER (1874-1879) w
Pub. & Ed. 1874-1879 Rev. Chas. W. Quick
    PPRE   1874-1879
               continued as

EPISCOPAL RECORDER AND COVENANT (1880-1881) w
Pub. 1880-1881   Covenant Publishing Co.
    PPRE   1880-1881
                 continued as

EPISCOPAL RECORDER (1882†) w m
Pub. 1882-1885   Rev. H. S. Hoffman
      1887-1888   Dr. Samuel Ashurst
      1888-1896   Reformed Episcopal Publication Society
      1896-1936   Episcopal Recorder Co.
      1936-1941   James W. Armstrong
Ed. 1887-1888   Dr. Samuel Ashurst
      1908-1936   Rev. W. A. Freemantle
      1936-1940   Bishop R. W. Peach
      1940-1941   Bishop H. D. Higgins
    PP   1912 Aug. 22
                1918 Nov. 7
    PPRE   1882†

EPISCOPAL REGISTER (1870-1884) w
Pub. 1870-1884   McCalla & Stavely
Ed. 1870-1882   McCalla & Stavely
      1882-1883   S. D. McConnell, C. G. Currie
      1883-1884   Rev. W. F. C. Morsell
    PPL   1874 Jan. 24-Feb. 21, Mar. 7-Nov. 28
                 1875 Jan. 2-May 29, June 5-Oct. (2, 9)-Nov. 13, 27-1876 Jan. 1
                 1876 Jan. 15, 29-May (27), June 3-July 8, 22-(Nov. 11)-1877 May 26
                 1877 June 2-(16)-Dec. 1, 15-1878 Feb. 9
                 1878 Feb. 23-Mar. 2, 16-May 25, June 1-1879, Mar. 15
                 1879 Apr. 12-May 24, May 31-Nov. 8, 22-1880 Jan. 10
                 1880 Jan. 24-May 22

ERIN (1822-1823) sw * ♩

ETOILE AMERICAINE, L', see American Star

PHILADELPHIA COUNTY 53

EVENING BULLETIN, THE (1816†) d w sw rep.
    AMERICAN CENTINEL (Jan. 1, 1816-Aug. 25, 1816) sw
    Pub. 1816   Lewis P. Franks
    Ed. 1816   Peter Hay
      PHi ♦   1816 Jan. 1-Aug. 25
                      continued as
    AMERICAN CENTINEL AND MERCANTILE ADVERTISER, THE (Aug. 26, 1816-Mar. 6, 1824) d tw w
    Pub. 1816-1824   Jacob Frick & Co.
    Ed. 1816-1824   Peter Hay
    Weekly edition published entitled *The American Centinel,* April 13, 1818-1824
      P   [1820 June 20-1824 Mar. 6]
      PDoHi   1817 May 15
                      1818 Dec. 9
                      1821 Mar. 26, Apr. 17
      PHi ♦   1818 Mar. 3, (4, 5)-(19)-(30)-Apr. (1),-(3)-(17, 18), 27-May (4)-June (3)-(15)-Sept. (5)-Oct. (3), 6-(10)-(30)-Nov. 4, 6, 7, 10-(19), 23, (24), 25, 27-Dec. 4, 7, 8, 11-15, 17, 19-22, (24), 25, 28 (29-31)
                      1819 Jan. 1-(5), 6, 8-18, 21, 23-(27)-(30)-Feb. (11)-(13)-(17)-(19, 20)-(24, 25)-(27)-Mar. (2)-(12)-(15)-(17)-(19, 29)-(31, Apr. 1)-(13)-(24)-(28)-May (7)-(26)-June (12-15)-(17)-(21)-30-July 5, 7-(27)-Aug. (18)-(23)-Sept. (3)-(9-14)-(18-21)-(24, 25)-(28)-(30, Oct. 1)-(6, 7)-(11-14)-(19)-(25-27)-(30)-Nov. (13)-Dec. (2), 3, (6, 7)-9, (11-13)-(15-17)-(31)
      PNoHi   1823 Aug. 2
      PP ♦   d 1816 Aug. 26-28
                      1817 Oct. 28
                      1818 Feb. 28, Aug. 22, Nov. 11, Dec. 7
                      1819 Mar. 17, 18, Apr. 2, June 7, Aug. 21
                      1820 Jan. 20, Feb. 21, Mar. 3, 23-25, Apr. 4, 8, 20, 21, May 23, June 30, July 1, 3, 7, Oct. 2 Nov. 21, 22, Dec. 11, 15, 20
                      1821 Jan. 20, July 14, 24
                      1824 Jan. 24, Feb. 2, Mar. 1
              tw 1816 Aug. 29/30, 31/Sept. 2-5/6, 12/13, 28/30, Oct. 5/7, 8/9, 29/30, Nov. 12/13-16/18-19/20, 28/29, 30/Dec. 1, 8/9-17/18, 24/25, 28/30, 31/1817 Jan. 1
                      1817 Jan. 2/3, 7/8, 9/10, 14/15-18/20, 23/24, 25/27, 30/31, Feb. 8/10, 15/17, 18/19, Mar. 22/24, Apr. 19/21, May 1/2, 6/7, 22/23, 27/28, June 21/23-26/27, July 8/9, 10/11, 17/18, 24/25, 29/30, 31/Aug. 1, 5/6, 21/22, Sept. 6/8-11/12, 23/24, 30/Oct. 1, 4/6, 11/13, 30/31, Nov. 1/3, 6/7, 15/17, 20/21-26/27, Dec. 4/5-11/12, 18/19, 27/29
                      1818 Jan. 3/5, 8/9, 13/14, 24/26-29/30, Feb. 5/6, 9/10, 14/16, 19/20, 28/Mar. 2-12/13, 17/18, 19/20, 26/27, 28/30, Apr. 2/3, 14/15, 18/20, 21/22, 30/May 1, 9/11, 12/13, 16/18, 19/20, June 9/10, 13/15, 16/17, 20/22, 23/24, 27/29,

EVENING BULLETIN, *continued*

July 2/3, 7/8, 16/17, 21/22-28/29, Aug. 1/3, 4/5, 13/14, 18/19-22/24, 29/31, Sept. 5/7, 10/11, 12/14, 17/18, 22/23, 24/25, 29/30, Oct. 1/2, 3/5, 15/16, 22/23, 24/26-29/30, 31/Nov. 1, 5/6, 7/9-17/18, 19, 21/23-28/30, Dec. 1/2-12/14, 17-18, 19/21, 26/28, 31/1819 Jan. 1

1819 Jan. 2/4, 9/11, 16/18-21/22, 26/27, 28/29, Feb. 6/8-23, 24, Mar. 2/3-11/12, 20/22, 25/26, 27/29, Apr. 1/2, 3/5, 8/9, 10/12, 15/16, 22/23, 24/26, 29/30-May 8/10, 15/17, 18/19, June 1/2-5/7, 10/11-15/16, 22/23, 24/25, July 1/2-6/7, 13/14, Aug. 14/16, 17/18, 21/23, 24/25, Sept. 28/29, 30/Oct. 1, 9/11, 13/15, 16/17, Nov. 30/Dec. 1, 30/31

1820 Jan. 1/3, 4/5, 11/12-15/17, Mar. 18/20, May 11/12, 23/24, 27/29, 30/31, June 1/2-6/7, 10/12, 13/14, 22/23, July 1/3, Aug. 5/7, 26/28, Sept. 7/8, 12/13, 16/18, 30/Oct. 2, 17/18-26/27, 31/Nov. 1, 2/4, 7/8, 23/25

1821 Jan. 2/3-13/15, 18/19, 20/22-27/29, Feb. 6/7, 8/9, 15/16-20/21, 27/28, Mar. 1/2, 3/5-10/12, 20/21, 22/23, 27/28-Apr. 5/6, 12/13, 28/30, May 8/9, 17/18, June 2/4, 5/6, 9/11, 21/22, 26/27-30/July 2, 3/4, 19/20, 21/23, Aug. 14/15, 21/22-30/31, Sept. 15/17, Oct. 13/15, 23/24, 30/31, Nov. 1/3, 8/9, Dec. 15/17

1822 Jan. 3/4, 5/7, 10/11, 22/23, Feb. 7/8, 12/13, 16/18, 19/20, 26/27, Mar. 2/4, 12/13, May 14/15, 21/22, July 2/3, 13/15, 18/19, Aug. 20/21-31/Sept. 1, Oct. 3/4, 15/16, Nov. 2/4, 23/25, Dec. 7/9

1823 Mar. 13/14, 20/21, Apr. 5/7, 12/14, 17/18, 26/27, 29/30, May 3/5, 10/12, 20/21, June 19/20, July 7, 8, 9, 12/14, 15/16, 29/30, 31/Aug. 1, 5/6, 14/15, 21/22, 26/27, Sept. 9/10, 13/15, 20/22, 23/24, 30/Oct. 1, 30/31, Nov. 4/5, Dec. 27/29

1824 Jan. 6/7, 20/21, 31/Feb. 1, 6, 17/18, 19/20

PPL 1822 Jan. 1-11, 16-17, 19-Feb. 23, 26-28, Mar. 4-Dec. 31

1824 Jan. 1-31, Mar. 1-6, 8-Dec. 31

PWaHi 1821 July 21
PWcHi 1822 June 1

continued as

AMERICAN SENTINEL (Mar. 8, 1824-Apr. 9, 1847) d tw w
Pub. & Ed. 1824-1847 Peter Hay & Co.
Tri-weekly edition published, entitled *American Sentinel and Mercantile Advertiser,* March 8, 1824-1840.

P 1824 Mar. [8-1847 Apr. 6]
P-M-9 1833 Mar. 20
PCHi 1831 July 29
PDoHi ♦ 1830 Oct. 11
PEL ♦ w 1825 Feb. 14
d 1832 Jan. 17, Feb. 3-9, 11-22, 24, 27-Mar. 20, 22-Apr. 16, 18-25, 27-May 4, 7-July 4, 6, 10-19, 21-Aug. 1, 3-9, 11-Sept. 18, 20-Nov. 19, 22, 24-Dec. 31

1833 Apr. 18, 19

PHILADELPHIA COUNTY 55

               1834 Jan. 1-17, 20-Feb. 14, 17-Mar. 18, 20-Apr. 18, 21-May 7, 9-22, 24-July 2, 4, 7-12, 18-Nov. 13, 15, 18-29
               1835 Jan. 2-24, 27-Feb. 10, 12-Apr. 24, 27- May 13, 15-20, 22-Aug. 3, 5-27, 31-Sept. 16, 18-Nov. 17, 19-21, 24-Dec. 25, 28-31
               1836 Jan. 6-22, 25-Mar. 19, 22-28, 30-Apr. 9, 12-18, 20-25, 27-June 24, 27-Aug. 5, 8- 10, 12, 13, 17-Sept. 2, 5-9, 12-Oct. 1, 4-8, 11-Dec. 9, 12-31
               1837 Jan. 2-18, 20-Feb. 1, 3-8, 10-17, 20, 21, 23, Apr. 7, 10, 11, 13-May 4, 6-13, 16, 20-23, 29-June 5, 8, 9, 12-19, 21-24, 27-July 4, 6-11, 14-21, 24-Aug. 14, Sept. 2-5, 7-30, Oct. 4-14, 17-24, 28, 30, Nov. 2-9, 11-24, 27-Dec. 5, 8-21, 23, 25, 28-30
               1838 Jan. 1-4, 9-11, 13-19, 22-29, 31-Feb. 6, 9, 13-17, 20, 22-Mar. 7, 9-21, 23, 26, 27, 29-Apr. 6, 11-May 29, June 1, 4-11, 13-16, 19-22, 25-July 3, 6-13, 16-Aug. 25, Sept. 28-Oct. 4, 6-8, 10-12, Nov. 15, 17, 26-Dec. 7, 10-22, 25, 27
               1839 Jan. 17
PHHi   d 1845 Aug. 2-Nov. 29
PHi ♦   1826 Feb. 24
               1827 Jan. 15-(18, 19)-(22)-(26, 27)-(30)-Mar. 9, July (2)-4, 6, (7)-Aug. (6)-Sept. (4, 5)-29, Oct. 16, 17, 19-22, 25-27, 30, 31, Nov. (3-5)-8, 13, (14), 15
               1828 Mar. 6-8, 11-Apr. 14, 17, 18, 22-26, 29, 30, May 2, 5, 6, 8, 9, 12-14, 21-(24), 27, 30, June 4-12, 16, 17, July 7-9, 12, (14), 17-22, Aug. 6, 9, 13-21, 26-28, Sept. 1-12, 15-17, 19-26, 29-Oct. 6, 8-16, 18-24, 27-Nov. 1, 5, 8-14, 19, 20, 24, 28, Dec. 1, (2)-22, 24, (25), 27-29, 31
               1829 Jan. 1, 2, 5-(24)-(28)-(30), Feb. (2)-(27)-Mar. (6)-(10-11)-Apr. (8)-(10, 11)(-(15)-May 6, 8-(16)-21, 23-July 4, 7-13, 15-Sept. (5)-Oct. (1)-(3)-(24)-Dec. (23), 24, 25, 28-31
               1830 Jan. 1- Mar. (1)- Oct. (28)- Dec. 24, 27-31
               1831 Jan. (1)- (4)- (13)- Apr. (23)- June (4)-(24)-July 4, 6, Sept. (1-19)- Oct. (4)-(6-10)- (12)- Dec. (1, 2)- (7-13)- 16-31)
               1832 Oct. 25, 31
               1833 July 6, Sept. (25), Dec. (7), (16)
               1834 Jan. (16), Mar. 11, 26, July 14, Oct. 14, 18, 21
               1835 Feb. 28, Oct. 17
               1837 June 17, Sept. 5, 6, Dec. 9, 11
               1838 Feb. 22, 23
               1842 Aug. (6)
PHsHi   1838 Feb. 28, Mar. 1
PMilD   1824 Mar. 19
PNoHi   1823 Aug. 2
               1824 Sept. 21, 22
PP ♦   d 1824 Oct. 19
               1825 Apr. 1, June 8, Aug. 22, Dec. 12
          tw 1824 Mar. 8/9, 13/15, 20/22, 25/26, 30/31, Apr. 3/5, 8/9, 10/12-15/16, 27/28, June 5/7, 10/11,

EVENING BULLETIN, continued

			29/30, July 10/12, 20/21, 27/28, 29/30, Aug. 31/Sept. 1, 18/20-25/27, Oct. 7/8-14/15, 26/27, 28/29, Nov. 2/3, 4/5, 9/10-16/17, 27/29, 30/ Dec. 1, 4/6, 21/22, 25/27-30/31
		1825	Jan. 4/5, 6/7, 11/12, 25/26, Feb. 1/2, 5/7, 22/23, 24/25, Mar. 8/9, 10/11, 15/16, 19/21, 27/28, Apr. 12/13-21/22, May 12/13, 17/18-21/23, June 9/10, 18/20, 23/24-28/29, July 2/4, 12/13, 14/15, 23/25, Aug. 6/8, 18/19, 30/31, Sept. 3/5, 6/7, 13/14, 29/30, Oct. 20/21, Nov. 5/7, 8/9, 29/30, Dec. 3/5, 20/21, 29/30
		1826	Jan. 3/4, 7/9, Feb. 7/8, 9/10, 28/Mar. 1, 4/6, 18/20, 21/22, June 10/12, Sept. 12, Oct. 19/20, 26/27, 28/30, Dec. 7/8, 30/-1827 Jan. 1
		1827	Jan. 16/17, Feb. 13/14, 15/16, May 10/11, 30, June 23/25, July 6/8, 10/11, 31/Aug. 1, 2/3
		1828	Feb. 14/15, 16/18, 23/25, Mar. 8/10, 11/12, Apr. 12/14-17/18, 26/28, May 1/2, 6/7-10/12, 20/21-29/30, 31/June 2, 5/6, 7/9, 12/13, 26/27, July 22/23, 24/25, Aug. 9/11, 26/27, 30/Sept. 1, 6/8, 13/15, 27/29, Oct. 11/13
		1830	July 8/9
	d	1838	July 6
		1846	Jan. 14, Apr. 10, 21, May 29
PPiUD	d	1843	July 6-10
PPL		1825	July 30, Sept. 1-Oct. 22, Nov. 1-1826 May 24
		1826	May 26-31, Aug. 1-Sept. 20, 22-Oct 11, 13-31, Dec. 1-1827 Mar. 30
		1827	Apr. 2-Aug. 29, 31-1828 Mar. 4-1828 Aug. 26
		1828	Aug. 28-Oct. 13, 16, 17, 20-Nov. 17, 19-1829 Jan. 31
		1829	Feb. 3-Apr. 3, 6-11, 14-17, 20-June 8, 10, 11, 13-July 11, 14-17, 20-Nov. 26, 28-Dec. 31
		1832	Jan. 3-13, 16-18, 20-26, 28-Feb. 24, 27-29, Mar. 2-Apr. 6, 9-May 3, 5-17, 19-24, 26-June 30, July 2-10, 12-17, 21-Aug. 6, 8, 11-18, 21-25, 28, 30, 31, Sept. 3-11, 13-Oct. 15, 17-19, 22-29, 31-Nov. 8, 10-24, 27-Dec. 29
		1833	Jan. 1-June 8, 10-14, 17-July 12, 15-Sept. 6, 9-Nov. 9, 11-1834 Jan. 4
		1834	Jan. 7-Feb. 22, 27-Mar. 5, 7-26, 29-31, Apr. 2-3, 5-26, 29-May 1, 3-July 28, 31, Aug. 2-4, 18, 19, 22-Sept. 13, 16-19, 22-Nov. 3, 5, 7-13, 15-Dec. 1, 3-22, 24-27, 30, 31
		1835	Feb. 2-13, 16-Mar. 20, 23-Apr. 10, 14-21, 23-May 8, 11-22, 25-June 13, 16-July 16, 18-Sept. 11, 14-Oct. 10, 14-16, 19-30, Nov. 2-Dec. 21, 23-1837 May 30
		1837	June 1-1838 Jan. 15
		1838	Jan. 18-Dec. 31
		1839	Mar. 25, 27-29, Apr. 1-May 1, 3, 6-10, 13-June 7, 10-July 25, 27-Aug. 23, 26-Sept. 19, 22-Oct. 26, Nov. 1-16, 19-Dec. 25, 28-1840 Jan. 1
		1840	Jan. 3-17, Apr. 15, 16, 18, 21-25, 28-30, May 5-June 10, 12-Aug. 1, 3-Sept. 3, 5-Oct. 2, 5-27, 29, 30, Nov. 2-13, 16-Dec. 16, 18-1841 Mar. 2

PHILADELPHIA COUNTY 57

		1841 Mar. 4, 6-9, 11, 12
PW	d	1838 Mar. 6
PWaHi	d	1829 Aug. 13
PWbW		1836 Apr. 7
PWcHi	d	1846 June (5), (12), (17)
PWeT		1836 Mar. 22-25
		1839 May 22-25
PWalG		1834 Feb. 6

American Sentinel merged with *Cummings' Telegraphic Evening Bulletin,* April 11, 1847, and
continued as

CUMMINGS' TELEGRAPHIC EVENING BULLETIN, (Apr. 12, 1847-Apr. 9, 1851)
  Pub. 1847-1851   Alexander Cummings
    w 1847-1851; sw Oct. 30, 1850-1851)
  Weekly edition known as *Cummings' Weekly Telegraphic Bulletin.*
  Semi-weekly edition known as *Philadelphia Evening Bulletin for the Country.*

P		1850 June 1-1851 Apr. 9
PBL	♦	1848 Oct. 4-19, 21-Nov. 22, 24-Dec. 22, 26-29
		1849 Jan. 1-6, 9-May 5, 8-June 23, 26-Aug. 2, 4-1850 Feb. 1
		1850 Feb. 4-Mar. 20, 22-29, Apr. 1-26, 29-June 5, 7-July 3, 5-Dec. 11, 13-24, 26-1851 Feb. 8
		1851 Feb. 11-Apr. 9
PP	♦	1847 Apr. 12-1848 May 24
		1848 May 28, June 1-3, 5-1851 Apr. 9
PPBu		1847 Apr. 12-1851 Apr. 9
PPL		1847 July 16, Aug. 5, 6
		1850 Mar. 26, 28, Apr. 9, June 25, July 26, 27, Aug. 16, Sept. 2, 26, 28, Oct. 11, 28, Nov. 20, 22
		1851 Jan. 1-Feb. 4, 10, Mar. 29-Apr. 9

continued as

CUMMINGS' EVENING BULLETIN, (Apr. 10, 1851-Apr. 9, 1856) d
  Pub. 1851-1856   Alexander Cummings
  Ed. 1851-1856   Charles G. Leland, Casper Souder, Jr., Ernest C. Wallace
    d Apr. 10, 1851-June 30, 1856:
    sw Apr. 1851-1854; w Apr. 1851-Apr. 1856
  Weekly edition known as *Cummings' Weekly Bulletin.*
  Semi-weekly edition known as *Philadelphia Bulletin for the Country.*

P		1851 Apr. 10-1856 Apr. 9
P-M		1854 July 6
		1855 Feb. 3, July 16
PBL	♦	1851 Apr. 10-July 3, 5-Nov. 26, 28-Dec. 24, 26-1852 Jan. 2
		1852 Jan. 7-12, 14-Feb. 21, 24-Mar. 5, 7-30, Apr. 1-July 4, 6-Oct. 21, 23-Nov. 24, 26-Dec. 3, 5-24, 26-1853 Mar. 3
		1853 Mar. 5-May 13, 15-June 8, 10-July 3, 5-29, 31-Aug. 18, 20-Nov. 10, 12-14, 16-23, 25-Dec. 1, 3-18, 20-25, 27-1854 Jan. 8
		1854 Jan. 10-Feb. 10, 12-16, 18, 22-27, Mar. 1-24, 26-Apr. 3, 7-May 21, 23-June 20, 22-July 3, 5, 7-Sept. 12, 14-30, Oct. 3-Nov. 22, 24-29, Dec. 1-24, 26-1855 Jan. 22

EVENING BULLETIN, *continued*
                       1855 Jan. 24-Feb. 7, 9-Mar. 5, 7-May 9, 11-30,
                            June 1-23, July 25-Sept. 12, 14-Nov. 21, 23-
                            27, 29-Dec. 2, 4-11, 13-24, 26-1856 Feb. 26
                       1856 Feb. 28-Mar. 17, 19-Apr. 7
    PHi ♦   1851 May 17, Dec. 30
                       1852 Feb. 20, 28, Mar. 2, 9, 10, (15), 16, 29
                       1853 Jan. (21), Mar. 29, Apr. 1, 16, (18, 19), 20,
                            23, 30, May 10-12, 23, 25- (27, 28), 31, June
                            (3), 6, (11), 13, (16), (30), July 13-15, Aug.
                            4, 11, 20, 26, 30, Sept. (1), 5, 6, (15), (19,
                            20), 21, (24), 27, Oct. 5, 20
                       1854 Mar. 11, June 6, Aug. (14), Oct. 12
                       1855 Mar. (31), Aug. 23, Sept. 8, Nov. 17
        w   1855 July 4
                       1856 Feb. 15, 16, 21, Mar. 15, 17, (26)
    PNoHi   w   1851 Apr. 16, 30-May 21, June 4-18, July 2
        sw 1851 Apr. 17
    PP ♦   1851 Apr. 10-1854 Dec. 31
                       1855 July 1-1856 Apr. 9
    PPBu   1851 Apr. 10-1856 Apr. 9
    PPFfHi 1851 Aug. 29
    PPL   1851 Apr. 10-21, Nov. 26, 28-Dec. 31
                       1852 Feb. 19, Mar. 20
                       1853 Jan. 1-Dec. 31
                       1855 Jan. 1-1856 Apr. 9
                   continued as

DAILY EVENING BULLETIN, (Apr. 10, 1856-Apr. 19, 1870) d
  Pub. 1856-1859   Alexander Cummings
       1859-1860   Cummings and Peacock
       1860-1865   Peacock, Chambers & Co.
       1865-1868   Bulletin Association
       1868-1870   F. L. Fetherston
  Ed. 1856-1870   Charles G. Leland, Casper Souder, Jr., Ernest C.
                            Wallace, Francis Wells, Charles Clark, Gibson Peacock
    P   1856 Apr. 10-1865 Sept.
    P-M   1865 Apr. 15
    PBL ♦   1856 Apr. 10-Aug. 19, 21-Sept. 1, 3-Nov. 19, 21-
                            Dec. 14, 16-24, 26-1857 Jan. 21
                       1857 Feb. 13, 14, 17-Mar. 20, 22-24, 26-July 3, 5-29,
                            Sept. 17-Nov. 13, 15-27, Dec. 3-24, 26
                       1858 Jan. 3, 5-14, 16-Mar. 8, 10-Apr. 7, 9-22, 24-
                            May 8
    PCHi   1862 Sept. 4
    PDoHi ♦ 1856 Oct. 27
                       1860 Feb. 4, Nov. 30
                       1862 Sept. 23, Oct. 26
                       1865 Apr. 17, 18, 24
                       1866 June 8
        w   1857 Jan. 17, Mar. 14-28
    PHi ♦   1856 Apr. 19, May 30, Oct. 17, Nov. 1, Dec. (3)
                       1857 Jan. (1, 2) 3, (5-8), 9, 10, (12-16), 17, (19)-
                            (30, 31)- Feb. 4, 5, (6)- Mar. (12)-(16-18),
                            19, 20-22, (23, 24)-(27)-Apr. 3, 5- (20)- May
                            (1)-(18), Oct. (24) Dec. 12, (31)
                       1858 Aug. (5, 6), 7, 11, 13, (14), (17), 21, 27,
                            (28), Sept. (1), (4), (17)
                       1859 Jan. (1), 8, July 30, Aug. 1, Nov. (2)

PHILADELPHIA COUNTY   59

         1860 Jan. 14, 28, Feb. (2, 3), (6), Mar. 1, (2),
              10, (15), 17, 19, 22, 23, 30, 31, Apr. 9, (13),
              14, 17, 19, (21), 24, 26-30, May 3, 9, 12, 15,
              16, (17), 18, 21, 22, (23), 25-June 8, 11-14,
              16, (18), 19-22, (23), 25- July 3, 6-Aug. (9)-
              (13), 17, 20-Sept. 3, 5-(12)-14, 18, 25-28, Oct.
              1, (2), 3, (4), 5-17, 19-31, Nov. 8-10, 13-17,
              20-23, 26-28, 30- Dec. 12, 14-24, (26), 27-31
         1861 Jan. (1-5), 7, (8-10)-15, 18-22, 25, 26, 29,
              30, Feb. 1, 4, 9-12, 14, 15, 18, 20-22, 26, 28-
              Mar. 5, 9-20, 23, 27, 29- Apr. 14, 16, 18-20,
              23-27, 30- May 5, 7-10, 13, 15, 20-31, June
              (1), 3-6, 11, 12, 15-24, 26, 28, 29-July (3)-
              (9)-15, (17), 18-Aug. 13, 15, 16, 19- Sept. 11,
              14-25, 27- Oct. 7, 10-17, 22-26, 29- Nov. 15,
              18, 19, 21-23, 26, 27, Dec. 2-9, 12, 13, 16-23,
              26, 30-1862 Apr. 3
         1862 Apr. (4), 5-10, (11), 12- May (6)- July 3,
              5- Oct. (7)- Nov. 26, 28- Dec. 24- 1863 Apr.
              (10)
         1863 Apr. 11-29, May 1- July 3, 5-15, 17- Oct. 28,
              30- Nov. 25, 27- Dec. 24, 26-31
         1864 Jan. (1, 2) 4, (5, 6) 7- Mar. 3, 5,- (19, 21)-
              Apr. (16)- July 3, 5- Aug. 3, 5- Nov. 23, 25-
              Dec. (23), 24, 27-1865 Mar. (7, 8)
         1865 Mar. 9- Apr. (10)- May 31, June 2- July 3,
              5-(14)- Sept. 13, 15-Oct. (7)-22, 24- Nov. (6)
              Dec. 6, 8-24, 26-30
         1866 Jan. 1- (16), 17, 18, 21, 22, 24-31, Feb. 2-7,
              9-28, Mar. 3, 5, 7, 9, 10, (14), 16, 20-22, 24-
              27, 30, 31, Apr. 3-5, 7, 9, 12, (13), June 8, 11
PNoHi   d 1865 Apr. 3, 13
         1869 May 8
PP ♦   d 1856 Apr. 10-1859 June 30
         1860 Oct. 10, 11
         1861 Feb. 1, 20, 22, 23, Apr. 10, 12, 13, Oct. 25,
              Nov. 13
         1863 July 6, 7, Oct. 9
         1864 Oct. 12, 20, Nov. 9
         1865 Feb. 21, 24, Apr. 6, 7, 13, 15, 21, 27, May 2,
              3, 11
         1868 Mar. 30
         1869 July 22
PPBu   1856 Apr. 10-1870 Apr. 19
PPeS   1862 Sept. 15, 18
PPFfHi   1863 Aug. 18
           1865 Aug. 14
PPL   d 1856 Apr. 10-Dec. 27, 30, 31
           1861 Jan. 1-June 29, July 1-1862 Dec. 31
           1863 Jan. 13, 30-Feb. 4, 7-Mar. 13, 16-Apr. 2, 4-
                29, May 1-June 30, July 1-22, 24- Sept. 11,
                14-29, Oct. 1-Nov. 4, 7-13, 16-1864 Jan. 7
           1864 Jan. 9-Feb. 4, 6-Mar. 24, 26-Apr. 1, 4-June
                30, July 1, 2, 5-Sept. 3, 10-17, 20-Oct. 10,
                12-21, 24-Nov. 5, 9-16, 18-23, 26-Dec. 13, 20-31
           1865 Jan. 3-16, 18-Feb. 27, Mar. 1-13, 15, 20, 21,
                24-May 10, 12, 13, 16-31, June 2, 5- 9, 12-30,
                July 1-11, 13-25, 28-Oct. 19, 21-Dec. 6, 8-30
PPM   1861 Jan. 1-1870 Apr. 19

EVENING BULLETIN, *continued*
    PPot   1856 Aug. 27
              1859 Aug. 24
    PWcHi   1860 Aug. 17, Dec. 18
              1861 Feb. 27, Apr. 16, July 19, 22, 24, 25
              1862 Feb. 15, 18, 19, 24, 25, 27, Mar. 8, 24, May 1, 30, 31, Sept. 1, 4, 22, Oct. 8, 25, Nov. 7, Dec. 19
              1863 Feb. 9, July 3, Dec. 15
              1865 Apr. 15
              1866 Aug. 7
              1867 May 6
              1868 Aug. 15
    PWcT   1867 May 16
    PWalG   1868 Oct. 24
              continued as

EVENING BULLETIN, THE (Apr. 21, 1870†) d
Pub. 1870-1871   F. L. Fetherston
     1872-1889   Peacock, Fetherston & Co.
     1889-1895   Gibson Peacock Co.
     1895-1897   The Bulletin Co.
     1897-1924   William L. McLean
     1924-1941   The Bulletin Co.
Ed. 1870-1895   Gibson Peacock
     1908-1921   William Perrine
     1924-1929   William L. McLean
     1929-1937   Fred Fuller Shedd
     1937-1941   M. F. Ferguson
    PUB   1870 Apr. 21-1911 Dec. 31
              1912 Apr. 1-30
              1913 July 1†
    P   1927 Jan. -1932 June 30†
    P-M   1913 Jan. 22-24
    PBf   1881 Nov. 17
    PCHi   1897 Mar. 5
              1898 July 4
              1901 Sept. 7, 11, 12, 16-19, 21
              1914 Dec. 30
    PDoHi ♦ 1872 Jan. 1
              1875 July 3
              1876 Mar. 10, July 18, Oct. 11, Nov. 9, Dec. 4
              1881 Sept. 22-24
              1885 July 23
              1896 Feb. 22
              1899 Feb. 10, Sept. 9
              1901 Sept. 14
              1902 Oct. 23
              1907 Apr. 11
              1908 Oct. 5-11, Nov. 4, 18
              1911 May 13
    PHi ♦   1872 Nov. 21
              1873 Mar. 27, Aug. 19-21, Sept. 18
              1874 Sept. 5, (10)
              1875 Aug. 23, Oct. 14
              1876 May (10)
              1881 Sept. 22
              1882 Jan. 2-(12)-(17)-(30, 31)- Feb. 1, (2), 3, (4), 6-(17)- (20, 21), 22, (23), 24, (25), 27, (28)-Mar. 1-(7)-(23-25)-(29)- Apr. (1)-

PHILADELPHIA COUNTY   61

3, (4), 5-(12), 13-(26), 27, (28, 29), May 1-(4)-(8)-(31)- June (7)-(30)- July 3, 5- Aug. (10)-(16)-(19)-(22)-(26)-(30, 31)- Sept. (4)-(11, 12)-(15)-(20)-(23)-(27), 28, (29), Oct. (6)-(21), 22, 23, 25, (26)- Nov. (11)-(24)-29, Dec. 1, 4, (5)-(14, 15)-(23), 24, 26-(30)

1883 Jan. (1)-(6)-(9, 10), 11, (12)-(22)-(30- Feb. 1)-(20, 21), 22, (23)-Mar. (7), 8, 9, (10)-(16)-(24)- May (9, 10), 11, (12)-(20)- June (25)- July 3, 5-(9-11), 12-(28)- Aug. (4)-(11), 12, 13, (14, 15)-(27)- Sept. (25)- Nov. (26)- Dec. 24, 26-31

1884 Jan. 1-(4, 5)- Feb. (2)- March (26)-(28)- Apr. (4)- June (30, July 1)- 3, 5-(30, 31)- Aug. (22)-(26)-(29)- Sept. (20)-(27)- Oct. (14)-(31)-Nov. (6)-(18, 19)-26, 28-Dec. (1)- (20)-24, 26, 31

1885 Jan. 1-(10)-(13)-(21)- Feb. (4)-March (21- 24)-(26)-Apr. (4)-(11)-(21, 22)-(24, 25)- May (1, 2)-(11)-(16)-(25)-June (1)-(8)- July (2), 3, 6-(16)-Oct. (1)-Nov. 25, 27- Dec. 24, 26-(31)

1886 Jan. 1-(30)-July 3, 6-Sept. 28, 30-Dec. 24, 26-31

1887 Jan. 1-(5)-(10)-(14)-(21)-(29-Feb. 1)-(7)- (16, 17)-(21), 23-March (5) (-(24)-(26)- (29)-(31)-Apr. (5)-(9)-May (5)-June (22)- July (1), 2, 5-(29-Aug. 1)-(16)-Sept. 14, 16-Oct. (18)-Nov. (1)-(7)-(18)-23, 25- Dec. (6)-(8)-24, 27-(31)

1888 Jan. (2)-(11)-July 3, 5-(13)-Nov. (1)-28, 30-Dec. 24, 26-31

1889 Feb. 1-Apr. (30)-July 3, 5-Nov. 27, 29-Dec. 24, 26-31

1890 Jan. 1-(8)-(10, 11)-(16)-(18, 20)-Feb. (10)- (24)-March (1)-(5)-(10)-(22)-(25)-Apr. (1)-(9)-(14)-(16)-(21, 22)-(26)-(30-May (8)-(13)-June (5)-(9)-(19)-(30)-July 3, 5- Aug. (23)-Nov. 26, 28-Dec. (23), 24, 26, (27)-31

1891 Jan. 1-(9)-March (24)-May (4)-June (1)- July 3, 6-(15)-(29)-Aug. (25)-Oct. (30)- Nov. (2), 25, 27-(30)-Dec. 24, 26, 31

1892 Jan. 2-May (2)-July 2, (5)-Aug. (13)-(30)- Oct. (22, 24)-Nov. (18)-Dec. (3)-24, 27-31

1893 Jan. 3-(11)-(28)-(31)-Feb. (8)-June (16)- (30)-July 3, 5-Oct. (14)-(21)-(30)-Nov. (18)-29, Dec. 1-(13)-23, 26-30

1894 Jan. (2)-(26)-Feb. (16)-(22)-Apr. (30)- May (7)-June (7)-July 3, 5-Aug. (2)-(22)- Oct. (27, 29)-Nov. (6)-(20)-28, 30-Dec. (11)- 24- 26-31

1895 Jan. 2-July 3, 5-Nov. 27, 29-Dec. 24, 26-31

1896 Jan. (1-4), 6-(9)-(18, 20)-Feb. (6)-(24)- Mar. (2)-(24, 25)-Apr. (2)-(30, May 1)- (14)-(25)-(28, 29)-June (19)-(22)-July 3,

PENNSYLVANIA NEWSPAPERS

EVENING BULLETIN, *continued*

  6-(9)-(28)-Aug. (1-8) (31, Sept. 1)-Oct. (12)-(16)-Nov. (7)-(20)-25, 27-(30)-Dec. 24, 26-(31)
1897 Jan. (1-4)-(8-11)-(13, 14)-(23)-Feb. (1)-(4)-(11)-(27)-Mar. (3)-(11)-(13)-(31, Apr. 1)-(5)-(10)-May (10)-(14)-June (3)-(16)-(21)-(30, July 1)-(3), 6-(21)-Sept. (14)-Oct. (1, 2)-(22)-Nov. (19)-Dec. (8)-(13)-24, 27, (28)-31
1898 Jan. 1-Apr. (1)-May (2)-July (5)-Aug. (27, 29)-Oct. (1)-(6)-Nov. (16)-28, 30-Dec. 24, 27-31
1899 Jan. (2-6)-(16-19)-(21)-Feb. (1)-Mar. (8)-(10)-(14)-(20)-(24, 25)-(31)-Apr. (8)-July (1)-3, 5-Sept. (7)-(30)-Oct. (11)-(30, 31)-Nov. (11)-(15)-Dec. (18)-(20)-23, 26-(29, 30)
1900 Jan. 1-Apr. (10)-July 3, 5-Dec. 24, 26-31
1901 Jan. (1-7)-(31)-Feb. (14)-(18)-(25)-Mar. (5)-(25)-(30-Apr. 6)-(24, 25)-May (18)-(29)-June (1)-(14)-July (1-3), (5, 6)-(15)-Aug. (23)-Sept. (2)-Oct. (1-10)-(17)-(22, 23)-(25-28)-(31)-Nov. (7-15)-Dec. (4)-(6)-(12)-(20)-24, 26-(31)
1902 Jan. (1)-(7)-(15)-Feb. (6)-(17)-(24)-Mar. (1)-(5-7)-(13)-(17)-(19-22)-(25, 26)-(28-Apr. 1)-(11)-May (6)-(10)-(13)-June (20)-(30, July 1)-3, (5)-(14)-Aug. (4)-(7)-Sept. (18)-(30, Oct. 1)-(11)-Nov. (17)-(29)-Dec. (1)-24, 26-(31)
1903 Jan. 1-July 3, 6-Dec. 24, 26-31
1904 Jan. (1)-Feb. 29, Mar. 26-April (1)-May (21)-June (16)-(30, July 1), 2, 5-Aug. (11)-Oct. (1-4)-Nov. (29)-Dec. 24, 27-31
1905 Jan. (2)-Dec. 23, 26-30
1906 Jan. (1)-(8)-(15)-(31)-Mar. (31, April 2)-(17, 18)-June (27)-July (2), 3, 5, (6)-(20)-(28)-(30)-Aug. (13)-(18)-(24)-Sept. (29-Oct. 4)-(9)-(17)-(23)-(30)-Nov. (7)-(23)-Dec. (3)-24, 26-31
1907 Jan. (1)-(31)-June (29-July 2), 3, 5-Oct. (1, 2)-Dec. (31)
1908 Jan. (1-3)-(14)-Feb. (26)-Mar. (2)-(17)-(27-31)-Apr. (10)-(16)-(20, 21)-May (6)-June (30, July 1)-3, 5-Aug. (18)-Sept. (2)-(30, Oct. 1)-(28)-(31)-Nov. (30)-Dec. 24, (26)-31
1909 Jan. 1-Apr. (1)-(29, 30)-June 10-July (1)-(3), 6-(14)-(31)-Aug. (16)-(24)-Sept. (13)-17)-Oct. (1-6)-(30)-Dec. 24, 27-31
1910 Jan. (1)-(15)-(31)-Feb. (7)-(12)-(16)-(23)-Mar. (30)-Apr. (1-7)-May (6)-(30)-June (4)-(7)-(9, 10)-(14-17)-(25)-(30-July 2), (5)-(11)-(30)-Aug. (8-11)-(30)-Sept. (3)-(23)-(28)-Oct. (1-7)-(13)-(20)-(28)-Nov. (2)-(4)-(7, 8)-(11)-(22)-Dec. (10)-24, 27-(31)

PHILADELPHIA COUNTY 63

1911 Jan. (3)-(6)-(24, 25)-Feb. (8)-(21)-(23)-
Apr. (1)-(26)-May (10)-(25)-June (16)-
(21)-July 3, 5-Aug. (2, 3)-(7)-(17)-(19)-
(24)-Oct. (16, 17)-Dec. 23, 26-30
1912 Jan. 1-Feb. (12)-(15)-May (18)-July 3, 5-
Dec. (4)-(24), 26-31
1913 Jan. 1-(31)-Mar. (17)-Apr. (9)-(12)-(16-
18)-(24)-(29)-May (2)-(8)-(19)-(31)-June
(19)-July (1)-3, 5-(8)-Aug. (21)-Sept. (13)-
(29-Oct. 2)-(24)-Nov. (11)-(13)-Dec. (1)-
(8)-(10)-24, 26-31
1914 Jan. (1)-(12)-(22)-Feb. (14)-(16-19)-Apr.
(9)-(29)-July 3, 6-(13, 14)-(16)-Oct. (3)-
(7)-(23)-(31)-Nov. (20)-Dec. (16)-24, 26-
31
1915 Jan. 1-(18)-(20)-(29, 30)-Feb. (15)-(26)-
Mar. (3, 4)-(16)-Apr. (10)-(30, May 1)-
(6, 7)-June (12)-(22)-(28-30)-July (3), 6-
(23)-(31)-Aug. (30)-Oct. (1)-(4)-(21)-
Nov. (22)-(30)-Dec. (3)-(8, 9)-(13)-(15,
16)-24, 27-31
1916 Jan. 1-(24)-Mar. (21-28)-(31)-Apr. (29)-
May (27-31)-June (5-7)-July 3, 5-Oct. (30)-
Nov. (10, 11)-(16)-Dec. (1)-(6)-(16)-(18,
19)-(23), (26-30)
1917 Jan. 1, (2)-(5)-(8)-(12)-(26)-(30)-Feb.
(1)-(3)-(6)-(28-Mar. 2)-(6)-(14)-(21)-
(30, 31)-Apr. (3)-(5)-(7)-(10)-(20)-(23,
24)-May (1)-(26)-June (22)-July 3, 5-(13)-
(23)-Oct. (12)-(23)-Nov. (30)-Dec. (3)-
24, 26-(31)
1922 Apr. (12)
1936 June 15, 24
PHHi 1930 May 29-1932 Dec. 22
PLaF 1918 July 27†
PLaHi 1876 May 10
PP ♦ 1873 Apr. 2, 3, July 7, Aug. 22, 25-27, Sept. 1, 2,
6, 8-11, 13, 15, 16, 19, 23, Nov. 22
1874 Feb. 9, 12, May 30
1875 Aug. 10
1876 May 10-Nov. 20, Dec. 6
1877 July 26
1881 Aug. 29
1882 Feb. 27, Oct. 25, Dec. 20
1885 July 23
1887 Apr. 7
1888 Mar. 12-14, Apr. 25
1894 Mar. 29
1901 Jan. 22, 24, 26, Feb. 1, 2, Aug. 26, Sept. 9, 14
1912 June 1-1918 Aug. 31
1918 Oct. 2-7, 9-31, Nov. 2-10, 12-Dec. 24, 26-1919
Jan. 31
1919 Mar. 1-Apr. 30, June 1-1924 Jan. 31
1924 Mar. 1-1925 Apr. 30
1927 June 1†
PPeS 1923 Jan. 13
1928 Nov. 7
1932 Nov. 9

EVENING BULLETIN, *continued*
    PPiHi   1898 Apr. 12-1899 Mar. 27
    PPL   1874 Oct. 30
                 1875 Jan. 18
                 1876 Mar. 8
                 1878 Feb. 5
    PPM   1870 Apr. 21-1896 Apr. 30
                 1903 Mar. 1-1904 Dec. 31
    PPot   1884 Nov. 11-1886 Feb. 13
    PWcHi   1871 June 19
                 1875 Feb. 2, 13, June 11
                 1876 July 20
                 1881 Mar. 18, Apr. 8, May 7, 9, Nov. 12, 22
                 1882 June 27
                 1883 Aug. 24, 29, 30, Sept. 1
                 1888 Dec. 3
                 1911 Apr. 3
                 1912 Apr. 15-20, 25-27
                 1913 Feb. 13, Mar. 4
                 1916 Sept. 6
                 1918 Nov. 11
                 1925 Mar. 4
    PWcT   1899 Dec. 14-1918 Oct. 4, 14
    PWalG   1905 Oct. 3, 23, 27, 31, Nov. 4, 6-8

EVENING CALL, see Call

EVENING CHRONICLE (1787) tw sw ♦ #
    EVENING CHRONICLE: or, The PHILADELPHIA ADVERTISER
    (Feb. 6, 1787-May, 1787) tw ♦ #
  Pub. 1787   Robert Smith
      continued as
    EVENING CHRONICLE, THE (May, 1787-Nov. 1787) tw sw ♦
    # tw, Feb. 6, 1787-July 31, 1787; sw, Aug. 7, 1787-Nov. 7, 1787
  Pub. 1787   Robert Smith
                 James Prange

EVENING CRITIC, THE (1868-June 30, 1882||) d
    PDoHi   1882 June 30

EVENING EXPRESS, THE (1874-1877) d rep
  Pub. 1874-1875   The Express Publishing Co., W. Channing Nevin,
                           Reinstein & McClintock
       1875-1876   H. H. K. Elliott & Co.
  Ed. 1874-1875   W. Channing Nevin
       1875   William Moran
       1875-1877   Reinstein & McClintock
    % EVENING EXPRESS
      PCHi   1875 July 13
      PHi   1874 Oct. 8, 10, 12, Nov. 18
                  1875 Nov. 5
                  1877 June 8
      PP   1876 Oct. 9
      PPL   1874 Sept. 26, Dec. 14

PHILADELPHIA COUNTY 65

EVENING FIRESIDE, OR LITERARY MISCELLANY (1804 - 1806)
w
    EVENING FIRESIDE, OR WEEKLY INTELLIGENCER (Dec. 15, 1804-Dec. 28, 1805) w
    Pub. 1804-1805   Joseph Rakestraw
        PP   1804 Dec. 15-1805 Dec. 28
        PPL   1804 Dec. 15-1805 Dec. 28
        PWcHi   1805 Jan. 26, Sept. 7, 14, Nov. 9, 23

        continued as
    EVENING FIRESIDE, OR LITERARY MISCELLANY (Jan. 4, 1806-Dec. 27, 1806) w
    Pub. 1806   Joseph Rakestraw
        PP   1806 Jan. 4-Dec. 27
        PPL   1806 Jan. 4-Dec. 27
        PWcHi   1806 Jan. 4, 11

EVENING HERALD (1866-1912) d ind *
    EVENING HERALD (1866-1874) d dem
    Pub. & Ed. 1866-1871   Charles F. Reinstein & Co.
                 1871-1873   Dennis F. Dealy
                 1873-1874   Herald Publishing Co.
        PCHi   1868 Feb. 26
        PHi   1872 Mar. 20
                 1874 Oct. 3, Nov. 9, 10
        PU   1866 Aug. 27-1868 Dec. 8
                 1868 Dec. 10-1869 Dec. 31
        PWcHi   1873 July 25
        continued as
    PHILADELPHIA HERALD (1874-1876) d evg ind
    Pub. & Ed. 1874-1875   Herald Publishing Co.
                 1875   A. E. Smythe
        PHi   1876 May 10
        PPL   1875 Mar. 29
        continued as
    EVENING HERALD (1876-1877) d *
    Pub. & Ed. 1876-1877   A. E. Smythe
        P-M   1877 July 24
        PP   1876 Oct. 26 (Vol. 1, No. 1)
                 merged with the *Philadelphia Evening Chronicle*
        continued as
    PHILADELPHIA CHRONICLE-HERALD, THE, (1877-1885) d evg ind dem *
    Pub. & Ed. 1877-1884   Dennis F. Dealy
                 1884-1885   American Company
        PHi   1881 Sept. 21
        PP   1881 Sept. 22
        PPL   1878 Jan. 10, 15, 30, Feb. 16
        PPoHi   1884 Dec. 27-1885
        PSF   1881 Jan. 2
        PWalG   1878 Jan. 7

continued as
DAILY HERALD AND EVENING CHRONICLE (1885-1887)
    d dem
Pub. 1885-1887   Dennis F. Dealy
    PDoHi   1885 July 23
    PPoHi   1885 Dec. 15
    continued as
EVENING HERALD (1887-1893) d dem
Pub. 1887-1893   Herald Company
Ed. 1888   Daniel Gibbons
    PHi   1888 Jan. 24
    continued as
EVENING POST HERALD (1894) d ind ♦
Pub. 1894   Post-Herald Publishing Co.
    continued as
EVENING HERALD (1895-1912) d ind ♦
Pub. 1895-1912   Herald Publishing Co.
Ed. 1895-1903   Geo. E. Vickers
    1903-1908   S. S. Houston

EVENING ITEM, see Item

EVENING LEADER (1878-1879) d ♦
Pub. & Ed. 1878-1879   John Dunn

EVENING NEWS, THE (1838) d ♦
Pub. 1838   M. H. Andrews

EVENING NEWS, THE (1861), see Philadelphia Evening News

EVENING NEWS (1879-1883), see Daily News

EVENING PUBLIC LEDGER (Sept. 14, 1914-Jan. 5, 1942) d evg *
    EVENING PUBLIC LEDGER (Sept. 14, 1914-June 30, 1918) d evg *
Pub. 1914-1916   Public Ledger Company
Ed. 1916   P. H. Whaley
    PP   1914 Sept. 14-1918 June 30
    continued as
EVENING PUBLIC LEDGER, THE, and THE EVENING TELE-
    GRAPH, (July 1, 1918-Dec. 31, 1919) d evg *
Pub. 1918   Public Ledger Company
Ed. 1918   Cyrus H. K. Curtis and Associates
    PHi ♦   1919 May 9, 12, 13-(14)-(16), 17, 19-22
    PP   1918 July 1-Dec. 31
    continued as
EVENING PUBLIC LEDGER (Jan. 1, 1919-Jan. 5, 1942) d evg *
Pub. 1919-1936   Curtis-Martin Newspapers, Inc.
    1936†   Public Ledger, Inc.
Ed. 1919-1926   David E. Smiley
    1933-1939   C. M. Morrison
    1939-1940   Stanley Walker
    1940   George F. Kearney

PHILADELPHIA COUNTY 67

    1941   C. M. Morrison
    PP   1919 Jan. 1-1942 Jan. 5
                small token edition issued Jan. 6, 1942†
    PP   1942 Jan. 6†

EVENING REPORTER (1860) d
    Pub. 1860   J. R. Haldeman & Co.
        PHi   1860 Oct. 30 (Vol. 8, No. 262)

EVENING REPUBLICAN (1874-1880) d ♦
    Pub. 1878-1879 Charles F. Reinstein
         1879-1880 C. Leslie Reilly
    Ed. 1879-1880 C. Leslie Reilly

EVENING STAR, THE (July 4, 1810-1811||) d tw ♦
    Pub. 1810   White, M'Laughlin & Co.
        1810-1811 William F. M'Laughlin & Co.

EVENING STAR, THE (1839) d tw w
    Pub. 1839   Metcalfe, Bausman & Co.
    Ed. 1839   J. Bausman
        PHi   1839 May 4 (Vol. 2, No. 177)

EVENING STAR (1866-1900||) d ind *
    THE STAGE (Jan. 29, 1866-Apr. 2, 1866)
    Pub. 1866   John W. Forney, Jr.
        PP   1866 Mar. 3 (Vol. 1, No. 30)
                   continued as
    EVENING STAR (Mar. 27, 1866-Oct. 2, 1900||) d *
    Pub. 1866   Charles E. School
         1868   School & Blakely (John Blakely)
    Pub. & Ed. 1869-1888 School & Blakely
                  1889-1899 John Blakely
        P-M   1877 July 23
        PArdL   1898 Mar. 16
        PCHi   1867 June 4
        PDoHi   1883 July 23
                  1889 Oct. 2
        PEbHi   1866 May 1
        PEHi   1867 Aug. 31
        PHi   1866 Apr. 23, 26, May 5, June 8
                  1872 Mar. 11
                  1893 Nov. 15, 20
                  1894 May 21
        PP   1866 Sept. 12, Nov. 1
                  1867 Feb. 8, 11, Mar. 9, 27, Apr. 17, May 8, 13,
                        July 15, 26, Sept. 3, Oct. 10, 29, 31
                  1868 Mar. 24, May 29, June 19, July 24, Aug. 20,
                      Sept. 29
                  1869 Jan. 8, 20, 23, Feb. 23, 25, Mar. 25, 30, Apr.
                      12-14, 17, 19, July 26, Aug. 13, Sept. 14, 30,
                      Oct. 30, Dec. 9

EVENING STAR, *continued*

1870 Jan. 14, 21, 22, 26, Feb. 9, 26, Mar. 2, 11, Apr. 19, May 6, 7, 11, 28, 30, 31, June 7, July 5, 9, 11, 20, 27, Aug. 6, 10, 13, 17, 26, 30, 31, Sept. 15, 21, 28, Oct. 8, Dec. 17

1871 Jan. 10, 13, 30, Feb. 7-11, 15, 16, 23, 25, 28, Mar. 2, 10, Apr. 5, June 17, July 3, 10, 19, 22, Aug. 19, Oct. 9, 10, Nov. 10, 22, 27, Dec. 1, 14, 15, 18, 30

1872 Jan. 15, 20, 23, Feb. 7, 8, 12, 15-17, 27, Mar. 1, 6-8, 11, 16, 27, Apr. 1, 17, May 2, June 13, 15, Sept. 10, Oct. 12

1873 Jan. 2, 13, 19, Feb. 25, 27, Mar. 11, 15, 25, 29, Apr. 9, 24, 29, May 6, 7, 13, 21, 31, June 4, 6, 12, 19, 25, 28, July 3, 6-9, 15, 26, 27, 31, Aug. 2, 4, 6, 7, 12, 14, 16, 25, 28-30, Sept. 2, 4, 9, 20, 27, Oct. 3, 4, 14, 15, 22, 23, 30, Nov. 1, 5, 10-13, 15, 19, 21, 24, Dec. 2, 5, 6, 8, 12, 16, 20

1874 Jan. 12, 17, 19, 26, Feb. 3, 5, 7, 12, 14, 20, 26, Mar. 3, 6, 11, 18, 19, 23, 26, 28, Apr. 1, 3, 4, 6, 9, 17, 30, May 5, 21, 23, June 6, 23, 27, July 1, 6-8, 16, 18, 21, 22, 24, 29, 31, Aug. 3, 5, 7, 10, 12, 14, 17-21, 24, 26-29, 31, Sept. 1, 4, 5, 7, 9, 11, 12, 14, 16, 17, 19, 25, 26, 30, Oct. 1, 12, 19-21, Nov. 6, 11, 12, Dec. 9, 23

1875 Jan. 2, 5, 7, 9, 15, 16, 20, Mar. 4, 8, 10, 11, 16, 22, 31, Apr. 5, 10, 12, 14, 22, 23, 26, May 4, 22, 24, 25, 29, June 1, 4, 7, 10, 22-24, 26, July 3, 6-8, 12, 14, 22, Aug. 3-5, 7, 11, 13, 14, 16, 25, 27, 28, Sept. 1, 4, 8, 9, 11, 13, 14, 27, Oct. 5, 7, 9, 23, Nov. 19, 21, 31

1876 Jan. 5 10, 11, 14, 22, 25-27, 31, Feb. 1, 3, 4, 7-12, 14, 19, 21, 25, 28, Mar. 2, 4, 7, 13, 17, 22, 24, Apr. 5, 10, 13, 17, 24, 26 28, 29, May 5, 9, 18, 19, 22, 27, June 5, 6, 10, 12, 13, 16-18, 23, 30, July 5, 10, 12, 20, 28, 29, Aug. 11-12, Sept. 2, 12-14, 19, 22, 29, Oct. 3, 5, 9, 13, 16, 24, 26, 31, Nov. 4, 7, 11, 13-16, 18, 25

1877 Jan. 26, Feb. 15, Mar. 2, 5, 7, 8, 10, 12, 13, Apr. 25, Aug. 10, 11, 13, 24, Sept. 3, Oct. 1, 5, 13, 26, 27, 29-31, Nov. 1, 6, 8, 10, 12, 14, 16, 17, 21, 22, 26

1878 Jan. 21, Feb. 2, 15, 16, 18, 19, 21, 23, 25, 27, 28, Mar. 1, 5-8, 13, 18-23, 25-27, 29, Apr. 4, 6, 8, 11, 13, 15, 16, 18, 22, 24, 30, May 11, 16-18, 20, 21, 23-25, 27, 28, 31, June 3, 5-8, 11-13, 15, July 2, 5, 9, 11, 15, 17-19, 22, 23, Aug. 3, 5, 14, 26-31, Sept. 6, 7, 11, 13, 16, 17, 19, 21, 25, 30, Oct. 5, 7-12, 19, 22, 23, 25, Nov. 2, 8, 9, 12, 16, 18-20, 22, 25, 26, Dec. 6, 17, 28

1879 Jan. 6, 10, 11, 14, 17, 18, Mar. 3, 22, June 10-12, 14, 27, July 3, 10, 23, Aug. 12, 20, Sept. 3, 6, 10, 13, 15

PHILADELPHIA COUNTY 69

      1880 Apr. 22, May 28, June 1, 3, 10, July 14, 21, 28, Aug. 6, Sept. 24, Oct. 26, 29, Nov. 1, 2, 4, 6, 12, 13, 30, Dec. 2
      1881 Jan. 8, 15, 29, Feb. 4, 8, 26, Mar. 2, 4, 5, 10, 16, 30, 31, Apr. 20, May 31, July 2, 5, 15, 16, 19, 21, 26, 27, Aug. 2, 8, 11, 16, 17, 19, 22, 24, 31, Oct. 4, 10, 12, Nov. 30, Dec. 1, 2, 4-9, 15, 16, 19, 20, 22, 24, 28
      1882 Jan. 4, 6, 7, 21, Mar. 7, 16, 17, 23, 25, 27, 30, Apr. 5, 14, 27, May 15-17, 20, 24, June 1, 3, 7, 14, 15, 21, 28, July 1, 3, 8, 10, 13, 14, 17, 19, 21, 29, Aug. 7, 9, 14, 19, 23, 24, 29, 30, Sept. 1, 5, 7-9, 11, 13, 14, 16, 18, 21, 26, 28, 30, Oct. 2, 6, 7, 9, 11-13
      1886 July 1-Dec. 31
      1896 Jan. 1-June 23, 25-30
  PPL   1867 July 29-1868 Apr. 8
      1868 Apr. 10-1874 July 16
      1874 July 18-1875 Mar. 26
      1875 Mar. 29-1878 Nov. 21
      1878 Nov. 23-1881 Sept. 24
      1881 Sept. 27-1882 Oct. 23
      1882 Oct. 25-1888 Oct. 26
      1888 Oct. 30-1892 July 5
      1892 July 7-Dec. 31
      1893 July 1-Sept. 12, 14-1894 Dec. 31
      1895 July 1-1898 Feb. 9
      1898 Feb. 11-1900 Oct. 2
  PPot   1884 Nov. 8, 11, 16
      1885 July 23
      1886 Nov. 3
  PU   1867 July 30-1885 June
      1886 Jan.-June
      1887 Jan.-1894 June
  PWcHi 1879 Apr. 25

EVENING STAR (1908†) d evg rep
 Pub. 1908-1936 Starr Printing Co.
 Ed. 1908-1936 Henry Starr Richardson
  PUB   1908 Dec. 9†
  P-M   1913 Jan. 22-24
  PDoHi 1908 Dec. 9
  PP   1914 Aug. 5
      1915 Jan. 1
      1928 May 2
      1931 Mar. 12-1933 Oct. 21
      1933 Oct. 24†

EVENING STAR AND DAILY ADVERTISER, see Philadelphia Evening Star and Daily Advertiser

EVENING TELEGRAPH (Jan. 4, 1864-July 1, 1918) d ind rep *
 Pub. 1864-1865 J. Barclay Harding and Charles E. Warburton
   1865-1896 Charles E. Warburton
   1896-1912 Barclay H. Warburton
   1912-1914 John T. Windrim
   1914-1918 Evening Telegraph Publishing Co.

EVENING TELEGRAPH, *continued*

Ed:	1865-1896	Charles E. Warburton
	1865-1866	J. Mason Grier
	1865-1911	Watson Ambruster, Edward J. Swartz, Wm. J. Clark, George W. Allen, Julie de Margurettes, J. Luther Ringwalt, Alexander K. McClure, Edwin K. Hart, Joseph Marshall
	1911-1914	George A. Waite
	1914-1916	John J. Collier
	1917-1918	Herman L. Collins
P-M		1865 Apr. 10, 15
		1876 Sept. 29
		1913 Jan. 22-24
PBf		1881 Apr. 22, Nov. 18
PCHi		1868 Apr. 15
PDoHi		1864 May 17
		1865 Apr. 10, 20
		1876 June 6, 15, 16, 24, July 1, Oct. 19, 26, Dec. 30
		1885 July 23
		1901 Sept. 7, 13, 14
		1907 June 5
		1908 Sept. 30, Oct. 5-10, Nov. 4, 17, 18
PHi		1864 Jan.-June
		1865 Dec.-1916 Dec. 30
		1917 June-Oct.
PHHi		1914 Mar. 19
PLaHi		1876 May 10
PMcC		1876 Aug. 10
		1877 June 18, 21
PNoHi		1869 Sept. 20
PP		1864 Jan. 4, 6, 8-11, 14, 15, 17-21, 23-Feb. 25, 27-May 5, 7-12, 14-18, 20-28, 31, June 1-16, 18-20, 27-Dec. 31
		1865 Apr. 3, 15, Dec. 1-6, 8-30
		1866 Jan. 1-Dec. 31
		1867 Jan. 1, 2, 4-Dec. 31
		1868 July 1-1870 Dec. 30
		1871 Jan. 2-June 30
		1872 Sept. 2-30
		1873 Jan. 2-1876 Dec. 30
		1877 Feb. 1-Dec. 31
		1878 Jan. 2-Dec. 31
		1879 Jan. 2-1880 Dec. 31
		1881 Jan. 3-Dec. 27
		1882 Jan. 2-Dec. 30
		1883 Jan. 2-1887 Dec. 31
		1888 Jan. 3-1891 May 25
		1891 June 1-Dec. 31
		1892 Jan. 1-30, Mar. 1-Dec. 31
		1893 Jan. 3-1894 Dec. 31
		1895 Jan. 2-Dec. 31
		1896 Jan. 2-Oct. 26, Nov. 2-Dec. 31
		1897 Jan. 1-Dec. 31
		1898 Jan. 3-Dec. 31
		1899 Jan. 3-1901 Dec. 26
		1902 Jan. 1-1910 Feb. 1
		1910 Feb. 3-Mar. 3, 5-29, Apr. 1-1911, Jan. 27

PHILADELPHIA COUNTY 71

	1911 Feb. 1-1917, July 31, Sept. 1-29
	1918 May 25-June 22, 25, 27, 28
PPB	1905 Oct.
PPeS	1872 Oct. 9
	1901 Sept. 19
PPiHi	1897 Mar. 4
	1898 Apr. 30
PPL	1873 Jan. 23, 24, 28-Mar. 26, 28-July 3, 7-9, 11-15, 18-22, 24, 29, 31, Aug. 1-Oct. 3, 6-Dec. 29
	1874 Jan. 2-Mar. 9, 11-24, 26-Apr. 2, 4-June 5, 8-22, 24-Aug. 7, 31-Sept. 3, 25-Oct. 29, 31-Dec. 4, 7-11, 14-1875 June 26
	1875 June 29-Aug. 17, 19, 23-1876 Feb. 21
	1876 Feb. 23-May 9, 11-25, 27-June 7, 9-July 21, 24-28, 31-Aug. 3, 5-10, 12-22, 24-Sept. 14, 16-27, 29-Nov. 8, 11-29, Dec. 1-5, 7, 8, 11-1877 June 14
	1877 June 16-1878 July 25
	1878 July 27-Dec. 6, 9-1879 Feb. 3
	1879 Feb. 5, 6, 8-May 29, 31-June 13, 16-20, 23-July 22, 24-Sept. 12, 15-19, 22-Oct. 15, 17-Nov. 17, 19, 20, 22-26, 28-Dec. 23, 26-1880 Feb. 13
	1880 Feb. 16, 17, 20-Mar. 15, 17-24, 26-Apr. 1, 3-10, 13-26, 28-May 8, 11-June 11, 14-21, 23-30, July 3, 6, 8, 9, 12-22, 24-Aug. 6, 9-17, 19-24, 27-Sept. 13, 15-Oct. 20, 22-Nov. 5, 8-1881 Feb. 1
	1881 Feb. 3-Mar. 22, 24-29, 31-Apr. 29, May 2-4, 6-June 22, 24-July 20, 22-Sept. 23, 27-Nov. 11, 14-17, 20-1882 Mar. 10
	1882 Mar. 13-May 9, 11-July 13, 15-Aug. 28, 30-Oct. 23, 25-Nov. 29, Dec. 1-1883 Jan. 27
	1883 Jan. 30-Feb. 13, 15-17, 20-Apr. 3, 5, 6, 9-13, 16-21, 25-May 10, 12, 15-June 13, 15, 16, 19-27, 29-Nov. 28, Dec. 1-1884 Mar. 29
	1884 Mar. 31, Apr. 1-8, 10-17, 19-29, May 1-5, 8-10, 13, 14, 17-21, 24-June 4, 16-21, 24-27, 30, July 2, 3, 7-Sept. 22, 24-Dec. 23
	1885 Jan. 7, 9-Feb. 13, 16-Mar. 14, 17-26, 28-May 13, 16-27, 29-Sept. 1, 3-12, 15-25, 28-Oct. 1, 3-7, 9, 14, 16-25, 27-1886 Feb. 3
	1886 Feb. 6-Nov. 24, 26-1887 Nov. 23
	1887 Nov. 25-1888 May 1
	1888 May 3-21, 23-25, 28-Nov. 27, 29-Dec. 11, 13-1890 July 31
	1890 Aug. 2-Nov. 4, 6-1891 Aug. 3
	1891 Aug. 5-Sept. 18, 21-Nov. 25, 27-1892 July 5
	1892 July 7-Aug. 2, 4-Sept. 9, 12-14, 16, 19-1893 Jan. 16
	1893 Jan. 18-Feb. 8, 10-Mar. 28, 30-Sept. 1, 4-16, 19-Nov. 29, Dec. 1-30
	1894 Jan. 1-Feb. 3, 6-Mar. 14, 16-Sept. 15, 18-28, Oct. 1-1895 May 3
	1895 May 6-June 12, 14-17, 19-Nov. 2, 5, 7-22, 25-1896 Apr. 8
	1896 Apr. 10-Dec. 31
PPot	1868 Oct. 6
	1870 Aug. 30
	1886 Feb. 10, 13
	1893 Jan. 27

EVENING TELEGRAPH, *continued*
        PSF   1881 Sept. 27
        PSuHi   1889 Nov. 11
        PWcA   1865 Apr. 15
        PWcHi 1864 Sept. 27
                  1865 Feb. 6, Apr. 3, 15, 17, 18, 20-22, 25-27, 29, May 19, 20, July 5, 7, Nov. 14
                  1866 Jan. 18, Sept. 17, Oct. 1
                  1867 May 8
                  1871 Dec. 5
                  1873 Nov. 10
                  1874 July 28, Nov. 25
                  1875 Feb. 13, 15, Sept. 13, 20, 22
                  1876 May 10, June 8, July 29, Aug. 30, 31, Sept. 2, 4, 25
                  1879 Sept. 27
                  1881 May 7, 11-14, July 2, 5, Sept. (7), Nov. 9, 11-15, 21, 26, Dec. 31
                  1882 June 27, July 26, Aug. 29
                  1883 Aug. 16-18, 23, 24, 28-Sept. 1, 3
                  1884 July 11
                  1888 Nov. 14
                  1901 Sept. 14, 17
                  1904 June 30
                  1908 Sept. 30
                  1912 Apr. 16, 17, 19
                  1913 Feb. 13, Dec. 6
        PWcT   1865 Nov. 14
                  1867 May 8
                  1901 Sept. 4
                  1908 Sept. 30
        PWalG 1905 Oct. 27, 30
                  absorbed by the *Evening Public Ledger,* July 2, 1918

EVENING TIMES (July 15, 1908-Apr. 14, 1914||) d ind
    Pub. 1908-1914   Frank A. Munsey
           1909   W. R. Fairfield
    Ed. 1909   H. J. Taft
        P   1910 June-1911 Sept. 30
        P-M   1913 Jan. 22
        PDoHi   1908 Oct. 5-10, Nov. 4, 18, Dec. 13
        PHi   1908 July 15 (Vol. 1, No. 1)
                       1909 Dec. 26
        PP   1908 July 15-1910 July 14
                       1910 Oct. 15-1914 Apr. 14
        PWcHi   1910 Feb. 10

EVERY SATURDAY (1889-1892) w ind ♣
    Pub. & Ed. 1889-1890 Curtis E. Blissinger
                    1890-1891 William Thompson
                    1891-1892 C. C. Thompson & Co.

EXCHANGE AND TRADE REGISTER (Mar. 9, 1842-Dec. 7, 1842||)
w com *
    Pub. 1842   Storms & Morgan
        PBL   ♦   1842 Aug. 10, 17, Sept. 14

PHILADELPHIA COUNTY   73

EXHIBITOR, THE (1877) &
    Pub. 1877   Hoag, Sherrard & Co.
    Ed. 1877   Mrs. E. S. Baden
        PWcHi   1877 June 9, July 14

EXPERIMENT (1834) d *

FAIR, THE (Oct. 15, 1844) d
    Pub. & Ed. 1844   Franklin Institute
        PHi   1844 Oct. 21, 29

FAIR PLAY, see Uptown, The

FAIRHILL WEEKLY, see Oakdale Weekly

FAIRMOUNT TELEGRAM (1916-1931) w &
    Pub. 1918-1931   Fairmount Telegram Co.
    Ed. 1918-1931   John F. Niland
        PP   1927 June 27

FALLS ADVERTISER AND RIVERSIDE GAZETTE (Falls of Schuylkill) (1879-1885) w ind &
    Pub. & Ed. 1879-1882 William G. Middleton & Co.
                   1882-1884 William B. N. Gifford
                   1884-1885 Eli S. Brasy

FALLS STAR (Falls of Schuylkill) (1883-1885) w &
    Pub. 1883-1884 Watson & Vose
           1884-1885 Star Falls Publishing Co.
    Ed.   1883-1884 Warren Watson

FAMA (1762) &
    Pub. 1762 Anton Armbruster

FAMILIEN JOURNAL (1876-1886) w for &
    Pub. & Ed. 1876-1880 F. Lisiewski and A. Schulte
                   1880-1881 Journal Publishing Co.
                   1881-1886 William Regenspurger

FAMILY CALL, see Call

FAMILY HERALD (1882) w &
    Pub. 1882 Covenant Publishing Co.

FAMILY MESSENGER AND NATIONAL GLEANER (1836-1851)
  w bw sm *
    SALMAGUNDI, NEWS OF THE DAY (Jan. 2, 1836-Dec. 29, 1836)
      bw *
    Pub. 1836   Charles Alexander
        PPL   1836 Aug. 3

continued as
AMERICAN WEEKLY MESSENGER (Jan. 4, 1837-Dec. 27, 1837)
w
Pub. 1837   Charles Alexander
PBL   1837 Feb. 22, May 10, 24, Aug. 9
PHi   1837 Jan. 4-Dec. 27
continued as
ALEXANDER'S WEEKLY MESSENGER (Jan. 3, 1838-Feb. 1844)
w *
Pub. 1838-1844   Charles Alexander
PAtM   1841 Apr. 14
PBL   1839 Feb. 13
PHi   1838 Jan. 3-Dec. 31
     1843 Jan. 4-Nov. 29
PNoHi   1839 Nov. 13
PWcHi   1842 Feb. 23
     1843 Feb. 8, July 19
continued as
ALEXANDER'S EXPRESS MESSENGER (Feb. 1844-Dec. 30, 1846)
w *
Pub. 1844-1846   Charles Alexander
P-M   1845 Sept. 17
PDoHi   1846 Apr. 8
PNoHi   1845 June 11, 18, July 2, 9, 23, 30, Nov. 12, 19
     1846 Jan. 14-Feb. 18, Mar. 11, 18, Apr. 8-July 1, 22-Dec. 30
PPCHi   1844 May 15
PPiUD   1844 Mar. 6, Oct. 26
PWcHi   1844 July 10
     1845 Dec. 3
continued as
ALEXANDER'S PICTORIAL MESSENGER (Jan. 6, 1847-Nov. 1, 1848) w *
Pub. 1847-1848   Charles Alexander
1848   S. D. Patterson
PHi   1848 Oct. 25
PNoHi   1847 Jan. 6-May 26, June 9, Aug. 4, Sept. 1, Oct. 6-Nov. 3, 24-Dec. 8
     1848 Jan. 26, Feb. 9, 23, Apr. 19, May 10, July 19
PPL   1847 Jan. 9-Apr. 3
Merged with *Philadelphia Saturday Gleaner*, and title changed to
FAMILY MESSENGER AND NATIONAL GLEANER (Nov. 8, 1848-Apr. 16, 1851) w *
Pub. 1848-1851   S. D. Patterson
P-M   1848 Nov. 8
PNoHi   1849 Feb. 21, June 6, July 11, Aug. 1, Oct. 24, Nov. 7, 28
     1850 May 1, 15, July 3-Aug. 28, Sept. 11-Dec. 25
     1851 Jan. 1-Mar. 12, Apr. 16

FARMER'S REGISTER, THE   (Apr. 18, 1798-Dec. 19, 1798) w
Pub. & Ed. 1798   Snowden & McCorkle
PPL   1798 June 6-20, July 25, Aug. 15-29, Nov. 14-Dec. 19

PHILADELPHIA COUNTY 75

FEDERAL GAZETTE AND PHILADELPHIA DAILY ADVERTISER, THE, see Philadelphia Gazette and Commercial Intelligencer, The

FEDERAL GAZETTE AND PHILADELPHIA EVENING POST, THE, see Philadelphia Gazette and Commercial Intelligencer, The

FELTONVILLE WEEKLY (Sept. 7, 1938†) w assoc
    Pub. 1938 Sept. 7 Ralph Hafner and Edward Singer
    Ed. 1938 Sept. 7 Ralph A. Hafner
    PUB   1938 Sept. 7†

FERRETT (1891-1893) w ♪
    Pub. 1892-1893   E. E. Walton & Co.
    Ed. 1892-1893   E. E. Walton

52ND AND GIRARD AVENUE NEWS, see Northwest News

FINANCIAL BULLETIN (1895-1913) d & e ♪ *
    Pub. 1898-1900   Printing Telegraph News Co.
          1900-1908   Warner H. Jenkins
          1908-1913   Financial Bulletin Co.
    Ed. 1900-1908   Warner H. Jenkins
          1911-1912   Frank Tyson
          1912-1913   George McDade

FINLAY'S AMERICAN NAVAL AND COMMERCIAL REGISTER (1795-1798) sw #
    AMERICAN NAVAL AND COMMERCIAL REGISTER, THE (Nov. 25, 1795-Dec. 1795) sw #
    Pub. 1795   Samuel Finlay
        (John Ormrod and Ephraim Conrad)
        PPL   1795 Nov. 25, 29, Dec. 1, 9, 16
        continued as
    FINLAY'S AMERICAN NAVAL AND COMMERCIAL REGISTER (Dec. 28, 1795-May 1, 1798||) sw #
    Pub. 1795-1796   Samuel Finlay (Godfrey Deshong)
        1796-1798   Samuel Finlay
        PPL   1795 Dec. 28
              1796 Jan. 1-9, 16-Feb. 2, 9-23, Mar. 4, 11-18, 29-Apr. 5, 12-June 21, 28-July 12, 19, 22, 29, Aug. 5-16, 23-1797 Jan. 4
              1797 Jan. 21-Mar. 7, 14-31, Apr. 11-14, 25, May 5-9, 16-26, June 2-Aug. 15, 22-Sept. 12, 22-Oct. 10, 20-Nov. 10, 17-Dec. 8

FIRST AND THIRTY-NINTH WARD NEWS (1888-1926) w Ind
    FIRST WARD NEWS (1888-1897) w ♪
    Pub. & Ed. 1890-1897   George O. Skipper
        continued as
    FIRST AND THIRTY-NINTH WARD NEWS (1898-1926) w ♪
    Pub. & Ed. 1898-1911   George O. Skipper
                1911-1926   Mary Skipper

FITZGERALD'S CITY ITEM, see Item

FORBICE (1901-1937)   w for ♦
  Pub. 1917-1937   Forbice Printing Co.
  Ed. 1917-1937   V. Terracciano

FORECAST (Falls of Schuylkill) (1900-1925) w local ♦
  Pub. & Ed. 1915-1925   Ernest E. Carwardine

FORNEY'S PROGRESS, see Progress

FORNEY'S WAR PRESS, see Press

FORNEY'S WEEKLY PRESS, see Press

FORTIETH WARD LEADER (1914-1922) w ind ♦
  Pub. 1916-1922   Leader Publishing Co.
  Ed. 1916-1922   John C. Deindorfer

FORWARD (1882†)   w rel
  Pub. 1898-1924   Presbyterian Board of Education
       1924-1941   Board of Christian Education of Presbyterian Church in the U. S. A.
  Ed. 1898-1914   J. R. Miller
       1914-1939   John T. Faris
       1939-1941   P. H. Miller
  PP   1911 Nov. 18
               1912 Apr. 13, Dec. 28
               1913 Jan. 11, Mar. 15, 29
               1917 Apr. 21-May 12, June 2, 30, July 7-Sept. 22, Nov. 3-Dec. 29
               1918 Jan. 5-Mar. 23, Apr. 6, 20-Nov. 2, Dec. 28
               1919 Feb. 22, Mar. 22-May 10, 24-June 14, July 26
               1920 June 5, Oct. 9, Dec. 10, 31
               1921 Jan. 1-Apr. 9, 23-May 21 (June 4-25), July 9, Aug 27, Sept. 3, 24-Oct. 15, 29-Nov. 26, Dec. 17
               1922 Jan. 21-28, Feb. 11-18, Mar 4-Apr. 8, 22-May 27, June 10-July 1, 15-29, Sept. 2, Oct. 28-Dec. 2, 23
               1923 Jan. 13-Feb. 3, 24, Mar. 24, Apr. 7-28, May 12-26, June 9, 23, 30, Sept. 1, 8, 22-Oct. 6
               1924 Apr. 12, May 10, Aug. 16-23, Sept. 20
               1925 Apr. 11, June 13, July 25-Aug. 22, Sept. 19
               1926 Feb. 6, 20, Mar. 27, May 15, June 12-19, July 3-10, Aug. 14-21, Sept. 4, Oct. 16, 23-30, Dec. 4, 18
               1927 Jan. 1, 15-29, May 7-July 16, Aug. 6-Nov. 26
               1929 Sept. 28, Nov. 9
               1931 Mar. 21, Apr. 18, July 25, Nov. 14, 21
               1932 Mar. 19
               1933 June 17, July 1-29, Aug. 12, Dec. 9
               1935 Sept. 18, Nov. 16, Dec. 7, 21
               1936 Jan. 4, 11, Sept. 19, Nov. 7, 21, Dec. 5
               1937 Jan. 23-July 3, 17, Aug. 7, Sept. 18, Oct. 2, 16-30, Dec. 4-25
               1938 Jan. 8-Apr. 2
               1939 Apr. 15, May 27
               1940 May 18, June 8
  PPPHi   [1900 Jan. 6-1901 Dec. 28]

PHILADELPHIA COUNTY   77

FOX CHASE CHRONICLE (1886-1891) w ♩
   Pub. & Ed. 1886-1887 Chronicle Publishing Co.
             1887-1890 Frank C. Benson
             1890-1891 Suburban Publishing Co.

FOX CHASE TIMES (1891-1892) w ♩
   Pub. & Ed. 1891-1892 E. H. Rosenberger

FRANKFORD AND HOLMESBURG GAZETTE, see Frankford Gazette

FRANKFORD BULLETIN (1938†) w ind ♩
   Pub. 1939-1941 Peerless Publishing Co.
   Ed. 1939-1941 E. L. Wagner

FRANKFORD CRITIC (1889-1891) w ind ♩
   Pub. & Ed. 1889-1891 Jacob B. Detweiler

FRANKFORD DISPATCH (June 22, 1878-Oct. 31, 1941) w ind rep
   Pub. 1878-1897 T. B. Foulkrod
        1897-1901 Mrs. George M. Taylor
        1901-1908 Dispatch Publishing Co.
        1908-1938 B. Hepworth & Co.
        1938-1941 Associated Philadelphia Community Newspapers
   Ed. 1878-1897 T. B. Foulkrod
       1878-1880 B. C. Tillinghast
       1897-1901 Mrs. George M. Taylor
       1901-1941 Benjamin Hepworth
   PUB   [1935-1941]
   PDoHi   1932 July 1
   PHi   1909 Sept. 17
   PP   1922 Nov. 10
              1927 Nov. 11
              1928 Jan. 6
              1929 Feb. 8-1941 Oct. 31
   PPFfHi   1914 Jan. 1-1917 June 1
              1917 July 20-1920 Apr. 30
              1920 May 14-1923 Dec. 7
              1923 Dec. 21-1928 July 20
              1928 Aug. 3-Oct. 19, Nov. 2-1929 Sept. 27
              1929 Oct. 25†
              merged with *Frankford Gazette*

FRANKFORD GAZETTE AND FRANKFORD DISPATCH (1868†)
w local ind * asso
    HOLMESBURG WEEKLY GAZETTE (1868-1873) w ♩ *
   Pub. & Ed. 1868-1873 W. F. Knott
      PHi   1869 May 8, 15, 22
                1871 Aug. 19
               continued as
    FRANKFORD AND HOLMESBURG GAZETTE (1874-1875) w *
   Pub. & Ed. 1874-1875 W. F. Knott
               continued as
    FRANKFORD GAZETTE (1876-1888) w *
   Pub. & Ed. 1876-1883 W. F. Knott
            1883-1888 James France
      PPFfHi   1876 July 1, 8

continued as
GAZETTE (FRANKFORD) (1889-1893) w ♦
Pub. & Ed. 1889-1893 James France
    continued as
NORTH PHILADELPHIA GAZETTE (1895-1915) w
Pub. & Ed. 1895-1915 James France
 PPFfHi 1909 Sept. 24-1915
    continued as
FRANKFORD GAZETTE (1916-Oct. 31, 1941) w
Pub. & Ed. 1916-1931 James France
 Frankford Gazette also published a daily edition, 1879-1880.
 PUB   1934 July 6-Dec. 21
 PP   1926 July 1, Oct. 1
      1929 Feb. 8-1941 Oct. 31
 PPFfHi 1916-1941 Oct. 31
    merged with *Frankford Dispatch* and
    continued as
FRANKFORD GAZETTE AND FRANKFORD DISPATCH, THE (Nov. 7†)
 Ed.   1941 Edward B. France
 PP   1941 Nov. 7†

FRANKFORD GLEANER, see Frankford News Gleaner

FRANKFORD HERALD (1845-1914||) w ind rep *
 Pub. 1871-1905 William W. Axe
   1905-1908 Heirs of Estate of William W. Axe
   1908-1910 George W. Baker
   1910-1914 Frankford Herald Publishing Co.
 Ed. 1871-1905 William W. Axe
   1905-1908 Estate of William W. Axe
   1908-1912 George W. Baker
   1912-1913 Robert T. Taylor
 PDoHi   1895 Dec. 7
 PHi   1876 Dec. 2 (vol. 23, No. 35)
 PP   1894 June 9
      1901 May 11
      1905 June 24

FRANKFORD NEWS GLEANER (1882†) w ind
 FRANKFORD GLEANER (1882-1891) w ♦
 Pub. & Ed. 1882-1891 George W. Henry
 NEWS GLEANER (1891-1934) w
 Pub. & Ed. 1891-1924 George W. Henry
  PPFfN   1897 Dec. 1
       1920-1924
  PWcHi 1896 Oct. 21
    continued as
 FRANKFORD NEWS GLEANER (1925-1941) w
 Pub. & Ed. 1925-1939 George W. Henry
     1939-1941 T. P. C. Henry
  PP   1935 Mar. 21†
  PPFfN   1925
  PUB   1927 Jan. 6†

PHILADELPHIA COUNTY 79

FRANKFORD REGISTER (1895-1904) w ind ♦
Pub. & Ed. 1900-1904   Harry S. Donat

FRANKFORD WEEKLY MESSENGER AND GENERAL ADVERTISER (Apr. 27, 1810-) w
Pub. & Ed.   William Coale
PPFfHi   1810 May 18 (Vol. 1)

FRANKLIN GAZETTE (Feb. 23, 1818-1824) d tw w sw dem % # *

Pub. 1818-1819   Richard Bache
       1819-1824   Bache & Norvell
       1824   John Norvell
d-evg   Feb. 23, 1818-Nov. 20, 1824‖
w   Apr. 11, 1818-June 28, 1820, 1826
tw   Feb. 23, 1818-Mar. 27, 1819‖ As: *Franklin Gazette (for the Country)*
sw   Mar. 28, 1819-Nov. 1824 As: *Franklin Gazette (for the Country)*
P   d   1819 Aug. 23-1820 Dec. 30
P-M   d   1818 July 13
PBL ♦   d   1818 Apr. 18-21, 23-25, May 11, 12, 14, 16, 18, 21-23, 25, June 19
         d   1820 Sept. 8, 9, Oct. 26-Dec. 1
         d   1821 Feb. 23, Mar. 1-9, 13-19, 21, 22, 27-29, 31, Apr. 2-14, 17-26, 28-May 15, 17-31, June 4-28, 30, July 3, 5-27, 30-Aug. 29, 31
         d   1822 Apr. 24, May 11, 13-16, 18, 20-25, 27, 28, Oct. 5
         d   1823 June 26, 30, July 1, 3, Sept. 3
         d   1824 Feb. 21, 23-28
PDoHi   d   1818 Mar. 10-13
           1819 Apr. 14
           1822 Oct. 9
         tw 1818 Mar. 10/11, 12/13, Apr. 17/18, May (1/2), June 10/11, 17/(18), 26/27, July 3/4, 8/9, 29/30, 31/Aug. 1, 5/6, 7/8, Sept. 2/3, 9/10, 14/15, (-23) /24, Oct. 5/6 (-) 9/10, 14/15, 19/20-(23)/24, (28)/29, (30)/31, Nov. (2)/3, (6)/7, 16/17, 20/21, 25/26, Dec. 2/3, 23/24, 28/29, 30/31
           1819 Jan. 4-26, 29-Feb. 2, 5-Mar. 6, 15-22, 24, Apr. 10, 14, 21, May 19, 26, 29, June 2, 9, 12, 16, 24, 28, 31, Aug. 25, Sept. 4, 11, 15, Oct. 6
           1820 Feb. 26, Mar. 1
           1821 May 23, Aug. 11, 29, Dec. 1
           1822 Mar. 2, 16, 30-Apr. 24, May 4-18, June 5, 8, 15-29, July 10, Aug. 10-24, 31, Sept. 4, Oct. 9, Dec. 4-11, 18-28
           1823 Jan. 1, 4, 11, 15
           1824 Jan. 9, Apr. 9
PHi   1818 Feb. 23-1820 Dec. 30, 1824 July 27
PKiHi   1820 (Aug.)
PLaHi   sw 1821 Oct. 20-1823 Mar. 12
PNoHi   1818 Dec. 23
PP   d 1819 Mar. 23, 25, 27, 29-31, Apr. 1-2, 5-6
           1820 Nov. 16
           1824 Sept. 24, 25

FRANKLIN GAZETTE, *continued*
- sw 1819 Apr. 7, 10, 21, May 5, 22, 26, 29, June 2, 23, 30, July 3, 7, 10, 31, Aug. 18, 21, 25, Sept. 1, 4, 11, 15, 18, 25, Oct. 2, 6, 9, 27, Nov. 3, 10, 17, Dec. 4, 8, 11, 15
- 1820 Jan. 15, 19, Feb. 12, 16, 19, Mar. 22, 25, Apr. 5, 15, May 17, 20, June 3, 10, 24, July 1, 29, Sept. 2, 16, 27, 30, Oct. 7, 14, 21, Nov. 1, 4, 15, 18, 22, 25, 29, Dec. 2, 9, 13, 20, 23, 27
- 1821 Jan. 10, 13, 15, 24, Feb. 3, 17, 21, 24, 28, Mar. 3, 7, 14, 24, 31, Apr. 7, 11, 28, May 5, 9, 16, 23, 26, June 6, 16, 23, 27, 30, July 4, 7, 28, Aug. 15, 18, 29, Sept. 1, 5, 15, 22, Oct. 6, 10, 31, Nov. 3, 24, 28, Dec. 8, 12
- 1822 Jan. 2, 19, 26, Feb. 9, 13, 20, 23, 27, Mar. 9, 13, 20, Apr. 3, May 4, 8, 25, June 5, 8, 15, 22, 26, July 20, Aug. 10, 14, 21, 24, 28, 31, Sept. 4, 25, Oct. 9, 19, 26, Nov. 13, 23, 27, Dec. 21, 25, 28
- 1823 Jan. 1, 15, 18, 25, 29, Feb. 8, 22, Mar. 19, Apr. 2, 26, May 3, 7, 10, 17, 21, 24, July 19, 30, Aug. 6, 16, 27, Sept. 3, 8, 13, 20, Oct. 1, 4, 15, 18
- tw 1823 Oct. 20/21-24/25, 29/30-Nov. 5/6, 12/13-17/18, Dec. 16/17, 20/22, 23/24, 27/29, 30/31
- 1824 Jan. 6/7-10/12, 22/23, 24/26, 29/30, Feb. 5/6, 12/13, 14/16, 19/20-24/25, Mar. 9/10, 13/15, 16/17, 30/31, Apr. 8/9, 13/14-18/19, 22/23, 27/28, June 5/7-8/9, 17/18, 19/21, July 6/7, 8/9, 13/14, 17/19, 22/23, 27/28, Aug. 3/4, 5/6, 17/18, Sept. 4/6, 30/Oct. 1, 2/4, 12/13-16/18, 23/25, Nov. 2/3, 13/15, 16/17
- w 1826 Nov. 2
- PPiHi w 1820 June 7, 21, 28
- PPL 1818 Feb. 25, 26, Mar. 2-Sept. 11, 15-17, 19-Dec. 4, 7-1819 Mar. 8
- 1819 Mar. 10-31, Apr. 2-13, 15-23, 26-May 1, 4-27, 29-July 23, 26-Aug. 26, 28-Sept. 21, 23-Nov. 1, 3-27, 30-Dec. 3, 6-8, 11-27, 30-1820 Jan. 27
- 1820 Jan. 29-July 25, 27-Dec. 19, 21-30
- PPM 1821 Jan. 1-May 4
- PPot sw 1822 Dec. 21
- PWC 1820 Apr. (4)
- PWcHi sw 1820 May 20-Aug. 5, 12-26
- PWalG 1823 Oct. 1

Merged with *Aurora* and title changed to *Aurora and Franklin Gazette,* Nov. 22, 1824 (q.v.)

FRANKLINVILLE TIMES (1891-1898) w ind ♃
Pub. & Ed. 1892-1898 E. H. Rosenberger

FREAR'S CENTENNIAL BUDGET (1874) w ♃
Pub. & Ed. 1874 Thomas Frear

FREE LANCE (1932) w
Pub. 1932 J. A. Kilcullen, S. P. White, J. R. Donnelly
Ed. 1932 J. A. Kilcullen
- PP 1932 June 24-July 29
- PPNw 1932 June 24-July 29

PHILADELPHIA COUNTY 81

FREEMAN'S AND IRISH AMERICAN REVIEW (Aug. 10, 1889-Mar. 26, 1891||) w *
    Pub. & Ed. 1889-1891 Freeman Publishing Co.
        PPCHi   1889 Aug. 10-1891 Mar. 26

FREEMAN'S JOURNAL AND COLUMBIAN CHRONICLE, THE, see National Palladium and Freeman's Journal

FREEMAN'S JOURNAL AND PHILADELPHIA DAILY ADVERTISER, THE, see National Palladium and Freeman's Journal

FREEMAN'S JOURNAL AND PHILADELPHIA MERCANTILE ADVERTISER, THE, see National Palladium and Freeman's Journal

FREEMAN'S JOURNAL FOR THE COUNTRY, THE, see National Palladium and Freeman's Journal

FREEMAN'S JOURNAL, THE, or THE NORTH AMERICAN INTELLIGENCER (Apr. 25, 1781-May 16, 1792) w #
    Pub. 1781-1792   Francis Bailey
         1792   Joseph Scott
        P   1781 Apr. 25-1785 Apr. 13
        PAtM   1784 Aug. 11
        PDoHi   1781 Nov. 14, 28-1782 Jan. 9
            1790 Apr. 28
            1792 Mar. 21
        PHi   [1781 Apr. 25-1791 Dec. 31]
        PNorC   1787 Mar. 28
        PP   1785 May 29
            1788 Mar. 19
        PPAP   1781 Apr. 25-Sept. 5, 19-1783 Jan. 8
            1783 Jan. 21-Feb. 26, Mar. 12, Apr. 2-16, June 18, July 2, Aug. 6, Sept. 3-10, 24-Oct. 8, 10, 22-1784 June 16
            1784 June 30-Aug. 18, Sept. 1-Oct. 27, Dec. 1-8, 29
            1785 Jan. 5-12, Feb. 9, 23, Mar. 16, 30-June 29, July 13-Aug. 17, 31, Sept. 14-Oct. 26, Nov. 9-Dec. 7, 28
            1786 Jan. 4, 25-Mar. 29, June 7, 21-Sept. 27, Oct. 11, 25-Dec. 6, 20
        PPiUD   1785 Jan. 12-Oct. 4, 6-25, 27-Nov. 8, 10-Dec. 28 missing issues, Oct. 5, 26, Nov. 9
        PPL   1781 Apr. 25-1792 May 16
        PPot   1792 May 16
        PPotW   1792 May 16
        PRHi   1781 May 30
        PSuCo   1787 Mar. 28

FREIE PRESSE, DIE, see Philadelphia Freie Presse

FRIEND (Oct. 13, 1827†) w rel
    Pub. 1827-1830   John Richardson
        1830-1834   William Salter

	1834-1848	George W. Taylor
	1848-1866	John Richardson
	1867-1892	John E. Stokes
	1892-1913	Edwin P. Sellew
	1913-1929	Davis H. Forsythe
	1929-1930	William H. Pile's Sons
	1930-1941	Contributors to The Friend
Ed.	1827-1851	Robert Smith
	1851-1879	Charles Evans
	1879-1898	John H. Dillingham
	1898-1910	Edwin P. Sellew
	1913-1929	Davis H. Forsythe
	1929-1930	Margaret W. Rhodes
	1930	Richard R. Wood
	1930-1938	Richard R. Wood and Olive R. Haviland
	1938-1941	D. E. Trueblood and Richard R. Wood
PP		1827 Oct. 13-1897 July 17
		1901 July 20-1902 July 12
		1911 July 6-1918 Aug. 22
		1918 Sept. 5-1920 June 17
		1920 July 1†
PPL		1827 Oct. 13-1863 Dec. 6
		1864 Jan. 9-1870 Dec. 31

FRIENDS' INTELLIGENCER (1844†) w lit rel

FRIENDS' WEEKLY INTELLIGENCER (Mar. 30, 1844-Mar. 19, 1853)

Pub. 1844 Mar. 30-1845 Apr. 26 Chapman and Jones
    1845 May 3-1848 Mar. 25 John Richards
    1848 Apr. 1-1853 Mar. 19 William D. Parrish Co.

Ed. 1845 Mar. 30-1853 Mar. 19 Association of Friends
PP   1845 Apr. 5-1853 Mar. 19
PPFI   1844 Mar. 30-1853 Mar. 19
PSF   1844 Mar. 30-Sept. 21, Oct. 5-1845 Mar. 22
        1845 Apr. 5-1846 Jan. 10
        1846 Jan. 24-1847 July 31
        1847 Aug. 14-1850 Apr. 27
        1850 May 11-June 1, 15-July 13, 27-Nov. 30, Dec. 14-28
        1851 Jan. 11-June 7, 21-Aug. 23, Sept. 6-1853 Mar. 19
        continued as

FRIENDS' INTELLIGENCER (Mar. 26, 1853-Apr. 25, 1885)

Pub. 1853 Mar. 26-1861 Apr. 6 William W. Moore
    1861 Apr. 13-1862 Sept. 6 T. Elwood Zell
    1862 Sept. 13-1864 Mar. 5 Charles H. Davis
    1864 Mar. 12-1871 Feb. 25 Emmor Comly
    1871 Mar. 4-1885 Feb. 7 John Comly
    1885 Feb. 14-1885 Apr. 25 Friends' Intelligencer Association

Ed. 1853 Mar. 26-1885 Apr. 25 Association of Friends
PP   1853 Mar. 26-1862 Mar. 8
        1864 Mar. 12-1873 Sept. 6, 20-Oct. 11
        1873 Oct. 25-1882 July 22
        1882 Aug. 5-Oct. 21, Nov. 4-1883 May 5
        1883 May 19-Sept. 15, 29-1884 Jan. 26
PPFI   1853 Mar. 26-1870 Feb. 7

PHILADELPHIA COUNTY 83

   PSF   1853 Mar. 26-1859 June 25
         1859 July 9-1860 Aug. 11
         1860 Aug. 25-Sept. 22, Oct. 6-1868 Apr. 11
         1868 Apr. 25-Sept. 12
         1869 Jan. 6-1872 Aug. 10
         1872 Aug. 24-Sept. 14, 28-1885 Apr. 25
         Merged with the *Friends' Journal* and
         continued as
FRIENDS' INTELLIGENCER AND JOURNAL (May 2, 1885-Jan. 11, 1902)
 Pub. 1885 May 2   Friends' Intelligencer Association
 Ed. 1885 May 2-1893 May 20 Howard M. Jenkins
    1893 May 27-1894 Dec. 29 Jenkins, Hall, Longstreth and Hillborn
    1895 Jan. 5-1896 Dec. 26 Jenkins, Hall, Hillborn and Darlington
    1897 Jan. 2-1902 Jan. 11 Jenkins, Hall and Hillborn
   PSF   1885 Jan. 3-1902 Jan. 11
         continued as
FRIENDS' INTELLIGENCER (Jan. 18, 1902†)
 Pub. 1902 Jan. 18-1939 Dec. 30 Friends' Intelligencer Association
 Ed. 1902 Jan. 18-1902 Dec. 27 Jenkins, Hall and Hillborn
    1903 Jan. 3-1903 May 23 Lydia H. Hall and Rachel W. Hillborn
    1903 May 30-1906 Feb. 3 Hall, Hillborn, Elizabeth Lloyd and R. Barclay Spicer
    1906 Feb. 10-1908 June 6 Hall, Hillborn, Lloyd, Spicer and Elizabeth Powell Bond
    1908 June 13-1914 Aug. 29 Spicer, Bond and Lloyd
    1914 Sept. 5-1915 Apr. 3 Bond and Lloyd
    1915 Apr. 10-1921 Oct. 22 Henry Ferris
    1921 Oct. 29-1922 Dec. 30 W. H. Abel
    1923 Jan. 6-1939 Dec. 30 Sue C. Yerkes
   PP   1905 Jan. 7-1915 Dec. 25
         1918 Apr. 13-Sept. 14, 28, Oct. 12, 26, Nov. 2-16, 30, Dec. 28
         1919 Jan. 4-May 3, 24-June 14, 28-July 26, Aug. 9-Sept. 13, Oct. 11-Nov. 1
         1920 Jan. 31, Mar. 20-Apr. 3, 17, 24, May 29-June 19, July 3-24, Aug. 21, Nov. 20-Dec. 11
         1931 Jan. 3†
   PSF   1902 Jan. 18-1933 July 22, Aug. 5-1939 Dec. 30
         1940 Jan. 6-Dec. 28
         1941 Jan. 4-June 21

FRIENDS' JOURNAL (1873-1885) w rel
 Pub. & Ed. 1884-1885 Howard M. Jenkins
   PHi   1885 Mar. 26
merged with *Friends' Intelligencer,* 1885, and title changed to *Friends' Intelligencer and Journal.*

FRIENDS' WEEKLY INTELLIGENCER, see Friends' Intelligencer

FUGGETLENSEG (1923†) w ind for
   Pub. & Ed. 1927-1941 Aurel Aczel
      PUB   1926 July 23 (Vol. 3, No. 29)†
      PP   1928 Apr. 6†
      PPiHi   1926 July 23-1931 Oct. 31

FULLER'S LITERARY AND BUSINESS JOURNAL (1854 - 1856),
  see United States Journal

GALES' INDEPENDENT GAZETTEER (1782-1797) w sw d #
   INDEPENDENT GAZETTEER, THE: OR THE CHRONICLE OF
     FREEDOM (Apr. 13, 1782-Jan. 9, 1790) w sw d #
    w Apr. 13, 1782-Sept. 14, 1782;   sw Sept. 17, 1782-Dec. 17, 1782;
    w Mar. 29, 1782-Jan. 18, 1783;   sw Jan. 21, 1783-Mar. 22, 1783;
    w Mar. 29, 1783-Sept. 30, 1786;   d Oct. 7, 1786-Jan. 9, 1790)
  Pub. 1782-1783   Eleazer Oswald
      1783-1784   E. Oswald & D. Humphreys
      1784-1790   Eleazer Oswald
      P   w 1782 Aug. (24-Sept. 14), Dec. (21-1783 Jan. 18)
                  1783 Mar. (29-1786 Sept. 30)
           sw 1782 Sept. 17-Dec. 17
                  1783 Jan. (21-Mar. 22)
            d 1786 Oct. (7-1790 Jan. 9)
      PDoHi sw 1783 Feb. 11
              w 1783 Apr. 5, Oct. 11, Nov. 1, 15-Dec. 27
                 1784 Jan. 10, 17, 31-Feb. 14, 28-Apr. 24, May 8,
                     June 5-19, Oct. 23, Nov. 13
                 1785 Jan. 1, Apr. 2, Aug. 20, Dec. 3, 24
            d 1787 Apr. 23, May 3, Oct. 23, Nov. 26
                 1788 Mar. 17, Apr. 26, July 28, Aug. 7, 20
      PHi   w 1782 Apr. 13-Sept. 14, Dec. 21-28
                 1783 Jan. 4-18, Mar. 29-1786 Sept. 30
           sw 1782 Sept. 17-Dec. 17
                 1783 Jan. 21-Mar. 22
            d 1786 Oct. 24, 25, 30, 31, Nov. 3, 4, 7-10, 14-16, 23,
                    24, 28, Dec. 1, 7-9, 12, 14-30
                 1787 Jan. 2-1789 Oct. 6
                 1789 Oct. 27, 28, Nov. 3-5, 7, Dec. 9, 17, 22-25,
                    28-30
      PPAP   w 1782 June 29, July 20-Aug. 3, 17, 31-Sept. 14 Dec.
                    21-1783 Jan. 18
                 1783 Mar. 29, Apr. 12, 19, May 3, 17, 31, June 21,
                    July 5, 26-Aug. 16, 23-Oct. 18, Nov. 1, 15,
                    29-Dec. 27
                 1784 July 3, Sept. 4-18, Oct. 2, 23, 30, Dec. 18
                 1785 Mar. 12, Apr. 2-June (4)-Aug. 6, Sept. 3-
                    Dec. 31
                 1786 Jan. 4-Mar. 4, 18, Apr. 1-15, 29-May 20, June
                    3-July 22, Aug. 5-Sept. 30
           sw 1782 Sept. 17-21, 28-Oct. 1, 8-12, 19-Nov. 5, 12-
                    Dec. 17
                 1783 Jan. 21, Feb. 4, 15-22, Mar. 4-11, 18-22
      PPiUD w 1785 (Feb. 5-1786 Sept. 30)
              d 1788 July 5, 22

PHILADELPHIA COUNTY 85

                      1789 Jan. 16, Feb. 7, June 8, July 24, Aug. 22, 29, Sept. 12, 23, Oct. 8, 19, 20, 23, 26, 27, 29, Nov. 2, 4, 11, 13, 14, 18, 20-27, 30, Dec. 12, 19, 26
                      1790 Jan. 2-7, 9
PPL   w   1782 Apr. 13-Sept. 14, Dec. 21-1783 Jan. 18
                      1783 Mar. 29-Dec. 27
                      1784 Aug. 14-1786 Sept. 30
         sw 1782 Sept. 17-Dec. 17
                      1783 Jan. 21-Mar. 22
          d 1786 Nov. 17, 20, 21
                      1789 Oct. 7, 9-30, Nov. 2, 3, 5-1790 Jan. 4
                      1790 Jan. 6-9
PSF   d 1786 Oct. 7-1788 Oct. 6
                      continued as

INDEPENDENT GAZETTEER AND AGRICULTURAL REPOSITORY, THE (Jan. 16, 1790-Jan. 4, 1794) w #
Pub. 1790-1794   Eleazer Oswald
   P   1790 Jan. 16-1794 Jan. 4
   PDoHi   1792 Feb. 1-Apr. 4
   PHi   1790 Mar. 13, 27, Aug. 21, Oct. 9
                      1791 Jan. 1-Feb. 12, Mar. 5-19, Apr. 2, 16-May 7, June 18, July 9, Aug. 20, 27, Sept. 24, Oct. 1, 8, 29, Nov. 12, Dec. 17-31
                      1792 Mar. 17, Apr. 21, 28, May 19, June 9, 30, July 14, Aug. 18, 25, Sept. 8-Oct. 6, 20, Nov 3, 17, Dec. 15, 29
                      1793 Jan. 19, Feb. 2-9, 23, Mar. 30, Apr. 13-20
   PP   1793 Oct. 26, Dec. 7-1794 Jan. 4
   PPiUD   1790 Jan. 16-1794 Jan. 4
                      missing issues, 1790 Feb. 6-27, Mar. 20, Apr. 3-17, May 1, 15, 29, June 26, July 24-31, Sept. 4, 11, Oct. 16, 30-1791 Feb. 5
                      1791 May 7, 21, June 11, Oct. 6, Dec. 3, 10, 31-1792 Mar. 24
                      1792 Apr. 14, 21, June 2, Aug. 4, Oct. 20-1793 Dec. 28, 1794 Jan. 4
   PPL   1790 Jan. 16-1794 Jan. 4
                      continued as

INDEPENDENT GAZETTEER, THE (Jan. 11, 1794-Sept. 9, 1796) w sw #
Pub. 1794-1795   Eleazer Oswald
      1795-1796   Elizabeth Oswald
   P   1794 Jan. (11)
         sw 1794 Jan. 15-1796 Sept. 10
   PDoHi sw 1794 Nov. 1, 12
                      1795 June 6, 13-24, July 8, 11, 25, Aug. 5, 14-Sept. 2, 9, 19, Oct. 28
                      1796 Jan. 16, 20, 27, Feb. 13-20, Apr. 2, June 8-15
   PHi   sw 1794 Feb. 8, 22-26, Mar. 1-1795 Jan. 3
                      1795 Jan. 10-Feb. 21, 28-Mar. 14, 25-May 2, 9-July 22, 29-Sept. 5, 12-Nov. 28, Dec. 9-1796 Mar. 26
                      1796 Apr. 2-May 18, 25-July 9, 27-Aug. 6, 13-Sept. 3
   PP   sw 1794 Feb. 12, 22, Mar. 5, 8, 22, 26, Apr. 2, 30, May 21, Sept. 17, Nov. 5, 22, Dec. 3, 17, 20, 24
                      1795 Jan. 3, Feb. 21, 28, Mar. 28, Apr. 8, 25, May 9, Aug. 29, Sept. 23, Nov. 28, Dec. 3, 5, 9, 26

		1796 Jan. 6, Feb. 3, May 14, 25, June 15, 18, July 2, 6, 9, 13, 16, Aug. 13, 24
PPiUD	w	1794 Jan. 11
	sw	1794 Jan. 15-1795 Mar. 4
		missing issues, Jan. 25, Mar. 15, Apr. 2, May 3, June 25
PPL	w	1794 Jan. 11
		1795 Jan. 14-Feb. 4, 11-Mar. 18, 25-Apr. 4, 11-May 2, 9-13, 20-23, 30-June 6, 20-July 8, 15, 22-Aug. 22, 29-Sept. 2, 16, Oct. 7, 24-Nov. 7, 14-1796 Jan. 23
		1796 May 21, Aug. 31-Sept. 10

continued as

GALES' INDEPENDENT GAZETTEER (Sept. 16, 1796-Sept. 12, 1797) sw

Pub. 1796-1797	Joseph Gales
P	1796 Sept. (16-Dec. 30)
PDoHi	1796 Oct. 11-Nov. 22, 29, Dec. 2, 30
	1797 Jan. 10, 31, Feb. 3, 10, Mar. 3, 28, Apr. 7, 11, 18-May 12, 26, June 2-13, 20, 23, July 7, 11, 25, Aug. 8
PHi	1796 Sept. 16-Dec. 13, 23-1797 Feb. 3
	1797 Feb 14-24, Mar. 3, 7
PP	1796 Oct. 14, 28, Nov. 8, 11, 18, Dec. 13, 20, 30
	1797 Jan. 3, 10, 24, 27, 31, Feb. 3, 28, Mar. 7, 10, 14, 24, 28, Apr. 7, 14, 21, May 19, 23, June 2, 6, 30
PPL	1796 Sept. 16-20, 27, Oct. 7-Dec. 16, 23-1797 Jan. 24
	1797 Feb. 3-7, 14-Mar. 3, 10-June 30, July 7-18, 25-Aug. 22, 29-Sept. 1, 8-12
PWeHi	1797 July (7)

GAZETA NARODOWA (1911-1928) w ind for ♂

GAZETA LUDOWA (1916-1922) w ♂

Pub. 1916-1920	A. Lewandowski & Bro.
1920-1922	Polish National Publishing Co.
Ed. 1916-1920	A. Lewandowski & Bro.

continued as

GAZETA NARODOWA (1922-1928) w ♂

Pub. 1922-1928   Gazeta Narodowa

GAZETTE (FRANKFORD), see Frankford Gazette

GAZETTE, see Germantown Gazette

GAZETTE OF THE UNITED STATES, see United States Gazette

GAZETTE OF THE UNITED STATES AND DAILY ADVERTISER, see United States Gazette

GAZETTE OF THE UNITED STATES AND DAILY EVENING ADVERTISER, see United States Gazette

PHILADELPHIA COUNTY 87

GAZETTE OF THE UNITED STATES AND EVENING ADVERTISER, see United States Gazette

GAZETTE OF THE UNITED STATES AND PHILADELPHIA DAILY ADVERTISER, see United States Gazette

GAZETTE OF THE UNITED STATES FOR THE COUNTRY, see United States Gazette

GEMEINNUTZIGE PHILADELPHISCHE CORRESPONDENZ (1781-1790), see Neue Philadelphische Correspondenz

GENERAL ADVERTISER, see Aurora, The

GENERAL ADVERTISER AND POLITICAL, COMMERCIAL, AGRICULTURAL AND LITERARY JOURNAL, see Aurora, The

GENERAL POST-BOTHE UND DIE DEUTSCHE NATION IN AMERIKA, DER (Jan. 5, 1790-June 29, 1790) sw #
    Pub. 1790   Melchior Steiner for Charles G. Reiche
    Ed. 1790   F. C. Reiche
        PHi   1790 Jan. 5-June 29
        PRHi   1789 Nov. 27
                  1790 Jan. 5-June 29

GERMAN AND ENGLISH GAZETTE, see Hoch Deutsche und Englische Zeitung

GERMAN REFORMED MESSENGER, see Messenger, The

GERMANTAUNER ZEITUNG (Feb. 8, 1785-1799) bw w for
    Pub. & Ed. 1785-1787 Leibert & Billmeyer
                            (Peter Leibert & Michael Billmeyer)
                1787-1799 Michael Billmeyer
    PBMa   1793 Dec. 10, 17
    PHi ♦   1785 Feb. 22-May 31, July 12-Aug. 9, Sept. 6, Nov. 29-Dec. 13
               1786 Jan. 10-Feb. 7, Mar. 21, Apr. 18, Aug. 8-Sept. 19, Oct. 17-Dec. 26
               1787 Jan. 9-Sept. 18, Oct. 16-Nov. 27
               1788 Jan. 8-June 24, July 22-Dec. 9
               1789 Jan. 6-Dec. 22
               1790 Jan. 5-Dec. 28
               1791 Jan. 11-Dec. 27
               1792 Jan. 3-Dec. 25
               1793 Jan. 1-15
    PPeS   1790 Apr. 27
               1793 Dec. 10

GERMANTOWN BULLETIN (1901-1906) w local
    Pub. & Ed. 1904-1906   J. Owen Scott

GERMANTOWN BULLETIN (1928†) w
    GERMANTOWN BULLETIN (Oct. 31, 1928-Dec. 26, 1929) w
    Pub. 1928-1929   Paton & Fetterolf
    Ed.   1928-1929   Isaac M. Walker
         1929   William L. Paton
         PUB   1928 Oct. 31-1929 Dec. 26
         PP   1929 Sept. 12-Dec. 19
         PPGHi   [1928 Oct. 31-1929 Dec. 26]
                    continued as
    GERMANTOWN BULLETIN AND CHESTNUT HILL AND MOUNT AIRY HERALD (Jan. 2, 1930-Jan. 29, 1931) w
    Pub. 1930-1931   Paton & Fetterolf
    Ed.   1930-1931   Wm. L. Paton
         PP   1930 Jan. 2-1931 Jan. 29
         PPGHi   1930 Jan. 2-1931 Jan. 29
         PUB   1930 Jan. 2-1931 Jan. 29
                    continued as
    GERMANTOWN BULLETIN (Feb. 5, 1931-Oct. 22, 1940) w
    Pub. 1931-1938   Paton and Fetterolf
         1939 July 13-1940 Feb. 15   K. Scott Phillips
         1940 Feb. 22-1940 July 12   Margaret E. Roth
         1940 July 19-1940 Oct. 22   Howard A. Morris
    Ed.   1931 Feb.   5-1932 July   William L. Paton
         1932 Aug.   -1933 Apr.   13   A. Everett Morrison
         1933 Apr. 20-1933 May   25   William L. Paton
         1933 June 22-1934 June   21   I. M. Walker
         1934 June 28-1934 Dec.   13   Hobe Morrison
         1934 Dec. 20-1936 Jan.   2   Charles Herb Brown
         1936 Jan.   9-1936 May   14   Charles G. Super, Jr.
         1936 May 21-1938 Nov.   17   Seth L. Fetterolf
         1939 July 13-1940 Jan.   25   Stewart Phillips
         1940 July 19-1940 Oct.   22   Howard A. Morris
         PP   1931 Feb. 5-1937 Oct. 21, Nov. 4-1938 June 16
                    1938 June 30-Nov. 23
                    1939 July 13-1940 Jan. 25
                    1940 Feb. 15-June 21, July 5-Aug. 30
         PPGHi   1931 Feb. 5-1940 Oct. 22
         PUB   1931 Feb. 5-1940 Oct. 22

GERMANTOWN CHRONICLE, see Philadelphia Evening Chronicle

GERMANTOWN COMMERCIAL (1879-1880) w ind
    Pub. & Ed. 1879-1880   A. J. Merrill & Co.

PHILADELPHIA COUNTY 89

GERMANTOWN COURIER (1936†) w ind
    Pub. 1936-1941   Philadelphia Suburban Newspapers, Inc.
    Ed. 1936   William F. Valentine and Geane Geddes
        1937-1939   George Walker
        1939-1941   L. A. Thomason, Jr.
        PUB   1936 Dec. 6†
        PHi   1936 Dec. 4 (Vol. I, No. 1)
        PP   1938 Aug. 18, Sept. 8†
        PPGHi   [1936†]

GERMANTOWN DAILY CHRONICLE, see Philadelphia Evening Chronicle

GERMANTOWN GAZETTE (1878-1895) w rep ♦
    Pub & Ed. 1880-1884   Gazette Publishing Co.
        1884-1885   Smith & Holeckley
        1885-1895   Henry Smith

GERMANTOWN GUIDE, see Independent Gazette and the Germantown Guide

GERMANTOWN INDEPENDENT, see Independent Gazette

GERMANTOWN INDEPENDENT GAZETTE, see Independent Gazette

GERMANTOWN NEWS (Oct. 1898†) w ind-rep
    Pub. 1900-1939   William Willans & Co.
        1939-1941   Willans Publishing Co.
    Ed. 1900-1908   Thomas Willans
        1908-1916   Samuel B. Scott
        1916-1941   William Willans
        PUB   1931 Dec.†
        PHi   1903 July 30
            1924 June 19, July 3
        PP   1914 Dec. 31
            1918 Mar. 4
            1919 July 31
            1922 Sept. 7
            1925 June 11-25, Oct. 15, 29, Nov. 19
            1926 Feb. 11-Mar. 4, 18, Apr. 1-29, July 15, Sept. 2, Nov. 4-11
            1927 Jan. 13, Feb. 3, Mar. 3, 24-Apr. 28, June 9, July 21, Aug. 18-25, Sept. 15, 29-Oct. 6
            1933 Jan. 5, 12, Feb. 2-Mar. 16, 30, Apr. 13-Nov. 30, Dec. 14-1934 Mar. 29
            1934 Apr. 12†

GERMANTOWN REVIEW (1916-1928) w ind
    Pub. & Ed. 1919-1928   J. H. Ewing
        PHi ♦   1919 Nov. 12
            1920 Jan. 21, Feb. 18, Mar. 31, Apr. 7, 28-May 26, June 9-23, July 7-Aug. 11, Sept. (22)
            1921 Jan. 19

GERMANTOWN TELEGRAPH (Mar. 17, 1830†) w local *
VILLAGE TELEGRAPH, THE (Mar. 17, 1830-May 19, 1830) w
Pub. & Ed. 1830 Philip R. Freas
  PHi 1830 Mar. 17-May 19
  PPGHi [1830]
  PPL 1830 Mar. 17-May 19

    continued as

GERMANTOWN TELEGRAPH, THE (May 26, 1830-Jan. 5, 1831) w *
Pub. & Ed. 1830-1831 Philip R. Freas
  PHi 1830 May 26-1831 Jan. 5
  PPGHi [1830-1831]
  PPL 1830 May 26-1831 Jan. 5

    continued as

GERMANTOWN TELEGRAPH AND PHILADELPHIA AND MONTGOMERY ADVERTISER (Jan. 12, 1831-Dec. 25, 1839) w *
Pub. & Ed. 1831-1839 Philip R. Freas
  PDoHi 1833 Jan. 2
  PHi 1831 Jan. 12-1839 Dec. 25
  PPGHi [1831-1839]
  PPL 1831 Jan. 12-1834 May 27
    1834 June 10-July 1, 15-1836 Sept. 21
    1836 Oct. 12-1838 Apr. 24
    1838 May 8-1839 Dec. 25

    continued as

GERMANTOWN TELEGRAPH (Jan. 1, 1840†) w *
Pub. 1840-1883 P. R. Freas & Co.
  1883-1889 Henry W. Raymond
  1889-1901 Edwin K. Hart
  1901-1921 The Germantown Telegraph Publishing Co.
  1921-1938 Germantown Publishing Co.
Ed. 1840-1883 Philip R. Freas
  1883-1889 Henry W. Raymond
  1889-1901 Edwin K. Hart
  1902-1903 Samuel R. Warren
  1903-1904 Fred T. Williamson
  1904-1908 John Galloway
  1912-1941 John J. McDevitt, Jr.
  P   1889 July 3-1912 July 28
  PBL ♦ 1842 Aug. 17
  PDoHi 1852 Mar. 10, June 2-Aug. 4, 18-Oct. 13, Dec. 22-1853 Jan. 12
    1853 May 25-July 20, Aug. 10-Sept. 21, Dec. 7
    1854 Mar. 22, 29, Apr. 12, 26, May 3, June 7, 14, 28, July 5, 19, 26, Aug. 23, Nov. 15-Dec. 13, 27
    1855 Feb. 28-Mar. 14, Apr. 18, May 2, June 6, 27, July 11, Aug. 15, 29, Sept. 19-Oct. 31, Nov. 14, 28, Dec. 5
    1856 Jan. 9-23, Feb. 6-20, Mar. 5-19, Apr. 2, 9, 30, May 7, 28, June 18, Oct. 1, 15-29, Nov. 12-26, Dec. 24-1857 Jan. 21
    1857 Feb. 4, 18, 25, Mar. 18, 25, May 20, June 24, Aug. 19, 26, Sept. 9, 16, Nov. 11-Dec. 16

PHILADELPHIA COUNTY 91

1858 Jan. 6, 13, 27, Mar. 3, 24, Apr. 7, 14, 28, June 9, 16, 30, July 7, 28, Sept. 29-Oct. 20, Nov. 3, 10, 24-Dec. 22
1859 Jan. 5, 12, Mar. 2, 16, 23, Apr. 20, May 11, June 1-22, July 13, 27-Aug. 17, Sept. 7, 21, Oct. 5-26, Nov. 9, Dec. 7-28
1860 Jan. 4, 18, 25, Feb. 15, 29, Mar. 14, Apr. 4-May 2, June 6, 20, 27, Aug. 29, Sept. 12, Oct. 3, Nov. 7-Dec. 5, 19, 26
1861 Jan. 9, 16, 30-Mar. 13, June 5, 12, 26-July 17, 31-Sept. 11, Oct. 2, 9, 23, Nov. 20-Dec. 11, 25
1862 Jan. 8, 15, Feb. 12-Mar. 5, Apr. 2-May 28, July 2, 16, 23, Aug. 6, 13, Sept. 24, Oct. 1, 15-Dec. 31
1863 Jan. 7-Mar. 4, 18, 25, Apr. 8, 29-May 27, June 10-24, Aug. 19, 26, Sept. 9, 16, 30, Oct. 14, 21, Nov. 11-Dec. 9, 23-1864 Jan. 20
1864 Feb 17, Mar. 9, Apr. 27, May 18, June 1, 15, 29, July 27, Aug. 10, 17, 31, Sept. 7, 28-Oct. 19, Nov. 2, 16-30, Dec. 14, 28-1865 Jan. 11
1865 Jan. 25, Feb. 1, 15, 22, Mar. 29, Apr. 18, May 3, 24, July 26, Aug. 9-23, Sept. 27, Oct. 11, 18, Nov. 1, 8, 22, Dec. 6-1866 Jan. 17
1866, Feb. 14-Mar. 7, 28, Apr. 18, 25, May 30, July 11, Aug. 15, Oct. 17, 31, Nov. 21-Dec. 5, 19, 26
1867 Jan. 9, Feb. 13, Mar. 13, Apr. 10-May 1, June 5, 12, July 10, 31, Aug. 7, 28, Sept. 4, 11, Oct. 2, 16, 30-Nov. 13, Dec. 4, 11, 25
1868 Jan. 15-29, Apr. 8, 22, May 6, July 1, 29-Aug. 26, Oct. 28, Nov. 18, 25
1869 Feb 10, Mar. 3, June 2, Aug. 18, 25, Sept. 15, Oct. 6-20, Dec. 1
1870 Jan. 19, Feb. 2-16, Apr. 6, 27, June 29, July 27, Aug. 10-31, Oct. 19, Nov. 9, 30-Dec. 28
1871 Jan. 11, 25-Feb. 15, Mar. 1, 29, Apr. 5, Aug. 30, Sept. 13-27, Oct. 18, Nov. 22-Dec. 13
1872 Mar. 27, July 31, Sept. 25, Oct. 9, Nov. 6, 13, 27, Dec. 25
1873 Jan. 15, Mar. 12, Apr. 9, Dec. 3, 24
1874 Mar. 25, Apr. 1, 29, May 13-27, June 10, 24, July 1, Aug 26, Sept. 23, 30, Oct. 14, Nov. 25, Dec. 9, 16
1875 Jan. 6, Feb. 3, 10, Mar. 3, 10, Apr. 14-28, May 12-26, July 21, Sept. 1, 8, Oct. 6, 20, Nov. 3
1876 Jan. 19, Feb. 2, Mar. 1, 15, 29, May 3, 24, Aug. 2, 16, Sept. 13, Oct. 11, Nov. 29
1877 Jan. 10, 17, Feb. 14, 21, Mar. 28, Apr. 4, June 27, July 11, 25, Aug. 15, Sept. 5, 12, Oct. 17, 31-Nov. 14, Dec. 5
1878 Jan. 9, 23, Feb. 6, Mar. 13-27, Aug. 7, Oct. 16, 23, Nov. 13, 27, Dec. 18
1879 Jan. 22, Apr. 16, Nov. 5, 12, Dec. 17
1880 Jan. 21, 28, Mar. 3, Apr. 7, 14, Oct. 6, 27
1881 Feb. 2, May 25
1883 Mar. 6
1886 Feb. 24

PHi 1840 Jan. 1-1883 Aug. 15
PNazHi 1846 Jan. 7, 14
PNoHi 1844 June 26
1848 Nov. 8

GERMANTOWN TELEGRAPH, *continued*

        1849 Feb. 7, June 27, Aug. 1, Sept. 12
        1850 Mar. 27, Apr. 3, May 8, 15, June 12, 19, July 3, 10, 24, Aug. 21
        1851 Feb. 12, Mar. 12, 26, Apr. 9, June 4, July 2, Aug. 6, Sept. 24, Nov. 26
        1852 Jan. 21, Mar. 10, Apr. 7, May 12, June 2, 23
        1858 Jan. 20, Feb. 3, 17, Sept. 15

PP   1851 Mar. 26, Apr. 9, May 7-14, July 2-1852 Sept. 15
        1853 Oct. 12, Nov. 9
        1854 Jan. 18
        1858 Nov. 17
        1859 Sept. 21
        1863 July 15
        1865 July 19
        1868 July 22
        1874 Feb. 25
        1875 Dec. 8-1876 Apr. 12
        1876 Apr. 26-1877 July 11
        1877 July 25-1878 Sept. 18
        1878 Sept. 18, 25, Oct. 9-Nov. 6, 20-27, Dec 25-1879 Jan. 8
        1879 Feb. 12, Mar. 19, Apr. 2, 9, 23-Dec. 31
        1880 Jan. 7-Feb. 25, Mar. 10-1881 May 25
        1881 June 8-1882 Jan. 25
        1882 Feb. 8, Mar. 8, 29-Apr. 12, 26-May 3, 17-July 19, Aug. 2-1884 Aug. 6
        1884 Aug. 20-Sept. 17, Oct. 1-1885 Aug. 5
        1885 Aug. 19-1886 June 16
        1886 June 30, July 21, Aug. 1-Sept. 22, Oct. 13-1888 June 27
        1888 July 25, Aug. 22, Sept. 12-Oct. 17, 31, Nov. 14, 28, Dec. 12, 26
        1889 Jan. 9, 23, Feb. 6, 20-Mar. 6, Apr. 3, 17, June 19, July 3, 17, Aug. 7, 21, Sept. 4
        1890 Jan. 12
        1892 July 20, Aug. 3-10, 24, Oct. 26-Nov. 2, Dec. 23
        1893 Jan. 4
        1908 June 14
        1927 Apr. 1-22
        1929 Dec. 27
        1930 June 12†

PPeS 1851 June 11
        1852 Feb. 11-18, July 7
        1853 Mar. 23, May 18, 25, Aug. 31, Dec. 14
        1854 Jan. 4, 25, Feb. 1, Mar. 15, Sept. 6, 20, Nov. 1, Dec. 6
        1855 Jan. 24, Feb. 21, June 6, Aug. 1-8, Oct. 3, 17-31, Dec. 26
        1856 Jan. 2, 30, Apr. 2, May 21, July 9, Aug. 6, Sept. 10, 17, Dec. 3, 10
        1857 Feb. 4, Mar. 11-Apr. 1, Nov. 11, Dec. 16-30
        1858 Jan. 13, 27, Feb. 3, 24-Mar. 10, May 12, June 9, Aug. 18, Sept. 15-29, Oct. 27, Nov 24, Dec. 15, 29
        1859 Jan. 5, Feb. 29, Apr. 6, 20-May 4, June 22, Aug. 31-Sept. 14, Oct. 12, 26, Nov. 23, Dec. 7
        1860 Feb. 15, Mar. 7, 14, Apr. 18, 25, July 18

PHILADELPHIA COUNTY 93

                1861 Aug. 14
                1862 Jan. 29, Dec. 10
                1863 Jan. 21, Apr. 22, June 24-July 1, Oct. 4
                1864 Jan. 6, June 15-22, Aug. 24, Sept. 7, Oct. 19, Nov. 9, Dec. 21
                1865 Apr. 5, June 28, Aug. 30, Nov. 22, Dec. 20
                1872 Oct. 16, 23
                1877 Feb. 7
                1878 Jan. 30, Apr. 24, June 26, July 31-Aug. 28, Oct. 9, Dec. 11, 18
                1879 Feb. 5, Mar. 12, May 7, June 18-July 2, 23, 30, Aug. 27, Nov. 5
                1880 Jan. 7, Feb. 11, Mar. 3, 10, 24, 31
                1881 Apr. 27, Aug. 24, Sept. 21, Oct. 12, 26, Dec. 14, 28
                1882 Feb. 15, 22, Apr. 5, June 28, July 19, Sept. 27
                1883 Jan. 24, May 16, July 11, Aug. 15, Sept. 26, Oct. 17, 24
                1884 Feb. 20, Mar. 19-Apr. 2, 23, May 7-21, June 4, July 9, 23, 30, Aug. 13, Nov. 12
                1885 Jan. 7, 21, Mar. 25, Apr. 1, June 3-17, July 1-15, Aug. 12, Nov. 4, 16
                1886 Jan. 13-Feb. 10, 24-Mar. 31, Apr. 28, June 9, July 14, Aug. 11, 25, Sept. 8
PPGHi   [1840-1880], [1927†]
PPL   1840 Jan. 1-1841 Jan. 27
                1841 Feb. 10-1843 Feb. (1)-1857 Dec. 30
                1861 Mar. 13-1863 Mar. 4
                1863 Mar. 18-1865 Mar. 1
                1868 Mar. 11-(25)-1870 Dec. 21
                1871 Jan. 4-1872 Mar. (6)-1875 Feb. 24
                1881 Mar. 16-1883 Aug. 15
                1888 Dec. 12-26
                1889 Jan. 2-7, Feb. 13, Mar. 6-Apr. 3, 17
PWcA   1859 Feb. 9
PWcHi 1844 Oct. 16, 23
                1859 Feb. 9
                1861 Aug. 28, Oct. 16, 23
                1875 Dec. 8
                1876 Dec. 20
                1902 Mar. 21

GERMANTOWN WEEKLY INDEPENDENT, see Independent Gazette

GERMANTOWN TIMES (1877-1882) w ♣
    Pub. & Ed. 1879-1882 O. S. Fell & Son

GERMANTOWNER ZEITUNG, DIE, (1762-1777), see Pennsylvanische Staats Courier, Der

GIORNALE ITALIANO (1895-1921) w non-part for ♣
    Pub. 1920-1921   Italian News Company
    Ed. 1920-1921   Thomas Barra

GIRARD AVENUE NEWS (1890-1891) w ♣
    Pub. & Ed. 1890-1891 Myers & Price

GIRARD AVENUE NEWS, see North Central Bulletin

GLEANER (Frankford), see Frankford News Gleaner

GLOBE AND EMERALD: or, SATURDAY'S JOURNAL OF LITERATURE, POLITICS, AND THE ARTS (1824-1826) w
  GLOBE, THE (Aug. 21, 1824-Dec. 18, 1824) w
  Pub. 1824 J. Mortimer and J. E. Milford
  PHi   1824 Aug. 21-Oct. 23, Nov. 6-20, Dec. 4-18
    Merged with the *Emerald: or, Political, Literary, and Commercial Recorder of New York City,* Dec. 20, 1824, and title changed to
  GLOBE AND EMERALD: or, SATURDAY'S JOURNAL OF LITERATURE, POLITICS, AND THE ARTS (Dec. 25, 1824-Apr. 15, 1826) w
  Pub. 1824-1825 J. E. Milford
    1824-1825 H. H. Byrne, E. Milford, T. W. Clerke & J. Mortimer
    1825-1826 T. W. Clerke & Co.
  PLewL   1825 Jan. 22
        1826 Jan. 7-21, Feb. 4, 18, Mar. 4, 18, Apr. 1-15

GRAHAM'S SATURDAY MAIL (1853-1855), see Saturday Evening Mail

GRAPHIC (1892) w Negro ♦
  Pub. 1892 Romero Thomasso
  Ed. 1892 Thomas W. Swann

GRAPHIC NEWS (1933), see Tabloid, The

GREATER PHILADELPHIA KENSINGTON BULLETIN (1937†) w local
  KENSINGTON BULLETIN (1921-1933, Jan. 8, 1937, Apr. 20, 1938) w
  Pub. 1921-1930 Kensington Bulletin, Inc.
  Ed. 1921-1923 James A. K. Sinnot
    1930   John C. Moss
  % Greater Kensington Bulletin.
    PP   1929 Oct. 25-1933 Dec. 1
  Pub. 1937-1941 Peerless Publishing Co.
  Ed. 1937   Herbert Peterson
    PP   1937 Jan. 8-Dec. 23
        1938 Jan. 7, 21
        continued as
  GREATER PHILADELPHIA KENSINGTON BULLETIN (Apr. 22, 1938†) w
  Pub. 1938-1941 Peerless Publishing Co.
  Ed. 1938-1941 E. L. Wagner
    PP   1938 Apr. 22, May 13, June 17, 24, July 1, Oct. 14
        1939 Jan. 13, Mar. 3, 10, 24

GREENBACK HERALD (1875) w *
  PEOPLE AND ANTI-MONOPOLIST (July 4, 1875-July 25, 1875) w
  Pub. 1875 People Publishing Co.
  PHi ♦ 1875 July 4-25
       continued as
  PEOPLE (Aug. 1, 1875-Aug. 22, 1875) w
  Pub. 1875 People Publishing Co.
  PHi ♦ 1875 Aug. 1-22

PHILADELPHIA COUNTY 95

                continued as
GREENBACK HERALD (Aug. 29, 1875-Oct. 30, 1875||) w *
  Pub. 1875   Volkmar & Co.
        1875   Greenback Herald Association, Ltd.
        PHi   ◆   1875 Aug. 29-Oct. 30

GRIFFIN'S JOURNAL (1873-1900) sm m rel
  I. C. B. U. JOURNAL (1873-1892) sm
  Pub. & Ed. 1883-1892 M. I. J. Griffin
        PHi   ◆   1884 Aug. 15, Sept. 1, 15, Nov. 1, 15
                      1888 Mar. 15
        PPL   1873 July 15-Aug. 15, Oct. 1-Dec.
                continued as
  GRIFFIN'S JOURNAL (1893-1900||) m
  Pub. & Ed. 1893-1900 Martin I. J. Griffin
        PHi   ◆   1900 May
        PPL   1894 Jan.-Apr., Oct.-Dec.
                      1895 Jan.-Apr., July-Dec.
                      1896 Jan.-Sept., Nov.-1898 June
                      1898 Aug.-Nov.
                      1899 Jan.-1900 July

GROONG (Sept. 15, 1919†) w for
  Pub. 1925†   Groong Publishing Co.
  Ed. 1925†   K. Kavorkian
        PUB   1919 Sept. 15†
        PP   1932 May 27†

GROTJAN'S PHILADELPHIA PUBLIC SALE REPORT, see Philadelphia Public Sale Report

GRUND'S PENNSYLVANISCHER DEUTSCHER (Aug. 1, 1840-Mar. 13, 1841||) w for *
        PShH   1840 Aug. 1

GUIDE (1884-1888) w ♣
  Pub. 1886-1888   William Nuneviller & Co.
        1888   William R. Robeson
  Ed. 1886-1888   R. R. Shronk
        1888   William R. Robeson

GUIDE (1871-1926), see Independent Gazette and Germantown Guide

GWIAZDA (1902†) w for rep
  Pub. 1903-1932   Stephen Novaczyk
        1932-1941   Polish Star Publishing Co.
  Ed. 1903-1932   Stephen Novaczyk
        1932-1937   Francis Grzeskowiak
        1937-1941   Dr. Charles Wachtl
        PUB   1902 Aug. 14
                      1932 Aug. 7†
        PP   1926 Aug. 5
                      1927 Dec. 29†

HENRICH MILLERS PENNSYLVANISCHER STAATSBOTE
(1762-1779) w sw for #
WOCHENTLICHE PHILADELPHISCHE STAATSBOTE, DER
(Jan. 18, 1762-Dec. 29, 1767) w #
Pub. 1762-1767   Henrich Miller
Ed. 1762-1767   Henrich Miller & Carl Cist
  PHi   1762 Jan. 18-Dec. 31
            1767 Mar. 30, May 25
  PPG   1762 Jan. 18-Dec. 27
  PPL   1763 Mar. 7-1767 Dec. 29
        continued as

WOCHENTLICHE PENNSYLVANISCHE STAATSBOTE, DER
(Jan. 5, 1768-May 16, 1775) w
Pub. 1768-1775   Henrich Miller
Ed. 1768-1775   Henrich Miller & Carl Cist
  PHi   1768 Mar. 29
            1769 Dec. 19
            1770 May 22-1775 May 16
  PPeS   1774 Sept. (13)
            1775 Feb. (7)
  PPL   1768 Jan. 5-1775 May 16
        continued as

HENRICH MILLERS PENNSYLVANISCHER STAATSBOTE
(May 23, 1775-May 26, 1779||) sw w #
sw May 23, 1775-July 26, 1775; w July 30, 1776-May 26, 1779
Pub. & Ed. 1775-1779   Henrich Miller
    Suspended from Sept. 17, 1777 to Aug. 5, 1778
  PBMa   1778 Aug. 26
  PHi   sw 1775 May 23-1777 Aug. 13
            1778 Aug. 5-1779 Apr. 21
  PPL   sw 1775 May 23-1779 May 26

HERALD OF GOSPEL LIBERTY   (1811-1814) bw
Pub. 1811-1814   Elias Smith
Established in Portland, Maine, and continued in Philadelphia beginning with the issue of July 5, 1811. The last issue at Philadelphia was that of Jan. 21, 1814, atfer which it was removed to Portsmouth, N. H.
  P   1811 June 21, Aug. 16
  PHi   ♦ 1811 July 5-Aug. 2, Sept. 13-Nov. 22
  PPPHi   1813 Dec. 10
            1814 Jan. 21

HEROLD UND ZEITSCHRIFT, see Lutherischer Herold

HIBERNIAN (1894-1897) w ♦
Pub. & Ed. 1895-1897   Joseph D. Murphy, Thomas E. Logan and Charles J. Bigley

PHILADELPHIA COUNTY 97

HICKORY TREE, THE (Sept. 20, 1834) w
    PPFfHi   1834 Sept. 20

HIGH DUTCH PENNSYLVANIA HISTORIOGRAPHER, ETC., see Pennsylvanische Staats Courier, Der

HIGH GERMAN PENNSYLVANIA RECORDER OF EVENTS, ETC., see Pennsylvanische Staats Courier, Der

HOCH DEUTSCHE PENNSYLVANISCHE BERICHTE, see Pennsylvanische Staats Courier, Der

HOCH-DEUTSCHE PENNSYLVANISCHE GESCHICHT-SCHREIBER, ETC., DER, see Pennsylvanische Staats Courier, Der

HOCH DEUTSCHE PENNSYLVANISCHE JOURNAL, DAS (1743) w for
    Pub. 1743   Joseph Crellius

HOCH DEUTSCHE UND ENGLISCHE ZEITUNG, DIE (Aug. 10, 1751-Jan. 25, 1752||) * # bw for (Eng. & German)
    Pub. 1751-1752   Benjamin Franklin

HOLMESBURG WEEKLY GAZETTE, see Frankford Gazette

HOLMESBURG WORLD (1891-1892) w
    Pub. & Ed. 1891-1892 M. C. Blinsinger

HOME GUIDE (1894-1898) w Temperance
    Pub. 1896-1898   Home Guide Publishing Co.
    Ed. 1896-1898   C. L. Burnett

HOME JOURNAL AND CITIZEN SOLDIER (1837-1851) w *
    HOME JOURNAL (1837-1843)
    Pub. & Ed. 1837-1843 A. H. Diller
        P-M   1843 May 1
            The *Citizen Soldier* (q.v.) was absorbed to form
    HOME JOURNAL AND CITIZEN SOLDIER (Jan. 3, 1844-1851) *
    Pub. & Ed. 1844-1851 A. H. Diller
        PDoHi   1844 Jan. 3-May 29
        PPiUD   1844 Nov. 20

HOME NEWS (1887-1892) w
    Pub. & Ed. 1887-1892 M. C. Blinsinger

HOME PROTECTOR (1881-1883) w Temperance ♦
  Pub. & Ed. 1881-1883 E. M. Lester
              1883   Home Protector Publishing Co.

HOME WEEKLY AND HOUSEHOLD NEWSPAPER, see Philadelphia Home Weekly

HOPE'S PHILADELPHIA PRICE-CURRENT, AND COMMERCIAL RECORD (1804-1813) w #
  HOPE'S NEW PHILADELPHIA PRICE-CURRENT (Oct. 15, 1804-Mar. 4, 1805) w
  Pub. 1804-1805   Thomas Hope
      PHi   1804 Dec. 3
                   1805 Jan. 5-Mar. 4
                   continued as
  HOPE'S PHILADELPHIA PRICE-CURRENT, AND COMMERCIAL RECORD (March 11, 1805-Dec. 28, 1813) w #
  Pub. 1805-1813   Thomas Hope
      PHi   1805 Mar. 11-1811 Oct. 14
                   1813 Aug. 16-Nov. 22
      PPL   1805 June 10-1810 Dec. 31
                   1811 Oct. 21-1812
                   1813 May 24, June 14-Dec. 28

HOSPITAL REGISTER (1863-1865) w *
  This paper was printed and published at U. S. Army General Hospital (Saterlee), West Philadelphia.
  WEST PHILADELPHIA HOSPITAL REGISTER (Feb. 14, 1863) *
      PHi   ♦   1863 Feb. 14
      PP   1863 Feb. 14-Mar. 21, Apr. 25
              continued as
  HOSPITAL REGISTER (1863-Apr. 1, 1865||) *
      PHi   ♦   1863 Apr. 1-1865 Apr. 1
      PPot   1864 Jan. 9, May 14, 28, June 11, July 9, Aug. 3, Sept. 3, 10, Oct. 1, Nov. 5, Dec. 10

HUSTLER (Wissinoming) (1915-1927) w local ♦
  Pub. 1918-1927   Williams & Williams
  Ed. 1918-1927   Moritt G. Williams

HY SIRD (1926†) w for
  w Apr. 14, 1926-Nov. 1935; m Dec. 1935†
  Pub. 1927-1937   Hy Sird Publishing Co.
  Ed. 1928-1932   H. Kooyoomjian
       1932-1937   S. Soukiassian
      PUB   1926 Apr. 14†
      PP   1928 Jan. 4-Apr. 11, 25-1929 Sept. 18
                   1929 Oct. 2-1930 Apr. 23
                   1930 May 7-July 23, Aug. 6-1935 Mar. 6

I. C. B. U. JOURNAL, see Griffin's Journal

ILLUSTRATED FASHION BAZAR (1876-1877) w m ↓
Pub. & Ed. 1876-1877 David R. Doty

ILLUSTRATED NEW AGE (1863-1875) d w dem *
   AGE, THE (Mar. 25, 1863-May 5, 1863) d morn
   Pub. 1863   A. J. Glossbrenner & Co.
                   (Adam J. Glossbrenner, Francis J. Grund, William H. Welsh)
   Ed. 1863   Charles J. Biddle
     PDoHi   1863 Mar. 30
     PP   1863 Mar. 25-Apr. 4, 7-25
     PPL   1863 Mar. 25-May 2, 5
     PPM   1863 Mar. 25-May 5
     PU   1863 Mar. 25-May 5
                continued as
   DAILY AGE, THE (May 6, 1863-June 10, 1866) d w dem *
   d May 6, 1863-June 10, 1866; w June 6, 1863-June 1866
   Pub. 1863   A. J. Glossbrenner & Co.
       1863-1866 Welsh & Glossbrenner
       1866   Welsh & Robb
                   (James M. Robb)
                   Weekly editions published, entitled *Philadelphia Weekly Age,* 1863-1866; *Campaign Age,* 1864
     PDoHi   1863 July 27
                 1865 Apr. 5, May 1
     PHi   1863 July 1-17, 20-Sept. 26, 29-Oct. 6, 8, 10-30, Nov. 3, 4, 9-17, 19, 20, 23-25, 30-1864 Aug. 24
                 1864 Aug. 26-Sept. 29, Nov. 1-1865 Feb. 18
                 1865 Feb. 22-Mar. 24, 27-Apr. 19, 21-Oct. 9, 11-Nov. 3, 6-16, 18-Dec. 30
     PHHi   1865 Nov. 2
     PP   1863 June 23-Sept. 18, 21-Nov. 10, 11-24, 26, 28-Dec. 10, 12-26, 28-30
                 1864 Jan. 4-Feb. 5, 8-Apr. 18, 21-May 16, 18-July 4, 6-30
     PPAP   1869 Sept. 16
     PPeS   1865 Aug. 17
     PPL   1863 May 6-Aug. 6, 8-Sept. (19)-Nov. 26, 28
                 1864 Dec. 31
                 1865 June (1)-(23, 24)-July 4, 7, (8), 13, (14)-(24), 25, 28-Aug. (7), 8, 15, 17-23, 29, 31, Sept. (7), 11, 12, 14-(18)-20, 22, 24, 26-28, Oct. 20
     PPM   1863 May 6-1866 June 10
     PStrHi w 1864 June 21
     PU   1863 May 6-July 23, 25-Aug. 6, 8-18, 20-Sept. 2, 4-Oct. 9, 12, 20, 22-Nov. (12)-26, 28-Dec. 25, 28-1864 Jan. 4-(18)-(27)-(30)-Feb. (4) (22)-Mar. (1)-Nov. 4
                 1864 Nov. 7, 8, 10-14, 16, 18, 19, 22-(26)-Dec. (3)-26, 28-(31)
                 1865 Jan. 1-(28)-Mar. (11)-(22)-Apr. 19, 22, 25-June (1)-July 4, 6-Oct. (12)-(16)-(20)-Dec. 23, 27-1866 Jan. 1-(5)-(11)-16
                 1866 Jan. 18-Feb. (16)-May (18)-June 10

ILLUSTRATED NEW AGE, *continued*

    PWcHi   w 1863 Sept. 26
    PYHi   1863 Sept. 26-1864 Mar. 24
                continued as

AGE, THE (June 11, 1866-March 8, 1874) d w *
d June 11, 1866-Mar. 8, 1874; w June 9, 1866-Mar. 7, 1874 as *Weekly Age*

Pub. & Ed. 1866-1870 Welsh & Robb
               1870-1874 Robb & Biddle
Ed.   1871-1874 William H. Cunningham

    PCHi   1868 May 15
    PDoHi   1867 Nov. 25
                1872 May 4
           w 1866 Sept. 15
    PHi   1873 Aug. 18, 21
    PMilt   1866 Oct. 17
    PPCHi   1869 Sept. 16
    PPeS   1868 Oct. 8
    PPFfHi   1866 July 16, 27, 31
    PPL   1867 Mar. 25-Apr. 9, 13, 18-May (11)
                1869 May 28-June 1, 3-July 30, Aug. 2-Oct. 21, 23
                1870 Mar. 21, 23-Apr. 9, 12-July 6, 8-19, 21-Oct. 8, 11-Nov. 24, 26-1871 July 13
                1871 July 15-Sept. 28, 30-Oct. (2)-1872 Jan. 31
                1872 Feb. 2-Mar. 29, Apr. 1-July 1
                1873 Mar. 11, 13-Aug. 12, 14-22, 25-Dec. 25, 29, 31
                1874 Jan. 3-Mar. 7
    PPM   1866 June 11-1870 June 30
                1871 Jan. 1-1874 Mar. 8
    PPot   w 1866 Oct. 1
    PU   1866 June 11-Aug. 29, 31-Sept. 25, 27-Oct. 26, 28-Nov. 2, (5)-Dec. 10, 12-1867 Feb. 20
                1867 Feb. 22-Apr. (15)-May 25, 28-June 13, 15-Oct. (7, 8)-(14)-(22)-(28)-Dec. (4)-31
                1868 Jan. 2-(6)-Feb. (5)-May (4)-(16)-30, June 2-Sept. (4)-21-Nov. 7, 17-21, Dec. 1-10, 21-30
                1869 Jan. 1-Feb. 11, 13-(17)-May (5)-(18)-(21)-(24)-29, June 2, 4-21, 23-July 4, 7-15, 17-20, 22-Sept. 9, 11-Oct. 17, 19-(30)-Nov. (20)-Dec. (22)-(24)-1870 Feb. (16)-Mar. (23)-(30)-Apr. (8)-(21)-(25)-(30)-May (11)-(13)-(25)-June (11)-(13)-(16)-(25)-Sept. 26
                1870 Sept. 28-(30)-Oct. (3)-(6)-(11)-(20)-(22)-(26)-(28-30)-Nov. (1)-(7)-(9)-(12)-(14)-(21)-(23)-(30)-Dec. (12)-(19)-(21)-1871 Jan. (31)-Mar. 17
                1871 Mar. 19-Apr. 17, 19-26, 28-May (10)-(13)-(17)-(31)-June (1)-4, (6, 7)-(9, 10)-(12, 13)-(16)-(22)-(28, 29)-July (1)-(14)-(20, 21)-(24)-Aug. (1)-10, 12-(14)-(16)-(19)-(24)-Sept. (7-9)-(13-14)-Oct. (10)-(12)-(17)-(19)-(21)-(24)-Nov. (8)-(14)-(20-22)-(24, 25)-Dec. (2)-(16)-(27)-(29)-1872 Jan. (2)-(6)-(16, 17)-(20)-(25, 26)-(30)-Feb. (2)-(8)-(12, 13)-(21, 22)-(24-27), 28, Mar. (1)-(7)-(9)-(13), (15), 16, (18)-(23), 25, (26)-(29, 30)-Apr. (1)-(3)-(6)-(9)-(13)-(16)-(18)-(20)-(22)-(24)-(27)-(30)-May 1, 3, (4)-(6, 7)-(9, 10)-(13)-(17)-(18)-(22)-(25), 28-June (8)-(11)-13, (15), 17-

PHILADELPHIA COUNTY 101

                        22, 25-(26-29), July (6)-(29)-Sept. (4-12)-(16)-(18)-(20, 21)-Oct. (1)-(4, 5)-(8)-18, 21-(29, 30)-Dec. (2)-(12)-(14)-(16, 17)-(20, 21)-(23)-(28)-1873 Jan. (23)-Mar. (20)-(26)-(29)-Apr. (4, 5)-(8, 9)-(11)-(15-19)-(24)-(26)-May (8)-(10)-(24)-(28)-(31)-June 4, (6)-(11-13), (16-18)-(21)-(24, 25)-(27-30)-July (15)-Aug. 6, 8-(19)-(21)-(29-30)-Sept. (2)-(6-13)-(16, 17)-(19, 20)-(25, 26)-(30)-Oct. (1)-(3-8)-(10)-(13-15)-(21)-(28)-(31), Nov. 3, (4)-(12, 13)-(15)-(28)-Dec. (4)-(6)-11, (13-16)-(19-23)-(29, 30)-1874 Jan. (6)-(17), 20-(22), 24-(26, 27)-(29)-Feb. (4), 5, (7-9)-(12)-(16-24)-Mar. 2

    PWcHi   1868 Mar. 5, Oct. 31
             w 1869 Mar. 13
    PWalG   1868 May 18
                continued as
ILLUSTRATED NEW AGE (Mar. 9, 1874-Mar. 12, 1875) d w
d Mar. 9, 1874-Mar. 12, 1875; w Mar. 14, 1874-Mar. 12, 1875
    Pub. & Ed.   1874-1875   Robb & Biddle
                   1874-1875   E. Morwitz & Co.
    Ed.   1874-1875   William H. Cunningham
        PPL   d 1874 Mar. 9-June 4, 6-23, 26-July 8, 10-30
                      1875 Jan. 30
        PPM   d 1874 Mar. 9-1875 Mar. 12
           Absorbed by *The Times*, March 13, 1875

INDEPENDENCE, see Fuggetlenseg

INDEPENDENCE (1843) d * ♂

INDEPENDENT ADVOCATE (1891-1894) w Negro ♂
    Pub. 1892-1894   Timothy Foster
    Ed. 1892-1894   David S. Cincora and Timothy Foster

INDEPENDENT BALANCE, THE (Apr. 16, 1817-Dec. 22, 1832||) w ind *
    Pub. & Ed.   1817-1821   George Helmbold
                   1821-1832   L. P. Franks
        P   1820 Sept. 13-Dec. 20
        P-M   1818 Feb. 4
        PHi   1818 Apr. 8, May 6-20, June 3-July 15, 29-Nov. 25
                       1820 June 14-Aug. 30, Sept. 20-Oct. 4, Nov. 8-22, Dec. 6, 20-1821 Jan. 10
                       1821 Jan. 31-Mar. 28, Apr. 11-25
                       1825 Sept. 17
        PlewL   1825 Oct. 8-29
        PNoHi   1819 June 23
        PPiHi   1827 Mar. 31
        PPL   1829 Aug. 22
        PWcHi   1830 June 19

INDEPENDENT BALLOTS (1814-20)
        P-M   1820 Aug. 9

INDEPENDENT DEMOCRAT AND PROTECTOR OF AMERICAN INDUSTRY (July 26, 1834) w dem
    PNo   1834 July 26

INDEPENDENT GAZETTE, THE (Germantown) (1882-1926) w d ind rep
    GERMANTOWN INDEPENDENT (Oct. 2, 1882-Apr. 10, 1896) w d
    Pub. & Ed. 1882-1891   Horace F. McCann and J. A. Savage
                1891-1896   Horace F. McCann

The weekly edition from 1890-1894 was known as *Germantown Weekly Independent*.

A daily edition was begun Sept. 20, 1886, assuming the title of *Daily Independent* on Oct. 29, 1887; publication of this daily edition ceased in 1889.

    PP   w 1882 Oct. 7-1887 Sept. 30
           1890 Oct. 10-1891 Oct. 9, Nov. 6-1895 Oct. 25
           1895 Nov. 22-1896 Apr. 10
       d 1886 Sept. 20-1887 Oct. 27
           1887 Oct. 29-1888 Mar. 20
    PPGHi 1882 Oct. 7-1896 Apr. 10

continued as

GERMANTOWN INDEPENDENT GAZETTE (Apr. 17, 1896-1919) w

    Pub. 1896-1916   Horace F. McCann
         1916-1919   Germantown Independent Gazette Publishing Co.
    Ed. 1896-1916   Horace F. McCann
        1916-1919   Edward W. Hocker
    PP   1896 Apr. 17-1899 Feb. 10
                  1899 Feb. 24-1900 Sept. 28
                  1900 Oct. 12-1904 Nov. 4
                  1905 Jan. 6-1906 Sept. 14
                  1906 Sept. 28-1907 Dec. 6
                  1907 Dec. 20-1915 Feb. 12
                  1915 Feb. 26-July 9, 23-1916 Sept. 28
                  1916 Oct. 12, 26-1918 Feb. 28
                  1918 Mar. 14-1919 Feb. 13
                  1919 Mar. 20, 27-May 22, June 26, July 10, 17
    PPGHi   1896 Apr. 17-1919

continued as

INDEPENDENT GAZETTE, THE (Germantown) (1919-Dec. 2, 1926) w

    Pub. 1919-1921   Germantown Independent Gazette Publishing Co.
         1921-1926   Cornelius L. Wells
    Ed. 1919-1921   Frank Wilbur Smith
        1922-1926   Edward W. Hocker
    PP   1919 Dec. 25
                  1921 Mar. 3-Nov. 17, Dec. 8-1922 Feb. 2
                  1922 Feb. 23-Mar. 9, Apr. 20
                  1923 Jan. 11-Apr. 26, May 10-31, June 14, July 5, 12, Aug. 2-30, Oct. 11-Nov. 1
                  1924 Jan. 5-Feb. 21, Mar. 6-July 31, Aug. 14, 28, Sept. 4, Oct. 2-16, Nov. 6, 13, 27-Dec. 11
                  1925 Feb. 19-Mar. 12, 26-1926 Jan. 28
                  1926 Feb. 11-Mar. 25, Apr. 8, 15, 29-Nov. 18, Dec. 2

PPGHi [1919-1926]
merged with the *Guide* and continued as *The Independent Gazette and Germantown Guide.* (q. v.).

INDEPENDENT GAZETTE AND GERMANTOWN GUIDE, THE
(1871-1930) w sm m
GERMANTOWN GUIDE, THE (Dec. 21, 1871-Nov. 21, 1872) m sm
Pub. & Ed. 1871-1872 Walter H. Bonsall & Co.
PPGHi 1871 Dec. (21-1872 Nov. 21)
continued as
WEEKLY GUIDE (Nov. 30, 1872-Aug. 30, 1873) w
Pub. & Ed. 1872-1873 Walter H. Bonsall & Co.
PPGHi [1872 Nov. 30-1873 Aug. 30]
continued as
GUIDE (Sept. 6, 1873-Dec. 2, 1926) w
Pub. 1873-1913 Walter H. Bonsall & Co.
    1913-1915 Walter H. Bonsall
    1915 Estate of Walter H. Bonsall
    1915-1926 A. Hays Jordan
Ed. 1873-1881 Walter H. Bonsall & Co.
    1881-1882 William U. Butcher
    1882-1914 William H. Bonsall
    1914-1915 J. M. Bonsall
    1915-1926 A. Hays Jordan
% *Germantown Guide; Guide*
PP 1875 Dec. 4-1876 Oct. 28
1876 Dec. 9-30
1877 Jan. 20-June 23, Aug. 25-Dec. 29
1878 Jan. 5-May 4, June 22, Nov. 30, Dec. 21
1879 Mar. 8, Apr. 5-1881 Dec. 31
1882 Jan. 14, 28, Mar. 18, 25, Apr. 1, 15-22, May 13, June 3-Aug. 19, Sept. 2-Oct. 21, Nov. 4-Dec. 30
1883 Jan. 6-Dec. 29
1884 Jan. 12-Feb. 23, Mar. 15, 29, Apr. 12-19, May 3-24, June 28, July 19-Aug. 30, Sept. 13-1886 Feb. 6
1886 Mar. 6-June 19, July 10-Aug. 14, 28, Sept. 25, Oct. 16, 30-1888 June 23
1905 Feb. 22
1908 Feb. 22
1914 May 2, Aug. 15, Sept. 5, 19
1915 Jan. 2-1916 Dec. 30
1917 Jan. 6-Dec. 29
1918 Jan. 5-1919 May 10
1919 June 14, July 12-19, Aug. 2
1920 July 3
1922 Sept. 9
1924 June 28, Aug. 2-9, 30, Sept. 13, Oct. 4-11, 25, Nov. 1-15, Dec. 6
1925 June 13-27, Oct. 10, Dec. 19
1926 Jan. 1-Feb. 3, 5-Apr. 7, 9-21, 23-Nov. 24, 26-Dec. 2
PPFfHi 1913 Apr. 19, June 21, Aug. 30
1914 May 16, June 6, 20, July 4
1916 Nov. 4

        PPGHi   [1873 Sept. 6-1926 Dec. 2]
        PWcHi 1889 Mar. 2
                  1917 Feb. 3
                  Merged with the *Independent Gazette* (q.v.) to form
  INDEPENDENT GAZETTE AND GERMANTOWN GUIDE, THE
     (Dec. 9, 1926-1930) w
    Pub. 1926-1930   Gazette Publishing Co.
    Ed. 1926-1930   Robert D. Toune
        PP   1926 Dec. 9-1927 Oct. 27
                 1927 Nov. 10-1928 May 17
        PPGHi   [1926 Dec. 19-1928 May 17]

INDEPENDENT GAZETTEER, THE, see Gale's Independent Gazetteer

INDEPENDENT GAZETTEER AND AGRICULTURAL REPOSITORY, THE, see Gale's Independent Gazetteer

INDEPENDENT GAZETTEER: OR THE CHRONICLE OF FREEDOM, THE, see Gale's Independent Gazetteer

INDEPENDENT WEEKLY PRESS (Dec. 5, 1835-1836||) w ind
    Pub. & Ed. 1835-1836 Lewis C. Gunn
        PPL   1835 Dec. 5
        PWcHi   1836 Feb. 6

INDEPENDENT WHIG AND PHILADELPHIA GAZETTE, THE
  (1802) d ♪ #
    INDEPENDENT WHIG (Mar. 20, 1802) (Specimen Issue) d ♪
    Pub. 1802 Robert Cochran for Joseph Scott
        continued as
    INDEPENDENT WHIG AND PHILADELPHIA GAZETTE, THE
      (July 15, 1802-Aug. 4, 1802) d ♪
    Pub. 1802 William F. McLaughlin for Joseph Scott

INDUSTRIAL PROTECTOR, see National Independent and Industrial Protector

INGLESIDE (1880-1881) w ♪
    Pub. 1880-1881 Ingleside Publishing Co.

INSURANCE INTELLIGENCER, see Philadelphia Intelligencer

INTERES (1916-1923) w commercial for ♪
    Pub. 1916-1923 Polish Publishing Co.
    Ed. 1916-1923 Feliks J. Lewandowski

IRISH AMERICAN NEWS (ca. 1892) w ♪
    Pub. & Ed. 1892 R. G. Waters

IRISH-AMERICAN REVIEW (1898-1904) w ind ♪
    Pub. & Ed. 1904 J. P. McManus

PHILADELPHIA COUNTY 105

IRISH PRESS, THE (1918-1922) w
    Pub. 1918-1922   Joseph McGarrity
    Ed. 1918-1921   Patrick McCartan
        1921-1922   Joseph A. Sexton
        PHi ♦   1918 Aug. (31)
                1919 Feb. 1, Mar. 1, 8
                1921 May 7
        PP   1918 Mar. 23-1919 Mar. 8, 22, 29, Apr. 12-1922 May 6
        PPCHi   1918 Mar. 24, 30
                1919 Feb. 1, Nov. 29
        PVC   1918 Mar. 23-1922 May 6
    Incorporated with *Celtic Outlook,* July 1922

IRISH REPUBLICAN SHIELD AND LITERARY OBSERVER
    (July 1827-Sept. 15, 1833) w lit rep *
    Pub. & Ed. 1827-1833 George Pepper
        PP   1832 Sept. 15 (Vol. 5, No. 7)

IRISH STANDARD (1879) w ind ♦
    Pub. & Ed. 1879 Irish Standard Publishing Co.

ITALIA, L' (1874) w for ♦
    Pub. & Ed. 1874 L. G. Contri

ITALICA GENTE (1914-1929) w for rel ♦
    Pub. & Ed. 1917-1929 Italian Augustinian Fathers

ITEM (1847-1913) d w sun *
    Pub. 1847-1848   Thomas Fitzgerald, George G. Foster, John F. Carter, Robert L. Govett
        1848-1859   Thomas Fitzgerald
        1859-1875   Fitzgerald & Co. (Thomas Fitzgerald and his sons, Ritter, Harrington, Thomas H., Gilbert and Robert)
        1875-1877   Fitzgerald & Sons
        1877   Sun Publishing Co.
        1877-1895   Harrington Fitzgerald
        1895-1910   The Item Publishing Co.
        1910-1913   Harrington Fitzgerald
    Ed. 1847-1870   Thomas Fitzgerald
        1870-1875   Fitzgerald & Co. (Ritter, Harrington, Thomas H., Gilbert and Robert)
        1875-1877   Fitzgerald & Sons
        1877-1913   Harrington Fitzgerald
    Titles of weekly editions vary: *City Item for Town and Country, Fitzgerald's City Item, Philadelphia City Item, Weekly Item, Item.* Titles of daily editions vary: *City Item, All Day City Item, Philadelphia Item, Item, Sun, Evening Item.*
    Also, a Sunday edition published, entitled *Sunday Item.* Absorbed the *Pennsylvania Volunteer, Fireside Visitor* and *The Bazaar.*
        P-M-13   1913 Jan. 22
        PAiC   1909 Mar. 18
        PBL ♦   1847 Dec. 11
        PCHi   1870 Nov. 19
        PDoHi   1858 Dec. 11, 18, 25

			1859 Apr. 23
			1875 Sept. 29
			1885 July 23, 24
			1887 July 2, Sept. 16
			1889 June 25
			1894 Nov. 7
PHi	◆	w	1860 Jan. 28, Nov. 17
			1866 Feb. 10
		d	1874 Oct. 9-Dec. 3
			1889 June 5
			1881 Sept. 20
		sun	1886 Mar. 21
PP		w	1848 Sept. 23-1849 Mar. 17
			1849 Mar. 24-Sept. 15
			1881 Jan. 1-1883 Dec. 29
			1885 Jan. 3-24, Mar. 7-Apr. 25, May 16-Aug. 29, Oct. 3-Dec. 26
			1886 May 1-Dec. 25
			1887 Feb. 26-July 30, Aug. 13-Dec. 31
			1890 Jan. 4-June 14, July 5-1894 Jan. 13
			1894 Jan. 27-1897 June 26
		sun	1897 Jan. 3-June 27
			1900 Jan. 7-1910 Sept. 11
			1910 Sept. 25-1912 Mar. 17
			1912 Mar. 31-Dec. 29
		d	1900 Jan. 1-1912 Dec. 31
PPL			1847 Dec. 4
		sun	1874 July 5
PMcC		w	1876 Mar. 23-Apr. 6, 13
		sun	1876 Apr. 2
PWcHI		sun	1885 Aug. 9
		d	1892 Dec. 31

JACKSON STAR AND DAILY ORB (1834) d *

JACKSONIAN, THE (Apr. 22, 1844-Sept. 9, 1844||) w dem
    PPiUD   1844 Apr. 22, May 6-13, June 17-24, Aug. 5-19, Sept. 9

JEDNOSC (1916†) w rep ind for
  Pub. 1917-1920   F. J. Wendt
        1920-1925   William Wendt
        1925-1930   Estate of William Wendt
        1930-1941   B. S. Pluta
  Ed. 1917-1925   F. J. Wendt
        1930-1941   John J. Nowosielski
        PUB   1925 Jan. †
        PP   1929 Oct. 3†

JEDNOSK (1897) w for ♦
  Pub & Ed. 1897   L. R. S. Etter

JEWISH CHRONICLE (1921-1932) w ♦
  Pub. & Ed. 1925-1932   M. S. Gilles
      PPDr   [1922-1924]

JEWISH EXPONENT, THE (1887†) w
  Pub. 1887-1941   Jewish Exponent Publishing Co.

PHILADELPHIA COUNTY   107

    Ed. 1887 Apr.   15-1888 May 25   Henry S. Morais, Charles Hoff-
                                                     man, Melvin G. Winstock
         1888 June   1-1889 May 10   Henry S. Morais and Charles
                                                     Hoffman
         1889 May   17-1903   Charles Hoffman
         1903-1936   Felix M. Gerson
         1936-1940   David J. Galter
         1940-1941   Dr. Julius H. Greenstone
    PHi   1910 Mar. 4
    PP   1890 Jan. 3, Dec. 12, 26
               1891 Jan. 9, 16-23
               1892 Apr. 22, May 6
               1911 Oct. 20†
    PPDr   [1887-1941]
    PUB   1887†

JEWISH GAZETTE (ca. 1929) w Yiddish & English rep ♪
    Pub. 1929 Sarasohn & Sons

JEWISH MORNING JOURNAL, see Philadelphia Jewish Morning Journal and the Jewish Daily News

JEWISH PRESS (1890-1893) w Yiddish ♪
    Pub. & Ed. 1892-1893 Moses Freeman

JEWISH RECORD (1875-1885) w
    Pub. 1875-1885   Jewish Record Association
    Ed.   1875-1885   Alfred T. Jones
       PP   1881 Sept. 30
       PPDr   1875-1886 (vols. 1-23 complete)
       PPYMHA 1875 Mar.-1878 Apr.

JEWISH WORLD (1914†) d w Yiddish ind *
    Pub. 1914-1934   Jewish World Publishing Co.
           1934-1935   Fleisher-Byer Co.
           1935-1940   Jewish World Employees Association
           1940-1941   Jacob Ginsburg
    Ed.   1919-1934   Jacob Ginsburg
           1934-1935   Nathan Fleisher
           1935-1939   Nathan Kravitz
           1939-1940   Maurice Melamed
           1940-1941   Jacob Ginsburg
    PUB   1914 Feb. 1†
    PP   1926 Oct. 5
               1927 June 10†

JOURNAL (1873-1883) w ♪
    JOURNAL (1873-1874) w ♪
    Pub. & Ed. 1873-1874 Joseph Gibbons
          continued as
    PHILADELPHIA JOURNAL (1875) w ♪
    Pub. & Ed. 1875 Joseph Gibbons
          continued as
    JOURNAL (1876-1883) w ♪
    Pub. & Ed. 1876-1883 Joseph Gibbons
                  1883   Marianna Gibbons

JOURNAL (1877-1881) w
  Pub. & Ed. 1881 Henry W. Scott

JOURNAL (1888-1891) w
  Pub. & Ed. 1891 Journal Publishing Co.

JOURNAL (1895-1920) w ind
  Pub. & Ed. 1899-1903 Charles L. Manning
         1903-1908 Alfred Turner
         1908-1920 Cecil P. Turner

JOURNAL (1896-1899) w ind
  Pub. 1896-1899   Journal Publishing Co.
  Ed. 1896-1899   George W. Banks, T. C. Hamilton

JOURNAL (1898-1899) w non-political
  Pub. 1898-1899   R. H. Gordon

JOURNAL (Jan. 30, 1930-Oct. 20, 1932||) w
  Pub. 1932   Peerless Publishing Co.
     PP   1932 July 20-Oct. 20

JOURNAL (1936), see Journal of North Philadelphia

JOURNAL DES REVOLUTIONS DE LA PARTIE FRANCAISE DE ST. DOMINGUE (Sept. 27, 1793-Jan. 27, 1794) w #
  Pub. 1793-1794 Jan. Parent et Compagnie
     PHi ◆ 1794 Jan. 6, 10, 15, 20, 27

JOURNAL OF THE EXPOSITION (1874) m
  Pub. 1874 Ezra S. Badge
      Merged with, and title changed to *Centennial and Journal of the Exposition,* April, 1874

JOURNAL OF GREATER NORTHEAST PHILADELPHIA (1930†) w ind
  Pub. & Ed. 1936-1941 Louis Merget
     PUB   1930 Jan. 30†
     PP   1932 Aug. 5-1937 July 3, 30, Aug. 27, Sept. 10, 17

JOURNAL OF NORTH PHILADELPHIA (1934-1938||) w
  JOURNAL OF CENTRAL NORTH PHILADELPHIA (Apr. 26, 1934-July 18, 1935) w
  Pub. 1934-1935   J. Louis Stall
  Ed. 1934-1935   Joseph E. Moritz and Charles Johnson
     PP   1935 June 13
             continued as
  JOURNAL OF NORTH PHILADELPHIA (July 25, 1935-1938||) w
  Pub. 1935-1938   J. Louis Stall

PHILADELPHIA COUNTY 109

  Ed. 1935-1938 Joseph E. Moritz and Charles Johnson
   % From Jan. 30, 1936 to Mar. 26, 1936, it was called the *Journal*.
   On Apr. 3, 1936, *Of North Philadelphia* was added.
    PP   1935 July 25, Aug. 15-1936 Apr. 23, May 7-June 18,
          July 9, 23-Aug. 6
        1936 Aug. 27, Sept. 8-10, 24-1937 Mar. 4
        1937 Mar. 25-1938 Feb. 3

JOURNAL OF THE KNIGHTS OF LABOR (1880-1895) w labor ♦
  JOURNAL OF UNITED STATES LABOR (1880-1888) w ♦
  Pub. 1887-1888 Charles H. Lichman
     1888   General Assembly Knights of Labor
  Ed. 1887-1888 Charles H. Lichman
     1888   Adelbert M. Dewey
         continued as
  JOURNAL OF THE KNIGHTS OF LABOR (1889-1895) w ♦
  Pub. 1889-1895 General Assembly of Knights of Labor
  Ed. 1889-1893 Adelbert M. Dewey

JOURNAL OF THE TIMES (1898-1902) w ♦
  Pub. & Ed. 1899-1902 M. H. Goodin

JOURNAL OF UNITED STATES LABOR, see Journal of the Knights of Labor

JUDISCHES VOLKSBLATT (1894-1895) w rel ♦
  Pub. & Ed. 1894-1895 Maginitzky Bros.

JUSTICE (1888-1896) w single tax ♦
  Pub. 1890-1896 Justice Publishing Co.
  Ed. 1891-1896 H. V. Hetzel, I. L. Shoemaker and G. F. Stephens

KENSINGTON BULLETIN, see Greater Philadelphia Kensington Bulletin

KENSINGTON CRITIC (1894†) w local rep
  Pub. & Ed. 1903-1929 Fred Baumgaertel
        1929-1930 James Pitts
    PUB   1927 [Jan.-1931 Dec.]
         1932 Jan. 1†
    PP   1932 Aug. 12†

KENSINGTON LOCAL (1890-1920) w local ind ♦
  Pub. & Ed. 1899-1911 J. C. Davis & Theo. P. Stoll
        1911-1920 Theo. P. Stoll

KENSINGTON NEWS (Jan. 18, 1934†) w
  Pub. & Ed. 1934 John M. Doyle
            1934 A. D. Graham
       PUB   1934 Jan. 18-May 10, 24-31, June 21-Dec. 13
               1935 Apr. 18†
       PP   1934 Dec. 27-1935 Sept. 5
               1935 Sept. 26, Nov. 26, Dec. 12
               1936 Jan. 3-24, Feb. 27
               1939 Mar. 2†

KENSINGTON PRESS (1899-1905) w rep
  Pub. & Ed. 1899-1905 J. B. Farra

KENSINGTON SUN (1886-1889) w
  Pub. & Ed. 1886-1887 Sun Printing Co.
           1887-1889 J. B. Haslam

KENSINGTON SUN AND ENTERPRISE (1886-1890) w
  KENSINGTON ENTERPRISE (1886-1889) w
  Pub. & Ed. 1886-1887 Sun Printing Co.
           1887-1889 J. B. Haslam
      continued as
  KENSINGTON SUN AND ENTERPRISE (1890) w
  Pub. & Ed. 1890 Haslam Printing Co.

KENSINGTONIAN (1884) w
  Pub. & Ed. 1884 James H. Griffes

KENSINGTONIAN (1909-1922) w local
  Pub. 1910-1922 Kensington Board of Trade

KENSINGTONIAN (1925-1936) w
  Pub. 1925-1936 H. Raymond Morse
      PP   1935 Mar. 8-1936 July 17

KEYSTONE (1867-1906) w Masonic
  KEYSTONE (1867-1902) w
  Pub. 1867-1868 William A. Maas
       1868-1869 McCalla & Stavely
       1869-1888 Masonic Publishing Co.
       1888-1889 Samuel M. Steele
       1889-1902 Masonic Publishing Co.
  Ed. 1869   Rev. Robert H. Pattison
       1869   Richard Vaux
       1869-1888 Clifford P. McCalla
       1888-1893 Samuel M. Steele
     PHi ♦   1867 July 20-1868 July 11
                1886 Dec. 11
     PPL   1870 Apr. 2
                1876 Apr. 8
                1878 Feb. 9, Apr. 6

PHILADELPHIA COUNTY 111

     continued as
 KEYSTONE AND PENNSYLVANIA FREEMASON (1903-1904)
w ♢
 Pub. 1903-1904 Masonic Publishing Co.
 Ed. 1903-1904 W. A. McCalla
  PP   1903 Sept. 5-1904 July 9
     continued as
 KEYSTONE (1904-1906) w
 Pub. 1904-1906 Masonic Publishing Co.
 Ed. 1904-1906 John C. Yorston
  PDoHi 1904 Sept. 3
  PP   1904 July 16-Aug. 6, 20-Sept. 10, 24-Dec. 31
     1905 Jan. 7-May 6, 20-Sept. 23

KEYSTONE INDEPENDENT (1866-1875) w temperance ♢
 KEYSTONE GOOD TEMPLAR (1866-1873) w ♢
 Pub. & Ed. 1871-1872 Hendrickson & Cavna
     1872-1873 Theodore W. Cavna
     continued as
 KEYSTONE INDEPENDENT (1874-1875) w ♢
 Pub. & Ed. 1874-1875 Theodore W. Cavna

KEYSTONE INDEPENDENT (Feb. 7, 1888-1889) w
 Pub. 1888-1889 International Publishing and Printing Co.
  PWcHi 1889 Aug. 17

**KIRCHENBOTE, FUR DEUTSCHE EVANGELISCH—LUTHER-
ISCHE GEMEINDEN, DER** (March 31, 1900-Nov. 29, 1908) sm for rel
 Pub. 1900 March 31-1908 Nov. 29 at Philadelphia, by the German Lutheran Ministers Conference of Philadelphia
 Ed. 1900 March 31-1906 July 21 C. Goedel
   1906 Aug. 4-1908 Nov. 20 A. Spaeth
  PPK 1900 March 31-1908 Nov. 29

KNAPSACK, THE (Oct. 24, 1865-Nov. 4, 1865||) d *
 Ed. Riter Fitzgerald
 Published for two weeks in the interest of the Great Fair for the Soldier's and Sailor's Home.
  PDoHi 1865 Oct. 24-27
  PP   1865 Oct. 24-Nov. 4

KOVA (1905-1917) w Socialist for ♢
 Pub. 1905-1909 J. O. Shirvydas
   1909-1917 Lithuanian Socialist Federation
   1917 Lithuanian Federation Socialist Party
 Ed. 1905-1909 J. O. Shirvydas
   1909-1911 J. Baltrusauis
   1911-1912 J. B. Smelstalius
   1912-1917 K. Vidikos

KRITIK (1869) w for ♣
    Pub. & Ed. 1869 H. Engel & L. Gruel

KURYER FILADELFIJSKI (1916-1920) tw d for ♣
    DZIENNICK FILADELFIJSKI (1916) d ♣
    Pub. 1916   Polish Publishing Co.
                    continued as
    KURYER FILADELFIJSKI (1917-1920) tw ♣
    Pub. 1917-1920 Polish Publishing Co.
    Ed. 1918-1920 Julian Lewandowsky

LADIES' LITERARY PORTFOLIO (Dec. 10, 1828-July 10, 1830) w
    Pub. 1828-1830 Thomas C. Clarke
         1830   Elikan Littel & Brother
                      Jesper Harding
    Ed. 1828-1830 Thomas C. Clarke
        % *Literary Portfolio*
    PDoHi   1829 July 1, 29, Aug. 19
    PP   1828 Dec. 10-1829 Dec. 9
    PPL   1830 Jan. 7-July 1
    Merged with the *Philadelphia Album and Lady's Literary Register* to form the *Philadelphia Album and Lady's Literary Portfolio* (q.v.).

LADY'S DOLLAR NEWSPAPER, THE (1848-1850) sm
    Pub. 1849-1850 L. A. Godey
    Ed. 1849-1850 Fanny Linton
    PDoHi   1850 Jan. 1

LANCASTER AVENUE NEWS (1919†) w non-part
    Pub. 1928-1930 Lancaster Avenue Business Assoc.
    Ed. 1928-1930 Michael E. Brown
    PP   1936 Jan.†

LAST MINUTE DOINGS (1916-1920) w local
    LAST MINUTE DOINGS ON WALNUT STREET AND VICINITY (Aug. 29, 1916-Aug. 21, 1917) w
    Pub. 1916-1917 Last Minute Doings on Walnut Street Publishing Company
    Ed. 1916-1917 E. J. Berlet
    PP   1916 Aug. 29-1917 Aug. 21
                    continued as
    LAST MINUTE DOINGS (Aug. 28, 1917-1920) w
    Pub. 1917-1920 Last Minute Doings Publishing Company
    Ed. 1917-1920 E. J. Berlet
    PP   1917 Aug. 28-1917 Dec. 25
    PHi♦   1917 Dec. 18

LAW AND ORDER ADVOCATE (1882) w rel
    Pub. & Ed. 1882 Law and Order Advocate Co.
    PPL   1882 Nov. 11

LAWNDALE PRESS, THE (1922†) w
Pub. & Ed. 1922-1940 J. E. Stante
- PUB   1922 Oct. 28†
- PP   1935 Mar. 14-21

LEGAL GAZETTE (1869-1876) w
Pub. 1869-1876   King & Baird
Ed. 1869-1871   Silas W. Pettit and John H. Campbell
    1871-1875   John H. Campbell
    1875 Apr. 2-1876 Jan. 7   George P. Rich
    1876 Jan. 14-1876 Apr. 7   H. L. Carson, J. L. Jones and H. Castle
    1876 May 5   Charles T. Bonsall
- PHi   1874 Jan. 9
- PP   1869 July 2 (Vol. 1, No. 1)-1876 May 26
- PPBa   1869 July 2-1876 May 26

LEGAL INTELLIGENCER (Dec. 2, 1843†) w d
PHILADELPHIA LEGAL INTELLIGENCER (1843-1846) w
Pub. & Ed. 1843-1846   Henry E. Wallace
- PUB   1843 Dec. 2-1846 **Dec. 30**
- PHi   1843 Dec. 2-1846 Dec. 30
- PPBa   1843 Dec. 2-1846 Dec. 30
- PUL   1843 Dec. 2-1844 Feb. (21)-Oct. (8)-(29)-Nov. (5)-Dec. (10)-1846 Dec. 30

continued as

LEGAL INTELLIGENCER (1847-1941) w d
Pub. 1847   Henry E. Wallace
    1868-1869   King & Baird
    1869-1891   J. M. Power Wallace
    1891-1908   Edward P. Allinson
    1908-1933   H. W. Page
    1933-1941   Legal Intelligencer Corp.
Ed. 1847-1873   Henry E. Wallace
    1873-1881   Henry E. Wallace, Dallas Sanders and Henry C. Titus
    1881-1891   Dallas Sanders and Henry C. Titus
    1891-1892   Edward P. Allinson and Henry C. Titus
    1892-1895   Edward P. Allinson, Henry C. Titus and R. J. Monaghan
    1895-1898   Edward P. Allinson and Henry C. Titus
    1898-1908   Edward P. Allinson and Theodore B. Stork
    1908-1933   Howard W. Page and Associates
    1933-1936   Albert Branson Maris
    1936-**1941**   Harold C. Roberts
- PUB   1847 Jan. 6†
- PAiL   w1860 Jan. 6-1874 Dec. 25
- PDoC   1872 Jan. 6-1895 Dec. 27
- PEC   w1892 Jan. 1-Dec. 30
- PHi   1847 Jan. 6-1885 Dec. 25
- PNazHi   1851 Sept. 19
- PP   1850 Mar. 8†
- PPBa   1847 Jan. 6†
- PPL   1878 Jan. 18
- PPRD   1916 Jan. 1-July 21

LEGAL INTELLIGENCER, *continued*
    PToF   1877 Jan. 5-Dec. 28
                  1881 Jan. 7-1889 Jan. 11
                  1892 Jan. 1-1893 Mar. 3
    PUL   1847 Jan. 6-1848 Mar. (15)-1849 Mar. (30)-Dec. 14
                  1849 Dec. 28-1901 Mar. (1)-May (3)-(17)-Dec. (27)-1903 Jan. (2)-1934 Dec. 31†
    PWcHi   1869 Dec. 20
                  1880 Jan. 9-Dec. 31

LEGAL NEWS (1879) d legal ♣
    Pub. & Ed. 1879 Joshua T. Owen

LEVEL OF EUROPE AND NORTH AMERICA; or THE OBSERVER'S GUIDE (1794-1796) m for (English & French) ♣ #
    THE LEVEL OF EUROPE AND NORTH AMERICA (LE NIVEAU DE L'EUROPE & DE L'AMERIQUE SEPTENTRIONELLE) (Oct. 1, 1794-1795) m # ♣
    Pub. 1794-1795   William W. Woodward (Printer)
                              Pierre Egron
                              continued as
    THE LEVEL OF EUROPE AND NORTH AMERICA; OR THE OBSERVER'S GUIDE (1795-Jan. 27, 1796) m ♣ #
    Pub. & Ed. 1795-1796 Peter Egron and Tanguy (C. C. Tanguy de la Boissière)
                              Title page is followed by a second leaf, with the title of *The Observer of Europe and North America: or a Journal of Political Economy, Agriculture, Meterology, Commerce, Navigation, Manufactures, Arts and Sciences, etc., etc.*

LIBERA PAROLA (Apr. 20, 1917†) w ind for
    Pub. 1917-1938   A. Guiseppe di Silvestro
          1938-1941   A. J. di Silvestro
    Ed. 1918-1938   A. Guiseppe di Silvestro
        1938-1941   Leon Sacks
    PUB   1917 Apr. 20†
    PP   1932 May 28-Oct. 22, Nov. 5-Dec. 24
                  1933 Jan. 7-Dec. 23
                  1934 Jan. 6-1937 Dec. 18
                  1938 Jan. 1-Oct. 1, 15-Nov. 6, 20-Dec. 10, 24, 31
                  1939 Jan. 7-Sept. 16, 30-Oct. 28, Nov. 11-1940 Aug. 10
                  1940 Aug. 24-Sept. 14, 28-Nov. 30, Dec. 21
                  1941 Jan. 11-Apr. 19, May 13, 17, June 7-21, July 4-19, Aug. 2, 16-30, Sept. 13, Oct. 4, 11, 25, Nov. 22-29, Dec. 20
                  1942 Jan. 3†

LIGHT (1890-1891) w rel ♣
    Pub. 1890-1891   M. Rosenbaum, F. Winkleman and Reverend N. Mosessohn
    Ed. 1890-1891   Reverend M. Mosessohn

LINDLEY-OLNEY NEWS (Nov. 27, 1936†) w local
    Pub. 1936-1941   Herman M. Golove and Irving Goldberg
    Ed. 1936-1941   Rolfe Garrett
                          % Lindley News
        PP   1936 Nov. 27†

LITERARY GAZETTE OR JOURNAL OF CRITICISM, SCIENCE AND THE ARTS, THE (Jan. 6, 1821-Dec. 29, 1821)
    Pub. 1821   James Maxwell
        PHi ♦   1821 Jan. 6-Dec. 29 (Vol. 1, No. 1-52)
        PP   1821 Jan. 6-Dec. 29

LITERARY PORTFOLIO, see Ladies' Literary Portfolio

LITTLE GENIUS (May 1839||) d
        PPL   1839 Sept. 25

LOGAN ADVOCATE-NEWS (1912-1918) w local ♪
    Pub. 1917-1918   Logan Publishing Co.
    Ed. 1917-1918   Wilbur H. Zimmerman

LOGAN BEACON, see Beacon

LOGAN TIMES (Jan. 1914-May 26, 1933||) w
    Pub. & Ed. 1920-1933 United Suburbs Associated
        PP   1920 Nov. 5, 19, 26
                      1925 Oct. 16, Nov. 26
                      1926 Jan. 29-Feb. 19, Apr. 23, 30, May 14, July 2, 23, Aug. 6, 27, Sept. 10, 17, Oct. 1, 15, 22, Nov. 5-1927 Feb 4
                      1927 Feb. 18-Mar. 18, Apr. 15-May 6, 20, 27, June 17, 24, July 8-Oct. 28
                      1929 July 19-Sept. 20, Oct. 11-1930 Mar. 7
                      1930 June 20-July 18, Aug. 1-Sept. 26, Oct. 17-Dec. 5
                      1931 June 5, 19, July 3-Dec. 4
                      1932 Feb. 5-Apr. 29, May 20-27, Aug. 19
                      1933 May 26

LOYAL AMERICAN (1890) w ♪
    Pub. & Ed. 1890 Loyal American Publishing Co.

LUTHERAN, THE (1848-1941) m w rel
    MISSIONARY, THE (Jan. 1848-Dec. 1855) m
    Pub. 1848 Jan.-1855 Dec. at Pittsburgh
    Ed. 1848 Jan.-1855 Dec. William A. Passavant
        PGLS   [1848-1855]
        PPK ♦   1848 Feb.-1849 Dec.
                    Missing
                    1848 Apr.

continued as
MISSIONARY, THE (Jan. 3, 1856-Oct. 24, 1861) w
 Pub. 1856 Jan. 3-1857 Feb. 5 an Association at Pittsburgh
   1857 Feb. 12-1861 Oct. 24 W. S. Haven at Pittsburgh
 Ed. 1856 Jan. 3-1861 Oct. 24 William A. Passavant
  PA1Mu 1856 Jan. 3-1861 Oct. 24
  PGLS [1856-1861]
  PPK ♦ 1856 Jan. 3-1861 Oct. 24
  PPLP ♦ 1860 Jan. 5-1861 Oct. 24
    Merged with *The Lutheran and Home Journal* (q.v.)
    continued as
LUTHERAN AND MISSIONARY, THE (Oct. 31, 1861-Nov. 10, 1881) w
 Pub. 1861 Oct. 31-1881 Nov. 10 at Philadelphia
 Ed. 1861 Oct. 31-1867 June 27 Charles P. Krauth, William A. Passavant
   1867 July 18-1874 Nov. 12 C. W. Schaeffer, J. A. Seiss, G. F. Krotel, and W. A. Passavant
   1874 Nov. 19-1876 Oct. 26 F. Richards
   1876 Nov. 2-1879 Oct. 30 Jos. A. Seiss
   1879 Nov. 6-1880 Feb. 12 G. F. Krotel
   1881 Feb. 24-1881 Nov. 10 J. A. Seiss, G. F. Krotel, F. A. Muhlenberg, Samuel Laird
  PA1Mu 1861 Oct. 31-1874 Dec. 17
  PGLS [1861-1881]
  PPK ♦ 1861 Oct. 31-1881 Nov. 10
  PPL 1862 Oct. 9, 16
  PPLP ♦ 1861 Oct. 31-1881 Nov. 10
    continued as
LUTHERAN, THE (Nov. 17, 1881-Sept. 25, 1896) w
 Pub. 1881 Nov. 17-1896 Sept. 25 at Philadelphia
 Ed. 1881 Nov. 17-1883 Oct. 25 G. F. Krotel
  PGLS [1883-1896]
  PPK ♦ 1881 Nov. 17-1896 Sept. 25
  PPLP ♦ 1881 Nov. 17-1895 Dec. 26
    Merged with *Lutheran Church Messenger* (q.v.) and *The Workman* (q.v.) and continued as
LUTHERAN, THE (Oct. 1, 1896-Apr. 24, 1919) w m
 Pub. 1896 Oct. 1 a Committee under General Council at Philadelphia
   1896 Oct. 8-1897 Oct. 28 a Committee under General Council, Lebanon and Philadelphia date line
   1897 Nov. 4-1919-Apr. 24 Lutheran Board of Publication of General Council, Lebanon and Philadelphia date line
 Ed. 1896 Oct. 1-1907 May G. F. Krotel, G. W. Sandt
   1907 May -1919 Apr. 24 G. W. Sandt
  PA1Mu 1896 Oct. 1-1918 Dec. 26
    m 1896 Nov.-1903 Dec.
  PGLS [1896-1919]
  PP 1914 Dec. 24-1919 Apr. 24
  PPK ♦ 1896 Oct. 1-1919 Apr. 24

PHILADELPHIA COUNTY 117

    PPLP ♦   1896 Oct. 1-1919 Apr. 24
          m 1896 Nov.-1904 Oct.
            Merged with *Lutheran Church Work and Observer* (q.v.) and with *Lutheran Church Visitor* (a Southern publication) and continued as
LUTHERAN, THE (May 1, 1919-1941†) w
Pub. 1919 May   1-1941†   Board of Publication of the United Lutheran Church at Philadelphia (1921 June 9-1923 Oct. 25 carried New York and Philadelphia date line)
Ed. 1919 May   1-1920 Dec. 2   George W. Sandt
    1920 Dec.   9-1927 Dec. 27   George W. Sandt, Nathan R. Melhorn
    1928 Jan.   5-1941†   Nathan R. Melhorn
    PA1Mu   [1919 May 1-1940 Sept. 25]
    PGLS   [1919-1941]
    PHi ♦   1930 Aug. 7
           1931 Aug. 6
           1939 Nov. 15
    PHLC   1938-1941
    PP   1919 May 1†
    PPK ♦   1919 May 1†
    PPLP ♦   1919 May 1†
    PSeSu   [1936-1941]

LUTHERAN AND HOME JOURNAL, THE (1856-1861) m sm rel
   LUTHERAN HOME JOURNAL, THE (Jan. 1856-June 1860) m
   Pub. 1856 Jan.-1860 June   Lutheran Board of Publication at Philadelphia
            This paper was preceded by the *Evangelical Magazine and Christian Eclectic,* published monthly (place of publication does not appear) May 1853-Dec. 1854 or later
    PA1Mu   [1856-1858]
    PGLS   [1856-1860]
    PP   1858 Jan.-Dec.
    PPK ♦   1856 Jan.-1860 June
    PPLP ♦   1856 Jan.-1860 June
    PSeSu   [1856-1858]
            Title changed to
   LUTHERAN AND HOME JOURNAL, THE (July 6, 1860-Oct. 11, 1861) sm
Pub. 1860 July   6-1861 Oct. 11   at Philadelphia
Ed. 1860 July   6-1861 Oct. 11   Committee of Clergymen
    PGLS   [1860-1861]
    PPK ♦   1860 July 6-1861 Oct. 11
    PPLP ♦   1860 July 6-Dec. 21
            Merged with *The Missionary* under the title of *The Lutheran and Missionary* (see under "The Lutheran")

LUTHERAN CHURCH MESSENGER (1875-1896) m rel
   CHURCH MESSENGER (Oct. 1875-Dec. 1893)
   Pub. 1875 Oct. -1885 Sept.   J. B. Rath, F. W. Weiskotten, William Ashmead Schaeffer at Bethlehem (J. B. Rath until Aug. 1885)

```
               1885 Oct.  -1886 June    at Philadelphia
               1886 July  -1887 July    Church Messenger Association
                                        Allentown and Philadelphia date
                                        line
               1887 Aug.  -1892 May     at Allentown
               1892 June  -1893 Dec.    Association of Ministers in the
                                        Ministerium of Pennsylvania at
                                        Allentown
      Ed.      1875 Oct.  -1885 Aug.    J. B. Rath, F. W. Weiskotten, Wil-
                                        liam Ashmead Schaeffer
               1885 Sept. -1886 June    F. W. Weiskotten, William Ash-
                                        mead Schaeffer
               1879 Oct.  -Dec.         Published as unnumbered issues
      PGLS            [1875-1886]
      PPK    ◆        1875 Oct.-1893 Dec.
      PPLP   ◆        1879 Oct.-1892 Dec.
                      Missing
                      1881 Aug.
                      Title changed to
```

LUTHERAN CHURCH MESSENGER (Jan. 1894-Sept. 1896)
```
      Pub. 1894 Jan. -1896 Sept.        Association of Ministers in the
                                        Ministerium of Pennsylvania at
                                        Allentown
      PGLS            [1894-1896]
      PPK    ◆        1894 Jan.-1896 Sept.
      PPLP   ◆        1894 Jan.-1896 Sept.
                      Missing
                      1895 July
                      Merged with *The Workman* (q.v.) and *The Lutheran*
                      under the title of *The Lutheran* (q.v.)
```

LUTHERAN CHURCH WORK AND OBSERVER (1880-1919)   m
  w rel

LUTHERAN MISSIONARY JOURNAL (1880-Dec. 1907) m
```
      Pub. 1888 Jan.  -1900 Dec.        at York
           1901 Jan.  -1907 Dec.        Lutheran Publication Society
                                        at Philadelphia
      Ed.  1888 Jan.  -1889 Mar.        J. C. Zimmerman, Jacob A. Clutz,
                                        George Scholl, Mrs. E. S. Prince
           1889 Apr.  -1889 July        Jacob A. Clutz, George Scholl,
                                        Mrs. E. S. Prince
           1889 Aug.                    Jacob A. Cluz, George Scholl, Mrs.
                                        E. S. Prince, A. W. Lilly, W. S.
                                        Freas
           1889 Sept. -1889 Oct.        John W. Rice, George Scholl, H.
                                        H. Weber, Mrs. E. S. Prince
           1889 Nov.  -1900 Dec.        A. Stewart Hartman, George
                                        Scholl, H. H. Weber, Mrs. E. S.
                                        Prince
           1901 Jan.  -1901 Nov.        A. Stewart Hartman, George
                                        Scholl, H. H. Weber, Mrs. Kate
                                        Boggs Shaffer
           1901 Dec.  -1907 Dec.        A. Stewart Hartman, Marion J.
                                        Kline, H. H. Weber, Mrs. Kate
                                        Boggs Shaffer
```

PGLS   [1886-1907]
PPK ♦   1894 Jan.-1895 Dec.
          1897 Jan.-1898 Dec.
          1900 Jan.-Dec.
          1903 Jan.-1907 Dec.
PPLP ♦ 1888 Jan.-1891 Dec.
          1893 Jan.-1907 Dec.
          continued as

LUTHERAN CHURCH WORK (Jan. 1908-Mar. 1912) m
Pub. 1908 Jan.-1912 Feb.   at Philadelphia
Ed. 1908 Jan.-1909 Dec.   W. H. Dunbar, H. Studebaker, Charles S. Albert
     1910 Jan.-1910 Dec.   Charles S. Albert
     1911 Jan.-1912 Feb.   Charles S. Albert, W. H. Dunbar
  PGLS   [1908-1912]
  PPK   1908 Jan.-1912 Feb.
  PPLP   1908 Jan.-1912 Mar.
  PSeSu   [1908-1912]
          Merged with *The Lutheran World* (q.v.) and continued as

LUTHERAN CHURCH WORK (Mar. 7, 1912-Oct. 21, 1915) w
Pub. 1912 Mar. 7-1915 Oct. 21   a standing Committee of the General Synod, Harrisburg and Philadelphia date line (1913 June 19 changed to Harrisburg, Philadelphia and York date line)
Ed. 1913 June 19-1915 Oct. 21   Frederick G. Gotwald
  PAlMu   [1912-1915]
  PGLS   [1912-1915]
  PPK ♦   1912 Mar. 7-1915 Oct. 21
  PPLP ♦ 1912 Mar. 7-1915 Oct. 21
          Merged with *The Lutheran Observer* (q.v.) under the title of

LUTHERAN CHURCH WORK AND OBSERVER (Oct. 28, 1915-Apr. 24, 1919) w
Pub. 1915 Oct. 28-1919 Apr. 24   Harrisburg, Philadelphia and York date line
Ed. 1915 Oct. 28-1919 Apr. 24   Frederick G. Gotwald
  PAlMu   [1915-1919]
  PGLS   [1915-1919]
  PP   1915 Oct. 28-1916 Oct. 5
  PPLP ♦ 1915 Oct. 28-1919-Apr. 24
          Merged with *Lutheran Church Visitor* (a Southern publication) and *The Lutheran* under the title of *The Lutheran* (q. v.)

LUTHERAN OBSERVER, THE (1831-1915) sm w rel
LUTHERAN OBSERVER, THE (Aug. 1, 1831-July 15, 1833) sm
Pub. & Ed. 1831 Aug. 1-1833 July 15   John G. Morris at Baltimore, Maryland
          This paper was preceded by *The Evangelical Lutheran Intelligencer*, published monthly at Frederick, Maryland, Mar. 1826-Feb. 1831.
  PGLS   [1831-1833]
  PPK ♦   1831 Aug. 1-1833 July 15

PPLP ♦ 1831 Aug. 1-1833 July 15
PPPHi 1831 Aug. 15, Sept. 1
Succeeded by
LUTHERAN OBSERVER AND WEEKLY RELIGIOUS VISITER (Aug 24, 1833-Mar. 22, 1834) w
  Pub. 1833 Aug. 24-1834 Mar. 22   at Baltimore, Maryland
  Ed. 1833 Aug. 24-1834 Mar. 22   Benjamin Kurtz
    PGLS   [1833-1834]
    PPK ♦   1833 Aug. 24-1834 Mar. 22
              Missing
              1833 Sept. 21, 28
    PPLP ♦   1833 Aug. 24-1834 Mar. 22
              Title changed to
LUTHERAN OBSERVER AND WEEKLY LITERARY AND RELIGIOUS VISITER (Apr. 4, 1834-May 2, 1834) w
  Pub. 1834 Apr. 4-1834 May 2   at Baltimore, Maryland
  Ed. 1834 Apr. 4-1834 May 2   Benjamin Kurtz
    PA1Mu   1834 Apr. 4-May 2
    PGLS   1834 Apr. 4-May 2
    PPLP ♦   1834 Apr. 4, 18, May 2
             Missing
             1834 Apr. 11, 25
             Title changed to
LUTHERAN OBSERVER AND WEEKLY RELIGIOUS AND LITERARY VISITER (May 9, 1934-Dec. 29, 1837) w
  Pub. 1834 May 9-1837 Dec. 29   at Baltimore, Maryland
  Ed. 1834 May 9-1837 Dec. 29   Benjamin Kurtz
    PA1Mu   [1834-1837]
    PGLS   [1834-1837]
    PPK ♦   1837 Oct. 20-Dec. 29
             Missing
             1837 Oct. 27, Nov. 24, Dec. 8
    PPLP ♦   1834 May 9-1837 Dec. 29
             Missing
             1835 May 22, July 17-Aug. 21, Oct. 9
             Article added to title
LUTHERAN OBSERVER AND WEEKLY RELIGIOUS AND LITERARY VISITER, THE (Jan. 8, 1838) w
  Pub. 1838 Jan. 5   at Baltimore, Maryland
  Ed. 1838 Jan. 5   Benjamin Kurtz
    PA1Mu   1838
    PGLS   1838
    PPK ♦   1838 Jan. 5-1839 Aug. 9
             Missing
             1838 Jan. 26, Feb. 2, Mar. 9, 16, May 4, 11, Oct. 5-1839 Aug. 2
    PPLP ♦   1838 Jan. 5-1839 Aug. 16
             Title changed to
LUTHERAN OBSERVER, THE (Ca. June 5, 1840-Oct. 22, 1915) w
  Pub. 1856 Feb. 22-1861 Feb. 1   F. R. Anspach, George Diehl, T. Newton Kurtz at Baltimore
       1861 Feb. 8-1861 Dec. 27   F. R. Anspach, T. Newton Kurtz at Baltimore
       1862 Jan. 3-1862 Oct. 31   T. Newton Kurtz at Baltimore

PHILADELPHIA COUNTY 121

	1862 Nov.	7-1864 Oct. 14	G. Diehl, T. Stork, F. W. Conrad at Baltimore
	1864 Oct.	21-1866 Dec. 28	G. Diehl, F. W. Conrad at Baltimore
	1867 Jan.	4-1915 Oct. 22	Lutheran Observer Association at Philadelphia (1875 Aug. 13-1876 Dec. 15 carried Philadelphia and Lancaster date line; 1884 Oct. 17-1915 Oct. 22 carried Lancaster and Philadelphia date line)
Ed.	1842 Jan.	7-1858 Jan. 29	Benjamin Kurtz
	1858 Feb.	5-1861 Feb. 1	F. R. Anspach, George Diehl
	1861 Feb.	8	F. R. Anspach, B. Kurtz
	1861 Feb.	15-1861 June 21	F. R. Anspach, Theophilus Stork
	1861 June	28-1861 July 5	F. R. Anspach
	1861 July	12-1861 Dec. 27	F. R. Anspach, Benjamin Kurtz
	1862 Jan.	3-1862 Feb. 7	Committee of Clergymen
	1862 Feb.	14-1862 Oct. 31	Benjamin Kurtz, Theophilus Stork
	1862 Nov.	7-1864 Oct. 14	G. Diehl, T. Stork, F. W. Conrad
	1864 Oct.	21-1866 Dec. 28	G. Diehl, F. W. Conrad
	1867 Jan.	4-1869 Dec. 24	F. W. Conrad, T. Stork, E. W. Hutter
	1870 Jan.	7-1872 Apr. 12	F. W. Conrad
	1872 Apr.	19-1890 Dec. 26	F. W. Conrad, V. L. Conrad
	1891 Jan.	2-1898 Apr.	F. W. Conrad, V. L. Conrad, Sylvanus Stall
	1898 Apr.	-1899 Dec. 1	V. L. Conrad, Sylvanus Stall
	1899 Dec.	8-1901 May 3	M. H. Valentine, Sylvanus Stall
	1901 May	10-1915 Oct. 22	M. H. Valentine

PAlMu   1850 Dec. 27
            1852 Jan. 2-1863 Dec. 25
            1872 Jan. 5-1874 Dec. 13
PGLS   1915
PP   1910 Jan. 7
            1912 Jan. 5-1915 Oct. 22
PPK♦   1841 July 9-1915 Oct. 22
            Missing
            1841 Nov. 19
            1842 Aug. 5, Dec. 16
            1843 Oct. 13
            1847 July 9
            1848 Aug. 4
            1849 Sept. 14
            1850 Apr. 26, May 24, June 28, Oct. 25, Nov. 1
            1852 Feb. 13, May 14, and pages 1-2 of Dec. 31
            1856 Dec. 5, 19
            1857 Feb. 6
            1862 June 6, Nov. 28, Dec. 12
            1866 Apr. 6, June 8, 22-July 27, Sept. 14-Dec. 21
            1891 Dec. 4
            1907 Feb. 15, Apr. 26
PPLP ♦   1840 June 5-1915 Oct. 22
            Missing
            1850 Apr. 26
PSeSu   1903 Jan.-Dec.
            Merged with *Lutheran Church Work* under the title of *Lutheran Church Work and Observer* (q. v.)

LUTHERAN WORLD, THE (1892-Feb. 28, 1912) w rel
    Pub. 1909 Apr. 7-1912 Feb. 28   at Greenville, Pa.
    Ed. 1909 Apr. 7-1912 Feb. 28   David H. Bauslin, C. E. Gardner
      PGLS   [1895-1912]
      PPK ◆   1909 Apr. 7-1912 Feb. 28
          Merged with *Lutheran Church Work* under the title of *Lutheran Church Work* (see under *Lutheran Church Work and Observer*)

LUTHERISCHER HEROLD (1851†) sm w for rel
    LUTHERISCHE HEROLD, DER (1851-June 24, 1880) sm
      Pub. 1851   -1872 Feb. 17   Henry Ludwig at New York
          1872 Feb. 29-1872 Oct. 10   New York Ministers' Conference of the New York Ministerium at New York
          1872 Oct. 24-1880 June 24   New York Ministerium at New York
      Ed. 1851   -1872 Feb. 17   Henry Ludwig
          1872 Feb. 29-1875 June 17   G. F. Krotel
          In earlier years the paper was also referred to as *Der Herold*.
      PGLS   [1857-1880]
      PPK ◆   1869 Dec. 11-1871 Feb. 4
          1872 Feb. 29-1880 June 24
          Missing
          1869 Dec 26
          1870 Mar. 5, 19
          1871 Feb. 18-1872 Feb. 17
          1872 Apr. 11, Nov. 7, Dec. 5
          1873 Feb. 13
          Merged with *Lutherische Zeitschrift* (q. v.) under the title of

    HEROLD UND ZEITSCHRIFT (July 3, 1880-Dec. 28, 1895) w
      Pub. 1880 July 3-1886 Dec. 25   Brobst, Diehl & Co. at Allentown
          1887 Jan. 8-1895 Dec. 28   T. H. Diehl at Allentown
      PGLS   [1881-1895]
      PPK ◆   1880 July 3-1895 Dec. 28
          Missing
          1887 Oct. 8
          1890 Mar. 8
          1894 Dec. 15
          Continued as

    LUTHERISCHE HEROLD, DER (1896-Dec. 25, 1909) w
      Pub. 1907 Jan. 5-1909 Dec. 25   New York Ministerium at New York
      Ed. 1907 Jan. 5-1909 July 3   C. G. Fischer
          1909 July 10-1909 Dec. 25   Gustav H. Tappert
      PGLS   [1896-1898]
      PPK ◆   1907 Jan. 5-1909 Dec. 25
          Merged with *Lutherisches Kirchenblatt* (q. v.) and with *Kirchenblatt Der Canada—Synode* under the title of

DEUTSCHE LUTHERANER, DER (Jan. 6, 1910-Sept. 28, 1922) w
   Pub. 1910 Jan. 6-1917 Mar. 1   Philadelphia and New York date line
        1917 Mar. 8-1922 Sept. 28   Philadelphia date line
   Ed. 1910 Jan. 6-1922 Sept. 28   G. C. Berkemeier, H. Offermann
      PGLS   [1910-1922]
      PPK ♦   1910 Jan. 6-1922 Sept. 28
                  Missing
                  1922 July 20
      PPLP   1910 Jan. 6-1919 Dec. 25
                  1922 Jan. 26-Feb. 9, Mar. 9-June 1, 15-Sept. 28
                  Merged with *Lutherischer Zions—Bote* (published at Chicago) under the title of

LUTHERISCHER HEROLD (Oct. 5, 1922†)   w
   Pub. 1922 Oct. 5†   at Philadelphia
   Ed. 1922 Oct. 5-1924 Apr. 24   E. E. Ortlepp
        1924 May 1†   C. R. Tappert
      PGLS   [1922-1941†]
      PPK ♦   1922 Oct. 5†
      PPLP ♦   1922 Oct. 5†

LUTHERISCHES KIRCHENBLATT   (Jan. 5, 1884-Dec. 25, 1909) w
   Pub. 1884 Jan. 5-1884 Dec. 27   Pastors of the General Council at Philadelphia
        1885 Jan. 3-1909 Dec. 25   Pastors of the General Council at Reading (Reading and Philadelphia date line)
   Ed. 1903 June 27-1905 June 17   F. Wischan
        1905 July 1-1909 Dec. 25   H. Offermann
      PGLS   [1884-1909]
      PPG   1884 Jan. 5-1886 Sept. 25
                  1896 Jan. 4-1903 Dec. 26
      PPK ♦   1884 Jan. 5-1909 Dec. 25
                  Merged with *Der Lutherische Herold* and with *Kirchenblatt der Canada—Synode* under the title of *Der Deutsche Lutheraner* (see under *Lutherischer Herold*)

LUTHERISCHE ZEITSCHRIFT (1858-1880) sm w for rel
LUTHERISCHE ZEITSCHRIFT, JUGENDFREUND UND MISSIONSBLAETTER (Jan. 23, 1858-Dec. 22, 1866) sm
Pub. & Ed. 1858 Jan. 23-1866 Dec. 22 S. K. Brobst at Allentown
This paper was preceded by the *Lutherische Zeitschrift* published monthly at Allentown, pub. and ed. by S. K. Brobst, Nov. 1854-Dec. 1855
      PGLS   [1858-1866]
      PPK ♦   1858 Jan. 23-1866 Dec. 22
               Missing
               1863 Jan. 31
               1864 pages 1-2 of Oct. 1
               Continued as
LUTHERISCHE ZEITSCHRIFT, JUGENDFREUND, KIRCHEN- UND MISSIONSBERICHTE (Jan. 12, 1867-Feb. 13, 1869) w
Pub. & Ed. 1867 Jan. 12-1869 Feb. 13 S. K. Brobst at Allentown

    PGLS [1867-1869]
    PPK ♦ 1867 Jan. 12-1869 Feb. 13
         Continued as
  LUTHERISCHE ZEITSCHRIFT, ELTERNFREUND, KIRCHEN—
    UND MISSIONSBERICHTE (Feb. 20, 1869-Dec. 24, 1870) w
  Pub. & Ed. 1869 Feb. 20-1870 Dec. 24 S. K. Brobst at Allentown
    PGLS [1869-1870]
    PPK ♦ 1869 Feb. 20-1870 Dec. 24
         Continued as
  LUTHERISCHE ZEITSCHRIFT (Jan. 7, 1871-June 26, 1880) w
   Pub. 1871 Jan. 7-1872 Dec. 21 S. K. Brobst at Allentown
     1873 Jan. 4-1876 Dec. 23 S. K. Brobst & Company at Allen-
                   town
     1877 Jan. 6   Brobst & Diehl at Allentown
     1877 Jan. 13-1880 June 26 Brobst, Diehl & Company at Allen-
                   town
   Ed. 1871 Jan. 7-1872 Dec. 21 S. K. Brobst
     1873 Jan. 4-1876 Dec. 23 S. K. Brobst & Company
    PGLS [1871-1880]
    PPK ♦ 1871 Jan. 7-1880 June 26
        Missing
        1877 Aug. 18
        1878 July 20
        1880 Jan. 10, 12
        Merged with *Der Lutherische Herold* under the title
        of *Herold und Zeitschrift* (see under "Lutherischer
        Herold")

McMAKIN'S MODEL AMERICAN COURIER (1848-1851), see American Saturday Courier

MAGAZINE OF THE GERMAN REFORMED CHURCH, see Messenger, The

MAGYAR HIRADO (1914) w ind for ♦
  Pub. 1914 I. Weiss
  Ed. 1914 Alexander Berkovitz

MAIL, THE; or CLAYPOOLE'S DAILY ADVERTISER (June 1, 1791-Sept. 30, 1793||) d #
  Pub. 1791-1793 David C. Claypoole
  P   1791 June 1-1793 Sept. 30
  PHi   1791 June 1-July 29, Aug. 1-1792 Apr. 6
        1792 Apr. 8-Dec. 31
        1793 Jan. 9
  PPM   1791 June 1-1793 June 29
  Discontinued publication with the issue of Sept. 30, 1793. On Dec. 9, 1793, Claypoole joined in partnership with John Dunlap, publisher of *Dunlap's American Daily Advertiser* (see under *North American*)

MAMMOTH SATURDAY GAZETTE, (1849-1850), see Saturday Evening Mail

MANAYUNK ADVANCE, see Twenty-First Ward Advance

PHILADELPHIA COUNTY 125

MANAYUNK COURIER (Jan. 1, 1848-Mar. 18, 1848||) w
  Pub. & Ed. 1848 Richard Beresford
    PHi   1848 Jan. 1-Mar. 18

MANAYUNK REVIEW (Jan. 4, 1900†) w local
  Pub. 1904-1912   A. J. Graloff & Co.
       1912-1930   Review Publishing Co.
  Ed. 1904-1919   A. J. Graloff
       1928-1930   Charles Snyder
  PUB   1900 Jan. 4 (Vol. 1, No. 1)†
  PP   1923 Oct. 24, Nov. 7-14, 28
               1925 Mar. 11-25, Apr. 8-29, May 20-June 17, Sept. 30, Nov. 4-11, Dec. 9-16
               1926 Jan. 6-13, Mar. 21, June 20, July 11-24, Oct. 20, Dec. 22
               1929 Aug. 7, 18, Oct. 16, Nov. 10
               1930 Jan. 15-22, Feb. 5, Apr. 9-May 14, 28, June 11-July 2, 23-Sept. 3, 17-24, Oct. 1-8, 22-Dec. 17, 31
               1931 Jan. 7-Apr. 8, 22-May 13, 27-Aug. 5, Sept. 9, 23, Oct. 7-14, Nov. 11, Dec 9, 30
               1932 Jan. 13-27, Feb. 10-May 4, 18-June 15, July 6-20, Aug. 10, 24-Sept. 7, 21-Nov. 23, Dec. 7-14, 28
               1933 Jan. 4-18, Feb. 1-May 17, June 14-Aug 16, Sept. 6-Oct. 4, 18-25, Nov. 29, Dec. 6, 20-27
               1934 Jan 3-Feb. 7, 21-28, Mar. 21-Dec. 26
               1935 Jan 2†

MANAYUNK SENTINEL, ROXBOROUGH, FALLS OF SCHUYLKILL AND WISSAHICKON STAR (1870-1917) w ind rep
  ONCE-A-WEEK (Mar. 24, 1870-Mar. 31, 1870) w
    Pub. & Ed. 1870 Josephus Yeakel
      PHi   1870 Mar. 24-31
            continued as
  OUR ONCE-A-WEEK VISITOR (Apr. 7, 1870-Oct. 27, 1870) w
    Pub. & Ed. 1870 Josephus Yeakel
      PHi   1870 Apr. 7-Oct. 27
            continued as
  SENTINEL (Nov. 5, 1870-Apr. 30, 1871) w
    Pub. & Ed. 1870-1871 Josephus Yeakel
      PHi   1870 Nov. 5-1871 Apr. 30
      PP   1870 Nov. 5-1871 Apr. 30
            continued as
  MANAYUNK SENTINEL, ROXBOROUGH AND FALLS OF SCHUYLKILL GAZETTE (May 6, 1871-Oct. 31, 1879) w
    Pub. & Ed. 1871-1879 Josephus Yeakel
    Ed.   1878-1879 F. A. Lovejoy
      PHi   1871 May 6-1879 Oct. 31
      PP   1871 May 6-1879 Oct. 31
            continued as
  MANAYUNK SENTINEL, ROXBOROUGH, FALLS OF SCHUYLKILL AND LOWER MERION GAZETTE (Nov. 7, 1879-Oct. 21, 1880) w
    Pub. & Ed. 1879-1880 Josephus Yeakel
            1880   Manayunk Sentinel Publishing Co.

PHi 1879 Nov. 7-1880 Oct. 21
PP   1879 Nov. 7-1880 Oct. 21
continued as
MANAYUNK SENTINEL (Nov. 4, 1880-Oct. 28, 1886) w
Pub. & Ed. 1880-1882 Manayunk Sentinel Publishing Co.
           1882-1886 Josephus Yeakel
PHi 1880 Nov. 4-1886 Oct. 28
PP   1880 Nov. 4-1886 Oct. 28
continued as
MANAYUNK SENTINEL, ROXBOROUGH, FALLS OF SCHUYL-
KILL AND WISSAHICKON STAR (Nov. 4, 1886-Apr. 26, 1917) w
Pub. 1886-1890 Josephus Yeakel
     1890-1893 Yeakel & Donohugh
     1893-1908 William L. Donohugh
     1908-1917 F. A. Lovejoy
Ed. 1886-1888 Josephus Yeakel
     1888-1894 Frederick A. Lovejoy
     1894-1908 William L. Donohugh
     1908-1917 F. A. Lovejoy
PHi 1886 Nov. 4-1891 Sept. 24
PP   1886 Nov. 4-1917 Apr. 26

MANAYUNK STAR AND ROXBOROUGH GAZETTE (Feb 5, 1859-Aug. 9, 1862) w
Pub. & Ed. 1859   D. B. Potts
           1859-1860 James H. Scott
           1860-1862 J. Lewis Scott
PHi   1859 Feb. 5-1861 Dec. 21
           1862 Jan. 4-Aug. 9
PP   1859 Feb. 5-June 11, 25-July 9, 23-Dec. 31
           1860 Jan. 21-Dec. 29
           1861 Jan. 5, Feb. 2-Apr. 27, Oct. 19-1862 Jan 4

MARITIME JOURNAL (1885-1909) w ♂
Pub. 1885-1889 Journal Publishing Co.
     1889-1892 Samuel Macdonnell
     1892-1893 Macdonnell, Sproule & Co.
     1893-1901 Maritime Publishing Co.
     1901-1909 Samuel B. Macdonnell
Ed. 1893-1901 Samuel B. Macdonnell

MARKET JOURNAL (1870-1875) w ♂
PHILADELPHIA MARKET JOURNAL (1873) w ♂
Pub. & Ed. 1873 W. H. Kilpatrick
continued as
MARKET JOURNAL (1874-1875) w ♂
Pub. & Ed. 1874 B. Salinger
           1875 H. S. Parmalee

MARKET JOURNAL (1890-1892) w co ♂
Pub. & Ed. 1890-1892 Charles W. B. Marshall

MASONIC MIRROR AND AMERICAN KEYSTONE (1852-1854) w frat ♂
MASONIC MIRROR AND KEYSTONE (Jan. 7, 1852) w
Pub. & Ed. 1852 Leon Hyneman

PHILADELPHIA COUNTY 127

    PHi   1852 Jan. 7 (Vol. 1, No. 1)
                continued as
  MASONIC MIRROR AND AMERICAN KEYSTONE (Jan. 14, 1852-
    Dec. 27, 1854||) w
  Pub. & Ed. 1852-1854 Leon Hyneman
    PHi   1852 Jan. 14 (Vol. 2)-1854 Dec.

MASTRO PAOLA (1895-1919) w rep for ♦
  Pub. & Ed. 1907-1919 Joseph Bruno

MATTINO, IL (1914-1923) d morn ind rep for ♦
  MATTINO (1914-1921) d ♦
  Pub. & Ed. 1914 Pietro Jacovini
              continued as
  MATTINO, IL, (1922-1923) d ♦
  Pub. & Ed. 1922-1923 Pietro Jacovini

MECHANICS' FREE PRESS, see Philadelphia Times, People's Friend and Mechanics' Free Press

MECHANIC'S GAZETTE (Nov. 10, 1827-Mar. 8, 1828||) w
  Pub. 1828 Edmund Morris
    PDoHi   1828 Mar. 8

MEDICAL INDEPENDENT (1870-1871) w ♦
  Pub. & Ed. 1870-1871 William Paine

MEDICAL REPOSITORY (1871) w ♦
  Pub. & Ed. 1871 Stanley C. Hylton

MERCHANTS AND MANUFACTURING GUIDE (1879-1910) w m
  MERCHANTS' GUIDE (1879-1887) w ♦
  Pub. 1880-1887   Merchants' Guide Publishing Co.
                continued as
  MERCHANTS' GUIDE AND MANUFACTURERS' ADVERTISER
    (1888-1904) w ♦
  Pub. 1888-1904   Merchants' Guide Company
  Ed. 1896-1902   Lot P. Evans
        1902-1904   John L. Landis
                continued as
  MERCHANTS' GUIDE (1905-1909) w m
  Pub. 1905-1909   Merchants and Travelers Association
  Ed. 1906-1907   De Witt B. Lucas
        1908   Addison B. Burke
        1909   Addison B. Burke and Robert H. Price
        PP   1906 July 7
                    1907 Feb. 23

continued as
MERCHANTS AND MANUFACTURING GUIDE (1909-1910) m ♠
  Pub. 1909-1910   Merchants and Manufacturers Guide Company
  Ed. 1909-1910   George C. Calhoun

MERCHANTS' DAILY ADVERTISER, THE, see True American, The

MERCHANTS' JOURNAL (1869-1871) w ♠
  Pub. & Ed. 1869-1871 Watson & Co.

MERCURY (1890-1899) w ♠
  SUNDAY MERCURY (1890-1896) w soc ♠
  Pub. & Ed. 1892-1896 Harold S. Silberman
          continued as
  MERCURY (1897-1899) w rep ♠
  Pub. & Ed. 1897-1899 Harold J. Silberman

MERCURY AND SIFTINGS (Feb. 23, 1851-1891) w sun ind dem *
  SUNDAY MERCURY (Feb. 23, 1851-May 4, 1851) w ♠
  Pub. & Ed. 1851 Samuel C. Upham, H. H. Norcross, Robert D'Unger
          continued as
  UPHAM'S PHILADELPHIA SUNDAY MERCURY (May 11, 1851-Aug. 27, 1852) w ♠
  Pub. & Ed. 1851-1852 Samuel C. Upham, J. M. Willis and James G. Gibson, Jr.
          continued as
  SUNDAY MERCURY (Sept. 2, 1852-1890) w *
  % The Sunday Mercury, The Mercury, Philadelphia Sunday Mercury
  Pub. 1852-1856   Samuel C. Upham and George W. Jones
      1856-1860   Jones & Magill (James P. Magill)
      1860-1862   Jones & Taggart (John H. Taggart)
      1862-1865   William Meeser, George W. L. Johnson, Frederick W. Grayson
      1865-1880   William Meeser & Co.
                  (William Meeser & Frederick W. Grayson)
      1880-1881   Mercury Publishing Co. (Dr. Edward Morwitz, Pres.)
      1881-1888   Dennis F. Dealy
      1888-1890   Herald Company
  Ed. 1852-1860   L. A. Wilmer, James Rees, G. G. Foster, Emerson Bennett, E. W. C. Greene
      1860-1868   E. M. Woodward, Charles H. Graffen, F. W. Grayson
      1868-1880   William Meeser & Co.
      1880-1882   F. W. Grayson
      1888-1890   Daniel Gibbons
  P   1866 Jan. 7-1869 Dec. 31
                1871 Jan. 1-1876 Dec. 31
  PCHi   1872 Jan. 28
  PDoHi   1868 May 17
                1889 May 26, June 9
  PHi   1854 Apr. 16
                1855 Apr. 22, May 6, 13, 20, 27
                1860 Oct. (7), Dec. 2
                1861 July (7)

PHILADELPHIA COUNTY   129

	1865 May 7, Oct. 15
	1866 Apr. 15, 29, June 10
PJB	1889 June 9
PP	1855 Oct. 28
	1857 Feb. 1
	1858 June 13
	1859 Feb. 6, Apr. 17, May 22, Nov. 20
	1868 July 19-26, Sept. 20
PPFfHi	1853 Apr. 24
PPL	1856 Apr. 20
PPot	1888 July 22
PWcHi	1860 Apr. 29
	1864 May 22
	1875 Feb. 14

continued as

MERCURY AND SIFTINGS (1890-Jan. 18, 1891||)   w dem *
Pub. & Ed. 1890-1891   William A. Bobb and George A. Hincken
   PPeS   1891 Jan. 18

MESSENGER, THE (1827†) m sm w rel
MAGAZINE OF THE GERMAN REFORMED CHURCH, THE
  (Nov. 1827-Dec. 1831) m
  Pub. 1827 Nov.-1831 Dec.   Board of Missions at Carlisle
        1830 Jan.-1830 Dec.   D. May and B. Flory at York
        1831 Jan.-1831 Dec.   D. May at York
  Ed. 1827 Nov.-1829 Dec.   at the Theological Seminary
      PUB ♦   1828 Aug.
               1829 Jan.-1831 Dec.

continued as

MESSENGER OF THE GERMAN REFORMED CHURCH, THE
  (Jan. 1832-June 29, 1835)
m 1832 Jan.-1885 June 29; sm 1834 July 1-1835 June 29
  Pub. 1832 Jan.-1834 June   May & Glossbrenner at York
        1834 July 1-1835 June 29 Daniel May at York
      PUB ♦ m 1832 Feb.-May, July, Sept.-Nov.
             sm 1834 July 1-1835 June 15

continued as

WEEKLY MESSENGER OF THE GERMAN REFORMED
  CHURCH, THE (July 18, 1835-Dec. 29, 1847) w
  Pub. 1835 July 18-1847 Dec. 29 Board of Missions at Chambersburg
  Ed. 1835 July 18-1840 Nov. 4 Benjamin S. Schmeck
        1840 Nov. 11-1844 Jan. 31 Benjamin S. Schmeck and Samuel R. Fisher
        1844 Feb. 7-1847 Dec. 29 Samuel R. Fisher
      PUB ♦ 1835 July 18, Sept. 2-Dec. 16, Dec. 30
            1836 Jan. 6-Feb. 17, Mar. 2-Apr. 13, Apr. 27, May 4, 18, 25, June 22, July 13, 27-Aug. 10, 24-Dec. 28
            1837 Jan. 4-1838 Aug. 29, Sept. 19-Dec. 12, Dec. 26
            1839 Jan. 2-16, Feb. 20-Mar. 6, May 1-Dec. 11
            1840 Jan. 1-29, Feb. 12-Nov. 18, Dec. 2-30
            1841 Jan. 6-1843 Apr. 12
            1843 Apr. 26-1847 Dec. 29

continued as
WEEKLY MESSENGER (Jan. 5, 1848-Nov. 29, 1848) w
Pub. 1848 Jan. 5-1848 Nov. 29   Board of Missions at Chambersburg
Ed. 1848 Jan. 5-1848 Nov. 29   Samuel R. Fisher
   PUB ♦   1848 Jan. 5-Feb. 9, Feb. 23-May 17, May 31-Nov. 29
continued as
GERMAN REFORMED MESSENGER (Dec. 6, 1848-Aug. 28, 1867) w
Pub. 1848 Dec. 6-1864 Aug. 31   Board of Missions at Chambersburg
     1864 Sept. 7-1867 Aug. 28 Board of Missions at Philadelphia
Ed. 1848 Dec. 6-1848 Dec. 27   Samuel R. Fisher
     1849 Jan. 3-1852 May 26   Benjamin S. Schmeck and Samuel R. Fisher
     1852 June 2-1859 Mar. 9   Samuel R. Fisher and Samuel Miller
     1859 Mar. 16-1861 Nov. 27 Samuel R. Fisher and B. Bausman
     1861 Dec. 4-1867 Aug. 28   Samuel R. Fisher
   PAlHi   1860 Jan. 18
   PUB ♦   1848 Dec. 6-1849 Sept. 26
           1849 Oct. 10-1857 Sept. 2
           1857 Sept. 16-1861 Dec. 4
           1862 Jan. 1-Sept 10, 24-Oct. 15, 29-1863 June 17
           1863 July 15-1867 Aug. 28
continued as
REFORMED CHURCH MESSENGER (Sept. 4, 1867-Dec. 29, 1875) w
Pub. 1867 Sept. 4-1875 Dec. 29 S. R. Fisher & Co. at Philadelphia
Ed. 1867 Sept. 4-1869 Mar. 24 Samuel R. Fisher
     1869 Mar. 31-1871 Dec. 6   Samuel R. Fisher and Geo. B. Russell
     1871 Dec. 13-1875 Dec. 29 Samuel R. Fisher
   PUB ♦   1867 Sept. 4-1875 Dec. 29
   PNoHi   1868 May 27
   PP   1868 Jan.-Dec.
continued as
MESSENGER, THE (Jan. 5, 1876-Dec. 28, 1887) w
Pub. 1876 Jan. 5-1887 Dec. 28   S. R. Fisher & Co.
Ed. 1876 Jan. 5-1887 Dec. 28   P. S. Davis
   PUB ♦   1876 Jan. 5-1887 Dec. 28
continued as
REFORMED CHURCH MESSENGER (Jan. 4, 1888-Jan. 30, 1936) w
Pub. 1888 Jan. 4-1888 May 30   S. R. Fisher & Co.
     1888 June 6-1899 Dec. 28   Chas. G. Fisher at Philadelphia
     1900 Jan. 4-1901 Dec. 26   Lebanon and Philadelphia
     1902 Jan. 2-1936 Jan. 30   Philadelphia
Ed. 1901 Jan. 3-1917 Oct. 4   C. J. Musser
     1917 Oct. 11-1931 Jan. 1   Paul S. Leinbach and A. S. Bromer
     1931 Jan. 8-1934 Apr. 19   Paul S. Leinbach, A. S. Bromer, and Ambrose M. Schmidt
     1934 Apr. 26-1936 Jan. 30 Paul S. Leinbach and Ambrose M. Schmidt
   PUB ♦   1888 Jan. 4-1936 Jan. 30
   PP   1917 Aug. 2-9, 23-30, Sept. 6-20, Oct. 18, Nov. 1-8
           1919 Apr. 17-May 15

PHILADELPHIA COUNTY 131

                  1923 Mar. 29-June 28, Sept. 13-Nov. 8, 15, 29-Dec. 27
                  1924 Jan. 17-Mar. 27, Apr. 10-June 19, July 3-31, Aug.
                       14, 21, Sept. 4, 25, Oct. 2-30, Nov. 6, 20-27, Dec.
                       4-18
                  1925 Jan. 8-Feb. 5, Nov. 12
                  1926 Jan. 7-14, Feb. 11-25, Apr. 29-May 20, June 3-17,
                       July 8-22, Aug. 5, 19-Sept. 23, Oct. 7-Dec. 2, 16
                  1927 Jan. 27, Feb. 10-24, Mar. 3-31, May 5-June 2,
                       Aug. 4, Sept. 15, 22, Oct. 20, Nov. 3-Dec. 29
                  1928 Jan. 5-Feb. 23, Nov. 22, Dec. 6-27
                  1929 Jan. 3-10, 24-Nov. 21, Dec. 5-26
                  1930 Jan. 2, 16-Mar. 6, June 12-Aug. 21, Sept. 4-Oct.
                       2, 16-23
                  1932 July 14
                  1934 Sept. 20, Oct. 25, Nov. 8-Dec. 13, 27
                  1935 Jan. 3-Dec. 26
        PPPHi   1902 Jan. 2-1936 Jan. 30
                  Missing
                  1913 Jan. 9
                  continued as
MESSENGER, THE (Feb. 6, 1936†) w
Pub. 1936 Feb. 6-1941† at St. Louis, Mo.
Ed. 1936 Feb. 6-1939 June 29 Paul S. Leinbach, Philadelphia and
                                        Julius H. Horstman, St. Louis, Mo.
    1939 July 6-1941 Dec. Paul S. Leinbach
    PUB ♦ 1936 Feb. 6†
    PPPHi 1936 Feb. 6†

MESSENGER (1892-1893) w rep ♦
    Pub. & Ed. 1892-1893 W. L. Stanger and J. C. Shearer

MESSENGER OF THE GERMAN REFORMED CHURCH (1832-1835), see Messenger, The

METHODIST HOME JOURNAL (1867-1873) w ♦
    Pub. & Ed. 1867-1873 Reverend Adam Wallace

MIND AND MATTER (1878-1885) w rel
    Pub. & Ed. 1878-1885 J. M. Roberts
            PPL   1878 Nov. 30-1879 Nov. 29
                     1879 Dec. 13-1880 Oct. 9
                     1880 Oct. 23-Dec. (4)-1881 Nov. (26)-1882 July 15
                     1882 July 29-1884 Nov. 17

MINERVA (1795-1798), see Philadelphia Minerva

MISSIONARY, THE (1848-1855), see Lutheran

MOMENTO, IL (Jan. 27, 1917-May 3, 1919||) w Italian
    PP   1917 Sept. 29, Oct. 6, Dec. 8
             1918 Feb. 2, 16-23, Mar. 16-Apr. 27
             1919 Jan. 11-25, Feb. 15-May 3

MONITOR (1883-1886) w ♦
    Pub. & Ed. 1886 J. W. Van Slyke

MOORE'S PHILADELPHIA PRICE CURRENT OR TRADE NEWS AND SHIPPING LIST (Dec. 14, 1833-Jan. 17, 1835) w *
    PHILADELPHIA PRICE CURRENT OR TRADE NEWS AND SHIPPING LIST (Dec. 14, 1833) w
    Pub. & Ed. 1833   T. M. Moore
        PHi   1833 Dec. 14
                      continued as
    MOORE'S PHILADELPHIA PRICE CURRENT OR TRADE NEWS AND SHIPPING LIST (Dec. 21, 1833-Jan. 17, 1835) w *
    Pub. 1833-1835   T. M. Moore
        PHi   1833 Dec. 21-1835 Jan. 17
    Merged with *Philadelphia Price Current and Commercial Advertiser*, and title changed to *The Commercial List and Philadelphia Price Current*, Jan. 24, 1835 (see under *Commercial List and Maritime Register*)

MORAVIAN (Jan. 1, 1856-Dec. 30, 1858) w rel
    Pub. 1856-1858   Moravian Publishing Office
    Ed. 1856-1858   E. DeSchweintz, L. F. Kampman, F. F. Hagen
        P   1856 Jan. 1-Dec. 26
        PBM   1856 Jan. 1-1858 Dec. 30
        PNazHi   1856 Jan. 1, 11-Dec. 26
                      1857 Jan. 2-Dec. 25
                      1858 Jan. 1-Feb. 5, 19, Mar. 5-Apr. 9, 23, May 14-June 25, July 9-Nov. 5, 19-Dec. 30
    Moved to Bethlehem, Pa., Jan. 1, 1859

MORGEN GAZETTE, see Philadelphia Gazette Democrat

MORNING JOURNAL (Jan. 1-June 30, 1830) d * w
    Pub. & Ed. 1830   William Brown
        PU   1830 Jan.-June
    Weekly edition entitled *Saturday Morning Journal*. Merged with the *Philadelphia Inquirer*, July 1, 1830 (q.v.)

MORNING PENNSYLVANIAN (1832-1861) d w tw dem *
    PENNSYLVANIAN, THE (July 9, 1832-Dec. 4, 1855) d tw w *
    Pub. 1832-1855   Mifflin & Parry
                          J. M. Cooper
                          William Hope
                          * William McGill
                          William Rice
    Ed. 1832-1855   James Gordon Bennett
                          John W. Forney
                          Joseph C. Neal
                          J. M. Cooper
    Tri-weekly edition entitled *Pennsylvanian for the Country*, July 9, 1832-Dec. 1855.
    Weekly edition entitled *Pennsylvanian*, July 9, 1832-Nov. 25, 1854; *Dollar Weekly Pennsylvanian*, Dec. 2, 1854-1855.
    P   d   [1833 Jan. 21-1855 Dec. 14]
    P-M   1852 May 18

PHILADELPHIA COUNTY 133

```
PAtM        d  1851 Dec. 6-8, 13
PBL      ♦     1855 Oct. 22
PByL           1846 Oct. 6
PCHi        tw 1839 Jan. 3-Dec. 31
               1840 Jan. 2-Dec. 31
               1841 Jan. 2-Mar. 23, 30-May 18
               1842 Feb. 22
               1843 June 3, July 4, Oct. 3, 14, Dec. 2-30
               1844 Dec. 3-28
               1845 Jan. 2-30, Feb. 18, June 12, 19, 26, July 12, 21,
                    Aug. 5, 7, 16-28, Sept. 16, 23, Oct. 2, 7, 9, 23,
                    28, 30, Nov. 11, 13, 18, 22-29, Dec. 4, 13, 16, 27
               1846 Jan. 1-Feb. 12, 19-24, Mar. 3, 7, 12, 21, 24, 31,
                    Apr. 2-30, May 2-30, June 2, 6, 9, 13, 20, 23,
                    27, 30, July 2-30, Aug. 1, 4, 11, 13, 18, 20, 27,
                    29, Sept. 1, 3, 8, 10, 12, 15, 17, 22, 29, Oct. 1,
                    3, 8-17, 24, 29-Nov. 24, Dec. 1-12, 24, 26
               1847 Mar. 4, Apr. 6, May 25, 29, June 10, 19, 24, 29,
                    July 3, 5, 15, 20-31, Aug. 3-31, Sept. 4-23, 28,
                    Oct. 5-12, 21, 23, 28, 30, Nov. 2-30, Dec. 2, 14-25
               1848 Jan. 1, 8, Mar. 16, Apr. 8, 18, June 13, 29, July
                    6, Aug. 12, 22, 26, Sept. 16, 30, Nov. 23, Dec. 12,
                    19, 30
            w  1849 May 12, 26, June 2, 16, July 7, 21, 28, Aug. 11-25,
                    Sept. 1, 8, 22, Oct. 6, 20, Nov. 3, 17
               1850 Jan. 4, Feb. 9, Mar. 2, 23, Apr. 6-27, May 4-25,
                    June 1-15, 29, July 13-27, Aug. 3-31, Sept. 7-28,
                    Oct. 12-26, Nov. 2-23, Dec. 7-28
               1851 Jan 11-25, Feb. 1-22, Mar. 1, 22, Apr. 5-26, May
                    3-June 28, July 12-26, Aug. 2-30, Sept. 6, 13,
                    Oct. 4-18, Nov. 1-29, Dec. 13, 20
               1852 Jan. 10, Feb. 7-21, Mar. 6, 20, 27, Apr. 3, 17,
                    24, May 1, 8, 29, June 5-26, July 10, 24, 31, Aug.
                    7-28, Sept. 4, 11, 25, Oct. 2-23, Nov. 13-27, Dec.
                    4-25
               1853 Jan. 8, 15, 29, Feb. 5-26, Mar. 12, 26, Apr. 9,
                    May 7-28, June 4, 11, 25, July 2-30, Aug. 6-20,
                    Sept. 3, 17, 24, Oct. 1, 8, 22, Nov. 5-26, Dec.
                    3-31
               1854 Jan. 7, 21, Feb. 4-25, Mar. 4, 18, Apr. 1, 15, 29,
                    May 13-27, June 3-24, July 1, 8, 22-Aug. 12,
                    Sept. 16, 23, Oct. 21, Nov. 4-Dec. 2
               1855 May 12, July 25
PDoHi       d  1833 June 28
               1834 June 25
               1844 Feb. 5
PE          tw 1843 Jan. 3-Mar. 4, 9-Apr. 13, 20, 25-June 15, 20, 24-
                    July 6, 11-15, 20-22. Aug. 1-5, 10-19, 24-26, Sept.
                    2-7, 12-26, Oct. 3-21, 26-Nov. 16, 21-Dec. 28
PHi         d  1833 Jan. 1-1855 Dec. 4
PNeBr       d  [1831-1832]
PP          d  1832 Oct. 10
               1833 Dec. 7
               1839 Jan. 11
               1840 Jan. 1-1841 June 5
               1841 June 8-July 3, 7-1842 June 30
               1849 Oct. 10
PPeS        w  1841 July 24
```

MORNING PENNSYLVANIAN, *continued*

PPFfHi	d 1845	June 24, July 1, 3, 14
PPi	d 1846	Nov. 13-1853 Mar. 4
PPiUD	d 1840	Aug. 19, Sept. 4, 23
	1841	May 3
	1842	Mar. 24, Apr. 21, Nov. 18, 21, 24, 25
	1843	Jan. 9, May 6, Nov. 25, Dec. 9
	1844	Jan. 8, Mar. 15, June 29, Aug. 10, 12, 24, Oct. 5, Nov. 12
PPL	d 1832	July 19-Aug. 6, 8, 16, 18, 20-Dec. 15, 18-19, 27, 29-1834 Jan. 7
	1834	Jan. 9-10, 13-15, 17-22, 24-27, 29-Mar. 2, 5, 8-14, 17-June 30, July 2-31, Sept. 2-12, 15-30
	1835	Jan. 1-31, Feb. 4
	1837	Apr. 19, 21-24, 26-May 2, 10, 13-29, June 1-2, 7-9, 14, 19-22, 26-30, July 8-11, 13, Sept. 6, 8-29, Oct. 2-Nov. 14, 17, 18, 21-23, 25-Dec. 13, 15-27, 29-1838 Jan. 10
	1838	Jan. 12-23, 25-31, Feb. 2-May 10, 12-Aug. 14, 16-17, 21-24, 27-Nov. 5, 7, 8, 10-14, 16-Dec. 31
	1839	Mar. 25-July 29, Aug. 1-Sept. 14, 17-1840 Jan. 3
	1840	Jan. 6-Feb. 8, 12-Apr. 6, 8, 10-13, 16-18, 21-May 8, 11-June 17, (19)-Aug. 1, 5, 6, 8-27, 29-Sept. 5, 8-11, 14-Dec. 11, 14
	1843	Jan. 6, 8-10, 12-17 (19)-July 31, Aug. 2-31, Sept. 2-Oct. 3, 5-Dec. 21, 23-1844 May 3
	1844	May 6-June 5, 7-29, July 1-1845 Oct. 6
	1845	Oct. 8-Nov. 27, 29-31
	1846	Jan. 1-1849 Jan. 9
	1849	Jan. 11-Feb. 6, 8-June 15, 18-30, July 2-Sept. 11, 13-Oct. 5, 8-Dec. 25, 27-1851 Jan. (7)
	1851	May 15, 17-June 23, 25, 27, 29, July 3-Sept. 11, 16-Oct. 22, 24, 28-Nov. (13)-14, 17-1852 Mar. 27
	1852	Mar. 30-May 1, 4-6, 8-Nov. 25, 27-1853 July (1)-Dec. 31
	1854	June 13-Aug. 11, 21, 23, 28, Sept. 2, 6, 7, 9, Oct. 26-28, 31-Nov. 23, 25-Dec. 19, 21, 22, 25-29
	1855	Jan. 1-Feb. 7, 9-24, 26-May 5, 8-June 6, 8-29, July 2-7, 10-25, 27-Aug. 16, 18-20, 23-27, 30-Nov. 1, 5-13, 15-22, 24-Dec. 14
PToHi	d 1849	Feb. 19-Dec. 31
	tw 1846	June 1-1847 Oct. 21
PU	d 1846	Jan. 1-1855 Dec. 14
	tw 1854	Dec. (1)-1855 Dec.
	w 1854	Jan. (1-Nov. 25)
PW	d 1844	Mar. 6, 7, 8, 9
	1846	Mar. 7, 9, 10-11, 12
PWcHi	d 1840	Jan. 9
	tw 1840	Mar. 7, 14, 26
	d 1841	Dec. 17, 27
	tw 1841	Aug. 14, Sept. 9, 16, 21, 23, 28, Oct. 5, 7, 9-19, 23-Dec. 16, 21, 23, 30
	d 1842	Nov. 19, Dec. 3, 13
	tw 1842	Jan. 1-11, 15-Feb. 12, June 11, Aug. 4-30, Sept. 3, 6, 10-Nov. 17, 22-Dec. 1, 6-10, 15-31
	d 1843	Jan. 14, Mar. 14, May 16, Aug. 15, Sept. 2, Nov. 7, Dec. 12

PHILADELPHIA COUNTY 135

          tw 1843 Jan. 3-Feb. 18, 23-Mar. 11, 16-May 13, 18, 20, 25-June 1, 8-July 1, 6-Aug. 12, 17-Sept. 5, 9, 21, Oct. 7, 17, 31, Nov. 2, 7-Nov. 30, Dec. 7, 28
          d 1844 Feb. 10, 22
          tw 1844 Jan. 2-9, 13-Feb. 8, 13-20, 24, 27, 29, Mar. 5, 7, 12, 14, 19-30, July 27, Aug. 1, 6, 13, 17
          d 1845 Feb. 25, Mar. 4, 18, Apr. 4, 29, May 1
          tw 1845 Feb. 27, Mar. 1, 6-15, 20-Apr. 17, 22, 24, May 3-13, 17-June 5, 10, 28, Sept. 13, 18, 20, 25-30, Oct. 11, 16, 21, 25, Nov. 4, 6, 8
          d 1846 Mar. 26, Nov. 28
          w 1846 Aug. 15, Sept. 19-Oct. 10, 24-Dec. 19
          tw 1846 Feb. 5, Mar. 14, 28, July 28, Aug. 25, Sept. 24, Dec. 17, 22, 29, 31
          d 1847 Jan. 2-Dec. 11, 25
          tw 1847 Jan. 2-21, 26-Feb. 25, July 17, Sept. 2, 9, 21, 25, 30, Oct. 2, 7, 16, 19, Nov. 23, Dec. 7, 9, 11
          d 1848 Mar 23, May 27, June 7, Aug. 15, Sept. 6, Dec. 13
          w 1848 Jan. 1-29, Feb. 12-Dec. 16, 30
          tw 1848 Jan. 11-Feb. 3, 8-26, Mar. 7, 11, 14, 21, 25-Apr. 1, 11, 20, 22, 25, May 23, 25, June 1, 3, 6, 10, 17-27, July 1, 4, 11, 13-20, Aug. 1, 3, 5, 10, 19, 24, 29, Sept. 2, 5, 14, 19, 21, 23, Oct. 5-Nov. 18, 25-30, Dec. 5, 14, 16, 21-(28)
          d 1849 Jan. 6
          w 1849 Jan. 6-July 28, Sept. 1-Dec. 29
          d 1850 Mar. 29
          w 1850 Jan. 5-Mar. 16, 30-July 13, 27-Aug. 10, 24-Nov. 23
          d 1851 Aug. 25
          w 1851 Feb. 22-Mar. 8, 22-Aug. 30, Sept. 20-Oct. 4, 18, Nov. 8-Dec. 6, 20
          d 1852 Apr. 24, June 28, 29, July 2 (5), 8-(14), 15, 17, 20, (21), 23-(28)-Aug. 6, 9-12, 14, (19), 20, 23, 24, 30-Sept. 13, 15-Oct. 4, 6-12, 15, 18, 28, 29, Nov. 4, 11, 13, 15, 16, 19, 22, 23, 29, 30, Dec. 9, 30
          d 1854 June 17, July 25, 29, Aug. 12, Sept. 30
          w 1855 Jan. (6), Mar. 3, Apr. 21
PWeT   d 1838 Apr. 3-6
          1840 Mar. 30-Apr. 2
          continued as

DAILY PENNSYLVANIAN (Dec. 15, 1855-June 30, 1857) d tw w *

Pub. 1855-1857   Mifflin & Parry
                      J. M. Cooper
                      William Rice
Ed. 1855-1857   James Gordon Bennett
                      William McGill
                      William Rice

Tri-weekly edition entitled *Pennsylvanian for the Country,* Dec. 1855-1857
Weekly edition entitled *Dollar Weekly Pennsylvanian,* Dec. 1855-1857

P   d [1855 Dec. 15-1857 June 30]
PCHi   w 1855 Dec. 29

MORNING PENNSYLVANIAN, *continued*

    PHi   d 1855 Dec. 15-1857 June 30
    PJsK   d 1856 Oct. 22
    PPL   d 1855 Dec. 15-22, 25-1856 Jan. 25, 28-Mar. 1, 3-13, 15-May 17, 20, 21, 23-June 11, 13, July 1, 3-8, 10, 12-Aug. 23, 26-Sept. 17, 20-24, 26-27, 30-Oct. 2, 6-10, 13-(15)-16, 18-20, 22-25, 28-Nov. 5, 8-12, 14-17, 19, 20, 22-1857 Feb. 20
             1857 Feb. 23-Mar. 14, 17, 21, 24-Apr. 11, 14-June 11, 13-30
    PPot   w 1856 Oct. 25
    PU   d 1855 Dec. 15-1857 June 30
             tw 1855-1857
             continued as

PHILADELPHIA DAILY PENNSYLVANIAN (July 1, 1857-Dec. 31, 1857) d tw w

Pub. 1857   William Rice
Ed. 1857   William McGill
Tri-weekly edition entitled *Pennsylvanian for the Country*, July 1, 1857-Dec. 1857
Weekly edition entitled *Dollar Weekly Pennsylvanian*, July 1, 1857-Dec. 1857

    P   d 1857 July 1-Dec. 31
    PHi   d 1857 July 1-Dec. 31
    PPL   d 1857 July 1-12, 14-Nov. 26, 28
    PToHi   d 1857 July 2-Dec. 14
    PU   d 1857 July 1-Dec. 31
           tw 1857
           continued as

PENNSYLVANIAN (Jan. 1, 1858-May 7, 1859) d tw w *

Pub. 1858-1859   William Rice
Ed. 1858-1859   Edward G. Webb
                   S. D. Anderson
                   Dr. E. Morwitz
Tri-weekly edition entitled *Pennsylvanian for the Country*, Dec. 1855-1857
Weekly edition entitled *Dollar Weekly Pennsylvanian*, Jan. 1, 1858-May 1859

    P   d 1858 Jan. 1-July 31
    PHi   d 1858 Jan. 1-1859 May 7
    PPL   d 1858 Jan. 1-9, 12-Feb. 16, 18-May 6, 8-22, 25, July 1-Nov. 16, 22, 24-1859 Jan. 1
             1859 Jan. 14, 17-Feb. 14, 16-Mar. 25, 29-Apr. 2, 6, 11-13, 18, May 2-7
    PToHi   d 1858 Feb. 12-Dec. 6
    PU   d 1858 Jan. 1-1859 May 7
           tw 1858 Jan.-1859 May
           continued as

MORNING PENNSYLVANIAN, THE (May 9, 1859-Apr. 2, 1861) d tw

Pub. 1859 May 9-1860 July 28   Dr. E. Morwitz
     1860 July 30-1861 Apr. 2   John H. Brimner
Ed. 1859 May 9-1859 Sept. 12   Nimrod Strickland
     1859 Sept. 13-1860 Apr. 30   Geo. W. Baker
Tri-weekly edition entitled *Pennsylvanian for the Country*, May 1859-Dec. 1861.

PHILADELPHIA COUNTY   137

    Weekly edition entitled *Dollar Weekly Pennsylvanian,* May 1859-
    Dec. 1861
    PChaIS   d 1860 July 9
    PHi   d 1859 May 9-1861 Apr. 2
    PPL   d 1859 May 9, 10, 12-June 10, 13-30
    PPot   d 1860 July 3
    PPPHi   d 1860 May 5
    PToHi   tw 1859 May 14-1860 June 1
    PU   d 1859 May 9-1861 Apr.
                tw 1859 May-1861 Apr. 6

MORNING POST (1825) d ♦
    Pub. 1825   William White

MORNING POST (1836-1845) d *
    Pub. & Ed. 1836-1845 Bella Badger
        PBL   ♦   1845 June 7

MORNING POST (1867-1871), see Philadelphia Post

MORNING STAR (Oct. 5, 1837-Sept., 1838) d
    Pub. 1837-1838   J. Metcalfe & Co.
    Ed. 1837-1838   J. Bausman
        PPL   1838 Dec. 6
    Merged with the *People's Advocate* and title changed to *Morning
    Star and People's Advocate* (q.v.)

MORNING STAR AND PEOPLE'S ADVOCATE (1823-1838) sw d *

    PEOPLE'S ADVOCATE (July 9, 1823-Sept. 1838) w
    Pub. 1838   Joseph Metcalfe & Co.
        1838   Rackliff & King
    Ed. 1838   J. Bausman
        1838   Rackliff & King
        PBL ♦   1838 Aug. 30, Sept. 4
        PDoHi   1823 July 30, Aug. 2, Nov. 12
        PE   1838 Sept. 8
    Merged with the *Morning Star* to form
    MORNING STAR AND PEOPLE'S ADVOCATE (Oct. 2, 1838-
    Dec. 6, 1838) d *
    Pub. & Ed. 1838 Rackliff & King
        PBL ♦   1838 Nov. 26
        PPL   1838 Dec. 6

NATION, THE (1856) w ♦
    Pub. 1856   Crofut & Bigelow

NATIONAL ADVERTISER (Jan. 1850-Jan. 1853) sw
    Pub. James Gibbons
        PWcHi   1853 Jan. 12

NATIONAL ARGUS, see National Evening Argus

NATIONAL ATLAS AND TUESDAY MORNING MAIL, THE
(1836-1838||) w *
    NATIONAL ATLAS AND SUNDAY MORNING MAIL, THE
    (July 31, 1836-Sept. 1836) w *
    Pub. 1836   Samuel C. Atkinson
      PHi ◆   1836 July 31-Sept. 18
                continued as
    NATIONAL ATLAS AND TUESDAY MORNING MAIL, THE
    (1836-1838||) w *
    Pub. 1836-1838   Samuel C. Atkinson
      PHi ◆   1836 Oct. 4-1838 Jan. 28

NATIONAL BANNER AND PHILADELPHIA LITERARY GA-
ZETTE (Aug. 17, 1833-1835) w ♦ *

NATIONAL BAPTIST (1865-1894) w
    Pub. 1868-1869   American Baptist Association
         1869-1871   American Baptist Publication Society
         1871-1874   Bible and Publication Society
         1874-1885   American Baptist Publication Society
         1885-1891   Reverend H. L. Wayland
         1891-1893   National Baptist Publishing Company
    Ed. 1868-1872   Lemuel Moss
         1872-1891   Reverend H. L. Wayland
      PCAB   [1865-1894]

NATIONAL CHRONICLE (d 1822-Sept. 14, 1825||; tw Aug. 15, 1825-
Oct. 28, 1825||) *
    Ed. 1825   Stephen Simpson
      PBL ◆   tw 1825 Sept. 23, Oct. 28
    The tri-weekly edition of the *Columbian Observer* merged with the *National Chronicle* in 1825 (q.v.)

NATIONAL DAILY ARGUS, see National Evening Argus

NATIONAL ENQUIRER AND CONSTITUTIONAL ADVOCATE
OF UNIVERSAL LIBERTY, see Pennsylvania Freeman, The

NATIONAL EVENING ARGUS (1851-1861) d w dem *
    NATIONAL ARGUS (Feb. 15, 1851-May 10, 1851) d ♦
    Pub. & Ed. 1851   Joseph Severns & Robert F. Christy
                    continued as
    NATIONAL DAILY ARGUS (May 10, 1851-1852) d w *
    Pub. 1851-1852   Joseph Severns & Co.
                      Severns & McGill
      Weekly edition entitled *National Argus*
      PBL ◆   1852 Jan. 23
      PPL   d 1851 Feb. 15, May 10
                continued as
    NATIONAL EVENING ARGUS (1852-Nov. 10, 1861) d w *
    Pub. & Ed. 1852-1861   Joseph Severns & Co.
                            Severns & McGill

PHILADELPHIA COUNTY 139

        PBL ♦   d 1852 Jan. 23
        PPL   d 1852 Mar. 20
                  1856 Mar. 6, 19, Apr. 9
        Weekly edition entitled *National Argus*

NATIONAL FARMER (1871) w ♂
    Pub. 1871   Brinkloe & Marat
    Ed. 1871   W. G. P. Brinkloe

NATIONAL FORUM, see Daily Forum

NATIONAL GAZETTE (Oct. 31, 1791-Oct. 26, 1793||) sw #
    Pub. 1791-1793   Philip Freneau
    P   1791 Oct. 31-1793 Oct. 26
    PDoHi   1792 Aug. 15-Sept. 12, 19-29, Oct. 6, 10, 17, 20
                      1793 May 4-11, 18-June 1, 19, 26-July 13, Aug. 21,
                            28-Oct. 12, 26
    PHi   1792 Oct. 13
    PPAP   1791 ct. 31-1792 Oct. 27
    PPiUD   1791 Oct. 31-1793 Sept. 14
    PPL   1791 Oct. 31-1793 Oct. 26
    PU   1793 June 15

NATIONAL GAZETTE AND LITERARY REGISTER, THE (Apr. 5, 1820-Dec. 30, 1841) sw d tw # *
    Pub. 1820-1841   William Fry
          1841   J. Reese Fry and Edward Fry
    Ed. 1820-1836   Robert Walsh
    P   sw 1820 Apr. 5-Dec. 30
        d or sw 1820 Nov. 1-1824 June 28
                    1825 Jan. 5-1842 Jan. 1
    PAlHi   tw 1827 Jan. 2-16, 20-Feb. 8, 15-Apr. 12, 17-July 3,
                          7-Aug. 18, 23, 28-Sept. 18, 22, 25, 29-Dec. 25, 29
                    1828 Jan. 1-29, Feb. 2-Apr. 3, 8-May 10, 15-July 3,
                          8-Sept. 6, 11-Dec. 25, 30
                    1829 Jan. 1-Apr. 16, 21-June 25, July 2, 4-Dec. 24,
                          29, 31
                    1830 Jan. 2, Mar. 20, 25, 27, Apr. 1-8, 13, 17-May
                          4, 11-July 3, 8-Aug. 17, 21-Sept. 18, 28-Oct. 5,
                          12-26, 30-Dec. 16, 21-25, 30
                    1831 Jan. 1-Mar. 31, Apr. 5-May 24, 28-June 11, 16-
                          28, July 2, 9-26, 30-Aug. 20, 25-Dec. 29
    PAtM   1831 Apr. 5-30
    PBL ♦   sw 1820 Apr. 8-15, 22, 26, May 3, 6, 13, 20, 24, 31-Oct.
                      28
              d 1821 Mar. 28
              d 1825 Mar. 22
             tw 1825 July 12-26, Aug. 2-16, 23-Sept. 22, 27, Oct. 1-
                    Nov. 5, 10-22, 26, 29, Dec. 10-17, 24
             tw 1826 Jan. 5, 24, 26, Feb. 14, 16, Mar. 7, 9, 16
                  1828 May 29-June 5, 21, July 3, 19, Aug. 16, 28,
                    Sept. 4, 11, 27
                  1829 Mar. 17, Apr. 2, 4, 9-16, 21-May 12, 16-July 4,
                    9, 11, 18-Dec. 24, 29, 31
             tw 1830 Jan. 5-Feb. 27, Mar. 4-Apr. 13-July 3, 8-Aug.
                    17, 21-Dec. 25, 30

NATIONAL GAZETTE AND LITERARY REGISTER, THE, *continued*

     tw 1831 Jan. 4-Feb. 15, 22-Mar. 31, Apr. 5-May 31, June 11-July 2, 7-Sept. 24, Oct. 1-Dec. 10, 20-31
     tw 1832 Jan. 3-10, 14-21, Feb. 2-21, 25-Mar. 3, 8, 15-24, 29-May 24, 29-June 14, 21-July 3, 7-31, Aug. 4-Sept. 6, 11-Oct. 20
       1833 Feb. 5-Mar. 2, Apr. 9-16, 27
       1834 May 20, June 21, July 1, 3, 8-Sept. 9, 13-23, 30-Oct. 9, 16-28, Nov. 1-15, 20-25

PCarlHi tw 1823 Dec. 20
       [1824]
       [1827]
       1828 Aug. 16, 19, 21
       1838 Mar. 24, Apr. 7, 28, May 3, July 12, 17
       [1839]

PDoHi sw 1821 Jan. 6-17, 27-Feb. 3, 10-Aug. 4, 11-Sept. 19, 26-1822, Jan. 2-9
       1822 Jan. 30-June 5, 12-19, 26-Sept. 4, 11-28, Oct. 5-Nov. 13, 20, 23, 30
     d 1822 Jan. 1-3, 5-July 3, 5-Sept. 30, Oct. 2-Dec. 31
       1824 Mar. 24
     tw 1822 Dec. 3-24, 28, 31
       1825 Sept. 15
       1826 May 13
       1827 July 14, Aug. 1-Sept. 27, Oct. 2-Nov. 29, Dec. 4-11, 15-25, 29
       1828 Jan. 1-Mar. 29, Apr. 3-June 21, 26-July 3, 8-19, 26-31, Aug. 7-30

PEL   sw 1822 May 11, June 1, 22, Oct. 5
     tw 1834 May 3
PHaC sw 1820 Apr. 5-Oct. 28
PHi   d 1820 Nov. 1-Dec. 30
PLewL d 1828 Apr. 2
PNhE d or tw 1825 Oct. 1
       1826 Feb. 16, June 14
       1828 Dec. 20
       1829 Dec. 8
       1830 Feb. 19
PNazHi   1837 Mar. 6
PP   d 1825 July 28
       1827 Jan. 1-May 30, June 2-1829 Dec. 31
       1837 Dec. 30
       1838 Jan. 1-9, 13, 16, 20, Feb. 16, May 25, 28, July 23, 27, 30, Aug. 8, 10, 13, 15, 16, 18, 25, 27, Sept. 1, 3-5, 12-14, 17-22, 26, 27, Oct. 6, 9, 11-13, 15, 18-20, 22-24, 27, 29-Nov. 3, 5, Dec. 22, 24, 27, 29, 31
       1839 Jan. 9-12, 14-18, 21, 23-25, 28-Feb. 2, 5-8, 11-16, 18-23, 26, 27, Mar. 1-Apr. 12, 16-20, 22, 23, May 9, 10, 21, 22, 24, 28, 31, June 26, 27, July 5, 6, 11, 13, 15, 20, Aug. 5, 12, 23, 24, 26, 30, Sept. 3, 5, 12, 13, 16, 17, 23, 26
       1840 Jan. 1-Mar. 24, 26-Oct. 27, 29-Dec. 31
       1841 Jan. 2-Feb. 10, 13-Mar. 26, 29-Apr. 6, 8-16, 19-May 3, Oct. 7, 9-Dec. 31
     tw 1823 Dec. 5
       1824 Nov. 16

PHILADELPHIA COUNTY 141

		1829 Nov. 17
PPAT	d	1835 Jan. 1-1837, May 30
		1837 June 1-(30)-1838 Mar. 21
		1838 Mar. 23-1841, Dec. 30
PPF	d	1820 Nov. 1-1831, Dec. 31
	tw	1820 Nov. 1-1841, June 30
PPFfHi	d	1825 Oct. 18
PPi		1833 Feb. 21, Apr. 8, May 1, 16, 22, 31, June 13, 18, 19, 24, 26, 29, July 15, 18, 20, 25, Aug. 8, 14, 16, 17, 21, 23, 27, 29, 30, Sept. 3, 5-7, 9-11, 13, 14, 16-21, 24, 26-28, 30, Oct. 2-5
		1834 Apr. 5, 7-22, 26, May 21, June 16, 19, July 5, 7, 10, 19, 24, 26, 28, 30, 31, Aug. 5, 6, 8, 13, 15, 16, 18, 19, 22, 23, 25, 27-30, Sept. 2-6, 9-11, 13, 15-26, Oct. 9, 14, 16, 18, 20-27, 29-Nov. 1, 3-8, 11-20, 22, 24, 27, 29, Dec. 10-12
		1835 June 17, 22, 24, 27, 29, July 3, 6-8, Sept. 1-9, 11, 15
		1836 Jan. 13, 19, 21, 22, Feb. 19, 26, Mar. 2, 3, 5, 8, 10-12, 14, 15, May 4, 7, 11-14, 27, 30, June 1, 2, 4, 7, 10
PPiHi	d	1821 Jan. 18
	tw	1829 Mar. 10-1830 Apr. 1
		1831 Jan. 1-Dec. 31
PPiUD	d	1822 July 23-1823, Aug. 5
		1826 Jan. 2-Dec. 30
		1827 Jan. 1-1829 Dec. 31
	tw	1823 Jan. 7-1824 Dec. 30
		1840 May 16, 19, Aug. 29, Sept. 5
		1841 Feb. 16, 25
PPL	sw	1820 Apr. 5-Oct. 28
	d	1820 Nov. 1-1822 Dec. 13
		1822 Dec. 16-1823, Feb. 21
		1823 Feb. 24-July 9, 11-1825, May 21
		1825 May 24-1831 Jan. 13
		1831 Jan. 15-Mar. 31, Apr. 2-July 29, Aug. 1-Oct. 14, 17-Nov. 14, 16-Dec. 10, 14-31
	tw	1822 Dec. 3-1823, Jan. 9
		1823 Jan 14-24, (25)-Feb. (25), Apr. (1)-May (3), 5-15, 20-31, Aug. 2-1824, Apr. 15
		1824 Apr. 20-1826, Jan. 5
		1826 Jan. 10-Oct. 14, 19-1827, Apr. 12, 17-May 31
		1827 June 5-1828, June 7
		1828 June 12-July 1, 8-Aug. 23, 28-1829 Apr. 16
		1829 Apr. 24-1830, Aug. 12
		1830 Aug. 17-1833, Mar. 14
		1833 Mar. 19-Apr. 4, 9-1835, Apr. 16
		1835 Apr. 21-1837, Jan. 19
		1837 Jan. 24-1840, Jan. 4
PPM ♦		1820 Oct. 31/Nov. 1, 4, 8, 11, 15, 18, 22, 25, 29, Dec. 2, 6, 9, 13, 16, 20, 23, 27-30
		1821 Jan. 2, 5/6, 9/10, 12/13, 16/17, 19/20, 23/24, 26/27, 30/31, Feb. 2/3, 6/7, 9/10, 13/14, 16/17, 20/21, 23/24, 27/28, Mar. 2/3, 6/7, 9/10, 13/14, 16/17, 20/21, 23/24, 27/28, 30/31, Apr. 3/4, 6/7, 10/11, 13/14, 17/18, 20/21, 24/25, 27/28, May 1/2, 4/5, 8/9, 11/12, 15/16, 18/19, 22/23, 25/26, 29/30, June 1/2, 5/6, 8/9, 12/13, 15/16,

NATIONAL GAZETTE AND LITERARY REGISTER, THE, *continued*

19/20, 22/23, 26/27, 29/30, July 3/4, 6/7, 10/11, 13/14, 17/18, 20/21, 24/25, 27/28, 31/Aug. 1, 3/4, 7/8, 10/11, 14/15, 17/18, 21/22, 24/25, 28/29, 31/Sept. 1, 4/5, 7/8, 11/12, 14/15, 18/19, 21/22, 25/26, 28/29

1822 Jan. 1-Mar. 6, 8-Apr. 4, 6-May 29, 31, June 2-July 3, 5-Aug. 15, 17-Dec. 31

1823 Jan. 1-Mar. 27, 29-Dec. 31

1824 Jan. 1, 2/3, 5/6, 7/8, 9/10, 12/13, 14/15, 16/17, 19/20, 21/22, 23/24, 26/27, 28/29, 30/31, Feb. 2/3, 4/5, 6/7, 9/10, 11/12, 13/14, 16/17, 18/19, 20/21, 23/24, 25/26, 27/28, Mar. 1/2, 3/4, 5/6, 8/9, 10/11, 12/13, 15/16, 17/18, 19/20, 22/23, 24/25, 26/27, 29/30, 31/Apr. 1, 2/3, 5/6, 7/8, 9/10, 12/13, 14/15, 16/17, 19/20, 21/22, 23/24, 26/27, 28/29, 30/May 1, 3/4, 5/6, 7/8, 10/11, 12/13, 14/15, 17/18, 19/20, 21/22, 26/27, 28/29, 31/June 1, 2/3, 4/5, 7/8, 9/10, 11/12, 14/15, 16/17, 18/19, 21/22, 23/24, 25/26, 28/29, 30/July 1, 2/3, 5/6, 7/8, 9/10, 12/13, 14/15, 16/17, 19/20, 21/22, 23/24, 26/27, 28/29, 30/31, Aug. 2/3, 4/5, 6/7, 9/10, 11/12, 13/14, 16/17, 18/19, 20/21, 23/24, 25/26, 27/28, Sept. 1/2, 3/4, 6/7, 8/9, 10/11, 13/14, 15/16, 17/18, 20/21, 22/23, 24/25, 27/28, 29/30

1825 Jan. 1, 3/4, 5/6, 7/8, 10/11, 12/13, 14/15, 17/18, 19/20, 21/22, 24/25, 26/27, 28/29, 31/ Feb. 1, 2/3, 4/5, 7/8, 9/10, 11/12, 14/15, 16/17, 18/19, 21/22, 23/24, 25/26, 28/29, Mar. 1, 2/3, 4/5, 7/8, 9/10, 11/12, 14/15, 16/17, 18/19, 21/22, 23/24, 25/26, 28/29, 30/31, Apr. 1/2, 4/5, 6/7, 8/9, 11/12, 13/14, 15/16, 18/19, 20/21, 22/23, 25/26, 27/28, 29/30, May 2/3, 4/5, 6/7, 9/10, 11/12, 13/14, 16/17, 18/19, 20/21, 23/24, 25/26, 27/28, 30/31, June 1/2, 3/4, 6/7, 8/9, 10/11, 13/14, 15/16, 17/18, 20/21, 22/23, 24/25, 27/28, 29/30, July 1/2, 4/5, 6/7, 8/9, 11/12, 13/14, 15/16, 18/19, 20/21, 22/23, 25/26, 27/28, 29/30, Aug. 1/2, 3/4, 5/6, 8/9, 10/11, 12/13, 15/16, 17/18, 19/20, 22/23, 24/25, 26/27, 29/30, 31/Sept. 1, 2/3, 5/6, 7/8, 9/10, 12/13, 14/15, 16/17, 19/20, 21/22, 23/24, 26/27, 28/29, 30/Oct. 1, 3/4, 5/6, 7/8, 10/11, 12/13, 14/15, 17/18, 19/20

1826 Jan. 2-9, 11-Mar. 23, 25-May 13, 16-July 3, 5-Aug. 2, 5-Nov. 9, 11-Dec. 30

1827 Jan. 2, 3/4, 5/6, 8/9, 10/11, 12/13, 15/16, 17/18, 19/20, 22/23, 24/25, 26/27, 29/30, 31/Feb. 1, 2/3, 5/6, 7/8, 9/10, 12/13, 14/15, 16/17, 19/(20), 21 (22), 23/(24), 26/(27), 28/Mar. 1, 2/3, 5/6, 7/8, 9/10, 12/13, 14/15, 16/17, 19/20, 21/22, 23/24, 26/27, 28/29, 30/31, Apr. 2/3, 4/5, 6/7, 9/10, 11/12, 13/14, 16/17, 18/(19), 20/21, 23/24, 25/26, 27/28, 30/31, July 2/3, 4/5, 6/7, 9/10, 11/12, 13/14, 16/17, 18/19, 20/21, 23/24, 25/26, 27/28, 30/31, Aug. 1/2, 3/4, 6/7, 8/9,

PHILADELPHIA COUNTY 143

10/11, 13/14, 15/16, 17/18, 20/21, 22/23, 24/25, 27/28, 29/30, 31/Sept. 1, 3/4, 5/6, 7/8, 10/11, 12/13, 14/15, 17/18, 19/20, 21/22, 24/25, 26/27, 28/29, Oct. 1/2, 3/4, 5/6, 8/9, 10/11, 12/13, 15/16, 17/18, 19/20, 22/23, 24/25, 26/27, 29/30, 31/Nov. 1, 2/3, 5/6, 7/8, 9/10, 12/13, 14/15, 16/17, 19/20, 21/22, 23/24, 26/27, 28/29, Dec. 1/2, 3/4, 5/6, 7/8, 10/11, 12/13, 14/15, 17/18, 19/20, 21/22, 24/25, 26/27, 28/29
1828 Jan. 1-Dec. 31
d 1829 Jan. 1-7, 9-Apr. 16, 18-May 4, 6-June 2, 4-Aug. 5, 7-19, 22-Sept. 21, 23-29, Oct. 1-Dec. 16, 18
tw 1829 Jan. 1, 2/3, 5/6, 7/8, 9/10, 12/13, 14/15, 16/17, 19/20, 21/22, 23/24, 26/27, 28/29, 30/31, Apr. 2/3, 4/5, 6/7, 9/10, 11/12, 13/14, 16/17, 18/19, 20/21, 23/24, 25/26, 27/28, Mar. 2/3, 4/5, 6/7, 9/10, 11/12, 13/14, 16/17, 18/19, 20/21, 23/24, 25/26, 27/28, 30/31, Apr. 1/2, 3/4, 6/7, 8/9, 10/11, 13/14, 15/16, 20/21, 22/23, 24/25, 27/28, 29/30, May 1/2, 4/5, 6/7, 8/9, 11/12, 13/14, 15/16, 18/19, 20/21, 22/23, 25/26, 27/28, 29/30, June 1/2, 3/4, 5/6, 8/9, 10/11, 12/13, 15/16, 19/20, 22/23, 24/25, 26/27, 29/30, July 1/2, 3/4, 8/9, 10/11, 13/14, 15/16, 17/18, 20/21, 22/23, 24/25, 27/28, 29/30, 31/Aug. 1, 3/4, 5/6, 7/8, 10/11, 12/13, 14/15, 17/18, 19/20, 21/22, 24/25, 26/27, 28/29, 31/Sept. 1, 2/3, 4/5, 7/8, 9/10, 11/12, 14/15, 16/17, 21/22, 23/24, 25/26, 28/29, 30/Oct. 1, 2/3, 5/6, 7/8, 9/10, 12/13, 14/15, 16/17, 19/20, 21/22, 23/24, 26/27, 28/29, 30/31, Nov. 2/3, 4/5, 6/7, 9/10, 11/12, 13/14, 16/17, 18/19, 20/21, 23/24, 25/26, 27/28, 30/Dec. 1, 2/3, 4/5, 7/8, 9/10, 11/12, 14/15, 16/17, 18/19, 21/22, 23/24, 28/29, 30/31
1830 Jan. 2-(8)-Apr. 1, 3-8, 10-June 8, 10, 11, 14-28, 30-July 3, 6-(17)-Oct. (18)-Dec. (1)-31
1831 Jan. 3-Dec. 1931
1832 Jan. 2-Dec. 22, 24, 26-(31)
1833 Jan. 1-Apr. 4, 6-Dec. 31
d 1834 Jan. (1), (2)-(6), (7)-Mar. (21)-27, 29-Apr. (21)-Dec. 31
tw 1834 Jan. 2, 3/4, 6/7, 8/9, 10/11, 13/14, 15/16, 17/18, 20/21, 22/23, 24/25, 27/28, 29/30, 31/Feb. 1, 3/4, 5/6, 7/8, 10/11, 12/13, 14/15, 17/18, 19/20, 21/22, 24/25, 26/27, 28/Mar. 1, 3/4, 5/6, 7/8, 10/11, 12/13, 14/15, 17/18, 19/20, 21/22, 24/25, 26/27, 31/Apr. 1, 2/3, 4/5, 7/8, 9/10, 11/12, 14/15, 16/17, 18/19, 21/22, 23/24, 25/26, 28/29, May 2/3, 5/6, 7/8, 9/10, 12/13, 14/15, 16/17, 19/20, 21/22, 23/24, 26/27, 28/29, 30/31, June 2/3, 4/5, 9/10, 11/12, 13/14, 16/17, 18/19, 20/21, 23/24, 25/26, 27/28, 30/July (1), 2/(3), 7/8, 9/10, 11/12, 14/15, 16/17, 18/19, 21/22, 23/24, 25/26, 28/29, 30/31, Aug. 1/2, 4/5, 6/7, 8/9, 11/12, 15/16, 18/19, 20/21, 22/23, 25/26, 27/28, 29/30, Sept. 1/2, 3/4, 5/6, 7/8, 10/11, 12/13, 15/16, 17/18, 19/20, 22/23, 24/25, 26/27, 29/30, Oct. 1/2, 3/4, 6/7, 8/9, 10/11, 13/14, 15/16, 17/18, 20/21, 24/25, 29/30, 31/Nov. 1, 3/4, 5/6,

NATIONAL GAZETTE AND LITERARY REGISTER, THE, continued

                7/8, 10/11, 12/13, 14/15, 17/18, 19/20, 21/22, 24/25, 26/27, 28/29, Dec. 1/(2), 3/4, 5/6, 8/9, 10/(11), 12/13, 15/16, 17/18, 19/20, 22/23, 24/25, 29/30
         1835 Jan. 1-16, 19-Nov. 30, Dec. 26-31
         1836 Jan. 2-5, 14-27, 29-Nov. (1)-(9)-Dec. 31
         1837 Jan. (3)- Nov. 9, 11-Dec. (16)-30
         1838 Jan. 1-9, 11-Feb. 7, 9-(10)-18, 20-27, Mar. 1-Apr. 12, 14, 15, 17-May (1)-9, 11-29, 31-Aug. (1)-Nov. 12, 14-Dec. 31
         1839 Jan. 2-Dec. 31
         1840 Jan. 1-Dec. 31
PWcHi   d 1822 Aug. 20
      tw 1825 Sept. (28)
         1826 Mar. 7
       d 1828 Mar. 11
       d 1829 Feb. 5, June 30
      tw 1832 Feb. 2-11, 21, 25-Mar. 10, Nov. 20-24
      tw 1835 Jan. 27, Oct. 10, Dec. 1
      tw 1836 May 7
      tw 1839 June 27-July 4, 9-Dec. 24, 31
      tw 1840 Jan. 2-Apr. 7, 16, 21-June 13, 18-25, 30-July (23)-25-Aug. (27-29)-Sept. (1)-(10)-Dec. 24, 31
       d 1841 Jan. 18, 19
      tw 1841 Jan. 2-12, 23-Apr. 20, 23-May 13, 18-July 7, 10-Aug. 12, 17-Oct. 2

Merged with *Pennsylvania Inquirer,* and title changed to *Pennsylvania Inquirer and National Gazette,* Jan. 1, 1842 (see under *Philadelphia Inquirer Public Ledger*)

NATIONAL GAZETEER AND LITERARY RECORDER (Dec. 15, 1827-Dec. 25, 1830) tw
    PPi   1827 Dec. 15-1829 Mar. 7
               1830 Apr. 3-Dec. 25

NATIONAL INDEPENDENT AND INDUSTRIAL PROTECTOR (1870-1871) w ♩
    INDUSTRIAL PROTECTOR (1870) w ♩
    Pub. 1870 J. W. Cutter
    Ed. 1870 William Y. Leader
                continued as
    NATIONAL INDEPENDENT AND INDUSTRIAL PROTECTOR (1871) w ♩
    Pub. 1871 C. H. Leader & Co.

NATIONAL INDUSTRIAL REVIEW (1921-1928) w
    Pub. 1921-1922   National Industrial Review Publishing Co.
           1922   H. Harry McGill
    Ed. 1921-1922   James Carew
           1922   H. Harry McGill
    PP   1921 Oct. 19, 26, Nov. 2
         1922 Apr. 19-May 3, 17-Sept. 6, Dec. 6
         1924 Sept.
         1927 Sept., Dec.
         1928 Jan.

PHILADELPHIA COUNTY 145

NATIONAL MAIL   (Jan. 17-July 18, 1874||)   dem w
   Pub. & Ed. 1874 B. W. Lacy
      PJenkT   1874 Jan. 17-July 18

NATIONAL PALLADIUM AND FREEMAN'S JOURNAL   (1804-1828) d tw fed * #
   PHILADELPHIA EVENING POST, THE, (Feb. 20, 1804-June 11, 1804) d #
      Pub. 1804   William M'Corkle
         PDoHi   1804 Mar. 30*
         PHi   1804 Feb. 20-June 11
         PPAT   1804 Feb. 20-June 11
                     continued as
   FREEMAN'S JOURNAL, AND PHILADELPHIA DAILY ADVERTISER, THE (June 12, 1804-Nov. 30, 1808) d tw
     (d June 12, 1804-Nov. 30, 1808; tw Feb. 20, 1805-Nov. 30, 1808
     As: *Freeman's Journal for the Country, The*)
     Tri-weekly edition entitled *Freeman's Journal for the Country, The*
   Pub. 1804-1808 William M'Corkle
      P   d 1805 Dec. 24
               1808 Nov. 29
      PDoHi   d 1807 Apr. 11, Oct. 28-Nov. 7
      PHi   d 1804 June 12-1808 Nov. 30
      PLaHi   d 1805 June 6, 8, 20, 27, July 16, 18, 20, 30, Aug. 1, 3, 6, 8, 15, 24, 29, Sept. 3, 5, 7, 10, 19, 28, Oct. 3, 5, 8, 10, 12, 15, 19, 22 24 31, Nov. 5, 7, 9, 12, 14-16, 19, 21, 30, Dec. 3, 5, 10, 12, 19, 21, 24, 28, 31
                 1806 Jan. 4, 7, 9, 11, 18, 21, 22, 25, 30, Feb. 1, 4, 6, 8, 13, 18, 20, 22, 27, Mar. 1, 2, 4, 5, 11, 13, 18, 20, 21, 25, 26, 29, Apr. 1, 3, 4, 10, 17-22, 29, May 1, 2, 6, 8, 10, 15, 17, 20, 22, 24, 27, 29, 31, June 3, 5, 10, 12, 14, 17, 19, 21, 24, July 1, 3, 8, 10, 12, 17, 19, 22, 24, 26, 29, 31, Aug. 2, 5, 9, 14, 16, 19, 21, 23, 28, Sept. 2.
           tw 1805 June 5, 7, 19, 26, July 3, 15, 19, 24, 29-Aug. 7, 14, 23, 28, Sept. 2-9, 18, 27, Oct. 2-14, 18-23, 30, Nov. 4-13, 18, 20, 29, Dec. 2, 4, 9, 11, 18, 20, 23, 27, 30
               1806 Jan. 1-10, 17, 20-24, 29-Feb. 7, 12, 17-21, 28-Mar. 5, 10, 12, 17-Apr. 3, 9, 11, 15-18, 30, May 3-9, 14, 19-23, 28-June 2, 11-30, July 5-11, 16-Aug. 4, 8, 15-22, 27, Sept. 1
                 continued as
   FREEMAN'S JOURNAL AND PHILADELPHIA MERCANTILE ADVERTISER, THE (Dec. 1, 1808-Jan. 6, 1827) d tw sw *
     Pub. 1808-1810 William M'Corkle and James Elliot
         1810-1817 William M'Corkle
         1817-1823 William M'Corkle & Son
                    (Joseph P. Hamelin)
         1823-1824 William M'Corkle & Joseph Hamelin
         1824-1827 Joseph P. Hamelin
     Semi-weekly entitled *Freeman's Journal and Columbian Chronicle*
      P   1809 July 3-Dec. 30
               1814 Jan. 6

NATIONAL PALLADIUM AND FREEMAN'S JOURNAL, *continued*

              sw 1815 Jan. 3-1816 June 2
PDoHi   1808 Dec. 1-26, 28-31
                 1809 Jan. 2-Mar. 30, Apr. 1-July 4, 6-Nov. 30
                 1810 July 4
                 1811 Jan. 7-Apr. 12, 15-30, May 2-16, 18-July 4, 6-16
                 1813 Jan. 1-June 30, July 20, Aug. 18
                 1814 Oct. 24, 28-Nov. 7, 12-21, 23-29, Dec. 1-16, 19-21, 23, 24, 31
                 1815 Jan. 3-6, 11, 26, Feb. 14, 18, 20, 23-27, Mar. 20, 23, Apr. 4, 5, May 23, 25-29, June 24, July 11, 12, Aug. 7-15, 17-19, Sept. 20
                 1816 June 8, July 5, 20, 22, 26, 27
                 1817 May 10, July 7, 8, Aug. 7, 12, 13, 16, 18, 23, 28, Oct. 2
                 1818 Mar. 20, Apr. 8, Sept. 4, 9, 11-15, 21
                 1819 June 22, 23, 25, July 8, 9, 26, 30
                 1820 Aug. 23-29, 31-Sept. 2, 5, 6, Oct. 17, 19-31, Nov. 2-4
                 1826 July 10
PE   1810 Dec. 7
PEHi ♦ sw 1810 Jan. 30-Feb. 20, June 5-19, July 24, Aug. 14-Sept. 4, 11, 21, 25, Oct. 2-9, 26, 30, Nov. 6, 9, 20, 23, 30, Dec. 4, 14
                 1811 Sept. 11, Oct. 11, 22
PHi   1808 Dec. 1-1812, Dec. 31
                 1814 Jan. 1-Dec. 31
           sw 1813 Jan. 19
                 1814 Jan. 19
                 1815 Nov. 17
PP   1809 Mar. 15
                 1816 Dec. 5
                 1817 Dec. 4
                 1818 Sept. 29, Oct. 26, Nov. 18
                 1820 May 19, June 29, July 1, 12, Aug. 9, 17, 25, Sept. 29, Oct. 6, Nov. 2, 3, 8, Dec. 19
                 1821 Jan. 24
PPF   1821 Jan. 1-Dec. 31
PPiUD   1812 Dec. 9, 31
           sw 1813 Jan. 1-Dec. 31
PPL   1825 Mar. 2-1826 Jan. 23
                 1826 Jan. 25-Oct. 10, 12-1827 Jan. 6
PPM   1808 Dec. (1)-31
                 1809 Jan. 2-Mar. 16, 18-(29), 30, Apr. (1)-Aug. (28)-Sept. 7, 9-Dec. 22
                 1810 June 30/July 3-Dec. 31
                 1811 Jan. 1-Feb. (26)-June (25), July 1-Dec. 31
                 1812 Jan. 1-Feb. 26, (28)-Mar. 27, 30-June (13)-July (9)-(13)-(21)-30, Aug. 1-Dec. 25, 28-31
                 1815 Jan. 2-12, 14-Mar. 24, 27-Apr. 13, 15, Dec. 30
                 1816 Jan. 1-Dec. 20-31
PRHi   1809 June 16
                 1810 Mar. 15, 16, 20, 25, Apr. 17, 24, 27, May 1, 8, 15, 22, 23, 31, June 1, July 2, 9, 17, 20, 27, 28, Aug. 7, 10, 14, 21, 28, 29, Sept. 4, 10, 11, 14, 18, 21, 25, 27, 28, Oct. 2, 8, 9, 12, 16, 19, 23-30, Dec. 4, 7, 10, 11, 13, 17, 21, 26

PHILADELPHIA COUNTY 147

       1811 Mar. 15, Apr. 1, 5, 9, June 22
       1813 Jan. 1-8, 12, 14, 25, 29, Feb. 6-12, 16, 18-Mar.
         2, 5, 26, Apr. 6, 16, 19, 20, May 11, 14, 18, 25,
         June 10, 11, 22, July 9, 19
     sw 1814 Feb. 25, Mar. 15-Nov. 22, 29-Dec. 30
       1815 Jan. 3-Mar. 10
  PWbW sw [1814 Nov. 8-1815 July 14]
  PWcHi   1820 Nov. 6
  Absorbed the *City Register and Daily Advertiser,* Nov. 1, 1824
       continued as
  NATIONAL PALLADIUM AND FREEMAN'S JOURNAL (Jan. 8,
   1827-Apr. 8, 1828||) d * ♦
  Pub. 1827   James A. Jones
     1827   Jones & Greene
     1827-1828 James A. Jones
  Ed. 1827-1828 Charles G. Greene, James Athearn, James A. Jones

NATIONAL REVIEWER (1826) w ♦ *

NATIONAL UNION (1838) w ♦ *

NATIONAL UNION (June 4, 1864-Sept. 24, 1864) w
  Pub. & Ed. 1864 J. H. Vosburg
    PHi   1864 June 4
    PPot   1864 Sept. 24

NATIONAL WHIG (1839) w ♦ *

NATIVE AMERICAN (Apr. 11, 1844-July 26, 1866) d w *
  Pub. 1844-1866 Hector Orr
  Ed. 1844-1866 Samuel R. Kramer
   Weekly edition entitled *American Weekly Sentinel,* Aug. 2, 1845
    to Nov. 29, 1845
    PBL ♦   1844 July 17, Aug. 20, Sept. 5
    PHHi   1845 Aug. 2-Nov. 29
    PHi   1844 June 15, 26, July 30, Aug. 1, 12, Sept. 16
          1845 Feb. 22
    PPCHi   1844 June 1, 2, 4, 6-12, 15-17, 19-21, 24-July 4, 9,
          10, 13, 20, 23, 24, 26
    PWcHi   1845 Feb. 17

NATIVE EAGLE AND AMERICAN ADVOCATE (1845-1849) d *
  AMERICAN ADVOCATE, THE (1844-1845) d
  Pub. 1844-1845 William D. Baker
    PE   1845 Mar. 21
    PPiUD   1844 Oct. 26, 28
        merged with
  NATIVE EAGLE (1845) d *
  Pub. 1845   William Nichols
  Ed. 1845   Peter Sken Smith
    PBL ♦   1845 May 30 (Vol. 1, No. 22), July 31
        continued as
  NATIVE EAGLE AND AMERICAN ADVOCATE (1845-1849) d *
  Pub. & Ed. 1845-1849 William D. Baker, Peter Sken Smith, Henry
        H. K. Elliott

NATIVE EAGLE AND AMERICAN ADVOCATE, continued
  PHi 1846 June 3, Dec. 28
  PWcHi 1846 Oct. 10

NAZARENE AND UNIVERSALIST FAMILY COMPANION
(Jan. 4, 1840-Dec. 30, 1843||)
  Pub. 1840-1843 Gihon, Fairchild & Co.
  Ed. 1840-1843 Asher Moore, T. D. Cook, John Perry, John Gihon
  PPL   1842 Jan. 1-Mar. (19)-Oct. 8, 22-Dec. 24
      1843 Jan. 7-Nov. 11, Dec. 2-30

NEAL'S SATURDAY GAZETTE, see Saturday Evening Mail

NEAL'S SATURDAY GAZETTE AND LADY'S LITERARY MUSEUM, see Saturday Evening Mail

NEUE FREIE PRESSE (1886-1889) d morn for (English & German) rep ♦
  Pub. & Ed. 1889 J. E. Metzger

NEUE PHILADELPHISCHE CORRESPONDENZ (1779-1812) w sw for #
  PHILADELPHISCHES STAATSREGISTER (July 21, 1779-1781) w #
  Pub. 1779-1781 Steiner & Cist
       (Melchior Steiner and Carl Cist)
  PPAP 1779 July 21-Aug. 4
      1780 May 24
  PPeS 1779 Sept. 29
    continued as
  GEMEINNUTZIGE PHILADELPHISCHE CORRESPONDENZ
  (May 2, 1781-Oct. 1, 1790) w #
  Pub. 1781-1790 Melchior Steiner
  PHi ♦ 1781 July 18-25, Aug. (1)-(8)-(15)-(22)-(29)-Sept. (5)-(12)-(19)-1783 Feb. 4
      1783 May 27-Aug. 26, Sept. 9-Oct. 14, 28-Nov. 25, Dec. 9-30
      1784 Jan. 6-July 13, Sept. 28, Oct. 19-Nov. 2, 16, Dec. 14
      1785 Feb. (22), May 3, June 14
      1786 Jan. 10-Mar. 7, 21, Apr. 4-25, May 9, 23, Aug. 15-22, Sept. 3-Dec. 26
      1787 Jan. 9-Mar. 13, Apr. 17-June 26, July 17-24, Aug. 7-1788, Feb. 26
      1788 Mar. 11-Apr. 15, May 20-June 10, 24-Sept. 30, Oct. 14-21, Nov. 4-Dec. 16
      1789 Jan. 6-Feb. 10, May 26, June 23, Aug. 18, Sept. (1)-8, Oct. (13)-20, Dec. 22
      1790 June 1, Aug. 10
  PPAP 1783 Oct. 14-Dec. 2, 16, 23
      1784 Jan. 6-Mar. 16, Apr. 6-June 29, July 20-Aug. 3, 24-31, Sept. 14, Oct. 12-26, Dec. 21
      1785 Mar. 29, Apr. 5, 19-May 3, 17, 24, June 14, 21, July 5-Aug. 2, 16, 30, Sept. 6, Oct. 18, Nov. 8-22, Dec. 13, 27

PHILADELPHIA COUNTY 149

      1786 Jan. 3, 17-24, Feb. 7-14, Mar. 14, May 16, June 6-July 4, 25, Aug. 15-22, Sept. 12-19, Nov. 7-28, Dec. 19
      1787 Jan. 2, 16, Feb. 6
PPeS   1787 Nov. 27, Dec. 18
PPK   1781 Aug. 1, 29
      1782 June 12
      1783 Jan. 14, 21
      1786 Feb. 28, Mar. 7
      1789 Aug. 18, Oct. 13
      continued as

NEUE PHILADELPHISCHE CORRESPONDENZ (Oct. 1, 1790-Nov. 20, 1792) sw w #
Pub. 1790-1792 Melchior Steiner
  1792   Steiner and Kammerer
       (Heinrich Kammerer)
P   1791 Jan. 11-1792 Nov. 20
PHi   1790 Oct. 5-1792 Nov. 20
PPeS   1791 Jan. 4, June 3-14
      1792 June 5-July 24, Aug. 14-Sept. 4, Oct. 2
PPK   1792 Feb. 17
      continued as

PHILADELPHISCHE CORRESPONDENZ (Nov. 27, 1792-Apr. 1800) sw w #
Pub. 1792-1798 Steiner and Kammerer
  1798   Heinrich Kammerer, Jr., and Joseph R. Kammerer
  1798-1799 Joseph R. Kammerer & Co.
  1799-1800 Joseph R. Kammerer and George Helmbold, Jr.
  1800   George Helmbold, Jr.
Paper suspended from Sept. 18 to Nov. 13, 1798
P   1792 Nov. 27-1796 Dec. 30
PHi   1792 Nov. 27-1793 Sept. 6
      1793 Nov. 29, Dec. 17, 20
      1794 Jan. 4, Feb. 7, 14, 18, 25, 28, Mar. 4, 7, 11, 18, 28, Apr. 1, 4, 15, 22, 25, May 6, 16, 23, 30, June 13, July (8), Aug. 19, 26, Dec. 5
      1795 Jan. (16), 23, 30, Feb. 6, 24, Mar. 13, Apr. (10), 14, 24, June 5, 23, July 31, Aug. 1, 4, (14), Sept. 15, 29, Dec. (18), 25, 29
      1796 Jan. 1, 8, 12, (15), 19, Feb. 23, Mar. 18, 22, Apr. 22, May (20), June 7, 21, 28, July 1, 15, 19, Sept. 20, Oct. 7, Dec. 16, 30
      1798 May 1-1799 Dec. 31
      Missing:
      1798 Sept. 11
      1799 Mar. 26, Aug. 6, Dec. 17
PPeS   1792 Nov. 27-Dec. 24
      1793 Sept. 10
      1794 June 13, 27
      1795 Apr. 17, May 1-June 2, 12-16, 23-30, July 10-14
PPK   1794 Feb. 18, Aug. 19
      continued as

NEUE PHILADELPHISCHE CORRESPONDENZ (Apr. 1800-Aug. 25, 1812||) w #

NEUE PHILADELPHISCHE CORRESPONDENZ, *continued*
  Pub. 1800-1808 G. Helmbold and John Geyer
    1808-1812 John Geyer
  PBMa   1800 Dec. 24
  PHi   1800 Apr. 23, July 23, 30
  PNo   1802 Dec. 21-1809 Dec. 26

NEUE WELT, DIE, see Philadelphia Demokrat

NEW AGE (1895-1899) w free silver ♦
  Pub. & Ed. 1897-1899 Marvin G. Sperry

NEW AMERICAN, THE (1895)
  PWeT   1895 Aug. 2

NEW CENTURY FOR WOMEN, THE (May 13, 1876-Nov. 11, 1876||)
w
  Pub. Women's Centennial Committee, Woman's Building, International Exhibition, Philadelphia.
  PDoHi   1876 Sept. 30
  PHi ♦   1876 Aug. 26
  PP   1876 May 13-Nov. 11
  PWcHi   1876 May 13-Nov. 11

NEW CHRISTIANITY (1887-1889) w rel ♦
  Pub. 1887-1889 Swedenborg Publishing Association
  Ed. 1887-1889 B. F. Barrett and S. H. Spencer

NEW ENTERPRISES (1884-1886) w sw ♦
  Pub. & Ed. 1884-1886 A. C. Farley & Co.

NEW ERA, THE (Sept. 23, 1865-June 9, 1866||) w (Manayunk)
  Pub. & Ed. 1865-1866 William M. Runkel
    PHi ♦   1865 Sept. 23-1866 June 9

NEW ERA (1881-1917) w ind rep (Tacony) ♦
  NEW ERA (1881-1888) w ♦
  Pub. & Ed. 1885-1887 Watson & Mills
      1887-1888 Mills & Titus
      continued as
  TACONY NEW ERA (1889-1915) w ♦
  Pub. & Ed. 1889-1908 Mills & Titus
      1908-1914 W. W. Hall and William F. A. Titus
      1914   W. W. Hall
      continued as
  NEW ERA (1916-1917) w ind ♦
  Pub. & Ed. 1916-1917 W. W. Hall

NEW ERA (1900-1904) w labor ♦
  Pub. & Ed. 1903-1904 Edward Moore

PHILADELPHIA COUNTY   151

NEW WORLD, THE   (1796-1797)   td d #
   NEW WORLD, THE; or MORNING AND EVENING GAZETTE,
    THE (Aug., 1796-Oct. 22, 1796) td #
   Pub. 1796   Samuel Harrison Smith
       PHi   ◆   1796 Oct. 4 (Vol. 1, No. 87)
                   continued as
   NEW WORLD (Oct. 24, 1796-Aug. 16, 1797||)d #
   Pub. 1796-1797   Samuel Harrison Smith
       PCHi   1796 Nov. 19
       PHi   ◆   1796 Nov. 11, 14
                   1797 Jan. 4, 6, 7, Feb. 18, Mar. 8, 10, 18, 24, 28, 30,
                        31, Apr. 6, 12, 15, 17, 18, 20, 28, May 1, 8, 19,
                        22, 23, 26, 27, 29, 30, June 1-3, 6-10, 12, 13, 20,
                        26, 27, 29, 30, July 8, 12, 13, 15, 20, 21, 24
       PPL   1796 Oct. 25-Nov. 4, 7-9, 11-17, 21-Dec. 2, 5-7, 9-24,
                        27, 29-1797 Jan. 3
                     1797 Jan. 20, Feb. 7-Mar. 8, 10-24, 27, Apr. 5, 7-24,
                        26-May 16, 18-June 27, 29-July 11, 13-Aug. 2,
                        4-9, 14-16

NEWS   (1829) w ♦ *

NEWS   (1877)   d evg ♦
   Pub. 1877   F. A. Kauffman
   Ed. 1877   Audubon Davis

NEWS GLEANER,   see Frankford News Gleaner

NEWS-POST   (1912-1913) d evg ind ♦
   Pub. 1912-1913   Hamilton B. Clark
   Ed. 1912-1913   Marlene E. Pew

NICETOWN HERALD   (Oct. 1, 1935†) w
   Pub. & Ed. 1935   Harry Yudelson
       PUB   1935 Oct. 1†

NICETOWN SIGNAL   (1884-1903) w ♦
   Pub. & Ed. 1884-1903   Charles F. Kerbaugh

NICETOWN SUN   (1877-1905) w ind ♦
   Pub. & Ed. 1890-1905   Edwin A. Fricke

**NIVEAU DE L'EUROPE ET DE L'AMERIQUE SEPTENTRIO-
NALE,**   see Level of Europe and North America; or The Observer's Guide

NORD AMERIKA   (1873†) w for rel
   Pub. 1873-1874   Joseph Berndt
       1874-1875   German Publishing Society
       1875-1880   German Volksblatt Society
       1880-1884   Philadelphia Volksblatt Society
       1884-1893   Volksblatt Publishing Co. (In the interest of St.
                      Vincent's Orphan Asylum)
       1893-1898   Charles J. Young
       1898-1941   John Wiesler, Jr.

NORD AMERIKA, *continued*
    Ed. 1873-1898   Joseph Berndt
          1898-1903   John Wiesler, Jr.
          1903-1908   Joseph Berndt
          1936-1940   Joseph Gross
          1940-1941   A. L. Ellerkamp
    PUB   1873 Sept. 13†
    PP   1931 June 18†
    PPCHi   1884 Dec. 20
                      1885 Jan. 3
                      1887 Oct. 1-Nov. 12
                      1888 Mar. 17-Apr. 14
                      1889 Aug. 14
                      1890 Jan. 1-1900 June 30
                      1907 Mar. 28-1912 Mar. 28

NORTH AMERICAN   (1771-1925) d tw w * #
    PENNSYLVANIA PACKET; AND THE GENERAL ADVERTISER, THE (Oct. 28, 1771-Oct. 18, 1773) w #
    Pub. 1771-1773   John Dunlap
        PHi   1771 Oct. 28-1773 Oct. 18
        PPL   1771 Oct. 28-1773 Oct. 18
        PWcHi   1771 Oct. 28-1773 Oct. 18
                      continued as
    DUNLAP'S PENNSYLVANIA PACKET, or, THE GENERAL ADVERTISER (Oct. 25, 1773-Nov. 22, 1777) w sw #
    Pub. 1773-1777   John Dunlap
        P   1776 July 8
        P-M   1776 July 8
        PDoHi   1774 Oct. 24
                    1775 Jan. 21
        PHaC   1777 June 10
        PHi   1773 Oct. 25-1777 Nov. 22
        PPL   1773 Oct. 25-1777 Sept. 9
        PPot   1776 July 8
        PPotW   1776 July 8
        PScrG   1776 July 8
        PWcHi   1773 Oct. 25-Dec. 27
                    1774 Jan. 3-1776 May 6
                    1776 May 20-July 1, 15-Aug. 20, Sept. 10, 17, Dec. 18, 27
Nov. 29, 1777-June 18, 1778, because of the British occupation of Philadelphia, this paper was published under the title of *The Pennsylvania Packet,* or, *The General Advertiser,* at Lancaster, Pa.
                    continued as
    THE PENNSYLVANIA PACKET, or, THE GENERAL ADVERTISER (July 4, 1778-Oct., 1783) tw sw #
    Pub. 1778-1780   John Dunlap
            1780-1781   John Dunlap and David C. Claypoole
            1781-1783   David C. Claypoole
        P   1778 Feb. 18-Dec. 22
                    1781 Oct. 28-1784 Sept. 18
        PBMa   tw 1778 Dec. 8
                    sw 1780 Nov. 4-14, 28, Dec. 30
        PDoHi   tw 1778 July 16, Nov. 7, 14, 28
                    tw 1779 Jan. 9, Feb. 4, June 12, July 3, 24, Sept. 18

PHILADELPHIA COUNTY   153

                          sw 1780 June 13, 27, July 11, 15, 25, Aug. 5-15, 22-
                                    Sept. 5, 12, 19-Oct. 28, Nov. 4, 7
                          tw 1781 Jan. 1-8
                          tw 1784 Mar. 18
          PHi   1778 July 4-1783 Oct. 11
          PP   ♦   1777 Dec. 3, 17-24
                              1778 Sept. 8-29
                              1779 Aug. 28
          PPAP   1777 Nov. 29-1778 Feb. 4
                              1778 May 6, 23, June 3-10, Sept. 17-22, Oct. 29,
                                    Nov. 3, 12
                              1779 Jan. 2-9, (14), 19-Feb. 18, Mar. 6, 20-Dec. 30
                              1780 Apr. 6, Oct. 17, 21
                              1781 July 19, Aug. 4, 28, Nov. 20
                              1782 Feb. 16-Mar. 28, Apr. 2-6, 11-18, 23-June 20, 25-
                                    Aug. 6, 10-20, 24-Sept. 19, 24-1783 Jan. 28
                              1783 Feb. 6-Sept. 6, 11-16, 20-30, Oct. 2-14, 21-23,
                                    Nov. 4-11, 15-20, 25-Dec. 20, 25-1784 Feb. 12,
                                    (14)-Mar. 13
                              1784 Mar. 18-20, 25, Aug. 19, Sept. 2-4, 9, 14
          PPL   1777 Nov. 29, Dec. 17
                              1778 Jan. 7, 21-Mar. 11, 25-June 17, July 4-9, 14-18,
                                    30, Aug. 9, 18, 22, 27, Sept. 1-3, 12-15, 22, 26,
                                    Oct. 8, 13-15, 22, 27-Nov. 7, 19-21, 26-28, Dec.
                                    3-15, 21, 29-31
                              1779 Mar. 27, Apr. 1-May 1, 8-13, 18-June 1, 5,
                                    10-19, 24-July 13, 20-29, Aug. 3-5, 10-21, 26-
                                    Sept. 4, 9-16, 28-30, Oct. 5, 14, Nov. 13-23
                              1780 Jan. 1-Feb. 10, 15-Apr. 4, 8-July 25, Aug. 6-
                                    Sept. 12, 19-23, 30-Dec. 23, 30-1781 Jan. 9
                              1781 Jan. 23-Feb. 20, 27, Mar. 10-May 15, 22-July
                                    14, 19-Sept. 15, 20-25, 29-Oct. 25, Nov. 1-6,
                                    15-1782 Feb. 26
                              1782 Mar. 2-9, 14-May 9, 14-June 18, 22-Oct. 8, 12-
                                    Dec. 24, 28-31
                              1783 Jan. 21-Feb. 8, 13-Apr. 22, 26-May 24, 29-June
                                    12, 17-28, July 3-Sept. 20
          PWbW   1784 Apr. 1, May 20
          PWcHi   tw 1779 Jan. 2-Dec. 7, 11-30
                          tw 1780 Jan. 1-Apr. 4
                          sw 1780 Apr. 8-Sept. 12, 19-Dec. 30
                          tw 1781 Oct. 16-Nov. 15, 20-1784 Sept. 18
                              continued as
THE PENNSYLVANIA PACKET AND GENERAL ADVERTISER
     (Oct. 14, 1783-Sept. 18, 1784) tw sw #
Pub. 1783-1784   David C. Claypoole
          PHi   ♦   1783 Oct. 14-1784 Sept. 18
          PPL   1784 Jan. 3-6, 10, 15-17, 22-June 26, 29-Sept. 18
                              continued as
THE PENNSYLVANIA PACKET AND DAILY ADVERTISER
     (Sept. 21, 1784-Dec. 31, 1790) d #
Pub. 1784-1790   John Dunlap and David C. Claypoole
          P   1784 Sept. 21-1790 Dec. 31
          PCarlHi   1790 July 6, 15-17, Aug. 2, 3, 5-7, 11-14, 26, Sept.
                                    14, 18, 21, 24, 25, 29, 30, Oct. 1, 5, 9, Nov.
                                    4, Dec. 20, 22, 23

NORTH AMERICAN, *continued*

    PDoHi   1784 Nov. 5
                1785 Sept. 12, Nov. 2, 8, 10, 12, 14, 16, 23, 28, 30, Dec. 1, 5, 22, 24, 30, 31
                1787 Mar. 8, May 19
                1788 June 18
                1789 July 16
    PE   1788 Feb. 15
                1789 Aug. 11
    PEHi   1788 Aug. 26
    PHi   1784 Sept. 21-1790 Dec. 30
    PLaHi   1789 May 23-1790 May 21
    PLanA1 1784 Sept. 21
    PNoHi   1784 Sept. 21
    PP ♦   1784 Sept. 21
                1785 July 27
                1787 Sept. 13
                1788 May 5-1790 Aug. 24
                1790 Aug. 26-Dec. 31
    PPAP   1784 Sept. 23-30, Oct. 2-8, 12, 13, 16, 19-23, 26-Nov. 1, 3, 5, 8, 25, Dec. 3, 8, 15, 27, (29)
                1785 Mar. 7, 15, 19, 29, 31, Apr. 1, 4, 6-18, 20-May 7, 10-25, 27, 28, 30, 31, June 4-9, 11-20, 22-28, July 2, 4, 6-11, 18, 19, 21, 23-28, 30, Aug. 2, 3, 6-15, 17, 19, 22-25, 27-Sept. 1, 7-14, 16, 17, 19, 21-26, 28, 29, Oct. 1-6, 8, 11, 12, 14, 17-25, 27-29, Nov. 2-11, 14, 17, 19-24, 26-28, 30, Dec. 2-14, 16-26, 28, 29, 31
                1786 Jan. 2-12, 14, 17-28, 31, Feb. 22, 24-Mar. 1, 3, 4, 7-20, 22, 23, 25, 28-31, Apr. 3-5, 7-11, 13-22, 25-May 2, 4, 5, 8-June 2, 6, 7, 9, 10, 12, 13, 15-26, 28-July 3, 5-14, 18-21, 24, 26-Aug. 1, 3, 4, 7-12, 14-21, 23, 24, 26-Sept. 4, 6-18, 20, 21, 23, 26, 27, Oct. 2, 5-11, 14, 16, 18, 19, 23-25, 31, Nov. 2, 6-9, 11, 15-21, 27, 30-Dec. 5, 7, 12-25, 27, 29
                1788 Jan. 1-Feb. 11, 13-Mar. 6, 8-Apr. 5, 8-May 23, 26-June 23, 25-30, July 2-Oct. 23, 25-1789 Jan. 17
                1789 Jan. 20-Feb. 20, 23-Apr. 4, 6-June 2, 4-Nov. 14, 17-25, 27, 30, Dec. 1, 3-1790 Apr. 1
                1790 Apr. 3-June 5, 8-Dec. 31
    PPCHi   1784 Sept. 21
    PPeS   1784 Sept. 21
    PPiHi   1788 Jan. 16
    PPiUD   1784 Sept. 21
                1785 Jan.-1786 Dec. 30
                1787 Oct. 17-1789 Nov. 24
                1789 Dec. 24, 25
    PPL   1784 Sept. 21-1788 Jan. 18
                1788 Jan. 21-May 31, June 2-July 9, 11-Nov. 27, Dec. 1-1789 Jan. 14
                1789 Jan. 16-19, 21-24, 27-Mar. 2, 4-Apr. 4, 6-May 21, 23-Nov. 4, 6-Dec. 7, 9-12-1790 May 18
                1790 May 20-28, 31-Dec. 31
    PPM ♦   1784 Sept. 21-Dec. 31
                1785 Jan. 1-Sept. 20, 22-Dec. 31
                1786 Jan. 2-Sept. 20, 26-Dec. 30

PHILADELPHIA COUNTY 155

—	1787 Jan. 1-Sept. 18, 20-Dec. 31
	1788 Jan. 1-July 8, 11-Dec. 31
	1789 Jan. 1-May (26)-Dec. 31
PPot	1784 Sept. 21
	1786 Aug. 1, Sept. 21
PPotW	1784 Sept. 21
	1786 Aug. 1
PShS	1784 Sept. 21
PU	1785 Jan. 1-1787 Dec. 31
	1788 July-1790 Dec. 31
PWaHi	1788 Aug. 2
PWbW	1788 July 14
PWcHi	1784 Sept. 21-Dec. 31
	1785 Jan. 1-Oct. 13
	1787 July 12
	1788 Aug. 2

continued as

DUNLAP'S AMERICAN DAILY ADVERTISER (Jan. 1, 1791-Dec. 8, 1793) d #

Pub. 1791-1793	John Dunlap
P	1791 Jan. 1-1793 Sept. 14
PBMa	1792 Jan. 28-Feb. 1
PDoHi	1792 June 12
PHi	1791 Jan. 1-1792 July (16)
	1792 Nov. 9, 12, 16 (sup.)
	1793 June (4) (sup.), Dec. 7
PP ♦	1791 Jan. 1-1792 June 12
	1792 June 14-Oct. 12, 14-1793 June 30
PPAP	1791 Jan. 1-Apr. 29, May 2-1792 June 12
	1792 June 14-Oct. 12, 14-1793 June 29
PPi	[1792 Feb. 2-Aug. 1]
	1793 Jan.-June
PPiHi	[1793 Jan. 2-Sept. 14]
PPiUD	1791 Jan. 1-1793 May 11
PPL	1791 Jan. 1-1793 Sept. 14
	1793 Dec. 2-8
PPM ♦	1793 Jan. 1-Sept. 14, Dec. 2-8
PSuHi	1791 May 28
PU	1791 Jan. 1-1793 Dec. 8
PWcHi	1792 June 7, July 31
	1793 Jan. 15, 17, 19, 21, 22, 26, 28, 29, 30, 31, Feb. 1, 2, 4, 5, 6, 7, 8, 9, 11, 13, 16, 18, 19, 20, 21, 23, 26, 27, Mar. 12, 13 22, 23, 25, 29, 30, Apr. 3, 4, 6, 17, 27, 29, 30, May 1, 2, 4, 7, 15, 25, 31, **June 4, 26,** July 1, 2, 3, 4, 5, 6, 8, 9, 10, 11, 12, 13, 15, 16, 17, 18, 19, 20, 22, 23, 24, 25, 27, 29, 30, 31, Aug. 1, 2, 3, 5, 6, 7, 8, 9, 10, 13, 14, 15, 16, 17, 19, 20, 21 22, 23, 24, 26, 27, 28, 29, 30, Sept. 2, 3, 4, 5, 6, **7**

continued as

DUNLAP AND CLAYPOOLE'S AMERICAN DAILY ADVERTISER (Dec. 9, 1793-Dec. 31, 1795) d #

Pub. 1793-1795	John Dunlap and David C. Claypoole
P	1793 Dec. 9-1795 Dec. 31
PDoHi	1793 Dec. 19
	1795 Feb. 13, 26
PHHi	1794 Jan. 1-June 30

156   PENNSYLVANIA NEWSPAPERS

NORTH AMERICAN, *continued*

PHi	1793 Dec. 9-1795 Dec. 31
PMilHi	1794 Apr. 17
PP	1793 Dec. 13
	1794 Jan. 1-Mar. 6, 8-June 30
	1795 Apr. 2, 4, May 30, Sept. 22, 24
PPiHi	1793 Dec. 9-11, 13-17
PPL	1793 Dec. 9-1795 Dec. 31
PPM ♦	1793 Dec. 9-11, 13-31
	1794 Jan. 3-Feb. 19, 21-Dec. 31
	1795 Jan. 1-Dec. 31
PU	1793 Dec. 9-1795 Dec. 31
PWcHi	1793 Sept. 2-7, 9-14, Dec. 2, 5, 7, 9, 11, 13-23, 25-31
	1794 Jan. 2, 4, 9, 10, 11, 25, 29, Feb. 1, 3, 13, 14, 15, 26, Mar. 1, 6, 8, 15, 28, 29, 31, Apr. 2, 5, 7, 9, 10, 11, 12, 16, 19, 21, 23, 25, 26, 28, 30, May 1, 2, 3, 5, 6, 7, 9, 10, 14, 15, 17, 19, 20, 22, 27, 29, 31, June 2, 7, 9, 24, 25, 26, 27, 28, 30, Sept. 29

                         continued as

CLAYPOOLE'S AMERICAN DAILY ADVERTISER Jan. 1, 1796-Sept. 30, 1800)   d   #

Pub. 1796-1799	David C. Claypoole and Septimus Claypoole
1799-1800	David C. Claypoole
P	1796 Jan.-1797 Dec. 31
	1799 Jan. 1-1800 July 30
	1800 July 31
PDoHi	1796 June 27, 30, July 1
PEHi	1796 Jan. 19
PHi	1796 Jan. 1-1799 Dec. 30
	1800 June (21), Aug. 4
PP	1797 Mar. 6, July 1-31, Oct. 7, 16, 18-20, 24-26, Dec. 1, 5, 16, 19, 22
	1798 June 2, Oct. 29
PPF	1799 Aug. 10
PPiUD	[1796 Jan. 1-1799 Dec. 3]
PPL	1796 Jan. 1-May 3, 5-Aug. 4, 6
	1797 Jan. 1-Dec. 31
	1798 May 8, 10
	1799 Jan. 1-Dec. 31
	1800 Feb. 1, 4-Sept. 30
PPM ♦	1797 Jan. 2, 4-(28)-Feb. 15, 17-22, 24-Mar. 3, 7-Apr. (8)-June 5, 7-(9)-(16)-(26)-29, July 1-Aug. 21, 23-28, Sept. 1-5, 7-28, 30-Oct. 31, Nov. 2-Dec. 30
	1798 Jan. 1-May 8, 10-22, 24-Sept. 20, (24-Oct. 31)-Dec. 31
	1799 Jan. 1-Apr. 24, 26-June 19, 21-Oct. 10, 12-18, 21-23, 25-Dec. (17)-27
PU	1796 Jan. 1-1797 Dec. 31

                         continued as

POULSON'S AMERICAN DAILY ADVERTISER (Oct. 1, 1800-Dec. 28, 1839)   d   #   *

Pub. 1800-1804	Zachariah Poulson, Jr.
1804-1839	Zachariah Poulson

PHILADELPHIA COUNTY 157

P
    1800 Oct. 1-1808
    1809 Oct. 6-1811 Sept.
    1818-1822 Dec. 31
    1832 Oct. 12
    1834 Dec. 11

P-M
    1802 Apr. 22
    1804 Aug. 25
    1807 Dec. 18
    1832 Oct. 2

PAtM
    1800 Oct. 1, 2
    1811 Oct. 1
    1812 June 10, Nov. 7, 21

PBelC
    1807 Sept. 7

PBL ♦
    1818 Jan. 3-5, 8-13, 15-20, 22-27, 31, Feb. 3-7, 10-12, 14-16, 18-20, 23-Aug. 4, 6-Oct. 10, 13-16, 19-Nov. 18, 20-Dec. 31
    1837 May 9

PCHi
    1800 Nov. 18

PDoHi
    1801 Mar. 9
    1803 May 9-June 1, 27-July 2, 5, 6, 9, 11, 14, 16-Dec. 7
    1804 Dec. 22, 24, 25
    1805 Jan. 1-11, Feb. 5-Mar. 8, 18-26, Apr. 6-May 21, 31-June 12, 22-July 2, 4, 24, 31-Aug. 16, 19, 22, 27, 29, Sept. 2, Oct. 9-Nov. 19, 26-Dec. 12, 14-1806 Feb. 1
    1806 Feb. 4-Mar. 25, Apr. 3, 17, May 9, June 13, 17, 19-26, 30-July 9, 12-Aug. 5, 7, 8, 11-Sept. 3, 5-23, 25-27, 30, Oct. 2-Nov. 1, 4-1807 Feb. 21
    1807 Mar. 4-May 13, 15-June 22, 24-27, July 4, 8, 10-13, 22-Aug. 10, 17, 19-25, Sept. 3-5, 8-15, Nov. 17-28, Dec. 7-1808 Mar. 16
    1808 Mar. 24-Apr. 1, 4-23, 26-May 24, 30-June 2, 6-9, 13-16, July 5-Aug. 5, 11, 12, 16-18, 25-Oct. 8, 11, 13-15, 22-Dec. 8, 29-1809 Jan. 13
    1809 Jan. 16-Feb. 2, 4-Mar. 4, 18-Apr. 13, 24-May 20, 23, 24, 26, 29-July 8, 11-Aug. 4, 14-Oct. 9, 13, 28, Nov. 2-1810 Jan. 15
    1810 Jan. 17-20, 23-Feb. 7, 9-Mar. 1, 3-Apr. 12, 14-July 19, 21-Aug. 23, 28, 29, Sept. 1, 5, 6, 10, 14, 21, 22, 28, Oct. 4-9, 11, 13-27, 30-Nov. 28, Dec. 1-8, 26, 31
    1811 Jan. 9-17, Mar. 12, Apr. 8, 9, 11-22, 25-27, May 7, 9, 11-17, 20-June 7, 8, 11-13, 15-26, 28, 29, July 11, 15-20, 30, Aug. 2-20, 23, 26-30, Sept. 5, 7, 10-12, 14-19, 21-Oct. 5, 9-Nov. 12, Dec. 2-9, 12-14, 24, 27, 28, 31
    1812 Jan. 1, 20-Feb. 20, 24-Mar. 3, 5, 7-10, 12-17, 19-23, 26-Apr. 4, 13-June 3, 5-July 13, 17-24, 29, 30, Aug. 1-10, 14, 21-24, 27-Sept. 1, 4-10, 12, 15-18, 24, 25, Oct. 3-9, 17-24, Nov. 3-9, 11, 14-Dec. 11, 14-25, 28-1813 Jan. 23
    1813 Jan. 26-Feb. 5, 9-Mar. 8, 10-Apr. 24, 27-29, May 1-5, 7-June 8, 24-July 3, 9-21, 23-Aug. 10, 23, Oct. 5-8, 13, 18, 23-27, 29-Nov. 8, 11, 12, 15-17, 19, 22, 23, 25-27, Dec. 1-6, 9, 15-18, 21-31
    1814 Jan. 10-13, 15-17, 21, June 22, July 11, 15,

NORTH AMERICAN, *continued*

18-Aug. 13, 17-23, Sept. 2, 27, Oct. 1-3, 5-11, 13-Nov. 30, Dec. 8-31
1815 Jan. 2-7, 10-Feb. 10, 13-15, 17-Mar. 8, 10, 13-16, 18-24, 29, 30, Apr. 10-19, 24-May 3, 5, 6, 13-26, 29-June 8, 12, 14-17, 30-July 18, 20-Aug. 14, 16-Sept. 28, Oct. 2-4, 7, 10-14, 17-26, Nov. 6, 21, 24-Dec. 13, 15, 16, 30
1816 Jan. 2, 6-10, Feb. 15-23, 26-Mar. 11, 13-21, 26-Apr. 8, 10-May 3, 6-14, 27-June 3, 17, 22-24, 26-July 5, 8-27, Aug. 29-Sept. 13, Oct. 14-28, Nov. 22, 25-27, 29-Dec. 2, 5-17, 19-27
1817 Jan. 2, 21, Feb. 11, 15, 18-22, 25-Mar. 5, 7, 10-14, 17-29, Apr. 1-7, 10, 12, 15, 16, 18, 21, 22, 24, 26, 29, May 13, 15, 17-22, 24, June 9, 11, 18-20, 26, 28-30
1818 Mar. 7, 25
1820 Sept. 18
1821 Jan. 11, July 31, Aug. 2, 3, 8, Oct. 6
1824 Jan. 26
1827 Apr. 7
1828 Apr. 24
PEHi 1805 Aug. 17
1811 June 10, Sept. 9
1812 Sept. 2
1823 May 30
PHi 1800 Oct. 1-1839 Dec. 28
PNhE 1822 Jan. 16
PNoHi 1801 Dec. 22
1802 Sept. 21
PP 1803 July 2
1808 Jan. 1-Apr. 30
1816 July 31
1818 Jan. 2-Feb. 27, Mar. 1-Sept. 16, 18-Dec. 13, 19, 20, 27-29
1819 Jan. 2-Dec. 7, 12, 19, 26, 31-1820 July 19
1820 July 21-Sept. 11, 13-Dec. 31
1821 Jan. 2-June 20, 22, 24-Oct. 31, Nov. 2-4, 11, 18, 20-Dec. 5, 9, 15-17, 19-21, 23, 26-1822 Dec. 26
1822 Dec. 28-1823 Jan. 5
1823 Jan. 8, 12, 17-Oct. 8, 10, 12-Nov. 25, 30, Dec. 6-8, 14, 17-1824 Feb. 10
1824 Feb. 12-Mar. 9, 11-Apr. 27, 29-May 3, 5-12, 15, 16, 23, 30, July 10, 12-18
1825 Jan. 1-Sept. 2, 4-7, 9-13, 15, 17, 18, 20, 22-27, 29-1826 Feb. 24
1826 Feb. 26-July 6, 8-Aug. 2, 4-Dec. 22, 24, 29-31
1827 Jan. 2-1828 Feb. 27
1828 Feb. 29-Mar. 13, May 4
1833 Dec. 14
1838 Sept. 13
1839 June 28, July 1
PPAP 1817 July 1-3, 5, 7-12, 14-19, 21-26, 31, Aug. 6, 8, 14, 18, 22, 26-29, Sept. 1, 3-6, 8-13, 15-18, 20, 22-27, 29-Oct. 1, 3, 4, 6-11, 13-18, 20-25, 27-Nov. 1, 3-8, 10-15, 17-22, 24-29, Dec. 1-6, 8-13, 15, 17-20, 22-25, 27, 29-30

PHILADELPHIA COUNTY 159

PPAT	1830	Jan. 1-22, 25-Feb. 1, 13-25, 27-Mar. 10. 12-15. 17-24, 27-30, Apr. 1-5, 7, 8, 10-June 4, 7-19, 22-(24)-July 7, 10-14, 16-24, 27-29, 31-Sept. 2, 6, 7, 9-Nov. 6, 10-(12)-17, 19, 20, 23-Dec. 4, 7-(21)
	1831	Jan. (6)-10, (13), 19-21, 25-Feb. 1, 3, 7-Apr. 11, 13-20, 22, May 5, 9-12, 16-June 2, 4-11, 14-16, 18-July 6, 8, 9, 12, 13, 18, 19, 22-Aug. 5, 8, 9, 11, 12, 15-17, 19-25, 27-Sept. 3, 8, 13, 15-21, 23-27, 29-Oct. 12, 14-Nov. 3, 5-23, 25-30, Dec. 2-1832 Jan. (5)
	1832	Jan. 6, (7), 10-(14)-Feb. 9, 11-20, (22), 25-Mar. 3, 6-15, 17-27, 29-Apr. 23, 25, 26, 28, May 1-28, 30-June 21, 23-25, 27-July 4, 7-(18)-(25)-28, 31-Aug. 8, 10-13, 15-20, 22-Oct. (2)-31, Nov. 2-Dec. (8)-1839 Dec. 28
PPi	1819	June 2-Dec. 1
PPiHi	1806	Mar. 14
PPiUD	1800	Oct. 1-Dec. 31
	1812	May 30-1814 Dec. 31
	1817	Jan. 1-1818 Dec. 31
	1831	Jan. 1-June 18
	1832	Jan. 2-June 30, July 2-Dec. (18), 19-21
	1834	Jan. 1-1835 June 30
PPL	1800	Oct. 1-4, 9, 10, 13-18, 21, 22, 25-Nov. 1, 4-18, 20-28, Dec. 1-4, 6-17, 19
	1801	Jan. 1-1806 Dec. 31
	1809	Jan. 4, 6-1823 Dec. 31
	1825	Jan. 1-27, 29-Feb. 18, 21-Apr. 16, 19-July 7, 9-Sept. 28
	1827	Oct. 1-Nov. 29
	1830	Dec. 1-13
	1834	Jan. 2-16
	1835	Feb. 5-11, 13-Mar. 2, 4-May 26, 28-Dec. 28, 30
	1837	Feb. 6, 8-May 8
	1839	May 7-23, 25-Sept. 12, 14-Dec. 28
PPM ♦	1800	Oct. 2-1801 Sept. (29)
	1801	Oct. 1-1802 Jan. 26
	1802	Jan. 28-1805 Jan. (10)
	1805	Jan. 11-Sept. (9)-24, 26-1807 Jan. (6)
	1807	Jan. 7-1813 Sept. (30)
	1813	Oct. 1-1814 Sept. 9
	1814	Sept. 11-1815 Feb. (7-Mar. 25)
	1815	Mar. 27-May (25-June 17)-Sept. 30
	1818	Jan. 1-July (1-6)-Dec. (29)-31
	1819	Jan. (1-Feb. 12)-Dec. (31)
	1820	Jan. 1-Dec. 30
	1821	Feb. (23)-Dec. 31
	1822	Jan. (1)-Dec. (31)
	1823	Jan. 2-Dec. (24, 25)-(30)
	1824	Jan. (1, 2)-Dec. 30
	1825	Jan. 1-Dec. (30)
	1826	Jan. (4)-Dec. (28, 29)
	1827	Jan. 1-1828 Dec. 30
	1829	Jan. 1-Dec. 31
PPot	1809	Mar. 18
	1822	**Aug. 19**

NORTH AMERICAN, *continued*
- PU
  - 1802 Jan. 1-Dec. 31
  - 1806 July-Dec.
  - 1807 Sept.-Dec.
  - 1814 Jan. 1-1817 Dec. 31
  - 1819 Jan. 1-1829 Dec. 31
- PWbW
  - 1804 Sept. 7, Dec. 21
  - 1815 Nov. 2
- PWcHi
  - 1801 June 20, 27
  - 1804 Sept. 1-Dec. 8, 11-31
  - 1805 Jan. 1-21, 23-26, 29-Feb. 28, Mar. 6, 7, 9-13, 16-18, 20-27, 29, 30, Apr. 2, 3, 5-May 6, 8-22, 24-June 26, 28-July 5, 8-13, 16-Aug. 8, 10-31, Sept. 3, 6, 7, 10, 12-14, 17-24, 26, 28-Oct. 8, 10-12, 15-17, 21-24, 26, 29, 30, Nov. 1, 5-Dec. 17, 20-1806 Feb. 15
  - 1806 Feb. 18-Mar. 7, 10-May 12, 14-20, 22-June 9, 11-13, 17-19, 27-July 7, 9-23, 25, 28, Aug. 2, 5, 7, 11, 12, 15-Sept. 27, 30-Oct. 2, 4, 11-Nov. 24, 26-Dec. 3, 5-1807 Feb. 7
  - 1807 Feb. 10-14, 17-20, 23-27, Mar. 2, 4-10, 12-Apr. 30, May 2-June 27, 30-July 9, 11-16, 18- Sept. 11, 14-Oct. 23, 26-Dec. 31

  Poulson's American Daily Advertiser was sold to and merged with the *North American*

THE NORTH AMERICAN (March 26, 1839-Dec. 31, 1839) d w *
- Pub. 1839 S. C. Brace & T. R. Newbold
- Ed. 1839 S. C. Brace
  - PBL ♦ d 1839 Apr. 2-May 23, 25-Oct. 10, 12-17, 19, 22-Nov. 12, 14-Dec. 25, 27, 30, 31
  - PHi ♦ 1839 Mar. (27)-June 13, 15-July 18, 20-Aug. 22, 28-Sept. 25, 27-Oct. (24)-Nov. (1)-Dec. 31
  - PP 1839 Mar. 26-Dec. 31
  - PPL 1839 Oct. 2, 14

continued as

THE NORTH AMERICAN AND DAILY ADVERTISER (Jan. 2, 1840-Oct. 20, 1845) d tw w *
- Pub. 1840   S. C. Brace & T. R. Newbold
- 1840   C. G. Childs & T. R. Newbold
- 1840   C. G. Childs & Co.
- 1840-1842   Walter Colton & C. G. Childs
- 1842-1844   C. G. Childs & J. Reese Fry
- 1844-1845   C. G. Childs, J. Reese Fry and T. R. Newbold
- 1845   C. G. Childs & J. Reese Fry
- Ed. 1841-1842   Colton, Childs and Atwill

Absorbed the *Commercial Herald and Pennsylvania Sentinel,* 1840

- P   w 1840 May 23-1842 Sept. 2
- PBL ♦ d 1840 Jan. 2-9, 11-14, 16-Apr. 6, 8-24, 27, 29-May 5, 7-July 7, 9-Aug. 25, 27
       tw 1840 Jan. 9
        d 1841 Feb. 22, 24-26, Mar. 1-Apr. 20, 22-May 14, 17-June 8, 10-July 5, 7-Oct. 20, 23-Nov. 17
          1842 Jan. 5, 7-11, 13-Feb. 7, 9-14, 16-Mar. 8, 10-Apr. 11, 14, 16, 19-May 5, 7-30, June 1-3, 6-10, 14-July 4, 6-17, 19-Sept. 18, 20-Oct. 6
          1844 Mar. 2, 7, 12, 13, 16, 18, Apr. 16
          1845 Mar. 24, Apr. 15, 16, 18

PHILADELPHIA COUNTY 161

    PHi ♦   1840 Jan. (1)-9, 11-Apr. 28, 30-May 6, 8-11, 13, 14, 16-20, 22-28, June 1-20, 23-26, 29-July (10)-14, 16, 17, 20-24, (30), Aug. 1, 4, 8, 12, 15-17, 19-21, 24-Sept. (16)-24, 26-Oct. (8)-Dec. 31
           1841 Jan. 1-(11), (12), 14-(16), 19-Feb. (15), (16)-25, 27-Mar. (12)-(16)-24, 26-29, 31-Apr. 20, 22-May (1)-8, 11-14, 17-21, 24-June 2, 4-10, 12-18, 21-29, July (2)-5, 7-(10)-Aug. 13, 16-Sept. (28)-Oct. 21, 23-Nov. (4)-Dec. (1)-3, (6)-(16)-30
           1842 Jan. (1)-(3)-7, 10-Feb. 10, 14-21, 23-28, Mar. 3-7, 9-12, 15-22, 24-Apr. 2, 5-May 18, 20-23, 25-June 8, 10-July (4), 6-(15)-Aug. (1)-(20)-30, Sept. 2, (3)-6, 8-20, 22-Oct. (6)- Nov. (7)-14, 16-Dec. (1)-6, (8)-(10)-(13)-(26)-(31)
           1843 Jan. 2, (3), (4)-(7)-(9)-Feb. (6)-Mar. 8, 10-Apr. (12), 14-(21)-May (27)-July 13, 15-(19)-Aug. (1), 2, 4-(15)-18, 21-Dec. (15)-21, 23-30
           1844 Jan. (2), (3)-Feb. 28, Mar. 1-Apr. (11)-(13)-30, May 2-7, (9)-July 3, 8-(13)-Sept. 21, 24-Nov. 4, 6-8, 11-29, Dec. 6, (7)-(10), 12, 13, 16-(31)
           1845 Jan. 1-8, 10-May (26), (27)-June (21)-(27)-July (1)-Sept. 5, 8-Oct. 20
    PP   1840 Jan. 2, 3, 6-9, 11-1841 Sept. 25
           1841 Sept. 29-1845 June 30
    PPiUD 1843 Sept. 26
           1844 Oct. 16
    PPL   1840 Jan. 23, May 8, June 4, 27, July 20, 22-25, 29, Sept. 29
           1841 Feb. 19, 20, 22-24, Mar. 2-4, Apr. 20, Oct. 2, 5, Nov. 15
           1842 Apr. 16
           continued as

THE NORTH AMERICAN (Oct. 21, 1845-June 30, 1847) d morn; d evg; tw w *

Pub. & Ed.   1845-1846 George R. Graham, Alexander Cummings
                1846-1847 George R. Graham
                1847   Graham & McMichael (Morton McMichael)
P   1847 Jan. 4-June 30
PBL   ♦   d 1846 May 11
PHi   ♦   1845 Oct. 21-Dec. (17), (18), (19)-(31)
              1846 Jan. (1)-(29)-Mar. (14)-Apr. (13)-July (2)-(7)-Aug. 24, 27-Oct. (2)-Nov. (7)-Dec. (11)-(29)-(31)
              1847 Jan. (1)-(4)-(6), (7)-(9)-(23)-Feb. 2, 4-Mar. (9)-(27)-May (1)-(26)-30
    PP   d-morn 1846 Jan. 1-July 3, 6-Aug. 10, 12-Dec. 31
           d-evg 1846 May 12
              w 1847 May 5-June 30
    PPL   d 1846 Mar. 6-24, 26-Apr. 7, 9-28, 30-May 19, 21-27, 29-June 3, 5-19, 22-July 4, 7, 9, 10, 13, 16-Aug. 29, Sept. 1-16, 18-29, Oct. 1, 3-13, 15-28, 30-Nov. 3, 5-11, 13-18, 20-Dec. 2, 4-13, 19-21, 23-31
            1847 Jan. 1-Feb. 8, 10-17, 19-Mar. 22, 25-29, Apr. 1-6, 9-17, 20-28, 30-May 18, 20-June 1, 3-15, 17-30
    PWcHi   1846 May 25, Aug. 6
           merged with *United States Gazette* (q.v.) to form

NORTH AMERICAN, *continued*

NORTH AMERICAN AND UNITED STATES GAZETTE (July 1, 1847-April 15, 1876) d tw w *

Pub. 1847-1848 Graham & McMichael
    1848-1854 McMichael & Bird (Dr. Robert M. Bird)
    1854-1876 Morton McMichael
Ed. 1849-1854 Robert T. Conrad, Dr. Robert M. Bird, James S. Wallace, G. G. Foster
    1868-1876 Clayton M. McMichael

P   tw 1850 Feb. 13
      d 1847 July 1-1855 Dec. 31
       1868 Oct. 26
P-M   1847 Nov. 9, Dec. 17, 21, 24
       1865 Apr. 17, 19
PAg   1849 June-1851 May
PBL ♦   d 1852 July 13, 14, 16
PCHi   1861 Dec. 30
       1864 June 10, 11
PDoHi   1848 Apr. 5
       1849 Feb. 28
       1854 May 31
       1865 Apr. 10
       1867 Sept. 27
       1868 Apr. 5, Nov. 29
PLaN   1847 July 2-1848 Dec. 30
PLhT   w 1863 Aug. 19
       1864 Apr. 27
       1865 May 17, 24
       1869 May 19
PP   d 1847 July 1-1876 Apr. 15
      w 1847 July 7-Nov. 24
       1848 May 3
PPAt   d 1847 July 1-1876 Apr. 15
PPeS   w 1862 Oct. 15
       1864 Aug. 3
       1872 Oct. 2
PPi   1849 June-1851 May
PPL   d 1847 July 1-21, 23-29, (30)-Aug. 3, 5-31, Sept. 2-7, 10-14, 16-Oct. 20, 22, 23, 26-Nov. 2, 5-16, 18-27, 29-Dec. 22, 24-30
       1848 Jan. 1-10, 13-19, 21-Feb. 2, 4-Dec. 30
       1849 Jan. 1-Apr. 19, 21-May 11, 14-June 30, July 2-Nov. 27, 29-1850 May 16
       1850 May 18-23, 26-June 28, July 1-3, 6-9, 11-1852 June 28
       1852 June 30-1854 June 24
       1854 June 27-1855 May 22
       1855 May 24-1857 Aug. 25
       1857 Aug. 27-1858 Nov. 18
       1858 Nov. 20-1859 Feb. 1
       1859 Feb. 3-Apr. 28, 30-July 14, 16-Nov. 24, 26-Dec. 26, 28-31
       1860 Jan. 3-June 20, 22-July 14, 16-Aug. 23, 25-29, Sept. 1-Oct. 11, 13-Nov. 29, Dec. 1, 4-1861 Jan 21
       1861 Jan. 23-May 11, 14-1862 Jan. (29)-1863 Apr. 30
       1863 May 2-Aug. 20, 22-1864 Nov. 1
       1864 Nov. 3-24, 26-1865 Mar. 21

PHILADELPHIA COUNTY 163

	1865 Mar. 23-Apr. 11, 19, 22-June 1, 3-17, 21-27, July 1-7. 10-Nov. 2, 4-Dec. 7, 9-1866 Feb. 22
	1866 Feb. 24-July 13, 16-Sept. 27, 29-Nov. 29, Dec. 1-1867 Feb. 5
	1867 Feb. 7-23, 26-May 8, 10-July 23, 25-Sept. 27, 30-1866 Feb. 3
	1868 Feb. 5-July 22, 24-1869 June 15
	1869 June 17-Nov. 18, 20-Dec. 17, 20-1870 Mar. 23
	1870 Mar. 25-1871 Jan. 9
	1871 Jan. 11-Apr. 20, 22-1872 Nov. 28
	1872 Nov. 30-1873 Aug. 15
	1873 Aug. 18-Sept. 19, 22-Oct. 10, 13-1874 June 3
PPM ♦	[1848-1875]
	1874 June 5-1875 Mar. 26
	1875 Mar. 29-May 21, 24-July 9, 12-Sept. 9, 11-1876 Feb. 18
	1876 Feb. 21-Mar. 25, 28-Apr. 15
	d 1847 July 1-1849 Apr. 2
	1849 Apr. 4-June 30, July 2, Aug. 3, 6, Sept. 11, 13-1850 Jan. 17
	1850 Jan. 19-June 29, July 1-Dec. 12, 14, 31-1851 Jan 11
	1851 Jan. 14-22, 24-Feb. 27, Mar. 1-May 5, 7-Aug. 5, 7, Nov. 27, 29-1853 June 30
	1854 Jan. 1-10, 12-July 4, 6, 8-Nov. 23, 25-Dec. 30
	1856 Jan. 1-June 30
	1857 Jan. 1-31, Feb. 3-June 26, 29, Aug. 8, 11-21, 24-Sept. 24, 26-Oct. 12, 14-16, 20-27, 29-Nov. 26, 28-1858 Jan. 6
	1858 Jan. 11-20, 22, Feb. 13, 16-23, 25-Mar. 3, 5-8, 10-15, 18-Apr. 6, 8, May 19, 21, 24-July 5, 7-Sept. 14, 20-Oct. 6, 8-Dec. 30
	1859 Jan. 3-17, 19, 20, 22-Feb. 12, 15-Mar. 28, 30-May 4, 6-18, 20-24, 26-July 16, 19-Oct. 4, 6-1860 June 30
	1861 Jan. 1-June 30
	1862 Jan. 1-Nov. 26, 29-1863 Apr. 30
	1863 May 2-1865 May 26
	1865 May 29-Dec. 7, 9-25, 27-1866 July 3
	1866 July 6-1869 July 5
	1869 July 7-1873 Sept. 19
	1873 Sept. 22-1876 Apr. 15
	[1879-1907]
PPot	1866 Apr. 12
PU	1853 Jan. 1-Dec. 31
	1855 Jan. 1-Dec. 31
	1857 Feb. 1-1858 Mar.
	1858 May-1859 Nov.
	1860 Feb.-Apr., Sept.-Dec.
	1861 Feb.-Apr., July-1876 Apr. 15
PWcHi	d 1864 May 12
	1865 Apr. 15
	w 1865 Apr. 19
	d 1866 Apr. 3
	1868 Feb. 8, 10
	1869 Nov. 29
	1870 Sept. 17

NORTH AMERICAN, *continued*
                continued as
      THE NORTH AMERICAN (April 17, 1876-May 17, 1925) d tw *
  Pub. 1876-1890   Morton McMichael & Sons
                    (Clayton McMichael, Walter McMichael)
       1890-1896   Clayton McMichael
       1896-1899   Clayton McMichael & Sons
                    (Campell S. McMichael, Clayton F. McMichael)
       1889-1925   The North American Company
                    (1899 Thomas B. Wanamaker)
  Ed. 1890-1896   Clayton McMichael
       1896-1899   Clayton McMichael & Sons
       1899-1925   E. A. Van Valkenburg
       P   1885 Jan. 1-June 30
                    1900 Jan. 1-1925 May 17
       P-M   1883 Nov. 16
                    1913 Jan. 23-26, Feb. 4
       PAlHi   d 1918 Nov. 18
       PArdL   1925 May 17
       PBMa   1887 Sept. 15
       PCHi   1884 Sept. 20
                    1887 Sept. 15
                    1901 Sept. 11, 19
       PDoHi   1885 July 24
                    1887 Sept. 15
                    1901 Sept. 7, 9, 11, 12, 14, 16, 17
                    1903 Mar. 29
                    1904 July 3
                    1905 Sept. 22
                    1908 Oct. 4-11, Nov. 4, 17, 18, Dec. 10
                    1910 May 16-20
                    1911 Dec. 10-1912 Jan. 7
                    1912 Jan. 21-Mar. 17, 31-Dec. 5, 29-1913 Feb. 16
                    1913 Mar. 9, 16, 23, Apr. 6-June 29
                    1914 Feb. 8, 15, Mar. 8, Apr. 26, May 3-Dec. 20
                    1915 Jan. 3
       PHHi   1917 Mar. 5
       PHi ◆   1885 Jan. (1)-(5)-Mar. (23)-Apr. (16)-June (8)-
                          July (1)-(4)-Nov. (13), (14)-(27), (28), Dec.
                          (1)-11, 14-31
                    1886 Jan. 1-22, 25-(29)-Feb. (12), (13)-Mar. (12)-
                          Apr. (19), (20), (21), (22)-May (7)-July (1)-
                          27, 29-Sept. (1)-(18)-31
                    1887 Jan. (1)-(8)-Feb. (1), 3-(16), (17), (18),
                          (19)-(22)-Mar. 21, 23-Apr. (7)-(9)-(22)-(30)-
                          May (28)-June (7)-(11)-July (1)-Sept. 14,
                          (16)-Nov. (14)-Dec. (23)-31
                    1888 Jan. (2), (3)-Mar. (3)-(14)-(16)-Apr. (28)-
                          June (4)-(30)-July (2), (3), (4), (5), (6),
                          (7)-(9), (10), (11)-13, 16, (17), (18)-(26),
                          (27), (28)-(30)-Sept. (1)-(3), (4)-(10),
                          (11), (12)-(22)-Oct. (26), (27)-(29), (30),
                          (31), Nov. (1,), (2), (3)-(5), 6, 8-22, 24-Dec.
                          (3)-31
                    1889 Jan. (1), (2), (3)-(5)-(14), (15), (16), (17),
                          (18), (19)-(21), (22), (23), (24), (25)-(28),
                          (29), (30), (31), Feb. (1), (2)-(4), (5), (6),
                          (7)-(13)-(20), (21), (22), (23)-(25), (26),

(27), (28)-Apr. 13, 16-Aug. 9, 12-30-Nov. 13, 18-Dec. 31
1890 Jan. (1-May 31)-June (30), July (1), (2)-(4)-(9)-(18)-(24)-(31)-Aug. (5)-(16)-(18)- Sept. (1)-(24)-(26), (27)-(29), (30)-Oct. (6)-(9), (10), (11)-(20)-(27)-(30)-Nov. (5)-(11)-(14)-(19), (20)-(22)-(27)-(28), (29)-Dec. (1), (2)-(5)-(11)-(26)-(30), (31)
1891 Jan. (1), (2), (3)-(5), (6)-(27)-Feb. (2)-(9)-(13)-(16)-Mar. (14)-(16)-(23)-Apr. (30), May (1)-(13)-(25), (26)-June (15)-(29), (30), July (1), (2)-(9)-(31)-Aug. (8)-(31)-Sept. (7)-(9)-(30)-Oct. (14)-(21)-(23)-(28)-Nov. (28)-Dec. (16), (17)-(23)-(31)
1892 Jan. (2)-(4), (5), (6), (7)-(12)-(16)-(26)-(28), (29)-Feb. (6)-(12)-(27)-(29), Mar. (1)-(14)-(29) - May (19) - (23) - (25) - (27)-(31)-June (29), (30), July (1)-(11)-(18), 19, 21-(25)-(30)-Aug. (31)-Sept. (23)-Oct. (29)-Nov. 23, 25-Dec. (27)-(29)-31
1893 Jan. (2), (3), (4), (5), (6)-(16)-Feb. (15), (16), (17)-(22)-Mar. (1)-(30)-June 14, 16-(19)-(24)-July (1)-Sept. (7), 9-(22), 25-(27)-(30)-Oct. (26)-Nov. (20)-(24)-(28)-Dec. 15, 18-(30)
1894 Jan. (1), (2), (3)-Feb. 6, (8)-(20)-Mar. (29)-(27)-(30)-Oct. (26)-Nov. (20)-(24)-(28)-May 3, 5-June (5)-(27), (28), (29), (30)-July (2), (5)-(13)-Aug. 3, (6)-29, 31-Sept. (14)-26, 28, (29)-Oct. (6)-(20)-(24)-Dec. 8, 11-31
1895 Jan. (1), (2), (4), (5)-(28)-Feb. (16)-(19)-Mar. (27)-Apr. (24)-June (22)-(29)-July (1), 3, 5-(8)-Aug. (1), 3-(14)-Sept. (7)-Oct. (16)-18, 21-Nov. (20)-(30)-Dec. (6)-(16)-(21)-(23)-(30), 31
1896 Jan. (1), (2)-(11)-(13)-(16)-Feb. 5, 7-(10)-(15)-(19), (20), (21)-(27)-Mar. (13)-(30), (31)-Apr. (9), (10), (11)-(22)-(30)-May (21)-June (5), 8-(11)-(26)-(29), (30), July (1), (2), (3), (4), 7-(17), (18)-(21)-29, 31-Aug. (12), (13)-18, (20)-Sept. (12)-(24)-28, 30, Oct. 6, 8-(23)-(27)-Nov. (9)-Dec. (2)-(21), (22)-(29), (30), (31)
1897 Jan. 1-May 20, 22-Oct. 22, 25-Nov. 16, (18)-Dec. 31
1898 Jan. (1-Apr. 27), (29-Dec. 10), (13), (14), (16-30)
1899 Jan. (2-21)-Feb. (6), (7)-(27)-Mar. (23)-Apr. (3)-(7)-(10), 11, (13), (14)-(17)-(19)-(21)-(24)-(26)-(28)-May (5)-(8-13)-(16-June 1)-(28)-(30-July 7)-(13)-(22)-(27)-Sept. (1)-(30)-Oct. (2)-(12), (13)-(23)-(31)-Nov. (2)-(20-Dec. 8)-(12)-(14)-(20)
1900 Jan. 1-Feb. 24, Mar. 1-Apr. (2)-(13)-June 30
1901 Jan. (1)-(30), Feb. 1-Mar. (7)-Apr. (1), (2)-(9)-Oct. (1)-Dec. 31
1902 Jan. (1), (2), (3), (4)-Feb. (14)-Apr. (1)-(5)-June (30), July (1)-Aug. (1)-(16)-(18), (19), (20)-(25), (26)-(30)-Sept. (1)-(16)-

NORTH AMERICAN, *continued*

(18), (19), (20)-(25), (26)-(29), (30), Oct. (1)-(22)-Nov. (13), (14)-Dec. (26)-(30), (31)
1903 Jan. (1), (2), (3)-(5)-(31)-Feb. (25)- Mar. (2), (3)-(5)-(13)-Apr. (1)-(11)-(13)-(20)-(29), (30)-May (6)-(11)-(16)-(28)-June (30), July (1), (2)-(7)-(10)-(29)-Aug. (7)-(15)-Sept. (30), Oct. (1)-(8)-(12)-Dec. (11)-(30), 31
1904 Jan. (1), (2)-(4)-(16)-(19)-Feb. (15)-Apr. (1), (2)-(4), (5), (6)-(13)-(19), (20), (21)-(28)-May (2), (3)-(7)-(25)-(28)-June (7)-(13)-(21)-(29), (30), July (1)-(19)-27, 29-Aug. (10), (11)-(29)-Sept. (29)-Oct. (1)-(10)-(29)-Nov. (9)-(11)-Dec. (30), (31)
1905 Jan. (2), (3)-(17), (18), (19)-(26)-(30)-Feb. (16)-(20)-Mar. (3), 6-Apr. (1)-(4), (5)-(17)-May (6)-(19)-June (30)-July (5)-Aug. (7)-(29)-Sept. (29), (30)-Oct. (2-10)-(14)-(17)-(20)-Nov. (16)-(21)-Dec. (12), (13)-(15), (16)-(30)
1906 Jan. 1-(3), (4), (5)-(10)-Mar. (15), (16)-(21)-(24)-(28)-(31)-Apr. (5)-(11)-(19)-(27)-May (9)-(15)-(17)-(24)-(29)-June (28)-July (2) Aug. (24)-Sept. (4)-(7)-(19)-(21), (22)-(25)-(29)-Oct. (1), (2), (3)-(5)-(8)-(13)-(17)-(19)-(27)-(30), (31), Nov. (1), (2), (8)-(20)-Dec. (1)-(3)-(14)-(20), (21), (25), (26), (27)-(31)
1907 Jan. (1), (2)-(10)-(12)-(22)-(29)-Feb. (1)-Mar. (4)-Apr. (1), (2), (3), (4), (5)-(10)-(20)-June (15)-(26)-(29)-July (1)-(8), 10-(15)-(26)-Aug. (5)-Oct. (1)-Nov. (6), (7)-(11)-(18)-Dec. (13), (14)-(19)-(31)
1908 Jan. (1-Apr. 1)-May (30)-June (3-8-23) (July 1)-(27)-(31)-Aug. (8)-Sept. (30)-Oct. (14)-Nov. (6)-Dec. (31)
1909 Jan. (1), (2)-(4)-Mar. (31), Apr. (1-June 30)-July (9)-(23)-(30)-Aug. (12)-(16)-(25)-(31)-Sept. (2)-(16), (17)-(23)-(30), Oct. (1)-Nov. (30)-Dec. (4)-(10), (11)-(31)
1910 Jan. (1), (2)-(9)-(16)-(23)-(26)-Feb. (11)-Mar. (30), (31), Apr. (1), (2)-(4)-(7)-(8)-(15), (16)-(21), (22)-(28), (29)-June (4)-July (1)-Aug. (13)-Sept. (20), 25, Oct. (1)-(3)-(29)-Nov. (24)-Dec. (28), (29), (30), (31)
1911 Jan. 1-(16)-Feb. (14)-(20), (21)-(23)-Mar. (6)-(10)-(14)-(18)-(20), (21)-(25)-(27)-(29), (30), (31), Apr. (1)-June (1)-July (5)-Nov. (20)-(28)-Dec. (23)-31
1912 Jan. 1-(18)-Feb. (2)-(9)-Mar. (1)-(21)-(30)-May (18)-(28), (29)-(31)-June (1)-(3)-(28), (29)-July (1)-(3)-(15)-(20)-(31)-Oct. (3)-(25)-(30)-Nov. (21)-Dec. (14)-(16)-(21)-(26), (27), (28)-(30), (31)
1913 Jan. 1-Feb. (27)-Dec. 31
1914 Jan. 1-(26)-Dec. 31

PHILADELPHIA COUNTY 167

	1915 Jan. 1-Dec. 31
	1916 Jan. 1-Dec. 30
	1917 Jan. (1)-(11)-(18)-(28), (29)-(31), Mar. (1)-(11)-(19)-(24)-(26)-(31)-Apr. (8)-May (10)-Aug. (5)-Sept. (1)-12, 14-19, 21-28, Oct. 1-7, 9-(11)-(13)-(18)-27, 29-Nov. (1-Dec. 31)
	1918 Jan. (1)-(11)-(31)-Feb. (11)-Apr. (1)-(15)-May (4)-June (7)-July (1)-(8)-(16)-Aug. (6)-Sept. (19)-Oct. (1)-(15)-Dec. 31
	1919 Jan. (1-Apr. 1)-July (1)-Aug. (6)-Oct. (1)-Nov. (1)-(5)-Dec. (30), (31)
	1920 Jan. (1), (2), (3)-(15)-(23)-(29)-Feb. (7)-(20)-Mar. (18), (19)-(31), Apr. (1), (2)-June (28)-July (1)-(6)-(24)-(30), (31)-Aug. (5)-(9)-Sept. (16), (17)-Oct. (1), (2)- (15)-(29)-Nov. (12)-(18), (19)-(24)-Dec. (1)-(3)-(14)-(24)-(27), (28)-31
	1921 Jan. 1-Oct. (1)-(12)-(18)-(27)-Dec. (29)-31
	1922 Jan. 2-May (1)-(5)-Sept. (20)-Dec. 30
	1923 Jan. 1-Dec. 31
	1924 Jan. 1-Apr. (3)-(7)-(17), (18), (19)-(29)-May (1)-(15)-(17)-(28)-(31)-June (20)-Aug. 30, Sept. 2-Dec. 31
	1925 Jan. 1-Mar. (14)-May (17)
PLaF	1916 June 11
	1917 Apr. 7
PNazHi	d 1918 Nov. 12
PNoHi	1924 Feb. 4
PP	d 1876 Apr. 17-1878 Mar. 23
	1878 Mar. 26-Sept. 17, 19-24, 26-28, Oct. 2-Nov. 15, 18-Dec. 7, 10-1883 June 30
	1883 July 3-1884 Aug. 4
	1884 Aug. 6-11, 13-Sept. 15, 17-Dec. 19, 22-1893 Nov. 4
	1893 Nov. 7-1894 June 30
	1894 July 4-1896 June 27
	1896 July 1-1899 Apr. 29
	1899 May 2-1903 Oct. 13
	1903 Oct. 15-1925 May 17
PPAT	1876 Apr. 17-1888 Dec. 31
PPCHi	1887 Sept. 15
	1891 Apr. 14
PPeS	1897 Apr. 5
	1901 Sept. 14
	1908 Jan. 15-18, 20, 21
	1924 Feb. 4
PPi	1877 Feb. 6-1878 Apr. 26
PPL	d 1876 Apr. 17-June 24, 27-July 8, 11-Sept. 11, 13-1878 May 3
	1878 May 6-1879 Mar. 24
	1879 Mar. 26-1880 Mar. 1
	1880 Mar. 3-July 20, 22-Nov. 9, 11-1881 Jan. 20
	1881 Jan. 22-1882 Nov. 8
	1882 Nov. 10-1884 Apr. 21
	1884 Apr. 23-Aug. 15, 18-1885 Aug. 24
	1885 Aug. 26-1886 July 8
	1886 July 10-1887 July 22
	1887 July 25-1890 Nov. 20
	1890 Nov. 22-1892 **Apr. 6**

NORTH AMERICAN, *continued*
- 1892 Apr. 8-11, 13-July 29, Aug. 1-Nov. 29, Dec. 1-1893 July 20
- 1893 July 22-1894 June 25
- 1894 June 29-July 24, 26-1895 Aug. 24
- 1895 Aug. 27-Oct. 25, 28-1896 Feb. 20
- 1896 Feb. 22-June 16, 19-July 17, 20-Sept. 28, 30-Nov. 4, 6-1897 Dec. 6
- 1897 Dec. 8-1898 Mar. 11
- 1898 Mar 14-Apr. 26, 28-July 20, 22-1899 Jan. 19
- 1899 Jan. 21-May 13, 15-July 8, 11-Sept. 23, 26-Nov. 25, 28-Dec. 29
- 1900 Jan. 1-27, 31-Feb. 26, 28-Mar. 13, 15-Apr. 4, 6-21, 24-May 11, 14-29, 31-June 22, 25-Aug. 9, 11-Sept. 28, Oct. 1-8, 10, 12, 13, 16-29, 31-Nov. 5, 7-Dec. 29
- 1901 Jan. 1, 2, 4-Feb. 1, 4-8, 12-Apr. 4, 6-24, 26-May 6, 9-23, 26-Aug. 26, 28, 29, 31-Oct. 8, 10-19, 22-Nov. 4, 6, 8-20, 25-30, Dec. 3-5, 7-13, 16-27, 30-1902 Feb. 6
- 1902 Feb. 8-26, 28-Mar. 12, 14-18, 20-Apr. 18, 20-May 14, 16-19, 21-July 11, 13-Sept. 4, 6-10, 12-26, 28-Oct. 16, 18-27, 29-Nov. 23, 25-30, Dec. 2, 4-9, 12-15, 17-1903 Mar. 25
- 1903 Mar. 27-Aug. 13, 15-18, 20-26, 28-1906 Apr. 30
- 1906 May 2-1907 Aug. 13
- 1907 Aug. 15-Sept. 1, 3-Oct. 20, 22-30, Nov. 1-7, 9-1909 Apr. 18
- 1909 Apr. 20-Aug. 22, Oct. 19, 21-1910 June 20
- 1910 June 22-1911 May 1
- 1911 May 3-12, 14-1912 Apr. 29
- 1912 May 1-June 4, 6-July 24, 26-Sept. 24, 28-Oct. 14, 16-1914 Feb. 11
- 1914 Feb. 13-Sept. 10, 12-Oct. 9, 11-13, 15, 16, 18-1915 July 2
- 1915 July 4-12, 14-Dec. 12, 14-1916 Feb. 25
- 1916 Feb. 27-June 20, 22-Aug. 31, Sept. 2-1917 Mar. 11
- 1917 Mar. 13, 15-1918 Jan. 6
- 1918 Jan. 8-Nov. 12, 14-1919 Feb. 18
- 1919 Feb. 20-May 21, 23-June 18, 20-Aug. 1, 3-1920 Sept. 12
- 1920 Sept. 14, 16-1921 Mar. 8
- 1921 Mar. 10-Sept. 25, 27-1922 Apr. 4
- 1922 Apr. 6-May 14, 16-1923 Apr. 27
- 1923 Apr. 29-May 4, 6-13, 15-1924 Jan. 22
- 1924 Jan. 24, 25, Mar. 1-July 2, 4-Sept. 26, 28-Nov. 14, 16-Dec. 19, 21-1925 May 17

PPM ♦
- 1876 Apr. 17-1877 June 30
- 1877 July 2-1881 Dec. 24
- 1881 Dec. 27-1903 June 30
- 1903 Sept. 1-1904 June 30
- 1904 Nov. 1-1905 June 30
- 1905 Sept. 1-1906 Dec. 31
- 1907 Mar. 1-1908 Apr. 30
- 1909 Oct. 1-1913 Aug. 31
- 1913 Nov. 1-1915 Oct. 31
- 1916 Mar. 1-June 30

PHILADELPHIA COUNTY   169

```
                    1917 Mar. 1-Oct. 31
                    1918 Jan. 1-1921 June 30
                    1921 Aug. 1-1925 Apr. 30
       PPot         1887 Sept. 15
                    1888 Nov. 7
                    1890 July 4
       PShW         1908 July 13
       PU           1876 Apr. 17-1882 Dec. 10
                    1882 Dec. 11, 17-21
       PWcHi        1900 July 17
                    1901 Jan. 23, Mar. 14, Sept. 7, 10, 11, 14-21
                    1908 Oct. 4
                    1909 Feb. 7
                    1910 May 7
                    1912 Apr. 17-19, 27-29
                    1913 Feb. 14, Apr. 1
                    1917 Apr. 3, 7
                    1918 Nov. 11, 12
                    1919 May 15
                    1921 Mar. 3, 5
                    1923 June 12
                    1924 Feb. 4, 7
                    1925 May 15-17
       PWcT         1900 Sept. 11
                    1901 Sept. 7, 11, 14, 18, 19
       PWalG        1905 Oct. 1, 17, 30, Nov. 5, 6
                    1924 Apr. 14
                    1925 May 12-16
```

NORTH CENTRAL BULLETIN (1924-1932||) w
    GIRARD AVENUE NEWS (Dec. 5, 1924-Apr. 29, 1932) w
    Pub. 1924-1932   Publication Committee
    Ed. 1924-1932   George M. Himmelwright
        PP   1929 Sept. 5-1932 Apr. 29
                continued as
  NORTH CENTRAL BULLETIN (May 6, 1932-June 3, 1932||) w
    Pub. 1932   Herbert Hustler
        PP   1932 May 6-June 3

NORTH END GAZETTE (1892-1918) w rep
    Pub. & Ed. 1903-1917 Charles M. Carlin

NORTH KENSINGTON WEEKLY, see Oakdale Weekly

NORTH PENN CHAT, see Chat of North Penn

NORTH PHILADELPHIA GAZETTE, see Frankford Gazette

NORTH PHILADELPHIA GLOBE (1929†) w non-part
    Pub. 1936-1939   Globe Publishing Co.
    Ed. 1936-1939   John R. Quinan
        PUB   1929 Oct. 31†
        PP   1929 Nov. 7-29, Dec. 19, 23
                 1930 Jan. 2-Feb. 6, Mar. 6-20
                 1931 Apr. 2-1933 Jan. 12
                 1933 Jan. 26-Feb. 23, Apr. 6-July 6, 20†

NORTH PHILADELPHIA INQUIRER (1897-1901) w sun ind 🕯
Pub. & Ed. 1898-1901 Curtis E. Blinsinger

NORTH PHILADELPHIA JOURNAL AND ADVERTISER (1878-1880) w 🕯
Pub. & Ed. 1880 Henry W. Scott

NORTH PHILADELPHIA PRESS (1924-1932) w
    CENTRAL NORTH PHILADELPHIA NEWS (1924-1931) w
    Pub. 1924-1931 Somerset Printing Co.
    PP 1931 June 11-Nov. 25
    continued as
    NORTH PHILADELPHIA PRESS (1931-1932) w
    Pub. 1931-1932 Somerset Printing Co.
    PP 1931 Dec. 3-1932 Feb. 25
        1932 Mar. 10-24

NORTH PHILADELPHIA PROGRESS (1907-1918) w local 🕯
Pub. 1908-1918 Freed & Swift
Ed. 1908-1918 Newton E. Freed

NORTH PHILADELPHIA TRIBUNE (1893-1919) w local (Bridesburg) 🕯
Pub. & Ed. 1893-1919 Paul Blattenberger

NORTH PHILADELPHIA WORLD (1895-1913) w rep ind 🕯
Pub. & Ed. 1898-1913 Walter H. Henming

NORTHEAST BREEZE (1928†) w non-part
Pub. 1936-1938 Blaetz Bros., Inc.
Ed. 1936-1938 Adelaide M. Blaetz
  PUB 1928†
  PP 1940 June 6†

NORTHEAST NEWS (1894-1920) w ind local 🕯
Pub. & Ed. 1894-1896 Robert A. Balfour
          1896-1897 Nathaniel R. Bradner
          1897-1920 F. X. Rafferty
Ed. 1895-1896 Charles A. A. Young

NORTHEAST NEWS (May 30, 1927†) w local
Pub. 1935† Edward J. Doyle
Ed. 1935 Aug. 23-1936 Nov. 13 Martin J. Doyle
    1936 Nov. 20† Edward J. Doyle
  PUB 1927 May 30†
  PP 1935 Aug. 23-Sept. 6, 20-Nov. 8, 22-26
      1936 Feb. 7-July 31, Aug. 21, Sept. 4-Oct. 9, 23-Nov. 6, 20, Dec. 4-30
      1937 Jan. 22-Feb. 12, 26, Mar. 5, 19-July 23, Sept. 10-17, Oct. 1, 8, 22-Dec. 3

PHILADELPHIA COUNTY 171

      1938 Jan. 7-Feb. 18, Mar. 4-May 20, July 3-Aug.
      12, Sept. 9-1939 Jan. 13
      1939 Jan. 27-July 6, 20-1940 Jan. 11
      1940 Jan. 25†

NORTHEAST PHILADELPHIA BANNER (1897-1930) w local ♪
 Pub. 1900-1903 J. Wenceslas Woller
   1903-1930 Woller & Woller
 Ed. 1900-1908 J. Wenceslas Woller
   1908-1925 J. W. Woller
   1925-1930 Wenceslas Woller

NORTHEAST PHILADELPHIAN (1892-1908) w rep ♪
 Pub. 1893-1902 Nathaniel R. Bradner
   1902-1908 M. Bradner
   1908   N. R. Bradner
 Ed. 1893-1908 N. R. Bradner

NORTHEAST REVIEW (1922-1929) w sun ♪
 Pub. & Ed. 1922-1929 Harry C. Osborne

NORTHEAST WEEKLY (1899) w rep ♪
 Pub. & Ed. 1899 John W. Ford

NORTHERN ADVERTISER (1848-1854) w
 Pub. 1854 James Gibbons
  PHi   1854 Oct. 28 (Vol. 6, No. 49)

NORTHERN LIBERTIES REPUBLICAN (1909-1913) w sun rep ♪
 Pub. 1910-1913 Northern Liberties Publishing Co.

NORTHWEST INDEPENDENT-NEWS (1889-1930||) w local ♪
 NORTHWEST INDEPENDENT (1889-1910) w ♪
 Pub. 1904-1905 W. B. Smith
   1905-1910 Louis C. Macaran
 Ed. 1904-1905 Oliver M. Shedd
   1905-1910 Louis C. Macaran
      continued as
 NORTHWEST INDEPENDENT-NEWS (1911-1930||) w ♪
 Pub. & Ed. 1911-1930 Louis C. Macaran

NORTHWEST NEWS (1890-1904) w ♪
 Pub. & Ed. 1895-1898 A. C. Wherry
     1898-1901 Winchell & Thompson
     1901-1904 T. A. Winchell

NORTHWEST NEWS (1935†) w
 52ND AND GIRARD AVENUE NEWS (July 25, 1935-Jan. 31, 1936)
 w local
 Pub. & Ed. 1935-1936 Robert S. Linderman and J. A. Kilcullen
  PP   1935 July 25-Dec. 20
      1936 Jan. 3-10, 24-31

```
             PUB            1935 July 25-1936 Jan. 31
                            continued as
        NORTHWEST NEWS (Feb. 6, 1936†) w local
             Pub. 1936-1937     Robert S. Linderman and J. A. Kilcullen
                  1937-1938     Wm. Penn Association
                  1938†         Hymen Schwartz
             Ed. 1936-1937      J. A. Kilcullen
                 1937-1938      H. L. Dutkin
                 1938†          Philip R. Bucci
             NOTE: Two editions of this paper are published concurrently,
             one dated from Overbrook and Haddington, and the other 52nd &
             Girard Avenue.
             PP             1936 Feb. 6-20, Mar. 5-12, 26-Apr. 16, May 7-June
                                18, July 2-9, 30, Oct. 1, 22
                            1937 Jan. 14, 21, Feb. 25, Mar. 18, Apr. 8, 15, May
                                6, July 22-29, Aug. 4-Sept. 30, Oct. 21-28, Nov.
                                4-Dec. 30
                            1938 Feb. 10, Mar. 10-31, Apr. 8
             PUB            1936 Feb. 6†
```

NORTHWEST RECORD (1894-1907) w sw local ♣
   Pub. & Ed. 1898-1907   Northwest Record Publishing Co.
              1907   Daily News Co.

OAK LANE REVIEW (1887-1888) w
   Pub. & Ed.   MacNamara
   PHi   1888 May 7 (Vol. 2, No. 2)

OAKDALE WEEKLY (1888†) w
   Pub. & Ed. 1888-1890   Graves & Banks
              1890-1891   Stuart S. Graves
              1891-1939   Graves & Co.
   Ed.   1903-1939   Stuart S. Graves
              1939†   M. E. Ocker
   Suspended publication July 16, 1938. Resumed publication, Mar.
   10, 1939.
   Part of the edition is printed under headings *Fairhill Weekly*, *North
   Kensington Weekly*, and *Tioga Weekly*. Issued mainly for free
   distribution.
   PUB   1910 Jan. 1-1938 July 16
                 1939 Mar. 10†
   PP   1930 May 3-1938 July 16
                 1939 Mar. 10†

OBSERVATORE, L' (Aug. 6, 1905-May 26, 1906‖) sm for
   PPCHi   1905 Aug. 6-Sept. 2, Oct. 7-Nov. 4
                 1906 Jan. 6, Feb. 24-Apr. 21, May 26

PHILADELPHIA COUNTY 173

OBSERVER (1936†) w
    OBSERVER AND SPORTING NEWS (1936-1939) w
    Pub. 1938 July 26-1939 Jan. 1 Alexander Borden
    Ed. 1938 July 26-1939 Jan. 1 W. John Hamilton
      PP   1938 July 26-1939 Jan. 1
                continued as
    OBSERVER (Jan. 8, 1936†) w
    Pub. 1939 Jan. 8† Alexander Borden
    Ed. 1939 Jan. 8† W. John Hamilton
      PP   1939 Jan. 8†

OLD PENN WEEKLY REVIEW (1902-1918) w col
    OLD PENN (1902-1907) w
    Pub. 1904-1907   Alexander Borden
    Ed. 1904-1907   George E. Nitzsche
      PHi ♦   1906 Oct. 19
                1907 Nov. 2
                continued as
    OLD PENN WEEKLY REVIEW (1908-1918) w
    Pub. 1908-1909   Office of Publication
          1910 Jan. 15-1911 June 24 Edgar S. Smith
          1911 Dec. 2-1916 Feb. 14 University of Pennsylvania
    Ed. 1908-1910   George E. Nitzsche and Associates
        1910-1911   Edward B. Robinette
        1911-1914   Members of the University Staff
        1915-1916   George E. Nitzsche and Members of the University Staff
        1917   Edward R. Bushnell
      PHi ♦   1910 Jan. 15-June 18, Oct. 8-1911 June 24
                1911 Dec. 2-1912 June 22, Oct. 19, 26, Nov. 16-1913 Jan. 18
                1913 Feb. 1, 15-Apr. 5, 19-May 3, 17-31, June 14, 21, Sept. 27, Oct. 11-Nov. 29, Dec. 13
                1914 Jan. 10-24, Feb. 7, 14
                1915 June 5
                1916 Jan. 15, 22
                1917 June 29

OLNEY HERALD (1908-1914) w ind ♦
    Pub. & Ed. 1909-1914 W. W. Major

OLNEY TIMES (1910†) w ind non-part
    ROXBOROUGH SUBURBAN TIMES AND REVIEW (Jan. 4, 1910-Sept. 13, 1929) w
    Pub. 1910-1919   Isaac M. Walker
        1919-1924   Suburban Times
        1924-1929   Charles M. Carlin
    Ed. 1910-1919   Isaac M. Walker
        1919-1924   Frank N. Subers
        1919-1924   William Carlin
        1924-1929   Charles M. Carlin

        PP   1929 Feb. 7-Sept. 13
        PUB   1910 Jan. 4 (Vol. 1, No. 1)-1929 Sept. 13
                              continued as
OLNEY TIMES (Sept. 20, 1929†) w
   Pub. & Ed. 1930-1939 Harry C. Osborne
               1939-1941 W. E. Tanner and T. F. Reilly
        PUB   1929 Sept. 20†
        PP   1929 Sept. 20†

ONALLAS   (1907-1910) w for rel ♣
   Pub. 1908-1910   Latin Press Printing & Publication Co.
   Ed. 1908-1910   Rev. Alex. Varlaky

ONCE-A-WEEK, see Manayunk Sentinel, Roxborough, Falls of Schuylkill and Wissahickon Star

OPINIONE-IL PROGRESSO ITALO-AMERICANO, L',   (Jan. 6, 1906†) d morn ind rep for
   L'OPINIONE (Jan. 6, 1906-May 30, 1935) d rep
     Pub. 1906-1912   Opinione Italian Publishing Co.
          1912-1919   New York and Philadelphia Publishing Co.
          1919-1935   L'Opinione Italian Publishing Co.
     Ed. 1906-1912   Agostino De Biasi
          1912-1915   Pietro Gacovini
          1919-1920   Felice Reale
          1920-1931   C. C. A. Baldi
          1931-1933   Tommasco Giustiniane
          1933-1935   Vincenzo Giordano
   Published an evening edition under the title *Bollettino Della Sera*. A Sunday edition was started in 1927.
   Purchased by Generose Pope, of *Il Progresso Italo-Americano*, New York, Aug. 26, 1932, and merged with same June 2, 1935, and Philadelphia edition published at New York.
     PP   1927 June 1-July 8, 10-Sept. 29, Oct. 1-Nov. 5, 7-1928 Jan. 23
                      1928 Jan. 25-1935 May 30
     PUB   1906 Jan. 6-1935 May 30
                      continued as
   L'OPINIONE-IL PROGRESSO ITALO-AMERICANO (June 2, 1935†) d ind
   Pub. 1935-1941   Generose Pope
   Ed. 1935-1941   G. Vitrone
     PP   1935 June 2†
     PUB   1935 June 2, Aug. 5†

OPINIONE ITALIANO, L', see Popolo Italiano

ORB (Apr.-Aug., 1834) * ♣

ORCHESTRA   (1867-1871) w music ♣
   Pub. & Ed. 1871 T. N. Stack

PHILADELPHIA COUNTY 175

OUR COUNTRY (June 27, 1848) ir
    Pub. 1848   O. Wheelock
    PHi ♦   1848 July 4 (Vol. 1, No. 2)

OUR DAILY FARE (June 8, 1864-Sept. 11, 1865) d *
    Pub. 1864-1865   A Committee for the Great Fair in Philadelphia, comprising George W. Childs, Chairman, Thomas MacKeller, Wm. V. McLean, with an editorial committee of 10 men and 10 women.
    The object of this Journal was to preserve a record of the Fair Movement throughout the loyal States, in aid of the Sanitary Commission appointed by the Secretary of War June 9, 1861.

    PDoHi   1864 June 8, 10, 13, 15-17
    PHi   1864 June 15, 16
    PP   1864 June 8-1865 Sept. 11
    PWcHi   1864 June 8-11, 13-18, 20, 21
        1865 Sept. 11
    PWcT   1864 June 15, 16
    The last issue, Monday, Sept. 11, 1865, is a supplemental number.

OUR ONCE-A-WEEK VISITOR, see Manayunk Sentinel, Roxborough, Falls of Schuylkill and Wissahickon Star.

OVERBROOK MIRROR (Sept. 5, 1938†) w ind
    Pub. 1938-1941   C. Louise Chapman
    Ed. 1938-1941   Harry W. Hackett
    PP   1938 Sept. 26 (Vol. 1, No. 4)
        1940 May 29†

OVERBROOK OBSERVER (Sept. 16, 1929) w
    Pub. and Ed.   Clement H. Congdon
    PP   1929 Sept. 16

OVERBROOK PRESS, see addenda

PALMETTO FLAG (Mar. 30, 1861-Apr. 16, 1861||) w abol # *
    Pub. 1861   Town & Company
    Ed. 1861   Henry J. Brent
    PHi ♦   1861 Apr. 13

PAMPHLET (1885-1888) w comm ♂
    Pub. & Ed. 1887-1888   Pamphlet Publishing Co.

PATHFINDER (1869-1870) w advertising ♂
    Pub. & Ed. 1869-1870   Philadelphia Printing & Publishing Co.

PATRIOT AND SHIELD (Frankford) (1826-1832||) w * ♂

176   PENNSYLVANIA NEWSPAPERS

PATRYOTA   (1889†)   w   rep   non-part   for   *
   Pub. & Ed. 1890-1891   S. Stupski
              1891-1892   Teofil Wasowicz
              1892-1895   Sigma Slupeski
              1926-1940   T. Wasowicz & Co.
              1940-1941   Patroyta, Inc.
   Ed.   1926-1941   Gregory J. Kociel
              First official organ of the United Polish Societies.
              Claims to be the oldest Polish newspaper in America.
       PUB   1912 Jan. 5-Dec. 27
                1922 Jan. 6-Dec. 29
                1924 Jan. 4
                1928 Dec. 28
                1930 Jan. 3†
       PP   1927 June 3†

PELICAN, THE; PELICAN, LE   (1805-1807)   w   tw   for   #
   PELICAN, DER   (Oct. 28, 1805-June 3, 1806)   w   for   #
     Pub. 1805-1806   Joseph Forster
         PHi ♦   1805 Oct. 28
                   1806 May 19
                   continued as
   PELICAN, LE; PELICAN, THE; PELICAN, DER (June 17, 1806-
      Dec. 31, 1806)   tw   for   ♦   #
     Pub. 1806   P. J. Forster
                   continued as
   PELICAN, THE; PELICAN, LE (Jan. 6, 1807-Feb. 21, 1807)   tw
     for   ♦   #
     Pub. 1807   P. J. Forster

PELIKAN EDLER, DER,   (Jan. 6, 1807-Jan. 28, 1807)   w   for   #   ♦
     Pub. 1807   P. J. Forster

PELOSI'S MARINE LIST AND PRICE CURRENT   (July 11, 1791-Apr. 23, 1792)   w   ♦   #
     Pub. 1791-1792   Vincent M. Pelosi by Robert Aitken & Son, printers

PENN TOWNSHIP BANNER   (Dec. 4, 1830-June 15, 1833)   w
      PNoHi   1832 Sept. 15
      PPhoR   1830 Dec. 4-1833 June 15
      PWcHi   1832 July 14, Sept. 1, Oct. (20)

PENSIERO   (1901-1904)   w   for   ♦
   Pub. & Ed. 1901-1904   F. Ronca

PENNSYLVANIA OR WEEKLY ADVERTISER, THE, see Pennsylvania Journal and Weekly Advertiser, The

PENNSYLVANIA ADVERTISER AND WEEKLY ADVERTISER, THE, see Pennsylvania Journal and Weekly Advertiser, The

PHILADELPHIA COUNTY 177

PENNSYLVANIA CHRONICLE, AND UNIVERSAL ADVERTISER, THE (Jan. 26, 1767-Feb. 8, 1774) w #
 Pub. 1767-1769   William Goddard
         (William Goddard, Joseph Galloway and Thomas Wharton)
   1769-1770   William Goddard and Benjamin Towne
   1770-1774   William Goddard
   P   1767 Feb. 4-1770 Jan. 22
   PBL ♦   1768 Feb. 1-Mar. 28, Apr. 11-Aug. 15, 29-Dec. 26
         1769 Jan. 2-Apr. 17, May 1-Dec. 25
         1770 Jan. 1-15
   PDoHi   1768 Feb. 22, Apr. 18
   PHi ♦   1767 Jan. 26-1770 July 23
         1770 Aug. 6-1772 Dec. 12
         1772 Dec. 26-1773 Jan. 2
         1773 Jan. 16-Sept. 6, 20-1774 Feb. 8
   PP   1767 Jan. 26-Mar. 30, Apr. 13-June 22, July 6, 13, 27, Aug. 3, 10, 31, Sept. 7-Oct. 28, Nov. 9
         1768 Jan. 18
   PPi   1770 Jan. 29-1774 Jan. 10
   PPiUD   1767 Feb. 23-Dec. 28
         1768 Jan. 25-1769 Jan. 23
   PPL   1767 Jan. 26-1774 Feb. 8
   PPot   1767 Mar. 30
   PU   1768 Jan. 20-27
   PWcHi   1768 Aug. 29
   PPAP   1767 Jan. 26-1770 Jan. 22
         1771 Jan. 28-1772 Jan. 20

PENNSYLVANIA DEMOCRAT (Aug. 11, 1809-Nov. 25, 1810) dem w # *
 Pub. & Ed. 1809 Joseph Lloyd
     1810 Lewis P. Franks

  Titles vary: *The Pennsylvania Democrat,* Aug. 11, 1809 to Dec. 29, 1809; *Pennsylvania Democrat,* Dec. 29, 1809 to May 4, 1810; *The Pennsylvania Democrat,* May 26, 1810 to Nov. 25, 1810
  Paper suspended May 4, 1810, and re-established May 26, 1810.
  PDoHi   1809 Sept. 1, 22-Nov. 3, 24, Dec. 22
       1810 Jan. 5-Apr. 13, May 4, 26-June 23, July 19-Aug. 23, Sept. 20, Oct. 4, 23, Nov. 8, 25
  PHi   1809 Sept. 8
  PPL   1809 Aug. 11-1810 Nov. 8

PENNSYLVANIA EVENING HERALD AND THE AMERICAN MONITOR, THE, see Pennsylvania Herald and General Advertiser

PENNSYLVANIA EVENING POST AND DAILY ADVERTISER, THE (1775-1784) tw sw d #
 PENNSYLVANIA EVENING POST, THE (Jan. 24, 1775-July 31, 1781) tw Jan. 24, 1775-Sept. 23, 1777, Oct. 11, 1777-May 20, 1778, June 11, 1778-Jan. 4, 1779, sw Jan. 7, 1779-July 31, 1781||

Pub. 1775-1781   Benjamin Towne
Suspended Sept. 23, 1777 to Oct. 11, 1777; again suspended May 20 to June 11, 1778.
P   1777 Apr. 8
PDoHi   1775 Apr. 8
         tw   1776 Aug. 1
              1777 July 29, Aug. 7
              1778 June 11, July 14
         sw   1779 Apr. 23
              1781 Feb. 16
              1775 Mar. 23, 30, Apr. 4-July 1, 6-1776 Dec. 24
              1777 Jan. 4-Dec. 30
              1778 Jan. 2-Dec. 28
              1779 Jan. 9, Apr. 23, 30, May 29, June 12, July 16, 22, Aug. 2, Sept. 18
              1780 May 26, June 6, 12
PHi ♦   1775 Mar. 23, 30, Apr. 4-Dec. 30
              1776 Jan. 2-Dec. 31
              1777 Jan. 4-Dec. 30
              1778 Jan. 3-Dec. 28
              1779 Jan. 9, Apr. 23, 30, May 22, 29, June 12, July 16, 22, Aug. 2, Sept. 18
              1780 May 26, June 6, 12
PPAP   1775 Jan. 24-28, Feb. 2-May 6, 11-16, 20, Sept. 9, 14-23, 28-Oct. 3, 7-19, 28, Nov. 4-18, 23-Dec. 30
              1776 Jan. 2, 6-Mar. 28, Apr. 2-May 7, 11-July 18, 23-Aug. 13, 17-27, 31-Sept. 12, 17, 21-Oct. 17, 22-Dec. 31
              1777 Aug. 28, Sept. 13
              1778 Dec. 4
         sw   1779 Mar. 6
PPeE   tw   1777 Feb. 1
PPL   1775 Jan. 24-Feb. 2, 7-Nov. 7, 11-Dec. 30
              1776 Jan. 2-Dec. 28
              1777 Jan. 4-June 24, 28-Dec. 30
PPotW   1777 Jan. 28
              continued as
PENNSYLVANIA EVENING POST AND PUBLIC ADVERTISER, THE (Aug. 3, 1781-1783) sw #
Pub. 1781-1783   Benjamin Towne
P   1782 July 29-Sept. 13

continued as

PENNSYLVANIA EVENING POST AND DAILY ADVERTISER, THE (1783-Oct. 26, 1784||)   d sw ♦ #
Pub. 1783-1784   Benjamin Towne

PENNSYLVANIA FREEMAN, THE (1836-1854) w bw m fs
NATIONAL ENQUIRER AND CONSTITUTIONAL ADVOCATE OF UNIVERSAL LIBERTY (Aug. 3, 1836-Mar. 8, 1838) w *
Pub. 1836-1837   Benjamin Lundy
     1837-1838   Pennsylvania Anti-Slavery Society
Ed. 1836-1837   Benjamin Lundy
     1838   John G. Whittier
     PHi   1836 Aug. 3, 17-1837 Jan. 28

PPL	1837 Feb. 11-Aug. 31, Sept. 14-1838 Mar. 8 1836 Aug. 3-1837 May (20)-June 24 1837-July 8-1838 Mar. 8
PSF	1836 Dec. 10, 24 1837 Jan. 7-May 13, 27-Sept. 28, Oct. 12-Dec. 28 1838 Jan. 4-Mar. 8
PWcHi	1837 July 27 continued as

PENNSYLVANIA FREEMAN, THE (Mar. 15, 1838-1854) w sw m *
w Mar. 15, 1838-Jan. 11, 1844; bw Jan. 18, 1844-Dec. 26, 1845;
w Jan. 1, 1846-June 29, 1854; m 1842

Pub. 1838-1854	Pennsylvania Anti-Slavery Society
Ed. 1838-1844	John G. Whittier
1844-1854	J. M. McKim and C. C. Burleigh
P	1847 Jan. 1-Dec. 30
PDoHi	1839 Jan. 24, 31, Feb. 21, Mar. 7, 21, Dec. 12 1840 June 18, July 16-23, 30, Aug. 20, 27, Sept. 3, Oct. 29, Nov. 5-19, Dec. 3, 24, 31 1841 Jan. 7, Feb. 24, Apr. 7, June 16, 23, Nov. 10 1851 Nov. 6, 13, 27, Dec. 4 1852 Jan. 1-8, Feb. 12, 26, Mar. 18-25, Apr. 8, 29, May 6, 20, June 3, 12, July 3, 31, Oct. 23, Nov. 2, Dec. 9-1853 Jan. 27 1853 Feb. 3, 17, 24, Mar. 3, 24-Apr. 21, May 5-June 9 1854 May 4
PHi	1838 Mar. 15-1839 Aug. 29 1839 Sept. 12-1840 Sept. 3 1846 Jan. 1-1853 Dec. 29
PNoHi	1840 Jan. 2, May 28, Aug. 27 1851 July 17
PP	1844 Feb. 1, Apr. 10, 24, May 9, 23, July 18 1845 Jan. 3, Feb. 13, 27, Mar. 13, 27, May 22, June 5, 19, July 3, 17, 31, Aug. 7, 14, 28, Sept. 11, 25, Oct. 9, 23, Nov. 6, 20, Dec. 14, 18 1846 Jan. 15-Apr. 23, May 7-21, June 4-July 23, Aug. 6-Dec. 24 1847 Jan. 1-Apr. 8, 22-Dec. 30 1848 Nov. 9 1849 Feb. 1-Apr. 12, 26-July 19, Aug. 2-Sept. 27, Oct. 25-Nov. 1, 15-1850 Jan. 31 1850 Feb. 14, 21, Mar. 7-May 16, 30-Oct. 24 1851 Jan. 2-30, Feb. 13-June 5, 26, July 3, 17, 31, Aug. 7-Oct. 23, Nov. 6-Dec. 25 1852 Jan. 1-29, Feb. 12-Mar. 11, 25, Apr. 1-June 3, 26, July 3, 24, Aug. 14-Nov. 25, Dec. 9-23 1853 Jan. 6, 20, 27, Feb. 10-Mar. 3, 31, May 5-19, June 2, 16, 30, Aug. 4, Sept. 22, 29, Oct. 13, Dec. 22. 1854 Jan. 5, 19, Feb. 9, 23, Mar. 2-30, Apr. 13-27, May 11-June 29
PPL	1838 Mar. 15, Apr. 26, May 10-1839 Jan. 17 1839 Jan. 31-Oct. 5 1840 Sept. 10-1841 Dec. 29 1842 Feb.-Oct. 1844 Jan. 18-Dec. 5

PENNSYLVANIA FREEMAN, THE, *continued*

                1845 Jan. 2-1847 Aug. 12
                1847 Aug 26-1850 Dec. 19
                1851 Jan. 2, 16-23, Feb. 6-1854 June 29
    PSF   1854 Feb. 16
    PWcHi   1838 Mar. (15), Apr. 19, May 3, 24, 31, June 21, Aug. (9, 23), Oct. (18), Nov. (22)
                1839 Jan. (10), 17, Mar. (28)-July 4, 18-Aug. (15-29), Sept. 5, Dec. (19)
                1840 Apr. (9, 16), June 11, 25, July 23, Nov. 26, Dec. (17), 24
                1841 Jan. (7), Mar. 31, Apr. (7), May (26), July (21), Sept. 1, Oct. (20)
        m 1842 Feb., June, (Aug.), Oct.
        sm 1844 Apr. (25), May 23, June 6, 20, Aug. 22, Sept. 19, Oct. 24, Nov. 21, Dec. 5, 19
                1845 Jan. 16, 30, Feb. 13, Apr. 10, 24, June 5, July 3, Aug. 28, Sept. 11, Oct. 9, Dec. 4, 18
        w 1846 Jan. 1, 15, 22, Feb. 5, 12, Mar. 5-19, Apr. 2-16, 30-May 21, June 4, 18-July 2, 23-Aug. 13, 27, Oct. 1, 22, Dec. 10, 24
                1847 Jan. 14-Mar. 11, 25, Apr. 8-29, May 13, 20, June 3, 10, 24, July 1, 15-29, Aug. 12, 26-Sept. 30, Oct. 14, 21, Nov. 18, 25, Dec. 9, 16, 30
                1848 Jan. 6-Dec. 28
                1849 Jan. 4-July 12, 26-Nov. 1, 15-Dec. (20)-(27)-1850 Mar. 14
                1850 Mar. 28-1851 Dec. 18
                1852 Jan. 29, Feb. 12-Mar. 4, Apr. 1, 8, 29, May (6), 20, 27, July 3, Sept. 11, 18, Oct. 9-Nov. 6, Dec. 2, 9, 23, 30
                1853 Jan. 6-1854 June 1
                1854 June 15, 29
    PWcT   1838 May 31-1851 Dec. 18
                1852 Jan. 29-1854 June 29

PENNSYLVANIA GAZETTE, THE (1728-1815) w

UNIVERSAL INSTRUCTOR IN ALL ARTS AND SCIENCES, AND PENNSYLVANIA GAZETTE, THE (Dec. 24, 1728-Sept. 25, 1729) w #

  Pub. 1728-1729   Samuel Keimer
      PHi   1728 Dec. 24-1729 Sept. 25
      PPFfHi   1728 Dec. 24
      PPL   1728 Dec. 24

                continued as

PENNSYLVANIA GAZETTE, THE (Oct. 2, 1729-June 20, 1778) w #

  Pub. 1729-1732   Benjamin Franklin and Hugh Meredith
        1732-1748   Benjamin Franklin
        1748-1765   Benjamin Franklin and David Hall
        1766   David Hall
        1766-1772   David Hall and William Sellers
        1772-1778   Hall & Sellers
                      (William Hall and David Hall, Jr.)

Suspended publication between Nov. 1, 1765, and Nov. 14, 1765, and resumed Nov. 21, 1765. Again suspended Nov. 27, 1776, to Feb. 5, 1777. Again suspended after the issue of Sept. 10, 1777, and pub-

PHILADELPHIA COUNTY 181

lished as *The Pennsylvania Gazette* in York, Pa., from Dec. 20, 1777 to June 20, 1778.

P	1746 May 8-1778 June 20
PBL ♦	1750 Mar. 5
	1751 Mar. 15
	1752 Jan. 14-Feb. 4, 25, Aug. 6, Oct. 12
	1753 Apr. 12-26, June 28, July 19
	1754 Jan. 1, 15-Feb. 27, Mar. 19, Apr. 4-11, 25-May 16, 28-July 9, 23-Dec. 31
	1755 Jan. 7-Mar. 25, Apr. 3-Dec. (25)-1762 Jan. 14
	1762 Jan. 28-1763 May 19
	1763 June 2-Aug. 11, 25-Sept. 1, 15-Dec (29)-1765 Oct. 31
	1765 Nov. 21-1776 Nov. 27
	1777 Feb. 5-Aug. 20, Sept. 3, 10
PBMa	1745 Mar. 26
PDoHi	[1746]
	1755 Apr. 10, 17
	1756 Jan. 22, Feb. 5, 12, 26, Mar. 4, 25, Apr. 8
	1764 Sept. 13
	1775 Mar. 22, Apr. 26, July 5-12
	1776 Feb. 14, Sept. 4-18
	1777 Mar. 19, May 14
PHaC	1762 Dec. 9-1777 Aug. 13
	1777 Aug. 27-Sept. 10
PHi	1729 Oct. 2-1776 Nov. 7
	1777 Feb. 5-Sept. 10
	1778 May 9
PHartD	1773 Dec. 24
PMedD	1759 Mar. 22
PP	1732 June 19-26 (Reprint)
	1763 Mar. 17
	1768 Feb. 11, Sept. 1, 22, 29
	1769 Jan. 26, Mar. 23, May 25
	1772 Feb. 17, Mar. 24, 31, June 29, Nov. 11
PPAP	1743 Jan. 13-Feb. 24, Mar. 10-May 5, 19-Dec. 20
	1744 Feb. 2-Apr. 19, May 3-10, 24-Oct. 18, Nov. 1-Dec. 4, 25
	1746 Jan. 28, Feb. 11
	1768 Jan. 14-Sept. 29, Oct. 27-Dec. 19
PPeS	1753 Aug. 23
PPiUD	[1755 Jan. 7-1759 July 19]
	1761 Jan. 1-1770 Nov. 29
	1772 Jan. 2-1775 Dec. 15
PPL	1732 Dec. 28-1733 May 10
	1733 May 24-1735 Dec. 23
	1736 Jan. 6-1740 May 8
	1740 May 22-1742 Feb. (3)-Mar. (25)-1744 May (24)-Aug. (30)-1745 Oct. (24)-1746 Jan. (14)-Apr. (27)-1752 Aug. 27
	1752 Sept. 14-Oct. 19, Nov. 2-1753 May (10)-Sept. (20)-1755 May (29)-June (26)-1765 Oct. 13
	1765 Oct. 31, Nov. 21-1777 Apr. 16
	1777 Apr. 30-Sept. 30
PPM ♦	1753 May 10-Dec. 27
	1754 Jan. 1-Dec. 31
	1758 Jan. 5-Dec. 28

PENNSYLVANIA GAZETTE, THE, *continued*
      1759 Jan. 4-Dec. 27
      1760 Jan. 3-Dec. 25
      1764 Aug. (16)-Dec. 27
      1765 Jan. 3-Dec. 26
      1766 Jan. 2-Dec. 25
      1767 Jan. 1-Dec. 31
      1768 Jan. 7-Dec. 29
      1769 Jan. 5-Dec. 28
      1770 Jan. 4-Dec. 27
  PU   1737 Nov. 17-Dec. 8
      1739 Jan. 11-Sept. 27
      1748 Feb. 23, Nov. 3
      1749 Nov. 9
      1751 Mar. 28-1753 June 14
      1755 Feb. 4-1756 Nov. 25
      1758 Jan. 5-1760 Dec. 25
      1761 [Feb. 5-1763 Dec. 15]
      1764 Jan. 12-1767 Dec. 31
      1768 Mar. 31, May 5-12, July 7-14, Oct. 6, Dec. 1
      1769 Jan. 5-1776 Oct. 30
      1777 Feb. 5-Aug. 20
  PWcHi 1754 June 27
      1755 Sept. (18)
      1758 Aug. 31
  PYHi   1775 Mar. 1
      continued as
  PENNSYLVANIA GAZETTE AND WEEKLY ADVERTISER,
    THE (Jan. 5, 1779-Mar. 27, 1782) w #
  Pub. 1779-1782 Hall & Sellers
    P   1779 Jan. 5-1782 Mar. 27
    PBL ♦ 1779 Jan. 13-1782 Dec. 24
    PDoHi 1779 Sept. 29
        1780 Jan. 5, 19-Feb. 16, Mar. 1, 15-Apr. 19, May 3-June 21, July 5-12, 26, Aug. 9-Sept. 6, 27-Oct. 25, Nov. 29, Dec. 13-20
        1781 Jan. 3-10, 24-Feb. 14, May 9, June 6-20, July 1-Aug. 29, Nov. 14-Dec. 26
        1782 Jan. 2-Feb. 6, 20-May 15, 29-June 5, 19-26, July 10-24, Aug. 7, 14, 28-Dec. 24
    PHi   1779 Jan. 5-1782 Mar. 27
    PP   1780 Feb. 9, Mar. 15, June 21
        1781 Jan. 31, Feb. 21
        1782 Feb. 9, Mar. 6
    PPAP 1779 Jan. 5-Oct. 13, 27-Dec. 29
        1780 Jan. 5-19, Feb. 2-Dec. 27
        1781 Jan. 3-May 16, 30, June 6, 20, July 4-Aug. 15, 29-Sept. 19, Oct. 3-10, 24, Dec. 26
        1782 Jan. 2-Mar. 27
    PPL   1779 Jan. 5-1782 Mar. 27
    PU   1779 Aug. 4-18, Sept. 1, 29-Oct. 13, 27-Nov. 3
        [1780 Jan. 1-1782 Mar 27]
        continued as
  PENNSYLVANIA GAZETTE, THE (Apr. 3, 1782-June 19, 1782)
    w #
    Pub. 1782 Hall & Sellers
      P   1782 Apr. 3-June 19

PHILADELPHIA COUNTY 183

    PDoHi   1782 Apr. 3-May 15, 29, June 5, 19
    PHi   1782 Apr. 3-June 26
    PPAP   1782 Apr. 3-24, May 8-June 12
    PPL   1782 Apr. 3-June 26
    PU   1782 Apr. 3-June 26
    continued as

PENNSYLVANIA GAZETTE AND WEEKLY ADVERTISER, THE (June 26, 1782-Nov. 6, 1782) w #

Pub. 1782   Hall & Sellers
    P   1782 June 26-Nov. 6
    PBuE   1782 July 3
    PDoHi   1782 June 26, July 10-24, Aug. 7, 14, 28-Nov. 6
    PHi   1782 June 26-Nov. 6
    PP   1782 July 28
    PPAP   1782 June 26, Oct. 9, 23-Nov. 6
    PPL   1782 June 26-Nov. 6
    PU   1782 June 26-Nov. 6
    continued as

PENNSYLVANIA GAZETTE, THE (Nov. 13, 1782-Oct. 11, 1815) w #

Pub. 1782-1808 Hall & Sellers
    1808-1815 Hall & Pierie
    (George W. Pierie & William Hall, Jr.)

    P   1782 Nov. 13-1801 Oct. 22
    P-M   1787 Mar. 28, Apr. 4-18
        1790 Mar. 17, July 28-Sept. 15, 29-Oct. 27
    PBL ♦   1783 Jan. 1-1789 Dec. 30
        1790 Mar. 17, July 28-Aug. 18, Sept. 1-15, 29-Oct. 27
        1791 Jan. 5-July 6, 20-Dec. 28
        1792 July 11
        1793 Jan. 9, June 12, Aug. 14, Sept. 11, Nov. 20-Dec. 24
        1794 Jan. 8-29, Feb. 19-Mar. 12, 26, Apr. 16, 23, May 7-June 4, 18-Nov. 19, Dec. 10-24
        1795 Jan. 7
    PBMa   1793 Aug. 28
    PDoHi   1782 Nov. 13-Dec. 24
        1783 Jan. 1-Feb. 12, 26-Apr. 23, June 4-18, Sept. 24, Dec. 3-1784 Jan. 7
        1784 May 5, Sept. 8, Nov. 24
        1785 Feb. 9, Aug. 10
        1786 Jan. 4, Feb. 1, May 17, 24, July 19, Aug. 2, 9, Oct. 4, 11
        1787 Jan. 31, Mar. 28, Apr. 4, Aug. 22, Sept. 5
        1788 Oct. 15
        1789 Jan. 28
        1791 June 29
        1793 Mar. 6, Apr. 3, May 15
        1794 Jan. 29
        1800 Jan. 15
        1811 Oct. 30
    PHi   1782 Nov. 13-1790 Dec. 30
        1794 Jan. 1-1796 Dec. 31
        1799 June 5
        1801 Dec. 16
        1802 Mar. 31, Apr. 28, June 30, July 7, 21, 28

PENNSYLVANIA GAZETTE, THE, *continued*

      1803 Jan. 5, 19, Feb. 2, Mar. 9
      1807 Oct. 14
      1808 Dec. 21
      1811 Sept. 18-1815 Oct. 11
PMedD 1795 Dec. 16
PNoHi   1789 Aug. 26
PP   1784 July 28
      1785 Nov. 30, Dec. 7, 14
      1787 Jan. 3, Dec. 19
      1788 June 25, July 2, Oct. 15, Nov. 5, Dec. 12
      1789 Mar. 4, Apr. 1, Nov. 25, Dec. 2
      1790 Jan. 6, Feb. 10, 24, Mar. 17, 31, Apr. 14, 21, June 9, 30, Aug. 4, Sept. 15, 29, Oct. 6, 13, Dec. 1, 8, 15
      1798 Aug. 29
      1803 June 1
PPAP   1782 Nov. 13, Dec. 4-1783 Feb. 19-1783 Oct. 22, Nov. 5-12, Dec. 10
      1784 Jan. 21-June 16, July 14-Sept. 15, 29-Oct. 27, Dec. 8-15, 29
      1785 Jan. 12-Mar. 16, 30-May 4, 18-25, June 8-Aug. 17, 31-Oct. 19, Nov. 9, 23-30, Dec. 21-28
      1786 Jan. 25, Feb. 8, 22, Mar. 8, 22, June 7-Nov. 22, Dec. 6-27
PPi   1786
PPiUD [1783 July 2-1789 Dec. 30]
PPL   1782 Nov. 13, Apr. 3-1790 Sept. 15
      1790 Sept. 29-1792 Aug. 15
      1792 Aug. 29-1794 Mar. 19
      1794 Apr. 2-Aug. 6, Sept. 3-Oct. 22, Nov. 5-1795 Jan. 7
      1795 Jan. 21-May 13, June 3-Sept. 2, 16-Nov 11-(25)-Dec. 9, 23-1796 Jan. 13
      1796 Jan. 27, Feb. 10-May 18, June 1-1797 Jan. (4)-1799 Aug. 21
      1799 Nov. 13-1802 Nov. 17
      1802 Dec. 1-1804 Feb. 22
      1804 Mar. 7-Dec. 26
PRHi   1785 Aug. 3
      1786 Feb. 15
      1788 Feb. 20, Apr. 2, July 9
      1790 Feb. 10, June 16-30, July 7, 14, Aug. 11, Sept. 1-22, Oct. 20, 27, Nov. 3-24, Dec. 1-15, 29
      1791 Jan. 19, 26, Feb. 2, 16, 23, Mar. 2, 9, May 4
      1794 Jan. 15
PSF   1786 Jan. 11-1789 Dec. 30
PU   [1782 Nov. 13-Dec. 31]
      1783 Jan. 15-1788 Dec. 31
      1789 Jan. 21-1795 Dec. 30
      1796 Aug. 10, Oct. 26
      1800 Jan. 22-1801 June 3
      [1801 June 24-1802 Dec. 31]
      1804 Jan. 25-May 30
      1805 Mar. 20-1806 Sept. 27
PWcHi 1784 Jan. 28
      1790 Jan. 13, 20, Feb. 17-Apr. 14, May 12-June 2, July 12-Aug. 15, Sept. 1, 15, 29-Oct. 13, 27, Dec. 15, 22

PHILADELPHIA COUNTY 185

                   1797 Mar. 8
                   1798 Jan. 10
                   1802 Dec. 22
                   1803 Aug. 31
    PWcP   1798 Jan. 17, Mar. 21
                   1799 Feb. 13, Nov. 13
    PWcT   1784 Sept. 21
                   1790 Jan. 13-Dec. 22
                   1798 Jan. 10

PENNSYLVANIA GAZETTE, THE (Oct. 1, 1827-Apr. 14, 1828) d evg w *

    Pub. & Ed. 1827-1828 George Taylor & Co.
    Weekly edition published entitled *Saturday Pennsylvania Gazette*.
    P   d 1827 Oct. 6-1828 Apr. 8
    PHHi   w 1828 Feb. 16-May 17
    PLewL   w 1829 Mar. 14
    PPL   d 1827 Oct. 1-1828 Apr. 12
    PPoU   w 1827 Oct. 6-1828 Apr. 12
    PWeT   d 1828 Mar. 28, 31, Apr. 1
    Pennsylvania Gazette was absorbed April 14, 1828, by, and title changed to *Aurora and Pennsylvania Gazette.* (q.v.)

PENNSYLVANIA GAZETTE AND WEEKLY ADVERTISER, see Pennsylvania Gazette (1790-1835)

PENNSYLVANIA GERMAN RECORDER OF EVENTS, see Pennsylvanische Staats Courier, Der

PENNSYLVANIA HERALD AND GENERAL ADVERTISER, THE (Jan. 25, 1785-Feb. 14, 1788) sw tw fed #

    CAREY'S PENNSYLVANIA EVENING HERALD (Jan. 25, 1785-Feb. 8, 1785) sw
      (A free weekly supplement entitled "*Complete Counting House Companion*" was issued to the subscribers)
    Pub. 1785   Matthew Carey
        PHi   1785 Jan. 25-Feb. 8
        PPL   1785 Jan. 25-Feb. 8
                   continued as
    CAREY'S PENNSYLVANIA EVENING HERALD AND AMERICAN MONITOR (Feb. 12, 1785-Mar. 22, 1785) sw
      (A free weekly supplement entitled "*Complete Counting House Companion*" was issued to the subscribers)
    Pub. 1785   Matthew Carey
        PHi   1785 Feb. 12-Mar. 22
        PPAP   1785 Mar. 12-19
        PPL   1785 Feb. 12-Mar. 22
                   continued as
    PENNSYLVANIA EVENING HERALD, THE, AND AMERICAN MONITOR, THE (Mar. 26, 1785-May 28, 1786) sw
      (A free weekly supplement entitled "*Complete Counting House Companion*" was issued to the subscribers)

PENNSYLVANIA HERALD AND GENERAL ADVERTISER, THE, continued

Pub. Mar. 26, 1785-Apr. 9, 1785   Carey, Talbot and Spotswood (Christopher Talbot and William Spotswood)
Apr. 12, 1785-May 28, 1786   M. Carey & Co.

PDoHi   1785 June 18
PHi   1785 Mar. 29-Aug. 27, Sept. 3-1786 May 28
PPAP   1785 Mar. 29-May 4, 14-June 8, 15, 25-July 2, 9, 16, 20, 30, Aug. 6, 17, 27, Sept. 8-28, Oct. 1, 5, 15-22, 29, Nov. 2, 9-Dec. 7, 14-31
   1786 Jan. 4-Feb. 22, Mar. 4-11, 18-Apr. 22, May 6-20, 28
PPL   1785 Mar. 29-1786 May 28

continued as

PENNSYLVANIA HERALD, AND GENERAL ADVERTISER, THE (May 31, 1786-Feb. 14, 1788) sw tw
sw May 31, 1786-Feb. 2, 1788
sw May 31, 1786-Feb. 2, 1788
tw Feb. 5, 1788-Feb. 14, 1788
(A free weekly supplement entitled *"Complete Counting House Companion"* was issued to the subscribers until Feb. 2, 1788, after which date it became a separate publication, Feb. 5, 1788-Oct. 30, 1799 (q. v.) and was published by William Spotswood)

Pub. May 31, 1786-Feb. 10, 1787   M. Carey & Co.
Feb. 14, 1787-Feb. 2, 1788   W. Spotswood
Feb. 5, 1788-Feb. 9, 1788   Matthew Carey
Feb. 14, 1788   John M'Culloch

PAtM   1787 Oct. 2
PDoHi sw 1787 Jan. 13, Mar. 7, 10
PHi   1786 May 31-1788 Jan. 26
  w 1786 July 8, Dec. 9, 23
PPAP sw 1786 June 7-July 12, 19-Sept. 6, 13-Oct. 4, 14, 21, 25, Nov. 1, 11-Dec. 6, 13-27
   1787 Feb. 24
PPL   1786 May 31-1788 Feb. 14

PENNSYLVANIA INQUIRER, see Philadelphia Inquirer Public Ledger

PENNSYLVANIA INQUIRER AND DAILY COURIER, see Philadelphia Inquirer Public Ledger

PENNSYLVANIA INQUIRER AND MORNING JOURNAL, see Philadelphia Inquirer Public Ledger

PENNSYLVANIA INQUIRER AND NATIONAL GAZETTE, see Philadelphia Inquirer Public Ledger

PENNSYLVANIA JOURNAL, AND WEEKLY ADVERTISER, THE (1742-1793) w sw

WEEKLY ADVERTISER, OR PENNSYLVANIA JOURNAL, THE (Dec. 2, 1742-Dec. 16, 1742) w sw #
w Dec. 2, 1742-Dec. 16, 1742

Pub. 1742   Wm. Bradford
PHi   1742 Dec. 2-16

PHILADELPHIA COUNTY 187

continued as
PENNSYLVANIA JOURNAL AND WEEKLY ADVERTISER, THE (Dec. 21, 1742-Sept. 18, 1793) w sw #
- w Dec. 21, 1742-June 20, 1781
- sw June 23, 1781-Dec. 27, 1788
- w Dec. 31, 1788-Sept. 18, 1793

Pub. 1742-1766 William Bradford
1766-1778 William and Thomas Bradford
1778-1781 Thomas Bradford
1781-1782 Thomas Bradford and Peleg Hall
1782-1793 Thomas Bradford

Suspended from Nov. 27, 1776 to Jan. 29, 1777; again suspended from Sept. 17, 1777 to Dec. 23, 1778

Titles vary as follows: Dec. 21, 1742, *The Pennsylvania* or *Weekly Advertiser;* June 13, 1751, *The Pennsylvania Advertiser and Weekly Advertiser;* Jan. 30, 1766, *The Pennsylvania Journal and The Weekly Advertiser;* Dec. 23, 1778, *The Pennsylvania Journal and Weekly Advertiser;* May 17, 1780, *The Pennsylvania Journal and the Weekly Advertiser.*

P		1771 Apr. 25-1792 Dec. 27
P-M		1780 Apr. 30, Aug. 30
PBL ♦		1774 June 18
	w	1790 Jan. 6-Feb. 17
	sw	1790 Feb. 20-Apr. 7
	w	1790 Apr. 14-Dec. 8, 22, 29
		1791 Jan. 5-Dec. 7, 21, 28
		1792 Jan. 4-Feb. 8, 22-Dec. 26
PBMa		1772 Aug. 19-Dec. 30
		1773 Jan. 6-Sept. 22, Oct. 6-Dec. 22
		1774 Jan. 5-19, Feb. 9-Apr. 27, May 11-25, June 15-Nov. 30, Dec. 14-28
		Supplements issued 1773 June 10, 1774 May 14, 20, July 23, Sept. 16, 1775 Apr. 14
		1775 Jan. 4-Feb. 1, 15, Mar. 15-Apr. 19, May 3-July 26, Aug. 9-Sept. 27
PDoHi		1779 Feb. 3, Mar. 3, Nov. 3
		1780 July 19-Aug. 2, 23, Sept. 6, 13, 27-Oct. 4, 18, 25
	sw	1781 Nov. 3-24, Dec. 1
PHaC	w	1765 Apr. 18, 25
		1766 Jan. 9-23, Feb. 6
PHi		1742 Dec. 2-1775 Dec. 27
•		1776 Mar. 20, May 1-29, June 12, July 17, Aug. 28, Oct. 9, Nov. 6, 20
		1777 Apr. 20, July 9, Feb. 3-1793 Aug. 28
PP	w	1774 May 18-Sept. 28, Oct. 12-1775 Sept. 13
		1775 Sept. 27-Dec. 27
		1789 Feb. 18
		1793 Jan. 30
PPAP		1768 Jan. 7-Dec. 29
		1779 Jan. (13), 28, June 2
		1780 Feb. 23, May 24, 31, June 14, Oct. 11
		1781 Jan. 3-Dec. 26
		1783 Jan. 1-Feb. 8, 15-1784 Mar. 3
	sw	1784 Mar. 10-May 1, 15-26, June 2-19, 26-30, July 7-10, 17-Aug. 4, 14-Sept. 18, 25-Oct. 6, 13-27, Dec. 11-22

PENNSYLVANIA NEWSPAPERS

PENNSYLVANIA JOURNAL AND WEEKLY ADVERTISER, THE, *continued*

      1785 Jan. 1, 19-22, Feb. 12, Mar. 16-19, 26-30, Apr. 2-9, 16-May 11, 18-Aug. 20, 27-Oct. 1, 8, 15-26, Nov. 2, 9, 19-23, Dec. 3-17, 24-30
      1786 Jan. 28-Feb. 4, Mar. 4, 15, Aug. 21-Dec. 2, 9-30
  PPi w 1776 Sept. 11, 25
      1786 Feb. 4-Sept. 25
  PPiUD w [1757 Jan. 6-1759 Dec. 27]
      [1768 May 26-Nov. 10]
      1776 Mar. 6-June 5
      1783 Jan. 1-Dec. 31
  PPL w 1747 Jan. 1-1763 Dec. 31
      1765 Jan. 17-31, Feb. 18, Mar. 14-Apr. 11, 25-May 2, 16, 23, June 6-Sept. 19, Oct. 3-10, 24-31, Nov. 14-Dec. 9, 26
      1767 Jan. 1-Dec. 31
      1770 Jan. 1-1777 Sept. 17
      1779 Jan. 1-1793 Dec. 31
     w 1756 Apr. 15-22
      1757 Mar. 17-Apr. 14, Dec. 8
      1760 June 5, 26, July 3-10
      1762 Nov. 18-25, Dec. 2
      1765 Oct. 31
      1767 Apr. 30, Sept. 24
      1768 Jan. 7-28, Feb. 11, June 9-16, July 28, Dec. 22
      1769 Feb. 9, 23, Oct. 26, Dec. 28
      1770 Jan. 11, Mar. (22), Apr. 12, July 12-19, Aug. 2, Sept. 6
      1771 Jan. 17, July 25, Nov. 14, Dec. 12, 26
      1772 Aug. 19-26, Sept. 9-16, Dec. 16
      1773 Jan. 13, May 26
      1774 Apr. 6, June 1, 15, 29, July 27, Oct. 5, Nov. (16), 30, Dec. 21
  PRHi 1787 June 6, Sept. 5
  PWcHi 1776 Mar. 6
  PWcT 1776 Mar. 6

PENNSYLVANIA LEDGER, OR THE PHILADELPHIA MARKET DAY ADVERTISER, THE (1775-1778) w sw Tory

  PENNSYLVANIA LEDGER, THE: OR THE VIRGINIA, MARYLAND, PENNSYLVANIA AND NEW JERSEY WEEKLY ADVERTISER (Jan. 28, 1775-Nov. 30, 1776) w #
  Pub. 1775-1776 James Humphreys, Jr.
    Suspended from Nov. 30, 1776, to Oct. 10, 1777.
    PHi   1775 Feb. 4-Oct. 21
          1776 June 29, July 6, Aug. 24
    PPL   1775 Jan. 28-1776 Jan. 20
          1776 Feb. 3-Mar. 9, 23-June 29, July 13-Nov. 30
     continued as
  PENNSYLVANIA LEDGER, THE: OR THE WEEKLY ADVERTISER (Oct. 10, 1777-Nov. 26, 1777) w #
  Pub. 1777   James Humphreys, Jr.
    PHi   1777 Oct. 10-Nov. 28
    PPL   1777 Oct. 10, 22, 29, Nov. 5, 12, 19, 26
     continued as

PENNSYLVANIA LEDGER, THE: OR THE PHILADELPHIA MARKET DAY ADVERTISER (Dec. 3, 1777-May 23, 1778) sw #
   Pub. 1777-1778 James Humphreys, Jr.
      PHi   1777 Dec. 3-(31)
               1778 Jan. 3-Feb. 28, Mar. 4-28, Apr. 1-May 23

PENNSYLVANIA MERCURY, AND PHILADELPHIA PRICE-CURRENT, THE (1784-1792) w tw

   PENNSYLVANIA MERCURY, AND UNIVERSAL ADVERTISER, THE (Aug. 20, 1784-July 19, 1791) w tw #
      w Aug. 20, 1784-Dec. 28, 1787
      sw Jan. 1, 1788-July 19, 1791

   Pub. 1784-1791 Daniel Humphreys
     P   sw 1790 Dec. 30-1791 July 19
     PDoHi   1784 Aug. 20, Nov. 5, Dec. 31
     PHi   w 1784 Aug. 20-1785 Feb. 25
               1785 Mar. 11-1786 Sept. 8
               1786 Sept. 22-1787 Dec. 28
           sw 1788 Jan. 19-26, 31, Feb. 7, 14, 21-Mar. 11, 15, 20-22, 29, Apr. 3, 8-12, 17-26, May 3, 8, 24, 31, June 10, 21-26, July 3, 8-24, 29-31, Aug. 7-Sept. 6, 16, 20, 25-Oct. 7, 21-Nov. 15, 20, 25-27, Dec. 2
               1789 Jan. 1-Feb. 26, Mar. 3-Apr. 28, May 2-Dec. 31
               1790 Feb. 27-June 12, 17-1791 Jan 20
               1791 Feb. 3, 12-Apr. 2, 7-July 19
     PPAP   1784 Aug. 20-27, Sept. 10, 24, Oct. 15, Dec. 3
               1785 Mar. 4, 18, Apr. 1, May 27, June 10, 24, July 1, 22, Aug. 12
     PPL   1784 Aug. 20-1790 Dec. 30
     PPoT   1788 May 15
               1789 Aug. 27
     PPotW   1788 May 15
               1789 Aug. 27 (Contains George Washington's answer to an address given in his honor)
           continued as
   PENNSYLVANIA MERCURY, AND PHILADELPHIA PRICE-CURRENT, THE (July 21, 1791-Mar. 1, 1792) w tw #
      tw July 21, 1791-Jan. 3, 1792
      w Jan. 5, 1792-Mar. 1, 1792

   Pub. 1791-1792 Daniel Humphreys
     P   1791 July 21-Sept. 24, Oct. 1-22
     PPL   1791 Sept. 15
     PHi   1791 Sept. 24, Oct. 1-22, 27, 29, Nov. 3, 5, 8, 19, 24, 26, 29, Dec. 3, 8

PENNSYLVANIA MERCURY AND UNIVERSAL ADVERTISER, THE (1775), see Story and Humphrey's Pennsylvania Mercury and Universal Advertiser

PENNSYLVANIA PACKET AND DAILY ADVERTISER, THE,
see North American

PENNSYLVANIA PACKET OR GENERAL ADVERTISER, THE,
see North American

PENNSYLVANIA PACKET AND GENERAL ADVERTISER, THE, see North American

PENNSYLVANIA SENTINEL, THE (1830-July 25, 1837) d
    Pub. & Ed. 1830-1837   John R. Walker
    PBL ♦   tw 1837 July 8, 10
    Merged with the *Commercial Herald* and title changed to *Commercial Herald and Pennsylvania Sentinel.* (q.v.)

PENNSYLVANIA STATE GAZETTE (PENNSYLVANISCHE STAATS GAZETTE), see Philadelphia Gazette Democrat

PENNSYLVANIA STATE ZEITUNG (1895-1897) w Hebrew ♦
    Pub. 1895-1897   Raphael Fleet
    Ed. 1895-1897   C. Malitz

PENNSYLVANIA STATESMAN (Jan. 12, 1851-1852||) d
    P   1851 Mar. 7
    PHi   1851 Nov. 13 (Vol. 24, No. 4781)
    PPL   1852 Jan. 12

PENNSYLVANIA VOLUNTEER (1849-1850) w ♦
    Pub. 1849-1850   Lambert W. Holland
    Ed. 1849-1850   John H. Taggart
    Absorbed by *Item* (q.v.)

PENNSYLVANIA WEEKLY NEWS AND RADIO PRESS (1934)
w dem
    PENNSYLVANIA WEEKLY NEWS (Jan. 20, 1934-May 13, 1934) w
    Pub. & Ed. 1934   Paul M. Gottlieb
    PP   1934 Jan. 20-May 13
        merged with *Radio Press* (q.v.) to form the
    PENNSYLVANIA WEEKLY NEWS AND RADIO PRESS (May 18, 1934-Sept. 30, 1934) w
    Pub. 1934   Paul M. Gottlieb
    PUB   1934 May 18-Sept. 30
    PP   1934 May 18-July 8, 22-Aug. 26, Sept. 9-30

PENNSYLVANIA WHIG, THE (Aug. 13, 1831-Oct. 3, 1832) sw *
    Pub. & Ed. 1831-1832   Stephen Simpson
    PHi ♦   1831 Aug. 13-1832 Aug. 8, Oct. 3

PENNSYLVANIAN, see Daily Pennsylvanian

PENNSYLVANIAN, THE, see Morning Pennsylvanian

PENNSYLVANIAN FOR THE COUNTRY, see Morning Pennsylvanian

PHILADELPHIA COUNTY 191

PENNSYLVANISCHE BERICHTE, see Pennsylvanische Staats Courier, Der

PENNSYLVANISCHE CORRESPONDENZ, DIE (1797-1800) sw w #
   Pub. 1797-1800 Henrich Schweitzer
      PHi   1799 Dec. 27
      PNazHi   1798 Jan. 2
      PNo   sw 1799 June 21-Aug. 20, 27, Oct. 25-Nov. (19)-26

PENNSYLVANISCHE GAZETTE, DIE, ODER DER ALLGEMEINE AMERICANISCHE ZEITUNG-SCHREIBER (Feb. 3, 1779-July 1779||) w #
   Pub. 1779   John Dunlap
      PHi   1779 Feb. (3)

PENNSYLVANISCHE STAATS COURIER, DIE (1739-1778) m quar bw w for #
   HOCH-DEUTSCH PENNSYLVANISCHE GESCHICHT-SCHREIBER ODER SAMMLUNG WICHTIGER NACHRICHTEN AUS DEM NATUR—UND KIRCHEN—REICH (Aug. 20, 1739-Oct. 1745)
     quar m #
         quar Aug. 20, 1739-1741
         m 1741-Sept. 16, 1745
   Pub. 1739-1745 Christoph Saur
     PHi   1739 Aug. 20
                  1742 Feb. 16
                  1743 Apr. 16-1745 Sept. 16
     PNazHi   1739 Aug. 20
     PPLp   1743 Dec. 16-1745 Sept. 16
             continued as

   HOCH-DEUTSCH PENNSYLVANISCHE BERICHTE (Oct. 16, 1745-May 16, 1746) quar m #
   Pub. 1745-1746 Christoph Saur
     PHi   1745 Oct. 16-1746 May 16
             continued as

   PENNSYLVANISCHE BERICHTE (June 16, 1746-Apr. 9, 1762) m sm bw #
   (m June 16, 1746-Mar. 16, 1748; sm Apr. 1, 1748-Oct. 16, 1756; bw Aug. 21, 1756-Apr. 9, 1762)
   Pub. 1746-1758 Christoph Saur, Sr.
        1758-1762 Christoph Saur, Jr.
     PHi   1746 June 16-1748 Apr. 16
                1748 May 16-June 16, July 16-Aug. 16, Sept. 16-Oct. 16, Nov. 16, Dec. 16
                1749 Jan. 16, Feb. 16-Mar. 16, Apr. 16-June 16, July 16-Sept. 16, Oct. 16-Dec. 16
                1750 Jan. 16-Feb. 16, Mar. 16, Apr. 16-1752 Aug. 16
                1752 Sept. 16-Dec. 16
                1753 Apr. 1-June 1, Aug. 1-16, Oct. 16
                1754 Jan. 16-Feb. 16, Mar. 16-Apr. 1, June 16, July 16-Sept. 1, Nov. 16-1755 Feb. 1

PENNSYLVANISCHE STAATS COURIER, DER, *continued*

                1755 Mar. 1-Dec. 16
                1756 Jan. 16-Dec. 25
                1757 Jan. 8-Dec. 24
                1758 Jan. 7-Dec. 23
                1759 Jan. 5-Dec. 7
                1760 Feb. 15, 29, Mar. 28, Apr. 25, May 23, June 6, Aug. 1
                1761 Jan. 2, Feb. 13, Mar. 27-Apr. 24, May 22-Nov. 20, Dec. 18
                1762 Jan. 29, Apr. (9)
    PPAP   1747 July 16-Nov. 16
                1753 Jan. 1-Dec. 31
                1754 Nov. 16
                1757 Apr. 16
    PPeS   1755 Oct. (16)
                1759 Feb. (2, Apr. 27, June 22, Aug. 31, Nov. 9)
                1760 Mar. (28, June 6)
                1761 June (5, July 31, Oct. 9)
                continued as

    GERMANTOWNER ZEITUNG, DIE (1762-1777) bw w
  bw Apr. 10, 1762-Mar. 19, 1776; w Mar. 20, 1776-Oct. 3, 1777

    Pub. 1762-1776   Christoph Saur
         1776-1777   Christoph Saur und Sohn
         1777   Christoph Saur, Jr., und Peter Saur
    PBiH   1777 Feb. 26
    PDoHi   1762 June 17
    PHi   1766 Aug. 7
                    1771 Nov. 7
                    1773 Feb. 25, July 29
                    1774 Apr. 21, Sept. 22
                    1775 Apr. 20
                    1776 Mar. 20, Sept. 11
                    1777 Mar. 12-19
                    continued as

  PENNSYLVANISCHE STAATS COURIER, DER (Oct. 8, 1777-June 17, 1778||) w

    Pub. 1777-1778   Christopher Saur, Jr., und Peter Saur
    Published at Philadelphia during the British occupation.
    PHi ♦   1778 Feb. 11

PENNSYLVANISCHE STAATS GAZETTE, see Philadelphia Gazette Democrat

PENNY POST (Jan. 9, 1769-Jan. 27, 1769||) tw
    Pub. and Ed.   Benjamin Macom
    PPL   1769 Jan. 9-27

PEOPLE (1871-1872) w ♦
    Pub. 1871-1872   Charles F. Reinstein
    Ed. 1871-1872   Wm. H. Van Nortwick

PEOPLE (1887-1905) w prohibition ♦
    Pub. & Ed. 1887-1905 People Company

PHILADELPHIA COUNTY   193

PEOPLE, THE   (1875), see Greenback Herald, The

PEOPLE, THE (1902-Oct. 27, 1909) w society
    Pub. 1902-1909   Drexel Biddle
    Ed. 1902-1909   Zinn Gould
        PWalG   1905 Oct. 6-27

PEOPLE AND ANTI-MONOPOLIST, THE, see Greenback Herald, The

PEOPLE'S ADVOCATE, see Morning Star and People's Advocate

PEOPLE'S ADVOCATE AND WESTERN JOURNAL OF COMMERCE (1870-1875) w ♦
    PEOPLE'S ADVOCATE (1870-1874) w ♦
    Pub. & Ed. 1874 Advocate Publishing Co.
                continued as
    PEOPLE'S ADVOCATE AND WESTERN JOURNAL OF COMMERCE (1875) w ♦
    Pub. & Ed. 1875 Advocate Publishing Co.

PEOPLE'S LEDGER (ca. 1868-1869) w ♦
    Pub. & Ed. 1868-1869 John S. Downing

PEOPLE'S LEDGER (1871-1879) w ♦
    Pub. & Ed. 1876-1878 Herman K. Curtis
            1878-1879 Selden Brothers

PEOPLE'S OMNIBUS   (Oct. 23, 1852) w ♦ *

PEOPLE'S PRESS (1915-1920) w socialist
    Pub. 1916-1920   Socialist Party of Philadelphia
    Ed. 1916-1920   Charles W. Ervin
        PHi ♦   1916 July 22 (Vol. 2, No. 1), Dec. 30

PERSONAL LIBERTY (1921-1925) w anti-prohibition ♦
    Pub. 1921-1925   Waller & Co.
    Ed. 1921-1925   William A. Waller

PETIT FIGARO (Mar. 2, 1889) w for
    Pub. 1889   P. Albert de Tramasure
        PPL   1889 Mar. 23

PHILADELPHIA ADVERTISER AND CITY GAZETTE (Mar. 30, 1830) w
        PHi ♦   1830 May 4 (Vol. I, No. 6)

PHILADELPHIA ABEND GAZETTE, see Philadelphia Gazette Democrat

PHILADELPHIA AFRO AMERICAN (1892†) w Negro
Pub. 1941 The Afro-American Company
Ed. 1941 Levi Jolley
Note: This paper was established in Baltimore, Md. In 1929 the Philadelphia office was opened and a Philadelphia edition has been published since that time.
PDoHi 1938 Jan. 22
PP 1940 Oct. 19-1941 Feb. 1
1941 Mar. 8, 15, Apr. 19, May 3-17, Aug. 16†

PHILADELPHIA ALBUM AND LADIES' LITERARY PORTFOLIO (1826-1834)
ALBUM AND LADIES' WEEKLY GAZETTE, THE (June 7, 1826-May 30, 1827) w
Pub. & Ed. 1826 Thomas Cottrell Clarke
PHi ♦ 1826 June 7-1827 May 30
PP 1827 Jan. 31-Apr. 11, 25-May 16
continued as
PHILADELPHIA ALBUM AND LADIES' LITERARY GAZETTE (June 6, 1827-July 3, 1830) w
Pub. & Ed. 1827-1829 Thomas Cottrell Clarke
Pub. 1830 Jesper Harding
Ed. 1830 Robert Morris
PDoHi 1829 July 1, 29, Apr. 19
PHi ♦ 1827 June 6-1829 May 27
1830 Jan. 2-July 3
PLewL 1827 Apr. 25-Dec. 26
1828 Jan. 9-23, Feb. 6-May 21, June 4-Aug. 20
PP 1827 June 6-1830 July 3
PPL 1830 Jan. 2, 23-Mar. 13, 27-Apr. 24, May 8, 22, June 5-July 3
Merged with *Ladies' Literary Portfolio* to form
PHILADELPHIA ALBUM AND LADIES' LITERARY PORTFOLIO, THE (July 10, 1830-1834) w
Pub. 1830-1834 Jesper Harding
Ed. 1830-1834 Robert Morris
PDoHi 1831 Jan. 22-Dec. 31
1833 Jan. 5, 26, Feb. 2-23, Mar. 9, 16, Apr. 6, 20, May 25, June 15, 22
PHi ♦ 1830 July 10-1834 Dec. 27
PP 1830 July 10-Dec. 25
PPL 1830 July 17-Aug. 28, Sept. 11-Dec. 25
1831 Jan. 1-8, 22, Feb. 5-Mar. 19, Apr. 2-30, May 14, 28-Oct. 15, 29-Nov. 1, Dec. 3-31
1832 Jan. 14-Feb. 4, Mar. 3, 17-Apr. 28, May 19-June 9, 23, July 14-21, Aug. 4-25, Sept. 8-22, Oct. 6-20, Nov. 10, Dec. 1, 22-29
1833 Jan. 5-June 15, 29-July 20, Sept. 14-21, Oct. 5-12, 26, Dec. (7), 28
Absorbed by the *Pennsylvania Inquirer and Daily Courier*

PHILADELPHIA AURORA, see Aurora

PHILADELPHIA COUNTY   195

PHILADELPHIA BREVITIES   (July 20, 1932-Nov. 23, 1932||)   w
   Pub. 1932   Philadelphia Brevities Corp.
   Ed. 1932   Donald F. Tracey, Walter Gold, M. Martin
      PP   1932 July 20 (Vol. 1, No. 1)-Nov. 23

PHILADELPHIA BRIEFS   (Dec. 6, 1932-July 4, 1934||)   w
   Pub. 1932-1934   Bis Publishing Co.
   Ed. 1932-1934   M. Martin
      PP   1932 Dec. 6 (Vol. 1, No. 1)-1934 June 27

PHILADELPHIA BULLETIN FOR THE COUNTRY,   see Evening Bulletin

PHILADELPHIA BUSINESS JOURNAL,   see United States Journal

PHILADELPHIA CALL,   see Call

PHILADELPHIA CHRONICLE-HERALD,   see Evening Herald

PHILADELPHIA CITY ITEM, THE,   see Item

PHILADELPHIA COMMERCIAL LIST AND PRICE CURRENT,
see Commercial List and Maritime Register

PHILADELPHIA COMMERCIAL TIMES   (1869-1877)   w

   Pub. 1869-1877   Wallington & Co., Philadelphia
      PHi ♦   1876 Dec. 30 (Vol. 7, No. 40)
               1877 Jan. 20
      PP   1875 Mar. 4

PHILADELPHIA COMMONWEALTH   (1873-1875)   w   dem   ♦
   Pub. & Ed. 1873-1875   W. H. White

PHILADELPHIA COURIER-JOURNAL   (1932)   w   Negro
   Pub. 1932   Philadelphia Courier-Journal Publishing Co.
   Ed. 1932   H. Homer Starks
      PP   1932 Aug. 6 (Vol. 1, No. 1), 14, 21

PHILADELPHIA DAILY EAGLE   (May 6, 1845)   d
   Pub. 1845   William Nichauls
   Ed. 1845   Peter Sken Smith
      PBL ♦   1845 Aug. 8

PHILADELPHIA DAILY NEWS   (1830-1869)   d   w   whig   *
   DAILY NEWS (1830-1847)   d   *
   Pub. & Ed. 1830-1847   John P. Sanderson
      PBL ♦   1839 May 9, 22, 25, 27, 29, 31, June 6, 7, 13-21

PHILADELPHIA DAILY NEWS, *continued*
Merged with *Daily Chronicle* (1847) to form
DAILY NEWS AND CHRONICLE (June 1847-May 16, 1848) d w *
  d June 1847-May 16, 1848
  w Dec. 23, 1847-May 16, 1848 as *Dollar Weekly News*
  Pub. & Ed. 1847-1848   John P. Sanderson
    PLaHi   1847 Sept. 7, 25, Oct. 11, 15, 22, 23, 27, 28, 29, Nov. 2,
                    4, 5, 8, 9-11, 15, Dec. 9, 17
                 1848 Jan. 3, 5, 7, May 16
    PWcHi   1848 Feb. 25, Mar. 20
              continued as
DAILY NEWS (1848-1858) d w *
  d June 1848-Sept. 1858
  w June 1848-Sept. 1858 as *Dollar Weekly News*
  Pub. & Ed. 1848-1849   John P. Sanderson
             1849-1850   John P. Sanderson & Co.
             1851   Paxon & Killinger
             1851-1858   Joseph R. Flanigen
  Ed.   1849   R. J. Conrad
    PBL ♦   1848 Oct. 2, 3
                 1849 Jan. 27, 29, Feb. 3, Nov. 30
                 1850 July 10
                 (1852 Jan. 26-28, 30-Feb. 21, 24-Mar. 17, 19-Apr.
                    10, 13-Apr. 24), July 16
    PCHi   1855 Oct. 3
    PDoHi   1854 Nov. 21
                 1856 Oct. 28
    PHi ♦   1856 Aug. 30, Sept. 1, 3, 9, Oct. 8, 10, 11, 18, 25,
                    Nov. 5-8, 10-13, 15, 22, Dec. 1, 3, 4, 11-13, 15,
                    29-31
                 1857 Jan. 2, 3, 10, Mar. 17, 30, June 23
    PLaHi   1848 Aug. 21, 26, 29, Sept. 2, 7, 11, 13, 21, 23, 26,
                    29, Oct. 3, 5, 13, Nov. 8 (extra ed., election)
    PP   1849 Sept. 28, Oct. 1, 4-23, 25, 26, 28-Nov. 2, 4-16,
                    19, 21-24, 27-Dec. 3
    PPFfHi   1849 Dec. 29
    PPL   1851 Mar. 25, Dec. 10
    PPot   1850 May 17
    PShH   1848 Aug. 28
                 1858 Aug. 27
    PSuHi   1858 Apr. 3
    PWcHi   1850 Feb. 9
                 1852 July 3
                 1854 June 24
              continued as
PHILADELPHIA DAILY NEWS (1858-1869) d w *
  Pub. & Ed. 1858-1869   Joseph R. Flanigen
  Weekly edition entitled *Dollar Weekly News*
    PCHi   1868 May 22
    PHi ♦   1859 Jan. 1, July 4
                 1860 Mar. 27
                 1861 Mar. 5, July 16
                 1865 Mar. 29, June 23, 29, Oct. 3
                 1866 May 5
    PMe   w 1861 Jan. 16, July 31
    PNoHi   1859 Apr. 11

PHILADELPHIA COUNTY 197

                      1865 Mar. 6, Apr. 1
    PP   d 1861 Jan. 4
    PPFfHi   1860 Aug. 24, Sept. 19, 28, Oct. 4, 10
                    1861 May 17
    PPL   d 1869 Mar. 15
              w 1869 Mar. 18
    PPot   1860 Jan. 27
    PPotW   1860 Jan. 27
    PShH   1858 Sept. 14
              w 1858 Oct. 28
                1859 June 30
                1860 May 31
                1861 May 9
    PStrHi   1860 Oct. 3, 12
                1868 June 2
    PWcHi   1860 Oct. 12
                1868 June 2

PHILADELPHIA DAILY PENNSYLVANIAN, see Morning Pennsylvanian

PHILADELPHIA DAILY RECORD (1859-1861) d ♦
  Pub. 1859-1861 Cyrus S. Haldeman & Co.

PHILADELPHIA DAILY REGISTER (Sept. 5, 1847-Sept. 4, 1854||) d
*
    Pub. 1847-1851   W. H. Sickels
        1851-1854   Moran & Sickels
        1854   William Birney
    Ed. 1854   William Birney, Henry J. Gibbs, E. W. Capron,
                      Charles Nordhoff, T. M. Coleman
    Title varies: *Philadelphia Evening Register; Daily Register*
    PHi   1851 Sept. 5-Nov. 1
    PWcHi   1854 Aug. 11

PHILADELPHIA DAY (1875), see Day, The

PHILADELPHIA DEMOKRAT (Aug. 28, 1838-May 9, 1918) d for
  PHILADELPHIA DEMOKRAT (Aug. 28, 1838-Aug. 21, 1840) d
    Pub. 1838-1839   Burkhardt and Rothenstein
        1839-1840   L. A. Wollenweber
    PPG ♦   1838 Aug. 27-Dec. 7, 10-17
                  continued as
  DEMOKRAT, DER (Aug. 22, 1840-Jan. 14, 1843) d tw
    Pub. 1840-1843   L. A. Wollenweber
    PPeS   1843 Mar. 9
    PPG ♦   1842 Jan. 1-Dec. 31
                  continued as
  DEMOKRAT UND ANZEIGER DER DEUTSCHEN, DER (Jan. 15, 1843-1847) d
    Pub. 1843-1847   L. A. Wollenweber
    PPG ♦   1844 Jan. 3-June 27

PHILADELPHIA DEMOKRAT, *continued*
              continued as
       PHILADELPHIER DEMOKRAT (1847-Dec. 31, 1853) d
    Pub. 1847-1852   L. A. Wollenweber
          1852-1853   John S. Hoffman
          PPG ♦   d 1847 Sept. 2-14, 16-Oct. (17)-(23-25)-30, Nov. 2, (3)-Dec. 3, 6-1848 Jan. 8
                          1848 Jan. 11-Feb. (15)-29, Mar. 27-Apr. (10)-12, 14-May 5, 8, June 22, 24-28, July 1-(12)-14, 17-22, 25-27, 29-Aug. 23, 25-30, Sept. 2-29, Oct. 2-(7)-12, 14-19, 21-25, 28-Nov. 21, 23-27, 9-Dec. 16, 19-30
                          1849 Jan. (3)-17, 19-27, 30, Feb. 9-Mar. 8, 10-27, Apr. 2, 3, 5-28, May 1-22, 24, 26-28, 30-June 11, 13-23, 26-(30)
                          1850 Jan. 1-29, Feb. 1-5, 7-Mar. 4, 6-8, 11-26, 28-Apr. 29, May 2-(4-7), 9-11, 14-(17)-20, 22, June 22, 25-(26)-July 1, 4-10, 12-19, 22, 24-Sept. 2, 4-(12-14), (18-21)-Nov. 8, 11-29, Dec. 2-6, 9-(19), (21), 24-27, 30, 31
                          1851 Jan. 1, 2, 4-(11)-31, Feb. 3-Apr. (7)-May (5)-(13)-(23)-June 30, July (3-7), (19), 22-31, Aug. 2-22, 27, 29-Sept. (2)-13, 16-27, 30-Oct. 4, 7, (8)-11, 14-(18)-30, Nov. 3-6, 8-11, 13, 18-(29), Dec. 2-5, 8-12, 15-22, (24)
                          1852 Jan. 1-16, 19-Feb. 10, 12-(16)-(23)-Mar. 11, 13-24, 26-Apr. 9, 12-(17)-May 10, 12-(15)-(18)-June (21-23)-(26)-July (1, 2)-(5)-Aug. (28)-Sept. 3, 6-(11)-(30)-Oct. (25)-Nov. (4)-Dec. 31
                          1853 Jan. 1-(25)-Feb. (18)-Mar. (7)-June (10)-(25)-(29)-30, July 4-(23)-Sept. (3), 5-Oct. (1)-(20)-Dec. (20)-(23)-29, 31
          PPot   1848 Sept. 9
              continued as
      PHILADELPHIA DEMOKRAT (Jan. 2, 1854-1918) d w sun
    Pub. 1854 Jan. 2-1873 July 9   Hoffman & Morwitz
          1873 July 10-1897 Oct. 5 Morwitz & Co.
                      1897-1908   Philadelphia Democrat Publishing Co.
                      1908-1918   German Daily Gazette Publishing Co.
    Ed.   1868-1873   Dr. E. Morwitz
                      1889-1891   Dr. G. Kellner
                      1909   Max Heinrici
    Sunday edition published entitled *Neue Welt* (Aug. 24, 1856-June 16, 1908)
    Weekly edition published entitled *Vereinigte Staaten Zeitung* (1845-1908)
        PDoHi   1885 July 24
        PPDe   1907 Nov. (1)-1918 May (8)
          sun   1907 July 28-1908 Apr. (3)
        PPeS   1907 Dec. 21 (Anniversary issue)
        PPG ♦   1854 Jan. (2)-(18)-(19)-Apr. (5)-(12)-May (22)-June 6, 8, (9)-15, 17-July (1)-(29)-(31)-Aug. (2)-10, (12)-(19)-(31)-Sept. (2)-(6, 7)-(9)-12-Oct. (6, 7)-(9)-(14)-Dec. (16)-(20, 21)-**(28)-(30)**

PHILADELPHIA COUNTY 199

1855 Jan. 3-(8)-Mar. (29)-June 30, July (4)-(21)-23, 25, Nov. (27)-Dec. (3)-(5)-(8)-(21, 22)-(25)-(31)
1856 Jan. (1)-(22)-May (20)-June (2)-(5)-(10)-(30), July 8-Aug. 11-Dec. (27)
1857 Jan. (1)-Feb. (12)-May 10-(30)-June (1)-(15)-(23)-(27-30)-July 3-(10)-Aug. (10)-(31)-Dec. (21)-31
1858 Jan. 1-Feb. 15, 17-Mar. (9)-May (12-17)-(19)-June (16)-(19)-(25)-(30)-July (7, 8)-Oct. (7)-Nov. (18)-Dec. 23
1859 Jan. (1)-Feb. (9)-(11)-Mar. (5-7)-(30)-June (25)-(30)-July 9, 20-(22)-(25)-(30)-Sept. (23, 24)-(29)-Oct. (11)-Nov. (9)-Dec. (8)-(13)-(20)-(22-31)
1860 Jan. 2-(10-12)-(27)-Feb. (1)-Mar. (1-6)-(29)-(31)-Apr. (2)-(6-9)-May (1)-3-June (2)-30, July 9-Aug. (8)-(15)-(20)-Sept. (15)-Oct. (20-22)-(25)-Nov. (1)-(17)-Dec. (18)-(21)-(27)-29
1861 Jan. 3-(4)-(11, 12)-(24)-Feb. (8)-(12)-(16)-(22)-Mar. (7)-(25)-Apr. (2)-30, May (3)-June 17, 19-Aug. (2)-(5)-(7)-(9-14)-(16-23)-(28)-Sept. (2)-(5-7)-(10)-(12-14)-(18-20)-(25-28)-Oct. (1-4)-(8)-(18)-(21)-(29)-Nov. (5, 6)-(9)-(12)-(29)-Dec. 31
1862 Jan. 1-Feb. (17)-Apr. (8)-May (2)-(29)-June (18)-(28)-July (14)-(21)-Aug. (6)-(22)- Sept. (2)-(6)-(11, 12)-(15)-(20-22)-Oct. (31)-Nov. (8)-Dec. (10)-(13)-(16)-31
1863 Jan. 2-Apr. (22)-(24)-(29)-June (6)-(16)-(28), July (1)-Aug. (3)-Oct. (29)-Nov. (16)-Dec. (8)-(21)-(31)
1864 Jan. 1-Oct. (10)-Dec. 31
1865 Jan 2-(16)-(31) - Apr. (25) - Sept. (20) - Dec. (2)-31
1866 Jan. 1-May (17)-June 6-(29)-July 3-Aug. 14, 16-Oct. (6)-Dec. 31
1867 Jan. (1)-Feb. (9)-(15)-May (18)-June 17, 19-July (12, 13)-Oct. (4)-(8)-(19)-(28)-Dec. 31
1868 Jan. 4-(14)-Feb. (7) - (17) - Mar. (10) - Apr. (11)-May (15-20)-June (23-26), July (1)-(18)-Oct. (23)-Nov. (7)-Dec. 31
1869 Jan. 1-(25-27)-(29)-Feb. (11)-(15)-July (12)-(15)-Aug. (3)-(20)-Dec. (8)-(20)-1870 Apr. (9)-1876 July 1
1876 July 4-1887 Dec. 31
1888 July 2-Dec. 31
1889 July 1-1893 June 28
1893 July 1-1902 Dec. 31
1903 July 1-1904 Dec. 31
1905 July 1-1907 Dec. 31
sun 1856 Aug. 24-1857 June 28
1879 Jan. 12-1907 June 30
PPL 1856 Apr. 11, 12, 21, 28, May (2)
PU 1887 Jan. (2)-Dec. 11
sun 1888 Jan. 15-Dec. 2
1889 Jan. 6-Dec. 29

PHILADELPHIA DEMOKRAT, continued
PUB   1908 June 16-1918 May 8
Philadelphia Demokrat merged May 9, 1918, with *Philadelphia Morgen Gazette* and title changed to *Philadelphia Gazette-Demokrat* (q.v.)

PHILADELPHIA DISPATCH, see Sunday Dispatch

PHILADELPHIA EVENING BULLETIN, see Evening Bulletin

PHILADELPHIA EVENING BULLETIN FOR THE COUNTRY, see Evening Bulletin

PHILADELPHIA EVENING CHRONICLE   (1868-1877)   d w *
    GERMANTOWN CHRONICLE (Nov. 7, 1868-Nov. 13, 1869) w
  Pub. 1868 Nov. 7-Nov. 21   Chronicle Association at Germantown, Philadelphia
    1868 Nov. 28-1869 Feb. 20 Clement Tingley, Jr.
    1869 Feb. 27-Sept. 11   Samuel W. Meixell
    1869 Sept. 18-Oct. 30   Lewis R. Hamersley
    PHi   1868 Dec. 26 (Vol. 1, No. 8)
          1869 Oct. 18
    PP   1868 Nov. 7-1869 Oct. 30
    PPiUD 1869 Apr. 30
      continued as
  DAILY CHRONICLE, THE (Nov. 15, 1869-Apr. 15, 1871) d
  Pub. 1869 Nov. 15-1870 Mar. 26 L. R. Hamersley & Co.
     1870 Mar. 28-1871 Apr. 15 G. Wharton Hamersley
  The Daily Chronicle of Germantown was first issued on Monday morning, Nov. 15, 1869.
    PP   1869 Nov. 15-1871 Apr. 15
      continued as
  GERMANTOWN DAILY CHRONICLE, THE (Apr. 17, 1871-Apr. 30, 1874) d
  Pub. 1871-1874 G. Wharton Hamersley
    PP   1871 Apr. 17-1872 Nov. 5
          1873 May 6-1873 Nov. 5
      continued as
  PHILADELPHIA EVENING CHRONICLE (May 1, 1874-Nov. 27, 1877) d
  Pub. 1874-1877 Dennis F. Dealy, at Philadelphia
    PHi ♦ 1874 Oct. 9, 10, 14, Nov. 9, 10, 16, 18
          1876 May 30
    PP   1876 Dec. 6
    PPL   1874 Sept. 26, 28, Oct. 3
          1875 Mar. 29
          merged with *Evening Herald*, 1877 and title changed to *Philadelphia Chronicle-Herald* (see under *Evening Herald*)

PHILADELPHIA EVENING ITEM, see Item

PHILADELPHIA COUNTY 201

PHILADELPHIA EVENING JOURNAL (May 2, 1842-Jan. 3, 1843||)
  d *
      Pub. & Ed. 1842   Reuben M. Whitney & Winthrop Atwill
                 1843   Reuben M. Whitney
        PBL ♦   1842 Aug. 4
        PPiUD   1842 May 4, Sept. 2, 3, 14, 20, 21, 24, 28, 30, Oct. 4,
                     1843 Jan. 3
                     8, 13, 14, 17, 21, 25, 26, 28-31, Nov. 2, 9, 26, Dec. 10

PHILADELPHIA EVENING JOURNAL (Apr. 12, 1856-July 5, 1863||)
  d *
      Pub. & Ed. 1856-1863   Albert D. Boileau
                   1863   Charles N. Pine & A. E. Lewis
        PCHi   1862 Oct. 25
        PHi   1856 Apr. 12-Dec. 31
                 1857 Jan. 1-Oct. 9, 12-1859 Oct. 11
                 1861 Jan. 28-Apr. 11, Oct. 12-1862 Apr. 11
        PP   1863 Feb. 25
        PPeS   1856 Apr. 29
        PPL   1862 Dec. 1
                 1863 July 2
        PPot   1857 May 11, June 12
                 1858 Mar. 25, 27, 29
                 1860 July 28, 30, 31, Aug. 1
        PPotW   1857 May 11, June 12
                 1858 Mar. 25, 27, 29
                 1860 July 28, 30, 31, Aug. 1

PHILADELPHIA EVENING NEWS (1861)
    Pub. 1861 J. R. Flanigan
    % *The Evening News*
        PHi   1861 Jan. 5 (Vol. 1, No. 153)
                    Jan. 26 (Vol. 2, No. 15)

PHILADELPHIA EVENING POST, THE, see National Palladium and Freeman's Journal

PHILADELPHIA EVENING REGISTER, see Philadelphia Daily Register

PHILADELPHIA EVENING STAR AND DAILY ADVERTISER, THE (1835-40) d *
    EVENING STAR AND DAILY ADVERTISER, THE (June 10, 1835-Jan. 1836) *
    Pub. 1835-1836   Sloanaker & Worrall
        PBL ♦   1835 Aug. 17-19, 22, 26, 28, Sept. 1, 2, 4-10, 12, 14, 18-22, 25-30, Oct. 5, 15, 16, Dec. 23, 28
                 1836 Jan. 1
                 continued as
    PHILADELPHIA EVENING STAR AND DAILY ADVERTISER, THE (Jan. 1836-Aug. 31, 1840||) *
        PBL ♦   1836 Apr. 26, 28, 30, May 2, 11, 14, 19-25, 27-31, June 2, 3, 7, 11, 13, 15
        PHi   1839 May 4
        PPot   1839 Oct. 14

PHILADELPHIA FAIR-ZEITUNG (Dec. 7, 1870-Jan. 2, 1871) ir for
Pub. 1870-1871 "Deutsch-Patriotischen Hülfs-Verein"
Ed. 1870-1871 O. Seidensticker
M. R. Muckle
F. Tiedemann
This paper was published by the German-Patriotic Aid Society, for the aid of wounded widows and orphans of German soldiers, killed in the war between Germany and France.
    PHi ♦   1870 Dec. 7 (Vol. 1, No. 1)-31 1871 Jan. 2

PHILADELPHIA FINANCIAL JOURNAL (1895-1940) d
    PHILADELPHIA FINANCIAL NEWS (Aug. 11, 1895-Apr. 23, 1901) d
    Pub. & Ed. 1895-1901   C. W. Barron
        PPN   1898 Aug. 1-1899 Apr. 30
                1899 Sept. 1-1900 Sept. 30
                1901 Feb. 1-Apr. 23
        continued as
    PHILADELPHIA NEWS BUREAU (Apr. 24, 1901-Apr. 28, 1929) d
    Pub. 1901-1929   Estate of C. W. Barron
    Ed. 1928-1929   H. W. Bartlett
        PP   1920 July 31, Dec. 21
                1921 Jan. 21, Mar. 14, 24
                1924 Mar. 11, 14, 26, Apr. 7, 10, June 5, July 24, Aug. 11, 19, 26
                1925 Jan. 21, Nov. 7, 14
                1926 May 4, Aug. 10, 11, Oct. 15, Nov. 25, Dec. 4
                1927 Mar. 9, 14
                1928 May 15-29, 31-June 14, 16-1929 Apr. 28
        PPN   1901 Apr. 24-Dec. 31
                1902 July 1-1903 July 31
                1904 Jan. 1-1929 Apr. 28
        continued as
    PHILADELPHIA FINANCIAL JOURNAL (Apr. 29, 1929-June 29, 1940) d
    Pub. 1929-1930   Estate of C. W. Barron
            1930   Hugh Bancroft
            1930-1940   Philadelphia News Bureau
    Ed. 1929-1937   H. W. Bartlett
        PUB   1929 Dec. 31†
        PP   1929 Apr. 30-1940 June 29
        PPL   1934 Dec. 31†

PHILADELPHIA FREIE PRESSE (1848-1887) d for rep
    Pub. & Ed. 1868-1880   F. W. Thomas & Sons
                    1880-1887   Freie Presse Publishing Association
                Sunday editions published: *Sonntags Blatt und Familien Journal*, 1857 to 1874; *Sonntags-Blatt, der Freien Presse*, 1877 to 1885.
                Weekly edition published *Die Republikanische Flagge*, 1856-1887.
        PHi   sun 1858 June 20-1859 Dec. 25
                      1860 Jan. 1-June 10
        PPG   d 1849 Jan. 1-July (11)-1850 Dec. (31)
                    1851 Jan. 7-Dec. (31)

1852 Jan. (13)-Dec. (30)
1853 Jan. 1-Nov. (25)-1854 Dec. (29)-(31)
1855 Jan. 1-1856 Nov. (6, 7)-1857 Mar. 7
1857 Mar. 9-May (3)-1858 May (27)-Dec. (31)-1859 Dec. 31
1860 Jan. 2-Oct. 8, 10-1861 Jan. (1)-Dec. (31)-1864 Jan. (18)-Feb. (13)-(17-22)-June (4-12)-(17)-July (1)-Aug. (29)-Dec. (29)
1865 Jan. 2-Feb. (6)-Mar. (7, 8)-(24)-1866 Jan. (2)
1866 Jan. 3-Mar. (3)-May 24, 27-1867 May 24
1867 May 26-1868-Dec. (31)
1869 Jan. (4)-June (30)-1870 Dec. 28
1871 Jan. 3-1887 Dec. 31
sun 1859 June 19-1861 June 10

PHILADELPHIA GAZETTE AND COMMERCIAL INTELLIGENCER, THE (Mar. 8, 1788-Nov. 3, 1845) tw sw d fed

FEDERAL GAZETTE AND PHILADELPHIA EVENING POST, THE (tw Mar. 8, 1788-Apr. 24, 1788; d Oct. 1, 1788-Mar. 31, 1790) #

Pub. & Ed. 1788-1790 Andrew Brown
P   d 1789 Aug. 27-1790 Mar. 31
PHi   d 1788 Oct. 1-Dec. 31
PPL   d 1788 Oct. 1-1789 Jan. 17
          1789 Jan. 20-Oct. 15, 19-1790 Mar. 31

continued as

FEDERAL GAZETTE AND PHILADELPHIA DAILY ADVERTISER (Apr. 1, 1790-Dec. 31, 1793) d #

Pub. & Ed. 1790-1793 Andrew Brown
P   1790 Apr. 1-1793 Dec. 31
PAtM   1790 July 13
               1791 Nov. 14
               1792 Apr. 26-May 1
PDoHi ♦   1792 Jan. 28
               1793 Oct. 25
PHi ♦   1790 Dec. (18)
               1791 Jan. 5, 24, July 7
               1792 Feb. (11), Mar. 31, Dec. 25
               1793 Mar. 7, July 9, 15, Sept. 4, 7, 25, Oct. 3, 26, Nov. 19, Dec. 24, 31
PNoHi   1791 Jan. 20
               1792 Jan. 2-Aug. 31
PP ♦   1791 Apr. 25, June 29, 30, July 8, 9, 11
               1792 Aug. 21
PPiUD   [1792 Jan. 4-Aug. 31]
PPL   1790 Apr. 26, 28-May 10, 12-15, 18-June 26, July 1-27, 29-1791 Dec. 21
               1791 Dec. 23, 27, 29-31
               1792 Jan. 2-25, 27-Apr. 5, 7-27, 30-May 21, 23-1793 Mar. 6
               1793 Mar. 8-28, 30-Dec. 31

continued as

PHILADELPHIA GAZETTE AND UNIVERSAL DAILY ADVERTISER (Jan. 1, 1794-June 17, 1800) d #

Pub. & Ed. 1794-1797 Andrew Brown
           1797-1799 Andrew Brown, Jr.
           1799-1800 Brown & Relf (Samuel Relf)

PHILADELPHIA GAZETTE AND COMMERCIAL INTELLIGENCER, THE, *continued*

P	1795 Jan. 22-1796 Dec. 31
PAg	1795 July-1796 Dec.
PBL ◆	1795 Apr. 29-Dec. 24, 26, 31
PDoHi ◆	1794 July 15
	1795 Feb. 25, 28, Nov. 5
	1796 Mar. 31, May 21
	1800 Feb. 27
PHaC	1795 Apr. 20
	1798 Jan. 1-June 30
PHi	1794 Jan. 1-1796 Dec. 31
PLaHi	1794 Feb. 6
PP ◆	1794 Aug. 16
	1795 Feb. 18
	1797 July 21, Sept. 6, 7, Nov. 21
	1798 May 16, 30
	1800 Mar. 28, Apr. 16, May 1
PPF	1799 Jan. 2-Feb. 26, 28-Mar. 21, 23-Apr. 24, 26-May (27)-June 15, 17-July (23)-Aug. 26, 28-Sept. 28, Oct. 1-18, 21-Nov. 21, 23-Dec. (13)-31
PPi	1795 July-1796 Dec.
PPiUD	[1798 Jan. 12-1800 June 17]
PPL	1794 Jan. 1-1797 Feb. 9
	1797 Feb. 11-Mar. 8, 10-15, 17-Apr. 21, 24-May 22, 24-June 15, 17-21, 23-July 11, 13-15, 18, 19, 21-Aug. 5, 8, 9, 11-23, 25-29, 31-Sept. 4, 7-11, 18-20, 22-28, 30
	1798 Jan. 1-May 8, 10-1800 June 17
PPM ◆	1794 Jan. 1-Feb. 1, 4-June 30

continued as

PHILADELPHIA GAZETTE AND DAILY ADVERTISER (June 18, 1800-Dec. 31, 1802) d #

Pub. & Ed. 1800-1801   Brown & Relf
             1801-1802   Samuel Relf

PAg	1802 Jan.-Dec.
PCarlHi	1800 Aug. 25-30, Sept. 7-22, 24-26, Oct. 2-15, 18-Nov. 24
PHi	1802 Jan. 1-Dec. 31
PP ◆	1800 July 9, 30, Aug. 15, 18, 19, 21, 26, 30, Sept. 2, 4, 19, Oct. 16, 17, 27, 28, Nov. 1, 5, 6, 10, 11, 13, 15, 18, 19, Dec. 1, 20, 22, 24, 27, 29, 30
	1801 Jan. 1 15, 17, 22, Feb. 16, 21, Mar. 9, Apr. 7, 9, 10, May 7, 8, 13, 20, 31, June 2, 4, 6, 9, 10, 15, 16, 21, 25, July 24, 25, 30, Aug. 6, 22, 25, Sept. 9, 19, 22, 29, Oct. 3, 7, 9, 23, 24, 26, 29-31, Nov. 3, 4, 6, 7, 9, 23-27, Dec. 5, 29, 30
	1802 Jan. 14, 19, 26, 28, Feb. 10, 12, 24, Mar. 2, 3, 6
PPi	1802 Jan.-Dec.
PPiUD	[1800 June 18-1802 June 26]
PPL	1800 June 18-1801 June 19
	1801 June 22-Dec. 18, 21-1802 Feb. 25
	1802 Feb. 27-Mar. 12, 15, 16, 18-Oct. 27, 29-Dec. 31

continued as

RELF'S PHILADELPHIA GAZETTE AND DAILY ADVERTISER (Jan. 1, 1803-Mar. 17, 1823) d sw # *

PHILADELPHIA COUNTY 205

    Pub. & Ed. 1803-1823   Samuel Relf
               1823   Stevenson Smith and Wm. M. Gouge
         Country edition published, entitled *Philadelphia Gazette*,
         1803-1823.

P		1803 Aug. 18
		1804 Jan. 4-1805 Dec.
		[1810 Jan. 1-Dec. 31]
		[1812 Aug. 1-Dec. 31]
		[1816 Jan. 1-Dec. 31]
		[1818 Jan. 1-Dec. 31]
P-M		1805 Feb. 25
PDoHi ♦	d	1804 Dec. 11
		1807 Jan. 20, Feb. 6, 9-Mar. 12, 14-26, 28-May 30, June 2-27, 30-Nov. 5
		1808 Jan. 1-4, 6, 8-26, 28-Mar. 16, 18-May 28, 31-June 4, 7-Dec. 3, 6-22, 24-31
		1813 July 10
		1820 Apr. 8, 22
PHi		1803 Aug. 2-Nov. 30
		1804 Jan. 1-1805 Dec. 31
		1811 Jan. 1-1812 Mar.
		1814 Apr. 28, May 2, July 25, Aug. 12, 27
		1818 Jan. 1-1819 Dec. 31
		1821 Jan. 1-Dec. 31
PLaHi		1816 July 24
PNazHi		1811 Nov. 8
PP ♦	d	1803 July 4 (sup), Aug. 23
		1807 July 1-16, 18-Sept. 14, 16-Oct. 16, 19, 21-Dec. 31
		1818 Jan. 1-14, 20-24, 27-Feb. 3, 5, 10, Mar. 6, 9-June 17, 19, 21, 24, 30
		1819 July 31
		1820 Jan. 27, Mar. 21, 29, Apr. 14, 26, July 3, Nov. 7, Dec. 14, 28
PPAP		1812 Jan. 12-Mar. 26, 28-May 15, 18-June 11, 13-18, 20, 22, 24-30, July 2, 3, 6-22, 24-29, 31-Aug. 19, 21-Nov. 2, 4-27, 30-Dec. 31
PPiHi		1803 Apr. 27
PPiUD		[1807 Jan. 1-Dec. 31]
		[1811 Apr. 21-May 18]
		1812 Mar. 9, Dec. 3, 29
PPL	d	1803 Jan. 1-Apr. 7, 9-July 4, 6-Sept. 16, 19, 21-Oct. 19, 21-1804 Mar. 29
		1804 Mar. 31-1805 Feb. 26
		1805 Feb. 28, Mar. 2-23, 26-Apr. 1, 3-5, 8-11, 13-May 30, June 1-3, 5-Oct. 25, 29-1806 Jan. 25
		1806 Jan. 28-Dec. 26, 31-1807 Apr. 7
		1807 Apr. 9-June 24, 26-Dec. 10, 12-1808 May 13
		1808 May 16-Dec. 8, 10-1809 Aug. 24
		1809 Aug. 26-1810 Apr. 19
		1810 Apr. 21-July 13, 16-1811 Jan. 1
		1811 Jan. 3-Apr. 11, 13, 19-Oct. 1, 3-1812 Aug. 27
		1812 Aug. 29-1816 Apr. 11
		1816 Apr. 13-1820 Aug. 1
		1820 Aug. 3-Nov. 10-1823 Feb. 25
		1823 Feb. 27-Mar. 17
PPM ♦		1804 Jan. 2-(13)-Feb. 15, 17-Mar. (2)-29, (31)-Apr. (13)-(26)-May (8, 9)-(21)-(24)-(30)-June (6)-(9)-July (20)-(23)-Aug. (4)-(9)-(22)-

PHILADELPHIA GAZETTE AND COMMERCIAL INTELLIGENCER, THE, *continued*

                        (25)-(28)-Sept. (7, 8)-(12)-(22)-Nov. (24)-Dec. (1)-(12)-Dec. 31
                      1806 Jan. 1-Dec. 31
                      1808 Jan. 1-1811 Dec. 31
                      1813 Jan. 1, 8, 29, Feb. 17, Mar. 9, 15, 17, Apr. 3, 8, May 20, Oct. 8, 16, 18, 22, 26-28, Nov. 12, 18, 23
                      1814 Feb. 1, Oct. 15, Dec. 20
                      1815 Apr. 12, 19, July 6, 29, Aug. 16, 19, 21, 22, Oct. 9, 29, Nov. 1-4, 14, 30, Dec. 27, 29
                      1816 Jan. 1-6, 9-24, 26-Mar. 14, 16-19, 21, 22, 26-Apr. 6, 10, 11, 13-20, 22-Nov. 21, 23, 25-1818 Dec. 31
                      1820 Jan. 1-1822 Dec. 31
    PPot   1808 Feb. 9
    PRHi   [1815 Jan. 1-1818 Dec. 30]
    PWaHi   1821 July 30, 31
    PWcHi   1808 Nov. (25)
                    continued as

PHILADELPHIA GAZETTE AND DAILY ADVERTISER, THE (Mar. 18, 1823-Sept. 22, 1833) d *

Pub. & Ed. 1823-1833   Stevenson Smith
            1833   Wm. H. Gouge
    PBL ♦   1828 Jan. 9
                    1831 Aug. 15
                    1832 July 9
    PDoHi ♦   1826 July 7
    PEL ♦   1828 Jan. 9
                    1831 Aug. 15
                    1832 July 9
    PHi   1827 Feb. 14, 20, 22, Mar. 12
                    1833 Jan. 1-Sept. 22
    PLewL   1833 Apr. 18
    PPiHi   1828 Apr. 17, May 8
    PPL ♦   1823 Mar. 18-1824 Feb. 13
                    1824 Feb. 16-1825 July 13
                    1825 July 16-18, 20-Sept. 19, 21-Nov. 10, 12-1826 May 5
                    1826 May 8-1827 Jan. 3
                    1827 Feb. 1-17, 20-July 3, 5-Sept. 28, Oct. 2, 30, Nov. 1-1829 Nov. 27
                    1829 Nov. 30-1830 Jan. 6
                    1830 Jan. 8-Feb. 6, 9-15, 17-June 17, 19-Aug. 9, 11-1831 Apr. 20
                    1831 Apr. 22-1832 June 29
                    1832 July 2-28, 31-Aug. 16, 18-Sept. 3, 5-Oct. 12, 15-1833 Jan. 2
                    1833 Jan. 4-9, 11-17, 19-Mar. 6, 8-May 31, June 3-Aug. 6, 8-Sept. 22
    PPM ♦   1826 Jan. (2)-Feb. 17, 20-Mar. 31, Apr. 3-15, 24-May 3, 5-June 26, 28-July 18, 20-22, 25-Aug. 16, 18-Oct. 13, 16-(18)-24, 26-Dec. 23-(30)
                    1827 Jan. 1, 3, 4, 6-12, 15-24, 26-30, Feb. 1-5, (7)-10, 19, Mar. 2-21, 24-(31)-June 21, 25-July 3-7, 24, 30-Aug. 10, 13-Dec. 19, 21-24-31
                    1828 July 1-Dec. 31
                    1829 Jan. 1-Mar. 27, 30-Aug. 26, 28-Dec. 31

1830 Jan. 1-June 24, 26-Dec. 31
1831 Jan. 1-Apr. (20)-May 23, 25
continued as
PHILADELPHIA GAZETTE AND UNIVERSAL DAILY ADVERTISER (Sept. 23, 1833-Nov. 30, 1834) d
Pub. & Ed. 1833-1834   Wm. H. Gouge
          1834   Samuel Coate Atkinson
P   1834 Mar. 1-Nov. 30
PHi   1833 Sept. 23-Dec. 31
PPL   1833 Sept. 23-Nov. 13, 15-Dec. 4, 6-1834 Apr. 9
                  1834 Nov. 28

Absorbed *Commercial Intelligencer* and title changed to
PHILADELPHIA GAZETTE AND COMMERCIAL INTELLIGENCER, THE (Dec. 1, 1834-Nov. 3, 1845) d *
Pub. 1834   Samuel Coate Atkinson
     1834-1845   Condy Raguet
     1834   Robert T. Conrad
P   1834 Dec. 1-1836 May 3
PHi   1844 July 1-Dec. 31
                  1845 June 6, July 1-Nov. 3
PP   1841 July 1-Dec. 31
                  1842 Jan. 1-Feb. 11, 13-Mar. 2, 4-16, 18-Apr. 12, 14-May 29, 31-June 30
                  1843 Jan. 1-Dec. 30
                  1844 Jan. 1-June 29
PPiUD   1841 Oct. 13, Nov. 1
                  1842 Apr. 18
PPL ◆   1834 Dec. 1-10, 12-19, 22, 23, 26-1835 Jan. 9
                  1835 Jan. 12-21, 23-27, 29-Mar. 3, 5-Apr. 1, 3-May 28, 30-Oct. 14, 16-1836 Jan. 16
                  1836 Jan. 18-Apr. 5, 7-16, 19-Aug. 26, 29-Nov. 14, 16-Dec. 28
                  1837 Jan. 2-14, 17-Oct. 3, 5-1838 Feb. 3
                  1838 Feb. 6-10, 13-19, 21-May 3, 5-1840 Mar. 31
Absorbed by the *North American*, 1845.

PHILADELPHIA GAZETTE-DEMOCRAT (Jan. 25, 1879†) d w sun for *
    PHILADELPHIA NEUE ZEITUNG (Jan. 25, 1879-Jan. 24, 1880) d
Pub. 1879-1880   Carl Theodore Mayer
PPDe   1879 Jan. 25-July (7, 8)-(11-15)
                  1880 Jan. 24
PPF   [1879 Jan. 25-1880 Jan. 24]
PPG ◆   1879 Jan. 25-1880 Jan. 24
                  continued as
    PHILADELPHIA GAZETTE (Jan. 26, 1880-July 11, 1880) d
Pub. 1880   Carl Theodore Mayer
PPDe   1880 Jan. 26-Mar. 13, 16-July 11
PPF   1880 Jan. 26-July 11
PPG ◆   1880 Jan. 26-July 11
                  continued as
    PHILADELPHIA GAZETTE UND REPUBLIK (July 12, 1880-Sept. 20, 1880) d
Pub. 1880   Carl Theodore Mayer
PPDe   1880 July 12-Sept. 20
PPF   1880 July 12-Sept. 20
PPG ◆   1880 July 12-Sept. 20

PHILADELPHIA GAZETTE-DEMOCRAT, *continued*

continued as

PHILADELPHIA GAZETTE (Abend Ausgabe) (Sept. 21, 1880-Nov. 27, 1892) d eve morn

Pub. & Ed. 1880-1891   Carl Theodore Mayer
           1891-1892   German Daily Gazette Publishing Co.

Philadelphia Abend Gazette Sept. 4, 1890-June 30, 1891
Philadelphia Morgen Gazette Apr. 12, 1890-Oct. 29, 1891
Morgen Gazette Oct. 30, 1891-Nov. 27, 1892

PPG ◆   1890 Sept. 4
          1891 Mar. 6, 10-June 30
PUB   1890 Sept. 4-(30)-Oct. 16, 18-27, 29-Dec. 10, 12-17, 19-24, 26-31
          1891 Jan. 2-May 6, 10-Sept. 30

continued as

PHILADELPHIA MORGEN GAZETTE (Nov. 28, 1892-May 9, 1918) d sw sun

Pub. 1892-1918   German Daily Gazette Publishing Co.
Ed. 1892   Max Heinrici

Sunday edition, *Philadelphia Sonntags-Gazette,* first issue Nov. 27, 1892

Weekly edition published *Pennsylvanische Staats Gazette,* 1896-1918.

PPDe   1894 Jan. 1-30, Feb. (1-Apr. 7)-June 30
         1895 Oct. 1-Dec. 31
         1900 Jan. 11, Feb. 7, Mar. 19
         1901 Jan. 5, Feb. 26
         1902 June 2-30, Nov. 14
         1903 Feb. 2, Apr. 9, June 22, Sept. 23
         1904 Jan. 1, Apr. 25, Aug. 6, Sept. 8, Dec. 29
         1905 Mar. 11, July 11, Sept. 7, 11, Oct. 7
         1906 May 3-8, 19, 22, 28, 31; Dec. 24, 26
         1907 Jan. 17, 19, 21; Mar. 19, 20; May 27, 29; June 12, 28

sun 1892 Nov. 27-1893 Jan. (1)-Mar. 5
      1893 Mar. 19-Apr. 9, 23-May 21, June 11, 18, July 2-Aug. (6)-1894 Mar. 11
      1894 Mar. 25-June (17)-Oct. (7-21)-1895 Feb. 3
      1895 Feb. 24-Apr. (28)-June (30)-1896 May (31)-July (19, 26)-Aug. (16)-1898 Sept. (25)-Oct. (2-23)-Nov. (6-20)-1899 Mar. 26
      1899 May 7-Sept. 24, Nov. 5-Dec. (31)-1900 Feb. 11
      1900 Mar. 4-Apr. (15)-July (1, 8)-Aug. (19)-Sept. (30), Oct. 14-Dec. 16, 30-1901 Feb. (3, 10)-(24)-June 30
      1901 Oct 6-1904 July (3)-Sept. (11)-1905 Jan. (22)-Feb. (26)-June (11)-Oct. (1)-1906 Feb. (11)-Mar. (4)-1908 Jan. (5)-June 14

PPG ◆ 1894 Jan. 1-June 30
        1895 Oct. 1-1900 Mar. 19
        1901 Jan. 5; Feb. 26
        1902 June 2-30; Nov. 14
        1903 Feb. 2; Apr. 9; June 22; Sept. 23
        1904 Jan. 1; Apr. 25, Aug. 6, Sept. 8, Dec. 29
        1905 Mar. 11, July 1, Sept. 7, 11, Oct. 7
        1906 May 3-8, 19, 22, 28, 31, Dec. 24, 26
        1907 Jan. 17, 19, 21, Mar. 19, 20, May 27, 29, June 12, 28

PHILADELPHIA COUNTY 209

Philadelphia Morgen Gazette merged with *Philadelphia Democrat,* May 9, 1918
continued as
PHILADELPHIA GAZETTE-DEMOCRAT (1918†) d for
Pub. 1918-1933 Philadelphia Gazette Publishing Co.
   1933-1937 Gustav Mayer
   1937-1939 Louis Mayer
   1939-1941 Philadelphia Gazette Publishing Co.
Ed. 1918-1933 Gustav Mayer
   1933-1939 E. Kiefer
   1939-1941 Louis Mayer
  PUB   1918 May 9-(19)-(26)-Sept. (22)-Nov. (29)-1919 Jan. (2)-Feb. 6
     1919 Feb. 8-28-Aug. 30, Sept. 1-Nov. (1)-Dec. (31)
     1920 Jan. 1-22, (24-25)-May (1)-(10)-(13)-1921 Mar. (26)-Apr. (24)-(27)-Nov. (7)-(9)-(11)-(13)-(15)-(17)-(19)-(21)-(23) - (25) - (27)-(29)-Dec. (1)-(3)-(4)-(9)-(11)-(15)-(17)-(19)-(21)-(23)-(25)-(27)-(29)-(31)-1922 Jan. (11), 26
     1922 Jan. 28-Aug. (7)-Oct. (31), Nov. (1)-Dec. (3)-1923 Feb. (28)-May (1)-(13)-July (1)-1926 Jan. (1)-June (20)-Nov. (1)†
  w   1921 Nov. 23-1923 Mar. 14
    1923 Apr. 4-25, May 9-Sept. 19, Oct. 3-Dec. 12, 26
    1925 Jan. 7-Mar. 25, Apr. 8-May (6)-1927 Sept. 21
  sun   1927 Sept. 25-Dec. 25
    1928 Jan. 8, 22-Mar. (13)-June 17, July 1, 15-Aug. 5, 19-1929 Nov. 17
  PP   1927 June 1, 3-25, 27-Sept. 3, 5-Oct. 11, 13-19, 21-Dec. 2, 4-12, 14-Dec. 31
    1928 Jan. 1, 3-Aug. 26, 28†

PHILADELPHIA GUIDE (1864-1870) w ♦
  Pub. & Ed. 1870 E. L. Pearson

PHILADELPHIA HERALD, see Evening Herald

PHILADELPHIA HERALD (Dec. 26, 1863-Jan. 2, 1864) w
  PHi ♦   1864 Jan. 2 (Vol. 1, No. 2)

PHILADELPHIA HEROLD (1894†) w ind non-part for
VEREINS UND LOGEN ZEITUNG (Jan. 6, 1894-Jan. 10, 1925) w for
Pub. 1902-1908 Central Newspaper Union
   1908-1916 Adolph Timm
   1916-1924 Graf & Breuninger
Ed. 1902-1916 Adolph Timm
   1916-1924 Graf & Breuninger
Vereins Und Logen-Zeitung merged Jan. 17, 1925, with, and changed title to *Philadelphia Herold.*
  PUB   1917 Jan. 10
  PCHi   1894 Feb. 9
  PLaF   1894 Jan. 6, 10
    1925 Jan. 17
  PPGHi   1894 Jan. 6
    1911 Nov. 18

PHILADELPHIA HEROLD, continued
    PPph   1911 Nov. 25
                    1925 Jan. (6)-Jan. 10
                    continued as
    PHILADELPHIA HEROLD (Jan. 17, 1925†) w
      Pub. 1925-1938   Graf & Breuninger
            1938-1939   Herold
            1939-1941   William B. Graf & Sons
      Ed. 1925-1928   Graf & Breuninger
            1929-1941   William B. Graf
      PUB   1925 Jan. 17-1927 Dec. 31
                      1929 Jan.†
      PLaF   1935 Nov. 2-1936 Apr. 18†
      PP   1927 Dec. 31
                      1928 Feb. 7, 21-Apr. 28, May 12-1929 July 6
                      1929 July 20-Sept. 21, Oct. 5-Dec. 14, 28-1936 July 8
                      1936 July 22†
      PPCo   1928 Jan.-Dec.

PHILADELPHIA HOME WEEKLY (1843-1869) w lit *
    DOLLAR NEWSPAPER, THE (Jan. 25, 1843-1864) w *
      Pub. 1843-1855   A. H. Simmons & Co.
            1857-1864   William M. Swain & Co.
            1864   George W. Childs
      PHi ♦   w 1846 May 27, July 29
                      1847 Sept. 29
                      1848 Mar. 8
                      1849 Mar. 14, 21
                      1850 Dec. 11
                      1853 Apr. 20
                      1855 Apr. 12, 19, 26
                      1857 Jan. 14, 21, Feb. 4, 11, Apr. 1, May 27
                      1862 Aug. 27, Dec. 24
                      1863 June 24
                      1864 May 11, July 27, Aug. 24, Sept. 14
      PP   1851 Mar. 26
                      1852 Jan. 14, 21, Feb. 18-Mar. 24
                      1853 Jan. 5, 19-Aug. 24, Sept. 7-Dec. 28
                      1862 Mar. 5
                      continued as
    HOME WEEKLY AND HOUSEHOLD NEWSPAPER, THE (1864-1865) w *
      Pub. 1864-1865   George W. Childs
      PHi ♦   1865 Apr. 12, 26, May 24
                      continued as
    PHILADELPHIA HOME WEEKLY (1866-1869) w *
      Pub. & Ed. 1866   George W. Childs
      PHi ♦   1866 Feb. 7, Nov. 7

PHILADELPHIA INDEPENDENT (May 10, 1931†) w ind Negro
      Pub. 1936-1941   Philadelphia Independent, Inc.
      Ed. 1936-1938   F. W. Woodward
            1938-1941   R. H. Jones
      PHi ♦   1933 Dec. 3
      PP   1935 Jan. 6, Feb. 3†
      PUB   1931 May 10†

PHILADELPHIA COUNTY 211

PHILADELPHIA INQUIRER PUBLIC LEDGER (1807†) # *
DEMOCRATIC PRESS (1807-1829) d tw w
Pub. 1807-1829   John Binns
    tw Mar. 27, 1807-Nov. 30, 1829|| as: *Democratic Press for the Country* from June 29, 1807;
        d June 29, 1807-Nov. 30, 1829||;
    w Nov. 26, 1807-Nov. 26, 1829|| as: *Weekly Democratic Press*
This was the first paper published in the United States using the word "Democratic" in the title.
Issue of June 12, 1819, was a one-sheet issue.

P		d 1807	May 20-1821 Aug. 29
		1826	June 24, 26
		tw 1807	July 13-1808 Jan. 8
		1810	Nov. 17-1820 Dec. 30
		[1826]	
P-M		1807	May 18
		1826	June 24, 26
PBelC		1807	Sept. 5, 8
		1816	Apr. 4-6
		1818	Apr. 2
PBL ♦		d 1811	Sept. 14-Oct. 2, 4-16, 19-Nov. 6, 9-18, 20-30, Dec. 4-10, 12-20, 23, 24, 26-31
		1812	Jan. 2-13, 15-Feb. 3, 5, 6, 10, 12-26, 28, Mar. 2-12, 14-18, 21-26, 28-31
		1823	Sept. 4, 12, 13, Oct. 16, Nov. 5
		tw 1827	Dec. 15/17, 18/19
PCarlHi		1813	July 8, 9
		1816	July 18, 19
PDoC		1813	Apr.-Sept.
PDoHi		d 1807	Oct. 14-17, 20, 23-31, Nov. 3-5, 7
		1808	Mar. 11, Sept. 22, 23
		1819	Nov. 16, Dec. 30
		1820	Feb. 11, 12
		1824	Apr. 5, 6, 23, 30
		1825	Mar. 28, Apr. 27, May 18, June 1
		1827	Sept. 6
		w 1813	Mar. 22/25, July 5/8
		1814	June 6/9, July 5/7
		1815	Mar. 13/16, Apr. 24/27, May 22/25, June 19/22, July 17/20, Nov. 6/9, Dec. 4/7
		1818	Aug. 3/6
		1819	Aug. 26/29
		1820	Sept. 25/28
		1821	Mar. 19/22
		1824	July 5/8
		1825	Feb. 7/10, Apr. 25/28, Dec. 12/15
		1827	Apr. 28, Sept. 8, Oct. 27
		1828	Jan. 12, Feb. 2-23, May 10, Aug. 16, Oct. 4, 18, Nov. 8, Dec. 20, 27
		1829	Jan. 3, 10, 24-Feb. 7
		tw 1821	Mar. 3/5, 27/28-Apr. 3/4, Sept. 25/26, 29/Oct. 1, 13/15
		1824	Apr. 27/28, 29/30, May 4/5-13/14, June 3/4-8/9, 12/14, 19/20, 24/25, 26/28, July 1/2, 3/5, 8/9, Aug. 10/11-19/20, Sept. 18/20, 21/22, 30/Oct. 1, 9/11, 12/13, Nov. 4/5, Dec. 4/6-9/10, 16/17, 21/22, 23/24, 28/29

PENNSYLVANIA NEWSPAPERS

PHILADELPHIA INQUIRER PUBLIC LEDGER, *continued*
- 1825 Jan. 22/24, Mar. 1/2, 26/28, Apr. 9/11-16/18, 21/22, 26/27, 28/29, May 12/13, 19/20-28/30, June 4/6-July 5/6, 9/11-21/22, 28/29, Aug. 16/17-27/29, Sept. 1/2-10/12, Oct. 1/3-13/14, 18/19-22/24, 27/28-Nov. 3/4, 10/11, 15/16, 17/18
- 1826 Mar. 16/17
- 1828 Dec. 4/5

PHi ◆ d 1807 Mar. 27-1808 Nov. 5
- 1808 Nov. 8-1809 Feb. 3
- 1809 Feb. 6-Mar. 3, 6-Aug. 11, 13-1810 Feb. 14
- 1810 Feb. 19-23, 27-Mar. 9, 12-May 17, 19-Oct. 3, 5, 6, 9-1811 Apr. 6
- 1811 Apr. 9-Aug. 30, Sept. 2, Dec. 31
- 1813 Jan. 2-June 29
- 1814 Jan. 3-June 27, July 11-15, 20-23, 26-Aug. 17, 19-Sept. 12, 14, 16-Nov. 10, 12-Dec. 16, 19-1815 June 5
- 1815 July 1-24, 26-Sept. 29, Oct. 2-10, 12-Dec. 14
- 1816 Jan. 1, 2, 4-Sept. 8, 10-Dec. 13, 16-1817 Apr. 3
- 1817 Apr. 5-1820 Jan. (3)-1821 Feb. 6
- 1821 Feb. 8-1822 Apr. 3
- 1822 Apr. 5-1823 Jan. 20
- 1823 Jan. 22-27, 20-1824 June 28
- 1825 Jan. 1-Dec. 31
- 1826 Jan. 3-July 22, 25-29, Aug. 1-Nov. 27, 29-1827 July 30
- 1827 Aug. 1-1828 Apr. 3
- 1828 Apr. 5-June 28, July 1-Oct. 30, Nov. 1-1829 Nov. 30

PLaHi 1813 Aug. 20, 21
PLewL w 1828 Nov. 29
PMe 1808 Apr. 6
PNoHi 1816 Jan. 11, 12
     1818 Jan.-1820 Feb.
     tw 1820 Feb. 10/11
     d 1822 Dec. 5, 6
     1825 Sept. 1, 2

PP d 1811 Apr. 13, May 1, 8, 10-June 10, 12-15, 19, 20, 27-29, July 1, 2, 5, 6, 8-18, 27, 31, Aug. 14, 17, 19-21, 27, 28, Sept. 11, 20, 21, 23, 24, 26, 28, 30, Oct. 1, 2, 4-12, 16, 17, Nov. 11, 19, 20, 23, 25, 27-30, Dec. 2-21, 23, 24, 27, 31
- 1812 Jan. 7, 8, 11, 13, 15, 16, 20-22, 25, 28, Feb. 1, 3-5, 15, 17-20, 26, Mar. 2, 12, 19, 21, 23, 31, Apr. 2-4, 6, 15, 20, 22, 23, May 18, 19, 24, 26-29, June 1-6, 19, 20, 22, 25-27, 29, 30, July 1-3, 6, 7, 9, 14, 18, 20-24, 31, Aug. 1, 3-6, 10, 11, 14, 21, 24-27, 29, Sept. 3-5, 7-10, 14, 16, 17, 21, 23, 29, 30, Oct. 2, Nov. 3-10, 17, 20, 24-26, 30, Dec. 3, 4, 16-19, 21, 30
- 1813 Jan. 1, 4, 12, 19, 21-23, 29, Feb. 2, 10-26, Mar. 3, 5, 8, 11, 13, 29, 30, Apr. 1, 2, 5-7, 9, 10, 12-15, 21, 27, May 24, 27, 29, 31-June 11, 16-18, 22-July 3, 7-19, 21-23, 26-31, Aug. 2, 4, 6, 7, 9-30, Sept. 2, 3, 10, 25, 28, Oct. 6, 8, 9, 13, 15, 19, 23, Nov. 8, 11, 15, 24-Dec. 1, 4, 5, 31
- 1814 Jan. 5, 7, 10-Feb. 5, 7, 10-22, 24-26, 28-Mar. 12, 21, 26, Apr. 6, 12-14, 23, 25-27, 29, May 4, 5, 10-

PHILADELPHIA COUNTY 213

                 13, 16-19, 24-26, 30 June 3, 4, 7, 28, July 14, 15, 18, Aug. 4, 15, 27, Sept. 10, 19, 20, 24, 27, 28, 30, Oct. 3-7, 11-15, 17, 19-22, 24-Dec. 2, 8, 9, 12, 15, 16, 20, 26, 28, 30
          1815 Jan. 5, 9, 20, 25, 28, Feb. 3, 4, 7, 8, 10, 13-15, 18, 24, Mar. 4, 7, 9, Apr. 17, 19-22, 24, 25, 29, May 4, 10, 20, June 9, 20, July 14, 19, 27-29, Aug. 1-3, 5, 7, 9, 11, 12, 15-18, 21, 24, 26, 30, 31, Sept. 1, 2, 6-9, 12, 14, 18, 19, 23, 29, Oct. 4, 5, 9-13, 19, 23, 25, 28, 30, Nov. 2, 4, 8, 11, 13, 16, 17, 21-25, 27, 29, 30, Dec. 1, 2, 4, 5, 7, 11-13, 15, 16, 18, 20, 21, 26, 30
          1816 Jan. 10, 15, 16, 19, Feb. 5, 8-10, 12-15, 17, 20-22, Mar. 6, 9, 10, 12-16, 18, 20-23, 26-30, Apr. 2, 3, 8-10, 13, 15, 16, 18, 20, 22, 25, May 2, 7, 11, 13, 16, 17, 22, 23, 25, 27-29, June 1, 3-7, 10, 12, 14, 18, 21, July 1, 5, 6, 11, 12, 15-17, 22, 24, 27, 31, Aug. 5-7, 14, 17, 19
      d 1816 Aug. 23, 26, 28, Sept. 2-7, 10-13, Oct. 10, 18, 24, 26, Nov. 15, 16, 27, 30, Dec. 4, 5, 9, 11, 12, 17
          1817 July 12, 24, Oct. 20
          1818 Aug. 26
          1819 Feb. 24, Dec. 9
          1820 Feb 29, Mar. 1, June 27, Nov. 2, 16, 25
          1822 Apr. 19
          1825 July 11
   tw 1814 Aug. 27/29
          1816 Dec. 19/20, 21/23, 26/27-31
          1817 Jan. 1, 4/6, 11/13, Feb. 6/7, 11/12, 13/14, 15/17, Mar. 29/31, Apr. 8/9, 10/11, 24/25, May 3/5, 6/7, 10/12, 20/21, 23/24, 29/30, June 3/4, 7/9, 14/16, 17/19/ 26/27, July 3/5, 6/7, 10/11, 12/14, 15/16, 26/28-31/Aug. 1, 16/18, Sept. 4/5, 11/12, 16/17, 20/22-25/26, Oct. 1, 4/6, 11/13, 21/22, 25/27-Nov. 1/3, 15/17, 25/26, 29/Dec. 1, 4/5, 7/9-12/13, 27/29
          1818 Jan. 1/2, 10/12, 15/16, 29/30-Feb. 2, 3/4, 7/9, 19/20, 26/27, Mar. 5/6-12/13, 17/18, 28/30, 31/ Apr. 1, 7/8-16/17, 21/22, 25/27, 28/29, May 2/4, 7/8, 14/15, 19/20, June 2/3, 6/8-27/29, July 11/ 13, 16/17, 23/24, 28/29-Aug. 6/7, 11/12, 13/14, 18/19, 22/24, 29/31, Sept. 3/4-10/11, 17/18, 22/ 23, 24/ 25, 28/29, Oct. 3/5, 6/7, 10/12, 15/16, 22/ 23, 24/26, Nov. 3/4, 7/9-14/16, 19/20-Dec. 1/2, 5/7-10/11, 17/18, 22/23, 26/28, 31/1819 Jan. 1
          1819 Jan. 12/13, 16/18-23/25, Feb. 9/10, 11/12, 16/ 17, Mar. 2/3-11/12, 18/19, 23/24, 25/26, 30/31-Apr. 6/7, 17/19, May 1/2, 4/5, 13/14-18/19, 22/ 24, June 3/4,19/21, 24/25-July 1/2, 6/7-22/23, 27/28, 29/30, Aug. 12/13, 17/18-21/23, Sept. 14/15-25/27, Oct. 5/6, 7/8, 16/18, 19/20, 26/27, 30/Nov. 1, Dec. 7/8, 26/27
          1820 Jan. 6/7, 11/13, 18/19, 25/26, Feb. 5/7, 10/11, 12/14, 19/21, Mar. 9/10-14/15, 18/20, 23/24

PPeS   w 1819 June 12
PPi   [1810]
PPiHi   1811 [Jan. 1-Dec. 31]
PPiUD 1811 Apr. 19, May 3, 10, 17, June 22-1812 Jan. 9

214 PENNSYLVANIA NEWSPAPERS

PHILADELPHIA INQUIRER PUBLIC LEDGER, *continued*

	1813 Jan. 2-Dec. 31
PPL	1813 June 12, Nov. 2
	1815 Jan. 11-Feb. 20, 23-May 30
	1818 Feb. 4-7, 10-13, 16, 18-Mar. 19, 23-Apr. 14, 16-Aug. 10, 12-Oct. 20, 26-Nov. 18, 20-Dec. 31
	1819 Jan. 2-Feb. 9, 11-16, 18, 19, 24-Aug. 19, 21-Sept. 21, 23-Oct. 11, 13-Nov. 22, 24-Dec. 22, 24-1820 Jan. (1)-25
	1820 Jan. 27-Mar. 30, Apr. 1-June 15, 17-July 3, 6-Oct. 3, 5-9, 11-13, 17-Nov. 1, 3, 6-Dec. 7, 9-20, 22-29
	1821 Jan. 1-Mar. 8, 10-Apr. 19, 21-Sept. 8, 11-Oct. 5, 9-12, 14-25, 27-Dec. 26, 28-1822 Jan. 2
	1822 Jan. 7-30, Feb. 1-Apr. 4, 6-29, May 1-Dec. 31
	1823 Apr. 1-May 26, 28-Dec. 31
	1825 Jan. 1-Feb. 4, 7, 8, 10-25, 28-Mar. 31, Apr. 2-8, 11-May 30, June 1-Oct. 29, Nov. 1-15, 17-23, 25-1826 July 22
	1826 July 25-1827 Feb. 7
	1827 Feb. 9-May 7, 9-16, 18-June 9, 12-July 24, 26-Sept. 7, 10-Nov. 2, 5-Dec. 6, 8-12, 14-24
	1828 Jan. 2-31, Feb. 4-July 31, Aug. 2-15, 18-Sept. 24, 26-Dec. 31
PPM	1813 Jan. 2-Dec. 31
	1816 Jan. 1-June 29
	1826 Jan. 3-Dec. 30
	1827 Jan. 1-Dec. 27
	w [1826]
PPot	d 1813 Oct. 7
	1815 Apr. 25, 26
	1829 Feb. 28, Mar. 2, May 23, 25
	w 1826 Apr. 22
PToHi	w 1816 Apr. 4
PWbW	1821 Sept. 8
PWcHi	w 1810 Oct. 8/11
PWeT	1822 Mar. 20
	1824 Mar. 30-Apr. 2

absorbed by the *Pennsylvania Inquirer* and continued as

PENNSYLVANIA INQUIRER (June 1, 1829-July 1, 1830) d
Pub. & Ed. 1829 John Norvell and John R. Walker
        1829 Nov.-1830 Jesper Harding
  P   1829 July 20, 30
  PP ♦ 1829 June 1
  PPI   1829 June 29-1830 July 1
  PPL   1829 June 1-22, July 1-18, 21, 24-Nov. (11)-Dec. 4, 7-1830 Jan. 5
          1830 Jan. 7-30
  PPot 1930 Apr. 29, 30

merged with the *Morning Journal* (q.v.) to form

PENNSYLVANIA INQUIRER AND MORNING JOURNAL (July 2, 1830-June 1, 1834) d
Pub. & Ed. 1830-1834 Jesper Harding
  P   1833 Dec. 20-1834 June 30
  PBL ♦ 1830 Dec. 25
           1831 Jan. 29
           1832 Sept. 18

PHILADELPHIA COUNTY 215

  PE   1834 May 10-12, 14-June 1
  PEL ♦   1830 Dec. 11, 25
        1831 Jan. 29
        1834 Jan. 29
  PP   1831 Jan. 1-June 29
  PPI   1830 July 2-1834 June 30
  PPL   1830 July 2-Sept. (7, 8)-14, 16-27, 29-Nov. 3, 5-9, 11-1831 Feb. 23
        1831 Feb. 25-Mar. (29)-Apr. (2)-22, 25-May 21, 24-26, 28-June 14, 16-(20)-22, 24-July 2, 5-Aug. 10, 12-Sept. 30, Oct. 3-(24)-26, 28, 31-Nov. 7, 9-18, 21-25, 28-Dec. 2, 5-14, 16-30
        1832 July 2-4, 6-(17)-19, 21-Nov. (1)-Dec. (3)-(7)-(19)-31
        1833 Feb. 1-Mar. 9, 12-Apr. 19, 22-July 4, 6-19, 22-Oct. (1)-Nov. (1)-Dec. 20, 23-25, 27-1834 Jan. (1, 2)-May 31
  PPM   1831 Apr. 4, 6-June 14, 16-July 5, 7-Oct. 19, 21-Dec. 17, 20-26, 28-31
        1833 Jan. 1-3, 5-12, 14-Apr. 18, 20-May 16
  PWcHi   1832 Jan. 7, 14, 21, Feb. 18, Mar. 3
        merged with *Daily Courier* (q.v.) to form

PENNSYLVANIA INQUIRER AND DAILY COURIER (June 2, 1834-Jan. 3, 1842) d
Pub. & Ed. 1834-1842 Jesper Harding
  P   1834 July 1-1838 Aug. 30
        1839 Nov. 21
        1840 June 12
  PE   1834 June 2-July 1, 4, 7-21, 23-29, 31-Aug. 9, 13, 15-Sept. 3, 5-Oct. 16, 18-31, Nov. 3- Dec. 9, 11-20, 23, 25, 27-1835 Feb. 2
        1835 Feb. 5-20
  PHi ♦   1834 June (2)-July (22)-(31)-Aug. (15)-(26)-Nov. 11, 13-(17)-(21)-Dec. 2, 4-(25)-31
        1835 Jan. (1)-Feb. 11, 16-Apr. (8)-July 4, 7-Aug. 1, 4-Sept. 22, 24-Oct. (2)- 16, 19-Nov. 4, 6-(10)-14, 17-(21)-Dec. 25, 29-31
        1836 Mar. 1-Apr. 13, 15-May 4, 6-July 13, 15, 16, 19-Nov. (1, 2)-Dec. (5, 6)- 26, 28, 30, 31
        1837 Jan. 2-Mar. (1)-Apr. 25, 27, 29, May 3, 5-June (2)-July (1)-4, 7-18, 20-24, 26, 27, 29-Sept. 5, 8-11, 13-19, 21-Oct. 10, 12-20, 23, 24, 27-Nov. 1, 6-8, 10-15, 17-20, 22-Dec. 30
        1838 Jan. 1-Apr. 23, 25-July (2)-4-(12)-26, 28-Sept. 17, 19-(25), 28, Oct. 1-11, 13-(15)-Nov. 12, 14-Dec. 31
        1839 Jan. 10-31, May 1-28, 30-June 29, July (2-8)-Sept. 9, 11-14, 17-Dec. 31
        1840 Jan. 3, 4, 8-10, 14-27, 29-June 2, 4, 6-Aug. 8, 11, 13, 14, 17-19, 21-Sept. 4, 7-(19)-Nov. (21)-28, Dec. 1-14, (16), 18-31
        1841 Jan. 1, 4-27, 29-Feb. (8)-Mar. 6, 9-Apr. 20, 22-May 14, 17-June (9)-July 5, 7-20, 22-Aug. 11, 13-17, 19-Sept. (27)-Oct. 15 (18)-Dec. (2)-1842 Jan. 13
  PP ♦   1840 Jan. 1-1842 Jan. 3
  PPCHi   1835 July 9
  PPi   1834 July 1-1842 Jan. 3
  PPL   1834 July 1-July 3, 7-Aug. (6, 7)-Dec. (15)-(31)

PHILADELPHIA INQUIRER PUBLIC LEDGER, *continued*

              1835 Mar. 27-June 30
              1836 Apr. 7-May (3)-June 3, 6, 8-July (11)- 30, Aug. 2-(8)-Sept. 30, Oct. 31-Nov. 4, 7, 9-Dec. 31
              1837 Jan. 4 (5)-Feb. 17, 20-28, Mar. 2-31, Apr. 4, 6-29, May 2-27, 30-June 30, July 3-(7)-(10)-(14)-31, Aug. 3-12, 15, 16, 18-31, Sept. 4-(13, 14)-Oct. (2), 4-10, 12-31, Nov. 2-Dec. 30
              1838 Jan. 2, 3, 5-(11), 12, 15, 27, 30, Feb. 1-Mar. (21)-Apr. 30, May 2-31, June 2-(16)- 30, July 3, 4, 6, 9-25, 27-Aug. 11, 14-17, 20-Oct. 1, 3, 5-(22)-Dec. 31
              1839 Dec. 14
              1840 Apr. 23, 24, 27, 28, May 15, 16, June 9, July (25)
              1841 Jan. (1)-4, 6-Apr. 13, 15-20, 22-May 14, 17-June (18)-30
PPM ◆   1841 Jan. 2-(12)-Mar. (20)-May 13, 17-July 5, 7-15, 17-Aug. 28, (31)-Sept. (13)-15, 17-Oct. (12, 13)-19, 21-Nov. (1)-Dec. (18)-24, 27-31
              1842 Jan. 3
PPot   1839 Oct. 16
PW   1840 Mar. 21, 28, Apr. 4, 7
PWcHi   1837 Nov. 7
              merged with *National Gazette and Literary Register* (q.v.) to form

PENNSYLVANIA INQUIRER AND NATIONAL GAZETTE (Jan. 4, 1842-April 1, 1860) d

Pub. & Ed. 1842-1855 Jesper Harding
           1855-1859 Jesper Harding and William W. Harding
           1859-1860 William W. Harding

           A weekly edition was published 1843-Dec. 26, 1846, *Philadelphia Saturday Inquirer;* Jan. 2, 1847-Oct. 28, 1847, *Philadelphia Saturday Gleaner.*

P   1844 Mar. 20-1850 Aug. 22
PBL ◆ w 1845 Dec. 6
PDoHi ◆   1859 Sept. 6, Oct. 24
PHi ◆   1842 Jan. 4-(18)-Feb. 9, 11-Mar. 1, 3-14, 16-Apr. 1, 4-May (14)-June 6, 8-18, 21-(24)-July 9, 13, 14, 16-19, 21, 22, 25-30, Aug. 4-(8)-11, 13, 16-(23)-Sept. 12, 17, 19, 21, 22, (26)-29, Oct. 1-10, 12-17, 19, 20, 24, 26-Nov. 2, 7, 8, 11, 12, 16-19, (22)-Dec. 5, 7-12, 16, 19-23, 26, 28-30
              1843 Jan. 2, 3, 5-Feb. (7)-Apr. 24, 26-June 20, 22-Oct. (12)-Nov. 18, 21-Dec. 21, 23-25, 27-30
              1844 Jan. 1-Feb. 29, Mar. 2-(26)-Apr. (18)-May (2)-June 29, July 3-Oct. 24, 26-Dec. (3)-(18)-(28)-31
              1845 Jan. 1-(4)-(31)-Mar. (1)-(21)-Apr. (7)-May (17)-June 12, 14-(28)-(30)-July 4, 6-Aug. (2)-(9)-Sept. (5)-Nov. 27, Dec. 1-31
              1846 Jan. 1-(23)-(26)-May (23)-June (23)-Aug. 4, 6-Oct. (20)-Nov. (27)-Dec. 25, 28-31
              1850 Jan. (1)-Feb. (8)-Apr. (5)-May (1)-June (3, 4)-July 4, 6-30, Aug. 1-Dec. 12, 14-31
              1852 Jan. (3)-22, 24-May (24)-July 5, 7-(24)-Nov. (4)-(25)

PHILADELPHIA COUNTY 217

    PHsHi   1842 Mar. 21-1846 Mar. 13
    PLhT   w 1847 Jan. 9-Mar. 13, 27-Apr. 3, June 12
    PP   ♦ d 1842 Jan. 4-June 1
                  1846 May 7
                  1849 Oct. 18
                  1854 Oct. 27, Nov. 13, 15, 16
              d 1854 Oct. 27, Nov. 13, 16, 23
                  1855 Apr. 30
                  1856 Feb. 29, May 29, Aug. 14, Oct. 7-11
                  1857 Feb. 20, May 4, June 20, 24, 26, July 14, Dec. 19
                  1858 Apr. 3, 10, 12, 14, 16, 27, May 1, 3, 5, 6, 10, 11, 13, 15, 18, 22, 24, 26, 28, June 2, 5, 11, 14, 15, 18, 19, 21-23, 25, 26, July 15, 17, 23, 28, 31, Aug. 3, 4, 6, 7
                  1859 Feb. 28, Mar. 2, July 7, 9, 11, 13, 14
    PPI   1842 Jan. 4-1860 Apr. 1
    PPiUD   1843 Oct. 16
                  1844 Sept. 6, Nov. 27
    PPL   1844 Jan. (1-3)-Apr. (25)-Dec. (31)
                  1846 Jan. 1-Feb. (19)-July 2, 4-Aug. 25, 27, 29-Sept. 1, 7-Dec. 31
                  1847 Jan. 9, Mar. 13, 27-Apr. 3, July (1, 2)-Nov. 25, 27
                  1848 Jan. (3, 4)-Oct. (13)
                  1849 Jan. (1-3)-Aug. (28)-Oct. (24)-Dec. 31
                  1850 July 1-Dec. (31)
                  1852 July (1, 2)-Dec. (31)
                  1853 Jan. (9)-Aug. (26)-Dec. (30)
                  1854 Jan. 2-Feb. (4)-July (1)-Nov. 15, 17-Dec. (3)-1855 Mar. 1
                  1855 Mar. 3-July (2)-Dec. (29)-(31)
                  1856 Apr. 24, 28, 30, May 3, July (1, 2)-(7)-Nov. 20, 22-1857 June (3)-July (2)-Oct. (5-6)
                  1857 Nov. 26, 28-Dec. (17)-(29)-(31)
                  1858 Jan. (1)-June (29, 30)-July 2, (3), Nov. (21)-18, 20-(27)-1859 Jan. (1-3)-July (1)-Oct. (29)-1860 Jan. (2)-Feb. 20
                  1860 Feb. 22-Mar. 31
    PPM ♦   1842 Jan. 4-May (16)-July 2, 6-Sept. (2)-25, 27-Oct. (2)-Dec. 26, 28 (30, 31)
                  1843 Jan. 5-Feb. (10, 11)-Mar. (6)-July 4, 6-Nov. (1)-Dec. (4)-21, 23-(27, 28)
                  1844 Jan. (8)-11, (13)-(15)-Feb. (9)-(14)-(29)-Mar. (18)-(21)-23, 26-May (8)-July 4, 6-Sept. (18-23)-(26)-Oct. (18)-Nov. (1)-Dec. 2, 4-(11)-(23-28)
                  1845 Jan. 3-June 27, 29-Sept. 19, 21-Nov. 27, 29-Dec. 31
                  1846 Jan. 1-(5)-Apr. 25, 29-May (29)-July (10)-Nov. 26-Dec. (30), 31
                  1847 Jan. (1, 2)-Feb. (5, 6)-Mar. (1)-May (17)-June (1)-(3)-(25)-July 5, 7-Aug. (1)-Nov. 25, 27-Dec. 31
                  1848 Jan. 1-Nov. 23, 25-Dec. 29
    PPoT   1849 Oct. 26
                  1851 Dec. 9
    PStP   1847 July 1-Dec. 30
                  1848 Jan. 1-Dec. 30
                  1849 Jan. 1-Dec. 31

PHILADELPHIA INQUIRER PUBLIC LEDGER, *continued*

PWcA		1844 Jan. 13, 16, 18, 19, 23, 27
PWcHi	d	1842 Apr. (4)
	tw	1842 May 14
		1843 Dec. 2
		1845 Feb. 18

continued as

PHILADELPHIA INQUIRER (April 2, 1860-April 15, 1934)   d   tw

Pub.	1860-1889	William H. Harding
	1889-1911	Inquirer Company (James Elverson)
	1911-1927	Philadelphia Inquirer Company
	1927-1929	James Elverson, Jr.
	1929-1932	The Philadelphia Inquirer Company
	1932-1934	Curtis-Martin Newspapers, Inc.
Ed.	1860-1887	William H. Harding
	1915-1934	Charles Heustis
	1934	John T. Custis
P	d	1861 Mar. 23-1864 Oct. 1
		1865 Apr. 24
		1881 Oct. 5-1893 Dec. 31
		1894 Jan. 1-1934 Apr. 15
P-M	d	1862 Apr. 21
		1864 June
		1865 Apr. 10, 17
		1876 Sept. 29, Nov. 10, 11, Dec. 18
		1877 July 23
		1878 June 20
		1881 July 4, Sept. 24
		1882 July 1, Oct. 25
		1884 Aug. 11
		1885 Aug. 4, 10, 22
		1886 Jan. 11
		1913 Jan. 23-26
PAlHi		1861 Apr. 23, 29, Sept. 5
PArdL	d	1862 May 12
		1926 June 1
		1928 June 9, 15, 29, Nov. 7
		1932 July 2, Sept. 1, Nov. 9
		1933 Jan. 6, 8
		1934 Feb. 7
PBf		1861 May 20
PBK	d	1862 Jan. 6, Feb. 21, 22, Mar. 3-6, 10, 11, 14-18, 21, 22, 26-31, Apr. 1-5, 9-30, May 1-8, 12, 13, 16, 17, 26, 27, 29, June 2-5, 13, 14, 18, 19, 25-30, July 1, 4-12, 16, 17, 25-31, Aug. 1, 2, 15, 18, 19, 22, 23, Sept. 8, 9, 12, 13, 19, 20, Oct. 1-4, 13, 14, 17, 18, 27, 28, Nov. 3, 4, 7, 8, 14, 15, 21, 22, 28, 29.
		1863 Feb. 9-12, 23, 24, Mar. 2, 3, 9-14, 18, 30, 31, Apr. 1, 2, 8-11, 29, 30, May 8, 9, 13, 14, 29, 30, June 5-9, 12, 13, 22, 23, July 1, 2, 8, 9, 13-28, Aug. 3, 4, 7-11, 18, 28, 29, 31, Sept. 1-3, 9-15, Oct. 24, Dec. 26
	d	1864 Mar. 7, 8, 14, 15, 17-22, 25-28, 29-31, Apr. 4, 5, 11-14, 18-21, May 2-7, 13, 14, 18, 19, 25, 26, 30, 31, June 1, 2, 13-16, 22-25, July 11, 12, 29, 30
		1865 Apr. 28, 29, May 5-13, 22, 23, 26-31, June 1, 9-13, 16-30, July 1

PHILADELPHIA COUNTY   219

		1869 Aug. 27, 28
		1875 Feb. 16
		1876 Apr. 24, May 16-18, 22-27, June 6, 9, 12, 14, 16, 20, 22, Sept. 4-7, 11, 13, Nov. 28, Dec. 7, 15, 22
		1877 Jan. 1, 12, 17, 23, Feb. 1-5, 7, 10, 20, 22, 24, 27, 28, Mar. 3, 10, 15, 26, Apr. 2
PBloHi		1865 Apr. 18-20
		1889 May 1, 2, June 1-7
		1901 Sept. 7, 9, 14-17, Nov. 18, 19
		1921 Nov. 12
		1923 Aug. 12
PBMa		1895 Apr. 21
PCarlHi		1909 Feb. 21
PCC		1861 July 24
		1929 June 1
PCHi		1861 Aug. 1-24, 26-Sept. 21, 23-31
		1876 July 4
		1878 Aug. 28
		1901 Sept. 7, 8, 11, 12-20
PDoHi ♦		[1861 Sept. 5-Dec. 31]
		1862 Sept. 16, 26, Oct. 24, Nov. 8
	d	1863 Feb. 18, Dec. 29
		1864 June
		1865 Feb. 6, 9, Apr. 13, 15, 17, 19, 21, 24, 29
		1866 Apr. 6, 13
		1876 Apr. 6, July 5
		1881 Sept. 26
		1885 July 24
		1890 Feb. 8
		1893 June 26
		1894 Jan. 26
		1900 Nov. 25
		1901 Sept. 7
		1902 Mar. 11
		1908 Nov. 4, 18
PEHi	d	1865 Apr. 25
PHHi	d	1860 June 11
		1865 Apr. 17
		1897 Feb. 3
		1898 Aug. 14
PHi ♦		1860 June (9-11)-16, July 2-4, 6-Sept. (18)-25, 27-Oct. (30)-Nov. (30)-Dec. (1')-31
		1861 Jan. (1)-(8)-Feb. (22)-Aug. 15, 18-Nov. (11)-1862 Apr. (2)-(11)-Sept. (18)-(30-Oct. 1)-(29)-Dec. (2)-25
		1862 Dec. 27-1863 Jan. (12)-Feb. (2)-July 1
		1863 July 3-Aug. 5, 7-1864 Apr. 2
		1864 Apr. 11-July (4), 5, (6)-(15)-(29)-Sept. (27)-Oct. 4, 6-(14)-(21)-Nov. 8, 11, 14, 15, 17-(19)-Dec. (1)-1865 Jan. (13)-Mar. (16)-Apr. (4)-(19)-(21-22)-May 16
		1865 May 18-July 4, 6-Sept. 1, 4-Nov. 20, 22-Dec. 1, 4-13, 15-25, 27-1866 Jan. 14
		1866 Jan. 6-Feb. (21)-Apr. (21)-Nov. (13)-Dec. 25, 27, (28), 29-1867 Jan. (24)-July 4
		1867 July 6-Sept. 16, 18-Dec. 25, 27, (28)-1868 Feb. **(27)-Mar. 9**

PHILADELPHIA INQUIRER PUBLIC LEDGER, continued

1868 Mar. 11-(16)-Apr. (9, 10)-13, 15-May (9)-(13)-June (12)-July (27)-Aug. (6)-Oct. (8)-(12)-Dec. 25, 27-1869 Mar. (5)-Apr. 30
1869 May 2-(19)-30, June 1-(21)-July 5, 7-19, 21-Aug. 10-18, 20-Sept. (8-9), 12, 15-19, 21, 22, 26, 29-Oct. 1, 3, 5, 7, 8, 10, (11), 12, 15, 17, 19, 21, 23, 24, 26, 28, 31, Nov. (2)-(4)-7, 11-(22-23)-(27)-Dec. (1), 3-(9)-(13)-19, 21-(25), 26, 28-1870 Mar. (5)-(9)-(14)-May 5
1870 May 7-(24)-July 4, 6-(20)-Oct. (6)-16-28-30-Dec. 26, 27-1871 Apr. (7)-May 15
1871 May 17-(31)-June 19-(27)-July 5, 7-Aug. 6, 8-11, 14-(19)-Dec. 25, 27-1872 Jan. 9
1872 Jan. 11-29, Feb. 1-Mar. (5)-Apr. 15, 17-23, 25-(27)-May (18)-(27)-June 23, 25-July 4, 6-Aug. 31-Sept. 3-Nov. (29)-Dec. 25, 27-1873 Mar. (14, 15)-July (18)-Sept. (20)-Nov. (8)-Dec. 25
1873 Dec. 27-1874 Feb. (28)-Mar. 23
1874 Mar. 25-May (13), Oct. 1-(5)-15, 17, 22, 24-1875 Feb. (20)-Mar. (22)-Apr. (2)-(6)-(9)-(24)-May (10)-(27)-June (3)-7
1875 June 9-July (5)-Aug. (24)-Sept. (10, 11), (13)-Nov. 16, 19-Dec. (10)-(27)-1876 Feb. (22)-1878 Jan. (28)-Oct. 6
1878 Oct. 8-Nov. (7)-(23)-1879 Jan. (31)-May (12)-Nov. (22)-1880 July (13)-Oct. (30)-Nov. (2, 3)-Dec. 27
1880 Dec. 29-1881 Jan. (3-7)-8-(15)
1881 Jan. 16, (17-19), 20-July (4-9)-Sept. (24)-1882 Mar. (1)-Apr. (18)-Sept. (19)
1882 Sept. 20, (21)-Oct. (30), 31, Nov. (1)-Dec. (30)-1883 June (15, 16)-(25-July 9)-10-Aug. (3-6))-7-(30)-1884 Aug. 13
1884 Aug. 15-Dec. (30-1885 Jan. 8)-9-(23, 24)-25-June (20)-July (1, 2)-Oct. (15)-Nov. (14)-Dec. (9)-(31-1886 Jan. 2)-(8)-(14)
1886 Jan. 15, (16)-June (19)-(29-July 1)-Sept. (9)-Nov. (8)-(12, 13), 14-17, (18), 19-Dec. (24, 25), 26-(31-1887 Jan. 1)-Feb. (16)-Mar. (8)-(26)-May (2)-Aug. (10-12)-13-(27)-Oct. (1)-Dec. (17)-26-(27-1888 Jan 2)-3-Mar. (7)-Apr. (3, 4)-June (21)-(25-27)-(30-July 4), 5-(27, 28)-Nov. (30)-Dec. (14)-1889 Mar. (5)-Apr. (11-13) 14, (15-22)-May (1-3)-July (15)-Nov. (30)-1890 Jan. (1)-Mar. (22), 23
1890 Mar. (24)-Apr. (5)-(12)-(19)-(26)-May (1-3)-(10)-(14) - (17) - (24) - June (23-25), 26, (27)-Oct. (24)-(27)-1891 May (1)-July (27)-Aug. 29
1891 Sept. 2-1892 Apr. (30-May 2)-(28)-Sept. (1)-1893 Sept. (2)-Oct. (3)-1894 Jan. (6)-Feb. (1)-May (21)-July 3-Aug. (31-Sept. 1)-1895 Jan. (1, 2)-(23)-Feb. (2)-Mar. 29
1895 Apr. 31-June (29)-30-July (4)-(25)-Aug. 1-Oct. (1)-1896 Mar. (28)
1896 Mar. 29, 30, Apr. (1)-(4)-May (16)-June (18)-29, July (1, 2)-(18)-(30)-Aug. (4)-(20)-

(27)-Sept. 29, Oct. 2-Dec. (12)-1897 Jan. (1-4)-
(27)-Feb. (20)-Mar. (31-Apr. 2)-June (30, July
1)-3-Sept. (29-Oct. 2)
1897 Oct. 3, (4), 5, (6)-Dec. (31)-1898 Jan. (4)-
(7)-Mar. (25-28)-(31-Apr. 2-9)-May (5)-June
(8)-(23, 24)-(29-July 4)-(30)-Aug. (5, 6)-
(10)-(30)-Sept. 29
1898 Oct. (1-18), 19-Nov. (26)-Dec. (15)-1899 Jan.
(2-5)-Feb. (9)-Mar. 29
1899 Apr. (3-24)-June (6-9)-(27-July 6)-Sept. 29,
Oct. (2, 3)-(31)-Dec. (30-1900 Jan. 5)-(24)-
Feb. (5)-(28)-Mar. (9)-(30-Apr. 19)-May
(12-18-June (21)
1900 June 22, (23-July 3), 4, (5)-Sept. (29-Oct. 12)-
(20)-Nov. (1, 2), 3, (5), 6-(30)-Dec. (14)-
24-(25-1901 Jan. 1)-2-(4)-(21)-24(30)-Feb.
(12)-(19)-Mar. (30)
1901 Apr. 2-May (9)-June (29-July 4)-5-Oct. (1-7)-
8-(12), 13, (14, 15), 16, (17)-(28)-Nov. (2)-
(6)-(9)-(11)-(16)-(20)-Dec. (25, 26), 27,
(28)-(31-1902 Jan. 2)-(7)-(12)-Feb. (7)-(11,
12)-Mar. 30
1902 Apr. (1-4)-5-(18)-(25)-(28)-May (30, 31)-
June (27, 28), 29, (30-July 2)-(8)-29-Aug.
(14)-Sept. (29-Oct. 8)-Nov. (6), 7, (8), 9, (10,
11), 12-(17, 18)-(27)-Dec. (25-1903 Jan. 1)
1903 Jan. (13)-(22)-(30)-Mar. (31, Apr. 1)-July
(3)-(11)-Oct. (1)-Dec. (14)-1904 Jan. (1-4)
1904 Jan. 5, (6, 7)-Feb. (9)-(29)-Mar. (5)-(9)-
(31-Apr. 6)-May (5)-June (6)-(July 1-9)-Aug.
(11)-Sept. (6)-(15)-(19), 20 (21)-(27)-(30)-
Oct. (1-12)-(29)-Nov. (19-22)-(25-30)-Dec.
(6, 7)-(14)-Dec. (31)
1905 Jan. (2)-Feb. (7)-(23)-Mar. (31-Apr. 6)-(21)-
May (23)-July (3-5)-Aug. (12)-Nov. (16)-
Dec. (30-1906 Jan. 6)
1906 Jan. 7-(10)-(20)-(23)-(31, Feb. 1)-(3)-(8-10)-
(23)-(27)-Mar. (1)-(17)-Apr. (9)-May (24,
25)-June (1, 2)-(12, 13)-July (2)-(14)-(27)-
Sept. (15-17)-Oct. (1, 2)-(11)-(15), 16, (17)-
(20), 21, (22), 23, (24)-Nov. (5, 6)-(9)-Dec.
31
1907 Jan. (1-8)-(19)-(25)-Feb. (13)-Mar. (9)-(28)-
Apr. (1-6)-(10, 11)-(13)-(23)-May (18)-June
(12)-(22)-(29)-July (1)-(8)-(23)-Aug. (16)-
Sept. (4), 5, (6, 7)-(24, 25)-(30-Oct. 5), 7-
(22)-Nov. (1)-(7)-(11, 12)-(15)-(25)-Dec.
(13)-(24), 25, (26), 27, (28), (30-1908 Jan. 4)
1908 Jan. (6-9)-(23)-Feb. (3)-(27)-Mar. (31, Apr.
1)-July (1, 2)-(10)-(14)-(17, 18)-(23-Aug. 1)-
Sept. (15)-(30)-Oct. (1)-(30, 31)-Nov. (14-
16)-Dec. (5)-(11)-(31-1909 Jan. 7)
1909 Jan. 8-Apr. (1, 2)-May (19, 20)-June (28), 29,
(30)-Dec. (22)-Dec. 31
1910 Jan. (1)-Mar. (24)-Apr. (1)-(27)-May (16)-
July (1-5)-(16-Aug. 6) - (11) - (25 - 30) - Sept.
(23)-Oct. (1)-(7)-Nov. (17)-Dec. 31
1911 Jan. 2-(7)-Feb. (27)-Mar. (18-20)-(31)-Apr.
(22)-June (30-July 1)-(18)-Aug. (12)-Sept.

PHILADELPHIA INQUIRER PUBLIC LEDGER, *continued*

      (4)-(14)-Oct. (2, 3)-(7)-(20, 21)-Nov. (30)-
      Dec. (7)-(23)-1912 Mar. 23
    1912 Mar. (25, 26)-Apr. (23)-May (31)-Sept. (18)-
      Oct. (1)-Dec. (14)-(25)-1913 Jan. 2
    1913 Jan. 1-(3, 4)-(7, 8), 9, (10)-Mar. (13)-(21)-
      July (25)-Oct. (21)-Nov. (29)-Dec. (4)-(9)-
      (31-1914 Jan. 2)
    1914 Jan. 3-(26)-May (14)-Aug. (27)-Nov. (28)-
      Dec. (11)-(18, 19)-1915 Jan. 11
    1915 Jan. (12)-(16)-May (19)-June (26)-July (2)-
      (8)-Aug. (26)-Dec. 31
    1916 Jan. (1-3)-Feb. (11)-(14, 15)-Mar. (10)-Apr.
      (19)-(28)-May (1)-(10)-June (9)-(21)-Aug.
      (1)-Sept. (8)-Oct. (2-4)-Dec. (30), 31-1917
      Jan. 9
    1917 Jan. (10, 11)-(21)-(27)-Feb. (1)-(21)-Mar.
      (15)-(21)-(28, 29)-Apr. (1)-(9)-(12)-(15)-
      (30)-June (5, 6)-(9)-July (8)-Sept. (1, 2)-
      Oct. (7)-17, 19-(23)-27, 29

PHsHi   d 1864 Oct. 28, 31
PLaF   1897 Dec. 20, 31
      1898 Jan. 3-7, 10-14, 16-21, 24-28, Feb. 4, 7, 20-25, 27,
        28, Mar. 1, 3, 6-11, 13-18, 20, 27, Apr. 3, 4, 8, 10,
        17, 25, May 1, 8, 15, 16, 22, 29, June 5, 9, 12, 19,
        26, July 10, 17, 24, 26, 28, 31, Aug. 7, 14, 21, 28,
        Sept. 11, 18, 25, 30, Oct. 2, 9, Dec. 17, 23, 27
PLewL   d [1861]
       [1862]
PLhT   d 1862 Nov. 8
      1863 Aug. 29, Sept. 11
      1865 Apr. 19, 25, May 13
PMcC   d 1876 May 24
PMontHi   d (1864 Nov. 26)
PNazHi   1865 Apr. 18, 20, 26
      1921 Nov. 16
PNeB   d 1861 June 11, 22, July 23, Sept. 28, Nov. 7, Dec. 28
      1862 Mar. 10, Apr. 2, 3, 5, 9-11, May 7, 13, 17, June
        3, 4, 10, 28, July 1, 4, 19, Aug. 27, Sept. 6, Oct.
        14, Nov. 8, 17, Dec. 27
      1863 Jan. 27, Feb. 11, May 30, June 2, 13, 17, 19, 20,
        25-27, 29, July 4, Aug. 20, Sept. 5, 11, 19, Oct. 3
PNoHi   d 1861 May 2, 3, 16, 23-26, 28, 29, 31-June 3, 6, 8-22,
        24-Aug. 2, 4-18, 20-Dec. 2, 4
      1862 Apr. 30
      1865 Feb. 1, Apr. 10, 17-26, 28, 29, Oct. 19
      1876 May 10
PP ♦   d 1860 Apr. 3-1862 Mar. 31
      1862 Apr. 16, May 12, July 21, 22
      1863 Apr. 14, 17, May 5, July 6-Dec. 31
      1864 Feb. 20, Oct. 8, Dec. 27
      1865 Mar. 6, 29, Apr. 4, 10, 11, 13-May 25, 27, 31-
        June 13, 15-21, 23-29, July 4, 7, 8, 17, 25, Nov. 6
      1866 Feb. 23, 24, July 20
      1867 Aug. 31
      1868 Mar. 31, May 6
      1870 Jan. 5-June 27
      1871 Aug. 1-31
      1874 Feb. 21

PHILADELPHIA COUNTY 223

                  1875 Jan. 1-Mar. 31, May 1-Dec. 26
                  1876 Jan. 1-31, Mar. 1, June-Dec.
                  1878 Mar. 30, June 4
                  1880 July 1-Dec. 31
                  1881 Jan. 1-June 30, July-Dec. 30.
                  1882 Jan. 1-June 30
                  1883 Jan. 1-Dec.
                  1884 Jan.-June, Aug. 11
                  1889 Mar. 1-1890 Apr. 13
                  1890 Apr. 15-Dec. 30
                  1891 Jan. 1-Oct. 31, Dec. 1-1892 Feb. 29
                  1892 Mar. 1-Dec. 30
                  1893 Jan. 1-Dec. 30
                  1894 Jan. 1-June 30, July 7-Dec. 31
                  1895 Jan. 1-Dec. 30
                  1896 Jan. 1-Dec. 30
                  1897 Jan. 1-Dec. 30
                  1898 Jan. 1-Oct. 30, Dec. 30
                  1899 Jan., Mar.-Dec.
                  1900 Jan. 1-Dec. 30
                  1901 Jan.-Dec.
                  1902 Jan. 1-1916 Dec. 31
                  1917 Feb. 1-July 31
                  1924 June 1-1925 Mar. 31
                  1926 Jan. 1-1934 Apr. 15
PPeS   d 1860 May 19
                  1862 Jan. 21-Apr. 3, 9-17, July 18, 22, 26, Sept. 13, 22-
                        Oct. 11
                  1865 Apr. 17, 19, 20-22, 24-26, June 17
                  1890 June 26, Nov. 20
                  1897 May 15
                  1928 Nov. 8
                  1929 Oct. 24
                  1930 Mar. 9
                  1932 Nov. 9-13
PPFfHi   d 1865 Feb. 20, Apr. 17, 21, 24, May 20
                  1867 Nov. 29
PPI   1860 Apr. 2-1933 Apr. 15
PPiHi   1862 Jan. 1-June 30
                  1863 Nov. 19
                  1864 May 13
PPL   d 1860 June 11, 14, 16, 28, 30-July (2, 3)-Aug. (25)-
                        Oct. 31, Nov. 21, Dec. 10, 12-15, 18-1861 Jan.
                        (1)-Feb. (23)-Aug. 9
                  1861 Aug. 12-19, 21-Sept. 25, 27-1862 June 30
                  1862 Nov. (17)
                  1863 Jan. 1-(5)-Feb. 27, Mar. 2-June (17)-July (1)-
                        1864 Mar. (7)-(17)-Aug. 13
                  1864 Aug. 16-Nov. 15, 17-Dec. (27)
                  1865 Jan. 18, Apr. 15-20, 22-June 24, 27-29, July 4-6,
                        11, 15, 18, 22-25, Dec. 6
                  1866 Jan. (1)-1869 July 1
                  1869 July 3-Dec. (31)-1870 Jan. (3)-(21)-Mar. (25)-
                        May (31)-June (16)-(31)-Dec. 31
                  1871 Jan. 2-Oct. 31, Dec. 1-30
                  1872 Mar. 15-Dec. 7
                  1873 Jan. 1-1875 Aug. 31
                  1875 Oct. 1-1876 June 30
                  1877 Jan. 1-1880 June 30

PHILADELPHIA INQUIRER PUBLIC LEDGER, *continued*

          1881 Jan. 1-1888 Dec. 31
          1889 Mar. 2-1916 Dec. 31
          1929 Jan. 1-1934 Apr. 15
PPM ♦
          1860 May 1-July 14, 16-Dec. 31
          1861 Jan. 1-Mar. 28, 30-June 14, 17-20, 24-Nov. 30, Dec. 3, 5-31
          1862 Jan. 1-29, 31-Mar. 29, Apr. 1-29, May 2-July 29, Aug. 1-Dec. 31
          1863 Jan. 1-July 31, Aug. 4-Dec. 7
          1864 Jan. 1-Apr. 30, May 10-Dec. 31
          1865 Jan. 2-Apr. (14, 15)-May (5)-July (3)-(14)-(17)-Sept. (25)-Oct. (14)-Nov. (4)-Dec. 30
          1866 Jan. 1-June (18)-Nov. 29, Dec. 1-31
          1867 Jan. 1-24, 26-Feb. 12, 14-Mar. 15, 18-June 6, 8-14, 17-July 15, 17-Dec. 2, 4-31
          1868 Jan. 1-Mar. (4)-July (1)-29, 31-Sept. 29, Oct. 1-Dec. (3)-(25)-(29)-31
          1869 Feb. 1-Mar. 19, 22-Apr. 29, May 1-(10)-July 2, 5, 7-Nov. 18, 20-Dec. (2)-31
          1870 Jan. 1-Mar. (8)-Dec. 31
          1871 Jan. 2-14, 17-25, 27-Sept. (1)-Dec. 30
          1872 Jan. 1-Feb. 28, Mar. 1-May (1)-Aug. (12)-Sept. (18)-(23)-(28)-(30)-Oct. 7, 9-Nov. 28
          1873 Jan. 1-22, 28, 31, Feb. (1)-Apr. 11, 14-May (28)-July 11, 14-Aug. 2, 5-(11)-Sept. 23, 25-Dec. 31
          1874 Jan. 1-July 22, 24, (25)-31, Aug. 3-27, 29-Nov. 6, 9-28, Dec. 1-4, 7-31
          1875 Jan. 1-Mar. (20)-24, 26-July 28, 30-Sept. (30)-Dec. 31
          1876 Jan. 1, 4-19, 21-26, 28-31, Feb. 2-Mar. 11, 14, 16-May (2)-(22)-June (15)-22, 24-July 11, 13-20, 22-Aug. (5)-Sept. (1)-4, 6-Nov. 20, 22-Dec. (30)
          1877 Jan. 1-June 28, 30-Aug. 15, 17-Dec. 31
          1878 Jan. 1-Apr. 30
          1881 Jan. 1-Sept. (1)-Oct. 18, 20-Dec. 31
          1882 Jan. 2-Sept. (1, 2)-Dec. 30
          1883 Jan. 1-31, Feb. 2-Dec. 31
          1884 Jan. 1-May 31, June 3-July 8, 10-12, 15-Nov. 5, 7-Dec. 31
          1885 Jan. 1, (2)-Apr. (23)-(30)-June (22)-Dec. 31
          1886 Apr. 1-July (10)-Sept. (1, 2)-Dec. 31
          1887 Jan. 1-Feb. (4)-(14)-Apr. (29)-Aug. 31
          1888 May 1-Dec. (1)-31
          1889 Jan. 1-Dec. 31
          1890 Jan. (1)-Apr. (30)-May (24)-Dec. 31
          1891 Jan. (1)-Apr. (30)-Aug. (30)-Sept. (1-Oct. 12)-Dec. (30), 31
          1892 Jan. 1-Apr. (29)-May (2)-Aug. (29-31), Sept. (2-4)-Nov. (7)-Dec. (30, 31)
          1893 Jan. 1-Dec. 31
          1894 Jan. 1-Aug. (31, Sept. 1)-Nov. (11)-Dec. (5)-(22)-31
          1895 Jan. (1)-Apr. (1-3)-Sept. (30)-Dec. 23
          1896 Jan. 1-July (1-4)-Dec. 31
          1897 Jan. (1)-June (29, 30)
          1902 Mar. 1, 3-Apr. (30)-May (3-5)-(21-24)-(29,

PHILADELPHIA COUNTY 225

                           30)-July (1, 2)-(4)-30, Aug. 1-(31-Sept. 2)-Oct. (31-Nov. 2)-Dec. (30, 31)
                1903 Jan. (1-4)-Feb. (27, 28), July 1-Nov. (1)-Dec. 30
                1904 Jan. 1-Mar. (5)-May (25)-June (1)-July (1)-(10)-(20)-Sept. (29)-Oct. (16)-Nov. (7)-(27)-Dec. (31)
                1905 Jan. (1)-Mar. (1-3)-Apr. (23-May 1)-July (1)-Sept. (1)-Nov. (1)-(20-22)-Dec. 31
                1906 Jan. (1-9)-Mar. (1-7)-Aug. 31, Nov. (1, 2)
                1907 Jan. (1-3)-Feb. 28, May 1-30
                1908 Mar. (1-8)-Apr. (30)
                1910 Jan. 1-1913 June 30
                1913 Aug. 1-1916 June 30
                1916 Sept. 1-1920 Apr. 30
                1920 July 1-1921 May 31
                1921 Dec. 31
                1922 Jan. 1-31, Apr. 1-30, Dec. 31
                1923 Jan. 1-1928, Oct. 31
                1928 Dec. 31
                1929 Jan. 1-1934 Apr. 15

PPoHi   d 1865 July 2-Sept. 16
PPot   d 1861 June 5, 17, 27, Sept. 14, Oct. 12, Nov. 6, 16, 20
                1862 Jan. 18, Feb. 13, Mar. 1, 13, 15, 26, 29, Apr. 12, Sept. 2-4, 11, 13, 17, 19, 20, 25
                1863 Apr. 7, Sept. 5, Oct. 3
                1864 June 14, Nov. 21
                1865 Apr. 10, 15, 17-21, 24, 26, May 3, 5, 6, 8, 15, 18, 19, 25, 29, 31, June 3, 12, 26, 28, July 4, 7, Aug. 4
                1869 Nov. 1
                1870 July 26
                1871 Sept. 28
                1881 Sept. 20
                1886 Nov. 3
                1887 Sept. 17
                1888 July 5
                1890 June 24-26
                1892 June 11
                1893 Mar. 5
                1896 June 19, 30, July 1-6, 8-13
PRHi   d 1861 Apr. 22-July 31
PSF   d 1865 Apr. 21, 22, 24-29
                1881 Sept. 27
PShH   1874 Aug. 14, Sept. 12
PSuHi   d 1865 Apr. 20
                1872 Nov. 12
PU   d 1862 Jan. 1, 2, 10, 14, 21, 22, 27-Feb. 1, 4-6, 8, 12-28, Mar. 3, 5-Apr. 3, 5-May 7, 9-July 26, 29-Nov. 15, 18-1863 Jan. (3-5)-(7)-(9)-(12-15)-(17)-(20)-Feb. (24)-(27)-Mar. (24)-Aug. 1
                1863 Aug. 4-1864 July 6
                1864 July 8-29, Aug. 20, 23-27, 30-Sept. 2, 3, 6, 7, 9, 12-17, 20-Oct. 10, 12-26, Nov. 7, 8, 19, 22-1865 Mar. 3
                1865 Mar. 6-Apr. 3, 5-10, 12-May 15, 17, 19-June 9, 12-19, 21-27, 29-July 8, 11, 13, 14, 17-Aug. 18, 21-25, 28-Sept. 15, 18-21
PVfHi   1865 Apr. 3

PHILADELPHIA INQUIRER PUBLIC LEDGER, *continued*

PW   d 1862 July 4-Dec. 31

PWbW   d 1861 June 4, 5, 8, 10-12, 18, 22, 26, 28, July 3, 20, 27, Aug. 16, Sept. 2, 3, 5, 6, 9-14, 21, 24, 30, Oct. 1, 3, 5, 7-12, 14, 15, 17, 19, 21-26, 28-30, Nov. 15, Dec. 7, 13, 14, 15-24, 28-31

                 1862 Jan. 1, 2, 4-20, 22-31, Feb. 1-7, 19, 21-24, Mar. 1, 8-10, 12-17, 19-21, 23, 25-31, Apr. 1-13, 15, 17, 20, July 18-31

                 1864 May 1-2, 15-18, 20-29, 31, June 1-13, 15-30, July 1, 3-15, 17-21, 23-29, Aug. 1-8, 13, 14, 16-31, Sept. 2-30, Oct. 1-12, 14-17, 19-23, 27-31, Nov. 1, 2, 4-28, Dec. 1, 2, 4, 5, 7-9, 11-13, 18, 19, 21-26, 28, 30

                 1865 Jan. 1-13, 15-19, 21-31, Feb. 1, 2, 4-28, Mar. 1-12, 14-20, 22-29, 31, Apr. 1-5, 7-9, 11-14, 16-30, May 1-7, 9-17, 19-31, June 1-6, 8-30

PWcHi   d 1860 May 28, June 14, 16, July 20, Aug. 1, 7

                 1861 Jan. 10, 11, 24-26, 28-Feb. 1, 4-(9)-Mar. (23), 28, 30-Apr. (26)-May 21, 23-(27), 31, June 3, 11, (12), 13, 22, 25, 26, 28, July 3-9, 11, 13-15, 17, 22-Aug. 15, 17-Sept. (16), Oct. 3, 9, 12, 18, 19, 22, 23, 25, (26-28), 30, 31-Nov. 2, 9, 14, 16, 18-(22), 25-(30), Dec. (2)-23, 27

                 1862 Jan. 1-7, 9-17, 20-25, 28-Feb. 8, 11-18, 20-Apr. 2, 4, 7-9, 11, 12, 15, 16, 18, 19, 22, 25 (28, 29), May 1, 5, 7-17, 21-(29), 30-June (11), 12-19, 21, 24, 25-July (15), 16-(26), 28, 30-Aug. 1, 4-(6), 7, 8, (11), 12-(23), 26, 27, 29-Sept. (13), 15-(20), 22-Oct. (11), 14, 16, 17, 20, 21, 23-28, 30, 31, Nov. 5, 8, 13-17, 21-26, 28-Dec. 3, 6-10, 12-(25), 26-31

                 1863 Jan. 2, 3, 6-(27), 28-Feb. (17), 18-27, Mar. 2-May 7, 9-June (6), 8-(16), 17-Sept. 3, 5-Nov. 20, 23-Dec. (7), 8-(28), 29, 31

                 1864 Jan. 1, 12, 14-Feb. 25, Mar. 1, 2, 4, 11-19, 22-25, Apr. 9, 11, 14, 16-(22), 23, 27, 30, May 3, 5-11, 14-16, 18-(23), 24, 28, June 6, (9)-(13), 16, 17, 20, 21 (25), 27, July 4, 5, 9-13, 27, Sept. 12, Oct. 7-12, 14, 15, 18-Nov. (30), Dec. 1-8, 23, 24, 26, 28, 31-1865 June 5

                 1865 June 7, (14), 15 (21), 23, 27-July 4, 7, (8, 10), 12, 13 (15)-17, 19 (20), 21, 24, 26, 29, Aug. 4, 5, 14, 16, 18, Sept. 16, 30, Oct. 2, 4-6, 9, 11, (16)-(18), 23, 24, 29

                 1866 Jan. 6-12, 26-29, 31-Feb. 5, 10, (13), 17-(22), 24-Mar. (1)-Apr. (3), 5, (7), (12), 13 (16)-(18), 20 (21)-23, 27-30, May 2-(7), 12, 15 (17)-22, 24, 25, 28-30, June 1-(4)-7, 13, 15, 16 (21), 22 (23)-27, 29-July 11 (13), 20-23, 30, Aug. 1, 7, 9, 10, 13, 16 (17), 18-(22)-24, 27, 29 (31), Sept. 4-7, 10, 15, 19, 20, 24-26, 28-Oct. (1)-(3), 5 (8)-10, 12-23, 25-27, 31-Nov. 2, 5, 7, 9-13, 15-(28), Dec. (1)-25, 28, (29)-1867 Jan. 1

                 1867 Jan. 4, (5), (7), (9-11), 15, 18, 19, 23-(29)-Feb. 16, 19, 21-26, 28-Mar. (2), (14), 18-20, 22-(26), 30-Apr. 30, May 2, (3)-21, (23)-27, 29-

June 6, 8-12, 15-17, 19-21, 24-July 4, 8-17, 20-
Sept. 6, 12-24, 27-Oct. 5, 8-(21)-(26)-Nov. (2)-
(5)-12, 14-21, 23-26, Dec. 3-18, 20-23, 30
1868 Jan. 2-6, (11), (15), (17), (18)-20, 22, (23),
25-(30), Feb. 10, 12-18, 20 (22)-Mar. (4)-(13)-
(16)-(20), 23-Apr. 13, 15-(28)-30, May 9, 12,
13, 15, 18-(20), (22), 23, 27, 28, 30-June 1, 5,
8, (9), 13-(17)-20, (25)-(27, 30, July 4, 6, (9)-
22, 25-28, 30-Aug. 1, 4-6, 10, 12, 20, 22, 26-
Sept. 3, 7-22, 24, (25), Oct. 7-(14), 16, 19-(24),
28, 29, 31-Nov. 2, 5, 6, 13, 14, 19, 20, 30, Dec.
2-5, 9, 12, 17-19, 22, 24, 25, 28-1869 Jan. 1
1869 Jan. 5, 7, 8, 13, 14, 16-19, 25, 26, 28, 30, Feb.
3-4, 6-11, (13)-15, 22, 24, 25, Mar. 2, 5, (6)-8,
13-22, 24, 26-29, 31, Apr. 1, 3-7, 9-(13), 14, 16
(19)-21, 23, 30, May 3, 5, 6, 8, 11-13, 19-21, 24-
26, June 5-9, 12-16 (29), July 3-5, 8, 9, 12-(14),
15, 19, 20, 27, 29-(31)-Aug. (2), 7, 11, 12,
17-19, 28-30, Sept. 2, 6-11, 20, 22-27, 30-Oct. 4-
(12)-14, 21, 25-(28)-Nov. 1, 3, 4, 6-9, 12-16, 18,
20, 29-Dec. 6, 8, 9, 13, 15, 17-20, 24-28, 31
1870 Jan. (1), 3, 4, 6, 7, 11, 18, 21, 22, 25, 27, 28,
Feb. 2, 5, 9, 23, 24, 26, Mar. 2, 4, 5 14, 15,
23-25, 29, 31-Apr. 4, 8-12, 14, (15)-21, 23, 27-29,
May 4, 10, 11, 14-18, 25, 28-June 6, 9, (10), 13-
15, 21, 22, 24, July 2, 6, 8, 9, 12-25, 27, 28,
Aug. (6)-9, 11-(13), 22, 30-Sept. (3), 7-13,
16-(29)-Oct. 3, 6, 7, 10-13, 15, 19, 21, 25, 27,
28, 31, Nov. 1, 4-7, 9-(16)-21, 24-26, 29-Dec. 3,
6-9, 12, 13, 15, 17, 20, 28-30
1871 Jan. 2, 3, 5, 9, 10, 12, (13, 14)-(16)-(18)-21,
24-27, Feb. 3, 17-(20)-23, (25)-27, Mar. 1, 2,
4-(17), 20-24, 27-Apr. (3)-5, 21-24, 26-28, May
6, 10, 11, 13, 17-22, 24-26, 29-June (5)-(12)-16,
19-21, 24-30, July 4, 5, 7-(10, 11)-12, 14-(21)-
25, 27, 29-31, Aug. 2-4, 7-(10)-11, 15, 28, 30-
Sept. 11, 13, 14, Oct. 10, (13), 21, 24, Nov. 6-9,
11, 14, 15, 17-24, 27-30, Dec. 13
1872 Feb. 14, 15, 17, (21), 22, 24-27, Mar. 1, 4, 5,
9, 18, (21), (26), 27, 30-Apr. 2, 29, Aug. 10,
Oct. (3), 8, 10, 15, 18, 23, Dec. 2, (3), 4, 6, (9),
13, 14, 23, 28, 30
1873 Jan. 4, 21, Feb. 4, Apr. (26)
1874 Feb. 13, Mar. (19), May 20, Sept. 1, Nov. 6-10,
14, 17, 19, 25-27, 30-Dec. (2), 17, 18, 23-25, 29-
1875 Jan. 1
1875 Jan. 4, 7, 9, (13)-15, 18-20, 25, 27, 29, Feb. 2,
10-16, 22, 25, 26, Mar. 1, 3-(5), 9, 11, 20, 24,
(26), 30, Apr. 3, 6, 15-20, 22, 23, 26, 28, 29,
May (1)-3, 5, 7, 10, 15-17, 19, 20, 22, 28-June
(1), 2, 5-(7, 8), 9, (11), 14, 18, 19, 22, (26),
(29), July (1), 5, 7, 9, 12-16, (21), 24-26, 28-
(29)-31, Aug. (4), 5, 7, 10, 14-17, 19, 21, 26,
(28)-(30), Sept. 1, 2, 8, 10-(14), 18, 21, 22,
25, 28, 30, Oct. 1, (4), 5, 9, 12-22, 25, 29, (30)-
Nov. 2, 5, 16, (19), (24), Dec. 3, (6)-10, 13,
15, 16, 29, 31
1876 Jan. 1, 4, 24, 26, 27, Feb. 8, 11, 12, Mar. 4-7,
10-17, 22, 23, 27, 28, 30, 31, Apr. 6, 7, 18-20,

PHILADELPHIA INQUIRER PUBLIC LEDGER, *continued*

                       22-26, May 6, 10, 11, 13, (19), 24, 25, 29, June 1, 3-5, 19, 30, July (1), 6, 8, 11-13, 17, 22, (24)-26, (29), Aug. 3, 12, 17-(22)-24, 28-30, Sept. 6-9, 12-14, 25, 26, 30, Oct. 5 (10), (13), 16, 17, 19, 21-24, 26, 28-31, Nov. (4), 8, 9, 16-(23), (24)-27, 29, 30, Dec. (2)-(6)-14, 18, 20, 21, (25)-28, 30
                1877 Aug. 29
                1878 Aug. 6
                1881 May 10-(13), 14, June 24, July 4-6, 8, 9, Sept. 20-23, 27, Nov. 11, 14, 23, 25, Dec. 20-23, 26, 27
                1882 Jan. 2, 4, 6, 9-11, 13, Feb. 28
                1883 July 5
                1894 Mar. 19, May 21
                1901 Sept. 14, 16, 19
                1913 Feb. 14
                1918 Nov. 11
                1927 June 12
    PWcT   d 1861 Nov. 16, 23
                1862 May 17, June 3, 9, 10, 12, Aug. 16, Sept. 16, Oct. 4, Nov. 8
                1864 Dec. 28
                1865 Nov. 23
                1866 Mar. 4-May 22
                1901 Sept. 14, 19
    PWG   d 1860 Oct. 13
    PYHi   d 1865 Apr. 17, 18, 20, 21, 24, May 27, July 8
                1867 Aug. 12
                1901 Sept. 9-14, 17-20
                merged with the *Public Ledger* (q.v.) to form the

PHILADELPHIA INQUIRER PUBLIC LEDGER (April 16, 1934†)

Pub. 1934   Curtis-Martin Newspapers, Inc.
      1934-1940   The Philadelphia Inquirer Company
      1940   M. L. Annenberg
Ed. 1934-1941   John T. Custis
    PUB   1934 Apr. 16†
    P   1934 Apr. 16-1935 Feb. 28
    PArdL   1934 Nov. 17
                1935 Feb. 14, Mar. 28
                1939 Jan. 15
    PDoHi   1936 May 27
    PHi ♦   1934 May 1-(6)-July (22)-(25)-Aug. (19)-Oct. (21)-Nov. (3)-(10)-(16)-(18)-Dec. (16)-(30)-1935 Apr. 9.
                1935 Apr. (10), 11 (12)-(28)-June (2)-(26)-Oct. (21)-Nov. (2)-1936 Feb. 12
                1936 Feb. (13)-Apr. (19)-July (27)-Aug. (21)-Nov. (24)-Dec. 3, 5, 6, (7)-(13)-1937 Feb. 6
                1937 Feb. (7)-(24)-(28)-Mar. (22)-Apr. (4, 5)-(10)-(14)-(26)-May (14)-June (17)-July 2, 4-Oct. (10)-(20)-(28)-Nov. (4)-(21)-(30)-Dec. (1)-(6)-1938 Feb. 27
                1938 Feb. (28)-June (6)-July (27)-Oct. (28)-1939 Feb. 13
                1939 Feb. (14)-(28)-Mar. (3)-Apr. (10)-(13, 14)-(23)-June (4)-(11)-July (15)-(23)-(29)-Aug.

PHILADELPHIA COUNTY 229

```
                    (13)-Nov. (16)-(19)-(29)-Dec. (11), 12, (13)-
                      (17)-1940 Mar. 12
                 1940 Mar. (13)-July (6)-(17)-(23)-Aug. (2)-(8)-
                      Sept. (25)-(30)-Oct. (5)-(18)-(31)-Nov. (22)-
                      1941 Jan. 4
                 1941 Jan. (5), 6, (7)-(18)-(29)†
     PLaF        1936 Mar. 19†
     PP    ♦     1934 Apr. 16†
     PPL         1934 Apr. 16†
     PPM         1934 Apr. 16†
     PPTU        [1936 July-Dec.]
                 [1937 Jan.-June, Aug.-Dec.]
                 1938 Jan. 1†
     PSeSU       1937 Sept. 1†
     PU          1934 Apr. 16†
     PWcHi       1938 June 22
                 1939 Jan. 31
```

PHILADELPHIA INTELLIGENCER (1857-1878) sm m
    INSURANCE INTELLIGENCER (Jan. 31, 1857-Dec. 28, 1861) sm
    Pub. 1857-1861   George C. Helmbold
        PHi   1857 Jan. 31-1861 Dec. 28
                  continued as
    PHILADELPHIA INTELLIGENCER (1862-1878) sm m
        sm Jan. 4, 1862-1868, m 1869-Nov. 1878||
    Pub. 1862-1868   George C. Helmbold
        1869   Orrin Rogers
        1870-1878   George C. Helmbold
        PBMa   1869 Sept., Oct.
        PHi   1862 Jan. 4-1878 Nov.

PHILADELPHIA ITEM, see Item

PHILADELPHIA JEWISH MORNING JOURNAL AND THE JEWISH DAILY NEWS (1900†) d
    PHILADELPHIA JEWISH MORNING JOURNAL (1900-1929) d
    Pub. 1908-1914   Jacob Ginsburg
        1914-1929   Jewish Journal Publishing Co.
    Ed. 1908-1914   Jacob Ginsburg
        1928-1929   B. Brown
        PPJMj   1913 Jan. 1 (Vol. 12, whole No. 3456)-1922 Apr. 30
                  continued as
    PHILADELPHIA JEWISH MORNING JOURNAL AND THE JEWISH DAILY NEWS (1930†) d
    Pub. 1930-1941   Jewish Journal Publishing Co.
    Ed. 1930-1934   B. Brown
        1934-1941   Charles Jaffe
        PP   1931 July 24-Dec. 18, 21-1932 Jan. 29
                  1932 Feb. 1-Sept. 21, 23-Oct. 12, 25, Nov. 3-10, 13-Dec. 2, 6-18, 20-23, 30-1933 Jan. 8
                  1933 Jan. 19-Feb. 20, 22, 24, 27-Mar. 2, 5-17, 20-May 29, June 4-21, 23-July 30, Aug. 1-30, Sept. 1-Dec. 27, 29-1934 Feb. 20
                  1934 Feb. 22-27, Mar. 2-Apr. 10, 12, 13, 16-19, 22-1935 Dec. 10
                  1935 Dec. 12-1936 Aug. 10

PHILADELPHIA JEWISH MORNING JOURNAL AND THE JEWISH DAILY NEWS, continued

     1936 Aug. 12-Sept. 4, 7-15, 20-23, 25-Oct. 15, 18-23, 27, 29-Nov. 13, 17-Dec. 24, 27, 28, 30, 31
     1937 Jan. 1-June 1, 3-29, July 1-Sept. 5, 10-14, 16, 17, 22-26, 28-Oct. 8, 11-1938 Apr. 24
     1938 June 26, 28-July 10, 12-17, 19-Nov. 8, 10-1939 Jan. 25
     1939 Jan. 27, 30-1941 May 5, 7-23, 26-Dec. 14, 16†

PHILADELPHIA JEWISH TIMES (1925†) w

  Pub. 1925-1929 Philadelphia Jewish Times Publishing Co.
     1929-1934 David Alter
     1934-1941 Joseph H. Biben
  Ed. 1927-1929 Joseph Herbach
     1929-1930 Iss Kricheff
     1930-1931 William Winger
     1931-1934 Herman M. Paris
     1934-1940 Joseph H. Biben
     1940-1941 A. C. Biben
  PUB   1926 Apr. 30-1928 Jan. 6
         1929 June 4†
  PP   1928 May 11†
  PPDr   [1925-1941]

PHILADELPHIA JOURNAL (1875), see Journal

PHILADELPHIA LEGAL INTELLIGENCER, see Legal Intelligencer

PHILADELPHIA LIBERALIST, see Southern Pioneer and Evangelical Liberalist

PHILADELPHIA MAIL (1866-1875) w co-operative ♦

  Pub. 1874-1875 Walter Lackey & Co.
     1875   C. Leslie Reilly
  Ed. 1874-1875 C. Leslie Reilly

PHILADELPHIA MAIL (ca. 1870-1871) d evg ♦

  Pub. & Ed. 1870-1871 Le Fevre, Bond & Co.

PHILADELPHIA MAIL AND UNIVERSAL LITERARY AND GENERAL ADVERTISER (w Mar. 30-Aug. 1830; m Sept. 1830-May 1833||) *

  Pub. 1830   E. Littell
  Also known as *Philadelphia Mail*
    P-M   1832 July
    PHi ♦   w 1830 Apr. 20
         m 1830 Dec.
    PW   1831 Nov.

PHILADELPHIA MARKET JOURNAL (1873), see Market Journal

PHILADELPHIA MERCURY (Sept. 29, 1827-Apr. 11, 1829||) w

  P-M   1828 Dec. 27
  PBL   1829 Feb. 14, Apr. 11
  PLewL 1828 Feb. 23

PHILADELPHIA COUNTY 231

PHILADELPHIA MERCURY AND EVENING JOURNAL (1842-May 23, 1844||) d *
    Pub. 1842-1844   Severns & Magill
        PBL   1843 Apr. 13
        PWet   1844 Mar. 25-28

PHILADELPHIA MINERVA (Feb. 7, 1795-July 7, 1798) w lit #
    Pub. 1795-1796   Woodruff & Pechin (Archibald Woodruff & William Pechin)
        1796-1797   John Turner
        1797-1798   William T. Palmer
    Absorbed by Samuel F. Bradford for his *True American and Commercial Advertiser,* and issued as a weekly supplement, entitled *Dessert to the True American,* 1798.
        PHi   1796 Feb. 6-1798 Jan. 20

PHILADELPHIA MIRROR, THE (Jan. 11, 1840) w lit
    Pub. & Ed. 1840-   W. B. Rogers
        PP   1840 Jan. 11

PHILADELPHIA MIRROR (1858-1859), see Philadelphia Public Mirror

PHILADELPHIA MORGEN GAZETTE, see Philadelphia Gazette Democrat

PHILADELPHIA MORNING POST (July 4, 1863) d *
        P-M   1863 July 4
        PHHi   1863 July 4
        PPot   1863 July 4

PHILADELPHIA MORNING TIMES (Mar. 27, 1855-Oct. 12, 1857||) d *
    Pub. 1855-1857   J. Barclay Harding
        PEHi   1857 July 7, 9, 15, 16, 20, 30, 31
        PWcHi   1857 Mar. 18

PHILADELPHIA NATIONAL FORUM, see Daily Forum

PHILADELPHIA NEUE ZEITUNG, see Philadelphia Gazette Democrat

PHILADELPHIA NEWS BUREAU, see Philadelphia Financial Journal

PHILADELPHIA OBSERVER, THE (1813†), see Christian Observer

PHILADELPHIA OBSERVER (Dec. 6, 1863-Jan. 10, 1864||) w
    Pub. & Ed.   Richard Meade Bache
        PHi ♦   1863 Dec. 13

PHILADELPHIA PATRIOT (1869-1870) w dem
    Pub. 1869-1870   M. K. Pierce
    Ed. 1869-1870   Charles N. Pine

PHILADELPHIA POST (1867-1878) d rep *
    MORNING POST (1867-1870) d *
    Pub. 1868-1871   John M. Carson, Morning Post Publishing Co.
        1871   Philadelphia Post Publishing Co.

PHILADELPHIA POST, *continued*

Ed.	1867-1868	John D. Stockton
	1867	John Russell Young, James Rankin Young, James McConnell
	1868-1871	John M. Carson
PCHi		1869 Apr. 20
PHi ◆		1868 Jan. 29
		1869 Apr. (2), Oct. 26
PMilt		1869 Oct. 23
PPiHi		1869 Oct. 26
PPL		1867 Oct. 8-1868 Apr. 1
		1868 Apr. 4, 6-14, 16-May 2, 4-1869 Jan. 19
		1869 Jan. 21, 25-Feb. 27, Mar. 2, 4-11, 15-Apr. 5, 7-May 13, 15-July 3, 7-1870 Dec. 26
		1870 Dec. 28-1871 Jan. 7
PPM		1867 Dec. 14-1868 Dec. 15
		1869 Jan. 1-1871 June 30
PWcHi		1868 Mar. 5
	continued as	

PHILADELPHIA POST (Jan. 9, 1871-Oct. 15, 1878||) d sun *
Sun. 1878 as *Sunday Post*

Pub.	1871	Philadelphia Post Publishing Co.
Ed.	1871	John M. Carson, Joseph H. Paist
PPL		1871 Feb. 1-Aug. 31, Sept. 14-1872 Feb. 29
		1872 Aug. 1-31, Sept. 14-Oct. 15
PPM		1871 Jan. 9-June 30

PHILADELPHIA PRESS, see Press

PHILADELPHIA PRICE CURRENT, see Commercial List and Maritime Register

PHILADELPHIA PRICE CURRENT AND COMMERCIAL ADVERTISER, see Commercial List and Maritime Register

PHILADELPHIA PRICE CURRENT: OR TRADE NEWS AND SHIPPING LIST, see Moore's Philadelphia Price Current; or Trade News and Shipping List

PHILADELPHIA PROGRAMME (1863-1865) d
Pub. & Ed. 1863-1865 Henry R. Hellier
    PHi ◆   1864 May 2, 13 (Vol. 2, No. 278)
               1865 Aug. 9

PHILADELPHIA PROGRESS, see Philadelphian (West Philadelphia)

PHILADELPHIA PUBLIC MIRROR (Apr. 7, 1858-1859||) d sun
    PDoHi   1858 Apr. 18 (Vol. 1, No. 2)

PHILADELPHIA PUBLIC SALE REPORT (1812-1827) w comm # *
    GROTJAN'S PHILADELPHIA PUBLIC SALE REPORT AND GENERAL PRICE CURRENT (May 11, 1812-Sept. 10, 1825) w #

PHILADELPHIA COUNTY 233

    Pub. & Ed. 1812   May 11-1825 Apr. 25 Peter A. Grotjan
              1825   May 2-1825   Sept. 10 L. Krumbaar
       PHi ♦   1812 May 11-Sept. 5
                   1814 Sept. 19-1819 Feb. 8
                   1819 Mar. 1-1820 Apr. 24
                   1820 June 26, July 10-1821 Feb. 12
                   1821 Feb. 26-1823 Sept. 8
                   1824 May 3-June 28, July 12-Aug. 2, 16-1825 Apr. 25, May 2-Sept. 10
       PP   1815 May 1
       PPAP ♦   1812 May 11-1820 Apr. 24
                continued as
    PHILADELPHIA PUBLIC SALE REPORT (Sept. 17, 1825-Apr. 28, 1827||) *
    Pub. & Ed. 1825 Sept. 17-1826 Oct. 28 L. Krumbaar
              1826 Nov. 4-1827 Apr. 28 William Stavely
       PHi ♦   1825 Sept. 17-1827 Apr. 28
       PPL ♦   1826 Jan. 28-Mar. 18, Apr. 1, 15-Aug. 5, 19-1827 Apr. 21

PHILADELPHIA RECORD, see Record, page 273

PHILADELPHIA RECORDER, see Episcopal Recorder

PHILADELPHIA REPOSITORY AND RELIGIOUS AND LITERARY REVIEW (1841) w rel
    Pub. 1841   Orrin Rogers
    Ed. 1841   William H. Gilder
       PHi ♦   1841 June 19 (Vol. 1, No. 51)

PHILADELPHIA REPOSITORY AND WEEKLY REGISTER
(Nov. 15, 1800-Dec. 29, 1804) #
    Pub. & Ed. 1800 Nov. 15-1801 Jan. 31 Ephraim Conrad
              1801 Jan. 10-1804 Jan. 7 David Hogan
              1804 Jan. 14-1804 Dec. 29 John W. Scott
                 This publication was sold Dec. 29, 1804 to a new publisher who continued it strictly as a magazine entitled *The Repository and Ladies Weekly Museum Magazine.*
       PCHi   1803 Feb. 12
       PP   1801 June 27-July 11, 25, Aug. 8-15, Sept. 5, Nov. 14-Dec. 26
                 1802 Jan. 2-Dec. 25
       PPot   1803 Mar. 5
       PWcHi   1803 Feb. 12

PHILADELPHIA REVIEW (1871) w ♦
    Pub. & Ed. (1871) A. D. Woodward & Co.

PHILADELPHIA SATURDAY BULLETIN, see Evening Bulletin

PHILADELPHIA SATURDAY BULLETIN AND AMERICAN COURIER (1856-1857), see Evening Bulletin

PHILADELPHIA SATURDAY COURIER, THE, see American Saturday Courier

PHILADELPHIA SATURDAY GLEANER, see Philadelphia Inquirer Public Ledger; also Family Messenger and National Gleaner

PHILADELPHIA SATURDAY HERALD, see Commercial Herald and Pennsylvania Sentinel

PHILADELPHIA SATURDAY INQUIRER, see Philadelphia Inquirer Public Ledger

PHILADELPHIA SATURDAY MUSEUM, see Saturday Evening Mail

PHILADELPHIA SATURDAY NEWS AND LITERARY GAZETTE (July 2, 1836-Jan. 5, 1839) w *
    Pub. 1836-1839   L. A. Godey & Co.
    Ed. 1836-1839   Joseph C. Neal, Morton McMichael
    Merged with *Atkinson's Saturday Evening Post* (q.v.)
    P   1836 Dec. 31-1838 Aug. 11
    PHi ♦   1838 Jan. 20

PHILADELPHIA SCHWABISCHER MERKUR, see Schwabischer Merkur

PHILADELPHIA SONNTAGS-GAZETTE, see Philadelphia Gazette-Democrat

PHILADELPHIA STANDARD (1875) * ↓

PHILADELPHIA SUN (1871) w ↓
    Pub. & Ed. 1871   Stokes & Co.

PHILADELPHIA SUNDAY ATLAS (Nov. 7, 1858-May 5, 1861||) w
    Pub. 1858-1859   George G. Thomas & Co.
         1859-1861   George G. Thomas
    PHi ♦   1860 Nov. 18 (Vol. 1, No. 1)
    PPL   1858 Nov. 7-1861 May 5

PHILADELPHIA SUNDAY ITEM, see Item

PHILADELPHIA SUNDAY MERCURY, see Mercury and Siftings

PHILADELPHIA SUNDAY TIMES, see Taggarts Sunday Times

PHILADELPHIA TAGEBLATT (Nov. 19, 1877†) d for ind *
    Pub. 1877-1918   Tageblatt Publishing Assoc.
         1918-1933   Philadelphia Tageblatt Publishing Co.
                       (Gustav Falkenstein, Pres.)
         1933-1938   Gustav Mayer
         1938-1940   Herman Lemke
         1940-1941   Philadelphia Gazette Publishing Co.
                       (Louis Mayer, Pres.)
    Ed. 1908-1918   L. Werner
       1918-1920   August F. Herbert

PHILADELPHIA COUNTY 235

    1920-1929   E. A. Thomaser
    1929-1933   Richard Schaffer
    1933-1940   Herman Lemke
    1940-1941   Louis Mayer

Sunday edition was first entitled, *Sonntags Zeitung des Tageblatts* (1879) and later changed to *Sonntags Blatt* (1879†)

PUB   d 1927 Jan.-Mar. (2)-Apr. (17)-(28)-(May 25-June 5), (7-11)-Sept. (5)-Oct. 7, 9-Dec. (11)-(30)-31
    1928 Oct. 1-1929 June 30
    1929 Oct. 1-1930 Mar. 25
    1930 Mar. 27-Apr. 8, 10, (11)-(13)-(17)-(25)-(27)-May (7)-(11)-(18)-(23)-(31)-June (1)-(8)-(15)-July (3)-19, 21, 24-26, 28-Sept. (16)-(28)-1931 Feb. (16)-Mar. (31)-Apr. (12)-(24)-1932 Apr. (3)-(17)-May (1)-(31)-Aug. 7
    1932 Aug. 9-21, 23-1933 July 5
    1933 July 7-1934 Feb. 27
    1934 Mar. 1†
    sun [1930 July 27-1934 Feb.], Mar. 1†

PHi   1906 Jan. 25

PP   d 1917 Aug. 3, 10, 21-30, Sept. 12
    1927 June 1-13, 15-30, July 1-Aug. 8, 10-Sept. 11, 13-Dec. 29, 31
    1928 Jan. 1-Feb. 6, 8-11, 13-Mar. 19, 21-1929 May 16
    1929 May 18-Dec. 10, 12†

PPG   d 1877 Nov. 19-1886 Nov. 17
    1886 Nov. 22-1890 Nov. 18
    1891 Apr. 1-1892 July 31
    1892 Aug. 3-1897 Nov. 14
    1897 Nov. 18-1899 July 31
    1900 Apr. 1-July 31
    1901 Jan. 1-1904 June 30
    1904 Oct. 1-1907 Aug. 28
    1907 Sept. 1-1908 Dec. 31
    1909 May 1-Aug. 31, Sept. 3-1911 Sept. 30
    1912 Jan. 1-1916 Dec. 31
    1917 July 1-1924 Dec. 31
    1925 Apr. 1-1926 Mar. 31
    1926 July 1-Dec. 31
    1928 Jan. 1-Sept. 30
    1929 July 1-Sept. 30
    w 1879 Sept. 7-Dec. 28
    1880 Jan. 4-1885 July 26
    1885 Aug. 9-1886 Nov. 14
    1886 Nov. 28-1893 July 30
    1893 Sept. 2-Nov. 5, 19-1895 Nov. 10
    1895 Nov. 24-1900 July 29
    1901 Jan. 6-1904 June 26
    1904 July 10-1906 June 24
    1906 Oct. 7-1908 Dec. 27
    1909 May 2-1911 Sept. 24
    1912 Jan. 7-1916 Dec. 31
    1917 July 1-1921 Dec. 25
    1922 Jan. 6-1924 Dec. 28
    1925 Apr. 5-1926 Mar. 28
    1926 July 4-1928 Sept. 30
    1929 July 9-Sept. 29

PHILADELPHIA TEUTSCHE FAMA (1749-1751) for ♣
    Pub. 1749-1751   Franklin & Bohm (Benjamin Franklin and Johann Bohm). Referred to in 1749 and 1750 as *Bohm's Fama* and *Bohm's Philadelphier Teutsche Fama.*

PHILADELPHIA TIMES, PEOPLE'S FRIEND AND MECHANICS' FREE PRESS (1828-1835) w *
    MECHANICS' FREE PRESS (Jan. 12, 1828-Apr. 23, 1831) w *
    Pub. & Ed. 1828-1831   Committee of the Mechanics' Library Co. of Philadelphia
    PHi   1828 Apr. 12-July 5, 19-1829 July 4, 18-1831 Jan. 15
        1831 Jan. 29-Apr. 23
    PPL   1830 Jan. 9-Oct. 16, 30-1831 Jan. 1
    PPM   1828 Apr. 12-Aug. 23, Sept. 6-Oct. 18, Dec. 13-1829 Mar. 21
        1829 Aug. 1-8, 22, Sept. 12-Dec. 19
        1830 Jan. 2-23, Feb. 6-Dec. 25
    continued as
    PHILADELPHIA TIMES, PEOPLE'S FRIEND AND MECHANICS' FREE PRESS (Apr. 30, 1831-1835) w *
    Pub. 1831-1834   Committee of the Mechanics' Library Co. of Philadelphia
    1834-1835   Joshua Johnson & Co.
    Title varies: *Philadelphia Times Mechanics' Free Press and Working Man's Register.*
    PHi ♦   1834 Oct. 18
        1835 Oct. 17

PHILADELPHIA TRIBUNE (1867-1870) w ind ♣
    Pub. & Ed. 1867-1870   E. James & Co.

PHILADELPHIA TRIBUNE (Nov. 2, 1884†) w ind rep Negro *
    Pub. 1884-1886   Richard A. Sneads
        1886-1891   Christopher J. Perry
        1891-1894   John W. Harris
        1894-1922   Christopher J. Perry
        1922-1923   Estate of Christopher J. Perry
        1923†   Philadelphia Tribune Co.
    Ed. 1884-1886   Richard A. Sneads
        1886-1891   Christopher J. Perry
        1891-1903   John W. Harris
        1903-1908   Christopher J. Perry
        1908-1915   John W. Harris
        1928†   E. Washington Rhodes
    PUB   1884 Nov. 2†
    PEHi   1919 Nov. 15
    PP   1924 Apr. 26
        1925 Nov. 28
        1927 May 26-Aug. 18, Sept. 1-1928 Aug. 30
        1928 Sept. 13-1929 Dec. 12
        1930 Jan. 2†

PHILADELPHIA UNDERWRITER (1869-1875) w insurance ♣
    Pub. & Ed. 1874-1875   S. E. Cohen

PHILADELPHIA COUNTY 237

PHILADELPHIA UNITED IRISHMEN (1869-1870) w
    Pub. & Ed. 1869-1870 C. Leslie Reilly

PHILADELPHIA VOLKSBLATT (1872-1898) d w for
    Pub. 1872-1874 Joseph Berndt
          1874-1875 German Publishing Society
          1875-1876 German Volksblatt Society
          1876-1889 Philadelphia Volksblatt Society
          1889-1893 Volksblatt Publishing Co.
          1893-1898 Charles J. Young
    Ed. 1872-1887 Dr. Joseph Berndt
         1895-1896 Joseph Berndt, E. W. Ditges
    Weekly edition entitled *Nord Amerika.*

PHILADELPHIA WEEKLY AGE, see Illustrated New Age

PHILADELPHIA WEEKLY MAIL (1866-1870) w comm
    Pub. & Ed. 1868-1870 C. Leslie Reilly

PHILADELPHIA WEEKLY PRESS, see Press

PHILADELPHIA WEEKLY TIMES (1857) w   *

PHILADELPHIA WEEKLY TIMES (1877-1902), see Times

PHILADELPHIA WOCHENBLATT (1855) w for
    Pub. 1855 William Rosenthal

PHILADELPHIAN (1825-1836), see Christian Observer

PHILADELPHIAN (West Philadelphia) (1877-1902) w local ind
    PHILADELPHIA PROGRESS (West Philadelphia) (May 8, 1877-Dec. 2, 1878) w
    Pub. & Ed. 1877-1878 John D. Avil, James Miller
              continued as
    WEST PHILADELPHIA PUBLIC TELEPHONE (Dec. 14, 1878-1884) w
    Pub. & Ed. 1878-1883 Avil & Torrey
             1883-1884 John D. Avil & Co.
             continued as
    TELEPHONE (West Philadelphia) (1884-1898) w
    Pub. & Ed. 1884-1886 John D. Avil & Co.
             1886-1898 Avil Printing Co.
    Ed.   1884-1898 John D. Avil
             continued as
    PHILADELPHIAN (1898-June 7, 1902) w
    Pub. 1898-1899 Avil Printing Co.
         1899-1901 Telephone Publishing Co.
    Ed. 1898-1899 John D. Avil
    PP   1899 Sept. 2, 16

PHILADELPHIAN (West Philadelphia), continued
    PU   1899 Dec. 30
              1900 Mar. 10, 24-1902 June 7

PHILADELPHIAN, OR LUTHERAN CHURCH VISITOR, THE
(Jan. 2, 1867-Dec. 16, 1868) sm rel
    Pub. 1867 Jan. 2-1868 Dec. 16 at Philadelphia
    Ed. 1867 Jan. 2-1867 Dec. 18 C. W. Schaeffer
          1868 Jan. 1-1868 Dec. 16 C. W. Schaeffer, Jacob Fry
        PPK ♦   1867 Jan. 2-1868 Dec. 16

PHILADELPHIER DEMOKRAT UND ANZEIGER DER DEUTSCHEN, see Philadelphia Demokrat

PHILADELPHIA'ER TELEGRAPH, UND DEUTSCHES WOCHENBLATT (1825-1831) sw for *
    AMERIKANISCHER CORRESPONDENT (Jan. 5, 1825-Dec. 30, 1829) sw
        Pub. 1825-1829   John George Ritter
              1829   Gossler & Blumer
        Ed. 1825-1829   Dr William Schmidt
             1829   J C. Gossler
        PHi   1829 Aug. 19-Dec. 30
                      continued as
    PHILADELPHISCHER CORRESPONDENT UND ALLGEMEINER DEUTSCHER ANZEIGER (Jan. 2, 1830-Dec. 29, 1830) sw
        Pub. 1830   Gossler & Blumer
        PHi   1830 Jan. 2-July (10)-Aug. 7
                      continued as
    PHILADELPHIA'ER TELEGRAPH, UND DEUTSCHES WOCHENBLATT (Jan. 3, 1831-Dec. 31, 1831) sw *
        Pub. & Ed. 1831   Alexander A. Blumer, N. W. Ecke
        PHi   1831 Feb. 16-Dec 14

PHILADELPHIER WOCHENBLAT, DAS (1790-1794) w for #
    CHESTNUTHILLER WOCHENSCHRIFT, DIE (Dec. 15, 1790-1794) w #
        Pub. 1790-1794   Samuel Saur
        PPL   1790 Oct 8 (prospectus issue), Dec. 15-1793 Aug. 13
                      continued as
    PHILADELPHIER WOCHENBLAT, DAS (1794) w ♦
        Pub. 1794   Samuel Saur

PHILADELPHISCHE CORRESPONDENZ, see Neue Philadelphische Correspondenz

PHILADELPHISCHE STAATS REGISTER (July 21, 1779-Oct. 25, 1781||), see Neue Philadelphische Correspondenz

PHILADELPHIA COUNTY

PHILADELPHISCHE ZEITUNG (May 6, 1732-June 24, 1732) w for #
    Pub. 1732   Benjamin Franklin
    Ed. 1732   Louis Timothee
    PHi   1732 May 6, June 24

PHILADELPHISCHE ZEITUNG, VON ALLERHAND AUSWAR-TIG-UND EINHEIMSCHEN MERCK-WURDIGEN SACHEN (July 12, 1755-Dec. 31, 1757) bw
    Pub. 1755-1757   Benjamin Franklin, Anthon Armbruster, William Smith
    Ed. 1755-1757   Rev. Johann F. Handshuh
    PHi   1755 Sept. 6, Nov. 27
                          1756 Mar. 6, Sept. 23, Dec. 30
                          1757 Jan. 14, Feb. 11-Mar. 14, Apr. 15-Nov. 18, Dec. 17-31

PHILANTHROPIST (1835-May 28, 1836) w, see Saturday Chronicle and Mirror of the Times

PILOT (1907-1908) w ind Negro ♪
    Pub. & Ed. 1907-1908 James S. Stemons

PIONEER, see American Pioneer and Fireman's Chronicle

PLAIN DEALER (Oct. 18, 1848) w dem
    Pub. 1848   Hamilton & Forney
    Hamilton and Forney were also the publishers of the *Pennsylvanian*, however, there is no volume and number on this paper, and no statement to indicate any connection with the "Pennsylvanian" except the fact that Hamilton and Forney were publishers of both. A campaign paper advocating the election of Lewis Cass and William O. Butler, Democratic candidates for President and Vice President.
    PP   1848 Oct. 17

PLEDGE AND STANDARD (Sept. 1838-1848) w
    Pub.   T. L. Sanders & Co.
    PBL   1848 Sept. 9
    PHi   1846 Sept. 5 (Vol. VIII, No. 46)
    PWcHi   1846 July 25

POLITICAL AND COMMERCIAL REGISTER (July 2, 1804-May 17, 1820||) d fed. #
    Pub. 1804-1820   Major William Jackson
    Title varied: *Commercial and Political Register*
    PAtM   1812 Apr. 7, June 22
    PDoHi   1809 June 16
                    1813 Nov. 16
    PHi ♦   1804 July 2-Aug. 30, Sept. 1-Oct. 19, 22-Dec. 31
                    1805 Jan. 2-May 20, 22-Sept. 16, 18-Nov. 15, 18, 19, 21-Dec. 6, 9-31
                    1806 June 9

POLITICAL AND COMMERCIAL REGISTER, *continued*
                        1807 Jan. 1-Feb. 4, 6-Mar. 25, 28-July 31, Aug. 27-Sept. 18, 21-Oct. 1, 5-Dec. 31
                        1809 May 15, Oct. 21
                        1810 Nov. 19
                        1811 Jan. 11, Apr. 2, 6
                        1813 Apr. 13, May 4, July 6-8, 10-Aug. 25, 28-Sept. 6, 8-Oct. 7, 9-Nov. 12
                        1814 Jan. 1-July 21, 23-Aug. 17, 19-Nov. 3, 5-Dec. 31
                        1815 Jan. 2-May 20, 23-July 24, 26-Aug. 24, 26-Nov. 2, 6-Dec. 30
                        1816 Jan. 1-23, Feb. 5-Apr. 23, 25-July 1, 3-Nov. 15, 18-Dec. 31
                        1817 Jan. 4-Feb. 5, 7, Mar. 8-13, 15-17, 19-24, 26-Apr. 3, 7-11, 14-16, 18-May 7, 9-20, 22-29, 31-Sept. 8, 10, 12-Dec. 31
                        1818 Oct. 19, 21, 23, 28, 29, 31-Nov. 2, 21-23, 26, 27, 30, Dec. 14, 18, 28
                        1819 Jan. 4, 8, 30, Feb. 3, 8, 9, 12, 15, 16, 19, 20, Mar. 3, 4, 16, 22, 24, 25, 27-31, Apr. 5-7, 12-15, 24, Oct. 22, 25, 29, Nov. 4, 9-12, 16, 18, 19, 22-25, 27, 30, Dec. 2-8, 10-16, 20, 22, 23, 29-31
                        1820 Jan. 3-5, 7-10, Mar. 8, May 9, 11, 12, 15-17
PLaHi   1805 Sept. 7-1808 Aug. 25
PP   1808 May 12-Aug. 2, 4-30
PPAP   1818 Feb. 23
PPiUD   1810 Jan. 1-Apr. 30
PPL   1804 July 2-1807 Mar. 26
                1807 Mar. 28-1811 Nov. 8
                1811 Nov. 11-1812 Mar. 26
                1812 Mar. 28-July 29, 31-Nov. 6, 9-21, 24-Dec. 31
PPM ♦   1805 July 1-Dec. 31
                1806 Jan. 1-Apr. 3, 5-June 30
                1808 July 1-Dec. 25, 27-31
                1809 Jan. 2-Dec. 30
                1810 Jan. 1-Mar. (2)-June (30)-July 1, 3, 5-Dec. 31
                1811 Jan. 1-Apr. 11, 13-July (2), 3, 6-Oct. 4, 6-Dec. 31
                1812-1816 June 29
PRHi   [1813 Jan. 4-Dec. 30]
PWcHi   1804 Sept. 14, Oct. 30
                1809 June 19

POPOLO ITALIANO   (1935†) d morn rep for
    L'Opinione Italiano was started by former employees of *L'Opinione*. Title was changed so as not to cause any confusion with the Philadelphia edition of *"L'Opinione, Il Progresso Italo-Americano,"* published at New York (q.v.)
    OPINIONE ITALIANO (June 2, 1935-June 8, 1935) d
      Pub. & Ed. 1935   Remo Zuecca
      PP   1935 June 2-8
                      continued as
    POPOLO ITALIANO (June 9, 1935†) d
      Pub. & Ed. 1935-1941 Remo Zuecca
      PUB   1935†
      PP   1935 June 9†

PHILADELPHIA COUNTY   241

PORCUPINE'S GAZETTE (1797-1799) d w #
    PORCUPINE'S GAZETTE AND UNITED STATES DAILY AD-
      VERTISER (Mar. 4, 1797-Apr. 22, 1797) d #
    Pub. & Ed. 1797 William Cobbett
        PBL ♦   1797 Mar. 4-Apr. 22
        PHi   1797 Apr. 21
        PPL   1797 Mar. 14-Apr. 22

                continued as

    PORCUPINE'S GAZETTE (Apr. 24, 1797-Oct. 26, 1799) d w tw #
    Pub. & Ed. 1797-1799 William Cobbett
                Weekly editions from Sept. 6, 1799 to Oct. 26, 1799,
                were published in Bustleton.
                Tri-weekly edition, entitled *The County Porcupine*,
                1798-1799.
        P   1798 Mar. 16-1799 Feb. 19
            tw 1798 July 5-Nov. 28
        P-M   1797 June 16
        PArdL   1797 Aug. 8
        PBL ♦   1797 Apr. 24
                   1798 Mar. 3
        PDoHi   1797 May 20, June 15
                   1798 May 23, June 12
                   1799 Mar. 30, July 9
            tw 1799 Feb. 23, 25
        PE   1798 July 5-1799 Sept. 27
        PHi ♦   1797 June 1, 3, 8, 14, 17, 20, 26, 30, July 1, 3, 6,
                      11, 13, 21, 31, Aug. 12, Sept. 1, 2
                   1798 Mar. (5)
        PLewL   1797 Aug. 2-Dec. 29
        PP   1798 May 26, June 1, Oct. 4, 10, 20, Dec. 10, 21
                   1799 Jan. 1, 28, Apr. 18, July 20
        PPL   1797 Apr. 24-1798 Mar. 22
                   1798 Mar. 24-Apr. 10, 12-28, May 1-22, 24-1799 Apr. 5
                   1799 Apr. 8-June 22, 25-July 20, 23-Oct. 11
        PPot   1798 Dec. 19
        PPotW   1798 Dec. 19
        PWcHi   1798 Oct. 3
        PWpHi   1798 Jan.-June

POST   (Aug. 2, 1884-Nov. 8, 1884) w
    Pub.   W. U. Hensel at Philadelphia and Lancaster
        PLaN   1884 Aug. 2-Nov. 8
        PWcHi   1884 Oct. 4

POST   (May 5, 1930-July 3, 1931||) w
    Pub. & Ed.   William Jordan
        PP   1930 Oct. 22-1931 June 3

POULSON'S AMERICAN DAILY ADVERTISER, see North American

PRAVDA (1902†) sw w (July 2, 1937-Jan. 8, 1938) non-part for *
- Pub. 1923-1941 Russian Brotherhood Organization
- Ed. 1923-1925 Dr. S. Pysh
  - 1925-1926 S. Zsendasiuk
  - 1926-1936 Simeon S. Pysh
  - 1936-1941 John Dzwonczyk
- PUB 1902 Mar. 11†
- PP 1927 Nov. 1†

PRESBYTERIAN, THE (1831†) w rel
PRESBYTERIAN, THE (Feb. 16, 1831-June 11, 1925) w %
- Pub. 1831 Feb. 16-1834 May 1 Russell & Martien at Philadelphia
  - 1834 May 8-1836 Apr. 14 William S. Martien at Philadelphia
  - 1836 Apr. 23-1845 June 28 William S. Martien, Philadelphia and New York date line
  - 1845 July 5-1849 Sept. 1 William S. Martien, New York and Philadelphia date line
  - 1849 Sept. 8-1852 Mar. 20 William S. Martien, Philadelphia and New York date line
  - 1852 Mar. 27-1864 Dec. 31 William S. Martien & Company, Philadelphia and New York date line
  - 1865 Jan. 7-1873 Sept. 13 Alfred Martien & Company, Philadelphia and New York date line
  - 1873 Sept. 20-1899 Jan. 18 Mutchmore. & Company, Philadelphia and New York date line
  - 1899 Jan. 25-1902 Jan. 8 The Presbyterian Publishing Company, Philadelphia and New York date line
  - 1902 Jan. 15-1925 June 11 The Presbyterian Publishing Company, Inc., Philadelphia date line.
- Ed. 1831 Feb. 16-1832 Nov. 14 John Burtt
  - 1832 Nov. 28-1834 Jan. 2 James W. Alexander
  - 1872 June 29-1873 Sept. 13 M. B. Grier
  - 1873 Sept. 20-1877 Nov. 3 M. B. Grier, S. A. Mutchmore
  - 1891 Apr. 15-1898 Dec. 28 M. B. Grier, S. A. Mutchmore, W. W. McKinney
  - 1899 Jan. 4-1899 Feb. 15 M. B. Grier, W. W. McKinney
  - 1899 Feb. 22-1899 May 24 W. W. McKinney
  - 1899 May 31-1901 Feb. 27 Robert Alexander, W. W. McKinney
  - 1901 Mar. 6-1905 Sept. 27 W. W. McKinney, Clara Augusta Alexander
  - 1911 June 21-1912 Jan. 17 David S. Kennedy, Walter A. Brooks, Clara A. Alexander
  - 1912 Jan. 24-1912 Nov. 27 David S. Kennedy, Clara A. Alexander
  - 1912 Dec. 4-1915 Oct. 14 David S. Kennedy, Clara A. Alexander, D. J. Burrell
  - 1915 Oct. 21-1918 May 30 David S. Kennedy, Samuel G. Craig
  - 1918 June 6-1923 Dec. 27 David S. Kennedy
  - 1924 Jan. 3-1925 June 11 David S. Kennedy, ed.; William L. McEwan, Maitland Alexander, Samuel G. Craig, Clarence E. Macartney, J. Gresham Machen, assoc. eds.
- r-M 1831 Apr. 13
  - 1836 Apr. 7
  - 1838 May 5, 12

PHILADELPHIA COUNTY 243

PDoHi	1833 Mar. 27
	1840 Dec. 12
PE	1841 Sept. 4, 18
PEL ♦	1831 Mar. 9
	1832 Jan. 18
	1833 June 5, 19-Aug. 7, 21-1836 May 21
	1836 June 4-1839 June 29
	1839 July 13-1847 Apr. 24
	1847 May 8-15, 29-1848 July 1
	1848 July 15-Aug. 19, Sept. 2-1856 Mar. 27
	1858 Mar. 20
PHi ♦	1859 Dec. 10
PLewL	1834 Jan. 2-1836 Apr. 4
	1836 Apr. 25-1837 Apr. 7
	1837 Apr. 21-1841 May 29
	1841 June 12-1849 Dec. 29
	1850 Mar. 2, Apr. 6, June 8, 22-1852 Dec. 25
	1853 Jan. 22
PNoHi	1833 July 31, Oct. 30
	1835 Sept. 3
	1837 Sept. 30
	1838 June 30, Dec. 1
PP	1831 Feb. 23-28
	1832 Feb. 15-July 18, Aug. 1-1836 Apr. 23
	1836 May 7-June 25, July 9-Aug. 13, 27-Sept. 17, Oct. 8, Nov. 5, 19, 26, Dec. 3, 10, 24, 31
	1837 Jan. 7-1839 May 30
	1839 Apr. 13-June 29, July 13-Dec. 28
	1840 Jan. 4-1843 Dec. 23
	1844 Jan. 6-1846 Feb. 28
	1846 Mar. 7-July 18, Aug. 1, 8, 15, 29, Sept. 5-Nov. 21, Dec. 5-26
	1847 Jan. 16-Sept. 18, Oct. 2-Dec. 25
	1848 Jan. 1-1861 Oct. 19
	1861 Nov. 2-Dec. 28
	1862 Jan. 4-1865 Oct. 7
	1865 Oct. 21-Dec. 30
	1866 Jan. 6-1874 Feb. 28
	[1874 Mar. 7 (Vol. 44, No. 10)-1878, 1891, 1900-1911, 1913, 1915-1919, 1922-1924, 1926-1927, 1929-1930, 1934-1935]
PPiHi	1859 May 7
	1863 Nov. 7
	1864 Feb. 27, Mar. 12-26, Apr. 23, May 7, June 4-25, July 2, 23, 30, Aug. 6, 21, Sept. 3, 24, Nov. 12, 26, Dec. 3
PPPHi ♦	1831 Feb. 16-1925 June 11
	Missing
	1887 Jan. 1, July 23
	1890 May 14
	1891 Sept. 16, Dec. 9
	1894 May 30
	Merged with *The Herald and Presbyter* and continued as

PRESBYTERIAN AND HERALD AND PRESBYTER, THE
(June 18, 1925-May 13, 1926) w

PRESBYTERIAN, THE, *continued*

Pub.	1925 June 18-1926 May 13	The Presbyterian Publishing Company Inc., Philadelphia and Cincinnati date line
Ed.	1925 June 18-1926 May 13	D. S. Kennedy, Samuel G. Craig, eds.; F. C. Monfort, assoc. ed.

PPPHi ◆ 1925 June 18-1926 May 13

title changed to

PRESBYTERIAN, THE continuing HERALD AND PRESBYTER, THE (May 20, 1926-Dec. 25, 1930) w

Pub.	1926 May 20-1930 Dec. 25	The Presbyterian Publishing Company Inc., at Philadelphia
Ed.	1926 May 20-1928 Sept.	D. S. Kennedy, Samuel G. Craig, F. C. Monfort
	1928 Oct.-1930 Jan. 30	Samuel G. Craig, ed.; D. S. Kennedy, assoc. ed.
	1930 Feb. 6-1930 Feb. 27	A. Mackenzie Lamb, David S. Kennedy, E. P. Whallon, Clara A. Alexander
	1930 Mar. 6-1930 Dec. 25	W. Courtland Robinson

PPPHi ◆ 1926 May 20-1930 Dec. 25

title changed to

PRESBYTERIAN, THE (Jan. 1, 1931†) w

Pub.	1931 Jan. 1†	The Presbyterian Publishing Company Inc., at Philadelphia
Ed.	1931 Jan. 1-1932 Feb. 25	W. Courtland Robinson
	1932 Mar. 3 and 10	W. Courtland Robinson, ed.; Edward P. Whallon, Anna I. McKinney, assoc. eds.
	1932 Mar. 17-1934 May 10	W. Courtland Robinson, David S. Kennedy, Edward P. Whallon, Anna I. McKinney
	1934 May 17†	Stewart M. Robinson, ed.; Anna I. McKinney, asst. ed.

PPPHi ◆ 1931 Jan. 1†

PRESBYTERIAN BANNER, THE (June 12, 1852-Nov. 10, 1855) w

Pub.	1852 Sept. 18-1854 Dec. 30	Philadelphia, New York, Baltimore date line
	1855 Jan. 6-1855 Nov. 10	Philadelphia, Chicago, New York, Baltimore date line
Ed.	1852 Sept. 18-1855 Nov. 10	David McKinney

A preliminary issue was published on June 12, 1852; editor not stated. On Nov. 17, 1855, it merged with *The Presbyterian Advocate* of Pittsburgh under the title of *Presbyterian Banner and Advocate*, published at Pittsburgh (Branch office at Philadelphia mentioned until Dec. 13, 1865). On March 10, 1860, the paper reassumed the name *Presbyterian Banner* with title varying. *The Presbyterian Banner* was continued until Dec. 16, 1937, when it merged into *Pageant,* a monthly magazine by the Board of Christian Education of the Presbyterian Church, published from Jan. 1938 until Dec. 1938 at Chicago, with editorial offices at Philadelphia.

PEL ◆ 1852 Dec. 11-25

1853 Apr. 23-May 7, 28-June 11, Aug. 13, 20, Sept. 3-Nov. 26, Dec. 10-24

PHILADELPHIA COUNTY 245

```
                          1854 Jan. 7-Apr. 22, May 20-June 17, July 8, 22-
                            1855 Jan. 27
                          1855 Feb. 10-24, Mar. 17-May 19, Sept. 1
      PHi     ◆           1854 June 17
      PPPHi   ◆           1852 June 12, Sept. 18-1937 Dec. 16
```

PRESBYTERIAN GUARDIAN, THE (Oct. 7, 1935†) sm m rel
(sm Oct. 7, 1935-June 26, 1937 and Jan. 10, 1940†; m July 1937-Dec. 1939)

```
      Pub. 1935 Oct. 7-1936 June 1      The Presbyterian Constitutional Cove-
                                          nant Union at Philadelphia
           1936 June 22-1937 Apr. 24   The Presbyterian Guardian Publish-
                                          ing Company at Philadelphia
           1937 May 15†                 The Presbyterian Guardian Publish-
                                          ing Corporation at Philadelphia
      Ed.  1935 Oct. 7-1936 Aug. 17    H. McAllister Griffiths
           1936 Sept. 12-1937 Jan. 9   J. Gresham Machen, Ned B. Stone-
                                          house
           1937 Jan. 23-1937 June 26   Ned B. Stonehouse
           1937 July-1937 Sept.        Charles J. Woodbridge
           1937 Oct.-1940 Nov. 25      Edwin H. Rian, Leslie W. Sloat, Ned
                                          B. Stonehouse, Murray Forst Thomp-
                                          son
           1940 Dec. 10-1941 Mar. 10   John P. Clelland, John Patton Gal-
                                          braith, Edwin H. Rian, Leslie W.
                                          Sloat, Ned B. Stonehouse, Murray
                                          Forst Thompson
           1941 Mar. 25-1941 June 10   John P. Clelland, John Patton Gal-
                                          braith, Edwin H. Rian, Leslie W.
                                          Sloat, Ned B. Stonehouse
           1941 June 25†               John P. Clelland, John Patton Gal-
                                          braith, R. B. Kuiper, Edwin H. Rian,
                                          Leslie W. Sloat
      PPPHi   ◆   1935 Oct. 7†
```

PRESBYTERIAN JOURNAL, THE (1875-1904), see Westminster, The

PRESBYTERIAN OBSERVER, THE (1873-1895‖) w rel %
This paper was established in 1873. Beginning 1880, Jan. 1 or before, it was published at Baltimore as *The Baltimore Presbyterian.* On July 20, 1882 its title was changed to *The Presbyterian Observer.* From 1887, May 12, until 1888, May 31, it was published Baltimore and Washington date line.

```
      Pub. 1888 June 7-1893 June 22    Presbyterian Publishing Company,
                                          Philadelphia, Baltimore, and Wash-
                                          ington date line
           1893 June 29-1895 July 25)  Presbyterian Publishing Company,
              or later)                   Philadelphia date line
      Ed.  1888 June 7-1889 May 30     S. A. Mutchmore and Horace M.
                                          Simmons
      PPPHi   ◆   1880 Jan. 1-1895 July 25
```

PRESBYTERIAN STANDARD, THE (1861-1866 or later) w rel
THE STANDARD (Mar. 21, 1861-May 23, 1861) w
   Pub. 1861 Mar. 21-1861 May 23   at Philadelphia

PRESBYTERIAN STANDARD, THE, *continued*
    Ed. 1861 Mar. 21-1861 May 23 Alfred Nevin
         PPPHi ♦ 1861 Mar. 21-1861 May 23
              Merged with *The Presbyterian Expositor* of Chicago
        continued as
    STANDARD, AND PRESBYTERIAN EXPOSITOR, THE (May 30, 1861-July 10, 1862) w
    (Note: From May 30, 1861 until Nov. 14, 1861 only the subtitle appears as *The Standard and Presbyterian Expositor,* while the main title continues as *The Standard;* on Nov. 21, 1861 the main title also is changed to *The Standard and Presbyterian Expositor.*)
    Pub. 1861 May 30-1861 Aug. 15 at Philadelphia
          1861 Aug. 22-1862 June 5 Alfred Nevin (from Sept. 5, 1861), Philadelphia and Chicago date line
          1862 June 12-1862 July 10 Alfred Nevin, Philadelphia date line
    Ed. 1861 May 30-1861 Aug. 15 Alfred Nevin
          1861 Aug. 22-1862 Mar. 20 Alfred Nevin, ed.; George Morton, assoc. ed.
          1862 Mar. 27-1862 July 10 Alfred Nevin
         PPPHi ♦ 1861 May 30-1862 July 10
        continued as
    THE PRESBYTERIAN STANDARD (July 17, 1862-Jan. 27, 1866 or later) w %
    Pub. 1862 July 17-1865 Oct. 26 Alfred Nevin, Philadelphia date line
          1865 Nov. 11-1866 Jan. 27) Chicago and Philadelphia date line
          or later)
    Ed. 1862 July 17-1864 Dec. 22 Alfred Nevin
          1864 Dec. 29-1865 Oct. 26 Alfred Nevin, ed.; Alfred Taylor, assoc. ed.
          1865 Nov. 11-1866 Jan. 27) Alfred Nevin, F. Senour
          or later)
         PPPHi ♦ 1862 July 17-1866 Jan. 27

PRESBYTERIAN WEEKLY (Jan. 2, 1873, or Dec. 1872-Feb. 26, 1874) w rel
    Pub. 1873 Jan. 2 or 1872, Dec.-1874 Feb. 26 John B. Kurtz (issue of Jan. 2, 1873, possibly also succeeding issues prior to March 13, 1873, at Philadelphia do not mention publisher)
    Ed. 1873 Jan. 2 or 1872, Dec.-1874 Feb. 26 Alfred Nevin
          Beginning March 5, 1874 the *Presbyterian Weekly* was published at Baltimore, Maryland. May 7, 1874, the article was added to the title: *The Presbyterian Weekly,* and on July 10, 1879, the title was changed to *The Baltimore Presbyterian.*
         PPPHi ♦ 1873 Jan. 2, Mar. 13, 20, 27, May 8, July 31, Aug. 14, 21, 28, Oct. 30, Dec. 4, 11, 18, 25
              1874 Jan. 1, Feb. 26, also 1874 Mar. 5-1879 Dec. 25 (incomplete)

PRESS (Aug. 1, 1857-Oct. 1, 1920) d tw w
    Pub. 1857-1878 John W. Forney
          1878-1920 The Press Co.

PHILADELPHIA COUNTY 247

 Ed. 1857-1878 John W. Forney
    1857-1877 Dr. R. Shelton Mackenzie
    1865-1869 Charles G. Leland
    1879-1880 Edward McPherson
    1880-1908 Charles Emory Smith
    1908-1917 Samuel C. Wells
    1917-1920 Alden March

Weekly editions (1857-1905) were published under the following titles: Aug. 15, 1857, *The Weekly Press;* Nov. 16, 1861, *Forney's War Press;* Nov. 11, 1865, *Forney's Weekly Press;* Oct. 20, 1877, *Weekly Press;* Jan. 5, 1878, *The Press Weekly Edition;* Dec. 27, 1879, *The Weekly Press;* July 8, 1880, *The Philadelphia Press;* July 22, 1880, *The Philadelphia Weekly Press;* Nov. 17, 1881, *The Philadelphia Press;* Jan. 26, 1882, *The Philadelphia Weekly Press;* Dec. 21, 1882, *Weekly Philadelphia Press;* Feb. 4, 1885, *Weekly Press, Sunday Press,* 1865-1867, 1881-1920.

 P   d 1857 Aug. 1-1920 Oct. 1
       w 1874 Jan.-1877 Dec. 22
        1888 Mar. 11-1889 Dec. 18
 P-M   d 1863 Feb. 13
        1865 Apr. 15, 17
        1876 Sept. 29, Nov. 10, 11
        1877 July 23
        1879 Dec. 27
        1881 July 4, Sept. 22, 29
        1882 July 1, Oct. 22-29
        1885 Aug. 5
        1889 June 1-16
        1913 Jan. 23-26, 29
       w 1886 Feb. 10
 PAlHi sun 1885 Aug. 9
       d 1919 Sept. 9, 10
 PAltHi w 1865 Mar. 24
 PBf   d 1867 June 12
        1879 Mar. 10
        1881 Jan. 2, Sept. 29, Nov. 15-19, Dec. 16
       w 1865 Mar. 18
        1866 Mar. 21
 PBloHi d 1880 May 22
        1885 July 24-Aug. 8, 10, 11
        1886 June 2, 3
        1887 June 29, Nov. 11, 12
        1888 Mar. 13-16
        1889 Mar. 5, Apr. 20, 23, 25, 30, May 4, 13, 25
        1916 June 12, 14, 17, 21
 PBMa   1882 Oct. 22
        1897 Apr. 14, 28
 PCHi   d 1861 July 10
        1864 June 7
        1881 Sept. 15
        1882 Oct. 22, 25, 26
        1887 Apr. 27
        1888 Mar. 15
        1897 May 4, 5
        1901 Sept. 16, 19
       w 1876 May 13
 PDoHi d 1857 Nov. 19-1859 Apr. 19
        1862 Apr. 14, July 21
        1864 Jan. 11, Oct. 17

PRESS, *continued*

		1865 Feb. 10, 11, Apr. 20, 22, 24, 28, 29, Oct. 23
		1866 May 23, July 2
		1867 Sept. 18
		1869 Oct. 12, 15
		1874 Jan. 1
		1876 May 11, Oct. 12, 15
		1881 Sept. 20, 23, 24, 26, 27
		1882 July 16
		1885 July 24, Aug. 9, Dec. 12
		1888 Oct. 18, 26, 28
		1887 June 22, Sept. 15, 16, 17, 18
		1888 Mar. 9, 10, 12, 13-16, June 16, Aug. 27, Sept. 30, Oct. 26, 30, Nov. 6
		1889 Feb. 4, 5, 26, Mar. 3, 4, 5, Apr. 30, May 1, 2
		1892 Mar. 27
		1901 Sept. 14
		1904 Nov. 13
		1908 Oct. 4-11 (Founder's Week), Nov. 4, 18
		1920 Oct. 1
	w	1862 Aug. 16
		1865 Apr. 22
PEHi	d	1869 Aug. 28
PEr	d	1899 Jan.-1920 Sept. 30
PHHi	d	1874 Jan. 1
		1880 Apr. 7, 24
		1897 Feb. 3
		1909 Feb. 23
		1912 Jan. 1
	sun	1919 Nov. 21
PHi ♦	d	1857 Aug. 1-Nov. 26, 28-Dec. 25, 28-31
		1858 Jan. (1)-(8, 9), (11, 12), 13, (14, 15), 16-(22)-(25)-Feb. (3)-(5)-Mar. (9)- (19, 20), (22-24)-(29-31)-Apr. (21, 22)-May (8)-(14)-17, 19, (20)-June (2)-18, 21, (22)-July 5, 7, (8)-(17)-(19, 20), 21-Dec. 31
		1859 Jan. (1)-Feb. (4)-19, 22-July 4, 6-Aug. 4, 6-Dec. (20)-(23)-(29, 30), 31
		1860 Jan. (2, 3), 4-July (2, 3), 4, 6-(24)-Sept. (18)-(22)-Oct. (29)-Nov. (23)-Dec. (3, 4)-(10)-(21)-(25), 27-(31)
		1861 Jan. 1-(8)-(17)-Feb. (22)-Apr. (18, 19)-(29)-May (2, 3)-June (29), July (1)-Sept. (7)-Oct. (12)-(18)-Dec. 25, 27-31
		1862 Jan. 1-July (1)-Dec. 25, 27-31
		1863 Jan. 1-Mar. (2)-(18)-(20, 21)-(24, 25)- Apr. (1)-(4)-(8)-(11)-(14)-July (1, 2)-(7)-(24)-(27)-31-Aug. (3, 4)-(8)-(12, 13)-(20, 21)-(26)-(31)-Sept. (10, 11)-(15)-(23)-(28)-(30)-Oct. (2)-(5-13)-(22)-(26)-Nov. (10, 11)-(19)-(24)-(27)-Dec. (3)-(21)-31
		1864 Jan. 1-July 4, 6-Dec. 31
		1865 Jan. 2-June (30)-July 4, 6-Dec. 25, 27-31
		1866 Jan. 1-(10)-Mar. (16)-Apr. (3)-June (27)-July (16)-Sept. (2-4)-Oct. 15, 17-Dec. 15, 17-25, 27-(31)
		1867 Jan. 1-7, 9-(11)-14, 16-28, Feb. 1-(11)-22, 25-Mar. (1), 2, 4-6, 8, 11-19, 21, 26-28, Apr. 1-(3), 4, 8, (9)-13, 16-(18)-20, 23-(29, 30), May 6,

PHILADELPHIA COUNTY 249

9-13, 16-(18), 21-June 3, 6-8, 11-15, 18, 19, 21-
(25)-July (1), 3, 4, 6, (7), 9, 10, 12, 15-17, 19,
20, 22-(24)-27, 29-Aug. 3 (5)-7, 9-17, 19-(22).
23, 25-28, Sept. 2-4, (8), 20-(24), 25, Oct. 2,
(3), (5), 7, 9-12, 14, 16-26, 28, (29), Nov.
2, 4, (5, 6)-8, 11-16, (18)-(20)-23, 25, (26),
27-30, Dec. 2-7, (9), 11-13, 16-21, 23-25, 27, 28,
30, 31
1868 Jan. (1-3), 4, (6), 7-(10, 11), 13, (14)-(16, 17),
18-(21, 22)-(25)-(30)-Feb. (4-8), 10, (11)-
(27)-29, Mar. 2-4, 6-(19), 21, 24-Apr. (7)-(14),
15, 17-22, 25-(27)-30, May 2, (5)-14, 16-22, 25-
(28), 29, June 1, 3, 4, (6), (8-9), 12-(20)-(22),
24-26, 29, July 2-7, 9, (10)-30, Aug. (3)-5, 7-
(12)-(31)-Oct. 2, 5, (6)-(19)-(30)-Nov. (2),
4-(10)-12, 14-(27)-Dec. (2), 4, 7-(10, 11),
(14)-(16), 21, 23-25, 28-31
1869 Jan. (1, 2), 5-(9), 12, 15-25, 27-(30)-Feb. (1),
2, 5-9, 13-17, 19, 22, 24-Mar. (1)-8, 10-(18),
22-24, 26-30, Apr. 1-12, 15-30, May 3-8, 11-18,
20, 21, 24-29, June 1-9, 11-16, 21, 22, 24-July
2, 5, 7-(15), 16, 19-(31), Aug. 2, 4-30, Sept.
1-4, 7-(20), 21, 24-Oct. 6, 11-19, 21-23, 26-Nov.
6, 9, 11-18, 20-26, (29)-Dec. (1), 2
1871 Aug. 24
1872 Nov. 13, 25, Dec. 20
1873 July 28, Aug. 20, Nov. 26, Dec. 3, 4, 31
1874 Feb. 2, 12, 14, 20, 22, Apr. 22, 23, June (6),
29-July 2, 30, Oct. 23, 26, (27), 29, Nov. 13
1875 Jan. 1, Feb. 23, Mar. 12, Apr. 20, Aug. 26,
27, Oct. 25, 26, Dec. 24
1876 Feb. (11), Mar. (4), (9), May (11), 30, June
6, 23, 24, 30, July 4, 5, Aug. 1, Sept. 5, 22,
26-29, Oct. 5, 6, Nov. 10, 16
1877 Jan. 1, Feb. 23, Apr. 23, May 10, 17, 18, June
16, July 3, 5, 11, Sept. 24, Oct. 19
1878 June 20
1879 Dec. (17)
1882 Jan. (2, 3)-(31)-Apr. (15)-(20)-(27)-May
(6)-(18)-July (1), (3-8)-Aug. (30)-Sept. (7)-
Oct. (2)-Nov. (27-Dec. 1)-30
1883 Jan. 1-(23, 24)-June (19)-(30), July (2)-(17)-
(19)-Aug. (31)-Dec. (31)
1884 Jan. 1-Feb. (11)-(13)-Mar. (1)-(17)-July
(1-5), 7-Aug. (14)-Sept. (1)-(11)-Oct. (13)-
(20-22)-(25), 27-(30)-Nov. (12)-(15), (17, 18)-
(24, 25)-Dec. (8)-31
1885 Jan. (1, 2)-Feb. (13, 14)-(18)-(27, 28)-Mar.
(7)-(14)-Apr. (11)-(18)-June (27)-(July 1)-
(4)-(11)-(18)-(24)-Sept. (18)-(25, 26)-Oct.
(10)-(16-17)-(24)-(30, 31)-Nov. (4)-(7)-
(14), (16)-(20, 21), (23)-(28), Dec. 1, (2)-(4,
5)-(12)-(19)-(23)-(29-31)
1886 Jan. (1, 2)-(9)-(16)-(23)-(26)-(30)-Feb. (5,
6)-(10)-(13)-(17)-(20)-(27)-Mar. (2)-(6)-
(13)-(20)-(27)-Apr. (3)-(10)-(17)-(24)-May
(1)-(8)-(15, 16)-(22)-(29)-June (3)-(5)-
(12), (14)-(19)-(26)-(30-July 3)-(7)-(10)-
(13, 14)-(23, 24)-(31)-Aug. (28)-Sept. (25)-

PRESS, continued

Oct. (17-19)-Nov. (6)-(19)-Dec. (18)-(21)-(27)-(30, 31)
1887 Jan. (1)-(7)-(22)-(26)-(29-Feb. 2)-(4, 5)-(9)-(12)-(16)-(19)-May (31)-June (13)-(30-July 1)-Sept. (19)-Dec. (24), (26)-(31)
1888 Jan. (2, 3)-(6)-Feb. (1, 2)-(4)-(8)-Mar. (9)-(20-22)-(24), (26)-(28)-Apr. (2)-(4-6)-12-13)-May (4)-(7)-(10)-(16, 17)-(19)-June (16-19)-(21)-(25-28)-(30), July (2)- (13)-Dec. 31
1889 Jan. (1)-Feb. (4)-(16)-Mar. (30)-Apr. (30, May 1)-June (10)-(13)-Aug. (31)-Oct. (18)-(30, 31)-Dec. (31)
1890 Jan. (1)-(3)-(24)-Feb. (4)-(12)-(22)-Apr. (17)-May (1)-(10)-June (30)-Sept. (1, 2)-(19)-(27)-Oct. (1)-Nov. (28)-Dec. (5)-(18)-(20)-(26)-31
1891 Jan. (1-10)-(17)-(23-27)-(30-Feb. 2)-(5-7)-(14-17)-(21-23)(27, 28)Mar. (3)-(7)-(14-17)-(21)-(24-28)-(31)-Apr. (4)-(7)-(11)-(20, 21)-(25)-(29, 30), May (2)-(6)-(9-11)-(16)-(23)-(30)-June (5, 6)-(11)-(13)-(19, 20)-(23, 24)-(26)-July (3-7)- (21)-Aug. (29-Sept. 1)-Nov. (4-6)-(13, 14)-Dec. (21)-31
1892 Jan. (1)-(15)-(18-20)-(27)-Mar. (26)-(30-May 2)-(4, 5)-(14)-June (2)-(6)-(10, 11)-(20-22)-Aug. (16)-(31-Sept. 2)-(23)-Nov. (2)-(19)-Dec. (9)-(17)-(24)-(31)
1893 Jan. 2-Feb. (13)-Mar. (7)-Apr. (18)-(27, 28)-June (27, 28)-July (30)-Aug. (16)-Sept. (1-4)-Oct. (12)-(14)-(18)-(31-Nov. 3)-(7)-(10)-(13-15)-Dec. (5)-(7)-(27-30)
1894 Jan. (1)-(3)-(6-8)-(20)-(27-30)-Feb. (1-3)-(6-13)-(15)-(17-20)-(26-Mar. 3)-(6)-(10-13)-(15-17)-(22, 23)-(26)-(28)-Apr. (2-6)-(9-30)-May (4, 5)-(11)-(14, 15)-(17)-(30)-June (18)-July (3, 4)-(6, 7)-(10)-(12)-(23)-(30)-Aug. (1)-(4-6)-(11)-(28, 29)-(31, Sept. 1)-Oct. (6-8)-Nov. (2)-Dec. (12, 13)-(15)-(19, 20), (26, 27)-(29-31)
1895 Jan. (1-3)-(10)-(12-16)-(22-25)-(31)-Feb. (5)-(15, 16)-(23)-(26-Mar. 1)-(14-Apr. 15)-(29, 30)-May (3)-(6-10)-(31)-June (3), (10)-(25, 26)-(29-July 5)-(9)-(23)-(31)-Aug. (17)-(27, 28)-(31)-Sept. (4)-(10, 11)-(17)-(25-Oct. 2)-(7)-(24)-Nov. (12)-(29)-Dec. (11)-(21)-(24)-(30, 31)
1896 Jan. (1-7)-(15)-(27, 28)-(30)-Feb. (11, 12)-(14)-(24)-Mar. (2-7)-(16)-(24)-(30-Apr. 1)-May (1)-June (4)-(9)-(11)-(24, 25)-(30-July 6)-(18)-(23)-Aug. (7)-Oct. (1)-(19)-(27, 28)-Nov. (2)-(27)-Dec. (12-16)-31
1897 Jan. (1)-(4, 5)-(11)-Mar. (1)-(31, Apr. 1)-May (14)-June (25-July 2)-Aug. (4)-(23)-Sept. (30, Oct. 1)-Dec. (4)-(30, 31)
1898 Jan. (1-4)-Mar. (1)-(3)-(28)-Apr. (1)-(4, 5)-(22)-(28)-May (6)-June (30-July 4)-(14)-Aug. (31)-Sept. (2)-(30, Oct. 1)-(18)-

PHILADELPHIA COUNTY 251

(22)-(29)-Nov. (25)-Dec. (5)-(19)-(27)-(29-31)
1899 Jan. (2-4)-(11, 12)-(17-19)-(28)-(31, Feb. 1)-(6)-(18)-(25-27)-Mar. (1-3)-(6)-Apr. (1)-(4)-May (1, 2)-(15)-(18-20)-June (1)-(30, July 1)-(11)-Aug. (1)-(7)-(11)-Oct. (2-4)-(13)-(26)-Nov. (21-23)-Dec. (13)-30
1900 Jan. (1)-(8)-Mar. (26)-(29)-(31-Apr. 2)-June (19-21)-(30)-Oct. (1)-(19)-Nov. (10)-(26)-Dec. (27-31)
1901 Jan. (1)-(3)-Mar. (2-5)-(29-Apr. 1)-June (3)-July (1, 2)-Aug. (21-Sept. (24)-Oct. (1)-Nov. (9-11)-(20)-(30)-Dec. (23)-(30), 31)
1902 Jan. (1-6)-(8)-Feb. (5)-(7, 8)-(13)-Mar. (3)-(10)-(26-Apr. 11)-June (30)-Dec. 31
1903 Jan. (1-16)-(28)-Feb. (16)-(18)-(28)-Mar. (3)-(6, 7)-(14-Apr. 6)-(25)-(28, 29)-May (13, 14)-July (1)-(15)-Aug. (13) (25)-Sept. (28-Oct. 1)-(19)-(31)-Nov. (14)-Dec. (12)-(31)
1904 Jan. 1-(16)-Apr. (1)-(23)-(29)-May (6)-June (22)-(30-July 7)-(11, 12)-Sept. (27)- (30-Oct. 10)-(24)-(31-Nov. 3)-(5-7)-(10)-(23)-Dec. (14)-(21-31)
1905 Jan. (2, 3)-(16)-Mar. (31)-May (24, 25)-July (1)-Oct. (19)-Nov. (3)-(Dec. 2, 30)
1906 Jan 1-Feb. (6)-Mar. (31-Apr. 2)-June (30-July 3)-Aug. (29)-Sept. (27-Oct. 1)-(29)-Nov. (2)-(22)-Dec. (31)
1907 Jan. (1)-(8)-Mar. (25-Apr. 2)-July (1)-Aug. (10)-(14)-Sept. (4)-(18)-(20, 21)-(24-30)-Dec. 31
1908 Jan. 1-Apr. (1)-(28)-May (12)-July (1-13)-Aug. (6)-Oct. (1, 2)-(8)-Nov. (27)-(30)-Dec. 31
1909 Jan. 1-Mar. (26)-June (1)-Aug. (16, 17)-(19)-Dec. 31
1910 Jan. (1)-Mar. (30)-July (1)-(12-14)-Sept. (24-Oct. 1)-Dec. (29-31)
1911 Jan. 2-Mar. (8)-(17)-July (13)-Oct. (28)-Nov. (22)-Dec. 30
1912 Jan. 1-Feb. (14)-Apr. (3)-Dec. 31
1913 Jan. 1-Feb. (18)-May (3)-June (30)-July (31)-Aug. 11, 13-Dec. 31
1914 Jan. 1-Dec. 31
1915 Jan. (1)-Apr. (2)-May (21-24)-July (15)-(30)-Dec. (16)-31
1916 Jan. 1-(27)-(31)-Apr. (8)-May (13)-Oct. (2)-Dec. (27-30)
w 1857 Nov. 14-28
1860 Sept. 8
1861 Mar. (9), Nov. 16-Dec. 21
1870 June (17)
1873 Dec. 20
1876 Mar. 4, May (13)-Sept. (2)-Dec. 9, 30
1881 Sept. (29)
sun 1876 May 30,. June 6, July 4
1884 Mar. 9-(16)-23
1885 Aug. (2, 9)
1887 Sept. (18)

PRESS, *continued*

```
                    1889 June 2
        PHoHi   d   1865 May 24
        PJsK    w   1857 Aug. 15
        PLaF    d   1857 Aug. 1-1873 Dec. 30
        PLaL    d   1867 Aug. 13
                    1876 Feb. 7, June 17
                    1877 Feb. 6, 16, 19, 20, 23, Mar. 1, 3, May 8, 9
                    1878 May 8, 9, June 18
                    1888 Apr. 14, Dec. 30
                    1893 Jan. 15
        PLhT    d   1861 Aug. 13, 1890 May 17
                w   1862 July 5
                    1876 Sept. 30
        PMcC    d   1877 June 18, 22
        PMe     sun 1897 Jan. 10
                w   1860 Jan. 7-1861 June 26
                    1862 Apr. 12
                    1863 Oct. 19
                    1864 Aug. 4
        PP      d   1857 Aug. 3-1877 June 29
                    1877 July 2-21, Aug. 7-Sept. 29, Oct. 5-Dec. 27
                    1878 Jan. 1-1920 Oct. 1
                w   1857 Aug. 15-1858 Dec. 18
                    1859 Jan. 22-July 30, Aug. 13-1860 Dec. 22
                    1861 Jan. 5-1862 Dec. 27
                    1863 Jan. 24-Apr. 11, May 23-1864 Dec. 3
                    1867 Jan. 12-26, Apr. 6-1868 Mar. 21
                    1869 Jan. 2-1874 Dec. 12
                    1875 Jan. 2-1889 Nov. 13
                    1889 Nov. 27-Dec. 25
                    1891 Jan. 7-1894 Dec. 26
                    1897 Jan. 6-1905 June 14
        PPeS    d   1860 Feb. 2, Mar. 21
                    1861 Spt. 2-1862 Aug. 30
                    1862 Oct. 4
                    1863 Feb. 12, Mar. 12
                    1866 Sept. 12, Dec. 8
                    1884 June 23, Oct. 18
                    1889 June 1-11, 15
                    1890 Mar. 15
                    1897 Dec. 4
                w   1867 Oct. 19, 26
                    1868 Nov. 21
                    1869 Jan. 9, 23
                    1870 July 9
                    1872 Oct. 12, 26
                    1878 Oct. 19
        PPFfHi  d   1859 Apr. 12
                    1863 May 16, June 20
        PPi     d   1858 Jan. 4-1880 July 3
                    1880 July 5-1920 Oct. 1
        PPiHi   d   1876 July 5
                    1898 Apr. 21, 23, June 4, 11, July 18
                    1899 Mar. 28
                w   1857 Nov. 21
                    1862 May 31, Aug. 30, Oct. (11, 18, Nov. 1), 29
                    1863 Sept. 12
```

PHILADELPHIA COUNTY 253

PPL d 1863 Apr. 4, 21, 28, 30-May 5, 7-12, 15-25, 27, 28, 30-June 15, 17-July 4, 7-22, 25, 28-Aug. 6, 8-Oct. 7, 9-17, 20-30, Nov. 3-14, 17, 19-24, 26-Dec. 2, 4-8, 10-15, 18, 19, 22-1864 Feb. 3
1864 Feb. 5-22, 25, 27-Mar. 28, 31-Oct. 22, 25-28, 31, Nov. 2-5, 8-24, 26, 29-Dec. 26, 28-1865 Jan. 25
1865 Jan. 27-31, Feb. 2-27, Mar. 1-3, 6-24, 27-May 19, 22, 24-June 28, July 1-7, 10-Aug. 26, 29, 30, Sept. 1-6, 11-15, 18-Oct. 19, 21-27, 30-Nov. 22, 24-1866 May 9
1866 May 11-June 26, 28-July 3, 6, 8-Sept. 5, 7-12, 15-18, 20-Oct. 5, 7, 8, 10-19, 21-Nov. 22, 24-1867 May 3
1867 May 5-June 13, 15-27, 29-Sept. 7, 9-14, 16-1868 June 18
1868 June 20-27, 30-July 6, 8-Aug. 19, 21, 24-Sept. 9, 11, 12, 15-Dec. 24, 28-1869 Feb. 2
1869 Feb. 4-Apr. 28, 30, May 3-7, 10-31, June 2-Aug. 2, 4-Sept. 18, 21-Oct. 26, 28, 30-Dec. 23, 25-1870 Sept. 17
1870 Sept. 20-Oct. 7, 10-25, 27-Nov. 11, 14-Dec. 14, 16, 17, 20-26, 28-1871 June 24
1871 June 27-1872 June 15
1872 June 18-28, July 1-Nov. 14, 16-1873 Jan. 18
1873 Jan. 21-Apr. 17, 19-May 13, 15-23, 26-June 11, 13-Aug. 6, 8-Nov. 24, 26-1874 Feb. 26
1874 Feb. 28-Mar. 6, 9-June 15, 18-Sept. 17, 19-Nov. 18, 20-1875 Feb. 17
1875 Feb. 19-24, 26-Aug. 4, 6-Sept. 23, 25-1876 Feb. 8
1876 Feb. 10, 12-May 5, 9, 11-20, 23-June 2, 5-July 7, 10, 11, 13-25, 28-Sept. 7, 9-14, 16-20, 22-Nov. 1, 3, 4, 7-Dec. 7, 9-1877 Jan. 4
1877 Jan. 6-July 17, 19-1878 Aug. 2
1878 Aug. 5-Oct. 3, 5-11, 14-1879 Apr. 24
1879 Apr. 26-Oct. 14, 16-Dec. 13, 16-1880 Jan. 26
1880 Jan. 28-Feb. 23, 25-Mar. 19, 22-June 16, 18-July 26, 28-Sept. 25, Oct. 8-Nov. 9, 11-1882 Jan. 2
1882 Jan. 4-1884 Apr. 11
1884 Apr. 14-17, 19-1885 Feb. 4
1885 Feb. 6-Aug. 24, 26-1890 July 1
1890 July 3-1891 June 26
1891 June 28-1892 Aug. 5
1892 Aug. 7-19, 21-1893 Apr. 9
1893 Apr. 11-Aug. 16, 18-Oct. 9, 11-1894 May 22
1894 May 24-1895 Mar. 7
1895 Mar. 9-Oct. 18, 20-1896 Mar. 10
1896 Mar. 12-17, 20-1897 Dec. 22
1897 Dec. 24-1898 Oct. 25
1898 Oct. 27-Nov. 3, 5-1899 Mar. 2
1899 Mar. 4-16, 18-Apr. 21, 23-26, 28-Dec. 13. 15-1900 Jan. 16
1900 Jan. 18-Feb. 13, 15-Mar. 2, 4-15, 17-20, 22-Apr. 14, 16, 18-June 5, 7-23, 25-Oct. 30, Nov. 1-1901 Jan. 15
1901 Jan. 17-Feb. 19, 21-Sept. 13, 15-Oct. 3, 6-1902 Jan. 4
1902 Jan. 6-Apr. 3, 5-May 15, 18-1903 June 3

PRESS, *continued*

                1903 June 5-Oct. 5, 7-1904 July 31
                1904 Aug. 2, 4-Sept. 18, 21-1905 Oct. 27
                1905 Oct. 29-1906 Jan. 19
                1906 Jan. 21-Mar. 29, 31-Apr. 16, 18-June 6, 8-Aug. 3, 5-Sept. 14, 16-Oct. 17, 19-Nov. 23, 25-1907 Jan. 3
                1907 Jan. 5-Feb. 15, 17-Nov. 25, 27-Dec. 3, 5-1908 June 7
                1908 June 9-July 1, 3-13, 16-1909 Mar. 17
                1909 Mar. 19-Apr. 22, 24-Aug. 2, 4-1910 July 25
                1910 July 27-Nov. 23, 25-28, 30-1911 Feb. 8
                1911 Feb. 10-Mar. 10, 12-June 13, 15-1912 Jan. 1
                1912 Jan. 3-Mar. 15, 17-Apr. 9, 11-25, 27-May 9, 11-June 17, 19-Sept. 2, 4-24, 26-Oct. 1, 3-29, 31-Nov. 13, 15-Dec. 31
PPM   d 1857 Aug. 1-1904 Oct. 31
                1905 Jan. 1-1920 Sept. 25
PPot   d 1863 Apr. 6
                1871 July 5
                1873 Jan. (Sup)
                1880 June 7-10
                1884 June 3, 7, Nov. 1-18
                1885 Mar. 5, Apr. 5, 9, July 24-26, Oct. 21, Dec. 1, 5
                1886 Feb. 10-13, June 3, July 1, Aug. 19, Sept. 6, Oct. 17
                1887 Jan. 18, 19, Sept. 12-17
                1888 Mar. 13-16, 23, Apr. 1, 8, 26, May 2, June 4, 16, 18-30, July 2-10, 12, 20, Aug. 4, 6, 8-12, 22, Sept. 5, 8, 11, 17-19, 22, 30, Oct. 13, 20, Nov. 14, 17
                1891 Feb. 15
PPoU   d 1876 Jan. 1-Dec. 31
PRHi   d 1859 Jan. 1-June 30
PSF   d 1881 Sept. 26
PShH   d 1876 Sept. 28
                1877 Dec. 14
PStfHi   d 1866 Oct. 31
PSuHi   d 1864 Sept. 8-1869 Dec. 14
                1889 Dec. 21-1890 Dec. 12
PToHi   d 1858 Jan. 5-May 27
                1861 May 2-Sept. 28
                1862 Apr. 1-June 26
            w 1860 Jan. 7-1861 Aug. 3
PU   d 1861 July 1-Dec. 31
                1865 Oct. 16-1866 Oct. (6)-1867 June 30
                1868 Jan. 1-Apr. (25), 28-May (2-4)-June 30
                1869 Jan. 1-1870 June 30
                1874 Jan. 1-12, 14, 15, 17-27, 29-Feb. 14, 17-Mar. 9, 11-May 15, 18-22, 25-27, 29-June 22, 24-July 27, 29-Dec. 9, 11-25, 28-1875 Jan. 11
                1875 Jan. 13-30, Feb. 2-12, 15, 16, 18, 22-Apr. (10), May (26)-June 10, 12-July 28, 30, Aug. 2-31, Sept. 2-21, 23-28, 30-1876 Feb. 26
                1876 Feb. 29-Mar. 6, 8-30, Apr. 1-26, 28-June 30, July 3-Aug. 8, 10-Sept. 15, 18-27, 29-1877 Feb. 26
                1877 Feb. 28-Mar. 7, 9-Apr. 25, 27-May 12, 15-21, 23-29, 31-July (11)-(14-17)-Aug. 20, 22-25, 28-

PHILADELPHIA COUNTY 255

       Oct. 2, 4-Nov. 19, 21-Dec. 5, 7-25, 27-1878 Jan. 10
    1878 Jan. 12-Mar. 2, 5, (6), 8-11, 13-15, 18-Apr. (30)-May 16, 18-June 12, 14, 15, 18-1879 Feb. 18
    1879 Feb. 21-24, 26-Apr. 14, 16-23, 25-Aug. 19, 21-Sept. 26, 29-Dec. 9, 11-1880 Jan. (10)-(31)-Feb. (7)-(14)-(21)-(28)-Mar. (15)-May 29
    1880 June 1-July 3, 5-31, Aug. 5-Sept. 18, 21-Oct. 1, 4-(9)-Dec. (7)-27, 29-1881 Jan. (1)-27
    1881 Jan. 29-Mar. (1)-1882 Jan. 9
    1882 Jan. 11-Feb. 21, 23-Oct. 31, Nov. 2-Dec. (6)-23, 27-30

PWaHi d 1857 Aug. 6-1858 Aug. 8
    1893 Jan. 28
PWbW d 1857 Sept. 2, 9, 21, Nov. 7, 30, Dec. 5, 11, 12, 16, 22
    1858 Feb. 4, Mar. 9, 11, 18, 19, 22, 23, 25, 27, Apr. 3, 8, 24, Oct. 6, 30, Nov. 12, 13, 15-20, 22-26, 29, Dec. 1, 2, 6, 9-11, 13, 15-18, 20, 23-25, 27-31
    1859 Jan. 1-11, 13, 14, 16-26, 29, Feb. 22, 24-27, Mar. 2-9, 11-15, 17-20, 26, Apr. 4, 6, 8-12, 14, May 2, 4-22, 24, 26, 28, June 6, 8-13, 19, 20, 23, 26-30
    1860 Jan. 2-July 4, 6-31, Aug. 1-Sept. (1)-7, 9-30, Oct. 1-28, Dec. 1-9, 11-16, 18-21, 25, 27-31
    1861 Jan. 1-7, 9-27, 30, Feb. 1, 3, 6, 8-10, 12, Mar. 19, 21, Apr. 3, 5-23, 25, 26, 28, May 26, 29, June 29, July 2-7, 10, Aug. 13, 15, 17, Sept. 9, 15-29, Oct. 3-7, 9-11, 13, 18-25, 27, Dec. 25, 27-31

PWcA d 1865 Apr. 15
    1869 Apr. 13 (Surrender of General Lee to General Grant)

PWcHi d 1857 Nov. 13
    1858 Aug. 25
    1860 Mar. 1, 2, Nov. 12
    1861 Apr. 25, Oct. 25, Nov. 1
    1862 Feb. (10), July 4, 26, 28, 30
    1863 June 15, Aug. 28, Nov. 20
    1864 Mar. 4, May 10, June 8, Sept. 19, Oct. 3, Dec. 31
    1865 Apr. 4, 10, 14-22, May 6, 26, June 1, 3, 17, 21, July 6, 10, 28, Nov. 13
    1866 Jan. 9, Feb. 13, Apr. 14, May 1, 4, 8, 13, 29, June 9, 16, July 3-5, Sept. 17, Nov. 17
    1867 Jan. 23, Feb. 23, 24, Apr. 29, May 13, June 11, July 4
    1868 Feb. 7, 24, Mar. 5, 25, Oct. 2, 17
    1869 Mar. 27, Apr. 13, Nov. 2, Dec. 25
    1870 May 10, Sept. 17
    1871 May 16, Aug. 2, Sept. 22
    1873 Feb. 11, Aug. 21, Nov. 3, 22
    1874 Aug. 21
    1875 July 15, 17
    1876 Jan. 1, Feb. 23, May 10-12, June 27, July 3-5, Sept. 28, 29, Nov. 13
    1877 Jan. 1, 16
    1878 Sept. 3, Dec. 30
    1879 Dec. 17
    1880 Aug. 31, Oct. 8, Nov. 3

PRESS, *continued*

1881 Mar. 9, May 8, June 19, Aug. 20, Sept. 22, Oct. 11, Nov. 12, 22, 25, Dec. 19-21, 23, 25, 27, 29
1882 Jan. 2, 3, 6, 9, 10, 13, Oct. 22, Dec. 5
1883 Sept. 10, Oct. 27
1884 Mar. 10, June 5-7, July 11, 18, 19
1885 Apr. 29, July 24, 25, 30, 31, Aug. 5, 7, 8
1886 Mar. 29, Apr. 3, May 11, July 1, Sept. 2, 6, 11, Oct. 1-8, 14, 19, 21, 22, 26, 28, 29, Nov. 1-3, Dec. 25
1887 Jan. 1, 29, Sept. 15-17
1888 Mar. 13, 14, Apr. 26, May 2, 23, 24, June 8, 26, July 4, Aug. 22, Sept. 27, Oct. 3, 6
1889 June 1-6, 8-12, 14, Dec. 5
1890 Jan. 15
1892 July 12, 27, 28
1894 Mar. 19, 20
1895 Nov. 27
1896 Apr. 12, June 19
1899 Oct. 27
1900 July (17)
1901 Sept. 7, 14, 18, 20
1906 Apr. 19-26
1909 Apr. 7
1913 Feb. 14
1919 Mar. 16, July 14, Nov. 7, 8
1920 Oct. 1

PWcHi w 1859 Mar. 12
1861 Nov. 16-1862 Aug. 9
1862 Aug. 30, Sept. 6, 20-Nov. 23
1870 Apr. 10
1871 Mar. 11
1872 Oct. 26-Nov. 9
1873 Feb. (15), July 12
1876 Jan. 1, May 13, July 8, Sept. 30
1885 Feb. 11, June 3, Sept. 30, Oct. 28, Nov. 18, Dec. 16
1886 Feb. 10, 24, Mar. 3, 10, Oct. 20
1887 Mar. 2, Aug. 24, Oct. 5
1888 May (2), Nov. 21
sun 1881 Sept. 22, Dec. 29
1882 Jan. 4, Oct. 25
1883 Aug. 26, Sept. 2
1885 Aug. 9
1887 Mar. 13, 27-Apr. 10, 24, May 15, 22
1888 Apr. 8
1889 June 2-16, Dec. 29
1894 May 27

PWcP d 1867 Dec. 30, 31
1868 Jan. 1

PWcT d 1865 Nov. 13
1866 May 1, 8, 13, June 16, July 4, 5
1867 Jan. 1, Feb. 24, May 13, July 4, 5
1876 Jan. 1, Feb. 23, May 11, July 3, 4, 5
1878 June 20
1896 Apr. 12
1901 Sept. 7, 14

PWalG d 1892 Oct. 30

PHILADELPHIA COUNTY 257

     d 1905 Oct. 27
  PYHi d 1858 Feb. 1-Apr. 6, 8-June 10, 12-1859 July 30
     1881 July 3, Aug. 27, Sept. 20-27
     1882 Feb. 28, July 1
     1901 Sept. 14, 18, Oct. 29
     1902 Feb. 28
     1903 Jan. 1-May 18
     Sold to *Public Ledger,* 1920

PROFESSIONAL AND SPORTING WORLD (1873) w
  Pub. & Ed. 1873 Robert B. Caverly

PROGRESS (WEST PHILADELPHIA) (1877-1878) w
  Pub. & Ed. 1877-1878 John D. Avil

PROGRESS (1878-1885) w
  Pub. & Ed. 1878-1881 John W. Forney
      1882-1885 Forney Publishing Co.
  Ed.   1884-1885 John W. Forney, Jr.
   % In 1878 *Progress* was known as *Forney's Progress.*
  P   1878 Nov. 16-1882 Nov. 4
  PCHi 1878 Nov. 16
  PGrT 1878 Nov. 16-1880 July 10
  PU   1878 Nov. 16-Dec. 28
     1879 Jan. 4-Nov. 8

PROGRESSIVE ADVERTISER (1916-1920) w progressive (Roxborough)
  Pub. & Ed. 1916-1920 C. B. Helms

PROGRESSIVE LABOR WORLD (1917†) w
  Pub.   1917-1932 Frank Feeney
  Ed.   1917-1932 Royd Morrison
  Pub. & Ed. 1939-1941 G. T. Simmons
    Progressive Labor World was suspended from 1932 to 1939.
  PP   1919 Aug. 14, Oct. 9, Nov. 20
     1920 Aug. 5, 12, Sept. 30, Oct. 7, Dec. 9
     1921 Apr. 7, 28, May 28-July 7, 21, 28, Aug. 18, Nov. 10, Dec. 1
     1922 Jan. 26, Feb. 16, Mar. 9-16, Apr. 13, May 11-July 20, Aug. 3-10, 24-Sept. 7, 21-28, Oct. 12-Nov. 2, 23-1923 Mar. 8
     1923 Mar. 29-Apr. 5, 19, May 3, June 28, July 12, Nov. 15-22
     1925 Aug. 27
     1926 Jan. 7
     1928 Apr. 5
     1929 May 2, 16, 29-June 13, 27, July 25, Aug. 22-29
     1930 Jan. 30, Feb. 6, Mar. 3-24, May 1, July 10, Sept. 25, Oct. 9, Nov. 6, Dec. 4
     1931 Mar. 19†
  PUB 1919 Mar. 19†

PROTESTANT EPISCOPALIAN AND CHURCH REGISTER, see Banner of the Cross

PROTESTANT REVIEW (1901-1908) w ♦
Pub. & Ed. 1903-1908 Reverend Wilson Delaney

PROTESTANT STANDARD (1878-1899) w anti-Romanist ♦
Pub. 1878-1899 F. G. Bailey
Ed. 1878-1891 Reverend James A. McGowan
    1891-1899 F. G. Bailey

PRZYJACIEL LUDU (1898-1924) w rep ind for ♦
Pub. 1898-1904 William Wendt & Son
    1904-1908 I. T. Wendt
    1908-1912 William Wendt & Son
    1912-1916 William Wendt
    1921-1922 Polish National Publishing Co.
    1922-1924 J. Lastowski
Ed. 1898-1904 William Wendt & Son
    1904-1912 I. T. Wendt
    1912-1916 F. J. Wendt
    1922-1924 J. Lastowski

PUBLIC ADVOCATE (1883-1884) w ♦
Pub. 1883-1884 Advocate Printing House
Ed. 1883-1884 F. Woods

PUBLIC JOURNAL (1920-1930) w rep Negro ♦
Pub. 1920-1930 Public Journal Publishing Co.
Ed. 1920-1930 Arthur H. Lynch

PUBLIC LEDGER (1836-1934) d morn ind *
    PUBLIC LEDGER (Mar. 25, 1836-Sept. 10, 1836) d
      PArdL   1836 Mar. 25
      PAtM   1836 Mar. 25
      PBL ♦   1836 Mar. 25
      PBMa   1836 Mar. 25
      PByW   1836 Mar. 25
      PCarlHi   1836 Mar. 25
      PCC   1836 Mar. 25
      PCHi   1836 Mar. 25
      PDoHi ♦   1836 Mar. 25
      PEHi   1836 Mar. 25 (reprint)
      PHaC   1836 Mar. 25
      PHHi   1836 Mar. 25
      PHi ♦   1836 Mar. 25-29, 31-May (6)-June (7)-30, July 3-(24)-Aug. (15)-Sept. 10
      PMcC   1836 Mar. 25
      PNoHi   1836 Mar. 25
      PP ♦   1836 Mar. 26-Sept. 10
      PPAT   1836 Mar. 25
      PPCHi   1836 Mar. 25
      PPeS   1836 Mar. 25
      PPFfHi   1836 Mar. 25
      PPi   1836 Mar. 25-Sept. 10
      PPL   1836 Mar. 25, Apr. 25-June 1, 6-Sept. 10
      PPot   1836 Mar. 25
      PPotW   1836 Mar. (25)
      PWaHi   1836 Mar. 25

PHILADELPHIA COUNTY 259

   PWcHi 1836 Mar. 25
   PWmT 1836 Mar. 25
        Merged with the *Daily Transcript* and
        continued as
PUBLIC LEDGER AND DAILY TRANSCRIPT (Sept. 12, 1836-Aug. 11, 1902) d morn

Pub. 1836-1855 Swain, Abell & Simmons
  1855-1861 Swain & Abell
  1863-1864 William M. Swain & Co.
  1864-1894 George W. Childs
  1894-1902 George W. Childs Drexel
Ed. 1836   Russell Jarvis
  1838-1864 Washington L. Lane
  1888-1893 M. V. McKean
  1893-1894 George W. Childs
  1893-1902 George W. Childs Drexel, L. Clarke Davis
NOTE: See also *Dollar Newspaper, Home Weekly & Household Newspaper,* and *Philadelphia Home Weekly,* papers in which the same publishers were interested.

   P   [1844]-1860 Feb. 8-15
        1860 Mar. 7, Sept. 5, Nov. 28, Dec. 12-1861 (Jan.-July 3)
        1862 July 2-23, Sept.-Nov. 19, Dec. 3-17
        1863 Jan. 2-8, Mar. 14, 25, Apr. 8-15, May 27, July 3-10, Sept. 9, Dec. 23
        1876
        [1889-1902]
   P-M   1864 Mar. 28
        1876 Mar. 13, June 3, Sept. 29, Oct. 20, Nov. 10, 11
        1877 May 18, June 22, July 5, 23, 24, 25, Oct. 4, 5, Nov. 28, Dec. 31
        1878 May 31, Sept. 11, 14, Oct. 24, 25
        1879 Jan. 4, 16, Dec. 13, 15, 16, 18, 19
        1881 July 4
        1882 Feb. 28, Oct. 23, 24, 28
        1884 Aug. 11
        1885 June 18, 23, 24, July 24, 25, 27, 31, Aug. 1, 3, 4-8, 10, 22, Sept. 5, Oct. 30
   PAg   1851 Mar.-Sept.
   PArdL 1863 July 6
   PBK   1854 June 28, July 5, Aug. 23, 30, Sept. 6, 13
        1861 Feb. 27, Mar. 13, 20, June 5, Nov. 20
        1862 Apr. 2, May 7, 21
   PBL ♦ 1837 May 18
        1838 Mar. 16, July 20, Aug. 28
        1839 May 10, 15
        1842 Aug. 29-Oct. 13, 15-24, 26-Nov. 22, 24-30, Dec. 2-22, 24-26, 28, 29, 31
        1845 Mar. 27-Apr. 2, 4-28, 30-May 22, 26-28, 30-June 17, 19-Sept. 3, 5-23, Oct. 14, 15, 18-20, 22-Dec. 15, 17-20, 23-1846 Jan. 13
        1846 Jan. 15, 17, 19-Feb. 2, 4, Mar. 26-June 4, 6-Aug. 31, Oct. 19-Nov. 11, 13-Dec. 5, 8-24, 28-1847 Jan. 4
        1847 Jan. 6-15, 19-Feb. 9, 11-Dec. 29, 31-1848 Jan. 18
        1848 Jan. 20-Mar. 29, Apr. 1-June 20, 22, 24-July 4, 6-Aug. 28, 30-Sept. 28, 30-Nov. 24, 27-Dec. 1, 4-1849 Feb. 2

PUBLIC LEDGER, *continued*

 1849 Feb. 6-Nov. 28, 30-1850 Apr. 1
 1850 Apr. 3-June 8, 11-21, 24-Nov. 29, Dec. 2-1851 Mar. 26
 1851 Mar. 28-May 29, 31-June 27, 30-Nov. 19, 21-28, Dec. 1-1852 Jan. 12
 1852 Jan. 14-20, 22-Feb. 25, 27-Mar. 19, 22-Apr. 19, 21-23, 26-May 13, 18-Aug. 10, 12-Nov. 17, 19-1853 Jan. 15
 1853 Jan. 18-June 7, 11-27, July 9-Dec. 6, 9-1854 Feb. 23
 1854 Feb. 25-May 9, Aug. 21-Nov. 14, 16-1855 Jan. 5
 1855 Jan. 8-29, Feb. 1-June 12, 14-23, July 19-Sept. 7, 10-Nov. 30, Dec. 3-1856 Mar. 3
 1856 Mar. 5-Sept. 4, 6-Oct. 23, 25-1857 June 22
 1857 July 27-Aug. 21, 24-Sept. 30, Oct. 2, 3, 6-Nov. 23, 25-Dec. 10, 14-1858 Jan. 16
 1858 Jan. 19-Sept. 20

PBMa 1892 Dec. 7
 1894 Feb. 3, 5
 1897 Apr. 28
 1900 Apr. 24, May 3

PChalK 1848 Aug. 21, Sept. 16
PChalS 1848 Aug. 21, Sept. 16
 1861 Feb. 22, 25, 26-28

PCHi 1853 Aug. 21, Dec. 28
 1878 Oct. 1
 1888 Mar. 13
 1893 Apr. 22
 1899 Feb. 15
 1900 Feb. 22
 1901 Sept. 14, 20

PDoHi ♦ 1840 Mar. 10
 1841 Feb. 27
 1843 Mar. 2
 1846 Mar. 2
 1847 Nov. 23
 1848 July 25
 1850 Feb. 23
 1851 Jan. 1, 22-1852 Jan. 7
 1853 Jan. 12-1854 Dec. 27
 1855 Jan. 24, 31, Feb. 21, May 2, 23, 30, 31, June 6, July 11, Aug. 1, Sept. 12, Oct. 24, Nov. 28, Dec. 26
 1856 Jan. 9-Dec. 31
 1861 Apr. 23, 24, June 26, July 6, Aug. 6, 9, Dec. 10, 30
 1862 Jan. 23, Apr. 14, 15, July 5, 9, Oct. 3
 1863 July 6
 1865 Apr. 10, 22, 24, June 6
 1866 Aug. 7, 20, Sept. 7
 1867 Jan. 16, May 29, Sept. 18, Nov. 13
 1868 Mar. 24
 1869 Mar. 4
 1870 Dec. 5
 1871 Aug. 26
 1873 Jan. 20, July 14, 15
 1875 July 6

PHILADELPHIA COUNTY 261

     1876 May 8, 10, June 24, July 3, 4, 5, 15, 21, Sept. 4, 29, Nov. 11
     1877 Jan. 1, 26, Feb. 23, Mar. 5, 6, 31, Apr. 11, 14, 21, May 10, 11, 18, July 5, 24
     1878 Mar. 2
     1881 Mar. 5, July 4, 5, Sept. 20, 21, 26, Oct. 3
     1882 Oct. 23
     1884 July 30
     1885 July 24
     1887 Sept. 16, 17, 19
     1894 Feb. 3, 5
PEbHi   1847 Dec. 29
PEL ♦   1842 Mar. 3-Aug. 30, Sept. 1-Oct. 10, 13, Nov. 3, 5-Dec. 20, 22-1843 Jan. 12
     1843 Jan. 14-Mar. 2
     1876 Jan. 1-Dec. 30
     1847 July 21-1849 Feb. 7
     1867 June 20
     1897 Feb. 3
PHi ♦   1836 Sept. 11-19, 21-Oct. 24, Dec. 30
     1837 Jan. 2-Mar. 29, 31-May (6)-June (7)-30, July 3-(24)-Aug. (15)-Sept. 19, 21-Oct. 24, 26-Dec. 30
     1838 Jan. 1-Mar. (9)-May 21, 23-Sept. 11, 20, Dec. 31
     1839 Jan. 1-Mar. (2)-(29)-Sept. (28)-Dec. 31
     1840 Jan. 1-May (9)-29-June (29)-July (20)-Aug. (1)-Sept. (15)-Dec. 31
     1841 Jan. 1-Mar. (16)-Apr. (1)-May (10)-June 2, 4-July 5, 7-Dec. 31
     1842 Jan. 1-20, 22-Mar. (4)-Apr. (21)-May (9)-June (30), July 2-Aug. (13)-Dec. 31
     1843 Jan. 2-Dec. 30
     1844 Jan. (1, 2)-(27)-Apr. (29)-May (1)-(21)-Dec. 31
     1845 Jan. 1-Dec. 31
     1846 Jan. 1-Feb. (14)-(25)-Oct. (17)-Dec. 31
     1847 Jan. 1-July 5, 7-Dec. 31
     1848 Jan. 1-Dec. 30
     1849 Jan. 1-Dec. 31
     1850 Jan. 1-Feb. (25)-Mar. (25)-29, Apr. 1-Oct. 7, 10-Dec. 27, 30
     1851 Jan. 1-(13, 14)-Feb. (10)-Apr. (24)-June (26)-July (23)-Dec. 31
     1852 Jan. 2-Feb. 7, 10-May (8)-July (27)-Dec. (31)
     1853 Jan. 1-May (12)-July (1)-Aug. (30)-Dec. (31)
     1854 Jan. (2)-(18)-Feb. 17, 20-(24)-Sept. (25)-Nov. (22)-Dec. 30
     1855 Jan. 1-Feb. (9)-(22)-June (1)-Oct. (11)-Dec. (1)-31
     1856 Jan. 1-Feb. (29)-Mar. 22, July (1)-(14)-Nov. (1)-Dec. (12)-(30), 31
     1857 Jan. 1-(8, 9)-(17)-Feb. (3)-(17)-(25, 26)-Mar. (10)-(21)-(26)-Apr. (11), (13)-(21, 22)-(29)-May (2)-June (16)-(24)-(26)-July 6, 8-(22)-(25)-(30)-Sept. (17), 18, 21-25, 28-Oct. (9)-(19)-(30)-Dec. (9)-(16)-31
     1860 Jan. (14-17)-(20-25)-(27)-(30)-Feb. (2, 3), 6-8, (10)-18, 22, 23, 25-Mar. 1, 3, 6, 8-(17)-21, 23, 24, 28-Apr. 3 (5, 6), (9), 10, (14), 16-18,

PUBLIC LEDGER, *continued*

(20)-23, (26, 27)-(30)-May (3, 4)-(7)-(9)-11, (14), (16), 17, (21, 22), (24), 26-(28), 30, Nov. 1-3)-(6, 7)-(9, 10), 12, 14, 16-(20)-(23, 24)-(27, 28)-(30)-Dec. (3)-(14)-31

1861 Jan. 1-Feb. (22, 23)-Mar. (9)-(25)-Nov. (1, 2)-Dec. 31
1862 Jan. (1)-May (28)-June (7)-July (1)-Nov. (27)-Dec. 31
1863 Jan. (1)-July (1, 2)-Nov. 28, Dec. 1-31
1864 Jan. 1-July 27, 29-Aug. 18, 20-Oct. 19, 21-Dec. 31
1865 Jan. 2-(31, Feb. 1)-Apr. (1)-(7-18)-(20-24)-(28)-June (13)-(28-July 1)-(7)-(11, 12)-(22)-Aug. (26)-Sept. (23-27)-(30)-Oct. 6, 9-Nov. 21, 23-Dec. 30
1866 Jan. (2)-(22)-Mar. (15)-(23, 24)-Apr. (9)-May (15-17)-(29, 30)-June (30-July 3)-(13)-18, 20-Aug. (13, 14)-(16)-(21-30)-Sept. (29)-Oct. 13, 16-Nov. (5)-(24, 25)-(31)
1867 Jan. (1-5)-(9-14)-(18)-(26)-Feb. (2-16)-Mar. (7)-(19, 20)-(28)-Apr. (11)-May (1)-June 26-July (1-4)-Aug. (15)-Sept. (2)-(14)-(25)-Dec. (11)-31
1868 Jan. (1, 2)-(4)-Feb. (5)-(29)-Mar. (10)-Apr. (28)-May 30, June 2-(22), 23, 25-July (1, 2)-28, 30-Aug. 18, 20-Oct. 14, 16-Dec. (19)-(31)
1869 Jan. (1)-Mar. (20)-(22)-Apr. (7)-(28)-June 3, 5-July (1), (2)-5, 7-Dec. 31
1870 July (1), (2)-Sept. (12)-(26)-(27), 29, (30)-Oct. (26)-Nov. (10)-Dec. 31
1871 Jan. (2), (3), (4)-(28)-30, Feb. 1-Mar. (7)-(18)-July (1)-(3), 4-(27)-(31)-Aug. (2)-Oct. 5, 9-Dec. (13)-30
1872 Jan. (1)-Mar. (13)-May (11)-July (1)-31, Aug. 2-6, 8-14, 16-Sept. 5, 7-12, 14, 17-Oct. (8)-12, 15-Nov. 8, 11-26, 28, 30-Dec. 4, 6-(12)-(28)-31
1873 Jan. (1)-(14)-Feb. 1, 4-10, 12-(15), 18-Mar. (11), (12)-(29)-Apr. (12)-May 17, 20-July (24)-(28)-Aug. 5, 7, 9-(20)-Sept. (2)-(17)-23, 25-(27)-Oct. (1)-(7)-Nov. (26)-Dec. 31
1874 Jan. (1)-Apr. (17)-July (1)-(22)-(30)-Aug. (15)-Dec. 11, 14-(31)
1875 Jan. (1), (2)-4, 7-(9)-May 21, 24-July (1), (2)-(19)-(29)-Aug. (11)-(16)-30, Sept. 1-3 (7)-15, 17-Oct. 4, 6-(29)-Nov. (9)-(29)-Dec. (3)-(18)-(31)
1876 Jan. (1)-(3), (4)-Mar. (18)-(25)-Dec. 30
1877 Jan. 1-(29)-Mar. (26)-Apr. (23)-July (10), (11)-(14)-Aug. (22)-Sept. (24)-Dec. (24), (25), (26), (27)-31
1878 Jan. 1-(29), (30)-Mar. (13)-Apr. (22)-May (20)-(23)-July (2), (4), (5)-Aug. (3)-(8)-(31)-Sept. (25), (26), (27)-Dec. 31
1879 Jan. 1-June (2)-(10), (11)-Sept. (24)-Dec. 31
1880 Jan. 1-Mar. (25)-Sept. (24), (25)-Dec. 31
1881 Jan. 1-June (4)-Aug. (19)-Dec. 31
1882 Jan. 2-Feb. (13)-Aug. (1), (2), (3)-Dec. (26)-30

PHILADELPHIA COUNTY 263

1883 Jan. 1-Mar. (26)-Dec. 31
1884 Jan. 1-Mar. (25)-May (7)-July (1), (2)- (24)-
Aug. (2)-(7), (8), (9)-Dec. 31
1886 Jan. (1)-Mar. (5), (6)-(8)-(13)-July (1)-Aug.
(31)-Oct. (2)-Dec. 31
1887 Jan. (1)-(25), (26)-(29)-Mar. (1), (2), (3)-
Apr. (6)-(20)-June (30)-Dec. 31
1888 Jan. 1-1889 Dec. 31
1890 Jan. 1-Dec. 31
1891 Jan. (1), (2), (3)-(5), (6), (7), (8), (10)-
(12)-Feb. (5)-(17)-Mar. (30)-Apr. (14)-(30),
May (1), (2)-(11)-(20)-July (1)-(6)-(13)-
Aug. (24)-(31), Sept. (1-30)-Oct. (21)-(23)-
Nov. (9), (10), (11), (12)-(24-30)-Dec. 31
1892 Jan. (1), (2)-(4)-7, 9-(14), (15), (16), (19)-
(27)-Feb. (3)-(13)-(16)-20, 23-(27)-Mar. (3)-
(29)-(31), Apr. (1)-(4), (5), (6)-(12)-(18)-
30, May 3-(7)-(13)-June 9, 11-(18)-22, 24-(30),
July (1), (2)-(4), (5), (6)-(15), (18)-(21)-
25, 27-Aug. (4)-(17)-Sept. (6), (7)-(29), (30),
Oct. (1)-Nov. (24)-Dec. 6, 8-(14)-16, 19-(31)
1893 Jan. (3)-18, 20-Mar. 31-July (1)-Aug. (18)-
Sept. (5), (6)-(9)-(26)-(29), (30)-Dec. 30
[1895 Jan. 1-Dec. 31]
[1896 Jan. 1-Dec. 31]
[1897 Jan. 1-Dec. 31]
1899 Jan. (2-6)-(12)-(16)-(19)-Feb. (7)-(22)-(28),
Mar. (1)-(25)-(28), (29)-(31), Apr. (1-July
1)-(3)-(7)-(10)-(31)-Aug. (23), 26-Sept. (1-
4)-(25)-(30)-Oct. 2-(26)-(31), Nov. (1)-(13)-
(24)-Dec. (30)
1900 Jan. [1-Dec. 31]
1901 Jan. [1-Dec. 31]
1902 Jan. [1-Aug. 10]

PHoHi   1874 Sept. 11
PHsHi   1874 Sept. 11
PLaHi   1837 Mar. 19
        1839 Dec. 31
        1841 Apr. 9
        1860 Dec. 31
PLaN   1848 Sept. 25-1849 Apr. 28
PLewL   1844 Apr. 30
PLhT   1850 Feb. 27
        1858 Sept. 1, 8
        1860 Nov. 21
PMcT   1875 Jan. 11, 13, 14
PMe   1876 May 24
PNhF   1846 Nov. 4
PNoHi   1837 Mar. 27-July 4, 6-1838 Mar. 27
        1839 Feb. 18, Mar. 23, Sept. 3, Oct. 12
        1840 Mar. 16, Nov. 3
        1841 Apr. 13, May 31, June 2-5, 8-14, 22
        1847 Aug. 11-Sept. 1
        1855 July 11, Oct. 17
        1860 Mar. 7
        1862 Jan. 8
        1863 Jan. 27, July 6
        1868 Dec. 7, 9, 14, 31
        1869 Jan. 2-5, 18, 30, Dec. 1

PUBLIC LEDGER, *continued*

                1876 May 9-18, 22-June 1, 3-22, 24-30
                1879 Aug. 7

PP ◆   1836 Sept. 11-Oct. 7, 10-29, Nov. 1, 2, 4-Dec. 15, 17, 20-30
                1837 Jan. 2-6, 9-12, 14-Feb. 3, 6-10, 13-27, Mar. 1-15, 17-27, 29, 31, Apr. 1, 4, 6-18, 22-25, 27-May 6, 9-17, 20-July 13, 15-24, 26, 27, 31, Aug. 1, 3-9, 11, 17-23, 28, 29, 31-Sept. 5, 7-13, 15-26, 29, 30, Oct. 2, 4, 5, 7-16, 19, 20, 24, 26, 28, 30, Nov. 1, 6-9, 11, 13, 15-24, 27, 28, 29, Dec. 1-4, 6-8, 11-13, 16-19, 21-25, 28, 29
                1838 Jan. 1-8, 10-22, 24-Feb. 1, 3-15, 17, 21-Dec. 31
                1839 Jan. 1-1840 Aug. 31
                1840 Sept. 2-5, 8-Dec. 25, 28-31
                1841 Jan. 1-Mar. 26, 29-July 5, 7-Dec. 31
                1842 Jan. 1-Mar. 31, Apr. 2-15, 18, Dec. 31
                1843 Jan. 2-1847 Mar. 24
                1847 Apr. 1-1849 Jan. 29
                1849 Jan. 31-Feb. 10, 13, Mar. 12, 15-Nov. 13
                1850 Nov. 15-Dec. 30
                1851 Jan. 1-24, 27-31, Feb. 3-28-1853 Feb. 7
                1853 Feb. 9-12, 15-Mar. 2, 4-1855 Mar. 13
                1855 Mar. 15-Dec. 31-1858 Apr. 14
                1858 Apr. 16-Aug. 30, Sept. 1-1859 Feb. 9
                1859 Feb. 11-Sept. 23, 26-Dec. 31
                1860 Jan. 2-1865 May 26
                1865 May 29-1866 Aug. 30
                1866 Sept. 1-1886 Jan. 29
                1886 Feb. 1-1889 Oct. 30
                1889 Nov. 1-1890 Sept. 24
                1890 Sept. 30-1891 Mar. 24
                1891 Mar. 26-Sept. 16, 25-1902 Aug. 10

PPAT   1887 Jan. 1-1902 Aug. 10

PPCHi   1876 July 4
                1883 June 4, 6
                1884 Jan. 30, Feb. 12, 18, Mar. 4, 6-10, 17, 26, Apr. 2, 3, 9, 15, 17, 23, Sept. 20
                1885 Sept.
                1887 Aug. 20
                1888 May 11
                1889 May 10, Nov. 12, 14, 15
                1890 July 1
                1891 Apr. 1, July 20
                1892 Jan. 25

PPeS   1845 Apr. 30, June 25
                1846 Feb. 18-25, Mar. 11, Apr. 9
                1862 Oct. 25
                1865 Dec. 6
                1870 Mar. 28
                1873 Nov. 8
                1890 Nov. 24

PPFfHi   1850 July 9
                1853 May 3
                1860 Mar. 30, Nov. 1
                1863 Sept. 9, 30
                1864 Mar. 30

PHILADELPHIA COUNTY 265

	1865 Jan. 18
	1885 July 24
PPI	1836 Sept. 11-1902 Aug. 10
PPiHi	1849 Apr. 25, Oct. 11
	1854 Nov. 22
	1861 Mar. 27, May 11, 29, June 12
	1862
	1864 Jan. 27, Feb. 3, 24, Mar. 2, 9, 30, Apr. 6, 20, 27, May 4, 25, June 1-22, July 6, 27, Aug. 3, 10, 24, Sept. 2, 9, 28, Oct. 5-19, Nov. 16, Dec. 7, 14
	w 1865 Jan. 18-Feb. 8
	1897 Mar. 5-1902 Aug. 10
PPiUD	1838 Aug. 4
	1840 Dec. 14
	1841 Aug. 17, Oct. 7, Dec. 15, 22, 31
	1842 Nov. 25, Dec. 1, 3
	1844 Feb. 29, Apr. 17, 19, June 20, Aug. 23, 30, Sept. 9, Oct. 5, 9, 22, 23, 26, Dec. 9, 10, 18, 19
PPL	1836 Sept. 11-15, 17-Nov. (25)-1837 Oct. 24
	1837 Oct. 26-1838 Apr. 20
	1838 Apr. 23-27, 30-May 14, 16-Sept. (26)-1839 Sept. 30
	1839 Oct. 2-1842 Jan. 20
	1842 Jan. 22-Mar. (24)-1844 Jan. (1-4)-May (1)-1847 Dec. 31
	1848 Jan. 3-Dec. 2, 5, 6, 8-(22)-1850 Aug. (9)
	1850 Aug. 10-(14)-(28)-Sept. (18)-1851 Jan. (1-Mar. 18)-June (10-12)-Nov. 15
	1851 Nov. 18-1852 Jan. (6)-Feb. 3
	1852 Feb. 5-(14)-(17)-Mar. (22)-Apr. (10)-(17)-24, 27-(31)-June (4)-(8-11)-(14-18)-(21)-July (9)-(12-14)-(16-22)-(24-27)-(29)-Aug. (2-12)-(14)-(21)-(28)-1853 Jan. (11)-(17, 18)-(20)-Apr. (25)-May 4
	1853 May 6-June (3)-(20)-July (18)-Oct. 15-Dec. 26, 28-1854 Jan. (2)-Apr. (28)-May (5)-(8)-(15)-31
	1854 June (2)-(9)-(22)-July (7)-(12)-25, 27-Aug. (3), 5, 8-(24)-Sept. (12-14)-1855 June 21
	1855 June 23-Oct. 2, 4, 6-1856 Jan. 4
	1856 Jan. 7, 10, 11, 14-Apr. 5, 8-June 28, July 1-19, 22-1857 Jan. 7
	1857 Jan. 9-June 13, 16-Sept. 19, 22-1858 July 15
	1858 July 17-(30)-Oct. 5, 7-1860 Jan. 5
	1860 Jan. 7-Mar. 21, 23-Apr. 13, 17-May 4, 7-Aug. 9, 11-13, 15-Dec. 15, 19-(31)
	1861 Jan. 8, 10-26, 29-Apr. 23, 25-June 20, 22, July 4, 6-Dec. 10, 12-1862 July (8)-21
	1862 July 23-Nov. 29, Dec. 2-1863 Jan. 2
	1863 Jan. 5-Mar. 5, 7-1864 Jan. 9
	1864 Jan. 12-Feb. (24)-June 21, 23-1865 Jan. (3)-5
	1865 Jan. 7-Apr. 18, 20, June 19, 22-July 15, 19-1866 Feb. 13
	1866 Feb. 15-Mar. 13, 15-May 28, 30-June 30, July 2-17, 19-Sept. 18, 20-Oct. 16, 18-Dec. 5, 7-8, 11, 14-31
	1867 Jan. 2-9, 11-16, 18-Mar. 25, 27-May 10, 13-1868 Jan. 1

PUBLIC LEDGER, *continued*

1868 Jan. 3, 6-Mar. 5, 7-Aug. 15, 18-21, 25-Sept. 12, 15-(21)-Oct. 20, 23-Nov. 6, 25, 27-1869 Mar. (30)-Apr. 7
1869 Apr. 9-28, 30-Mar. 3, 5-Sept. 18, 21-Nov. 12, 15-Dec. 21, 23-1870 Feb. 21
1870 Feb. 23-Mar. 7, 9-(16)-Apr. 1, 4, 5, 7-May 6, 9-27, 30-June 7, 9-July 19, 21, 23-Sept. 10, 13-1871 Jan. 3
1871 Jan. 5-Mar. (15)-June 30, July 3-Aug. 24, 26-1872 Jan. (1)-July 1
1872 July 3-Sept. (25)-Dec. 14, 17-31
1873 Jan. 2-Feb. 13, 15-Mar. 25, 27-July 10, 12-Sept. 5, 8-(24)-29, Oct. 1874 Feb. (3)-Mar. 5
1874 Mar. 7-20, 23-May 12, 14-28, 30-June 8, 10-July 9, 11-Aug. 1, 4-13, 15-Sept. 12, 15-21, 23-Oct. 12, 14-Dec. 8, 10-1875 May 10
1875 May 12-(22)-June 29, July 1-Aug. 12, 14-16, 18-1876 May 17
1876 May 19-June 8, 10-13, 15-28, 30-July 4, 6-31, **Aug. 2,** 4-Sept. 15, 18-Nov. 4, 7-Dec. 28
1877 Jan. 1-June 30, July 2-Aug. (6)-1878 Jan. (1)-Apr. (1)-June 29
1878 July (1)-19, 22-1879 Dec. 30
1880 Jan. 1-June (30)-Sept. 15, 17-1881 June 2
1881 June 4-(23)-Aug. (24)-1882 July 19
1882 July 21-Dec. 30
1883 Jan. 2-Apr. 28, May 1-June 30, July 2-1884 Apr. 16
1884 Apr. 18-June 24, Nov. 17, 19-1885 Mar. (16)-26
1885 Mar. 28-Aug. 17, 19-24, 26-(29)-Dec. (7)-1886 **Mar. 15**
1886 Mar. 17-1887 Nov. (7)-Dec. (8)-1888 Jan. (2)
1888 July 2-Dec. (29), 31-1889 Feb. (16)-June (4)-(29)-July (1)-1890 July (1)-(10)-1891 Jan. (1)-1892 June 29
1892 July (1)-Aug. (12)-Sept. (9)-Nov. 19, 22-1893 Jan. 2-(3)-5
1893 Jan. 7-Apr. 22, 24-July (1)-Sept. 25, 27-1894 Mar. (20)-1896 Mar. (6)-9
1896 Mar. 11-26, 28-May 4, 6-June 4, 6-18, 20-24, 26-Sept. 23, 25-1897 Apr. 12
1897 Apr. 14-1898 Jan. (1)-June 8
1898 June 10-Aug. 8, 13-Nov. 2, 4-1899 Feb. 9
1899 Feb. 11-22, 24, 27-Mar. 10, 13-24, 27-Apr. 12, 14-May (6)-8, 10-June 30, July 7-Oct. 2, 4-Nov. 29, Dec. 1-1900 Mar. 31
1900 Apr. 2-May 21, 23-June 12, 14-July 27, 30-Oct. 12, 15-30, Nov. 1-14, 16-27, 29-Dec. 3, 5-23, 26-28
1901 Jan. 1-1902 Aug. 10

PPM
1841 Feb. 23-1843 Dec. 9
1844 Jan. 9, 15, 17, 19-Apr. 6, 9-11, 13-23, 25-27, 30-May 6, 9-June 1, 8, 11, 12, 14-July 4, 6-11, 13-16, 19-Aug. 1, 5-8, 10, 12, 14, 16, 17, 20-Sept. 4, 6, 7, 10-12, 17-19, 21-Oct. 1, 7, 9-Nov. 12, 14-22, 25-30, Dec. 3-24, 27-1850 June 29
1850 July 2-1855 Dec. 27
1856 Jan. 1-1860 Dec. 31

PHILADELPHIA COUNTY 267

	1861 Jan. 3, 5, 9, 14, 19, Feb. 6, June 4, 13, 15, 18, 22, July 1-4, 8, 10, 13-17, 20-Aug. 14, 19-26, 28-29, 31-1868 June 30
	1870 Jan. 1-Dec. 31
	1891 Jan. 1-1894 Sept. 24
	1895 Jan. 1-1897 Sept. 24
	1898 Jan. 1-1900 Sept. 24
	1900 Nov. 26-1901 Nov. 26
	1901 Dec. 26-1902 Aug. 10
PPoT	1858 July 26, Aug. 28
	1860 July 10
	1888 Nov. 7
	1895 May 28
PPTU	1849 Apr. 25-28, May 4, 5, 11, 12, 18, 19, 25, 26, June 1, 2, 8, 9, 15, 16, 22, 23, 29, 30
	1850 Jan. 1, 5, 7, 12, 14, 19, 21, 26, 28, Feb. 2, 4, 9, 11, 16, 18, 23, 25, Mar. 2, 4, 8-11, 16, 18, 22, 26, 30-Apr. 4, 6, 8, 12, 13, 19, 20, 26, 27, May 3, 4, 10, 11, 17, 18, 24, 25, 31, June 1, 5-10
PSF	1881 Sept. 6-27
	1882 Oct. 4
PStP	[1847]-1849
PSuHi	1846 Sept. 24, 25
	1867 Apr. 2
PToHi	1846 Jan. 7
	1855 May 7
	1856 Feb. 11, 25
	1857 Jan. 28
PU	1845 Mar.-1846 Mar.
	1847 Apr.-1848 Mar. 1
	1848 Mar. 27-1851 Sept. 22
	1852 July-1864 Dec.
	1865 Mar. 25-1875 Sept.
	1876 Mar.-1877 Mar. 31
	1877 Sept.-1879 Mar.
	1898 Jan.-1900 Dec.
PVfHi	1865 Apr. 3
PWbW	1864-1894
	1898 Apr. 27-Aug. 31
PWcA	1844 Jan. 13, 16, 18, 19, 23, 27
PWcHi	1837 May 6
	1839 Apr. 23
	w 1840 Aug. 22
	1843 Apr. 10
	w 1844 Jan. 13, 16, 18, 19, 23, 27
	w 1845 Sept. 10
	w 1846 May (20)
	w 1847 Jan. 6, 13, Mar. 24, July 7-28, Aug. 11, Sept. 1, 15, Oct. 6, 13, Nov. 3, Dec. 1-29
	w 1848 Jan. 5, 19-Mar. 22, June (7), July 19, Sept. 20, Dec. 6, 13, 27-1849 Jan. 3
	w 1849 July 11, Aug. 29
	w 1850 Apr. (3), May (22), Nov. 20, 27, Dec. 25
	w 1851 May 14, June 25, Aug. 6, 20, Oct. 29, Dec. 31
	w 1852 Jan. 7, Mar. 17, 24, May 2, June 2, Oct. 6-27
	w 1854 May 3, 10, Aug. 23, Sept. (6, 13), Oct. 12, Dec. 13, 20
	w 1855 Mar. 7, Oct. 10, 31, Dec. **(26)**
	w 1856 Jan. (2), Feb. **(27)**

PUBLIC LEDGER, *continued*

                w 1857 Jan. 28, Apr. (15), Nov. 25
                w 1858 May 10, June 23
                w 1859 Dec. 7
                   1861 Mar. (6)
                   1846 Apr. 18
                   1848 July 8
                   1849 Jan. 9, June 1
                   1850 Aug. 7
                   1851 Oct. 18, Dec. 26, 27
                   1852 June 5
                   1854 Jan. 3
                   1856 Sept. 13, Dec. 19
                   1860 July 10, Oct. 8
                   1861 June 21, Oct. 10
                   1862 July 4
                   1863 July 15
                   1867 May 6, 16
                   1868 Feb. 8-(11), 12-18, 21-24, 28-Mar. 2, 4, 6-13, 17-Apr. 18, 21-May 19, 21-June 11, 19-July 21, 23-Aug. 1, 4-7, 10-21, 24, 25, Sept. 1-5, 8-22, (24)-Oct. 7, 13-(26), 28-Nov. 12, 14-Dec. 29
                   1869 Jan. 7-11, 13-(21)-27, Feb. 8, 9, 11-23, 25-Mar. (10)-(31), Dec. 28
                   1873 Sept. 27
                   1874 Apr. 28
                   1875 May 22
                   1876 Aug. 15
                   1878 May (18)
                   1881 Oct. 22
                   1882 Aug. 18, Dec. 29
                   1883 Jan. 29
                   1886 Mar. 25
                   1891 Jan. 16
                   1893 June 23, 28, July 17, Aug. 3, 7, 11, Oct. 2, 3, 5
                   1899 Sept.
                   1901 Sept. 7, 14, 17-20
                   1902 May 23
        PWcT   1846 July 15
                   1857 Nov. 25
                   1867 May 16
                   1900 Sept. 11
                   1901 Sept. 14, 18, 19
        PWfF   1848 July 26
                   [1855-1866]
        PYHi   1865 Apr. 3
                   purchased the *Times* and
                   continued as

PUBLIC LEDGER AND PHILADELPHIA TIMES (Aug. 12, 1902-Jan. 13, 1913) d morn *

    Pub. 1902-1906   Public Ledger Company
                                (Adolph S. Ochs, Pres.)
          1907-1913   George W. Ochs
    Ed. 1902   George W. Childs Drexel
          1902-1904   L. Clarke Davis
          1903-1910   A. C. Lambdin
          1903   W. A. Gordon

PHILADELPHIA COUNTY 269

1906	N. B. Hale
1908-1913	George W. Ochs
1908-1909	J. A. Graham
1910-1913	Alan Cunningham
1910-1913	G. Warfield Hobbs
1910-1913	David E. Smiley

NOTE: *Public Ledger and Philadelphia Times* appeared on the "logotype" from Aug. 12, 1902-Nov. 13, 1902, although it was carried on the editorial masthead until Jan. 13, 1913.

P	[1902 Aug. 12-1913 Jan. 13]
PCHi	1902 Aug. 12
	1908 Oct. 10, 11, 18
	1909 Apr. 25, Nov. 6
	1910 May 10
	1912 May 10, Dec. 1, 15
PDoHi	1908 Oct. 18-25, Nov. 4, 8, 18
	1909 Mar. 14
PHHi	1910 July 4
	1911 Feb. 12, Nov. 26
	1912 May 3, 26
PHi ♦	1902 (Aug. 12-Sept. 30), Oct. (2-Nov. 13), 14-Dec. (31)
	1903 Jan. (1-Dec. 31)
	1904 Jan. (1-Sept. 30), Oct. (5-Dec. 31)
	1905 Jan. (1-Dec. 31)
	1906 Jan. (1-Dec. 31)
	1907 Jan. (1-Mar. 31), Apr. (2-Oct. 1), (3-Dec. 31)
	1908 Jan. (1-Dec. 31)
	1909 Jan. (1-Dec. 31)
	1910 Jan. (1-Mar. 24), (26-Dec. 31)
	1911 Jan. (2-Dec. 30)
	1912 Jan. 1-(25)-(31)-Mar. (16)-(20)-Apr. (4)-(16)-(27)-May (27), (28)-Sept. (28)-(30)-Oct. (18)-1913 Jan. 13
PLaF	1912 Oct. 27
PLaHi	1909 Jan. 11
PNazHi	1907 Oct. 4
PP	1902 Aug. 12-1913 Jan. 13
PPAT	1902 Aug. 12-1913 Jan. 13
PPiHi	1902 Aug. 12-1913 Jan. 13
PPL	1902 Aug. 12-1913 Jan. 13
PPM	1902 Aug. 12-24, Sept. 24-1905 Nov. 30
	1906 Mar. 25-1907 Jan. 24
	1907 May 25-July 25
	1908 Jan. 1-July 24
	1910 Jan. 1-13
PU	1902 Sept.-1913 Jan. 13
PVC	1908 Aug. 9-Dec. 6
PWcHi	1903 Dec. 27
	1904 Apr. 7, 8
	1906 Feb. 18
	1908 Oct. 8
	1910 May 7, Sept. 29
	1911 Feb. 26, Apr. 2, May 7, 19
	1912 Apr. 28
PWG	1905 Oct. 22

continued as

PUBLIC LEDGER (Jan. 14, 1913-May 17, 1925) d morn *

PUBLIC LEDGER, *continued*

    Pub. 1913-1925   Public Ledger Company (Cyrus H. K. Curtis, Pres.)
    Ed. 1913-1914   George W. Ochs
          1913-1925   David E. Smiley
          1914-1924   Cyrus H. K. Curtis and Associates

NOTE: From Oct. 2, 1920-Nov. 7, 1920, the *Public Ledger and The Press* appeared on the "logotype" although the editorial masthead merely contained the title *Public Ledger*.

P	[1913 Jan. 14-1925 May 17]
P-M	1913 Jan. 23-26, 29
PB	1913 July 4
PArdL	1917 Nov. 28, 30
	1925 Jan. 24, Feb. 4
PBloHi	1915 May 5-1916 June 7
PCarlHi	1913 July 13
PCC	1913 July 4
	1915 Mar. 25
	1924 Dec. 1, 7
	1925 Mar. 1
PCHi	1913 July 4
PDoHi	1913 Dec. 7, 14, 21, 28
	1914 Jan. 18-25, Feb. 1, 8, May 31, Sept. 13, Oct. 25
	1924 Feb. 17
PEr	[1920 Oct. 2-1925]
PHHi	1916 Sept. 3
PHi	1913 Jan. 14-Feb. (1)-(6)-(10), (11)-Mar. (27)-Apr. (30)-May (12)-Aug. (13)-(29), (30)-Sept. (15)-Oct. (1)-(22)-(28)-Nov. (21)-Dec. 31
	1914 Jan. (1), (2), (3)-(5)-(12)-Feb. (25)-Mar. (6), (7)-(11)-Oct. (21), (22)-(24)-(26), (27)-(31)-Nov. (17)-(30)-Dec. (15), (16)-(31)
	1915 Jan. 1-Oct. (1)-Dec. (31)
	1916 Jan. 1-Feb. (14)-Aug. (8)-Dec. 30
	1917 Jan. (1-Mar. 1)-(4)-(6)-(8)-(10-12)-(14-16)-(19), (20)-(23)-(30), (31)-Apr. (3)-(7)-(10)-(11)-(16)-(24)-May (3)-(6)-(8, 9)-(22)-June (1-3)-(8)-July (1)-(4)-(9)-(22)-Aug. (2)-(29)-Sept. (29)-Oct. (14)-17, 19-25, 27, 29-Nov. (1), (2)-(30)-Dec. (28)-(31)
	1925 Jan. 1-May 17
PJT	1913 July 4
PLaF	1913 July 4
	1914 July 27-29, Aug. 2, 5, 11, 13, 15, 16, 21, 23, 28, 30, Sept. 2, 4
	1916 Mar. 5, 6, 12, June 4, 11
	1917 Feb. 11, Mar. 4, Apr. 1-9, Aug. 26
	1918 Apr. 28, Aug. 25, Sept. 1, 2, Oct. 27, Nov. 5, Dec. 1, 15, 22
	1919 Jan. 5, June 24, Nov. 9
	1920 May 16, 23, Sept. 19
	1924 Nov. 23, Dec. 7
	1925 Mar. 1, 10
PNazHi	1918 Nov. 7, 8, 10, 13, 14
	1921 Nov. 13
PP	1913 Jan. 14-1925 May 17
PPAT	1913 Jan. 14-1925 May 17

PHILADELPHIA COUNTY 271

    PPeS   1919 Aug. 25, Oct. 12
                       1920 Jan. 25, Feb. 8-22, Mar. 21, July 12
                       1921 Feb. 20, Mar. 5
                       1924 Nov. 18
    PPI   1913 Jan. 14-1925 May 17
    PPi   1920 Sept.-1925 May 17
    PPiHi   1913 Jan. 14-1916 May 7
    PPL   1913 Jan. 14-1925 May 17
    PPM   1913 Jan. 14-1919 Dec. 31
                       1920 Feb. 1-1925 May 17
    PU   1913 Jan. 14-1925 May 17
    PWcHi   1913 Feb. 14-1916 Feb. 12
                       1918 Apr. 30, May 30, June 30, Aug. 31, Oct. 12, 16,
                           Nov. 11, 12
                       1920 Oct. 2, Nov. 3
                       1923 Aug. 10, 11
                       1924 Feb. 4
    PWcT   1918 Apr. 30, May 30, June 30, Aug. 31, Oct. 11, 14
                       1919 May 8
                       merged with the *North American* and
                       continued as

PUBLIC LEDGER AND NORTH AMERICAN (May 18, 1925-Oct. 31, 1927) d morn *
Pub. 1925-1926   Public Ledger Company
                      (Cyrus H. K. Curtis, Pres.)
    1926-1927   Curtis-Martin Newspapers, Inc.
                      (Cyrus H. K. Curtis, Pres.)
Ed. 1925-1927   David E. Smiley
    NOTE: This title was carried on both the "logotype" and the editorial masthead.
    P   [1925 May 18-1927 Oct. 31]
    PEr   [1925 May 18-1927 Oct. 31]
    PHi   1925 May 18-Sept. (8)-Oct. (22)-Nov. (16, 17)-
                     Dec. (4)-(12)-31
    PP   1925 May 18-1927 Oct. 31
    PPI   1925 May 18-1927 Oct. 31
    PPi   1925 May 18-1927 Oct. 31
    PPL   1925 May 18-1927 Oct. 31
                   1927 Oct. 31
    PPM   1925 May 18-July 1, Sept. 1-1927 Oct. 31
    PU   1925 May 18-1927 Oct. 31
    PWcHi   1927 Jan. 17
                   continued as

PUBLIC LEDGER (Nov. 1, 1927-Apr. 15, 1934) d morn ind
Pub. 1928-1934   Curtis-Martin Newspapers, Inc.
                      (Cyrus H. K. Curtis, Pres.)
                      June 21, 1933, John C. Martin, Pres.
    P   [1927 Nov. 1-1934 Apr. 15]
    PArdL   1928 Apr. 21
                   1929 Mar. 4
                   1932 May 21, Nov. 9
                   1933 Dec. 5
                   1934 Feb. 15, Apr. 5
    PCHi   1934 Apr. 14, 15
    PDoHi ♦   1930 Mar. 9
                   1934 Apr. 14, 15
    PEr   [1927 Nov. 1-1934 Apr. 15]

PUBLIC LEDGER, *continued*
    PHi ♦
        1927 Jan. 1-Dec. 31
        1928 Jan. 2-Dec. 31
        1929 Jan. 1-Aug. 31, Sept. 2-Nov. 30, Dec. 2-31
        1930 Jan. 1-May 30, June 2-Dec. 31
        1931 Jan. 1-Feb. 28, Mar. 2-May 30, June 1-Oct. 30, Nov. 2-Dec. 31
        1932 Jan. 1-Dec. 31
        1933 Jan. 2-Apr. 29, May 1-Dec. 31
        1934 Jan. 1-Apr. 15
    PLaF
        1933 Oct. 15
        1934 Feb. 25
    PP   1927 Nov. 1-1934 Apr. 15
    PPAT   1927 Nov. 1-1931 Dec. 31
    PPeS   1928 Aug. 12, Nov. 7
    PPI   1927 Nov. 1-1934 Apr. 15
    PPi   1927 Nov. 1-1928 Aug. 1
    PPL   1927 Nov. 1-1932 Apr. 30
    PPM   1927 Nov. 1-1928 Oct. 31
                1928 Dec. 1-1934 Apr. 15
    PU   1927 No. 1-1934 Apr. 15
    PWcHi 1934 Apr. 14, 15
        Merged with the *Philadelphia Inquirer* Apr. 16, 1934 continued as *Philadelphia Inquirer Public Ledger* (q. v.)

PUBLIC NEWS (1886-1892) w ♦
    Pub. & Ed. 1891-1892 J. Herbert Boozer

PUBLIC OPINION (1871-1872) w ♦
    Pub. 1871-1872 G. Wharton Hamersly

PUBLIC RECORD, see Record

PUBLIC TELEPHONE, see Philadelphian (West Philadelphia)

PYTHIAN SHIELD (1889) w ♦
    Pub. & Ed. 1889 Stock & Hallman

QUAKER CITY, THE (Dec. 30, 1848-1850||) w *
    Pub. 1848-1850 Jos. Severns & Co.
    Ed. 1848-1850 Geo. Lippard
        PHi 1848 Dec. 30 (Vol. 1, No. 1), 1849 Dec. 29

QUAKER CITY (1870-1871) w ♦
    Pub. & Ed. 1870-1871 R. S. Pettit & Co.

QUAKER CITY BREVITY, see Tabloid

QUAKER CITY REVIEW (1878-1883) w ♦
    Pub. & Ed. 1883 L. Wade

QUILL (1886-1888) w prohibition ♦
    Pub. 1886-1888 Quill Publishing Co.
    Ed. 1886-1888 Rev. Oswald Congelton

PHILADELPHIA COUNTY

QUIVER (1893-1914) w local ♦
    Pub. & Ed. 1905-1909 George B. Cole
               1909-1911 Quiver Publishing Co.
               1911-1914 James J. Wray

QUIZZICAL REGISTER (Jan. 19, 1833-Apr. 6, 1833||) w
    Pub.   Tom & Jerry
       PHi ♦   1833 Jan. 26, Apr. 6

RADIO PRESS (1933-1934) w
    Pub. 1933-1934 Norman Publishing Company
    Ed. 1933-1934 Milton J. Feldman
        PP   1934 Mar. 10 (Vol. 1, No. 26)-May 11 (Vol. 2, No. 9)
                      On May 18, 1934, merged with *The Pennsylvania Weekly News* under the title of *The Pennsylvania Weekly News and Radio Press* (q.v.)

RADOTEUR, LE (1793) ♦
    Pub. & Ed. 1793 Chez le Rédacteur du Courrier Politique

RAG BABY (Aug. 16, 1879-Sept. 27, 1879||) w * Campaign paper
    Ed.   John G. Mills and Frank Higel
       PWcHi   1879 Sept. 27
       PWalG   1879 Sept. 13

REAL ISSUE (1930) ir
    Pub.   Bohlen, Phillips & Dorrance (Campaign Committee)
       PHi ♦   1930 Apr. (Vol. 1, No. 2)
       PP   1930 May 7, 16

RECORD (May 14, 1870†) d & sun
    PUBLIC RECORD (May 14, 1870-Apr. 30, 1877) d
    Pub. & Ed. 1870-1876 William J. Swain
        P-M   1876 Sept. 29, Nov. 10
       PHi   1870 May 14-1871 Jan. 14
                    1871 Jan. 17-31, Feb. 2, 3, 6-Apr. 7, 10-18, 20-29, May 10-Dec. 4, 6-29
                    1872 Jan. 1-Mar. 11, 13, 14, 16-May 14, 16-1873 Mar. 3
                    1873 Mar. 5-Apr. 2, 4, 5, 8-Nov. 13
       PP   1870 May 14-1871 May 13
       PPL   1875 May 17
       PPR   1870 May 14-1877 Apr. 30
       PWcHi   1870 Dec. 12
                continued as
    RECORD, THE (May 1, 1877-Oct. 11, 1879) d
    Pub. 1877-1879 Record Publishing Company
       PUB   1877 May 1-1879 Oct. 11
       PNoHi   1877 June 1
       PP   1877 May 1-1879 Oct. 11
       PWcHi   1879 Jan. 11
                continued as
    PHILADELPHIA RECORD, THE (Oct. 13, 1879†) d sun
    Pub. 1879-1890 William M. Singerly
          1890-1928 Record Publishing Company

RECORD, *continued*

	1928-1930	J. David Stern
	1930-1941	Philadelphia Record Company
Ed.	1879-1890	William M. Singerly
	1894-1898	William M. Singerly
	1898-1919	Theodore Wright
	1924-1928	John P. Power
	1928-1930	Melville F. Ferguson
	1930-1938	J. David Stern
	1938-1941	H. J. Saylor

Sunday edition first issued, June 25, 1882
Article dropped from title Nov. 11, 1931

PUB	1879 Oct. 13†
P	1885 June 1-1935 May 31
P-M	1879 Dec. 15, 17
	1881 July 4
	1884 May 1, Aug. 11
	1885 Aug. 10
	1913 Jan. 23-26
PArdL	1904 Apr. 15
	1924 Nov. 5
PBK	1892 Sept. 20
	1898 May 5, 6, 11, 16, 18-20, 27, June 3, 10, 14, 18, 24, 28, Aug. 26, 27, 29, 31, Sept. 1-3, 6, 15, 16, 18-20, 24, Oct. 10, 21
PBMa	1897 Apr. 28
PCC	1920 May 2, June 27
	1927 July 26
PCHi	1881 Sept. 20-22, 27
	1882 Jan. 26, 27, Oct. 4
	1901 Sept. 7-9, 11-16
	1910 Jan. 16
PDC	1898 Oct. 31
PDoHi	1881 July 2 (Reprint), 4, Dec. 31
	1882 Oct. 26
	1885 Mar. 5, July 24
	1886 Jan. 16
	1887 Sept. 16, 17
	1888 Aug. 28
	1894 Nov. 7, 8
	1901 Sept. 8, 14, 15
	1903 Jan. 18
	1908 Oct. 4, Nov. 4, 18 (Oct. 4-11 Founder's Week)
	1918 Sept. 14
	1920 June 13
	1936 June 23
PEr	1920 May 2-June 27
PHHi	1885 Mar. 26
	1897 Feb. 3
PHi	[1882 Jan. 2-1917 Oct. 31]
	1920 May 2, 9, 16, 23, 30, June 6, 13, 20, 27
PLaF	1933 Oct. 15†
PNazHi	1918 Nov. 8
	1936 June 23, 27, 28, Nov. 4, 5
PNoHi sun	1920 May 2-June 27
PP	1879 Oct. 13-1881 Nov. 12
	1882 May 15-1884 June 18
	1884 June 20-1894 Dec. 31

PHILADELPHIA COUNTY 275

	1895 Jan. 14-1896 Sept. 13
	1897 Nov. 14-1905 Jan. 30
	1905 Feb. 1-1915 May 16
	1915 June 1-1917 July 16
	1917 Aug. 1†
PPCHi	1888 Aug. 12
	1895 Aug. 9
	1896 Nov. 14
PPeS	1920 May 2-June 27
	1928 Nov. 6-8
	1932 May 14
PPiHi	1898 Sept. 28
PPL	1935 Feb. 28
PPM	1909 May 16, June 13
PPot	1885 July 24
	1886 Dec. 29
	1893 Jan. 28, Mar. 4
PPTU	1936 July 10-18, 20-24, 27-31, Aug. 1-7, 10-14, 17-21, 24-26, 28, 31, Sept. 1, 2, 4, 5, 8-12, 14, 16, 19, 21-25, 28-30, Oct. 1-6, 8, 9, 12-18, 20-24, 26-31, Nov. 2-15, 17-30, Dec. 1-31
	1937 Jan. 1-June 30, Aug. 1-Dec. 30
	1938 Jan. 1-Dec. 31
	1939 Jan. 1†
PSeSU	1938 Dec. 1†
PSew sun	1920 May 2-June 27
PSF	1881 Sept. 26-28
PSuHi	1892 Jan. 1
PUn	1920 May 2-July 2 (Golden Jubilee issue)
PWcHi	1880 Jan. 1-7
	1881 Mar. 7, May 13
	1882 Jan. 5, July 22
	1883 Aug. 29, (30)
	1889 June 2
	1890 Apr. 5
	1894 Mar. (19)
	1901 Sept. 6-16, 18-20
	1906 Jan. 7
	1909 May 16, June 13
	1911 Jan. 8
	1913 Feb. 14
	1919 June 27
PWcT	1906 Jan. 7
	1911 Jan. 8
PWalG	1905 Sept. 17, Oct. 15, 16, 22, 29, Nov. 5, 12

RECORDER,   see Episcopal Recorder

REFORMED CHURCH MESSENGER,   see Messenger, The

REFORMIERTE KIRCHENZEITUNG (1868-1873) w for ♣
    Pub. 1868-1869   Dr. S. R. Fisher
          1869-1873   Reformed Church Publication Board
    Ed. 1868-1873   J. G. S. Whittman

REGISTER, THE (Jan. 1, 1853) w A Gazette of the Protestant Episcopal Church in the United States
    Pub. & Ed. 1853 Jan. 1 at Philadelphia
        PHi ◆   1853 Apr. 9
        PPEHi   1853 Feb. 5, June 4, Dec. 3

RELF'S PHILADELPHIA GAZETTE AND DAILY ADVERTISER, see Philadelphia Gazette and Commercial Intelligencer, The

RELIGIOUS MESSENGER OF THE PHILADELPHIA CONFERENCE (1826) w
    Pub. & Ed.   1826 John Clarke
    PHi   1836 Dec. 28 (Vol 1, No. 52)

RELIGIOUS NEWS AND HOME GUIDE (1898-1902) w ♪
    RELIGIOUS NEWS (1898) w ♪
    Pub. & Ed. 1898 W. K. Fisher
        continued as
    RELIGIOUS NEWS AND HOME GUIDE (1898-1902) w ♪
    Pub. & Ed. 1898-1902 Wm. K. Fisher and James E. Lake

RELIGIOUS REMEMBRANCER, see Christian Observer

RELIGIOUS TELEGRAPH AND OBSERVER, see Christian Observer

RELIGIOUS WEEKLY (1911-1913) w ♪
    Pub. 1911-1913 Religious Weekly
    Ed. 1911-1913 Rev. Carl B. Baker

REPORTER (1886-1891) d morn comm ♪
    Pub. & Ed. 1891 R. H. Gordon

REPORTER (1903-1912) w ♪
    Pub. & Ed. 1906-1912 Alonzo F. Jenkins
    Ed.   1908-1912 A. A. Williams

REPUBLICAN (1900-1905) w rep ♪
    Pub. & Ed. 1901-1903 John Long
        1903-1905 John Riddele

REPUBLIKANER (1886-1888) d morn rep for ♪
    Pub. & Ed. 1886-1888 J. E. Metzger

REPUBLIKANISCHE FLAGGE, DIE, see Philadelphia Freie Presse

RETAILER (1884-1885) w anti-monopoly ♪
    Pub. & Ed. 1884-1885 John A. Haddocks

REVIEW (1902-1908) w local ♪
    Pub. 1902-1908 Review Publishing Co.

REVUE (1884-1888) w for ♪
    Pub. 1884-1888 Revue Publishing Co.

PHILADELPHIA COUNTY 277

ROOSEVELT DEMOCRATIC NEWS (1934-1935) pol
    PP   1934 Nov. 1
               1935 Oct. 22, 29

ROUGH AND READY (1848)
    Pub. at Philadelphia
    PHi   1848 Aug. 12 (Vol. 1, No. 1)

ROVER, THE, see Town Rover and Weekly Censor

ROXBOROUGH INDEPENDENT (1913-1920) w local
    Pub. & Ed. 1913-1916   Curtis E. Blinsinger
               1916-1920   Harold B. Tyson
    PP   1914 Dec. 10

ROXBOROUGH INTELLIGENCER (1875-1876) w ♦
    Pub. & Ed. 1875-1876   D. R. King

ROXBOROUGH NEWS, see addenda

ROXBOROUGH SUBURBAN TIMES AND REVIEW, see Olney Times

ROXBOROUGH TIMES, THE, see addenda

ROYAL PENNSYLVANIA GAZETTE, THE (Mar. 3, 1778-May 26, 1778||) sw #
    Pub. 1778   James Robertson
        PHi   1778 Mar. 3-May 26
        PPAP   1778 May 12
        PPL   1778 Mar. 3-May 26

SAINT PAULS TRI-WEEKLY PRESS (1862) tw
    PWcHi   1862 Sept. 3

SALMAGUNDI, NEWS OF THE DAY, see Family Messenger and National Gleaner

SATURDAY AMERICAN AND TEMPERANCE ADVOCATE (1844-1846) w ♦ *
    Pub. 1844-1845   Wm. Sloemaker
         1845   Lewis C. Levin
         1845-1846   Barrett & Jones

SATURDAY BULLETIN (Nov. 17, 1827-Dec. 29, 1832||) w *
    Pub. 1827-1832   Edmund Morris
    Ed. 1830-1832   John J. Smith
    Merged with the *Saturday Evening Post,* Jan. 5, 1833
    P   1831 July 30
    PBL ♦   1829 Aug. 1, Oct. 10, Dec. 12
                  1830 Jan. 16, Feb. 13, 20, Mar. 6, 13, Apr. 10, May 1-29, June 19, July 3-24, Aug. 21, Sept. 4-Dec. 25
                  1831 Jan. 1-8, Feb. 5, 19, March 19, 26, Apr. 2, 30, May 7
    PHHi   1830 May 28-1832 Dec. 22
    PPL   1830 May 15-1832 Dec. 29
    PW   .   1830 Dec. 11

SATURDAY CHRONICLE (1836-1842) w
    SATURDAY CHRONICLE AND MIRROR OF THE TIMES (May 21, 1836-May 28, 1836) w
    Pub. 1836   Benjamin Matthias and Joshua L. Taylor
        PBL ◆   1836 May 21
        absorbed the *Philanthropist* (q.v.) to form
    SATURDAY CHRONICLE, PHILANTHROPIST AND MIRROR OF THE TIMES (June 4, 1836-May 13, 1837) w
    Pub. 1836-1837   Benjamin Matthias and Joshua L. Taylor
        PBL ◆   1836 June 4, 18-July 2, 23-Oct. 15, Nov. 5-Dec. 10, 31
                  1837 Jan. 14, Feb. 18-Mar. 11, May 6, 20-July 1, 15, 22, Aug. 5, 26, Sept. 9-Dec. 30
        PHi ◆   1836 Dec. 31
        continued as
    SATURDAY CHRONICLE AND MIRROR OF THE TIMES (May 20, 1837-Nov. 13, 1841) w
    Pub. & Ed. 1837-1841   Benjamin Matthias and Joshua L. Taylor
        P   1841 Jan. 9-Nov. 13
        PBL ◆   1837 May 20-Dec. 30
                  1838 Jan. 6-Feb. 3, Mar. 10-June 2, June 23-28, Aug. 11, Dec. 15
                  1839 Mar. 2, Apr. 20-May 4, June 15, Sept. 7-28, Oct. 19-Nov. 16, Dec. 28
                  1840 Jan. 4-Feb. 8, 22-June 27, July 18-Aug. 1, 15, 22
        continued as
    SATURDAY CHRONICLE (Nov. 20, 1841-Oct. 1, 1842) w
    Pub. & Ed. 1841-1842   Benjamin Matthias and Joshua L. Taylor
        P   1841 Nov. 20-1842 Sept. 3
        PBL ◆   1841 Nov. 20
                  1842 Mar. 5
    Merged with *United States Saturday Post* and title changed to *United States Saturday Post and Chronicle*.

SATURDAY COURIER, see American Saturday Courier

SATURDAY EVENING MAIL (1842-1857) w *
    PHILADELPHIA SATURDAY MUSEUM (Dec. 1842-Oct. 5, 1844) w ◆ *
    Pub. & Ed. 1842-1844   Joseph C. Neal and Morton McMichael
                                Clarke & Fairman
                                Clarke & Van Wyck
        continued as
    NEAL'S SATURDAY GAZETTE AND LADY'S LITERARY MUSEUM (Oct. 12, 1844-Dec. 16, 1848) w *
    Pub. & Ed. 1844-1847   Joseph C. Neal & Morton McMichael
               1847-1848   Mrs. Jos. C. Neal
               1848   Cummings & Peterson, Clarke & Van Wyck
        PBL ◆   1847 Feb. 13, Mar. 6
                  1848 Jan. 1, 29, Feb. 5, 26, Apr. 8-29, May 27-June 3, July 22, Aug. 19, 26, Sept. 16, Oct. 7-21, Nov. 11, 18, Dec. 9

PHILADELPHIA COUNTY 279

       PHi   1845 Jan. 4-Dec. 27
       PP   1844 Oct. 12-1845 Oct. 11
       PWcHi   1845 Mar. 6, Nov. 1, 22, 29, Dec. 13, 20
                 continued as
NEAL'S SATURDAY GAZETTE (Dec. 23, 1848-Mar. 31, 1849) w *
Pub. & Ed. 1848-1849 Mrs. Joseph C. Neal
           1848-1849 Charles J. Peterson
       PBL ♦   1848 Dec. 23
                 1849 Jan. 6-20, Feb. 3, 10, 24, Mar. 3
       PDoHi   1849 Feb. 24
                 continued as
MAMMOTH SATURDAY GAZETTE (Apr. 7, 1849-Sept. 28, 1850) w
Pub. & Ed. 1849 Mrs. Joseph C. Neal
           1849 Charles J. Peterson
       PHi ♦   1850 July 6
                 continued as
SATURDAY GAZETTE (Oct. 5, 1850-Dec. 9, 1853) w *
Pub. & Ed. 1853 George R. Graham
       PDoHi   1851 June 21
       PHi ♦   1853 June 25
                 continued as
GRAHAM'S SATURDAY MAIL (Dec. 16, 1853-Feb. 3, 1855) w *
Pub. & Ed. 1853-1855 George R. Graham
       P-M   1854 June 3, July 15
       PLhT   1854 Apr. 15
                 continued as
SATURDAY EVENING MAIL (Feb. 10, 1855-1857) w * ♦
Pub. & Ed. 1855-1857

SATURDAY EVENING MESSENGER (May 3, 1856-June 28, 1856||)
w
       PPL   1856 May 24, June 28

SATURDAY EVENING REPUBLIC (1868-1891) w ♦ ind
   Pub. & Ed. 1886-1891 Charles H. Vary

SATURDAY GAZETTE (Apr. 19, 1823-May 24, 1824) w
       PHi ♦   1823 May 24

SATURDAY GAZETTE (1850-1853), see Saturday Evening Mail

SATURDAY GLEANER see Philadelphia Inquirer Public Ledger

SATURDAY GUILLOTINE (Apr. 29, 1820-1830||) w
   Pub. 1820-1830 Edmund Curl and Left-legged Jacob
       PHi ♦   1830 June 5

SATURDAY MORNING (1879-1892) w ♦
   Pub. & Ed. 1883-1892 H. A. Brainard

SATURDAY MORNING HERALD, see Commercial Herald and Pennsylvania Sentinel

SATURDAY MORNING JOURNAL (1830), see Morning Journal

SATURDAY NEWS AND LITERARY GAZETTE, see Philadelphia Saturday News and Literary Gazette

SATURDAY PENNSYLVANIA GAZETTE, see Pennsylvania Gazette, The

SATURDAY REVIEW AND REPUBLIC (1867-1898) w rep
    Pub. & Ed. 1867-1895 Harper & Brother
               1895-1898 Edwin Van D. Paul
    PHi ♦   1892 Dec. 3
    PP   1889 Nov. 2-1890 Feb. 1, 15-Oct. 15
              1890 Nov. 1-1891 Dec. 19 (except Jan. 10, May 10, July 25)
              1891 Dec. 26-1892 Sept. 23, Oct. 7-1894 Feb. 3
              1894 Feb. 10-17, Mar. 9-16, 30-1895
              1896 May 2-Aug. 29- (except July 11, 18, Aug. 15)
    PPCHi   1896 Sept. 5

SCANDINAVIAN VOICE (1891) w for ♦
    Pub. & Ed. 1891 Peter Ceder

SCHOOL, CHURCH AND HOME (1870-1877) w temp ♦
    Pub. 1875-1876   Charles Heritage
          1876-1877   H. Dixon Cooper
    Ed. 1875-1876   Charles Heritage
          1876-1877   S. M. Cooper & Sons

SCHWABISCHER MERKUR (1885-1888) w for
    PHILADELPHIA SCHWABISCHER MERKUR (Sept. 5, 1885-Mar. 10, 1888) w
    Pub. 1885-1888   C. Marius Baumann
    PPG   1885 Sept. 5 (Vol. 1, No. 1)-1886 Aug. 28
                      1887 Apr. 9-1888 Mar. 3
                      continued as
    SCHWABISCHER MERKUR (Mar. 17, 1888-July 14, 1888) w
    Pub. 1888   C. Marius Baumann
    PPG   1888 Mar. 17-July 14

SCOTT'S PHILADELPHIA PRICE-CURRENT, AND COMMERCIAL REMEMBRANCER (May 31, 1813-Nov. 22, 1813) w
    Pub. 1813   John W. Scott
    PHi ♦   1813 Aug. 16-Nov. 22
    PPL   1813 May 31-July 12

SCOTT'S WEEKLY PAPER (Aug. 15, 1846-1855) w *
    Pub. 1846-1855   Andrew Scott
    PPL   1853 Jan. 8

PHILADELPHIA COUNTY 281

SENTINEL (1870-1871), see Manayunk Sentinel, Roxborough, Falls of Schuylkill, and Wissahickon Star

SENTINEL (1884-1890) w ind Negro ♦
    Pub. & Ed. 1884-1890 G. W. Gardner

SERA, LA (1897-1909) d evg for ♦
    Pub. 1906-1908 La Sera Publishing Co.
        1908-1909 L. De Benedictis
    Ed. 1906-1909 L. De Benedictis

SESQUI-CENTENNIAL (1921-1923) w ind ♦
    Pub. & Ed. 1921-1923 J. Hampton Leonard

SHARP SHOOTER AND ANTI-FOGY (1854-1868) w sun
    Pub. 1868 First Progressive Christian Church
    Ed. 1868 Dr. S. M. Landis
        PDoHi 1868 Oct. 4, 11

SIGARETTA (Cigarette) (1915-1924) w sun humorous for ♦
    Pub. & Ed. 1915-1924 L. De Benedictis

SINGLE TAX HERALD (1915-1919) w single tax
    Pub. 1915-1919 Single Tax Herald Publishing Co.
    Ed. 1915-1919 Robert C. Maccaulay
        PHi 1915 Oct. 12

SOLDIER'S WEEKLY MESSENGER (Sept. 26, 1866-July 10, 1867||)
    w
    Pub. 1866-1867 Soldier Messenger Corp.
    Ed. 1866-1867 C. T. Collins
        PHi ♦ 1866 Sept. 26-Dec. 26
                1867 Jan. 2-May 22, June 5, 12-26, July 3, 10

SOLID ROCK HERALD (1901-1907) w ind rep Negro ♦
    Pub. 1906-1907 John Clinton, Jr.
    Ed. 1906-1907 Abel P. Caldwell

SONNTAGS BLATT, see Philadelphia Tageblatt

SONNTAGSBLATT DER FREIEN PRESSE, see Philadelphia Freie Presse

SONNTAGS BLATT UND FAMILIEN JOURNAL, see Philadelphia Freie Presse

SONNTAGS GAZETTE (1892-1918), see Philadelphia Gazette Democrat

SONNTAGS JOURNAL (1876-1916) w for ind
Pub. & Ed. 1876-1880 F. Lisiewski and A. Schulte
          1880-1881 Journal Publishing Co.
          1881-1916 William Regenspurger
    PPG   1888 Dec. 9-1909 Nov. 21

SONNTAGSZEITUNG (1871) w ind for ♣
Pub. & Ed. 1871 Muehleck & Scheu

SONNTAGS—ZEITUNG DES TAGEBLATTS, see Philadelphia Tageblatt

SOUTH-END RECORD (1891-1897) w ♣
Pub. & Ed. 1891-1897 Edward A. Glenan

SOUTH PHILADELPHIAN (1895-1919) w ind non-part rep ♣
Pub. & Ed. 1895-1919 James E. Lennon

SOUTH PHILADELPHIAN (Aug. 31, 1929†) w
   SOUTH PHILADELPHIA (Aug. 31, 1929-July 19, 1930) w
   Pub. & Ed. 1929-1930 William J. Morrow
      PUB   1929 Aug. 31-1930 July 19
      PP   1929 Aug. 31-1930 July 19
                continued as
   SOUTH PHILADELPHIAN (July 26, 1930†) w
   Pub. & Ed. 1930   William J. Morrow
      PUB   1930 July 26†
      PP   1930 July 26-1933 Mar. 24
                1933 Apr. 7-28, May 26-July 7, 21-Sept. 1, 15-1934 Mar. 2
                1934 Mar. 16-Apr. 6, 20-1935 Oct. 4
                1935 Oct. 18-Nov. 15, 29, Dec. 13-27
                1936 Feb. 7-21, Mar. 13, May 1, 15-1937 Nov. 5
                1937 Nov. 19-1938 July 29
                1938 Aug. 12, 26, Sept. 2, 23
                1939 May 19-June 2
                1940 Jan. 12, Feb. 2, May 24, June 7-14, 28

SOUTH PHILADELPHIA WORLD (1906-1913) w local ♣
Pub. & Ed. 1906-1913 James Hunter

SOUTHERN MONITOR (June 6, 1857-1860||) w *
Pub. & Ed. 1857-1858 J. B. Jones
      PHi   1857 June 6-1858 May 29
      PLewL   1857 June 6

SOUTHERN PIONEER AND EVANGELICAL LIBERALIST (1832-1836) w
   PHILADELPHIA LIBERALIST (June 9, 1832-June 13, 1835) w
   Pub. 1832-1835 Southern Convention of Universalist
   Ed. 1832-1835 Rev. Zelotes Fuller

PHILADELPHIA COUNTY 283

    P   1832 June 9-1833 June 1
    PHi   1832 June 9-1835 June 13
    PP   1833 June 8, 29-1834 Jan. 4
                  1834 Jan. 18-June 14
    PPFfHi   1834 Oct. 4, 18
                  1835 Jan. 10
    PPL   1832 June 9-1835 June 13
                  continued as
  SOUTHERN PIONEER AND PHILADELPHIA LIBERALIST
    (July 25, 1835-April 30, 1836) w
  Pub. 1835-1836   Southern Convention of Universalists
  Ed. 1835-1836   Rev. Zelotes Fuller
    PPL   1835 July 25-Aug. (29)-1836 Apr. 30
                  continued as
  SOUTHERN PIONEER AND EVANGELICAL LIBERALIST
    (May 7, 1836-July 9, 1836) w
  Pub. 1836   Southern Convention of Universalists
  Ed. 1836   Rev. Zelotes Fuller
    PPL   1836 May 7, 10, 28-June 25, July 9

SOUTHWARK GAZETTE, AND PHILADELPHIA CHRONICLE, THE (July 15, 1797-Aug. 1, 1797) tw ♪ #
  Pub. 1797   Timothy Montford

SOUTHWEST CHRONICLE, (1929-1934), see West Philadelphia Chronicle

SOUTHWESTERN TIMES (1887-1891) w ♪
  Pub. & Ed. 1887-1891 Wm. E. Bayer

SPIRIT OF THE PRESS, THE (Sept. 14, 1805-Oct. 1808) w n #
  Pub. 1805-1808   Richard Folwell
    PHi   1807 Aug.
    PPL   1805 Nov. 16

SPIRIT OF '76 (1837) d *

SPIRIT OF THE TIMES (1837-1851) d w dem *
  SPIRIT OF THE TIMES (1837-1847) d w *
    d Nov. 1837-July 21, 1847 w Sept. 14, 1844-Dec. 14, 1844||
  Pub. & Ed. 1837-1847 John S. Du Solle & Edward A. Penniman
    Weekly edition entitled *Weekly Times,* 1844
    P   [1838 June 29-1847 July 21]
    PDoHi   1844 May 17 (Extra)
    PHi   1838 June 23
                  1839 Jan. 15, 24, 30, Feb. 2, 11, 15, 19, June 10, July 6, 30, Aug. 17, 28, Sept. 9, Oct. 3, Dec. 30
                  1840 Jan. 25
                  1841 Mar. 26, May 6, June 8, July 15, Nov. 10, 27
                  1842 Jan. 1-Dec. 31
                  1843 Feb. 9, 15, Mar. 24, 25, May 18, 27, 29, June 10-15, 24, July 4, 22, Aug. 24, 25, Oct. 18, Nov. 9, 11, 13, 17

SPIRIT OF THE TIMES, *continued*
                1844 Feb. 5-7, 13, 14, Mar. 9, May 9, 16, 17, June 5, 22, 25, 26, July 1-1845 June 30
    PLaHi   [1839 Jan. 1-Dec. 31]
                1840 July 1
                1841 Dec. 31
    PNoHi   1839 Nov. 16
                1840 Feb. 22, May 29, June 12, 22, July 6-20, 22, 23, 25-Aug. 4, 7, 11, 14, 15
                1841 June 4-7, 9, 10, 12, 15, 16, 19
    PP   1839 July 29, Aug. 26
                1841 May 27, June 2, 7
    PPiUD   1841 July 16, Aug. 5, Sept. 21
                1842 Sept. 12, Nov. 11, 12
                1843 Aug. 30, Oct. 7
                1844 May 9, Oct. 7, 8-14, 16-18
    PWcHi   1844 Feb. 26
                merged with *Daily Keystone and People's Journal* (q.v.) to form

SPIRIT OF THE TIMES AND DAILY KEYSTONE (July 22, 1847-Dec. 25, 1849) d *
    Pub. & Ed. 1847-1848   Manuel M. Cooke
                1847-1849   Thomas B. Florence
                1849   A. H. Smith & Charles W. Carrigan
    P   [1847 July 22-1849 Nov. 29]
    PDoHi   1848 Oct. 7
    PHi ♦   1847 Oct. 20, 22, 26, 28
                1848. Jan. 27, Mar. 29, 30, Apr. 4, July 15, 29
    PLaHi   1847 Aug. 25
    PP   1848 Feb. 25
                1849 Oct. 31
    PPL   1847 July 22
                1849 Jan. 1-Dec. 25
    PWalG   1848 Nov. 27
                continued as

SPIRIT OF THE TIMES (Dec. 27, 1849-1854||) d *
    Pub. & Ed. 1849-1851   A. H. Smith & Charles W. Carrigan
    PBL   1850 Nov. 30
    PHi   1850 Oct. 9, Nov. 11
    PPL   1849 Dec. 27-31
                1850 Apr. 11, Sept. 9, Oct. 3, 5
                1851 Jan. 3, 4, 29, 30

SPIRIT OF THE TIMES (1883) w
    Pub. & Ed. 1883 George L. Myers and W. A. Gwynne ♦

SPORTING ITEM (1892) ♦
    Pub. & Ed. 1892 Fitzgerald & Sons

SPY AND PHILADELPHIA COUNTY COURIER (June 30, 1827) *

SPY IN PHILADELPHIA AND SPIRIT OF THE AGE, THE (July 6, 1833-Dec. 28, 1833) w *
    Pub. 1833   William Hill & Co.
    PHi   1833 July 6-Dec. 28

PHILADELPHIA COUNTY 285

STAGE, (1866) see Evening Star (1866-1900)

STANDARD, see Presbyterian Standard

STANDARD AND PRESBYTERIAN EXPOSITOR, THE, see Presbyterian Standard

STANDARD-ECHO (1891-1899) w undenominational Negro ⚫
    Pub. & Ed. 1891-1899 Abel P. Caldwell

STANDARD OF THE CROSS AND THE CHURCH (1844-1891) w rel ⚫
    Pub. 1844-1891   Walter E. Hering
    Ed. 1844-1891   Rev. W. C. French and W. B. French

STAR, see Gwiazda

STAR OF LIBERTY, THE (Oct. 6, 1812-Nov. 25, 1812) d w tw ⚫ #
    Pub. 1812   Britton Evans

STAR SPANGLED BANNER (1834) tw * ⚫

STORY & HUMPHREY'S PENNSYLVANIA MERCURY AND UNIVERSAL ADVERTISER (1775) w # ⚫
    PENNSYLVANIA MERCURY, AND UNIVERSAL ADVERTISER, THE (Apr. 7, 1775) ⚫ # w
    Pub. 1775   Story & Humphreys
                     (Enoch Story and Daniel Humphreys)
                     continued as
    STORY & HUMPHREY'S PENNSYLVANIA MERCURY AND UNIVERSAL ADVERTISER (Apr. 14, 1775-Dec. 22, 1775) w ⚫ #
    Pub. 1775   Story & Humphreys
                     (Enoch Story and Daniel Humphreys)

SUBURBAN PRESS (Feb. 7, 1929†) w
    Pub. 1929   Joseph H. Ewing
    Ed. 1929   A. C. Chadwick
        PUB   1929 Feb. 7†
        PP   1929 Feb. 7†

SUBURBAN TIMES AND REVIEW (Roxborough), see Olney Times

SUN (Oct. 1, 1829-Feb. 19, 1835) w anti-Masonic
    Pub. 1829-1833   J. Clarke and Chas. Thomson Jones
    Ed. 1829-1833   J. Clarke
    The issue of Oct. 1, 1829 was a proposal for publishing the *Sun*. Regular publication started Dec. 15, 1830
        P   1831 Dec. 15

SUN, continued
   PDoHi 1832 Nov. 29, Dec. 6
   PHi   1831 May 19-Sept. 15
        1833 May 2-1835 Feb. 19
   PLaHi 1829 Oct. 1

SUN (Aug. 11, 1831-Feb. 12, 1835) d
   P-M   1835 Feb. 12
   PLewL 1831 Aug. 11
        1832 Oct. 25

SUN (Feb. 12, 1877-Jan. 1884) d morn evg * ♦
  Pub. 1877   Sun Publishing Co.
   1877-1884 Harrington Fitzgerald
        merged with the *Item,* 1879 (q.v.)

SUN (North Philadelphia) (1877-1919) w local ♦
  Pub. 1910-1919 Sun Publishing Co.
  Ed. 1910-1919 Edwin A. Fricke

SUN (1886-1890) w ind ♦
  Pub. & Ed. 1886-1890 Camagys & Bro.

SUN (1890-1891) w sun ♦
  Pub. 1890-1891 Sun Publishing Co.
  Ed. 1890-1891 R. Ross MacIver

SUN, THE (May 5, 1843-June 30, 1857) d w *
d May 5, 1843-June 30, 1857; w 1843-1857 as *Dollar Weekly Sun*
% *Philadelphia Sun* and *The Daily Sun*
   Pub. 1843-1844 Lewis C. Levin
     1844-1845 William Sloanaker & Co.
     .1844   John Dainty & Co.
     1846-1847 Barnett & Jones
     1848   O. P. Cornman
     1849-1852 Wallace & Fletcher
     1852-1857 Joshua Fletcher
   Ed. 1843-1844 Lewis C. Levin
     1844-1845 William Sloanaker & Co.
     1849   James S. Wallace
     1852-1857 William D. Baker
   P   w 1847 June 10-Aug. 24
   PBL ♦ 1844 Jan. 6, May 4, 7
       1845 Mar. 29, June 17
       1846 July 7
       1847 Sept. 15
       1848 Aug. 9, Dec. 4
       1849 March 17
       1852 Jan. 26, 28, Feb. 9, Mar. 18, 31, July 15, 16, 19
   PCHi   1856 July 4
   PDoHi 1844 Oct. 26
       1847 Apr. 8, July 14
   PHi ♦ 1844 Oct. (16)
       1845 Jan. 2-June 26

PHILADELPHIA COUNTY

       1847 Nov. 24, Dec. (4), 6, 8
       1848 Jan. 1-June 30
       1849 Jan. 1-Dec. 31
       1853 Feb. 15
       1856 Nov. 5
       1857 Jan. 1-June 30
  PNoHi   1844 May 17, 22
       1845 Dec. 13
       1847 June 8
  PPFfHi   1852 Oct. 8
       1856 Oct. 30
  PPL   1847 Oct. 8
       1849 Nov. 16-29, Dec. 1-(17)
       1850 Jan. 1-Feb. 20, 22-July 4, 6-Dec. 25, 27-1851
         Sept. 1
  PShH   1843 May 18
       1847
  PWcHi   1844 May 11
       1852 July 3
       1856 Oct. 10
       1857 Oct. 24

SUN (1877-1879), see Item

SUN, THE (May 18, 1925-Feb. 4, 1928) d morn ind
  Pub. 1925-1928 Public Ledger Co.
  Ed. 1925-1928 David E. Smiley
  PP   1925 June 1-1928 Feb. 4

SUNDAY ARGUS (1879) w dem ♩
  Pub. & Ed. 1879 Jos. Severns & Co.

SUNDAY ATLAS, THE, see Philadelphia Sunday Atlas

SUNDAY DAWN (1871-1873) w ♩
  Pub. & Ed. 1871-1873 J. Trainor King

SUNDAY DELTA, THE (1853-) w ♩
  Pub. 1853   David S. Palmer

SUNDAY DISPATCH (May 14, 1848†) w *
  SUNDAY DISPATCH (May 14, 1848-Dec. 27, 1920) w
  Pub. & Ed. 1848-1869 Lawlor, Everett & Hincken
          (John Lawlor, Robert Everett, Elias Hincken)
      1869-1882 Everett & Hincken
      1882-1887 E. J. Hincken
      1887-1889 Sunday Dispatch Co.
      1889-1892 Leader Publishing Co.
      1892-1900 Dispatch Publishing Co.
      1900-1908 James L. Hall
      1908-1920 Dispatch Publishing Co.
  Ed. 1848-1890 Thompson Westcott
     1848-1890 James Kees

SUNDAY DISPATCH, *continued*

    1889-1892 W. Y. Leader
    1892-1920 James L. Hall
 P   1890 June 6-1912 June 30
 PCHi 1857 Aug. 2
 PDoHi 1857 Aug. 2
    1869 Dec. 5
    1871 Sept. 17
    1903 July 19
 PHi ♦ 1848 Oct. 15-1884 Mar. 23
    missing
    1848 Oct. 22
    1878 Oct. 20, 27
    1880 Oct. 31, Nov. 7
    1881 Feb. 6 ,Mar. 27, Apr. 3, 10, 24, May 1, Sept. 25, Oct. 2, 9, 23, 30, Nov. 6, 13
    1882 Jan. 29, Feb. 5, 12, 19, 26, Mar. 5, 12, 19, 26, June 25, Dec. 3, 31
    1883 Apr. 1-1884 Feb. 17
 PP   1848 May 21-1884 Dec. 28
    1917 Aug. 31
    1918 Dec. 29
 PPCHi 1869 Jan. 3-17, Feb. 7-29, Mar. 14-Apr. 11, May 2-July 4, 18-Aug. 1, Sept. 5-Oct. 17, 31-Nov. 7, 21-Dec. 26
 PPeS 1861 Nov. 17
    1882 Nov. 9
 PPFfHi 1853 Mar. 27
    1863 Mar. 8
 PPL 1848 May 14-1882 Dec. 31
    1905 May 7-1906 Jan. 28
    1906 Feb. 11-1908 Dec. 27
 PPM 1848 May 14, 1882 May 7
    [1860-1870]
 PUB 1848 May 14 complete to
    1849 May (13)-July (22)-Oct. (21) complete to
    1851 May (11)-June (15) complete to
    1859 May (2), 23 complete to
    1865 Apr. (23)-Dec. (10)-24 complete to
    1866 Jan. (21)-Apr. (15) complete to
    1889 Oct. 20
    1890 June 1-1920 Dec. 26
 PU   1867 Jan. 1-1869 Dec. 31
 PWcHi 1858 Mar. 28
    1862 June (1)
    1863 July 26
    1865 May 28
    1866 Sept. (2)
    1875 Mar. 28
    1876 Aug. (13)
    1886 Nov. 14
    continued as

PHILADELPHIA DISPATCH (Jan. 2, 1921-July 20, 1924) w
 Pub. 1921-1924 Dispatch Publishing Co.
  Ed. 1921-1924 John I. Dillion
  PUB 1921 Jan. 2-1924 July 20
  PP   1922 June 4
     1924 Mar. 4

PHILADELPHIA COUNTY 289

              continued as
    SUNDAY DISPATCH (July 27, 1924†) w
      Pub. 1924-1941   Philadelphia Dispatch Publishing Co.
      Ed. 1924-1938   John I. Dillion
           1938-1941   Bernard Haggerty
        % *Philadelphia Dispatch*
      PUB   1924 July 27†
      PP   1926 Apr. 4
                      1927 Sept. 11-1928 May 27
                      1928 June 10†
      PHi ♦   1940 Nov. 3

SUNDAY EVENING REPORTER   (1914-15) sun rep
      Pub. 1914-1915   C. Scott Richards
      Ed. 1914-1915   Edward J. Radcliffe
      PHi ♦   1915 Oct. 17

SUNDAY EVENING TIMES, THE (1913)
      PHi ♦   1913 June (29) (Vol. 5, No. 349)

SUNDAY GAZETTE, THE   (ca. 1831) w ♦
      Pub. 1831   Alexander Turnbull

SUNDAY GLOBE (1848-1852) w
    SUNDAY PAPER (Aug. 18, 1848-1849) w ♦
      Pub. 1848-1849   Robert F. Christy & Co.
      Ed. 1849   Dr. Thomas Dunn English
                          J. N. Willis Geist
              continued as
    SUNDAY GLOBE (1849-1852) w
      Pub. 1849-1852   Robert F. Christy & Co.
      Ed. 1849-1852   Dr. Thomas Dunn English
                          J. M. Willis Geist
      PHi ♦   1850 Sept. 13

SUNDAY GRAPHIC   (1890-1895) w ind ♦
      Pub. 1890-1893   Graphic Publishing Co.
           1893-1905   Josph F. Turner
           1895   Drexel-Biddle & Bradley Publishing Co.
      Ed. 1890-1893   J. Irving Dillon
           1893-1895   Josph F. Turner
           1895   A. J. Drexel Biddle & Alexander Bradley

SUNDAY HERALD   (1879-1881) w ♦
      Pub. 1879-1881   Andrew Moulton & Co.
      Ed. 1879-1881   George L. Myers

SUNDAY ITEM   (1847-1910), see Item

SUNDAY ITEM (1916-1931) w sun rep
  Pub. 1916-1918   James J. Wray
       1918-1926   Philadelphia Item Co.
       1926-1931   James J. Wray
  Ed. 1916-1931   James J. Wray
       PP   1928 May 6-1930 Nov. 30

SUNDAY LEADER (1870) w ♦
  Pub. & Ed. 1870   Wm. Y. Leader

SUNDAY LEADER (1876-1879) w ♦
  Pub. & Ed. 1877-1878   Robert M. McWade
            1878-1879   John Dunn

SUNDAY LEDGER, THE (ca. 1848-1853) w ♦
  Pub. 1848-1853   George W. Ward

SUNDAY MAIL AND EXPRESS (1891-1892) w ♦
  Pub. & Ed. 1891-1892   Harold S. Silberman

SUNDAY MERCURY (1851-1890), see Mercury and Siftings

SUNDAY MERCURY (1890-1896), see Mercury

SUNDAY MIRROR (1875-1883) w ♦
  Pub. 1880-1883   Wallis, Holah & Ashbrook
       1883   Wallis & Ashbrook

SUNDAY MORNING (1869-1870) w ind ♦
  Pub. & Ed. 1869-1870   J. R. Flanigan

SUNDAY MORNING TIMES, see Taggarts Sunday Times

SUNDAY NEWS (1884-1889), see Daily News (1879-1915)

SUNDAY NOVELTY (Nov. 25, 1855-Jan. 6, 1856) w
  Pub. & Ed. 1855-1856   D. M. Hardin Andrews and Fred H. G. Brotherton
       PHi ♦   1856 Jan. 6 (Vol. 1, No. 7)

SUNDAY PAPER, see Sunday Globe

SUNDAY POST, see Philadelphia Post

SUNDAY PRESS, THE (1853) w ♦
  Pub. 1853   James Mortimer

PHILADELPHIA COUNTY

SUNDAY PRESS (1865-1867) (1881-1920), see Press

SUNDAY PRESS AND MIRROR OF THE TIMES
(1874-1881) w ♦
    Pub. & Ed. 1874-1875 W. Broadman
               1875-1877 A. E. Smythe
               1877-1881 Dennis F. Dealy
               Merged with the *Philadelphia Press,* 1881 (q.v.)

SUNDAY REPUBLIC (Oct. 27, 1867-Nov. 18, 1888) w rep *
    Pub. 1867-1869 Dunkel, Hales & Co.
                     (Aaron K. Dunkel, Nathan S. Hales)
         1869-1879 Dunkel, Hales & Co.
                     (Aaron K. Dunkel, Nathan S. Hales,
                     Thomas S. Keyser, Thomas W. Swain)
         1879-1885 Hales, Keyser & Swain
         1885-1887 Thomas S. Keyser
         1887-1888 Sunday Republican Publishing Co.
    Ed. 1867-1869 J. R. Dunglison
        1885-1888 J. R. Dunglison
                     Anne E. McDowell
    P 1876 Oct. 22-1880 Oct. 10
    PHi ♦ 1868 June 21, 28
             1875 Aug. 8
    PP 1868 July 19, 26, Sept. 20
          1881 Sept. 25
          1888 Nov. 18
    PWcHi 1879 Nov. 23

SUNDAY REPUBLICAN (1893-1895) w rep ♦
    Pub. 1895 Sunday Republican Co.

SUNDAY SUN, THE (1836) w ♦
    Pub. 1836 Putman & Creamer

SUNDAY SUN, THE (1843) w ♦
    Pub. 1843 John Lawlor

SUNDAY SUN (Apr. 9, 1876-Apr. 1, 1877||) w
    Pub. & Ed. 1876-1877 John H. Fort
    PPL 1877 Apr. 1

SUNDAY TRANSCRIPT (1847-Sept. 12, 1937) w ind
    Pub. 1856-1857 Johnson Greene & Co.
                    (John S. Jackson, George W. L. Johnson, E. W. C.
                    Greene)

	1857-1861	John S. Jackson
	1861-1864	Greene & Co.
		(E. W. C. Greene and Thomas Hawkesworth)
	1864-1880	E. W. C. Greene
	1880-1894	Sunday Transcript Co.
	1899-1917	Transcript Publishing Co.
	1917-1918	J. S. Knight
	1918-1920	Jos. Broadnap
	1920-1933	Clement H. Congdon
	1933-1937	Long Publishing Co.
Ed.	1856-1894	E. W. C. Greene, George W. L. Johnson, Madame Julie de Margurettes, Edward G. Webb, Wm. M. Bunn, John Strafford
	1908-1914	F. G. Liggett
	1914-1916	S. Applebaum
	1916-1918	J. S. Knight
	1918-1920	Jos. Broadnap
	1920-1937	Clement H. Congdon

P   1864 Mar. 27
PHi ♦ 1860 Aug. 12
        1862 Sept. 14, Dec. 28
        1863 Jan. 4, Mar. 8
        1864 May 8, Sept. 18
        1865 Apr. 16, 23
        1917 July 22
PP   1859 Jan. 9, Feb. 6-13, Mar. 13, May 15
        1868 July 5, 19, 26, Aug. 30, Sept. 13, 20
        1918 June 2
        1920 May 9
        1924 Apr. 6
        1926 Apr. 6
        1929 June 16, Oct. 27, Dec. 29
        1930 June 5, Dec. 28
        1931 July 12, 26-1937 Sept. 12
PPeS 1862 Sept. 7
PPFfHi 1869 Feb. 14

SUNDAY TRIBUNE (Sept. 13, 1874-Sept. 5, 1875) w

Pub. & Ed. 1874-1875 William Moran
PP   1874 Sept. 13-Dec. 27
        1875 Jan. 3-31, Feb. 14, June 20-Sept. 5
PPL   1874 Sept. 13-1875 Jan. 31
        1875 Feb. 14, June 20-Sept. 5

SUNDAY WORLD (1876-1907) w rep

Pub. & Ed. 1876-1907 H. A. Mullen
PCHi   sun 1902 May 25
PDoHi sun 1881 July 3
PP   sun 1881 Sept. 25
PPot   sun 1884 June 8

SUPPORTER, OR DAILY REPAST, THE (Apr. 4, 1800-Nov. 10, 1800) d w *

Pub. 1800   John Nicholson
            (Isaac Ralston, Francis & Robert Bailey and Thomas Bedwell, printers)

PHILADELPHIA COUNTY   293

            PDoHi   1800 Apr. 23
            PPiHi   1800 Apr. 15

SVIT   (1897-1907) w for ♂
        Pub. 1906-1907   Alexander A. Nemolovsky

TABLOID   (1933-1934) w
        QUAKER CITY BREVITY (Mar. 31, 1933-Sept. 15, 1933) w
        Pub. & Ed. 1933   Walter Gold
            PP   1933 Apr. 14-Sept. 15
                          continued as
        GRAPHIC NEWS (Sept. 29, 1933) w
        Pub. & Ed. 1933   Walter Gold
            PP   1933 Sept. 29
                          continued as
        TABLOID NEWS (Oct. 6, 1933-Oct. 27, 1933) w
        Pub. 1933   Walter Gold
            PP   1933 Oct. 6-27
                          continued as
        TABLOID (Nov. 3, 1933-Feb. 2, 1934) w
        Pub. & Ed. 1933-1934 Walter Gold
            PP   1933 Nov. 3-1934 Feb. 2

TACONY NEW ERA   (1885-1915), see New Era

TACONY TIMES   (1925-1929) w rep ♂
        Pub. & Ed. 1925-1929 John B. Quinan

TAGEBLATT,   see Philadelphia Tageblatt

TAGGARTS SUNDAY TIMES   (1863-1901) w *
        SUNDAY MORNING TIMES (Dec. 6, 1863-Nov. 29, 1874) w *
        Pub. 1863-1869   Robert C. Smith & Co.
                          (J. Travis Quigg and Wardale G. McAllister)
            1869-1874   John H. Taggart & Son
        Ed. 1863-1869   F. T. S. Darley
             1869-1874   John H. Taggart & Son
            PCHi   1870 Sept. 18
            PHi   1869 Nov. 14-1874 Nov. 29
            PP   1865 Apr. 30
                          1868 July 19-26, Sept. 20
            PPeS   1865 Apr. 23
            PPL   1869 Nov. 14-1870 Sept. 4
                          1874 Nov. 29
            PPM   1870 Sept. 11-1874 Nov. 29
            PWcHi   1865 Apr. 16
                          continued as
        PHILADELPHIA SUNDAY TIMES (Dec. 6, 1874-Sept. 18, 1881)
            w *
        Pub. & Ed. 1874-1881 John H. Taggart & Son

TAGGARTS SUNDAY TIMES, *continued*
    PHi   1874 Dec. 6-1881 Sept. 18
    PPL   1874 Dec. 6-1881 Sept. 18
    PPM   1874 Dec. 6-1875 Nov. 28
                1876 Jan. 1-1881 Sept. 18
            continued as
    TAGGARTS PHILADELPHIA SUNDAY TIMES (Sept. 25, 1881-Nov. 16, 1884) w
Pub. & Ed. 1881-1884 John H. Taggart & Son
    PHi   1881 Sept. 25-1884 Nov. 16
    PPL   1881 Sept. 25-1884 Nov. 16
    PPM   1881 Sept. 25-1882 Nov. 19
                1883 Nov. 25-1884 Nov. 16
            continued as
    TAGGARTS SUNDAY TIMES (Nov. 23, 1884-Nov. 13, 1887) w ind dem
Pub. & Ed. 1884-1887 John H. Taggart & Son
    PHi   1884 Nov. 23-1887 Nov. 13
    PPL   1884 Nov. 30-1885 Mar. 29
                1885 Apr. 12-June 21, July 5-1887 Nov. 13
    PPM   1884 Nov. 30-1887 Nov. 13
            continued as
    TAGGARTS TIMES (Nov. 20, 1887-June 10, 1900) w ind dem *
Pub. & Ed. 1887-1893 John H. Taggart & Son
            1893-1896 John H. Taggart's Sons
            1896-1900 The John H. Taggart Publishing Co.
Ed.   1893-1896 Wm. M. Taggart
            1896-1900 Wm. M. & Harry E. Taggart
    PCHi   1893 Nov. 12
    PDoHi   1889 Jan. 27
                1890 Mar. 30
    PHi   1887 Nov. 20-1897 Oct. 31
    PPL   1887 Nov. 20-1900 June 10
    PPM   1887 Nov. 20-1900 June 10
            continued as
    TAGGARTS SUNDAY TIMES (June 17, 1900-1901) w
Pub. & Ed. 1900-1901 Samuel E. Hudson and Robert Haight
    PPL   1900 June 17-1901 Jan. 20
    PPM   1900 June 17-Oct. 28

TAUTA (The Nation) (1926-1927) w for ♪
    Pub. 1926-1927   Tauta Publishing Co.

TELEPHONE (1884-1898), see Philadelphian (West Philadelphia)

TEMPERANCE ADVOCATE AND LITERARY REPOSITORY (1841-1843) sm * ♪
    Pub. & Ed. 1841-1843 Lewis C. Levin
                          Samuel C. Atkinson & Co.
                          Absorbed by *Temperance Standard* and title changed to *Temperance Advocate and Standard*

TEMPERANCE ADVOCATE AND STANDARD
(1840-1844) w tw *
    WEEKLY STANDARD (1840-1841) w * ♦
    Pub. 1840-1841   Merrihew & Thompson, printers
                    continued as
    TEMPERANCE STANDARD (Dec. 9, 1841-July 1, 1843) tw *
    Pub. 1841-1843   Merrihew & Thompson, printers
    PWcHi   1842 Jan. 1
                    United with the *Temperance Advocate and Literary Repository*
                    continued as
    TEMPERANCE ADVOCATE AND STANDARD (1843-1844) sm * ♦
    Pub. & Ed. 1843-1844   Lewis C. Levin
                             Samuel C. Atkinson & Co.
                             United with *Saturday American* to form *Saturday American and Temperance Advocate* (q.v.)

TEMPLE OF REASON, THE (Feb. 14, 1801-Feb. 19, 1803||) w
    Pub. 1801-1802   Dennis Driscol
          1802-1803   Published for the Proprietors
                       Published in New York from Nov. 8, 1800-Feb. 7. 1801 when paper removed to Philadelphia
    P   1801 Apr. 29-Aug. 12

TICKLER, THE (Sept. 16, 1807-Nov. 17, 1813||) w
    Pub. 1807-1808   George Helmbold, Jr.
          1808-1812   George Helmbold
          1812-1813   Henry K. Helmbold
    Ed. 1807-1813   Toby Scratch'em J. R. S.
    P   1809 Mar. 11-1810 Jan. 31
    PDoHi   1807 Nov. 25
    PGHi   1812 Feb. 12
    PHi   1807 Sept. 16-1813 Nov. 10
    PHHi   1807 Nov. 25
                    1808 Nov. 23
    PLaHi   1808 Jan. 20-1810 Mar. 21
    PPot   1809 June 7
    PPotW   1809 June 7
    PRHi   1810 Sept. 26-Oct. 3
                    1811 Jan. 16-1812 Mar. 18
                    (1811 May 29)
                    (1812 Jan. 22, Feb. 26, Mar. 11)
    PYHi   1812 Feb. 12

TIMES (1876-1902) d w ind *
    Pub. 1876-1900   Frank McLaughlin
          1900-1902   Philadelphia Times Company
                       (1900, Charles Kindred, Pres.)
                     (1901-1902, Adolph S. Ochs, Pres.)
    Ed. 1876-1900   Alexander McClure
                     A weekly edition was published, *Philadelphia Weekly Times* (1877-1902)

TIMES, *continued*

    P-M
        1876 Sept. 21, Nov. 10, 11
        1879 Dec. 17
        1881 July 4, Sept. 24, Oct. 1
        1882 Oct. 25
        1883 Oct. 2
        1885 Mar. 5, 14, July 24, Aug. 10, Dec. 2
        1886 July 4
    PBf   1881 Mar. 29, Apr. 2, July 27
    PBloHi   1885 July 24
    PBMa   d 1897 Apr. 28
    PCHi   1884 July 24, Nov. 30
        1887 Sept. 16
        1888 Mar. 14
        1902 Aug. 11
    PDoHi   1876 Nov. 10
        1879 June 29
       w 1880 June 5
        1881 May 21, June 5, July 3, Sept. 21
        1882 Jan. 26, July 1
        1884 Mar. 30
        1885 Mar. 14, July 23, 24, Aug. 9
        1887 Sept. 15-18
        1888 Mar. 13, 15, 17, 18, June 7, 16
        1889 Mar. 3, May 1, June 6, 9, Sept. 10
        1893 June 25
    PEbHi   1889 June 1
        1899 Feb. 12
    PHi   1876 Jan. 1-1884 Dec. 31
        1901 Jan. 1-1902 Aug. 1
    PHHi w 1877 May 12
       d 1879 June 21
        1897 Feb. 3
    PMcC   1876 Jan. 28, May 11, July 5, 24, Aug. 9, 10, 21
    PMedD   1884 Nov. 30
    PMilt   1879 Mar. 28
    PMtHi   [1876 June 3-1877 Jan. 1]
    PNhF   1881 Apr. 5
        1887 May 1
    PP   1876 May 1-June 1, 3-31, July 2-3, 5-Aug. 27, 29-31, Sept. 29, Oct. 9
        1877 Jan. 1-9, 11-July 3, 5-31, Aug. 2-4, 7-22, 24-Oct. 1, 2, 4-Nov. 6, 8-10, 14-16, 19, Dec. 5, 7-10, 12, 14-21, 24-1878 Jan. 16
        1878 Jan. 18-20, 22-23, 25-Apr. 22, 24-May 9, 11-July 16, 18-Aug. 28, 30-Sept. 21, 23-28, 30-Oct. 11, 14-19, 21-24, 26, 28-30, Nov. 1, 2, 4-9, 11-16, 18-23, 25-Dec. 7, 9-14, 16, 19-21, 23-28, 30-1879 Jan. 10
        1879 Jan. 13-18, 20-25, 27-Feb. 1, 3-8, 10-15, 17-22, 24-Mar. 1, 3-8, 10-15, 17-22, 24-29, Apr. 1-5, 7-12, 14-19, 21-26, 28-29, May 2, 3, 5-9, 12, 13, 15-17, 19, 21-24, 26-30, June 2-7, 9-14, 16-21, 23-28, 30-July 5, 7-12, 14-19, 21-23, 25, 26, 28-Aug. 2, 4-8, 11-15, 18-23, 25-30, Sept. 1-6, 8-12, 15-20, 23-27, 29-Oct. 4, 6-9, 11, 13-18, 20-22, 24-27, 29-Nov. 1, 3-8, 10-15, 17-22, 24-29, Dec. 1-6, 8-13, 15-20, 22-27, 29-1880 Jan. 3

PHILADELPHIA COUNTY 297

           1880 Jan. 5-10, 12-17, 19-24, 26-31, Feb. 2-7, 9-14,
                16-21, 23-28, Mar. 1-6, 8-13, 15-20, 22-27, 29-
                Apr. 3, 5, 6, 8-10, 12-17, 19-24, 26, 28-May 1,
                3-8, 10-15, 18-22, 24, 25, 27-29, 31-June 4, 7-12,
                14-19, 21-26, 28-July 3, 5-10, 12-17, 19-24, 26-31,
                Aug. 2-7, 9-12, 14, 16-21, 23-28, 30-Sept. 4,
                6-11, 13-18, 20-25, 27-Oct. 2, 4-9, 11-16, 18-23,
                25-Nov. 6, 8-13, 15-20, 22-27, 29-Dec. 4, 6, 11,
                13-18, 20-25, 27-1881 Jan. 1
           1881 Jan. 3-8, 10-15, 17-22, 24-29, 31-Feb. 5, 7-9,
                11, 12, 14-19, 21-26, 28-Mar. 5, 7-12, 14-19, 21-26,
                28-Apr. 2, 4-9, 11-16, 18-23, 25-30, May 2-7,
                9-14, 16-21, 23-28, 30-June 4, 6-11, 13-18, 20,
                22-25, 27-July 2, 4-9, 11-16, 18-23, 25-Aug. 6,
                8-13, 15-20, 22-27, 29-Sept. 3, 5-10, 12-17, 19-24,
                26-Oct. 1, 3-8, 10-15, 16-22, 24-29, 31-Nov. 5,
                7-12, 14-19, 21-26, 28-Dec. 3, 5-10, 12-17, 19-24,
                26-1882 Jan. 7
           1882 Jan. 9-14, 16-21, 23-28, 30-Feb. 4, 6-11, 13-18,
                20-25, 27-Mar. 4, 6-11, 13-18, 20-25, 27-Apr.
                1, 3-8, 10-15, 17-22, 24-29, May 1-6, 8-13, 15-20,
                22-27, 29-June 3, 5-10, 12-17, 19-24, 26-July 1,
                3-8, 10-15, 17-22, 24-29, 31, Aug. 5, 7-12, 14-19,
                21-29, 31-Sept. 2, 4-9, 11-16, 18-23, 25-30, Oct.
                2-7, 9-14, 16-21, 23-28, 30-Nov. 4, 6-11, 13-18,
                20-25, 27-Dec. 2, 4-9, 11-16, 18-23, 25-1883 Mar.
                12
           1887 Sept. 15
           1889 June 27, Sept. 12, Dec. 16
           1890 Mar. 18, 19
           1891 Jan. 18
           1892 Feb. 12, Mar. 9, Aug. 17
           1893 Jan. 28, Dec. 20
           1894 Oct. 1-Dec. 31
           1897 Apr. 1-June 30, Oct. 1-1898 Mar. 31
           1901 Apr. 1-June 30
       sun 1888 Jan. 15
   d & sun 1901 July 1-Sept. 30
PPeS   1886 Oct. 12
           1890 Mar. 6
           1897 May 15
PPiHi   1879 Dec. 16
           1898 July 10
PPM   1875 Mar. 13-1879 June 30
           1880 Jan. 1-1890 Dec. 31
           1901 Jan. 1-Mar. 31
           1902 Jan. 1-Mar. 31
         w [1877 Mar.-1890 Feb.]
PPot   1902 Jan.-Mar. 31
           1881 Sept. 20
           1884 Nov. 5
           1885 July 24, Nov. 26
           1886 Nov. 3, 9
           1887 Sept. 11, 15, 16
           1888 June 16, 17, 24, Aug. 6, Nov. 7
           1894 Oct. 8, Nov. 7
PSF   1881 Sept. 27
PSuHi   1877 May 3-July 7, Sept. 8

TIMES, *continued*

PU
    1875 Mar. 13-1883 Apr. 12
    1893 Jan. 1-1895 Dec. 31

PWaHi   1893 Jan. 28

PWcHi
d 1875 May 27, Sept. 21, 22
    1876 Apr. 15, July 4, Aug. 26, Nov. 1, 3, 6, 8, 9-11, 14-18, 23-25, 27, 30, Dec. 4, 6, 7, 13, 16, 26-28
    1877 Jan. 1, 2, 4, 6, 8, 10, 11-13, 16, 18, 19, 23-25, 29, Feb. 1, 2, 5, 7-9, 12-21, 24-Mar. 9, 13, 15-17, 20, 21, 23-27, 29-Apr. 4, 7, 9-11, 19-May 3, 5-18, 21-25, 28-30, June 1-26, 28, 29, July 2-6, 10-Aug. 3, 7-10, 13-15, 18-24, 28-31, Sept. 4, 5, 7-12, 15-21, 25, 28, Oct. 1-22, 24, Nov. 1, 3, 5, 6, 8-13, 15, 16, 19-Dec. 12, 14-19, 21-1878 Feb. 11
    1878 Feb. 13-16, 19-27, Mar. 25-Apr. 15, 17, 19-25, May 2-4, 8, 16-21, 31, June 1-5, 7-18, 26, 28, July 1-5, 9, 11, 13, 16-19, 23, 29, 30, Oct. 4, 7, 11, 12, 15, 18, 23, 24, 28-30, Nov. 1-4, 8-16, 19-22, 27, 30-Dec. 9, 11-17, 19-31
d 1879 Jan. 1, 3-Feb. 20, 22-28, Apr. 12, 19, May 12, 21, 24, 28, 31, June 10, 14, 17-19, 23, 24, 26-28, July 5, 7, 12-15, Aug. 11, 13-16, 20, 22, 25-28, Sept. 1, 2, 4, 5, 23
    1880 June 9, Nov. 3, Dec. 11
    1881 Mar. 5, May 9, 14, June 11, Aug. 18, 19, Sept. 12, 20, 22, 23, Oct. 5
    1884 Apr. 3, 17, June 17
    1885 Aug. 27, Dec. 18
    1886 Mar. 26, Apr. 19, Nov. 3
    1887 Mar. 23, Sept. 17
    1888 Jan. 15, Mar. 13
    1889 Apr. 29, June 1-18
    1890 Mar. 15, Oct. 3, 7
d 1893 Apr. 28, 25
    1895 Sept. 14, Dec. 21
    1896 Sept. 29, Nov. 4
    1897 Jan. 27, Mar. 5, Apr. 27, 28, May 14, 15
    1898 Feb. 25, Mar. 29, Apr. 4, Oct. 25, 26
    1899 Apr. 3, June 10
    1901 Feb. 28, Mar. 30
w 1877 Apr. 7, May 5, 12, 26, July 21-1878 Jan. 19
    1878 Apr. 13, June 1
sun 1878 Nov. 24, Dec. 8, 15
    1879 Jan. 19, 26, June 15, Aug. 17, Dec. 21
    1881 July 3, Dec. 25
    1886 July 4, Oct. 3, Nov. 7
    1887 Apr. 10
    1889 June 2-16
    1890 Feb. 16
    1893 Mar. 19, Apr. 30, June 11
    1897 Jan. 31, May 16
    1898 May 15, Oct. 30, Dec. 25
    1901 Sept. 8-22
    1902 June 8, Aug. 10

PWcNW   1876 Nov. 11, 15

PHILADELPHIA COUNTY 299

        PWcT   1889 Mar. 3
                        1896 Feb. 23
                        1897 Dec. 5
                        1899 Apr. 6, Dec. 3
                        1900 Sept. 11
                        sold to *Public Ledger,* 1902

TIMES, THE [1859] bw
    Pub. 1859   Joel Cook, Jr. & Co.
                         Wetherill & School
        PHi ♦   1859 Nov. 2, 16, 30, Dec. 14

TIMES AND DISPATCH (Jan. 1, 1871)
    P-M   1871 Jan. 1

TIOGA GUIDE (1935-1936||) w
    Pub. 1935-1936   Tioga Press
    Ed. 1935-1936   W. E. Delk
    Suspended from Nov. 14, 1935 to Dec. 26, 1935.
    PUB   1935 Apr.-1936 Mar. 26
    PP   1935 Aug. 27. Sept. 26-Nov. 7
                1936 Jan. 2-Mar. 26

TIOGA NEWS (1904†) w local non-part.
    Pub. & Ed. 1904-1906   Curtis Newspaper Union
                 1906-1925   E. M. Gordon
                 1925-1930   C. E. McAfee
                 1931-1941   Margaret E. Ocker
                 % *Tioga Home News, Home News*
    PUB   1922 June 15†
    PP   1930 Dec. 5-1939 Dec. 21
                1940 Jan. 4†

TIOGA WEEKLY, see Oakdale Weekly

TOWN ROVER AND WEEKLY CENSOR (Apr. 26, 1845) w
    %   *Town Rover; The Rover*
    PDoHi   1845 June 14

TOWN TATTLER (Apr. 4, 1868) w
    Pub. 1868   Renshaw and Rees
    PHi   1868 Apr. 4 (Vol. I, No. 1)

TRANGRAM or FASHIONABLE TRIFLER (1810)
    Ed. 1810   Alex Coxe, Mordecai Manassas
        In the first issue it was explained to the reader that the title was adopted because a Trangram was a strange thing, an odd thing, curiously contrived.
    PHi   [1810]

TRUE AMERICAN, THE (1797-1818) d w #
    MERCHANTS' DAILY ADVERTISER, THE (Jan. 16, 1797-June 30, 1798) d #
    Pub. 1797-1798   Thomas Bradford
           1798   Samuel F. Bradford
           PHi   1797 Jan. 16-1798 June 30
           PPL   1797 Feb. 7
                    1798 June 12, 29

TRUE AMERICAN, THE, *continued*
            continued as
    TRUE AMERICAN AND COMMERCIAL ADVERTISER, THE
      (July 2, 1798-July 9, 1815)   d   w   #
    Pub. 1798-1801   Samuel F. Bradford
         1801-1813   Thomas Bradford
         1813-1815   Elliot & Stiles
                    (James Elliot and Thomas T. Stiles)
    absorbed *Philadelphia Minerva* and started a weekly literary supplement, entitled *The Dessert to the True American,* July 14, 1798-Aug. 19, 1799.
      PDoHi   1798 Aug. 10
                    1815 Jan. 10, Feb. 21, Mar. 2
      PHi   1798 July 2-1813 Dec. 31
          w   1798 Sept. 8-1799 Jan. 19
      PLaHi   1805 Apr. 29-1806 Sept. 3
      PP   1798 Sept. 3
                    1799 Mar. 2, July 11, 26, Nov. 5, 18, 23
                    1800 Jan. 18, Feb. 15, May 2
                    1804 Apr. 16
          w   1798 Sept. 8-Nov. 10
                    1799 Jan. 19, July 19
      PPF   1799 Feb. 27
      PPL   1798 July 2-24, 26-31
                    1804 Feb. 20-Mar. 29, 31-Oct. 6, 9, 11-Dec. 31
                    1805 Jan. 2-Feb. 9
                    1808 Apr. 11-14, 16-1809 May 18
                    1809 May 20-1810 Sept. 25
                    1810 Sept. 27-1811 Apr. 13
                    1811 Apr. 19-Dec. 21, 24-1812 Jan. 2
                    1812 Jan. 4-May 23, 26-July 10, 13-1813 May 21
                    1813 May 24-July 8, 10-Aug. 4, 16-1815 Jan. 11
                    1815 Jan. 13-Mar. 9, 11-23, 25-Apr. 12, 14-July 8
          w   (8 issues, no dates given)
      PPM   1801 July 1-Aug. 19, 21-Dec. 31
                    1802 Aug. 3-Dec. 31
                    1814 Feb. 5, 15, 22, Mar. 11, Apr. 14, 16, May 25, 27, Sept. 2, Oct. 6, 8, Nov. 11, Dec. 9, 15, 21, 22, 24, 28, 30, 31
                    1815 Jan. 2, 4, 5, 17, 20, 21, 27, Feb. 3, 4, 8, 10, 23, Mar. 4, Apr. 25, 26, 28, May 16, 23, 31, June 12, 21, 22, 29, July 8
      PRHi   1812 Sept. 25
            continued as

    TRUE AMERICAN, THE (July 10, 1815-Mar. 7, 1818)   d   w   #
    Pub. 1815-1816   Thomas T. Stiles
         1816-1817   Stiles & Miner
                    (Charles Miner)
         1817-1818   Smith & Cummins
                    (Thomas Smith and Ebenezer Cummins)
                    title varies between July 10, 1815 and Nov. 29, 1817
      PDoHi   1815 Aug. 30
                    1816 July 18, Aug. 6, Sept. 30, Nov. 4, 6
                    1817 Apr. 28, May 14, July 23
         sw   1816 Dec. 11, 14
                    1817 Jan. 22-Feb. 18, 26, Mar. 1, 8, 19-29, Apr. 19, 30, May 7, Aug. 3, 9-16, 23, 27, Sept. 6
                    1818 Feb. 11-Mar. 7

PHILADELPHIA COUNTY 301

        PP   1817 Dec. 8-1818 Mar. 7
        PPL   1815 July 10
                     1816 Apr. 6, 9, 13-May 31, June 3-Sept. 14-1817
                     1817 Apr. 5-1818 Mar. 9, Apr. 3
        PPM   1815 July 10-12, 14, 19, 21, 26, Aug. 5, 12, 14, 17, 19, 21, 24, 28, Sept. 20, Oct. 4, 5, 7, Nov. 3, 4, 15, 27, Dec. 8, 12, 20, 28, 29
                     1816 Jan. 2, 20, 25, Feb. 7, 16, 17, 21, 22, 24, Mar. 18, Apr. 24, 27, May 4, 9, 13, 14, 20, 24-27, June 1-12, 22-29, July 6- 11, 18, 20, 23-27, 31, Aug. 12, 23, 27, Sept. 3, 4, 11, 14, 17, 20, 21, 25, 27, Oct. 5-7, Nov. 12, 15, 26, Dec. 25
        PRHi   1817 Sept. 29-Nov. 26
        PWbW   d 1816 Dec. 12
                  sw 1816 Sept. 18-Nov. 20
                     missing
                     1816 Oct. 23-Nov. 13, 16
                     On March 7, 1818, the paper was united with the *United States Gazette,* to form a new paper called *The Union or United States Gazette and True American.*

TRUE SUN (1848) d
        Pub. 1848   Charles B. Barrett
        Ed. 1848   Peter Sken Smith and Charles B. Barrett
        PHi ♦   1848 Mar. (7) (Vol 1, No. 38), 10, 15 (30)

TURN ZEITUNG, DIE (Oct. 24, 1850-Oct. 15, 1855) w
        Pub. 1850-1855 W. Rapp
        PPG   1854 Nov. 2-1855 Oct. 15

TWENTY-FIRST WARD ADVANCE (Manayunk) (1887-1909) w
ind rep
        ADVANCE (Manayunk) (1887-1907) w
        Pub. & Ed. 1887-1907 D. W. Seltzer
        PHi ♦   1887 Nov. (9)-1888 Feb. 15
                     1888 Feb. 27-Apr. 11, 25-May 2, 16-1889 **Mar. 6**
                     1889 Mar. 20-Nov. 27, Dec. 11-1890 June 4
                     1890 June 18-Aug. 6, 20, Sept. 3-1891 Jan. (7)-Feb. 26
                     1891 Mar. 11-18, Apr. 1, 15, 29, Aug. 12, 26-Sept. 23
                     continued as
        TWENTY-FIRST WARD ADVANCE (Manayunk) (1908-1909) w
             ♦
        Pub. & Ed. 1908-1909 H. S. Hehno

TWENTY-SIXTH AND THIRTY-SIXTH WARD NEWS (1889-1920) w local ♦
        TWENTY-SIXTH WARD NEWS (1889-1892) w ♦
        Pub. & Ed. 1889-1892 George O. Skipper
                     continued as
        TWENTY-SIXTH AND THIRTY-SIXTH WARD NEWS (1900-1920) w ♦
        Pub. & Ed. 1900-1911 George O. Skipper
                1911-1920 Mary Skipper

UJSAG (News) (1914-1916) w for ♦
    Pub. & Ed. 1914-1916 Joseph Remenyi

UNION, THE, OR UNITED STATES GAZETTE AND TRUE AMERICAN, see United States Gazette

UNITED STATES AND DOLLAR NEWSPAPER (1837-Oct. 1, 1842) w *
    WEEKLY LEDGER (1837-Apr. 1841) w * ♦
        continued as
    UNITED STATES AND DOLLAR NEWSPAPER (Apr. 1841-Oct. 1, 1842) w * ♦
        Merged with the *Saturday Evening Post.*

UNITED STATES BUSINESS JOURNAL, see United States Journal

UNITED STATES COMMERCIAL AND STATISTICAL REGISTER, see Hazard's United States Commercial and Statistical Register

UNITED STATES GAZETTE (1790-1847) sw w d fed. * #
    GAZETTE OF THE UNITED STATES (Nov. 3, 1790-Sept. 18, 1793) sw * #
    Pub. 1790-1793   John Fenno
        First established in New York Apr. 15, 1789, and moved to Philadelphia, where it continued publication with the issue of Nov. 3, 1790.

P	1790 Nov. 3-Sept. 8, 1793
PDoHi	1792 Feb. 1-Apr. 4
PHi	1790 Nov. 3-5, 7-9, 11-Dec. 29
	1791 Jan. 1-11, 13-25, 27-Mar. 18, 20-Apr. 23, 25, 26, 28-Dec. 31
	1792 Jan. 4-May 30, June 1, 3-8, 10-15, 17-26, 28-July 6, 8-10, 12, 13, 15-20, 22-Aug. 21, 23-31, Sept. 2-11, 13-29
	[1793 Feb. 20-Sept. 18]
PP	1790 Nov. 3-1793 Sept. 14
PPiUD	1790 Nov. 3-1791 Apr. 27
PPL	1791 June 1-8, 15-Dec. 31
PRHi	1790 Nov. 3-1791 Apr. 27
	1791 May 7-1792 May 30

        Paper suspended from Sept. 18, 1793 to Dec. 11, 1793, because of yellow fever epidemic and poor business conditions.
        continued as
    GAZETTE OF THE UNITED STATES AND EVENING ADVERTISER (Dec. 11, 1793-June 11, 1794) d * #
    Pub. 1793-1794   John Fenno

P	1793 Dec. 11-1794 June 11
PHi	[1793 Dec. 11-31]
	1794 Jan. 2-June 11
PPL	1793 Dec. 11, 13-1794 Mar. 31
	1794 Apr. 2, June 11

PHILADELPHIA COUNTY   303

continued as
GAZETTE OF THE UNITED STATES AND DAILY EVENING
   ADVERTISER (June 12, 1794-June 30, 1795) d * #
Pub. 1794-1795   John Fenno
   P   1794 June 12-1795 June 30
   PDoHi   1794 July 5
   PHi   1794 June 12-1795 June 30
   PPAP   1794 July 31, Aug. 14, 18, 23, 26, 30, Oct. 21, Nov. 5,
                      6, 8, 10, 15
                  1795 Apr. 25, 29, May 16, June 16
   PPL   1794 June 12-1795 June 30
            continued as
GAZETTE OF THE UNITED STATES (July 1, 1795-June 30, 1796)
   d * #
   July 1, 1795 as *Gazette of the United States;*
   July 2, 1795-Jan. 5, 1796 as *Gazette United States;*
   Jan. 6, 1796-June 30, 1796 as *Gazette of the United States*
Pub. 1795-1796   John Fenno
   P   1795 July 1-1796 June 30
   PHi   1795 July 1-1796 June 30
   PP   1795 July 1-Dec. 31
   PPi   1795 July 1-1796 Dec.
   PPL   1795 July 2-Dec. 31
                  1796 Jan. 2-Mar. 16, 18-May 16, 23, 25, 26, 28, 31-
                      June 30
   PWcHi   1796 Mar. 14
            continued as
GAZETTE OF THE UNITED STATES AND PHILADELPHIA
   DAILY ADVERTISER (July 1, 1796-June 24, 1800) d sw * #
Pub. 1796-1798   John Fenno
   1798-1800   John W. Fenno
   1800   Caleb P. Wayne
   P   1796 July 1-1800 June 24
   PAtM   1799 Oct. 9
   PDoHi   1798 Nov. 12
   PHi   1796 July 1-Dec. 30
                  1797 Feb. 2, 3, 6, 7, Apr. 11, 15, July 1-1800 June 24
   PP   1796 July 1-Dec. 31
                  1798 Jan. 1-1800 June 27
   PPL   1796 July 1-7, 11-Aug. 29, Sept. 17-Oct. 19, Nov. 2,
                      4-Dec. 22, 24-30
                  1797 Jan. 2-24, 26, 28-Aug. 27, 29-1798 Oct. 3
                  1798 Oct. 5-9, 11, 12, 15-24, 26-31, Nov. 2-1799 Mar.
                      21
                  1799 Mar. 23-Apr. 24, 26-Aug. 26, 28-Oct. 15, 17-
                      1800 June 24
   PPot   1797 Oct. 18
   PPotW   1797 Oct. 18
   PWcHi   1799 Jan. 28, June 29, Aug. 28
            continued as
GAZETTE OF THE UNITED STATES AND DAILY ADVER-
   TISER (June 28, 1800-Nov. 1, 1801) d * #
   d June 28, 1800-Nov. 1, 1801;
   sw Aug. 10, 1801-Sept. 11, 1801 as *Gazette of the United States;*
   sw Sept. 14, 1801-Nov. 2, 1801 as *Country Gazette of the United
      States*

UNITED STATES GAZETTE, *continued*

P	d	1800 June 28-1801 Nov. 1
PHi	d	1800 June 28-1801 Nov. 1
PMedD	d	1800 Aug. 1
PP	d	1800 June 28-Dec. 31
	sw	1801 Aug. 7/10, 10/13, 14/17, 18/20, 21/24, 25/27, 28/Sept. 1, 1/4, 4/7, 8/11, 11/14, 15/17, 18/21, 22/24, 24/28, 28/Oct. 1, 2/5, 5/8, 9/12, 13/16, 16/19, 26/29, 30/Nov. 2
PPiUD	sw	1801 (Aug. 4-Nov. 2)
PPL	d	1800 June 28-Nov. 24, 26-1801 Apr. 2
		1801 Apr. 4-Oct. 31
PU	d	1801 Aug. 31, Sept. (7, 14, 21, 28), Oct. (5), (21-25)
	sw	1801 Aug. 10-Nov. 2

continued as

GAZETTE OF THE UNITED STATES (Nov. 2, 1801-Feb. 18, 1804)
d * #

   d Nov. 2, 1801-Feb. 18, 1804
  sw Nov. 6, 1801-Feb. 17, 1804 as *Gazette of the United States for the Country*

Pub. 1801-1802   for E. Bronson by Thomas Smith
      1802   Thomas Smith for the Proprietors (E. Bronson and Elihu Chauncey)
      1802-1804   by the Proprietors (Bronson & Chauncey)

P	d	1801 Nov. 2-1804 Feb. 9
PDoHi	d	1802 July 30, Oct. 6, 7, 20
		1803 Sept. 12, Oct. 17
		1804 Feb. 7, 9-17
PHi	d	1801 Nov. 2-1804 Feb. 18
PLaHi	d	1802 Aug. 3
PP	d	1803 Jan. 1-June 30
		1804 Jan. 1-Mar. 6
	sw	1801 Nov. 3/6, 7/10, 10/13, 13/17, 17/20, 24, 27, Dec. 1, 4, 8, 11, 18, 22, 24, 29
		1802 Jan. 1, 5, 8, 12, 15, 19, 22, 26, 29, Feb. 2, 5, 9, 12, 16, 19, 23, 26, Mar. 2, 5, 9, 12, 16, 19, 23, 26, 30, May 4, 7, 11, 14, 18, 21, 25, 28, June 1, 8, 11, 15, 18, 22, 25, 29, July 2, 6, 9, 13, 16, 20, 23, 30, Aug. 3, 6, 10, 13, 17, 20, 24, 27, 31, Sept. 3, 7, 10, 14, 17, 21, 24, 28, Oct. 1, 5, 8, 12, 15, 19, 22, 26, 29, Nov. 2, 5, 9, 12, 16, 19, 23, 26, 30, Dec. 3, 7, 10, 14, 17, 21, 24, 28, 31
		1803 Jan. 4, 7, 11, 14, 18, 21, 25, 28, Feb. 1, 4, 8, 11, 15, 18, 22, 25, 29, Mar. 1, 4, 8, 11, 15, 18, 22, 25, 29, Apr. 1, 5, 8, 12, 15, 19, 22, 26, 29, May 3, 6, 10, 17, 27, 31, June 3, 7, 10, 17, 21, 24, 28, July 8, 25, Aug. 2, 5, 9, 12, 16, 20, 23, 27, 30, Sept. 2, 6, 13, 16, 20, 23, 27, 30, Oct. 4, 7, 28, Nov. 4, 11, 18, 22, 29, Dec. 6, 9, 13, 20, 23, 27, 30
PPiUD	sw	1801 Nov. 11-Dec. 31
		1802 Jan. 1-Feb. 18, 20-Mar. 1, 3, 4, 6-Apr. 15, 17-May 3, 5-Aug. 26, 28-Sept. 7
		1803 Jan. 4-May 12, 14-19, 21-23, 25-June 13, 15, 16, 18-30, July 2-4, 6-11, 13, 23-28, 30-Aug. 18, 20-Sept. 7, 9-18, 20-22, 24-Oct. 10, 12-31, Nov. 2-24, 26-Dec. 1-16, 18-31
		1804 Jan. 1-Feb. 13, 15-17

PHILADELPHIA COUNTY 305

    PPL   d 1801 Nov. 2-1802 Apr. 15
                     1802 Apr. 17-1803 Jan. 7
                     1803 Jan. 10-1804 Jan. 24
                     1804 Jan. 26-Feb. 18
    PU   d 1801 Dec. (8, 14, 21, 28)
                     1802 Jan. 4, 11, Feb. 1, 8, 15, 22, Mar. 8, 22
               sw 1801 Nov. 6-Dec. 29
                     1802 Jan. 5-Dec. 31

                    continued as

UNITED STATES GAZETTE (Feb. 20, 1804-Mar. 7, 1818) d sw
* #
  d Feb. 20, 1804-Mar. 7, 1818;
  sw Feb. 21, 1804-Mar. 7, 1818 as *United States Gazette for the Country*
Pub. 1804-1805   for the Proprietors (Enos Bronson and Elihu Chauncey)
     1805-1807   for the Proprietor (Enos Bronson)
     1807-1818   Enos Bronson
Semi-weekly edition published, entitled *United States Gazette for the Country*
    P   d 1804 Feb. 20
                     1806 Dec. 30
              sw [1804 Feb. 21-1818 Mar. 8]
    P-M   d 1805 Aug. 16
    PAIR   d 1812 Jan. 2, June 20, July 6, 30, Sept. 14, Oct. 26, Dec. 2, 19
                     1813 Jan. 9, 23, Mar. 27, Apr. 7, Aug. 4, Sept. 18, 29, Oct. 30, Nov. 3, Dec. 8, 11
                     1814 Feb. 23, Mar. 14, May 4, Sept. 10
    PAtM   sw 1810 Oct. 4, 8, 11
                     1811 Apr. 18
                     1812 Apr. 27
    PBro   sw 1812 Nov. 8, 28
                     1817 Jan. 1
    PByL   d 1814 Nov. 2
              sw 1814 Nov. 2
    PCarlHi   sw 1813 (one issue)
                    [1814]
    PDoHi   d 1805 May 21, June 3, 4, 12, 24, July 1, 16, 17, Aug. 1, 12-14, 16, 19, 21-23, 26-28, 30, 31, Sept. 3-14, 17-24, 27-Oct. 8, 18-25, 28-Nov. 15, 18-22
                     1806 Jan. 2, 13-15, 17, 20, 22, 24-Feb. 5, 11, 12, 15-22, 27-Mar. 10, Sept. 20-23
                     1807 June 20, 29, July 27, Aug. 11-13, 15, 19-24, 26-Sept. 12, 16-23, 30-Oct. 6, 14-20, 23-Nov. 9, 21-Dec. 4, 17
                     1808 Apr. 19, July 20, Aug. 3, 9, 16, 19, 22, 24, 31, Sept. 2, 7, 10, 20, 21, 27, 30, Oct. 3, 5-8, 11-14
                     1809 Jan. 20, Oct. 24, 27, 30, Nov. 1, 4
                     1810 Feb. 28, Apr. 4, 6-9, 11-13
                     1811 May 13
                     1812 July 18, Nov. 13, Dec. 31
                     1813 Feb. 2, 4, Mar. 27, Oct. 20-26
                     1814 July 14
                     1815 Feb. 14, May 6, 8, 10-12, 16-19, June 28, Sept. 14

UNITED STATES GAZETTE, *continued*
           1816 Feb. 12, 15, July 20, 22, 26-Aug. 1
           1817 Oct. 20, 25, 30
           1818 Feb. 26
       sw 1805 Mar. 19, May 10
           1808 July 23
           1810 Mar. 12
           1812 Mar. 16
           1814 Oct. 15
           1815 June 3, July 15
           1816 Aug. 14
           1817 Oct. 1
PHi   d 1804 Feb. 20-1806 Dec. 31
           1807 July 1-1818 Mar. 8
       sw 1807
           1814 Oct. 15
           1815 Jan. 7-Sept. 30, Oct. 7-Dec. 27
PHoHi d 1813 Jan., Feb., July
PLaF   d 1813 Jan. 1-1915 Dec. 29
PLaHi sw [1805 Mar. 29-1806 Sept. 1]
PP   d 1804 Mar. 7-June 30, July 6, 12, 13, 18, 25, 26, Aug. 4
           1805 Jan. 1-1806 Dec. 31
           1807 July 1-1808 Apr. 9
           1808 Apr. 21, 28, May 26, 30, June 6, 9, 20, 23, July 1-1812 Feb. 8
           1812 Feb. 11-Apr. 17, 20, 21, 23-May 16, 19-June 30
           1813 Jan. 1-Dec. 31
           1814 Mar. 8-10, June 15, 26, Nov. 26
           1815 Jan. 1-Feb. 18, 21-Sept. 9, 12-1816 July 8
           1816 July 10, 12, 13, 16-22, 24-Sept. 7, 10-1817 Feb. 7
           1817 Feb. 10-1818 Mar. 24
           1818 Mar. 26-Aug. 4, 6-12, 17-27, 29-Sept. 19, 22-26, 29, Oct. 1-Nov. 16, 18-Dec. 30
       sw 1805 Jan. 1-June 28, July 5-Oct. 4, 11-Dec. 31
           1806 Jan. 3-Mar. 11, 18-21, 27-July 21, 28-Dec. 29
           1807 Jan. 1, 8-May 28, June 4-Oct. 12, 19-Nov. 9, 19, 26-Dec. 31
           1808 Jan. 4-Sept. 14, 21-24, Oct. 1-8, 15-Dec. 29
           1809 Jan. 2-July 10, 17-Dec. 28
           1810 July 1-Dec. 31
           1811 Jan. 3-Mar. 3, 11-18, 25-May 16, 23-Dec. 30
           1812 Apr. 2-16, 27, May 11-18, July 10, 27-Aug. 6, 13-20, 27-Sept. 3, 10-Oct. 22, 29-Nov. 16, 23-Dec. 12, 23-30
           1817 Jan. 1-Nov. 12, 19-Dec. 20, 26-31
           1818 Jan. 3-Mar. 7
PPi   sw 1813 Apr. 7-Dec. 8
PPiHi sw 1814 May 21, 28, June 8
PPiUD sw 1804 Feb. 21-Dec. 28
           1809 May 11-1810 Sept. 13
PPL   d 1804 Feb. 20-Mar. 29, 31-Oct. 9, 11-Dec. 31
           1805 Jan. 2-Feb. 9
           1808 Apr. 11-14, Dec. 16-1809 May 18
           1809 May 20-1810 Sept. 25
           1810 Sept. 27-1811 Apr. 13
           1811 Apr. 19-Aug. 26, 28-Dec. 21, 24-1812 Jan. 2
           1812 Jan. 4-May 23, 26-July 10, 13-1813 May 21
           1813 May 24-July 8, 10-Aug. 4, 16-1815 Jan. 11

PHILADELPHIA COUNTY

                    1815 Jan. 13-Mar. 9, 11-23, 25-Apr. 12, 14-1816 Apr. 6
                    1816 Apr. 9, 13-May 31, June 3-1817 Apr. 3
                    1817 Apr. 5-1818 Mar. 8
  PPot   sw 1806 Nov. 25
                  1808 Feb. 9
             d 1817 May 1
  PPoU   sw 1812 Aug.-Oct.
                  1814 Jan.-Apr.
                  1815 Jan.-Nov.
  PRHi   sw 1813 Jan. 29-Dec. 29
  PSom   sw 1812 Apr. 6-1814 Jan. 4
  PU   d 1812 Mar. 19, Aug. 11-Dec. 30
                  1813 Jan. 4-Aug. 9, 19-28, Oct. 4-8
                  1814 Jan. 4-Dec. 23
  PWbW   d 1814 Aug. 3-5, 7-9, 11, 12, 14, 15-31
                  1815 July 8-11, 13, 14, 16, 17, 18, 20, 21, 23-25, 27, 28, 30, 31
                  1816 Aug. 17-20, 22-31, Sept. 6, 8-10, 12-Dec. 31
                  1817 Jan. 1-Mar. 25, 27-May 20, 22-Aug. 26, 28-Sept. 16, 18-23, 25-Dec. 31
                  1818 Jan. 1-6, 8-Mar. 7
  PWcHi   d 1808 Apr. 19
                  1811 Mar. 18
              sw 1810 Oct. (11)
                  1815 Jan. 11
  PWeT   d 1812 Apr. 2, 14, 27, May 18, June 29, Aug. 20
              Merged with the *True American* (q.v.)
              to form

UNION, THE, OR UNITED STATES GAZETTE AND TRUE AMERICAN (Mar. 9, 1818-Mar. 31, 1823) d sw # *
  d Mar. 9, 1818-Mar. 31, 1823
  sw edition published, entitled *The Union.*
      United States Gazette and True American for the Country, Mar. 11, 1818-Mar. 31, 1823.
  Pub. 1818-1819   Bronson & Smith (Enos Bronson and Thomas Smith)
      1819   E. Bronson; for the Proprietors; for the Proprietor
      1819-1820   William Henry Sanford
      1820-1823   James G. Watts & Co. (George H. Hart)
  P   d [1820-1823]
              sw [1818 Mar. 11-1823 Mar. 31]
  P-M   d 1820 Nov. 3
                1821 June 19, Aug. 27
  PBL ♦   tw 1822 Oct. 1/2, Nov. 28/29, 30/Dec. 2, 3/4, 5/6, 7/9, 12/13, 14/16, 17/18, 19/20
  PDoHi   d 1818 Mar. 23, 24, 26-Apr. 4, 7-11, 14, 16-25, 28, 29, May 7, 9, 12-18, 20, 21, 23-27, July 25
                  1819 Jan. 13, Feb. 2, 3, 5, 6, 8-10, 13, Apr. 2, May 8, July 18, 22, 28, Aug. 4, 5, 7-9, 27, 28, 31, Sept. 1, 3, 4, 8, 11, 14, 15, 17, 21
              sw 1820 May 12
               d 1820 Aug. 18, 19, Sept. 4-19
                  1821 Oct. 29, 30, Nov. 6-9, 12-15, 21-23, 30, Dec. 5, 6
                  1822 Feb. 6, Apr. 30, May 1, Sept. 21-24
  PHi   d 1818 Mar. 9-1819 Dec. 31
                  1820 Sept. 1-1823 Mar. 31
              sw 1818 Mar. 11-Dec. 30
  PHsHi   d 1818 Aug. 1, 10

UNITED STATES GAZETTE, *continued*
PLaHi   sw 1818 Apr.-1822 Oct. 18
PNhE   d 1823 Feb. 19
PP   d 1818 Mar. 9-Aug. 4, 6-12, 17-27, 29-Sept. 19, 22-26, 29, Oct. 1-Nov. 16, 18-Dec. 30
           1820 Jan. 1-June 30
           1821 Apr. 1-1822 Mar. 3
           1822 Mar. 6-Dec. 31
        sw 1820 Feb. 4, 8, 11, 15, 18, 22, 25, 29, Mar. 3, 7, 10, 14, 21, 24, 28, 31, Apr. 4, 7, 11, 18, 21, 25, 28, May 2-5, 12, 16 19, 23, 26, 30, June 2, 6, 9, 13, 16, 20, 23, 27, 30, July 4, 7, 11, 14, 18, 21, 25, Aug. 1, 4, 8, 11, 15, 18, 22, 25, 29, Sept. 1, 5, 8, 12, 15, 19, 22, 26, 29, Oct. 3, 6, 13, 17, 20, 24, 31, Nov. 3, 7, 10, 14, 17, 21, 24, Dec. 1, 5, 8, 15, 19, 22, 25, 29
           1821 Jan. 2-Dec. 28
           1822 Jan. 4-18, 25, Feb. 5-19, 26-Mar. 8, 15-Apr. 5
PPL   d 1818 Mar. 9-Dec. 7, 9-25, 28-1819 Apr. 10
           1819 Apr. 13-May 1, 4-1821 Apr. 20
           1821 Apr. 23-May 15, 17-July 5, 7-Dec. 25, 27-1822 Apr. 5
           1822 Jan. 4-18, 25, Feb. 5-19, 26-Mar. 8, 15-Apr. 5
           1823 Jan. 1-Mar. 31
PWbW   d 1818 Mar. 10, 12, 13, 15-17, 19, 20, 22-24, 26, 27, 29-31
           1821 June 29, Aug. 10
           [1823]
PWcHi   d 1822 May 30, Aug. 10
        continued as
UNITED STATES GAZETTE (Apr. 1, 1823-June 30, 1847||) d sw w *
        d Apr. 1, 1823-June 30, 1847
        sw edition Apr. 1, 1823-June 30, 1847, entitled *United States Gazette for the Country;* w edition 1843-Apr. 3, 1849, entitled *Weekly United States Gazette;* tw 1823-1824, 1834-1835, entitled *The United States Gazette.*
        United States Gazette was absorbed by the *North American,* July 1, 1847 (q.v.).
Pub. 1826-1829   Hart & Chandler
     1829-1847   Joseph R. Chandler
P   sw [1823 Apr. 1-1847 June 30]
P-M   1830 July 20, 23
           1832 Jan. 19
           1833 Jan. 19
PB   1842 June 15
PBL ♦   d (1823 Apr. 14-July 24, Nov. 5)
           1824 Feb. 12-Apr. 9, Sept. 28
           1825 June 20, July 6-14, 16-Aug. 5, 8-15, 17, 22, 25-Sept. 5, 7, 9-22, 24-Oct. 29, Nov. 3, 11
           1826 Mar. 22, 29, Apr. 4, 13, 21, 26, May 3, 6, 10, 12-15, 17, 18, 20-27, 30-June 6, 8-20, 26, 27, July 1, 4, 6, 13, 18, 21, 22, 25, 26, 28-31, Aug. 2, 4, 7, 8, 12, 14-16, 19, 21, 24, 28-30, Sept. 13-19, 21-25, 27, 28, 30-Oct. 6, 12-16, 19, 21, 23-26, 28, Nov. 2, 4, 6, 8, 9, 11, 14, 15, 17, 18, 20
           1827 June 19, 22, July 3, Sept. 13, 25, Oct. 4, 8, 9, 19, 22, Nov. 19, Dec. 14, 20, 24, 25, 28, 31

PHILADELPHIA COUNTY 309

1828 Jan. 1, 7, June 6, 13, 24, 26, July 7, 8, 16, 18, 19, 23, 29, Aug. 5, 6, 13, 15, 18, 23, 26, 27, Sept. 1, 4, 11, 13, 16, 17, 19, 22, 27, Oct. 21
1829 Mar. 27-31, Apr. 2, 3, 6-10, 13-May 29, June 1-July 4, 8-Aug. 11, 12, 14-Dec. 17, 19-25, 28-31
1830 Jan. 2-Mar. 6, 9-11, 13-May 22, 25-June 29, July 1-5, 7-Oct. 12, 14-Nov. 11, 13-17, 19-Dec. 13, 15-30
1831 Jan. 1-Feb. 10, 12-23, 25-Mar. 2, 4-9, 11-16, 18-Apr. 1, 4-12, 15-July 4, 6-Aug. 2, 4, 5, 8, 11-16, 18-31, Sept. 2-5, 7-20, 22-Dec. 31
1832 Jan. 2-13, 16-26, 28-31, Feb. 2-15, 18-22, 24-Mar. 12, 14-June 6, 8-July 4, 7-Aug. 2, 4-30, Sept. 1-Oct. 15, Dec. 6-28, 31
1833 Jan. 1-3
1835 Mar. 18, July 22, Sept. 14
1836 Jan. 23, 25-29, Feb. 3-9, 12-18, 23-27, Mar. 1-4, 7, 8, 10, 11, 15, 17-23, 25-29, 31, Apr. 6-21, 27, 29, 30, May 4, 12, 14-June 3, 10-25, July 4, 6-Aug. 4, 6-26, 29-Sept. 2, 5, 7-12, 14-23, 26-28, 30, Oct. 1, 4-11, 13, 15-Nov. 17, 19-22, 24-Dec. 26, 28-1837 Jan. 18
1837 Jan. 20, 24, 26-Feb. 2, 7-20, 22-Mar. 8, 13, 15-18, 21-31, Apr. 3-10, 12-17, 19-May 9, 12-June 28, 30-July 4, 6-22, 25-28, 31-Aug. 4, 7-10, 12-Sept. 19, 22-Oct. 13, 16-23, 25-Nov. 9, 11, 13, 15-Dec. 6, 8, 11-19, 21-25, 27-1838 Jan. 13
1838 Jan. 16-31, Feb. 2-9, 12-14, 19, 20, 23-Mar. 1, 5, 6, 8-29, 31, Apr. 2, 11-27, 30-June 2, 5, 6, 8, 9, 12-21, 23-28, July 2, 6-12, 14-25, 27-Aug. 9, 13-25, 28-Sept. 12, 14-22, 25-27, 29, Oct. 1, 3, 4, 6-23, 25-27, 30-Nov. 10, 13-27, Dec. 28, 31-1839 Jan. 1
1839 Jan. 3, 4, 7-9, 14, 17-19, 28, Feb. 2, 14, 16-19, 22-Mar. 28, 30-Apr. 16, 18-23, 25-29, May 1-20, 22-July 3, 6, 10-Aug. 2, 5-17, 20-Sept. 4, 6-18, 20-Nov. 23, 26, 28-Dec. 7, 10-17, 19-25, 27-1840 Jan. 2
1840 Jan. 4-Feb. 11, 13-21, 24, 26-Mar. 20, 23-Apr. 7, 9-11, 14, 15, 17-30, May 2-June 2, 4-19, 23-July 7, 9-14, 16-24, 29, 30, Aug. 1-8, 11-24, 26-31, Sept. 2-24, 26-Oct. 2, 6-12, 14-22, 26, 27, 29-Nov. 2, 4-6, 9-18, 20-Dec. 2, 4-9, 12, 15-17, 24, 25, 30
1841 Jan. 4, 7-11, 13-20, 22-26, 28-Feb. 1, 3, 4, 6-12, 15-19, 22-Apr. 1, 3-14, 16-20, 22-May 6, 8-11, 13, 14, 17-21, 24-29, June 3-5, 9-18, 21-28, 30-July 5, 8, 30-Aug. 6, 9, 11, 19, 24-26, 28-Sept. 6, 8-18, 21-Dec. 8, 10, 13, 14, 17-20, 23-27, 29, 30
1842 Jan. 3, 7-11, 13, 15, 18-20, 22-25, 27, Feb. 1, 5, 9-16, 19-23, Mar. 1, 7, 9, 10, 15, 18, 19, 22, 23, 25, 28-30, Apr. 1-8, 11-22, 25-May 17, 19-23, 25-June 9, 11-27, 29-July 2, 6-25, 27-Aug. 17, 19, 20
sw 1844 Jan. 1, May 1
d 1845 Dec. 15

PENNSYLVANIA NEWSPAPERS

UNITED STATES GAZETTE, *continued*
- tw 1823 Apr. 12/14, 15/16, 17/18, 26/28, 29/30, May 1/2, 3/5, 6/7, 8/9, 10/12, 13/14, 17/19, 28/29, June 3/4, 5/6, 7/9, 10/11, 12/13, 14/16, 17/18, July 2/3, 11/12, 14/15, 16/17, 18/19, 21/22, 23/24, Nov. 4/5
- tw 1824 Feb. 12/13, 14/16, 17/18, 19/20, 21/23, 24/25, 26/27, 28/Mar. 1, 2/3, 4/5, 6/8, 9/10, 11/12, 13/15, 16/17, 18/19, 20/22, 23/24, 25/26, 27/29, 30/31, Apr. 1/2, 3/5, 6/7, 8/9, 10/12, 15/16, 17/19, 20/21, Apr. 22/23, 24/26, 27/28, 29/30, May 1/3, 4/5, 6/7, 8/10, 11/12, 13/14, 15/17, 18/19, 20/21, 22/24, 25/26, 27/28, June 3/4, 5/7, 8/9, 10/11, 15/16, 17/18, 19/21, 22/23, 24/25, 26/28, 29/30, July 1/2, 3/5, 6/7, 8/9, 10/12, 13/14, 15/16, 20/21, 22, 23, 24/26, 27/28, 29/30, 31/Aug. 2, 3/4, 5/6, 7/9, 10/11, 12/13, 14/16, 17/18, 19/20, 21/23, 26/27, 28/30, 31/Sept. 1, 2/3, 4/6, 7/8, 9/10, 11/13, 14/15, 21/22, 23/24, 25/27, 30/Oct. 1, 2/4, 5/6, 7/8, 9/11, 12/13, 14/15, 16/18, 19/20, 21/22, 23/25, 26/27, 28/29, 30/Nov. 1, 2/3, 4/5, 6/8, 9/10, 11/12
- tw 1833 May 13/14, 29/30, Dec. 13/14
- tw 1834 Mar. 28/29, May 28/29, 30/31, June 2/3, 13/14, Aug. 6/7, Dec. 1/2, 3/4, 8/9, 10/11, 17/18, 22/23, 24/25, 26/27, 29/30, 31/1835 Jan. 1
- tw 1835 Jan. 5/6, 7/8, Feb. 4/5, 18/19, 25/26, Mar. 25/26, Apr. 3/4, 8/9, 10/11, 22/23, 29/30, May 1/2, June 24/25, July 1/2, 3/4, 8/9, Aug. 3/4, 5/6, 12/13, 19/20, Sept. 2/3, Nov. 30/Dec. 1, 9/10

PBridE 1826 July 11
PBro sw 1842 June 15
PDoHi d 1823 Dec. 13, 16, 19
PE sw 1838 June 30
PEL ◆ sw 1831 Feb. 15, 18
  sw 1833 July 31, Sept. 14, 18, 25-Oct. 9, 26-Nov. 2, 13, 20, 27, Dec. 7, 14-21
  1834 Jan. 1, 29, Mar. 5, 12, 15, Apr. 2, May 24-Aug. 30, Sept. 6-Nov. 15, 22
  d 1834 Jan. 1-Mar. 1, 4-21, 24-Apr. 19, 22-May 7, 9-22, 24-July 4, 7-26, 29-Sept. 29, Oct. 1-15
  1835 Jan. 1, 2, 5-20, 22-Feb. 12, 14-Mar. 19, 23-25, 27-Apr. 25, 28-May 2, 5-20, 22-June 22, 24-Sept. 9, 11-21, 23-Oct. 16, 19, 21-Nov. 27, 30-Dec. 5, 8, 9, 11-15
  1836 Jan. 2-Feb. 22, 24-Mar. 23, 25-Apr. 2, 5-23, 26-May 4, 6-17, 19-30, June 1-10, 13-25, 29-July 1, 4-11, 13-30, Aug. 2-5, 9-22, 24-Sept. 8, 10-12, 14-26, 28, 29, Oct. 1-12, 14-Nov. 15, 17-23, 25-Dec. 15, 19-31
  d 1837 Jan. 12-17, 19-Mar. 7, 9, 11-29, 31, Apr. 3, 5-7, **10-28, May 1-3,** 5, 8-12, 16, 18, 20-23, 26, 29-June 1, 5, 6, 8, 9, 12-16, 19-23, 26, 28-July 26, 28-Aug. 1, 7-12, Sept. 1-8, 13, 16-18, 22-28, 30-Oct. 4, 6, 9-14, 17-25, 27-30, Nov. 1, 3-9, 11-20, 22-Dec. 7, 11, 13-15, 18-23, 28

PHILADELPHIA COUNTY 311

      d 1838 Jan. 1-4, 6-17, 19-24, 27, 30-Feb. 1, 3-5, 7, 9, 10, 13, 15-27, Mar. 2-16, 19-22, 24-27, 29-Apr. 19, 21, 24-May 21, 24-June 5, 7, 9-22, 25-29, July 2-3, 6-Aug. 15, 17-28, 31-Sept. 5, 20, 28-Oct. 18, 22, Nov. 15, 17, 20, 22, 26-Dec. 22, 25

PHi   1823 Apr. 1-1827 Apr. 30
      1828 Jan. 1-1841 Dec. 31
      1842 July 1-1847 June 30

PHoHi   sw 1833-1838
PJR   w 1847 Apr. 3
PLewL   1829 Aug. 27-Nov. 27, 29-Dec. 28
      1830 Jan. 1-Apr. 13, 20-July 27, Aug. 3-Oct. 8, 15-1831 Feb. 11
      1831 Feb. 13-Apr. 8, 19-July 2, 15-29

PNo   1835 Sept. 1
PP   d 1823 July 1-Nov. 13, 15-1824 Jan. 15
      1824 Jan. 17, 19-21, 23, Feb. 2-Mar. 5, 8, 9, 11-Apr. 14, 16, 19-May 6, 8-11, 13-27, 29, June 1-8, 10-Oct. 9, 12, 13, 15-1825 Feb. 18
      1825 Feb. 21-Aug. 6, 9-1826 Sept. 29
      1826 Oct. 2-Dec. 30
      1827 July 2-Dec. 31
      1828 July 1-Oct. 3, 6-13, 15-Dec. 13, 16-1829 May 9
      1829 May 11-June 29, July 1-Aug. 7, 10-13, 15-Dec. 17, 19, 21, 23-28, 31
      1830 Jan. 1-Dec. 31
      1831 Apr. 30, July 9
      1832 Dec. 25
      1834 Oct. 24
      1838 July 13, 24, 26, Aug. 1, 6, 7, 16, 17, 20, 22, 24, 25, 28, 30, Sept. 1, 3-6, 8, 10, 11, 13-15, 17-22, 27, Oct. 10, 12, 15, 16, 18, 20, 23, 24, 27, 29-31, Nov. 3, 5, 24, Dec. 24, 25, 28, 29
      1839 Jan. 9-12, 14, 18, 21-25, 28-30, Feb. 1, 2, 4-9, 11-16, 18, 19, 21, 23, 25-28, Mar. 2, 4-9, 11-16, 18-21, 23, 25-28, Apr. 1-4, 9-13, 15-19, 22, 23, May 7, 20-22, 25-28, 31, July 13, 17, 22, Aug. 2, 10, 12, 15, 16, 21-24, 27-30, Sept. 4-6, 9-11, 13, 14, 16, 19, 21, 23, 26
      1840 Sept. 10, 21
      1841 Jan. 1-12, 14-Apr. 8, 10-1842 Mar. 18
      1842 Mar. 21-June 29
      1845 July 1-Dec. 31
      1847 Jan. 14, 19, Feb. 1, 9, 11, 12, 14, 15, 18, 23, 24-26, Mar. 8, 12, 13, 17, 18, 23-26, 28, 29, Apr. 5, 8, 10-14, 17-23, May 1, 5-7, 9, 30-June 2, 4-25, 28, 29

PPAP   1834 Mar. 22
PPAT   1835 Jan. 1-1847 June 30
PPiHi   sw 1830 Nov. 9
      1836 July 30
PPiUD   1842 Mar. 19, Sept. 14, 15
      1843 May 29
      1844 Sept. 4

UNITED STATES GAZETTE, *continued*
   PPL   d 1823 Apr. 1-Oct. 21, 23-1826 Jan. 13
              1826 Jan. 16-27, 30-Feb. 3, 6-10, 13-24, 28-Mar. 3,
                   6-10, 13-17, 20-28, 30-31, Apr. 3-7, 10-15, 18-24,
                   26-28, May 1, 3, 4, 6-8, 10-15, 17-22, 24-Aug.
                   18, 21-Oct. 25, 27-Nov. 30, Dec. 2-6, 8, 11, 12,
                   14, 15, 18, 19, 21, 22, 25, 28, 29
              1827 Jan. 1-1829 July 4
              1829 July 7-1830 Nov. 19
              1830 Nov. 22-1841 May 14
              1841 May 17-1843 Dec. 21
              1843 Dec. 23-1847 June 30
   PPM   1824 Jan. 1-Dec. 31
              1844 Mar. 1-June 29, July 2-4, 6-Oct. 18, 21-Dec. 13,
                   16-1845 Dec. 17
              1845 Dec. 19-1846 May 26
              1846 May 28-Nov. 26, 28-Dec. 25, 28-31
              1847 Jan. 2-June 30
   PShH   sw 1842 July 30
   PSuHi   sw 1832 Mar. 13
              1833 Mar. 6
              1834 Aug. 2
   PDoHi   w 1845 Jan. 11-1846 Dec. 19
   PWcHi   1827 Nov. 1, 8, 22
              1829 Aug. 3, 8, 10, 17, 24, Sept. 7
   PWbW |1823|
              1824 Dec. 31
              1825 Dec. 30
              1826 Apr. 28, May 5
              1828 Jan. 29
              1829 Feb. 14-June 29
              1834 Apr. 19
              1836 Mar. 9
              1837 Feb. 1
   PWcHi   d 1830 Jan. 8
           sw 1833 Mar. 30
              1835 Mar. 27
            d 1839 Apr. 19
              1840 Nov. (23)
   PWeT   1832 Mar. 19, 24, 26, 27

UNITED STATES GAZETTE (VEREINIGTE STAATEN ZEITUNG) (1878-1908), see Philadelphia Demokrat

UNITED STATES GAZETTE FOR THE COUNTRY, see United States Gazette

UNITED STATES JOURNAL (1854-1877) w d
   PHILADELPHIA BUSINESS JOURNAL (1854) d ♦
   Pub. 1854   Fuller & Co.
   Ed. 1854   Zelotes Fuller
                    continued as
   FULLER'S LITERARY AND BUSINESS JOURNAL (1854-1856) d ♦
   Pub. 1854-1856   Fuller & Co.
   Ed. 1854-1856   Zelotes Fuller

continued as
BUSINESS JOURNAL AND TRAVELER (1856-1857) d
Pub. 1856-1857   Fuller & Co.
Ed. 1856-1857   Zelotes Fuller
    PPL   1856 Apr. 12
                  continued as
UNITED STATES BUSINESS JOURNAL (1857) d ♦ *
Pub. 1857   Fuller & Co.
Ed. 1857   Zelotes Fuller
                  continued as
UNITED STATES JOURNAL (1858-1870) d w *
Pub. 1858-1870   Fuller & Co.
Ed. 1858-1870   Zelotes Fuller
    PHi ♦   1863 Sept. 12
                  1866 Feb. 24
                  1867 June 1, July 6
    PMontHi   [1858 Jan.]
                  1869 May 1
    PPL   1869 May 1
                  continued as
UNITED STATES BUSINESS JOURNAL (1871-1874) w * ♦
Pub. 1871-1874   Fuller & Co.
Ed. 1871-1874   Zelotes Fuller
                  continued as
UNITED STATES JOURNAL (1875-1877) w ♦
Pub. 1875-1877   Fuller & Co.
Ed. 1875-1877   Zelotes Fuller

UNITED STATES RECORDER, see Carey's United States Recorder

UNIVERSAL GAZETTE, THE (Nov. 16, 1797-Sept. 11, 1800) w #
    Pub. 1797-1800   Samuel Harrison Smith
        Removed to, and continued publication, in Washington, Nov. 6, 1800.
        PDoHi   1797 Dec. 14, 21
                      1798 Mar. 8, Apr. 26, May 24-June 28, Sept. 6-Oct. 4
                      1799 May 30-Aug. 1, Oct. 3, 17, 24, Nov. 21
                      1800 Mar. 20, Apr. 3, June 5, 12
        PHi   1798 Jan. 11-Mar. 1, 15-Dec. 27
                      1799 Jan. 3, 17-Feb. 7, 21-Mar. 28, Apr. 11, 25-Nov. 14, 28-Dec. 19
                      1800 Jan. 2-June 26
        PP   1798 June 21, Sept. 6, Nov. 15
                      1799 Jan. 17-Mar. 7, 21-July 11, 25-Sept. 19, Oct. 3-1800 Sept. 11

UNIVERSAL INSTRUCTOR IN ALL ARTS AND SCIENCES, AND PENNSYLVANIA GAZETTE, THE, see Pennsylvania Gazette

UNIVERSE (1856-67) w
    CATHOLIC VISITOR (1856-1857) w ♦
        Merged with the *Catholic Herald* and
        continued as
    CATHOLIC HERALD AND VISITOR (1857-Dec. 26, 1863) w ♦
        continued as
    UNIVERSE (Jan. 2, 1864-Sept. 28, 1867||) w
        PPCHi   1864 Jan. 2-May 14, 28-Sept. 10, 24, Oct. 8-29, Dec. 24
                  1867 Sept. 7, 28

UNIVERSITY COURIER, THE (1891-1898) w
    Pub. 1891-1895   Students of the University of Pennsylvania
           1895-1898   University Courier Publishing Co.
    Ed. 1891-1898   Students of the University of Pennsylvania
       PU   1892 Nov. 11, 29-1893 June
                    1893 Oct. 11-1894 June
                    1894 Oct. 10-1895 June 12
                    1895 Sept. 25, Oct. 23

UPHAM'S PHILADELPHIA SUNDAY MERCURY, see Mercury and Siftings

UPTOWN, THE (1936-1937||) w
    FAIR PLAY (Nov. 6, 1936-Feb. 25, 1937) w
    Pub. 1936-1937   K. Scott Phillips
       PP   1936 Nov. 6 (Vol. 1, No. 1)-1937 Feb. 25 (Vol. 2, No. 8)
       PPL   1937 Jan. 28
                  continued as
    UPTOWN, THE (Mar. 4, 1937-June 24, 1937||) w
    Pub. 1937   K. Scott Phillips
       PP   1937 Mar. 4 (Vol. 2, No. 9)-June 24

VEREINIGTE STAATEN ZEITUNG (UNITED STATES GAZETTE), see Philadelphia Demokrat

VEREINS UND LOGEN ZEITUNG, see Philadelphia Herold

VERO (1886-1913) w ind rep for ♣
    VESUVIO, IL (1886-1911) w ♣
    Pub. & Ed. 1886-1909   Prof. F. G. Scannapieco
                  1909-1910   Leonardo Terrone
                  1910-1911   Il Vesuvio Printing & Publishing Co.
    Ed.   1910-1911   Leonardo Terrone
                continued as
    VERO (1912-1913) w ♣
    Pub. 1912-1913   Il Vesuvio Printing & Publishing Co.
    Ed. 1912-1913   Leonardo Terrone

VILLAGE TELEGRAPH, THE, see Germantown Telegraph

VOCE DELLA COLONIA (1893-1921) w d rep for ♣
    VOCE DELLA COLONIA, LA (1893-1905) w ♣
    Pub. & Ed. 1893-1905   Cerceo Bros. & Catalano
                  continued as
    VOCE DEL POPOLO, LA (1906-1916) d ♣
    Pub. 1906-1914   Italo-American Publication & Printing Co.
    Ed. 1906-1913   Dr. V. Cerceo
          1913-1914   Joseph A. Di Silvestro
                continued as
    VOCE DELLA COLONIA (1917-1921) w rep ♣
    Pub. & Ed. 1917-1921   Thomas Catalano

VOICE OF DEMOCRACY (1843)
    Pub.   A. M. C. Johnson
       PBL   1843 Dec. 25

VOICE OF THE NATION (PHOEBUS), see American Democratic Herald and Commercial Gazette

PHILADELPHIA COUNTY   315

VOLKS STIMME, DIE (May 1, 1925-1933||) w for *
    Pub. 1925-1933   E. A. Thomaser
        PPG   1925 May 1 (Vol. 1, No. 1)
                     1930 Mar. 26

VOLKSWAECHTER (1893-1894) w Hebrew ♦
    Pub. & Ed. 1893-1894   The Volkswaechter Publishing Co.

VORWARTS (1886-1887) sw for ♦
    Pub. 1886-1887   Vorwarts Publication Association

WAHRE UND WAHRSCHEINLICHE BEGEBENHEITEN (Feb. 24, 1766) for (Germantown)
    Pub. 1766   Christoph Saur
        PPES   1766 Feb. 24

WASHINGTON GAZETTE (Feb. 7, 1848-Apr. 3, 1848)
    Pub. & Ed.   George A. Latimer and George T. Donaldson
        PHi ♦   1848 Feb. 7-Apr. 3 (Vol. 1, No. 1-8)

WEEKLY ADVERTISER OR PENNSYLVANIA JOURNAL, THE,
    see Pennsylvania Journal and Weekly Advertiser

WEEKLY AGE, see Illustrated New Age

WEEKLY CALL, see Call

WEEKLY CHRONICLE AND BREWERYTOWN HERALD (1901-1939) w
        BREWERYTOWN HERALD (1901-1916) w ♦
    Pub. & Ed. 1901-1911   Bruno Wahl
                  1911-1916   William J. Wahl
                      continued as
    WEEKLY CHRONICLE AND BREWERYTOWN HERALD (1917-1939) w
        Pub. & Ed. 1917-1935   Wm. J. Wahl
        Pub.   1935 Apr. 13-1938 Jan. 29 Wm. J. Wahl
                  1938 Feb. 5-1939 Dec. 30   L. E. Wahl
        Ed.   1935-1936   L. E. Wahl
        PP   1934 Feb. 17, Mar. 10, 24-1935 June 29
                  1935 July 13-1936 Oct. 31
                  1936 Nov. 14-1937 Mar. 20
                  1937 Apr. 3-1938 Oct. 8
                  1938 Oct. 22-1939 Dec. 30

WEEKLY CONSTITUTIONAL UNION, see Constitutional Union

WEEKLY DEMOCRATIC PRESS, see Philadelphia Inquirer Public Ledger

WEEKLY DEMOKRAT, see Philadelphia Demokrat

WEEKLY FORECAST (Falls of Schuylkill) Apr. 1900-Nov. 20, 1913||) w
    Ed. and Prop.   Ernest E. Carwardine
    PHi   1913 Nov. 20 (Vol. 13, No. 34)

WEEKLY FORUM, see Daily Forum

WEEKLY GUIDE, see Independent Gazette and Germantown Guide

WEEKLY ITEM, see Item

WEEKLY LEDGER, see Public Ledger

WEEKLY MESSENGER, see Messenger, The

WEEKLY MESSENGER OF THE GERMAN REFORMED CHURCH, THE, see Messenger, The

WEEKLY NEW AGE, see Illustrated New Age

WEEKLY NEWS, see Evening News

WEEKLY NORTH AMERICAN, see North American

WEEKLY NORTH AMERICAN FARMER (ca. 1849-1850) w
    Pub. 1849-1850   Meyer & Strause

WEEKLY PRESS, see Press

WEEKLY PHILADELPHIA PRESS, see Press

WEEKLY PHILADELPHIA TIMES, see Times

WEEKLY PRICE CURRENT (1798) w
    Pub. 1798   James Humphreys

WEEKLY STANDARD, see Temperance Advocate and Standard

WEEKLY TIMES (1844), see Spirit of the Times

WEEKLY TIMES (1876-1902), see Times

PHILADELPHIA COUNTY 317

WEEKLY TRIBUNE, THE (1886)
    Pub. 1886   Chris. J. Perry, at Philadelphia
    PHi ♦   1886 Sept. 25 (Vol. 2, No. 47)

WEEKLY UNITED STATES GAZETTE, see United States Gazette

WEST PHILADELPHIA ADVERTISER AND JOURNAL (1877-Oct. 3, 1879||) w
    Pub. & Ed. 1877-1879   Thomas E. Bagg
    PP   1879 Oct. 3

WEST PHILADELPHIA BULLETIN (1903-1920) w local rep ♦
    Pub. & Ed. 1903-1920   James L. Waldin

WEST PHILADELPHIA CHRONICLE (1929-1936) w ind
    SOUTHWEST CHRONICLE (June 20, 1929-Aug. 31, 1934) w
    Pub. & Ed. 1929-1934   J. Dala Temple
                            Charles Rosenberg
        PUB   1929 June 20-1934 Aug. 31
        PP   1929 June 20-1934 Feb. 8
                    1934 Mar. 23, 30, Apr. 6-May 18, June 1-15, Aug. 17, 31
                    continued as
    WEST PHILADELPHIA CHRONICLE (Sept. 7, 1934-July 31, 1936) w
    Pub. 1934-1936   Charles Rosenberg
        PUB   1934 Sept. 7-1936 July 31
        PP   1934 Sept. 7-Nov. 9, 29
                    1935 Jan. 18-Mar. 8, Apr. 12, June 28-July 26, Aug. 9-Sept. 13, Nov. 1-Dec. 31
                    1936 Jan. 10-24, Feb. 14, 28-Mar. 6, 20, July 31

WEST PHILADELPHIA GUIDE (1908-1920) w local ♦
    Pub. & Ed. 1908-1920 Clement L. Burtnett

WEST PHILADELPHIA HERALD (1911-1912) w local ♦
    Pub. 1911-1912   West Philadelphia Co.
    Ed. 1911-1912   J. Mills Leslie, Jr.

WEST PHILADELPHIA HOSPITAL REGISTER, see Hospital Register

WEST PHILADELPHIA PRESS (1877-1908) w rep ♦
    Pub. & Ed. 1885-1888   Smallwood & Maull
                  1888-1890   Press Publishing Co.
                  1890-1892   Albert E. Story
                  1892-1894   Press Publishing Co.
                  1894-1903   A. E. Story
                  1903-1905   B. B. Lee
                  1905-1908   William Wheaton
                  1908   Preston B. Lee
    Ed.   1903-1905   John W. Shorten

WEST PHILADELPHIA RECORD (1900-1908) w local
    Pub. & Ed. 1906-1908 E. M. Smith

WEST PHILADELPHIA SATURDAY STAR (1860-1872||) w *

WEST PHILADELPHIA PUBLIC TELEPHONE, see Philadelphian (West Philadelphia)

WEST PHILADELPHIA TIMES (1924†) w rep
    Pub. 1924-1938 West Philadelphia Times, Inc.
    Ed. 1924-1925 W. Edwin Blair
          1925-1927 William A. Gordon
          1927-1938 Noel C. Albertson
    PUB   1924 Jan.†
    PP   1927 Dec. 30
                 1928 Jan. 6-Apr. 13, 27-May 25, June 8-Nov. 16, 30-1939 Jan. 19
                 1939 Feb. 2†

WEST PHILADELPHIA TRIBUNE (Nov. 16, 1933-Feb. 23, 1934||) w
    Pub. 1933-1934 West Philadelphia Tribune Co.
    Ed. 1933-1934 George Arthur Ried
    PP   1933 Nov. 16-1934 Feb. 23

WEST PHILADELPHIAN (1893-1919) w ind
    CYCLONE (1893-1897) w
    Pub. & Ed. 1893-1897 Mortimer Smallwood
                    continued as
    WEST PHILADELPHIAN AND CYCLONE (1898-1907) w
    Pub. & Ed. 1898-1907 P. C. Fossett
                    continued as
    WEST PHILADELPHIAN (1908-1919) ind
    Pub. & Ed. 1908-1919 P. C. Fossett

WEST PHILADELPHIAN (1921-1924) w local
    Pub. & Ed. 1921-1924 S. V. Sharp

WESTMINSTER, THE (1875-1910) w rel
    PRESBYTERIAN JOURNAL, THE (Dec. 30, 1875-Mar. 24, 1904) w %
    Pub. 1875 Dec. 30-1877 Dec. 6 J. Ford Sutton
          1880 Nov. 4-1883 Nov. 8 The Presbyterian Journal Company
          1883 Dec. 20-1889 Apr. 4 R. M. Patterson & Co.
          1889 Apr. 11-1893 Nov. 16 R. M. Patterson
          1893 Nov. 23-1904 Mar. 24 The Presbyterian Journal Company
    Ed. 1875 Dec. 30-1878 Jan. 17 Alfred Nevin and J. Ford Sutton
          1878 Jan. 24-1880 Aug. 19 Alfred Nevin
          1880 Nov. 4-1886 Dec. 30 R. M. Patterson
          1887 Jan. 6-1889 Feb. 28 R. M. Patterson, Ed.; Richard Montgomery, Assoc. Ed.

PHILADELPHIA COUNTY 319

    1889 Mar. 7-1889 Nov. 14   R. M. Patterson, Ed.; Richard Montgomery, Assoc. Ed.; J. Loughran Scott, J. M. P. Otts
    1889 Nov. 21-1893 Nov. 23   R. M. Patterson, J. Henry Sharpe, Richard Montgomery, J. Loughran Scott, J. M. P. Otts
    1893 Nov. 30-1894 Nov. 15   R. M. Patterson
    1894 Nov. 22-1898 Sept. 29   W. P. White and John McGill White
    1900 Jan. 18-1903 Aug. 13   W. P. White and J. L. Scott
    1903 Aug. 20-1904 Mar. 24   Henry Alexander Grubbs, Ed.; J. L. Scott, W. P. White, Assoc. Eds.

    PPPHi ♦   1875 Dec. 30-1904 Mar. 24
                   missing
                   1886 Sept. 30, Nov. 18
                   1896 July 9
                   succeeded by

WESTMINSTER, THE (Apr. 2, 1904-Oct. 8, 1910) w
    Pub. 1904 Apr. 2-1910 Oct. 8   The Holmes Press, Inc., Philadelphia and New York date line
    Ed. 1904 Apr. 2-1905 Dec. 30   Richard S. Holmes, Ed.; Henry A. Grubbs, Managing Ed.; J. L. Scott and W. P. White, Assoc. Eds.
    1906 Jan. 6-1910-Oct. 8   Richard S. Holmes, Ed.; J. L. Scott and W. P. White, Assoc. Eds.

    PPPHi ♦   1904 Apr. 2-1910 Oct. 8
                   missing
                   1909 July 23
                   On Oct. 6, 1910, *The Westminister* and *The Interior* of Chicago united, becoming *The Continent,* published at New York. On Apr. 29, 1926, *The Continent* was absorbed by *The Presbyterian Advance* of Nashville, Tennessee, which on Oct. 4, 1934, was succeeded by *The Presbyterian Tribune,* published in New York City until the present time.

WHIG CHRONICLE, THE (Oct. 1812-Dec. 23, 1812||) tw * #
    Pub. 1812   George F. Goodman
        PDoHi   1812 Oct. 16

WISSINOMING ADVANCE (1902-1908) w local ♦
    Pub. 1906-1908   Advance Publishing Co.

WISSINOMING SCHEDULE (1891-1892) w ♦
    Pub. & Ed. 1891-1892   Joseph G. Smith

WOCHENTLICHE DEMOKRAT, see Philadelphia Demokrat

WOCHENTLICHE PENNSYLVANISCHE STAATSBOTE, DER,
see Henrich Miller's Pennsylvanischer Staatsbote

WOCHENTLICHE PHILADELPHISCHE STAATSBOTE, DER,
see Henrich Miller's Pennsylvanischer Staatsbote

WOMAN'S ADVOCATE (Jan. 13, 1855-June 6, 1857||) w
This was the first woman's paper and was printed by women.
Ed. 1855   Miss Anne E. McDowel
    PDoHi   1855 Aug. 4-Sept. 1, 15, Oct. 6-20, Nov. 3-Dec. 15
                      1856 June 14, July 5, Sept. 20, 27, Oct. 11, 18, Nov. 22
                      1857 Mar. 21, June 6
    PNoHi   1855 July 28

WORKMAN, THE (Feb. 17, 1881-1896) w sm rel
w 1888 Feb. 9-1889, Feb. 7
    Pub. 1881 Feb. 17-1896   at Pittsburgh
    Ed. 1881 Feb. 17-1894, June   William A. Passavant
          1894 Aug. 2-1896   W. A. Passavant, Jr.
    PPK   1881 Feb. 17-1896 Jan. 30
                      Missing 1896 Jan. 2
    PPLp   1881 Feb. 17-1884 Feb. 7
                      1889 Feb. 9-Mar. 21, Apr. 18-May 30, June 27-1890 Jan. 23
                      Merged with *Lutheran Church Messenger* and *The Lutheran* under the title of *The Lutheran* (q.v.)

WORLD (as it is and as it should be), THE (Feb. 10, 1832-Dec. 28, 1833) w
    Pub. 1832-1833 June 15   T. W. Ustic, for The World Association, at Philadelphia
          1833 June 29-1833 Dec. 28   T. W. Ustic, for The Baptist Missionary Association, of Pennsylvania
    Ed. 1832 Feb. 10-1832 Dec. 29   Charles W. Denison
          1833 Jan. 5-1833 June 22   An Association of Gentlemen
    PHi ♦   1832 Feb. 10-1833 Dec. 28

WORLD, THE (Mar. 5, 1839-Oct. 9, 1839||) d pol *
    Pub. & Ed. 1839   Russell Jarvis
    PP   1839 Aug. 19 (Vol 1, No. 142), 26
    PPL   1839 July 12, Aug. 10, 29, Sept. 6, 19, Oct. 9
    PWcHi   1839 July 22

WYNNEFIELD FORUM (1936-1941†) w
    Pub. & Ed. 1941   S. Bakove, at Philadelphia
    PP   1941 Mar. 10, Apr. 7, 21-Aug. 18, Sept. 1-22, Oct. 6-20, Nov. 3†

YOUNG FOLKS NEWS (1868) w
    Pub. 1868   Alfred Martien, at Philadelphia
    Ed. 1868   Rev. Henry Reeves
    PHi   1868 Dec. 23 (Vol. 1, No. 2)

YOUNG REPUBLICAN (1908-1929) w rep
    Pub. 1908-1929   Young Republican Syndicate
    Ed. 1908-1929   Daniel T. McCool

PHILADELPHIA COUNTY 321

    PHi ♦   1911 Apr. 8
              1912 Aug. 7
              1913 Jan. 22
              1915 Sept. 1
              1916 Apr. 19, May 3, Dec. 6
              1917 July 11, Aug. 15
              1918 Apr. 24, Oct. 2
              1919 Jan. 15, Feb. 19, Sept. 13, Nov. 1
              1920 Jan. 21, Mar. 17, Apr. 14, June 9
    PP   1922 Mar. 22

YOUNGSTERS' WEEKLY NEWS   (Sept. 5, 1935-Apr. 23, 1936||) w
    PP   1935 Sept. 5-1936 Mar. 5, 19-23

ZUKUNFT, DIE (1748-1749) sm w for ♦
    Pub. 1748-1749   Godhart Armbruster

ZUKUNFT, DIE   (1884) w for ♦
    Pub. & Ed. 1884 Henry Grau

ZVAIGZDE (1901-1936) w for rel ♦
    Pub. 1909-1920   Lithuanian Catholic Publishing Co.
         1920-1936   A. Milukas & Co.

ADDENDA

CHRONICLE OF WYNNEFIELD, THE (May 10, 1941†) w
THE WYNNEFIELD COMMUNITY WEEKLY (May 10, 1941 June 14, 1941)
Pub. and Ed.　　Lester LaBove
　　　　　　　changed to
CHRONICLE OF WYNNEFIELD, THE (June 21, 1941†)
　　PP　　　　1941 May 10

OVERBROOK PRESS, w
Pub. and Ed.　　1930-1931　Oliver S. Powers
　　　　　　　1931　　　　Henry C. Shepard
Ed.　　　　　　1931-1932　Edward Gabell
　　PP　　　　1930 Dec. 4
　　　　　　　1931 May 28-Nov. 19, Dec. 4-24
　　　　　　　1932 Jan. 8-29

ROXBOROUGH NEWS (1895) w
Manager　　　1925-1926　George G. Gunn
Ed.　　　　　1926-1927　Cornelius L. Wells
　　　　　　1928　　　　Harold E. Hillmann
　　PP　　　1925 Oct. 7
　　　　　　1926 Jan. 6-13, Mar. 3-10, Apr. 28
　　　　　　1927 Feb. 16, Oct. 5, 26-Dec. 28
　　　　　　1928 Jan. 11-Mar. 14, 28

ROXBOROUGH TIMES, THE (Mar. 29, 1928) w
Pub.　　　1928 Isaac M. Walker and Cornelius L. Wells
Ed.　　　　1928 Robert D. Towne
　　PP　　1928 Mar. 29-Apr. 26, May 17, June 7, 21-28, July 12-Aug. 23, Sept. 6-Dec. 27